KU-426-587

THE CORRESPONDENCE OF
Alexander Pope

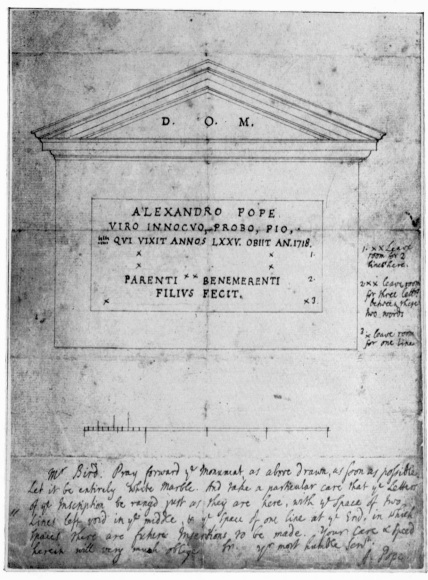

Facsimile of a letter to Francis Bird (reduced)

(Cf. ii. 26)

THE
CORRESPONDENCE
OF
Alexander Pope

EDITED BY

GEORGE SHERBURN

VOLUME II
1719–1728

OXFORD

AT THE CLARENDON PRESS

1956

Oxford University Press, Amen House, London E.C. 4

GLASGOW NEW YORK TORONTO MELBOURNE WELLINGTON
BOMBAY CALCUTTA MADRAS KARACHI CAPE TOWN IBADAN

———

PRINTED IN GREAT BRITAIN

CONTENTS

VOLUME II

Of the small number of letters found in this year two-thirds come from the Homer MSS. Many have to be dated by a dangerous amount of mere guess-work. Pope was much occupied in completing his translation of the *Iliad* and in settling his 'domestic economy' in Twickenham. It seems probable that he removed to Twickenham in March, and that he was speedily at work to find a house there for the Wortley Montagus, who were certainly living in the Piazza, Covent Garden, during this year. For the summer, with Sir Godfrey Kneller's aid they found in Twickenham and rented a house furnished. It proved so satisfactory that either it or another Twickenham house was purchased by Mr. Wortley in 1722. Saville House was theirs for some years thereafter. Sir Godfrey was possibly also trying to sell Mr. Wortley a house in town during this year—without success. Sir Godfrey readily became a friend of Pope's, and during the summer various friends visited the poet's new home. The fact that the Prince of Wales was now resident in Richmond was bound to increase the number of aristocratic personages in nearby Twickenham, and immediately Pope was caught up in the society of the place.

POPE *to* TERESA AND MARTHA BLOUNT[1]   [1719]

Homer MSS. Add. 4808

Dear Ladies,—I find myself obliged to dine to day at Battersea,[2] so that I can't meet you till you are at Parson's Green,[3] where I will not fail to be between five & s[ix] & stay till you come. If this letter does not find you in [   ] street, it will be left at Mrs Floyds. Pray think me with all sincerity Your most affectionate | most humble Servant, | A. Pope

London, 11 a clock.

*POPE *to* THE EARL OF BURLINGTON[4]

2 *February* 1718/19

Chatsworth

Feb. 2d 1718/19

My Lord,—I doubt not it will be a pleasure to your Lordship to know, that I have been unhappy in nothing so much this whole month, as in never being able to meet you. It is a sign my ways are very wrong,

---

[1] On this letter part of *Iliad* xxii was translated, a fact which should date it not later than June or July of 1719.

[2] In 1719 Craggs lived in Battersea. See the end of Craggs' letter to Pope, 1 Oct. 1719.

[3] Lord Peterborow lived in Parson's Green, and since *The Weekly Packet*, 23 May 1719, reports his departure for the Continent, the letter must come early in the year. His lordship seems consistently to use the spelling of his name here adopted.

[4] The letter dates Pope's final decision not to build a house in town.

when they are constantly contrary to yours. And the Knockers of both your Doors, in town & in country, can testify, if their Porters have not set down my name, how much I am injured. I am told your Lordship is going into the Country upon some journey to morrow, & lest the affair you sent to me about should be That of my building or not, I take this method of repeating what I said when last I had the honour of seeing you; That I readily resign the piece of ground intended for me, as not being yet prepard to build, & absolutely unwilling to retard the progress of the rest who are. I beg leave also to assure you, My Lord, that I think the Obligation as fully & strongly layd upon me, as if I had embraced the Favor you designed me. I take it further, as a Title to a future one; so that instead of obliging me Once, you will do it Twice, in the very same Affair. This is putting your Benefit out to use, & doubling it. Tho' you never design'd to be the greatest Usurer in the world, yet you really will be so, if all the Hearts of those you have to deal with, have as good a Fund as mine. I am, with the sincerest Esteem & Gratefulness, | My Lord, | Your most faithful, obligd, & | most humble Servant, | A. Pope.

*POPE to THE EARL OF BURLINGTON[1]

Chatsworth

[*3 February* 1718/19]

Chiswick, Tuesday.

My Lord,—I am unfeignedly concerned to be perpetually unfortunate in my hopes, & views, of waiting on your Lordship. This day I am engaged by Ladies, who are come out of town to dine here on an appointment of some days standing: I had promised to entertain 'em the only way I could, by a sight of your Gardens this Evening: for I was told you would certainly not be here at this time, but at Lord Carleton's in the Country. I now lye under a double *Distress*; but think the greatest, that of my being hinderd all day from seeing you. For the other, as to your Gardens, I beg your Lordships leave I may keep my promise, & send to ask it. If you stay all night I'll come personally to thank you; if not, I'l follow your Wheels to London, or stop you on the Road, or do any thing to see you; tho at present 'tis a great proof of my virtue, & ability to bear Satyr, since you have Twick'nam for your Subject. I'm sure you shall always have me for your Neighbor, where-ever I live; & always for | My Lord | Your most gratefull, most affectionate, most obedient Servant, | A. Pope.

I beg the Bearer may know | if I may carry my Company to the | Garden, what time in the after- | noone may be least inconvenient?

---

[1] This letter seems to follow that of 2 Feb. The 3rd was Tuesday. The letter contains the first mention of Twickenham as a future place of residence.

POPE *to* BROOME[1]   16 *February* 1718/19

Elwin–Courthope, viii. 41

London, Feb. 16, 1718

I think you ought to esteem it a piece of great friendship and trust, that I have not once thanked you yet for your continued favours. It is what no man would have omitted, who had the least doubt of your goodnature or kindness to him, and I assure you I did this on purpose to convince you, how far I was from being capable of taking ill of you your forgetfulness of me before. You see, dear sir, I have put myself upon equal terms with you. I am what the world, according to its shallow way of reasoning, calls an offender, and a careless fellow. But, to my consolation, we are both so; and so indeed, at one time or other, are all the honest undesigning men I know.

I cannot express to you how very much you oblige me in what you have done for my sake. You will, in the most literal sense, be such a friend to me as perseveres to the end. When that day of my deliverance from poetry and slavery shall arrive, as I guess it may this summer, I hope to conclude my long labour with more ease than triumph, better pleased with a conscientious discharge of all my debts and duties, than with any vain praise the world may give me. I shall retire a *miles emeritus*, and pity the poets militant who are to succeed me. I really wish them so well, that if my gains by Homer were sufficient, I would gladly found an hospital, like that of Chelsea, for such of my tribe as are disabled in the muses' service, or whose years require a dismissal from the unnatural task of rhyming themselves, and others, to death. Poor Gildon should have his itch and — cured together, and old Dennis not want good looking after, and better accommodation than poets usually meet with in Moorfields.[2]

Pray fail not to make my hearty services acceptable at Mrs. Marriot's. My friend Tom Smith much rejoiced me with an account of their design to part with Sturston, and live in London. They will find me a mere old fellow at their return hither, pursuing very innocent pleasures, building, planting, and gardening.[3] Study and amours are two vanities I have utterly left off. I have at this present writing no less than five houses, in different counties, through which I make a tour every summer. You will be welcome to all of them, and I heartily wish, about April or May, you could pass one or two months in this manner, with, dear Mr. Broome, your faithful and affectionate friend and servant.

---

[1] By this time Broome was well to do, and not so much interested in payment for his work on Eustathius as Elwin thought. Pope paid Jortin and the others who did this work: Broome and Parnell laboured as friends, and here Broome gets his thanks.

[2] The site of Bedlam.

Pope looks forward already to his Twickenham gardens.

*MRS. RACKETT to MRS. POPE[1] 22 March 1718/19

Homer MSS. Add. 4808

Hallgrove, Mar 22 1719

Madame,—Mrs Racket being in the depth of affliction for the loss of her poor little child desires me with her humble duty to you to acquaint you with it, hoping you will excuse her not writing herself, her sorrow being such at present, as she cannot put pen to paper, nor mention such a melancholy subject. The poor child was seized last monday with a violent fever which continued without the least intermission till saturday night when she died. Mr Racket has just got up having had a violent tedious fitt of the gout he is likewise in a great concern for this sad accident. both desire me to give their duty to you, love & service to Mr pope to whom also I beg mine may be acceptable

[*Written in left margin*:] Wishing you both many a happy Easter I am | Madame | Your Humble servant

JAMES GIBBS to POPE[2] [1719?]

Homer MSS. Add. 4808

Sir,—I had the honor of yours last night leate so Could not answear it sooner, I am obliged to goe out by tymes this morning, but to morrow if you will doe me the honor to call att my house by tymes, or if you'l be pleasd to send me word by the bearer if I may wait upon you, the designes shall be ready for you to aprove or disaprove of according as you shall finde them to your purpose, as for makeing me loose ane houre in your Company, I should always be proud of the honor of spending my tyme so aggreeably and belive me to be with all respect | Honored Sir | your most humble | and most obedient Servant | Ja Gibbs

Monday morning | 8 a cloke

*MRS. RACKETT to MRS. POPE[3] 19 April [1719]

Homer MSS. Add. 4808

Dear Mother—The somer coming on and the roads good [p]utts me in hopes I shall see you soon att Ha[llgr]ove   Mr Morris is goeing

---

[1] Written for Mrs. Rackett. The signature has been cut or torn away. Easter came on 29 Mar. 1719.

[2] The position of the letter in the Homer MSS. indicates that this letter probably was written in the spring or summer of 1719. The supposition, therefore, is that Gibbs, here at the beginning of his great vogue as architect, was making plans for changes in Pope's villa at Twickenham. Since the position in the Homer MSS. establishes only an *ante quem* date, the letter may refer to the house projected in 1718 in London.

[3] The position of the letter in the Homer MSS. makes the year 1719 probable.

and I shall have [a]n emty roome att your servis and an other [f]or
my brother if he will oblidg me with his [g]ood company   Mrs
Doune comes not this so[m]er   I shall be alone all somer if my
mother [R]ackett and you dont come to see me all heer [j]ine in reall
love and service | from Dear Mother | Your Dutyfull Daughter |
M Rackett

Aprill the 19

DR. ABEL EVANS *to* POPE[1]   13 *May* 1719

Homer MSS. Add. 4808

FRAGMENT

St John's oxon. | May 13th 1719.

Tis not that I forget you or disrespect You but Knowing you to be a
man of true Business I thought it too impertinent to trouble you with
any of mine. but now I understand you are at leisure have at you as
far as this half sheet will hold. in the first Place I am very well satisfy'd
you have done for me what you are able. & I heartily thank you &
beg your pardon & very much blush for having given you any trouble
of this Kind with a sort of men you Know as much what to make of
as I. I don't Know how they are in your Church but in ours to tell
you the truth all the Clergymen I ever yet saw are a sort of Ecclesiastical quelque choses that betwixt Common Honesty & Common
sense I Know not what to make of. they preach indeed practice
obedience their practise is active insolence & Impudent injustice. &
when the Layety use em as they use one another there will be an end
of 'em.

POPE *to* ———[2]   1 *June* 1719

Homer MSS. Add. 4808

London, June 1st 1719.

Sir—I received yours, with the inclosed Bill on Lord Molineax for
400 livres, but his Lordship hath not been in London this long time,
& they dont know at my Lord Cardigans (whither the Bill is directed)
when he will return, or which way I may apply about it? The Sum
is too small to be worth much trouble, & therfore if you could remit
Both this & the Year of the Life-rent, together, by a bill on some

---

[1] Part of the sheet is cut away. Pope has evidently been at work trying to get Evans a
rectory. As chaplain of his college he seems not to have been happy.

[2] A rent-charge on the Manor of Ruston in the East Riding of Yorkshire was a part of
the dowry of Pope's mother. The present letter presumably concerns the payment of this
charge and may be directed to the lord of the manor. In 1715 the Popes had considered,
apparently, selling the charge to the Vander Bempdens, who had property near Ruston.

Correspondent of yours who is surely to be met with, or on Mr Daniel Arthur here; it would be much more convenient. Upon your notice given, directed as usual, I will return you inclosed the Note you sent: & am | Sir | Your most humble Servant | A. Pope

I am very sorry to give you this second trouble but can't tell how to help it.

EDWARD WORTLEY MONTAGU *to* POPE[1]   [1719?]

Homer MSS. Add. 4808

Wedensday Evening.

Sir,—I am hindred by business from being at Twitnam either to morrow or Friday. So that Saturday will be the first day we can be there. I desire you will give Yourselfe the trouble of excusing us to Sir Godfrey for not coming sooner. I believe we shall accept of the kind offer of your house I am Sir | Your most Obedient | humble Servant | Edw. Wortley

SIR GODFREY KNELLER *to* POPE[2]   16 *June* 1719

Homer MSS. Add. 4808

Sir,—I am in Towne, and have Louck'd for beds, and bed steds, which must cost ten pounds. a year. when I promis'd to provide them. you had maid no Mention of the Towne rates, which I am to pay, and will be 5 pounds. a year at least and which wou'd be 15 pe annum whit the bedstead, and that house did let for 45. a year when I bought it, So that all I have laed out being neer 400 pounds woud be done for nothing—of which you will Consider, and let me Know. your mind. The stabels are fitted. as your Gentleman ordert them to be, and all the painting will be don, to Morrow or Thorsday. with whenscoating in the Quickesd Manner and best and If you can Stay till Satturday.

¹ The position of this note in the Homer MSS., as part of Book XXIII, forces it into the year 1719. Dr. Arbuthnot's midsummer letter to Pope speaks as if he had more than once come to Twickenham to see Lady Mary. Although this present letter is placed later in the Homer MSS., it seems probable that it came early in the summer when Lady Mary and her husband were looking for a house in Twickenham. This letter is found in Add. 4808, f. 183. The beginning of a letter, undated, from Pope to Sir Godfrey on f. 157 says, 'I just come from Lady Mary's who had sent word she was . . .' Pope was officiously helpful with regard to these housing problems.

² This letter refers, not to Pope's own house, which by this date should have been supplied with beds, but to a house which Kneller is renting to the Wortley Montagus, perhaps only for the summer. They later (1722) bought, and for some years used, Saville House in Twickenham. In an undated letter to her sister, the Countess of Mar, Lady Mary remarks, 'Mr. Wortley has purchased the small habitation where you saw me. We propose to make some small alterations.' Lady Mary was spending much time there before the purchase of the house. The remark about stables and the fact that the house was to be leased furnished indicate that Pope's villa is not in question.

the roomes shall be aired, and pray let me Know your pleasure about the beds and bedsteds: for them I can not provide, you may have 6. of which 2 are to have Courtins, for 10 pounds a year.—and am giving My Most humble respects to My Lady Mery Whorthly | Sir, | Your Most humble | and Most faithfull | Servent G Kneller

I thought one might have
such beds and bedsteds for
4 or 5 pounds a year, and which I woud have done If no rates payd

from Great Queen Street June the 16—1719

EDWARD BLOUNT *to* POPE[1]   [*June* or *July* 1719]

Homer MSS. Add. 4808

I am pleas'd in the thought of your being as much disappointed as my-self and the Company that waited and wish'd for you. I am engag'd at home partly by Company and partly by my not being so well as I would be to enjoy the pleasure of that Noble Lords Company you mention and yours when ever you are at leisure. If you can name any other day now or when you have better Consider'd of it, you need but send your Commands to | Dear Sir | Yours most Sincerely | E Blount.

Thursday. | ten a Clock.

LINTOT *to* POPE[2]   11 [*July*] 1719

Homer MSS. Add. 4808

Sir,—Please to read this sheet, that I may have it when I call to morrow, | Yours B. Lintot

Saturday the 11th | 1719

JACOB TONSON, JR. *to* POPE   11 *July* 1719

Homer MSS. Add. 4808

Sir,—Haveing Mislaid your Letter I have forgott the Name of the Book which yo[u] want, Be pleased to lett me know what the Book is, & I will Endeavour to procure it for You: I am Sir | Your most humble | Servant | Jacob Tonson.

11 July: | 1719.

---

[1] On the back of this note part of *Iliad* xxii is translated, and since the other letters used at the moment for Book XXII are dated June or July of this year, the probability is that this does also. It is no more than a probability, but the letter cannot postdate the summer during which the translation was made.
[2] In 1719 'Saturday the 11th' has to be either Apr. or July. The sheet in question should be from vol. v of the *Iliad*. The volume ended with Book XXI, which Dancastle's letter of 27 July indicates has not yet been transcribed for the press.

DR. ABEL EVANS *to* POPE[1]   26 *July* 1719

Homer MSS. Add. 4808

St Johns Oxon | July 26th 1719.

I shoud much sooner have sent you my acknowledgement & thanks for the very Kind reception I met with from you at your pleasant House at Twicknam but in truth it has been so very Hot that I coud neither write read or think but only Ly still swim or sleep & I am still so monstrously lazy that you must expect but a very short Letter from me. no gallantry or gayety but only a little down right good breeding & Civility. I hope this will find your good Mother settl'd in her Health as also your self as much as her age & your Constitution will permit if wishes had any Power in Medicine I coud soon make you both immortal for she very well deserves it for furnishing the world with you, & you have your self made your name immortal enough I wish only your Body might come in for a small share of that Noble Blessing if it only were for nine hundred & ninety nine years. I wish the same to your Good Friend the Dutchess. that she might live to teach people of Quality all the good qualitys in the world. I write as I talk & I speak as I think & am with great sincerity | Your most affectionate Freind & Servant | A Evans.

Address: To Mr Alexander Pope | at Mr Lintot's Bookseller | Fleetstreet | London |

Postmark: 27/IY

THOMAS DANCASTLE *to* POPE   27 *July* [1719]

Homer MSS. Add. 4808

Binf: July 27

At my return home last night out of Somersetshire I expected nothing less than that I should find a Severe Reprimand from you for my long neglect of Service. indeed I can not Sufficiently extoll your admirable Patience; But presume you have heard the Occasion of my long Ramble, I received, when in London, two letters in one Day, to acquaint me that my Nephew Carew was fallen down with the Small pox and was very desirous I would come to him, at first Sight I thought his Life in Some Danger, he had travell'd into Essex in the heat of Weather & was seiz'd the next day after he reach'd home, takeing the Distemper in this manner he had a very plentiful Share, more than I could have imagin'd, being almost as free from fat as Mr Pope himself. I left him in perfect Safty.

---

[1] Evans is the first friend to mention the hospitality of 'your pleasant house at Twicknam'. What duchess at this moment might be called Pope's 'good friend' is not clear. Elwin thought Buckingham, but it might be Hamilton. The only duchess known to be friendly to Evans was Sarah, Duchess of Marlborough, but Pope was probably not at this time her friend.

Your 21st Book will be ready before you can send me another & your Order how I may convey my Copy to you. I am now much at leizure to dispatch the whole set I wait your Comands & am | Dear Sir | Your most obliged | humble servant. | Tho: Dancast[le]

be pleased to present my humble service to mrs Pope my sister Moore & Molly Carew join with me in the same Request, & my bro: to you both

POPE *to* MRS. RACKETT   1 *August* [1719]

Homer MSS. Add. 4808

Twick'nham. August 1st

Dear Sister,—The business of this is to acquaint you with my intentions of sending for you with the Chariot on Thursday or Friday next, in order to get you hither. I have named the latest day that I could possibly allow you to stay from us, being obliged to lend the chariot upon a Journey on Saturday. We will take no denial, & therfore expect no Excuse, or Answer to the contrary from you. If I hear nothing, (as I hope I shan't) it shall certainly come one of the days abovesaid: So pray be in readiness. My hearty Love to you both, & my Mothers kindest remembrances. I am always | Dear Sister | Your affectionate Brother | A. Pope.

SIR GODFREY KNELLER *to* POPE[1]   [1719]

Homer MSS. Add. 4808

I belive ther will be Card playrs enoug, and we may do how we please. If you Come about 4: a Clock, you may see me paint. to Morrow I am Engaged to go to Harrow the Hill. with Company. being ever | Dear Frind | Your most | affectionat Serv't | G Kneller

Address: To | Mr Pope. | present

DR. ARBUTHNOT *to* POPE[2]   [*August* 1719]

Homer MSS. Add. 4808

FRAGMENT

London Thursday

I was out of town when your letter came but I am glad the contents were obeyd, by my Maids opening of it. I am as glad you are turnd

---

[1] The position of this letter in the Homer MSS. (as part of Book XXII) makes its probable date the summer of 1719.

[2] The Elwin–Courthope edition (x. 267) prints this fragment as from an unknown correspondent, but the handwriting is unmistakably that of Dr. Arbuthnot, who was a close friend of Lady Mary. The leaf has preserved the lower half of the postmark (AV), which gives the month. The position in the Homer MSS. suggests the year.

such a Bon Vivant. but you have so good a ham over against you, I
wonder you want any other. This is in the manner of your Conversation with Lady Mary for which you are so often reprimanded, &
never reformd; may I take the freedom to give her ladyship my most
humble respects. Ile tell you freely when I go to Twitenham it is to
pay my respects to her ladyship, & not to see you. for you never stay
a moment with me. I was busy all last week & shall be this too. but
next I hope to have the vision, tho I will not putt a profane Epithet
to it. Your Water Man unknown to me or my servant went to Mr
Guerney's, & has taken about 30 Shillings more of Spaw waters than
either I or my man knew off. pray enquire ab[ou]t this Matter & lett him

*EDWARD BLOUNT *to* POPE   30 *August* 1719
Ushaw College

Aberley. Aug. 30. 1719

Laudabunt alij claram etc:[1]

Let some the Booby Hatch, or Berlin Praise
Let others sing of Coaches close, or open chaise
Your Chariot will a better Theme afford,
If Phoebus, and your nine but give the word;
Like your Wheels my numbers then should Roll
And with a Lofty Head I'de Knock the Pole;
Nor Greece nor Rome like this e're Chariot drove
Fit for the Goddess or the God of Love:
For want of Talent proper Art and Time
For foolish Prose I quit the loosest Rhyme. etc.

Your Chariot put me in mind of Doctor Faustus or rather of Fortunatus's Cap. It's no matter which as long as my meaning is, to tell you,
that I had all I could wish for in it: I was guarded from Sun, Dust,
and wind and was carried with all imaginable ease both to me, and
my two four legg'd Companions, who went very merrily with me. If
I got a small touch of an Itch for Rhyming, that's not worth Complaining of. I took a dose of Bark and stop't it presently, and I am as
well and as free from it now as ever I was in my life, and I flatter my
self there is no danger that humour will return again: if it should, I
shall apply my self to you for a Remedy, that is, to be treated as an
impenitent Fellow.

Here is a parcell of Old Matrons, Stale Maids and some young
virgins, who remember my Friend Pope and love him.[2] The few lines

---

[1] Horace, *Carmina*, I. vii. I.

[2] These ladies were evidently some of them sisters of William Walsh, who remembered
Pope's visit to Abberley in 1707 and valued the lines in the *Essay on Criticism* (729-44)
which dedicated that poem to Walsh's memory.

you dedicated to the Memory of their Brother and your Friend, they value beyond any Monument of Stone or Brass.

At my return towards London I design to contrive being set down at your House, because I shall have many things to say to you, and nothing to displease you, nor me, if I keep clear off my Ague. I shall be glad to hear from you whilst I am at Mawley near Bewdly Worcestersh—to inform me of the Certainty of your being well at Twickenham about the 18th of next month, or thereabouts. My Cous: Bromley[1] owns he wants your 4th Volume, and Victoria[2] both your 3d and 4th; I shall put them in the way to have them safe: Having but just now mention'd it to them; I have stol'n this Scrap of time from a House full of good natur'd Folks that express a Friendly satisfaction in seeing me, and they give me a wellcome you like, which is, to be free to let you do what you have most a mind to. Just so it fares with me, to morrow I go from hence, and by the latter end of the week I propose being at Mawley to pass one week and then return from whence I came most truly and affly | Dear sir | Yours E. Blount. |

How dayes are out of Fashion, else I would send a Compliment to some people you know, who live within a Mile of an Oak.

I know not where I have got this small Itch of Rhyming, but as when people are stung with the Tarantula. they are play'd to, and dance till they are cur'd, so I have stirr'd about in my Rhymes till I am very well cur'd, and as free from the least humour tending to that distemper as ever I was in my life: I have tak'n the Bark, which I hope will prevent its return.

Address: To | Mr Pope | at his House | in Twickenham | Middx | By London.

MARTHA BLOUNT *to* POPE[3]   [*September* 1719?]

Homer MSS. Add. 4808

Sir,—We shall be at home all friday & expect you soon after dinner. Your dangers on the water that Night I can immagine, from what George[4] told us: the wine is Come saffe.

Address: For Mr Pope.

---

[1] William Bromley (1664–1732) was Walsh's heir. He was M.P. for Oxford, and in 1710 Speaker of the House.

[2] Mrs. Victoria Walsh (a sister of William?) is among the subscribers to the *Iliad*.

[3] The date is a guess, based on the fact that the verso of the note contains part of *Iliad* xxiii. Though unsigned the letter seems to be in Martha Blount's hand. She had the habit, one may note, of placing a semicolon under raised letters (M:).

[4] A servant of the Blounts.

*POPE to EDWARD WORTLEY MONTAGU[1]   [1719?]

The Pierpont Morgan Library

Sir,—I write this from Sr. Godfrys own mouth, who says that Austin his Surveyor (who lives in St. Albans street) assures him all that is wanting to the house may be done in 2 days: and that he has alredy orderd it to be accordingly mended. But that he is ingagd to another, to treat for Selling it outright, or at least for a long Lease; so that he cannot treat further about it, and absolutely refuses to let it till Christmass. These are his words. I can add no more but that I am, with true Esteem, | Sir your most obedient humble | Servant | A. Pope

Sir Godfry thinks Your Surveyors account very untrue, and says, he is well assurd, that his house is as strong as any whatsoever. Tuesday noone.

Address: To the Honourable | Mr Wortley Montagu | in the Piatza, | Coventgarden.

Endorsement: Mr. Pope.

LORD SHANNON (*for* CONGREVE) *to* POPE   [1719]

Homer MSS. Add. 4808

Ashley[2] thursday.

Sir,—By Candle light Mr Congreve wants a Scribe, he has not been well indeed, but will take the air your way to morrow morning. Don't let this be any restraint on you, for he is not Qualified for long visits. Since you were so kind to mention me in your letter, I hope you'l keep your promiss, and let me have the pleasure of seeing you here what day is most Convenient for you next weeke, and it will be a very great Satisfaction to Sir Your most humble servant | Shannon

Address: To | Mr Pope

CONGREVE *to* POPE[3]   [1719]

Homer MSS. Add. 4808

Ashley Monday.

Sir,—I had designd to have waited on you to day but have been out of order since Saturday as I have been most of the Summr. & as the

---

[1] For some years after their return from Constantinople the Wortley Montagus when in town lived in Covent Garden. Their removal to Cavendish Square, according to Professor Halsband, came pretty certainly in 1731. Hence the house in question in this letter is probably one in Twickenham. Later letters in the Homer MSS. indicate that this one falls in 1719.

[2] Ashley (Walton-on-Thames) was the seat of Richard (Boyle), Viscount Shannon, with whom Congreve was staying. For an additional Congreve letter see vol. v.

[3] The position of this letter in the Homer MSS. (part of Book XXIV) together with Congreve's phrase 'most of the summer' places it late in the summer of 1719. Lady Mary seems to be in Twickenham a part of the time.

days are now, unlesse I am able to rise in a Morning, it will be hard to go & Come & have any pleasure between the whiles the next day after I had known from you where Lady Mary was, I sent to know how she did but by her answer I perceive she has the goodnesse for me to believe I have been all this Summr here, tho' I had been here a fortnight when you came to see me. pray give her my most humble service if I can I will wait on you. I am Your | Most Obedient | humble Servant | Wm Congreve

†POPE *to* LORD BATHURST[1]   13 *September* [1719]
1737
                                                                  Sept. 13.

I believe you are by this time immers'd in your vast Wood; and one may address you as to a very abstracted person, like Alexander Selkirk,[2] or the Self-taught Philosopher.[3] I should be very curious to know what sort of contemplations employ you? I remember the latter of those I mention'd, gave himself up to a devout exercise of making his head giddy with various circumrotations, to imitate the motions of the cœlestial bodies. I don't think it at all impossible that Mr. L[4] may be far advanced in that exercise, by frequent turns toward the several aspects of the heavens, to which you may have been pleas'd to direct him in search of prospects and new avenues. He will be tractable in time as birds are tam'd by being whirl'd about; and doubtless come not to despise the meanest shrubs or coppice-wood, (tho' naturally he seems more inclin'd to admire God in his greater works, the tall timber: for as Virgil[5] has it, *Non omnes arbusta juvant, humilesque myricæ.*) I wish my self with you both, whether you are in peace or at war, in violent argumentation or smooth consent, over Gazettes in the morning, or

---

[1] This letter was first printed in the Roberts octavo of 1737; i.e. Pope's *Works*, vi (1737), 282–4. It was possibly first *published* in the quarto and folio editions of that year. Curll, in *Mr. Pope's Literary Correspondence*, v (1737), 226, printed the letter as addressed to Lord Bathurst, whose name Pope did not print in connexion with the letter. Warburton (1751) named Bathurst as addressee in a footnote. The only textual revisions Pope made in the letter occur in the folio and quarto of 1737, and are quite negligible except for the date, which there and there only appears as 23 Sept.—possibly a printer's error.

[2] The story of Selkirk had been a sensation in 1711 when he was brought back to England after having been marooned (1704–9) on Juan Fernandez. Interest was much revived in 1719 by the publication in April of *Robinson Crusoe.*

[3] The Title of an Arabic Treatise of the Life of Hai Ebn Yocktan.—Pope, 1737. There were various translations of this work into Latin or English in Pope's day. We know that Pope owned the English translation of Simon Ockley (1708) and he may have had a Latin version. In imitating the movements of the heavenly bodies Yocktan 'used a great many sorts of circular motion . . . sometimes walking or running a great many times round about his house or some stone, at other times turning himself round so often that he was dizzy'. This was one step in mystic contemplation of Divine Essence. The next involved abstracting oneself from all sense-perception and imagination, 'endeavoring to the utmost to think of nothing besides Him'.

[4] Probably Erasmus Lewis; possibly Bathurst's clerical friend Henry Layng, who later translated a passage in the *Odyssey* for Pope.   [5] *Eclogues*, iv. 2.

over Plans in the evening. In that last article, I am of opinion your Lordship has a loss of me: for generally after the debate of a whole day, we acquiesc'd at night in the best conclusion of which human reason seems capable in all great matters, to fall fast asleep! And so we ended, unless immediate Revelation (which ever must overcome human reason) suggested some new lights to us, by a Vision in Bed. But laying aside Theory, I am told you are going directly to Practice. Alas, what a Fall will that be? A new Building is like a new Church, when once it is set up, you must maintain it in all the forms, and with all the inconveniences; then cease the pleasant luminous days of inspiration, and there's an end of miracles at once!

That this Letter may be all of a piece, I'll fill the rest with an account of a consultation lately held in my neighbourhood, about de-signing a princely garden.[1] Several Criticks were of several opinions: One declar'd he would not have too much Art in it; for my notion (said he) of gardening is, that it is only sweeping Nature:[2] Another told them that Gravel walks were not of a good taste, for all of the finest abroad were of loose sand: A third advis'd peremptorily there should not be one Lyme-tree in the whole plantation; a fourth made the same exclusive clause extend to Horse-chestnuts, which he affirm'd not to be Trees, but Weeds; Dutch Elms were condemn'd by a fifth; and thus about half the Trees were proscrib'd, contrary to the Paradise of God's own planting, which is expressly said to be planted with *all trees*. There were some who cou'd not bear Ever-greens, and call'd them Never-greens; some, who were angry at them only when cut into shapes, and gave the modern Gard'ners the name of Ever-green Taylors; some who had no dislike to Cones and Cubes, but wou'd have 'em cut in Forest-trees; and some who were in a passion against any thing in shape, even against clipt hedges, which they call'd green walls. These (my Lord) are our Men of Taste, who pretend to prove it by tasting little or nothing. Sure such a Taste is like such a stomach, not a good one, but a weak one. We have the same sort of Critics in poetry; one is fond of nothing but Heroicks, another cannot relish Tragedies, another hates Pastorals, all little Wits delight in Epigrams. Will you give me leave to add, there are the same in Divinity? where many leading Critics are for rooting up more than they plant, and would leave the Lord's Vineyard either very thinly furnish'd, or very oddly trimm'd.

I have lately been with my Lord —[3] who is a zealous yet charitable

---

[1] The Royal Gardens at Richmond.—Curll, 1737. The garden of the Prince of Wales at Richmond. He rented the house and grounds in 1718, and purchased them in 1719.—Elwin.   [2] An expression of Sir T. H[anmer].—Warburton, 1751.
[3] Alludes to the Letter the Duke of *Chandos* wrote to Mr *Pope* on this Occasion.—Curll, 1737. (Curll seldom makes so wildly erratic a note as this. If the letter had had a year date, he could not have dragged the Duke of Chandos into the picture, as he could after 1731.)

Planter, and has so bad a Taste, as to like all that is good. He has a disposition to wait on you in his way to the Bath, and if he can go and return to London in eight or ten days, I am not without a hope of seeing your Lordship with the delight I always see you. Every where I think of you, and every where I wish for you. I am, &c.

FENTON *to* LINTOT   14 *September* 1719
Homer MSS. Add. 4808

September 14th 1719.

Mr Lintot,—Pray give my most humble Service to Mr Pope, & tell him I beg the favour of him to let me know when he comes to Town what morning I shall wait on him at his Lodgings, for I walk out in a morning so often, that I may otherwise lose an opportunity of seeing him.

———

Lib. 21. Ver. 132. The first part of Dacier's note is taken from Eustathius, but instead of Aurelius Victor & Dion, he quotes Herodotus, without mentioning the Book he takes it from.

Ver. 467. I cannot find that Eustathius assigns the same reasons that Mm[1] does, why Apollo & Neptune do not fight with one another. | Your humble Servant. | E. Fenton

I will endeavour to find out the passage above mention'd in Herodotus.

THOMAS VERNON *to* POPE[2]   [*September* 1719?]
Homer MSS. Add. 4808

Sunday noone

Sir,—There was Company here last night that would have bin very well pleased to see you. Assoon as I have dined I will wait upon you & if you please wee'le spend the afternoon in visitts. I am alwaies | Your Obedient humble | Servant | Tho: Vernon

Address: To A. Pope Esqr.

SIR GODFREY KNELLER *to* POPE[3]   [1719]
Homer MSS. Add. 4808

Dear Friend,—I hope your Genuos dos and will Know myn is with the Most acceptable and Most accomplisced Company to Morrow.

---

[1] Madame Dacier.

[2] The uncertain chronological placing of this letter is based solely on the dates of nearby letters used in Pope's translation. Thomas Vernon, Esq., of Twickenham Park, was Pope's landlord. This, the only note preserved from him to Pope, seems to indicate very friendly relations: the lack of correspondence is perhaps due to the proximity in which they lived. Vernon died in 1726.

[3] The position of this letter as part of *Iliad* xxiii and its possible relation to the letter from Craggs of 1 Oct. suggest a date in the autumn of 1719, possibly 30 Sept., if we relate

for My body is in no Condition, to stirr out not so much as out of
my bed as Yet. and, has had no rest these two Nights., but what it
snadches and gets, in thee day time, by fits. and I belive my left Lag
will be out of ordr a good wyle. pray give my hearty good will to the
Compa. for the deeds, and my most humble servis. being evr yours |
G Kneller

Address: To | Mr Pope | Present

JAMES CRAGGS *to* POPE[1]   1 *October* 1719

Homer MSS. Add. 4808

Cockpit, Octr the 1st 1719.

I was Yesterday out of town & came directly here this morning where
I received your letter enclosed in a very fine one from Sir Godfrey
Kneller, You'l easily imagine how much I am concerned at the Accident which has befallen him, but I comfort my self since his hand &
head which I could least have spared remain in their former vigour
& condition. I don't see why this misfortune is to be compleated by
the Loss of Dr. Arbuthnot's & your good company which you'l give
me leave to expect to morrow at Battersea, where we will drink
Sir Godfrey's health & make a new appointment against his recovery.
I am entirely Dear Sir | Your's | J Craggs.

POPE *to* MARTHA BLOUNT[2]   30 *October* [1719?]

Bowles, (1806), x. 8–10

October 30.

You must needs know, dearest Madam, how kindly, how very kindly,
I take your letter. I am sure there is scarce an hour in which I am not
thinking of you, and of every thing relating to you; and therefore
every least notice given me of you, is to me the most important news
in the world. I am truly concerned for your head-ach, and for your
finding the town disagreeable: but I hope both of these uneasinesses
will be transitory, and that you'll soon (even the very next day after
your complaint) find both yourself and the town mighty well again. I
do sincerely, and from my soul, wish you every pleasure and content-

---

it to the Craggs invitation. The spelling is perplexing. *Snatches* is for *snatches*, and *Compa.*
for *company*. Kneller's 'genius', but not his body, will be present tomorrow. The 'deeds'
remain obscure. Craggs took a house in Twickenham in the spring of 1720.

[1] This letter occurs at the very end of the MSS. of the *Iliad* (Add. 4808, f. 205). On the
back of it in Pope's hand is written: 'End the notes with a dedication to Mr. Congreve,
as a memorial of our friendship occasioned by his translation of this last part of Homer.'

[2] The year is pure guess-work. It might as well be 1718 as 1719, and other years are
possible. On 30 Oct. 1719 Sir George Thorold became Lord Mayor of London—a day later
to be celebrated as the day on which the action of *The Dunciad* took place—see *Dunciad*,
Bk. i, ll. 85–88.

ment the world can give; and do assure you at the same time, the greatest I can receive will always be in hearing of yours, and in finding, by your communicating it to me, that you know how much I partake of it. This will satisfy my conscience better, than if I continued to trouble you daily; though there is really no day of my life that I don't long to see you.

As to my health, I'm in a very odd course for the pain in my side: I mean a course of brickbats and tiles, which they apply to me piping hot, morning and night; and sure it is very satisfactory to one who loves architecture at his heart, to be built round in his very bed. My body may properly at this time be called a human structure. My mother too is fallen ill of her rheumatism, but was not the worse, but better, for your stay the other night. You left her in high humour with you. Pray give hers and my faithful services to your mother and sister.

Shall I congratulate or condole with you on my Lady Kildare's[1] account? I heartily wish her very happy with any able Divine, when-ever you have no mind to her company. I thank you for your kind admonition to consult the Doctor, and faithfully promise to take care of myself at your desire, whenever you'll take the least care of yourself at mine. You may be confident the master builder will come to survey your house the first day he is able: if he does not soon recover, I'll send to another, whom I believe I can find at Kensington.

Pray, have you heard farther of Bertie? I have not. I writ yesterday to Cleveland-court,[2] to deliver you what letters came from the Lottery-office. God give you good fortune (the best thing he can give in this world to those who can be happy). You know I have no palate to taste it, and therefore am in no concern or haste to hear whether I gain or lose. But I won't release you from your engagement of sending me word of the tickets, because every word of yours is unfeignedly a great satisfaction to | Yours, etc.

If I am not able to come soon to London, I will epistolize your sister speedily.

SIR GODFREY KNELLER *to* POPE[3]   [1719]
Homer MSS. Add. 4808

Dear Frind,—I find them Statues are so very fresh, being painted in three Collers, and ought to be near a fier, severall days, for as they are

---

[1] Elizabeth, dowager Countess of Kildare, had presumably lived near Mapledurham (at Caversham) during the childhood of the Blount sisters. She had married the 18th Earl in 1684, and he had died in 1707.   [2] Jervas's house.

[3] The position of the note in the Homer MSS. suggests that it dates from the autumn of 1719. The letter has a connexion with Pope's lines 'To Sir Godfrey Kneller, on his paint-ing for me the Statues of Apollo, Venus, and Hercules'. The lines are recorded, under the

it is impractick to put them were intend 'm¹ it woud be pitty, they shou'd take dust—Jinny stays heer 8 or 10 days and will not fail, of sending them when reddy, and I am (giving My hearty and humble servis to your deer Mother) dear Mr Pope | Your Most Sincere | and in reality humble | an faithfil Servent G Kneller

*POPE *to* [   ]²   [1719]

Homer MSS. Add. 4808

Sir,—I'm sorry to give you this trouble, which I'm forcd to, on account of a Letter directed to our Man at Mr Jervas's in Cleveland court, which I yesterday sent by one of your Servants from Twitenham. There was inclosed in it a Paper of great concern, which I find was never brought to my lodging; I beg you to inquire about it, & let it be given to the bearer, if possible, to night; If not, you'l extremely oblige me in sending the letter to morrow very early to me, it requiring haste. I beg you always to believe me with all esteem | Dear Sir | Your most faithfull | humble Servant | A. Pope.

Mr Jervas's in Cleveland Court:

Wensday 7 a clock.

*POPE *to* THOMAS DANCASTLE   9 *November* 1719

Yale University

After a Continuance of broken promises, both of your Brothers & your own, and after a vain Hope of seeing one or both of you at Twit'nam, these six weeks or more: I have yet the charity to forgive & write to you. I really am a hearty well-willer to you both, & truly glad at all times of any notice of your health & welfare. I hope the pain in your head which you usd to complain of, has not returnd upon you; if it does, why should you not come hither, and let me consult my Doctor about you? My present Employment is Gardening, tell your Brother I have taken 2 Acres of land last week³ & am in exceed-

title quoted, in the *Notebooks* of George Vertue (ii. 122) as published by the Walpole Society, xx (1932). Elwin printed them (iv. 452) under a somewhat different title. The three *grisaille* paintings were in Pope's will bequeathed to Lord Bathurst, and are still to be seen at Cirencester.

¹ He means, 'it is impracticable to put them where you intend 'em'.
² The chronological placing of this letter is inferred from the fact that it occurs almost at the end of the *Iliad*. The addressee can be hypothesized only wildly. His servant was supposed to have brought a letter to 'our man' (Frank Waters?) at Jervas's. Pope, arriving there (i.e. 'to my lodging'), finds the letter has not arrived. It contained a document which Frank was instructed by letter to convey to some other person. If the letter has been returned to Twickenham, Pope wants it sent back to Jervas's by his messenger. The addressee might be Mr. Wortley Montagu or any other friendly resident of Twickenham.
³ Evidently the ground for Pope's garden, lying across the highway from his house. The separation of house and gardens made the grotto essential as a means of easy access.

ing pain how to be deliverd of the Maggots I am in travail of. As to my poetical affairs, they lie neglected enough of conscience, yet not so totally forgot, but that I hope to finish the whole work by Christmass. The Book which precedes that you are now copying, is in the press; and so shall yours be, the moment you can conveniently send it. I congratulate You on your approaching Deliverance from this Slavery, which you have so heroically undergone thro' so many volumes: You have Fought it out as long as Hector himself, and at length have seen his Death. I promise you to Remember with gratitude the great Toils you have sufferd for my sake; I hope, long after I shall have forgot those of my own part of the Labour. Pray (dear Sir) accept of myne & my Mothers faithfullest services, make them agreable to your Brother, & think me always what I shall always be, | Your most affectionate & | obligd Friend & Servant | A. Pope.

Novr 9th 1719.

POPE *to* BROOME[1]   31 *December* [1719]

Elwin–Courthope, viii. 40

Twitenham, Dec. 31 [1718].

I deferred writing to you till I could inform you of the safe arrival of Eustathius. I cannot tell how many thanks I am to pay you, and therefore desire you will come up to tell me. The sooner I see you, the better for me, in January. The weather favours, and my particular leisure is this month,—which, to say truth, I cannot promise myself the next. I shall then be in the hurry of publishing the Homer, together with some hundred other accidentals, of which I will give you an account when I see you.

The place I am in is as delightful as you can imagine any to be, in this season; the situation so very airy, and yet so warm, that you will think yourself in a sort of heaven, where the prospect is boundless, and the sun your near neighbor.

Semperque innubilus æther,
Integit, et large diffuso lumine ridet.[2]

As a last unfailing motive to draw you here, I will tell Mrs. Betty Marriot such wonders of the enchanted bowers, silver streams, opening avenues, rising mounts, and painted grottos, that her very curiosity shall bring her to us, and then—see whether your lawful wife can keep you. Consider also the ease, the quiet, the contentment of soul, and

---

[1] Printed in Elwin–Courthope under the bracketed date of 1718; but Pope was not living at Twickenham at that time, nor was he about to publish any Homer early in 1719 as he was in 1720. The year seems surely 1719.

[2] Lucretius, iii. 21–22.

repose of body, which you will feel, when stretched in an elbow chair, mum for your breakfast, chine and potatoes for dinner, and a dose of burnt wine to give you up to slumbers in the evening, without one sermon to preach and no family duty to pay.

> O quid solutis est beatius curis?
> Cum mens onus reponit, et conjugali
> Labore fessus, venires larem ad nostrum,
> Desideratoque acquiesceres lecto![1]

Think and come. I say no more. | Yours most affectionately.

[1] Catullus, xxxi. 7–10 (obviously 'adapted').

This is not a very interesting year in Pope's career. The letters present, as usual, insoluble problems in dating, and concern South Sea speculation rather than literary work. In March Pope invested something like £500 in the stock, which he did not sell, influenced probably by his friend and neighbour, Secretary Craggs, who was backing the 'bubble'. During the year Craggs had a house in Twickenham, and for much of the year Fenton was living with him as tutor in literature, &c. Pope was making improvements in his villa and his garden, and such interests diverted him from writing. There is some reason to think that possibly the project of translating the *Odyssey* was vaguely contemplated before the end of the year. Notable is the evidence of increasing friendship with Atterbury, but the Blount sisters and Caryll remain the most frequent correspondents.

POPE *to* TERESA *or* MARTHA BLOUNT[1] [1720?]

Mapledurham

Madam,—I cannot but put you once more in mind of your Appointment on Sunday, but I find I cannot Return with you, & therfore let you know it, that you may, if you like it, fill up your Number in the Coach with any Body you would bring, as any one you like must of course be agreable to | Madam | Your most obliged & | obedient Servant | A. Pope.

Tuesday.

If you can drink nothing but Claret, you must bring a Bottle with you

POPE *to* LADY MARY WORTLEY MONTAGU[2] [1720?]

The Pierpont Morgan Library

Sunday

Indeed, dear Madam, tis not possible to tell you, whether you give me every day I see you, more pleasure, or more respect? And upon my

---

[1] This letter has been placed by Elwin as if written in 1720. It might obviously date from any year after Pope was in a position to entertain and (presumably) after the Blount ladies had left Mapledurham.

[2] Kneller, at Pope's instance, is preparing to paint Lady Mary, whom Pope is seeing now almost every day. Hence she is living in Twickenham, where, as other letters show, the sittings for the portrait took place. The year is deduced from the fact that the portrait is signed 'Sir Godfrey Kneller pinxt. 1720'. See George Paston (E. M. Symonds), *Lady Mary Wortley Montagu* (1907), p. 292.

word, when ever I see you after a day or two's absence, it is in just such a View as that you yesterday had of your own writings. I find you still better than I could imagine, & think I was partial, before, to your prejudice.

The Picture dwells really at my heart, and I have made a perfect Passion of preferring your present Face to your past. I know, & thoroughly esteem, Your Self of this year: I know no more of Lady Mary Pierrepoint, than to admire at what I have heard of her, or be pleasd with some Fragments of hers, as I am with Sappho's. But now —I can't say what I would say of you now—Only still give me cause to say you are good to me, & allow me as much of your Person as Sir Godfrey can help me to.

Upon conferring with him yesterday, I find he thinks it absolutely necessary to draw the Face first, which he says can never be set right on the figure if the Drapery & Posture be finishd before. To give you as little trouble as possible, he proposes to draw your face with Crayons, & finish it up, at your own house in a morning; from whence he will transfer it to the Canvas, so that you need not go to sit at his house. This I must observe, is a manner in which they seldom draw any but Crown'd Heads; & I observe it with a secret pride & pleasure.

Be so kind as to tell me if you care he shou'd do this to morrow at twelve. Tho' If I am but assurd from you of the Thing, let the manner & time be what you best like: Let every Decorum you please, be observ'd. I should be very unworthy of any favour from your hands, if I desird any at the expence of your Quiet, or Conveniency, in any degree.

I have just received this Pamphlet, which may divert you.

I am Sincerely | Yours. | A. Pope

Address: To the Right Honorable the Lady M. W. Montagu, at Twicken-ham.[1]

POPE *to* LADY MARY WORTLEY MONTAGU[2] [1720?]

Sandon Hall

              Thursday 9 a clock

Madam,—Sir Godfry happening to come from London yesterday, (as I did myself) will wait upon you this morning at twelve to take a sketch of you in your dress, if you'l give leave. He is really very good to me: I heartily wish you will be so too. But I submit to you in all things, nay in the manner of all things; your own pleasure, & your

---

[1] The address is taken from Dallaway, i. 57.

[2] The letter, undatable as it is, seems to follow logically in the series concerning Lady Mary's portrait. The text is from a transcript made by Professor Robert Halsband from the original at Sandon Hall.

own time. Upon my word, I will always take yours; & understand you as you would be understood; with a real respect & resignation when you deny me anything, and a hearty gratitude when you grant me any thing. Your Will be done! but God send it may be the same with mine!

   I am most truly Yours | A. Pope

   I beg a single word in | answer, because I am to | send to Sir Godfrey accordingly.

†POPE *to* JERVAS[1]   [1720?]

1735

Dec. 12, 1718.

The old project of a Window in the bosom, to render the Soul of Man visible,[2] is what every honest friend has manifold reason to wish for; yet even that would not do in our case, while you are so far separated from me, and so long. I begin to fear you'll die in *Ireland*, and that the Denunciation will be fulfilled upon you, *Hibernus es, & in Hiberniam reverteris*—I shou'd be apt to think you in *Sancho*'s case;[3] some Duke has made you Governor of an Island, or wet place, and you are administring Laws to the wild *Irish*. But I must own, when you talk of *Building* and *Planting*, you touch my String; and I am as apt to pardon you, as the Fellow that thought himself *Jupiter* would have pardon'd the other Madman who call'd himself his Brother *Neptune*. Alas Sir, do you know whom you talk to? One that had been a Poet, was degraded to a Translator, and at last thro' meer dulness is turn'd into an Architect. You know *Martial*'s Censure—*Præconem facito, vel Architectum.*[4] However I have one way left, to plan, to *elevate*, and *to surprize* (as *Bays* says.) The next you may expect to hear, is that I am in Debt.

   The History of my Transplantation and Settlement which you

---

[1] Published in all Pope's editions except 1735 a2. Pope's date for it—doubtless slapped on in 1735—is altogether impossible. Any time during the first half of 1720 is possible. The letter is not clearly a fabrication or a conflation of two or more letters. Pope writes at a time when he has lived for a year (vaguely defined!) at Twickenham and when he is at work editing Parnell's *Poems* (published in Dec. 1721, dated 1722) and composing an epitaph for Rowe (d. 6 Dec. 1718). Pope recalls nostalgically 'the old intercourse and conversation' with Jervas and others, and is thus reminded of their dead friends, whom he enumerates *as friends* rather than as men lately deceased. Garth died on 18 Jan. 1718/19 (after Pope's date of Dec. 1718), fifteen months after Parnell's death. Earlier lack of mention of Rowe's decease had evoked reproach from Jervas, and the interchange of such communication makes the interval between his death and Pope's reply to the reproach longer than six days. The memories of these three friends are pleasant and remote. Pope elsewhere showed awareness of the paradox of Garth's evident profound Christian spirit and his apparently complete unbelief.

[2] On the project of Momus for this window see Lucian's *Hermotimus*, 20.

[3] As early as this date Jervas was evidently interested in *Don Quixote*, which later he translated.   [4] Martial, v. 56. 11.

desire, would require a Volume, were I to enumerate the many projects, difficulties, vicissitudes, and various fates attending that important part of my Life: Much more should I describe the many Draughts, Elevations, Profiles, Perspectives, &c. of every Palace and Garden propos'd, intended, and happily raised, by the strength of that Faculty wherein all great Genius's excel, Imagination. At last, the Gods and Fate have fix'd me on the borders of the *Thames*, in the Districts of *Richmond* and *Twickenham*. It is here I have passed an entire Year of my life, without any fix'd abode in *London*, or more than casting a transitory glance (for a day or two at most in a Month) on the pomps of the Town. It is here I hope to receive you, Sir, return'd in triumph from Eternizing the *Ireland* of *this Age*. For you my Structures rise; for you my Colonades extend their Wings; for you my Groves aspire, and Roses bloom. And to say truth, I hope Posterity (which no doubt will be made acquainted with all these things) will look upon it as one of the principal Motives of my Architecture, that it was a Mansion prepar'd to receive you, against your own should fall to dust, which is destin'd to be the Tomb of poor — and — [1] and the immortal Monument of the Fidelity of two such Servants, who have excell'd in Constancy the very Rats of your Family.

What more can I tell you of my self? so much, and yet all put together so little, that I scarce care, or know, how to do it. But the very reasons that are against putting it upon Paper, are as strong for telling it you in Person; and I am uneasy to be so long deny'd the satisfaction of it.

At present I consider you bound in by the *Irish* Sea, like the Ghosts in *Virgil*,

> — Tristi palus inamabilis unda
> Alligat, & novies Styx circumfusa coercet![2]

and I can't express how I long to renew our old intercourse and conversation, our morning Conferences in bed in the same Room, our evening Walks in the Park, our amusing Voyages on the Water, our philosophical Suppers, our Lectures, our Dissertations, our Gravities, our Reveries, our Fooleries, our what not?——This awakens the memory of some of those who have made a part in all these. Poor *Parnelle, Garth, Rowe*! You justly reprove me for not speaking of the Death of the last: *Parnelle* was too much in my mind, to whose Memory I am erecting the best Monument I can. What he gave me to publish, was but a small part of what he left behind him, but it was the best, and I will not make it worse by enlarging it. I'd fain know if he be buried at *Chester*, or *Dublin*; and what care has been, or is to

---

[1] The texts of 1737–42 fill these blanks with 'Frank and Betty'; i.e. Francis Waters and Betty (his wife?).   [2] *Aeneid*, vi. 438–9.

be taken for his Monument, &c. Yet I have not neglected my Devoirs to Mr. *Rowe*; I am writing this very day his Epitaph for *Westminster-Abbey*[1]—After these, the best natur'd of Men, Sir *Samuel Garth*, has left me in the truest concern for his loss. His death was very Heroical, and yet unaffected enough to have made a Saint, or a Philosopher famous: But ill Tongues, and worse Hearts have branded even his last Moments, as wrongfully as they did his Life, with Irreligion. You must have heard many Tales on this Subject; but if ever there was a good Christian, without knowing himself to be so, it was Dr. *Garth*.

I am, &c.

POPE *to* TERESA BLOUNT[2]   [1720?]

Mapledurham

Madam,—Your Letter gives me a Concern which none, but one who (in spite of all accidents) is still a Friend, can feel. I'm pleased however, that any thing I said Explains my past actions or words in a better Sense than you took 'em. I know in my heart (a very Uncorrupt Witness) that I was constantly the thing I profess'd myself to be, to you; that was, Something better, I will venture to say, than Most people were Capable to be, to you, or any body else.

As for forgiveness, I am approaching I hope, to that time & condition, in which every body ought to Give it, and to Ask it, of all the world. I sincerely do so with regard to you: and beg pardon also for That very Fault, of which I taxd others, my Vanity, which made me so Resenting.

We are too apt to Resent things too highly, till we come to know, by some great misfortune or other, how much we are born to endure? And indeed, as for me, you need not suspect of Resentment, a Soul which can feel nothing but Grief.

I desire extremely to see you both again; yet I believe I shall see you no more; and I sincerely hope as well as think both of you will be glad of it. I therefore wish, you may each of you find all you desired I could be, in some one, whom you may like better to see. In the meantime I bear testimony of both of you to each other, that I have certainly known you, truly and tenderly each other's Friends, & wish you a long enjoyment of each others Love & affectionate offices. I am piqu'd at

[1] See Ault, *New Light*, pp. 146–55, for a history of the epitaph for Rowe. By the time the monument was put up, Pope had found it necessary because of too frequent solicitation to conceal his connexion with any epitaph.

[2] This is an impossible letter to place, since there were misunderstandings with the Misses Blount in 1718 and other years. A group of undatable Blount letters is placed here as possibly falling early in 1720 when Pope was in London, and when some of the group seem to have been written. Pope was presently again at work trying to aid the Blounts financially by speculation in South Sea stock.

your Brother, as much as I have Spirits left to be piqu'd at any one: And I promise you I will prove it, by doing every thing I can in your Service. | I am sincerely | Madam | Your most faithful | Servant | A. Pope

Address: To | Mrs Teresa Blount

POPE *to* TERESA BLOUNT   [1720?]
Mapledurham

Dear Madam,—I am agreeably waked by your billet, & shall be extreamly pleasd, & obligd to you both, if you will give me this Evening. If in this you sacrifice any other Company, it is really too much, & I beg you to add them to ours by appointing any body else to meet us. I'll call this morning however. My faithful Service to your Sister.

I am sorry I have not the pacquet, but if the inclos'd 7 will save you any trouble, I send 'em to be in the way. | I am, to both of you, | most truly your Servant | A. P.

Address: To Mrs Ter. Blount

POPE *to* [TERESA] BLOUNT[1]   [early 1720?]
Mapledurham

I take it kindly whenever you command any thing of me: I shall not want the Horses all day, being to have our party with Mrs Lepell. I wish to God I were as fitt to keep you company as those are who love you far less. Nothing can be so bitter to a tender mind as to displease most, where he would, (and ought in gratitude,) to please best. I am faithfully yours; unhappy enough to want a great deal of Indulgence; but sensible I deserve it less & less, from my disagreeable carriage. I am truly grateful to you for pardoning it so often, not able to know when I can overcome it, and only able to Wish, You could bear me better.

POPE *to* FRANCIS BIRD[2]   [1720?]
Arthur A. Houghton, Jr.

Mr. Bird: Pray forward the Monument, as above drawn, as soon as possible. Let it be entirely white Marble. And take a particular care

---

[1] Another undatable letter. Miss Lepell was staying with the Popes in Mar. 1720 for the benefit of her health. On 21 Apr. she was married to the Hon. John Hervey (after 1723 Lord Hervey), and the letter must antedate that event. Mrs. Lepell had been a friend for some time.

[2] Elwin's assumption that this letter referred to the monument to Craggs is due probably to the fact that the copy of *The Gentleman's Magazine*, liii (1783), 99, from which he took

that the Letters of the Inscription be rangd just as they are here, with
the Space of two Lines left void in the middle, and the Space of one
line at the End, in which Spaces there are future Insertions to be
made. Your care and Speed herein will very much oblige | Sir | Your
most humble Servant | A. POPE

Endorsement: Mr. Pope's Directions in | his own Handwriting for | his
Father's Monument.

*POPE *to* FORD[1]   5 *January* 1719/20

A. Merivale
                                               Twick'nham. Jan: 5th 1719.
Finding myself unexpectedly ingagd two or three days longer in the
Country, than I proposed when I saw you last: I beg the favour of
you not to appoint Sir William Stapylton till the beginning of the next
week, when I'l certainly be with you. If you have alredy sent a note
to Jervas's, be so kind as to inform me by Post, & If it be necessary
I'll come up as soon as I receive it. I have nothing to add, but that
your Glass pens write very well, & that the best use I can ever make
of any Pen, is to tell you how sincerely & affectionately I shall always
be | Dear Sir | Your faithfull & obedient | Servant | A. Pope

Address: To | Cha. Ford, Esqr. at Mr. | Hoyes's in Pall-Mall | present

CONGREVE *to* POPE[2]   20 *January* [1719/20]

Homer MSS. Add. 4808
                                               Surry street Jan: 20
I return you a thousand thanks for your letter about spaw water.
Dr Arbuthnot has orderd me at present to drink bath water. So I
Cannot expressly say when I shall want the spaw but if the person

his text, lacked the plate (see frontispiece). The plate is taken from *The Gentleman's Magazine*
because the original letter, fouled by folding, is in a less perfect condition. The monument was
executed as Pope directed, and the vacant spaces commemorate his mother and himself. To
indicate his own relation to the monument Pope required the addition of only two words:
et sibi.
    The date of the letter is uncertain: it should have been written shortly after his settlement
in Twickenham, and must antedate his difficulty with Lady Kneller over Sir Godfrey's
monument in the summer of 1725.
    1 Printed from a transcript kindly made by the owner. Pope's acquaintance with Sir
William Stapylton is not elsewhere noted.
    2 The year is uncertain. Pope had hoped to finish the *Iliad* before Christmas of 1719, but
his health was bad. On the verso of this note (ff. 192–3) is a part of Book XXIV. A letter
from John Hughes dated 22 Jan., without year, follows on ff. 195–6, and certainly dates
from 1719/20. Hence probably this from Congreve is 1720.

mentiond by you imports any quantity for himself at any time I shall
be glad to know of it. I am sorry You did not keep your Word in
letting me see You a second time. I am | always Dear Sir Your Most
Obedient | humble servant Wm Congreve

Address [apparently for this letter on fol. 193*v*]: To | Mr Pope | at his house
in | Twit'nam |

Postmarks: 20/IA PENY POST PAYD

---

*POPE *to* JOHN HUGHES*[1]   22 *January* [1719/20]

1772 (Duncombe)

Twickenham, Jan. 22 [1719/20]

Your letter found me, as I have long been, in a state of health almost
as bad as that you complain of; and indeed what makes me utterly
incapable of attending to any poetical task, even that of Homer. This
minute too I can scarce return you the civility of an answer, being in
the full operation of a vomit I have taken. I can only say, with sincerity, I am heartily concerned for your illness, and the more uneasy
with my own, in that it hinders me from serving you. I truly wish you
health and life, to enjoy that reputation and those advantages which
so much ingenuity, joined with so much virtue, deserves. As soon as
I am able to be in town, I will wait on you with the play, in which,
and in every thing else, I wish you all success. I am, dear Sir, Your
faithful and most obedient servant, | A. Pope.

JOHN HUGHES *to* POPE[2]   22 *January* [1719/20]

Homer MSS. Add. 4808

I am very sorry to hear of your ill health, & that my Message came
so unseasonably, as to give you so much trouble to answer it. I hope
by your mentioning your coming to town that You are on the mending
Hand, & that the Spring coming on will be favourable to You. If you
shoud not come in a Day or two I must beg your Return of the Copy,
which is much wanted, the time of acting drawing very near. Your
not being in a Condition to supply me with a Prologue is a great
Dissappointment to me, but I shoud much rather chuse that my Play
shoud want this Advantage, than put you to any trouble at present

---

[1] The date here may be supplied by Duncombe from Hughes's reply written on the same
day. *The Siege of Damascus*, Hughes's most famous play, was first acted 17 Feb. 1719/20.
See the next letter and those of 18 and 26 Feb.
[2] See the letter immediately preceding, to which this is obviously a reply.

which may be prejudicial to you, being with a true Respect Dear Sir |
Your most obedient humble | Servant | J Hughes

Red lyon Street Holborn | against East Street
    22. Jan. 1719.
Address [apparently for this letter on fol. 195*v*]: To | Alexander Pope Esq; |
    at his House at | Twickenham | Middx
Postmark: 23/IA

POPE *to* JOHN HUGHES   [*January* 1719/20]
1772 (Duncombe)

I return you the play sooner than I am willing to part with what I
like so extremely well, because you press it. Upon my word, I think
it every way worthy of you, and make not the least doubt but the
world will do you the justice you deserve in the acceptation of it:
I continue very much out of order, but must be forced to be in town
(well or ill) some days this week, upon indispensable affairs; when I
will wait upon you, and tell you my sincere thoughts, none of which
is more sincere than that I am truly | Your most obliged and | faithful
servant, | A. Pope.

MRS. POPE *to* HER SON[1]   [26 *January* 1719/20?]
Homer MSS. Add. 4808
                                        a letter from your Sister

My Deare,—Just now is Come and gone Mr mannock and Charls
Rackitt[2] to take his leeve of us, but being nothing in itt doe not send it,
he will not faile to Cole here one friday morning, and take Ceare to
Cearrie itt to mr Thomas Doncaster he shall dine wone day with
Mrs Dune in Ducke Street but the day will be unsirton, soe I thinck
You had better to send itt to me, he will not faile to Cole here, that is
mr mannock, Your Sister is very well but Your brother is not, There
Mr Blunt of mapill Durom is ded the Same day that mr Ingilfild died,
my Sirvis to mrs Blunts, and all that aske of me, I hope to here from

---

[1] The position of this letter in the Homer MSS. (f. 194*v*) indicates the end of 1719 or
very early 1720 as its date. It is one of the latest letters used in the *Iliad*. Thomas Hearne
in his *Collections*, vii. 92 and 107, records information to the effect that Charles Englefield
of Whiteknights died suddenly on Thursday, 21 Jan. 1719/20. The following Tuesday is
assumed to be the date of this letter. The report from Mapledurham was probably an error.
No such death has been discovered.
    One must not judge the social graces of any lady of Mrs. Pope's age by orthography.
Spelling was becoming standardized in her day; it was not so in her childhood.
[2] Charles Rackett is Pope's brother-in-law, and Mr. Mannock is probably the friend,
William Mannock, mentioned in Mrs. Rackett's will later and supposed to be the source of
such of Spence's *Anecdotes* as are signed 'Mr. Mannick'. Thomas Doncaster is doubtless the
old lady's variant of Dancastle.

You and that you are well, which is my dalye prayres, this with my blessing I am | Your loveing mother | Ed Pope

tuesday 12 a Clock

POPE *to* [MARTHA?] BLOUNT[1]   [*January* 1720]

Mapledurham

Dear Madam,—I find upon coming to town, that Mrs Robinson's Tickets are not giv'n out till to morrow. I hope this notice will arrive in time, before you are engag'd otherwise.

If you'll give this Bearer your Exchequer Orders for 500*l.* I'll get them Registerd, and the Interest receivd: this being a proper time to send 'em to the Exchequer.

I heartily wish you all the amusements & pleasures I must be (for a time at least) deprivd of. I beg you to think me not the worst of your Friends, who after so many Mistakes, and so many Misfortunes, am resolved to continue unalterably | Madam | Yours. A. P.

POPE *to* PRIOR[2]   [*February* 1719/20]

Longleat Prior Papers, vii

Sir,—I can find nothing to be objected or amended in what you favor'd me with, Unless you shou'd think the first Speech you put into your own mouth a little too long. It is certainly no Fault, & I don't know whether I should speak of it; but as a proof that I would, if possibly I was able, find something like a fault, to show my zeal, & to have the vanity of pretending, like Damon himself, to have Advis'd you. Pray accept my thanks for the Sight of 'em, & think me much more Pleasd than Vain (tho a little of both) to be | Your most faithful affecti|onate, humble Servant | A. Pope.

The Duke of Bucks desires to be of Our Party on Munday sennight.

Address: To | Mr Prior, in | Dukestreet, | Westminster.

Endorsement: Februy 1719/20

[1] The chronological placing of this letter is due to the assumption that it refers to a benefit for Mrs. Robinson of 2 Feb. 1720 at Drury Lane, where she had been perhaps the principal singer between the acts during the season. (This information is furnished by Professor Emmett Avery.) The reference to the Exchequer order would fit this speculative season also.

[2] The endorsed date is not in Pope's hand. The letter was printed in 1779 in *Gent. Mag.* xlix. 232. Elwin notes: 'This letter is described in the Index of Prior's Letters (Harley MS.), as "From Mr. A. Pope, returning the poem of Conversation with his opinion thereon." "Conversation" was published in 1720.'

POPE *to* CARYLL   [*February* 1719/20]
Add. 28618

Your[1] desire that I should tell you some news of the *beau monde* or from Parnassus, could not be expressed at a time when I am less capable to comply with it. I have not the least knowledge of any poetical affairs; I have not seen a play these twelve months, been at no assembly, opera, or public place whatever. I am infamously celebrated as an inoffensive unenvied writer, even by Curll himself. My friends have given me over, as to all wit & pleasure. I am the common topick of ridicule as a country putt; and if (once a month) I trudge to town in a horseman's coat, I am stard at, every question I ask, as the most ignorant of all rustics. But to tell you the whole truth, besides all this, I confess my unpoliteness proceeds directly from choice. I have lain under an impediment to all amusement and pleasure these many months, namely very great indispositions and such an alteration in my constitution as rather deserves to be called a ruin than a revolution. I have had no appetite or digestion a vast while, I have perpetual vomitings and nervous distempers upon me, with a dejection of spirits that has totally taken away everything (if I ever had anything) which could be called vivacity or cheerfulness. I have not half the taste I once had of any thing pleasing in this world, and those things that trouble me, I have double the satisfaction of. I was not a little troubled for poor Mr Englefield.[2] I have lost one or two more that I loved. I find few left that are worth loving. Yet I assure you if ever I see a virtue sprung up, or a good action done, it is the only thing that makes me content to live. I preserve with great constancy all the regards I ever had to my friends, and in particular to yourself. I rarely see any of 'em, but often recollect there are some such in the world, and that recollection renders me the better satisfied to be in it. I am very sincerely a well-wisher to your whole family, and at all times | Dear sir | Yours most faithfully | A: P:

POPE *to* [TERESA] BLOUNT[3]   [*c.* 2 *February* 1719/20?]
Mapledurham

Dear Madam,—Understanding that you are yet unfurnishd of a Ticket, I beg you will oblige me in the acceptance of this. I had sent it before, if I had not understood that you were sure of one. Pray let me make use of this opportunity of assuring you I am as much & as truly as ever I was | Your most faithfull & | ever obedient Servant | A. Pope

---

[1] Your] You *MS.*

[2] On the death of Charles Englefield see Mrs. Pope to her son [26 Jan. 1719/20].

[3] On the assumption that the ticket in question is for Mrs. Robinson's benefit, the letter falls about the date of that event—2 Feb. If it refers, as it well might, to a lottery ticket, it might fall in any of several years.

JAMES ECKERSALL *to* POPE[1]   [6–13 *February* 1719/20]

Homer MSS. Add. 4808

FRAGMENT

[   ] at £4 per Cent, and find they are 2 per Cent [   ] The Price
of South Sea has Continued to Ris[e since] I saw you, and does not
Vary above one or t[wo points] above and below £170. if you wou'd
have [stock at] about that price I will take the best Oppert[unity] to
get it at the lowest, but shall do Noth[ing till I] know your Resolution.

My Wife Joynes with me in kind Services to [your Mother] and
I must not forget Good Old Nurse; I [hope the] Country Air, Regular
hours, and the Care [of the] Old Gentlewoman will Re-establish your
H[ealth and] Strengthen your Constitution, which will [afford] great
Pleasure to all Your Friends, and pe[rticularly] to him that is with
Great Affection and Sin[cerity] | Your Most Obedient h[umble]
Servant | James [Eckersall]

*POPE *to* JAMES ECKERSALL[2]   14 *February* 1719/20

Arthur A. Houghton, Jr.

Feb. 14th

You are too Scrupulous in asking my Consent to any thing which
Mrs Eckersall has a mind to. To whose Inclination if you joyn your
own Consent, I assure you, you have mine. Therfore I leave the time
& price entirely to your judgment, or to her Liking. When I put the
Lottery orders into your hands, I knew they were at a discount. Pray
believe I am fully pleas'd with adventuring in so good company, &
shall not be displeas'd, whatever happens, any other wise than if it
makes the Lady think herself unfortunate in being Yok'd with a Poet.
I am hers & | Dear Sir | Your most faithful humble | Servant | A. Pope.

Address: To | James Eckersall, Esqr | with speed

---

[1] The letter, torn along the top and the right margin, is in Eckersall's hand, and the date
is determined from the fact that the second week in February is the only period in the
fantastic history of South Sea stock when the price hovered about 170. Since later letters
(14 and 21 Feb.) deal with unsold lottery orders, it is possible that here the first sentence
really read: 'I have tried to sell the lottery orders at £4 per Cent . . .'

One must note that, while in this and following letters of this period the subjects are
financial, there was a real friendship between Pope and his mother and the Eckersalls.
Eckersall, of Drayton, had been Clerk of the Kitchen and Gentleman Usher to Queen Anne
(so Elwin notes). He died in 1753, aged 74.

[2] This hardly seems a reply to the letter of 6–13 Feb., but it may well be a reply to a note
dispatched shortly after that, and now lost. It seems to fit a sequence between that letter and
that to Eckersall of 21 Feb. The dating is highly speculative.

POPE *to* JOHN HUGHES[1]   18 *February* 1719/20

1772 (Duncombe)

Twickenham, Feb. 18, 1719–20.

I have been much concerned not to have waited upon you as I designed, since you obliged me with your play. I am since much more troubled to hear of the continuance of your illness. Would to God you might live as long, as, I am sure, the reputation of your tragedy must! I am a fellow-sufferer with you, in not being able to see it played, having been and still being too much indisposed to go to any public place. But I could be extremely glad, some particular friends of mine had that pleasure I cannot enjoy: you would highly favour me in letting three or four ladies have a side-box, who have sent into the country to me, upon information that the boxes are disposed of by you. I am sorry to give you this trouble, when perhaps, for your health's sake, you should not have a moment's disturbance, and I could not send sooner, at this distance. Pray think I wish you all the success you deserve, and all the health you want.

I am, dear Sir, | Your most affectionate humble servant, | A. Pope.

POPE *to* JAMES ECKERSALL[2]   21 [*February* 1719/20]

The Historical Society of Pennsylvania

I daily hear such reports of advantages to be gaind by one project or other in the Stocks, that my Spirit is Up with double Zeal, in the desires of our trying to enrich ourselves. I assure you my own Keeping a Coach & Six is not more in my head than the pleasure I shall take in seeing Mrs Eckersall in her Equipage. To be serious, I hope you have sold the Lottery orders, that the want of ready mony may be no longer an Impediment to our buying in the Stock, which was very unlucky at that time. I hear the S. Sea fell since, & should be glad we were in: I also hear there is considerably to be got by Subscribing to the new African Stock, Pray let us do something or other, which you judge the fairest Prospect, I am equal as to what Stock, so you do but like it. Let but Fortune favor us, & the World will be sure to admire our Prudence. If we fail, let's e'en keep the mishap to ourselves: But tis Ignominious (in this Age of Hope and Golden Mountains) not to

---

[1] Mr. Hughes died the night before this letter was written, aged 42.—Duncombe, 1772.

[2] The year is easily assumed, and the dating at the end of the letter fixes the Sunday in question as either February or August. Since on the whole South Sea stock was rising sharply in February (from 137 to 182 in the first three weeks of the month) and, though absurdly high in August, tending to fall (900 to 800 approximately) at that time, the earlier month is the more plausible. In no other months of the year did Sunday fall on the 21st.

Venture. I am very truly your Lady's and | Sr | Your most obligd hum|ble Servant | A. Pope.

Sunday the 21st

Address: To James Eckersall Esqr | present

POPE *to* JABEZ HUGHES¹   26 *February* 1719/20

Arthur A. Houghton, Jr.

Febr. 26. 1719/20.

Sir,—I can't omit the acknowledgment I really think I owe your great Civility, especially at so melancholy, & affecting a moment, as that of your worthy Brother's death must have been to you. Indeed even his common Acquaintance must have known enough of him, to regret his Loss; and I most heartily condole with you upon it. I believe I am further obliged to you for his Play; which I rec'd yesterday, & read over again, with more Concern & Sorrow than I ever felt in the reading any Tragedy. The real loss of a Good Man may be calld a Distress to the World, & ought to affect us more than any Feign'd, or Ancient Distress, how finely drawn soever. I'm glad of an Occasion to give you under my hand this Testimony both how Excellent I think this Work to be, & how Excellent I thought the Author. I am with my hearty thanks to you, | Sir | Your most obligd & most hum|ble Servant | A. Pope.

Address: To Mr Jabez Hughes, | at Mr Hughes's house over | against East-street, in | Red Lyon Street.

Postmark: PENY POST PAYD [blurred except the first word]

Endorsement: The Essay on Man

POPE *to* JAMES ECKERSALL   2 *March* [1719/20]

Add. 32567 (Mitford transcript)

I give you this Second trouble (tho' I am ashamd of the first) to desire if you have not actually yet disposd of the Lottery orders, to let me have em sent before eleven or twelve to morrow morning to Mr Jervas's (your's & all if you please) for I believe I can sell 'em, or do what is equivalent. I'll add no more, but that my Mother & I joyn in our good Wishes for Mrs Eckersalls & your Welfare. I am always | Dear Sir | Your most obligd & most faithful | Servant   A. Pope.

Twickenham | March 2d | Wednesday Morning.

Address: To James Eckersall Esqr | with Speed.

---

¹ Jabez was the younger brother of the late dramatist. Jabez (d. 1731) was chiefly a translator. (*DNB*.)

AARON HILL *to* POPE[1]   [1720]

1720 (From the Preface to Hill's *Creation*)   •

Sir,—I am under the greatest Confusion I ever felt in my Life, to find
by your Letter, that I have been guilty of a Crime, which I can never
forgive *Myself*, were it for no other Reason, than that *You* have forgiven it. I might have learnt from your Writings the Extent of your
Soul, and shou'd have concluded it impossible for the Author of those
elevated Sentiments, to sink beneath them in his Practice.

You are generously moderate, when you mitigate my Guilt, and
miscall it a *Credulity*; 'twas a passionate, and most unjustifiable *Levity*,
and must still have remain'd unpardonable, whatever Truth might
have been found in its mistaken Occasion.

What stings me most, in my Reflection on this Folly, is, that I
know not how to *atone* it; I will endeavour it, however; being always
asham'd, when I have attempted to revenge an Injury, but never more
proud, than when I have begg'd Pardon for an Error.

If you needed an Inducement to the strengthening your Forgiveness, you might gather it from these two Considerations; *First*, The
Crime was almost a Sin against Conviction; for though not happy
enough to know you personally, your *Mind* had been my intimate
Acquaintance, and regarded with a kind of partial Tenderness, that
made it a little less than Miracle, that I attempted to offend you. A
sudden Warmth, to which, by Nature, I am much too liable, transported me to a Condition, I shall best describe in *Shakespear*'s Sense,
somewhere or other.

> Blind in th' obscuring Mist of heedless Rage,
> I've rashly shot my Arrows o'er a House,
> And hurt my Brother.———

A *Second* Consideration is, the Occasion you have gather'd to
punish my Injustice, with more than double Sharpness, by your
Manner of receiving it. The Armour of your Mind is temper'd so
divinely, that my mere *Human* Weapons have not only fail'd to pierce,
but broke to pieces in rebounding. You meet Assaults, like some expert

---

[1] In apology for his attack on Pope in the Preface to *The Northern Star* (1718) Hill prefixed to *The Creation* (1720) 'a Preface to Mr. Pope, concerning the Sublimity of the Ancient
Hebrew Poetry and a material and obvious Defect in the English'. Embedded in this Preface
is this letter, a 'duplicate' of one sent to Pope, possibly in 1718, but more probably shortly
before publication of the Preface of 1720. Pope's error in 1718 had been his doubt whether
a poem glorifying the Tsar (who was 'the Northern star') would please at a moment when
Russia seemed to be lining up with Sweden and the Pretender. Hill had put down this doubt
to professional jealousy.

This is the first of Hill's somewhat tedious correspondence with Pope. Its flattery is
typically excessive and doubtfully sincere. Hill had, on the other hand, a realistic appreciation
of Pope's lapses in behaviour.

Arabian, who, declining any Use of his own Javelin, arrests those which come against him, in the Fierceness of their Motion, and overcomes his Enemies, by detaining their own Weapons. 'Tis a noble Triumph you now exercise, by the Superiority of your Nature; and while I see you looking down upon the Distance of my Frailty, I am forc'd to *own* a Glory, which I *envy* you; and am quite asham'd of the poor Figure I am making, in the bottom of the Prospect. I *feel*, I am sure, Remorse, enough to satisfy you for the Wrong, but to *express* it, wou'd, I think, exceed even *your own* Power.

> Yours, whose sweet Songs can rival *Orpheus'* Strain,
> And force the wondring Woods to dance again,
> Make moving Mountains hear your pow'rful Call,
> And headlong Streams hang list'ning in their Fall.[1]

No Words can be worthy to come after these; I will therefore hasten to tell you, that I am, and will ever be, with the greatest Truth and Respect, | Sir, | Your Most Humble, | and Most Obedient Servant, | A. Hill.

POPE *to* HILL[2]   2 *March* [1719/20]

1751 (Hill)
                                                              March 2. 1731.

Sir,—I am extremely pleas'd with the Favour you have done me in sending me your Poem, and the more, as it gives me the Opportunity of assuring you I never did, or meant you, the least Injury; in which I should have fully satisfy'd you long since, had you ask'd me the Question. I remember, Mr. *Lintot* shew'd me a Piece of yours, of which (he said) you desir'd my Opinion: I was just then in a great Hurry, going a Journey out of Town upon Business for a few Days; and therefore told him I would call for it in a Day or two, to read carefully: However, I cast my Eye on some Parts of it, which I lik'd, and told him so. This was all, to the best of my Memory, that pass'd between us; and you may imagine it was some Surprize to me when I saw your Preface a very short time after. I think it incumbent on any well-meaning Man, to acquit himself of an ill-grounded Suspicion in another, who perhaps means equally well, and is only too credulous. I am sincerely so far from resenting this Mistake, that I am more displeas'd, at your thinking it necessary to treat me so much in a Style

---

[1] Adapted from Pope's 'Summer', ll. 81–84.

[2] Apparently this is a reply to the letter in the Preface to Hill's *Creation* (1720). The letter was printed in the *Collection of Letters . . . Written by Alexander Pope, Esq., and Other Ingenious Gentlemen to the late Aaron Hill* (1751) and reprinted by Bowles, Roscoe, and in the later Warton editions. Elwin corrected the error in the year date, made obvious by the postscript.

of Compliment as you do in your Letter. I will say nothing of the Poem you favour me with, for fear of being in the wrong; but I am sure, the Person who is capable of writing it, can need no Man to judge it. I am, with all Respect, | Sir, | Your most obedient | humble Servant, | A. Pope.

I receiv'd yours but four Days since, it being directed to *Chiswick,* where I have not liv'd this Twelve-month.

POPE *to* CARYLL   3 *March* [1719/20]

Add. 28618

Twitenham. March the 3.

I cannot but own you show yourself truly a Christian by your forgiving epistle, considering my manifold and really inexcusable offences. The truth is I have written to no body since I have so much to do, to write to everybody. This looks a little like a riddle, but you'll solve it when you reflect a poet writes to everybody in his labours, and pleasures I have had none. If I could have found time for any, I assure you one of the first had been to see you at Grinsted. I have yet a fortnight's work with Homer,[1] a vast deal with masons and gardeners,[2] and a deal of what I think more troublesome than all, in the management of my money affairs; for these new projects of government have in a manner overturned all my settlements.[3] Among the rest that unfortunately want ready money at this time, your humble servant is not the least in need, therefore your memorandum as to the interest is not unreasonable (tho' I myself had really forgot there was such a thing in the world between us) I would have you think, when I can forget to correspond with you on things far more pleasant & valuable to me than money, such as used to make the subject of our letters, I must not be in a capacity of remembring such trifles. However (that you may not think me so much a hermit tho' I'm never in town) pray inclose a bill for it on Mr Wright,[4] or any goldsmith you use.

[1] The last two volumes of the *Iliad* appeared 12 May 1720.

[2] A portico, possibly the grotto, and some enlargements of the villa were under way.

[3] The new projects of the government concerned the rival plans of the Bank of England (presented 27 Jan. and 1 Feb.) and of the South Sea Company—which last won out. Sir Robert Walpole favoured the project of the Bank, and so, after the South Sea panic, became the country's most respected financial expert.

[4] There exists in the possession of Mr. H. B. Vanderpoel an order from Caryll to Mr. Wright, Goldsmith in Covent Garden, to pay Mr. Alex. Pope 'the sum of eleven pounds'. It is dated 28 Feb. 1720 [1721], and represents the annual interest on a bond paid to Pope by Caryll for many years.

POPE *to* [TERESA] BLOUNT[1]   [6 *or* 13 *March* 1720]

Mapledurham

Sunday

Madam,—This is just to let you know, that being again in the City yesterday, I was obliged to stay so late, that I could not go home. So that if you have any thing to say to me, here I am; & here shall stay, till the matter of the annuities is decided; on purpose to do as you'l commission me. I expected some answer to my last.

Your other business is at last brought about. I have borrowed mony upon ours & Mr Eckersals Orders, and bought 500ll stock S. Sea, at 180. It is since risen to 184. I wish us all good luck in it, & am very glad to have done what you seemd so desirous of.

I am | Your most obedient & | Faithful Servant | A. Pope

My faithful Service | to your Mother and | Sister.

POPE *to* LADY MARY WORTLEY MONTAGU[2]

16 *March* [1719/20]

The Pierpont Morgan Library

Madam.—You received, I suppose, the Epistle Sir Godfrey dictated to me, which (abating some few flowers) was word for word. My own Concern that you should be setled in my neighborhood has since put me upon farther enquiryes, and I find there is a pretty good house in the Town, opposite to that which my Lord Will Pawlet has taken: Tis the same that Lord Coventry lately had. If Mr Wortley wou'd come & see it, he'l know all the particulars which I'm not able to give an exact account of, having sent you this notice the moment I heard of it. Tho still that which I believe you both would like best, is the house in the field I spoke to him about, & which I think the prettiest situated Thing imaginable.

---

[1] Pope has bought South Sea Stock at 180—a price reached first (according to reports in *The Weekly Packet*) on 4 Mar. 1720. The stock was now sky-rocketing, and reached 184 once or twice before the middle of the month, after which date it rose rapidly. Since the stock could be bought for 180 as late as Friday the 11th, this letter dates from either 6 or 13 Mar. (both Sundays), presumably the 13th.

[2] The year of this letter is perhaps doubtful. Mar. 1718/19 seems too early, since Pope himself was hardly established in Twickenham at that time. On the other hand, Sir Godfrey's message may be that embodied in the letter from Pope to Mr. Wortley Montagu beginning 'I write this from Sir Godfrey's own mouth'—here placed doubtfully in [Sept. 1719]. The fact that Gilbert, 4th Earl of Coventry, died 27 Oct. 1719 suggests that the house he 'lately had' might be available in the spring of 1720. One assumes that Pope's friends having hitherto leased a house are now ready to purchase.

Lord Bathurst told me you had given orders that the book of Eclogues[1] should be trusted to my hands to return it to you. I'm sensible of the obligation & had been the Faithfull Ambassador between you, had I not been forcd to leave the Town the minute he told me of it. I can't perform impossibilitys, therfore will not pretend to tell you the Esteem with which I always have been, & am | Dear Madam | Your most faithfull | humble Servant | A. Pope.

Twitnam, | March 16.

Address: To the Right Honble the Lady | Mary Wortley, in the Piazza | in Coventgarden, | London.

Postmark: 17/MR

Endorsement: Mr Pope.

*POPE *to* JAMES ECKERSALL   [21 *March* 1719/20]

Maine Historical Society

Munday.[2] 7 aclock | in the morning

I was extremely obligd to your Goodness in partaking my Infirmities, & enduring them so well the last time I saw you. I continu'd very ill till next morning, & then calld at your door (being in haste upon business) but you was not stirring. Soon after, before I left the town that day I was advised to make use of the Rise of the S. Sea Stock which was got above 200. & sell, then, and wait to buy again on the Coming of the Bill on Munday or Tuesday, when they expected some Ruffle on the debate. I left my desires with a Friend who was going into the City, being hugely joy'd at the thought of having got Mrs Eckersall at least some Coffee mony, notwithstanding all our rubs & impediments for want of getting rid of the Lottery orders (which still lye without the least hope that I can see of being sold) But I am now alarmd & vex'd again, on hearing of the prodigious & unexpected rise on Saturday night, not many hours after I gave my Commission. I have sent to my man (who was gone out of town for the Sunday) and can't tell yet whether he has sold it, or not, but am very uneasy about it. If he has, I shall be unfeignedly much more sorry to have got your Lady but fifty pound or thereabouts (when I hop'd, at least, to have gott her a Coach & six) much more sorry I say for that, than for my own part of the Loss. I will send, (or bring you if I am well enough) the first notice I have, & am most sincerely and | (with my

---

[1] The Eclogues are Lady Mary's *Court Poems*, published by Curll in 1716, and transcribed prettily by Pope and bound for her ladyship in red morocco. See Pope to Lady Mary in the autumn of 1717 (here, i. 441).

[2] The only 'Munday' when South Sea had supposedly got above 200 was the one bracketed as date here. On the 19th it passed 200, but if Pope's orders were too promptly carried out, he must have regretted it, for on the 21st stock opened at 187, and by the end of the week it had reached 300.

Mother's and my hearty respects to Mrs Eckersall) Dear Sir | Your most affectionate obligd Servant | A. Pope

Twickenham.

Address: To | James Eckersall Esqr | to be left at Mr Jervas's in | Cleveland court.

POPE *to* BROOME   24 *March* 1720

Elwin–Courthope, viii. 43

Twickenham, March 24, 1720.

Instead of the concern you express that we did not finish our index,[1] you should have told me how glad you were, and what thanks you gave to God for your signal deliverance from my hands and evil doings. I hope you are safely arrived at the haven of all men's hopes, the arms of your lady. I really envy her your company; to say more would look sinful. [2]I am seriously sensible of the kind expressions you use to me, and be assured I shall never forget the long and laborious things you undertook and discharged for my sake. It is really as reasonable that you should be congratulated on the finishing of my Homer, as I myself. I have had the flowery walks of imagination to expatiate in. It is a spirited and lively task, to be striving to raise oneself to the pitch of the most delightful of authors, while you have drudged in only removing the loads, and clearing the rubbish, heaped together by the negligence no less than by the industry of past pedants, whose very taste was generally so wrong, that they toiled most on what was least worth; and to undo what they raised, was the first thing to be done, in order to do anything to the purpose. As you had no share in the pleasant, and so large an one in the disagreeable part of the work, I think this to be acknowledged in the strongest terms, as it highly exalts the merit of your friendship to me, that your task was a task of so much more pains than even credit. It was Hercules in the stable of Augeas, when the same Hercules was capable of so many better and more glorious labours. I can say nothing that equals my sense of it, in short, and therefore shall say very little; but if you would tell me in what manner you have a mind I should mention it, I will gladly do it.

I beg you will not interpret my silence at any time as any forget-fulness or neglect of you. Indeed, my whole life is a scene of continued hurry, and spent in dependencies and civilities, of which, in this glut of company, there is no end. I hope, as indeed I have long hoped, to

---

[1] The indexes to the *Iliad* were elaborate. Broome's long help is here cordially recognized.

[2] The passage beginning here and running to the end of the paragraph (omitting the last half of the last sentence, beginning with 'but') is quoted by Broome in his letter to Fenton, 15 June [1728]. The rather generous conclusion of the paragraph Broome in his anger suppressed.

have some leisure soon, to collect myself again, and recompose the scatterings of a mind almost distracted by a thousand things, which it is impossible you should have a notion of. Then I may hope to seem, what I really am, a more diligent friend, and more thoughtful of those I value and am obliged to, among which number, pray be always so just to reckon yourself.

I have never once been able since to see Mrs. Marriot, or any of her family. I will go in quest of them the next time I can get to town. I have been very ill, and am now constantly engaged at home in attending a lady I have a true friendship for, who is here in hopes of a recovery by our air from a dangerous illness,—Mrs. Lepell.[1] I can add no more, having broke from company to write this, than that I shall be ever your most faithful, affectionate servant.

My mother and old nurse always remember you.

†POPE *to* THE HON. MRS. H[ERVEY][2]   [1720]

1737

All the pleasure or use of familiar letters, is to give us the assurance of a friend's welfare; at least 'tis all I know, who am a mortal enemy and despiser of what they call fine letters. In this view I promise you, it will always be a satisfaction to me to write letters and to receive them from you; because I unfeignedly have your good at my heart, and am that thing, which many people make only a subject to display their fine sentiments upon, a Friend: which is a character that admits of little to be said, till something may be done. Now let me fairly tell you, I don't like your style: 'tis very pretty, therefore I don't like it; and if you writ as well as Voiture, I wou'd not give a farthing for such letters, unless I were to sell 'em to be printed. Methinks I have lost the Mrs. L* I formerly knew, who writ and talk'd like other people, (and sometimes better). You must allow me to say, you have not said a sensible word in all your letter, except where you speak of shewing kindness and expecting it in return: but the addition you make about

---

[1] Mrs. Lepell in Apr. was privately married to the Hon. John Hervey, younger brother of Pope's friend Carr, Lord Hervey. Upon the death of Carr in 1723 the younger brother became Baron Hervey of Ickworth. After 1730, if not before, he and Pope were hostile, and in 1733 were violently lampooning each other in verse and prose. Lady Hervey naturally supported her husband in the quarrel.

[2] The Roberts octavo of 1737 (1737 a) gives us the closest indication of the identity of the addressee of this letter. The indication occurs only in the Table of Contents, not in the heading of the letter; for only in this table is the initial of her name given. The mention in the letter of the 'lost' Mrs. L*, suggests that Pope's friend Molly Lepell is now lost as the wife of the Hon. John Hervey, son of the Earl of Bristol and later known as Lord Hervey, Pope's enemy. The marriage was at first secret, and the letter seems written shortly after it. If her quoted remark about 'being but two and twenty' is to be taken seriously, the year of the letter should be 1722, since Miss Lepell was born in 1700; but the remark need not be too literally taken.

your being but two and twenty, is again in the style of wit and abomination. To shew you how very unsatisfactorily you write, in all your letter you've never told me how you do? Indeed I see 'twas absolutely necessary for me to write to you, before you continu'd to take more notice of me, for I ought to tell you what you are to expect; that is to say, Kindness, which I never fail'd (I hope) to return; and not Wit, which if I want, I am not much concern'd, because judgment is a better thing; and if I had, I wou'd make use of it rather to play upon those I despis'd, than to trifle with those I loved. You see in short, after what manner you may most agreeably write to me: tell me you are my friend, and you can be no more at a loss about that article. As I have open'd my mind upon this to you, it may also serve for Mr. H— who will see by it what manner of letters he must expect if he corresponds with me. As I am too seriously yours and his servant to put turns upon you instead of good wishes, so in return I shou'd have nothing but honest plain how d'ye's and pray remember me's; which not being fit to be shown to any body for wit, may be a proof we correspond only for our selves, in meer friendlyness; as doth, God is my witness, Your very, &c.

POPE *to* CARYLL[1]   [*c.* 1 *May* 1720]
Add. 28618

I have been in uneasiness for your health for some time past, being informed by Lady Guldeford some weeks ago of your fit of the gout: The fever I heard nothing of till I received your own letter, and am truly concerned at the long suffering you must have had, as well as danger you have been in. I shall be heartily glad to hear that your recovery is perfected, as soon as you can allow me that satisfaction. Your note on Mr Wright was received, & I enclose, as you desire, an acquittance. The question you ask about the fair lady's gains, & my own, is not easily answered. There is no gain till the stock is sold, which neither theirs nor mine is. So that, instead of wallowing in money, we never wanted more for the uses of life, which is a pretty general case with most of the adventurers, each having put all the ready money they had into the stock. And our estate is an imaginary one only: one day we were worth two or three thousand, and the next not above 3 parts of the sum. For my own particular I have very little in; the ladies are much richer than I, but how rich (as you see) there's no telling by any certain rule of arithmetic,

Pauperis est numerare pecus.[2]

---

[1] The letter is plausibly dated from the remark about the publication of Homer 'next week'. The last two volumes of the *Iliad* appeared on 12 May.

[2] Ovid, *Metamorphoses*, xiii. 824.

I am a little scandalized that you should so much as send a thought after the gains & advantages of this world, who seem to me, and have seem[ed] so long, to be so fairly advanced in the superior prospects of another. For such an one to say he has been always on the loosing side, I think is a great impropriety of expression; and nothing would have taken away my objection, so effectually as what you confess in the next period of your letter, how much convinced you are of that *faiblesse de l'homme*, of which there is so fine a treatise among the *Essais de Morale.*[1]

I am sensible of the kindness of that expression, where you assure me of the concerns you partook from finding me under a depression of spirits by my last letters. Indeed, I have very ill health, and have fewer spirits to support such a state that I used to have formerly. It really doubles my indisposition when those of my friends partake them, to whom I wish all that I want; and the best cordial I could have in my own illnesses, would [be] to hear they were well & happy, as I shall always wish yourself, and your whole family. I am | Dear sir | yours, as of old, | A: Po:

My Homer will be delivered out next week. You'll see, by some laborious indexes, what has retarded it so long.

POPE *to* ROBERT DIGBY[2]   1 *May* 1720

1735

May 1, 1720.

You'll think me very full of my self, when after a long Silence (which however to say Truth has rather been employ'd to contemplate of you, than to forget you) I begin to talk of my own Works. I find it is in the Finishing a Book, as in concluding a Session of Parliament, one always thinks it will be very soon, and finds it very late. There are many unlook'd for Incidents to retard the clearing *any publick Account*, and so I see it is in mine. I have plagued myself, like great Ministers, with undertaking too much for one Man, and with a Desire of doing more than was expected from me, have done less than I ought.

For having design'd Four very laborious and uncommon sorts of Indexes to *Homer*, I'm forc'd, for want of time, to publish two only; the Design of which you will own to be pretty, tho' far from being fully executed. I've also been oblig'd to leave unfinish'd in my desk

---

[1] *Essais de Morale* (1671 ff.) were by Pierre Nicole under the pseudonym of Sieur de Chanteresne. Others of 'Messieurs de Port Royal' may have contributed. There were translations into English in 1677 and 1696.

[2] Published in all Pope's editions except 1735 a2. The significant textual revisions are noted below.

ls of two Essays, one on the *Theology* and *Morality* of *Homer*,
her on the *Oratory* of *Homer* and *Virgil*. So they must wait
e Editions, or perish; and (one way or other, no great Matter
labit Deus his quoque finem.[1]

k of you every day, I assure you, even without such good
Memorials of you as your Sisters, with whom I sometimes talk of you,
and find it one of the most agreeable of all subjects to them. My Lord
Digby must be perpetually remember'd by all who ever knew him, or
knew his Children. There needs no more than an acquaintance with
your Family, to make all Elder Sons wish they had Fathers to their
lives-end.[2]

I can't touch upon the subject of filial Love, without putting you
in mind of an old Woman,[3] who has a sincere, hearty, old-fashion'd
respect for you, and constantly blames her Son for not having writ to
you oftner, to tell you so.

I very much wish (but what signifies my wishing? my Lady *Scuda-
more* wishes, your Sisters wish) that you were with us, to compare the
beautiful Contraste this Season affords us, of the Town and the Country.
No Ideas you could form in the Winter can make you imagine what
Twickenham is ⌜(and what your Friend Mr. *Johnson* of *Twickenham*
is)⌝ in this ⌜warmer⌝ Season.[4] Our River glitters beneath an unclouded
Sun, at the same time that its Banks retain the Verdure of Showers:
Our Gardens are offering their first Nosegays; our Trees, like new
Acquaintance brought happily together, are stretching their Arms to
meet each other, and growing nearer and nearer every Hour: The
Birds are paying their thanksgiving Songs for the new Habitations
I have made 'em: My Building rises high enough to attract the eye
and curiosity of the Passenger from the River, where, upon beholding
a Mixture of Beauty and Ruin, he enquires what House is falling, or
what Church is rising? So little taste have our common Tritons of
Vitruvius; whatever delight the ⌜true, unseen,⌝[5] poetical Gods of the
River may take, in reflecting on their Streams my *Tuscan* Porticos,
or *Ionic* Pilasters.

But (to descend from all this Pomp of Style) the best account ⌜I can
give⌝[6] of what I am building, is, that it will afford me a few pleasant
Rooms for such a Friend as yourself, or a cool situation for an hour

---

[1] *Aeneid*, i. 199.
[2] Lord Digby outlived several of his children, including the son to whom Pope is writing.
[3] Mrs Pope.
[4] Bracketed phrases were omitted in the quarto and folio of 1737. 'Mr. Johnson' is James
Johnstone (1655–1737), former joint Secretary for Scotland under King William. He was a
Scot and a Whig, and his taste in neither gardening, poetry nor politics pleased Pope. See
the affair of Mallet's play in letters of Dec. 1730. Pope mentioned Johnstone once or twice
in his poems ('Moral Essay I', l. 158; 'Imitation of Spenser').
[5] Bracketed words were omitted in editions of 1737–42.
[6] These words also were omitted in editions of 1737–42.

or two for *Lady Scudamore,* when she will do me the Honour (at this Publick House on the Road) to drink her own Cyder.[1]

The Moment I am writing this, I am surprized with the account of the Death of a Friend of mine; which makes all I have here been talking of, a meer Jest! Buildings, Gardens, Writings, Pleasures, Works, of whatever stuff Man can raise! none of them (God knows) capable of advantaging a Creature that is mortal, or of satisfying a Soul that is Immortal! Dear Sir, I am | Your most faithful Servant.

‡POPE *to* FENTON[2]   5 *May* [1720]

[1]737

May 5.

Sir,—I had not omitted answering yours of the 18th of last month, but out of a desire to give you some certain and satisfactory account, which way, and at what time, you might take your journey. I am now commissioned to tell you, that Mr. Craggs will expect you on the rising of the Parliament, which will be as soon as he can receive you in the manner he would receive a man *de belles Lettres,* that is, in tranquillity and full leisure. I dare say your way of life (which, in my taste will be the best in the world, and with one of the best men in the world) must prove highly to your contentment. And I must add, it will be still the more a joy to me, as I shall reap a peculiar advantage from the good I shall have done in bringing you together,[3] by seeing it in my own neighbourhood. Mr. Craggs has taken a house close by mine, whither he proposes to come in three weeks: In the mean time I heartily invite you to live with me; where a frugal and philosophical diet for a time, may give you a higher relish of that elegant way of life you will enter into after. I desire to know by the first post how soon I may hope for you?

I am a little scandalized at your complaint that your time lies heavy on your hands, when the muses have put so many good materials into your head to employ them.[4] As to your question, what am I doing? I answer, just what I have been doing some years, my duty; secondly

---

[1] Bowles informs us that Scudamore cider was made from an apple called by that name.

[2] In 1737 b the year is 1717; other editions have no year added to 5 May. But Fenton became Craggs's instructor in 1720, at which time Craggs took the house in Twickenham. In 1717 Pope was at Chiswick. For further complications see the letter to Jonathan Richardson placed in Feb.–Mar. 1732—and the footnotes to it, here iii. 270.

[3] Mr. Craggs had had no learned education: he wanted to improve himself in knowledge of that kind, and desired Mr. Pope to chuse him out a polite scholar, by whose conversation and instruction he might improve himself in letters. Mr. Pope recommended Mr. Fenton: but Mr. Craggs's untimely death prevented both from receiving the benefits of this connexion. —Warburton, 1751.

[4] The idleness of Fenton, who was left even more idle when Craggs died within twelve months, suggests a situation auspicious for the project of translating the *Odyssey.* Fenton very likely did as much on Pope's edition of Shakespeare as he did on the *Odyssey.*

relieving my self with necessary amusements, or exercises, which shall serve me instead of physic as long as they can; thirdly, reading till I am tired; and lastly, writing when I have no other thing in the world to do, or no friend to entertain in company.

My mother is, I thank God, the easier if not the better, for my cares; and I am the happier in that regard, as well as in the consciousness of doing my best. My next felicity is in retaining the good opinion of honest men, who think me not quite undeserving of it; and in finding no injuries from others hurt me, as long as I know my self. I will add the sincerity with which I act towards ingenious and undesigning men, and which makes me always (even by a natural bond) their friend; therefore believe me very affectionately | Yours, &c.[1]

*JABEZ HUGHES to POPE   16 *May* 1720

1772 (Duncombe)

London, May 16, 1720.

Sir,—There is something so singularly polite in your being pleased to honour me with the last volumes of your excellent "Homer", that I am impatient to return my thanks immediately for so acceptable a favour. I have often heard my dear brother mention your presenting him with the volumes which were published in his life-time, with much pleasure, as an obliging expression of friendship; but thus to complete your valuable gift to one, who never had the happiness of being personally known to you, is particularly genteel and kind.

I am the more touched with this unexpected regard, as proceeding from an author, who always appeared to me distinguished by a certain peculiar felicity and elegance of genius, from which the principal and inimitable graces of poetry arise; and though, from this prepossession, I believed your translation, when you began it, would be performed with great beauty and merit, I must own the success is beyond my expectation, and I am surprised to see with what vigour you have supported so long a labour; with what a wonderful warmth of imagination, a copiousness and power of expression, and fine harmony of numbers you have conducted it to the end. We know the privilege Horace indulgently allowed to Homer himself, in the length of so extended a course; but you have certainly waived it in the translation, and are "awake" through the whole.

In a word, sir, I congratulate you very heartily on your happy conclusion of this noble undertaking, by which you have enriched our

---

[1] The last two paragraphs of this letter, beginning 'As to your question . . .', are used neatly in a letter written to Richardson in Feb. or Mar. 1732. Evidently Pope was 'editing' this letter to Fenton at the time he wrote to Richardson, and saw how effectively these paragraphs could be used to suggest that the idle Fenton might approach Pope with a project of translation or might be induced to aid Pope with regard to Shakespeare.

tongue with an admirable version of the most celebrated poem of antiquity, and have acquired to yourself the immortality of your applauded author.

I am, Sir, | Your most obliged and obedient servant, | Jabez Hughes.

†ROBERT DIGBY *to* POPE[1]   21 *May* 1720

1737

May 21, 1720.

Your letter which I had two posts ago was very medicinal to me; and I heartily thank you for the relief it gave me. I was sick of the thoughts of my not having in all this time given you any testimony of the affection I owe you, and which I as constantly indeed feel as I think of you. This indeed was a troublesome ill to me, till after reading your letter I found it was a most idle weak imagination to think I could so offend you. Of all the impressions you have made upon me, I never receiv'd any with greater joy than this of your abundant good-nature, which bids me be assured of some share of your affections.

I had many other pleasures from your letter; that your mother remembers me is a very sincere joy to me; I cannot but reflect how alike you are; from the time you do any one a favour, you think your selves obliged as those that have received one. This is indeed an old-fashioned respect, hardly to be found out of your house. I have great hopes however to see many old-fashioned virtues revive, since you have made our age in love with Homer; I heartily wish you, who are as good a citizen as a poet, the joy of seeing a reformation from your works. I am in doubt whether I should congratulate your having finished Homer, while the two Essays you mention are not compleated; but if you expect no great trouble from finishing these, I heartily rejoyce with you.

I have some faint notion of the beauties of Twickenham from what I here see round me. The verdure of showers is poured upon every tree and field about us; the gardens unfold variety of colours to the eye every morning, the hedges breath is beyond all perfume, and the song of birds we hear as well as you. But tho' I hear and see all this, yet I think they would delight me more if you was here. I found the want of these at Twickenham while I was there with you, by which I guess what an increase of charms it must now have. How kind is it in you to wish me there, and how unfortunate are my circumstances that allow me not to visit you? if I see you I must leave my Father alone, and this uneasy thought would disappoint all my proposed pleasures; the same circumstance will prevent my project of many happy hours with you in Lord Bathurst's wood, and (I fear) of seeing you till winter,

---

[1] Printed in 1737 and thereafter reprinted without notable change.

unless Lady Scudamore comes to Sherburne, in which case I shall press you to see Dorsetshire as you proposed. May you have a long enjoyment of your new favourite Portico. Your, &c.

POPE *to* FORTESCUE[1]   24 *June* 1720

1797 (Polwhele, i. 323)

                                                        June 24, 1720.

I have a great many obligations to you, and I may say, the lampreys are of the fresh water, since they are very fresh and good. I am really piqued at the stocks, which put a stop, at present, to all trade and all friendship, and I fear all honour too. I am sure, however, they do you as little prejudice, and your morals, as any man's; your memory of your friends is proved by the good offices you continue to do them; and I assure you I heartily wish some occasion may offer itself of my proving to you my sense of this which I say. Pray, if it is possible to remember a mere word of course in such a place as Exchange Alley, remember me there to Gay, for any where else (I deem) you will not see him as yet. I depend upon seeing you here now the books are closed.[2] Dear Sir, adieu! | A. Pope.

Address: To Wm. Fortescue, esq. at Tom's coffee-house, in Devereux-court, near the Temple.

POPE *to* BROOME[3]   [1720]

Elwin–Courthope, viii. 43

                                                        Twitnam, Thursday

On Saturday last I received an open note from Mr. Lintot, that you were then in town, but were to be gone again on the Monday. I was engaged all Sunday here, and came to town on Monday night in order to go, as I was obliged, with the Duke of Buckingham to Tunbridge on Tuesday early, from whence I did not return till to-day, and came directly hither, not imagining till I was here, that you were yet in town, which Mr. Gay now tells me. Had I received any previous notice of your coming to London, I should not have failed seeing you there, if you would not have favoured me with a visit here. I hope, if this finds you in town, you will yet do so, for be assured you can see no man who is more yours than, dear sir.

---

[1] Elwin mistakenly says this letter was published by Pope in his quarto of 1737.
[2] The transfer books of the South Sea Company were closed on 22 June 1720.
[3] The letter is impossible to date surely, but since Gay was abroad in the summer of 1719, and since the Duke died early in 1721, it is probable that he took Pope to Tunbridge Wells in the summer of 1720.

POPE *to* FORTESCUE[1]   3 *July* 1720

The Pierpont Morgan Library

July the 3d 1720

From an Information given me by Mr Gay, correspondent with what I formerly heard from you, that Estates were yet to be had in Devonshire at 20 & 25 years purchace, I beg it of you as a particular Kindness to interest yourself so much in my affairs as to get (if possible) about the yearly value of two hundred ll. entirely, or in the parcells, (as it falls out & as to your Judgment shall seem meet.) If Mr Gay & I by this means become Effectually your Countrymen, We hope (in conjunction with you) to come in time to Represent Devonshire itself. To which happy County, fertile in its productions, abounding in its Witts, delicious in its Cyders, Be all honour, praise, & glory &c | I am ever sincerely | Dear Sir Yours. | A. Pope.

Address: To Wm Fortescue Esq

---

†ROBERT DIGBY *to* POPE[2]   9 *July* 1720

1737

Sherburne, July 9, 1720.

The London language and conversation is I find quite changed since I left it, tho' it is not above three to four months ago. No violent change in the natural world ever astonished a Philosopher so much as this does me. I hope this will calm all Party-rage, and introduce more humanity than has of late obtained in conversation. All scandal will sure be laid aside, for there can be no such disease any more as spleen in this new golden age. I am pleased with the thoughts of seeing nothing but a general good humour when I come up to town; I re-joyce in the universal riches I hear of, in the thought of their having this effect. They tell me you was soon content; and that you cared not for such an increase as others wished you. By this account I judge you the richest man in the South-sea, and congratulate you accordingly. I can wish you only an increase of health, for of riches and fame you have enough. Your, &c.

---

†POPE *to* ROBERT DIGBY[3]   20 *July* 1720

1735

July 20. 1720.

Your kind desire to know the state of my Health had not been unsatisfied so long, had not that ill state been the impediment. Nor should

---

[1] It is uncertain whether this unrealized project for investment is the result of gains from Homer or from the South Sea.   [2] Printed by Pope without revision, 1737–42.
[3] Published in all Pope's editions except 1735 a2.

I have seem'd an unconcern'd party in the Joys of your family, which
I heard of from Lady *Scudamore*, whose short *Eschantillon* of a Letter
(of a quarter of a page) I value as the short Glimpse of a Vision afforded
to some devout Hermit; for it includes (as those Revelations do) a
promise of a better Life in the Elysian Groves of *Cirencester*, whither
I could almost say in the style of a Sermon, the *Lord bring us all, &c.*
Thither may we tend, by various ways to one blissful Bower: Thither
may Health, Peace, and Good Humour, wait upon us as Associates:
Thither may whole Cargoes of Nectar (Liquor of Life and Long-
ævity!) by mortals call'd *Spaw-water*, be convey'd, and there (as *Milton*
has it) may we, like the Deities,

> On flow'rs repos'd, and with fresh garlands crown'd,
> Quaff Immortality and Joy—

When I speak of Garlands, I should not forget the green Vest-
ments and Scarfs which your Sisters promis'd to make for this purpose:
I expect you too in Green with a Hunting-horn by your side and a
green Hat, the Model of which you may take from *Osborne*'s Description of King *James* the First.[1]

What Words, what Numbers, what Oratory or what Poetry, can
suffice, to express how infinitely I esteem, value, love, and desire you
all, above all the Great ones⌐, the rich ones, and the vain ones⌐[2] of
this part of the World! above all the Jews, Jobbers, Bubblers, Subscribers, Projectors, Directors, Governors, Treasurers, &c. &c. &c. &c.
in saecula saeculorum![3]

Turn your Eyes and Attention from this miserable mercenary
Period; and turn yourself, in a just Contempt of these Sons of Mam-
mon, to the Contemplation of Books, Gardens, and Marriage.[4] In
which I now leave you, and return (Wretch that I am!) to Water-
gruel and *Palladio*.[5]

I am, &c.

---

[1] In his *Traditional Memoyres on the Raigne of King James* (1658) Francis Osborne had
written (p. 54) the passage Pope must have read shortly before writing: 'I shall leave him
dress'd to posterity in the colours I saw him in the next Progress after his Inauguration,
which was as green as the grasse he trod on, with a Fether in his Cap, and a Horne instead of a
Sword by his side: how sutable to his Age, Calling or Person, I leave to others to judge from
his Pictures . . .'

[2] The bracketed words are omitted 1737–42.

[3] This passage tends to arouse suspicion as to Pope's gains from his South Sea stock.

[4] *The Weekly Packet*, 6 Aug. 1720, announces the marriage of Lord Digby's second
daughter, Elizabeth, to the son of Sir Gilbert Dolben, which took place 4 Aug. at Sherborn
Castle.

[5] Vitruvius and (especially) Palladio were the great names in the austere classical tradition
of architecture praised by Lord Burlington, Pope, and others. We shall presently find Pope
describing his villa as 'Little Whitehall'.

†ROBERT DIGBY *to* POPE[1]   30 *July* [1720?]

1737

                                        Sherburne, July 30.

I congratulate you, dear Sir, on the return of the Golden-age, for sure
this must be such, in which money is shower'd down in such abundance upon us. I hope this overflowing will produce great and good
fruits, and bring back the figurative moral golden-age to us. I have
some omens to induce me to believe it may; for when the Muses
delight to be near a Court, when I find you frequently with a First-
minister,[2] I can't but expect from such an intimacy an encouragement
and revival of the polite arts. I know you desire to bring them into
honour, above the golden Image which is set up and worshipped, and
if you cannot effect it, adieu to all such hopes. You seem to intimate
in yours another face of things from this inundation of wealth, as if
beauty, wit, and valour would no more engage our passions in the
pleasurable pursuit of them, tho' assisted by this increase: if so, and if
monsters only as various as those of Nile arise from this abundance,
who that has any spleen about him will not haste to town to laugh?
What will become of the play-house? who will go thither while there
is such entertainment in the streets? I hope we shall neither want good
Satire nor Comedy; if we do, the age may well be thought barren of
genius's, for none has ever produced better subjects. | Your, &c.

ATTERBURY *to* POPE[3]   *August* 1720

Longleat Portland Papers, xiii (Harleian transcripts)

          Relating to Drydens | Tomb In August 1720.

Sir,—I have sent the Officer to view the Place and find, upon his
Report, that no Objection lyes against erecting a Tomb, where part
of the Screen of the Chappel next Cowley's Monument stands: but
there must be a smooth free Stone Wall behind it, both to Support the
Tomb backwards, and to remove the Eysore there would otherwise

---

   [1] Printed 1737–42, without revision.
   [2] Pope's neighbour, the younger Craggs.
   [3] In the Portland Papers at Longleat (xiii, f. 197) immediately following this letter is a
transcript of one from Atterbury to the Duke of Buckingham, who was moved, by Pope's
second line in his early epitaph for Rowe, to erect at his own expense a proper monument to
Dryden. Pope had written of Dryden's tomb:

              Beneath a rude and nameless stone he lies.

See Norman Ault, *New Light*, pp. 145–55. The letter to Buckingham is dated 8 Aug.,
and hence one assumes that the bishop wrote to Pope this present letter about that date.
Possibly it is slightly later, as Pope may already have approved the suggested site, and is now
asked 'to hasten the execution of the design'. The monument was 'first expos'd to publick
View' 23 Jan. 1720/1.—Johnson's *Lives of the Poets* (ed. Hill), i. 487.

be to those who go into that Chappel to see the Tombs, there: but I do not find, that the Extraordinary Expence of such a Stone Wall will come to so much as Ten Pounds; and such a Trifling Expence therefore is not to be regarded. All Doubts being remov'd (I know not how any came to be entertain'd) I wish you would now hasten the Execution of the Design, for some Reasons which did not occur to me when I saw you last. The mention of that naturally puts me upon acknowledging the Kindness of your last Visit as I do very heartily.

The Lamer, or the Lazyer I am, the more I must Value the Visits of any of my Friends, and particularly Yours.

You took a Memorandum or two with you, of which I shall have an Account at your Leysure, Chapman lys Clasp'd up for you, when I know whither to send it.¹ I wish you a pleasant Enjoyment of those after Summers, which I am going back to make the most of at Bromly. The Sun owes us a great deal of good Weather and if he's an honest Planet, will pay us. I hope his Septr & Octr will make amends for his June and July: and then I may happen to walk with you a Turn or Two in my Gallery this Winter without a Cane. Lame, or Well, in Bed, or in my Chair, in my Coach or in my Garden; I am every where and always | Sir | Your very affectionate & | humble Servant | Fr. Roffen.

POPE *to* LADY MARY WORTLEY MONTAGU

22 August [1720]

The Pierpont Morgan Library

Twick'nham. August 22d

Madam,—I was made acquainted late last night, that I might depend upon it as a certain gain, to Buy the South Sea-Stock at the present price,² which will certainly rise in some weeks, or less. I can be as sure of this, as the nature of any such thing will allow, from the first & best hands: & therfore have dispatched the bearer with all Speed to you. I am sincerely | Dear Madam | Your most faithfull | humble Servant | A. Pope.

Endorsement: Mr Pope.

¹ This may possibly mean that Chapman's *Odyssey* is ready to be sent either to Pope or to a collaborator. If so, the project concerning the *Odyssey* is under way earlier than one would have thought.

² This was bad advice to give Lady Mary. At the end of June the stock had touched 1000; by the date of Pope's letter it was hovering briefly above 800, and thereafter it steadily declined. If it was at this time that Lady Mary bought for M. Rémond, it is no wonder the results were tragic. By the end of September it had touched 200. Lady Mary had advice from Craggs as well as from Pope. See Wharncliffe, ii. 9.

POPE *to* CARYLL   19 *September* [1720]
Add. 28618
                                                        Twittenham. 19 Sept.
I received your two letters and am truly concerned to see (by your making use of the young lady's hand) the inability of your own by the gout.
I hope and heartily wish your speedy recovery. The extreme hurry everybody is now in about the stocks must plead the justest excuse that can
be made for my not waiting on you, as well as the litter[1] I am encompassed with by workmen, with whom my presence is but too necessary.

I delivered yours to the Secretary[2] with my own hands, and you
need not fear the addition of such a character as I know by long
experience how to give you. The business of it he said not a word to
me about. I am sorry I can't add to this short letter; for business
hinders me from saying a word more than this, That I am always |
Dear Sir | Your faithful friend and servant | A. P.

†POPE *to* ATTERBURY[3]   23 *September* 1720
1737
                                                          Sept. 23, 1720.
I hope you have some time ago receiv'd the Sulphur, and the two
volumes of Mr. Gay,[4] as instances (how small ones soever) that I wish
you both health, and diversion. What I now send for your perusal,
I shall say nothing of; not to forestall by a single word what you
promis'd to say upon that subject. Your Lordship may criticize from
Virgil to these Tales, as Solomon wrote of every thing from the cedar
to the hysop. I have some cause, since I last waited on you at Bromley,
to look upon you as a Prophet in that retreat, from whom oracles
are to be had, were mankind wise enough to go thither to consult you:
The fate of the South-sea Scheme has much sooner than I expected
verify'd what you told me. Most people thought the time wou'd come,
but no man prepar'd for it; no man consider'd it would come *like a
Thief in the night*, exactly as it happens in the case of our death. Methinks God has punish'd the avaritious as he often punishes sinners,
in their own way, in the very sin itself: the thirst of gain was their
crime, that thirst continued became their punishment and ruin. As for
the few who have the good fortune to remain with half of what they
imagined they had, (among whom is your humble servant) I would
have them sensible of their felicity; and convinced of the truth of old

---

[1] Elwin here errs in printing *letter*. The transcript for once is clear, and reads *litter*. The
litter is caused by the workmen.   [2] Secretary Craggs.
[3] Printed in all Pope's editions, 1737–42. A few negligible improvements in the text
were made for the quarto and folio of 1737. They do not appear in other editions.
[4] The quarto subscription edition of Gay's *Poems* had appeared in July. Atterbury did not
subscribe, and Pope has now made him a present of the volumes.

Hesiod's maxim, who after half his estate was swallowed up by the *Directors* of those days, resolv'd, that *half* to be *more than the whole.*[1]

Does not the fate of these people put you in mind of two passages, one in Job, the other from the Psalmist?[2]

Men shall groan out of the CITY, *and hiss them out of their* PLACE.

They have dreamed out their dream, and awaking have found nothing in their hands.

Indeed the universal poverty, which is the consequence of universal avarice, and which will fall hardest upon the guiltless and industrious part of mankind, is truly lamentable. The universal deluge of the S. Sea, contrary to the old deluge, has drowned all except a few *Unrighteous* men: but it is some comfort to me that I am not one of them, even tho' I were to survive and rule the world by it. I am much pleas'd with a thought of Dr. Arbuthnot's: he says the Government and South-sea company have only lock't up the mony of the people upon conviction of their Lunacy, (as is usual in the case of lunaticks) and intend to restore 'em as much as may be fit for such people, as fast as they shall see 'em return to their senses.

The latter part of your letter does me so much honour, and shews me so much kindness, that I must both be proud and pleas'd, in a great degree; but I assure you, my Lord, much more the last than the first. For I certainly know, and feel, from my own heart, which truly respects you, that there may be a ground for your partiality one way; but I find not the least symptoms in my head, of any foundation for the other. In a word, the best reason I know for my being pleas'd, is that you continue your favour toward me; the best I know for being proud, wou'd be that you might cure me of it; for I have found you to be such a physician as does not only *repair* but *improve*. I am with the sincerest esteem, and most grateful acknowledgement, Your, &c.

|| ATTERBURY *to* POPE[3]　　　　　　28 *September* 1720

Longleat Portland Papers, xiii (Harleian transcripts)

Bromly Wedn. aftern. | Septr 28th 1720.

⌐The Sulphur came sometime ago inclos'd in a Letter from Dr Arb.⌐ The Arabian Tales and Mr Gays Books, I reced not till Mund. night,

---

[1] Pope probably knew this, 'the most acute of all his [Hesiod's] sayings', from Cowley's Discourse 'Of Agriculture'. It is also found in Basil Kennet's *Lives and Characters of the Ancient Grecian Poets* (1697). Possibly Pope knew the original text.

[2] Pope is either adapting from memory or 'creating' Scripture. The first adaptation is based on Job xxiv. 12 and xxvii. 23. The Psalms offer no adequate source for the second sentence, but in the Douai version of Psalm lxxv. 6 we find the following about the 'foolish of heart': 'They have slept their sleep: and all the men of riches have found nothing in their hands.'

[3] Printed in all Pope's editions 1737–42. His texts omit the date, superscription, and the first sentence. They make a few negligible rhetorical improvements in later editions.

and together with them your Letter, for which I thank you. I have had
a fit of the Gout upon me ever since I return'd hither from Westminster on Sat. 7 night last. It has found its way into my Hands, as well
as Legs; so that I have been utterly incapable of writing. This is the
first Letter that I have ventured upon, which will be written, I fear,
Vacillantibus Literulis,[1] as Tully says, Tyro's Letters were after his
Recovery from an Illness. What I said to you in mine about the
Monument, was intended onely to quicken, not to alarm you. It is
not worth your while to know, what I meant by it, but when I see
you, you shall: I hope that may be at the Deanery, towards the End
of Octr by which time I think of Setling there for the Winter.
What do you think of some such short Inscription as this in Latin,
which may in a few words say all that is to be said of Dryden, and yet
nothing more than he deserves?

JOHANNI DRIDENO.
Cui Poesis Anglicana
Vim suam, ac Veneres debet
Et, si quâ in posterum augebitur laude;
Est adhuc debitura:
Honoris ergo P
JOHANNES: SHEFFIELD: Dux Buckingami &c.

To shew you, that I am as much in earnest in the affair, as you
your self something I will send you too of this kind in English; but not
to be imparted to any Creature living beyond your Self, If your design
holds of fixing Dryden's Name only below, and his Busto above—
may not these be graved just under the Name.

This Sheffield rais'd, to Dryden's Ashes just
Here fix'd his Name, and there his Lawrell'd Bust
What else the Muse in Marble might express
Is known already, Praise would make him less.

Or, instead of the 2 Last, these

Then cease to fill the Marble with his Praise
Ill Lines may lessen Worth that None can raise.

Or thus—

More needs not; where acknowledg'd Merits reign
Praise is impertinent, and Censure vain.

This you'll take as a Proof of my Zeal at least tho' it be none of my
Talents in Poetry. When you have read it over I'll forgive you, if you
should not once in your life time again think of it.

[1] Cicero, *Ad Familiares*, xvi. 15. 2.

And now Sir for your Arabian Tales.[1] Ill as I have been almost ever since they came to hand, I have read as much of them, as ever I shall read while I live. Indeed, they do not please my Tast: they are writ with so Romantick an Air, and allowing for the Difference of Eastern manners, are yet, upon any Supposition that can be made, of so wild and absurd a Contrivance at least to my Northern understanding, that I have not only no pleasure, but no patience in perusing them. They are to me like the Odd Paintings on Indian Screens; which at first glance, may Surprize and please a little, but when you fix your Eye intently upon them, they appear so extravagant disproportion'd, and Monsterous, that they give a Judicious Seer pain and make him seek for relief from some other Object. They may furnish the mind with some new Images: but, I think the Purchase is made at too great an Expence: for to read those two Volumes through, liking them as little as I do, would be a terrible Pennance: and to read them with pleasure would be dangerous on the other Side, because of the Infection. I will never believe, that you have any keen relish of them, till I find you write worse than you do, which I dare say, I never shall. Who that Petis de la Croix is the pretended Author of them, I cannot tell, but observing how full they are in the Descriptions of Dress, Furniture &c I cannot help thinking them the product of some Womans Imagination, and believe me I would do any thing but break with you, rather than be bound to read them over with attention.

I am sorry I was so true a Prophet in respect of the S. Sea—Sorry I mean, as far as your Losses concern'd, for in the general I ever was, and still am of Opinion that had that project taken root and flourish'd it would by degrees have overturn'd our Constitution. Three or four hundred Millions was such a weight, that whatsoever way it had lean'd, must have tombled down all before it—But of the Dead we must speak gently and therefore as Mr Dryden says somewhere Peace be to its manes!

Let me add one Reflection to make you easy in your Ill luck, Had you got all that you have lost beyond what you ventur'd (perhaps 7 or 8000ll) Consider that your Superfluous Gains would have sprung from the Ruin of several Familys that now want Necessarys. A Thought, under which a good and good Natur'd Man, that grew rich by such means could not, I perswade myself be perfectly Easy. Adieu! and believe me ever | affectionately Yours | Fr. Roffen.

---

[1] One cannot be certain just what these were. Petis de la Croix had published in French *Les Mille & un jours. Contes persans* (1710–12), and they were translated as *The Persian and Turkish Tales compleat* in two volumes by Ambrose Philips and William King (1714). For this work Pope paid his respects to Philips in his *Epistle to Dr. Arbuthnot*, l. 180. In 1720 Pope evidently thought better of these tales than did Atterbury, whose reaction annoyed Horace Walpole as late as 1798 (when new editions were appearing). See Walpole's *Letters* (ed. Toynbee), xiv. 140.

POPE *to* TERESA BLOUNT[1]   [1720]

Mapledurham

As the weather proves very blustring & uncertain, we would by no means give you all, the trouble or the Ceremony of taking leave of us. But my Mother will wayt upon You in a chariot, soon after dinner (if you are not otherwise ingagd) I am ingagd to be with Mr Craggs till five or six, after which I shall be very glad to pass the Evening with you, if you have nothing to do. But if you prefer coming hither, the same Chariot may carry you back. I beg you to do just what is most convenient to yourselves; for Ceremony is to no purpose, I think, either with those that are Friends, or with those that are not. We are very much | Your humble Servants.

Address: To | Mrs Teresa Blount.

POPE *to* CARYLL   28 *October* [1720]

Add. 28618

I am very sorry at what you say in respect to the Secretary. Since he spoke nothing about that matter to me, I concluded he had writ to you himself; and if he has not, it must be attributed doubtless to the great hurry and multiplicity of his affairs, or else to the immediate change of the value of estates, which fell just then with the stocks.[2]

Your doctrine of *selling out* was certainly the most true and important doctrine in the world; and success (which makes everything right) has proved it so. 'Tis not to be denied but every creature that did not sell out must never pretend to any moderation in desires of gain. And really people are become so little affected in that point that very few make any scruple to own as much. Indeed, I think all the morals that were among us, are gone; that is to say, all the pretences to morals. If ever a nation deserved to be punished by an immediate infliction from heaven, this deserves it; & I think it would be in high presumption upon God's mercy, to hope even He will turn all this, any way, to our good? There is no doubt He *can*; but whoever presumes to guess, much less point out, the way, must surely arrogate too much for any human blindness to make out, or see. For my part all I *see* is ruin and mischief: all I *wish* is quiet and resignation.

To give you a friendly part in my private concerns, and those of your other friends, I must just tell you, as to myself, that I am not

---

[1] This letter is vaguely placed by the mention of Craggs, who lived in Twickenham from the early summer of 1720 until the time of his death in Feb. 1720/21. One assumes that the blustering weather might punctuate a summer visit to Pope's neighbourhood, but it might come at any time when the poet could be engaged with Mr. Craggs.

[2] Elwin thinks this approach to Craggs concerned a wish to sell him some property, now that Craggs had done so well in the South Sea. It seems an acceptable hypothesis.

hurt by these times or fates, (which I think escaping well) and that
your relations the ladies in Bolton Street, are still gainers, even, at this
low ebb; and may be pretty considerable so, if there be but any moderate rise again.

I wonder you never mention my friend Mrs Cope, who it seems
is with you. You know my regard for that lady's person and interest,
and I'm therefore pleased to think you espouse them. Pray assure her
of my best good wishes and service. | Adieu | Dear sir | Your most
affectionate humble servant | A: P:

Twitenham: | Octr 28.

†ROBERT DIGBY *to* POPE[1]   12 *November* 1720

[1737]
Coleshill, Nov. 12, 1720.

I find in my heart that I have a taint of the corrupt age we live in.
I want the publick Spirit so much admired in old Rome, of sacrificing
every thing that is dear to us to the common wealth. I even feel a more
intimate concern for my friends who have suffered in the S. Sea, than
for the publick, which is said to be undone by it. But I hope the reason
is, that I do not see so evidently the ruin of the publick to be a consequence of it, as I do the loss of my friends. I fear there are few besides
your self that will be persuaded by old Hesiod, that *half is more than the
whole.* I know not whether I do not rejoyce in your Sufferings; since
they have shewn me your mind is principled with such a sentiment.[2]
I assure you I expect from it a performance greater still than Homer.
I have an extreme joy from your communicating to me this affection
of your mind;

Quid voveat dulci Nutricula majus alumno?[3]

Believe me, dear Sir, no equipage could shew you to my eye in so much
splendor. I would not indulge this fit of philosophy so far as to be
tedious to you, else I could prosecute it with pleasure.

I long to see you, your Mother, and your Villa; till then I will say
nothing of Lord Bathurst's wood, which I saw in my return hither.
Soon after Christmas I design for London, where I shall miss Lady
Scudamore very much, who intends to stay in the country all winter.
I am angry with her as I am like to suffer by this resolution, and would
fain blame her, but cannot find a cause. The man is cursed that has
a longer letter than this to write with as bad a pen, yet I can use it

---

1 Printed 1737-42 with practically no textual changes.
2 Warburton (1751), in a footnote to line 139 of Pope's *Imitation of the Second Satire of
the Second Book of Horace*, remarks: 'Mr. Pope had South-sea Stock, which he did not sell
out. It was valued at between twenty and thirty thousand pounds when it fell.' This estimate
of Pope's investment seems exaggerated.   3 Horace, *Epistles*, i. 4. 8.

with pleasure to send my services to your good mother, and to write my self your, &c.

POPE *to* BROOME   *December* [1720]

Elwin–Courthope, viii. 47   Sunday night, December [1720].

I am really afflicted at the ill news of your illness, which Mr. Lintot, who called here to-day and missed me, being engaged at Mr. Secretary's,[1] informed my mother was not yet over. If you can stay longer, I am persuaded a removal to our good air of Twickenham would do you service in your health, and no man living will be more welcome to me. I very much desire to see you, and am really not able, for engagements of no small consequence to me, to wait on you to-morrow. Believe me, without ceremony, but with all truth, yours most affectionately.

POPE *to* TERESA BLOUNT   11 *December* 1720

Mapledurham   Twitenham Decr 11th 1720.

Madam,—I send you this Christmas Present, which I hope you'l like, tho it is not so properly Brawn as I wish, for want of Horn. I can't be positive that twill be any great recommendation to *your Goûte*, to say it has the true Country-Taste, I can't tell but you may prefer even Town-Brawn to Country-Brawn, tho' more experienced persons of your Sex generally prefer the Rurall Brawn, as to the firmness of the Flesh, (I mean in Ploughmen, rather than Porters, ask Lady [   ][2] else?)

I found our House exactly like Noah's Ark in every thing, except that there's no propagation of the Species in it. As to the Waters, we ride above 'em as yett. The Prospect is prodigiously fine: It is just like an Arm of the Sea, and the Flood over my Grassplot, embraced between the two Walls, whose tops are only seen, looks like an open Bay to the Terras. The opposite meadow where you so often walked, is coverd with Sails, & not to flatter you, I feel the Flowers in it next Spring, will be rather attributed to the production of the waters, than of your Footsteps; which will be very un-poeticall after all. We see a new River behind Kingston, which was never beheld before; and that our Own House may not be void of Wonders, we pump up Gudgeons thro the Pipe in the Kitchen, with our water. Having finishd my description, I conclude Your most humble Servant.

Address: To | Mrs Teresa Blount, in | Bolton street, | These

---

[1] Secretary Craggs.
[2] Apparently only the initial of this lady was written down, but in opening the letter even the initial was, fortunately or unfortunately, torn away. A bit remains, suggesting the possibility that the letter was H.

POPE *to* CARYLL   12 *December* 1720

Add. 28618

Decr 12th 1720.

I had epistolized you long ago but in an expectation of your coming
to town, which was given to me by several hands. I was lately very
happy in an evening's conference with your son,[1] who, like all the
rest of his family, has an undoubted right to me, tho' I took it a little
ill he did not make use of it in making my cottage his habitation during
his stay at Twitenham. I was unfortunately at London, all but one
day, and I can't express how concerned I am, to have missed the
satisfaction of both Lady Mary's and his neighbourhood.[2] Nothing
can make it up but your own coming, which your last letter gave me
some hopes of, but Mr Caryll tells me you don't intend as yet to leave
the country. My present situation very much resembles Noah's ark,[3]
not only on account of the wide watery prospect of all the face of the
Earth overflowed round about me but also because I find myself and
little family, in a manner separated from all the world, without commerce or society, or without that which makes society and commerce,
money. The vast inundation of the S. Sea has drowned all, except a few
unrighteous men (contrary to the deluge), and it is some comfort to
me I am not one of those, even in my afflictions. 'Tis a serious satisfaction to me to reflect, I am not the richer for the calamities of others,
which (as the world has gone) must have been the case nine times in
ten. I protest to you I speak in earnest,[4] than to have been the greatest
the gainer with that reflection; and to convince you how much I'm
in earnest, I am really forced to desire you to order me the little you
owe me (if you can, to even it till Xmas), being in more necessity for
present money than I ever yet was. I'm much pleased with a thought
of Dr Arbuthnot's, who says the Government and South Sea Company
only have locked up the money of the people, upon conviction of their
lunacy (as is usual in the case of lunatics), and intend to restore 'em
as much as is fit for such people, as they see 'em return more and more
to their senses.

I am got to the bottom of my letter before I was aware: there's
a pleasure in writing or talking to you which I could indulge, but must
have mercy on you. I am constantly and faithfully | yours | A: P:

[1] Mr. Henry Caryll, who was in the service of the Duke of Lorraine, and had come to
England with the Duke's envoy, the Count de Begue.—Elwin.

[2] Lady Mary Caryll's mother, the Countess of Seaforth, lived in Twickenham.

[3] See Pope to Teresa Blount, 11 Dec. 1720. There are faint reminiscences of such floods
in the letters of Horace Walpole; e.g. (Toynbee ed.) iii. 309.

[4] The text here is obviously faulty. Possibly, as Elwin suggests, the scribe omitted a line
in transcribing. Thus it might read: 'I protest to you I speak in earnest [and though not a
gainer, would rather even have lost] than to have been the greatest the gainer. . . .'

In this year Pope's letters give us only fragmentary glimpses of his activities. A usual his time was chiefly spent at Twickenham (where his villa was being enlarged) with brief visits to London. In September he made a visit of indeterminate length to Oxford and Gloucestershire. His mother's health in the early summer was an excuse for not visiting Caryll, who seemed annoyed by the failure to visit and perhaps by other matters. The correspondence (as preserved) with Caryll and with the Misses Blount is notably less frequent this year. Pope's literary work concerns the edition of Shakespeare, the posthumously published *Poems* of Parnell (published in December), and the *Works* of the Duke of Buckingham, finally published in 1723. Pope's most notable poem of the year was his dedicatory *Epistle* to Robert, Earl of Oxford, printed in Parnell's *Poems*.

*POPE to JONATHAN RICHARDSON¹   [1721?]

Frank J. Hogan

I desire particularly to see you on Munday, for on Tuesday &c, I must be absent from home. I will set apart the whole day, & therfore pray dine with me. I am sorry your Son is still detained, I hope not by Indisposition. There are some strokes in your Letter that give me uneasiness, I hope not with too much cause, for little Evils we all must expect in the Course of this World, as it is constituted.

I am with truth Yours | A. Pope

Address: To Mr Richardson at | his house in | Queens Square | Bloomsbury.
Postmark: PENY POST PAYD.

*POPE to JONATHAN RICHARDSON²   [1721–44]

The Pierpont Morgan Library

Pray let me enjoy yours and your Sons agreable Conversation, in the place where I can have it most uninterrupted, (viz) Twickenham. This Saturday Evening, & Sunday all day & night, I will be there attending you. It is but turning your Horses heads towards me,

¹ Since it is undatable, this letter is placed at the beginning of the intimacy of Pope and the Richardsons—or thereabouts.
² This letter might be written at any time after Pope formed his acquaintance with Richardson, unless the reference to Hampstead limits its possible date. It is placed, lacking other information, at what is supposed to be the beginning of intimacy with the Richardsons.

instead of setting them towards Hampstead, to morrow afternoon. Believe me, no man is with more truth | Yours, | A. Pope.

Friday night.

Address: To | Mr. Richardson, at his | house in Queens Square | Bloomsbury.
Postmark: PENY POST PAYD.
Endorsement: Pope.

POPE *to* LADY MARY WORTLEY MONTAGU¹   [1721?]

The Pierpont Morgan Library

Mu[nday]

It is not in my [power] (dear Madam) to say what a[gita-]tion the two or three words I [wrote] you the other morning have gi[ven me.] Indeed I truly Esteem you, and [put my] Trust in you. I can say no more, & I know you would not have me.

I've been kept in town by a violent Headache, so that I might see You any time to day (except two, 3 or 4 aclock when I am ingaged to dinner) I should be pleasd & happy, More indeed than Any other Company could make me.

Your most faithful | obligd Servant | A. Pope

POPE *to* THE REV. GEORGE BERKELEY²   [1721?]

Robert H. Taylor

Sunday.

My Lord Bishop was very much concernd at missing you yesterday; he desird me to ingage you & myself to dine with him this day, but I was unluckily præingagd. And (upon my telling him I shoud carry you out of town to morrow & hopd to keep you till the end of the week) he has desird that we will not fail to dine with him the next Sunday, when he will have no other company.

I write you this, to intreat you will provide yourself of Linnen &

---

¹ The letter is obviously undatable. On the supposition (a wild one) that Pope's 'trust' in Lady Mary may be a phrase of consolation concerning her difficulties with M. Rémond (which Pope knew about and Mr. Wortley did not!) it may be placed in 1721. The square brackets indicate words missing because part of the upper right corner of the leaf is torn away. The emendations follow earlier texts made, perhaps, before the tearing occurred. Lord Wharncliffe notes that the letter is endorsed by Mr. Wortley Montagu 'Mr. Pope'.

² This letter was printed by John Duncombe in *Letters of John Hughes and other Eminent Persons* (1772). Duncombe dated the letter 1713, and in a footnote identified the bishop as Atterbury. Warton inserted the name of Atterbury in the text and gave [1722] as date. The date is difficult, but should probably fall in the period of Pope's residence in his Twickenham villa, when also he was more intimate with Atterbury. In 1722 Berkeley seems to have stayed in Ireland until December; and Atterbury was sent to the Tower in Aug. 1722. The year 1721 seems a plausible date. There is some reason to think that Berkeley was in London during the summer of 1721, and the dinner (if it took place) very likely fell in June or July, before Atterbury was crippled with the gout.

other necessaries sufficient for the week: for, as I take You to be almost the only Friend I have, that is above the little vanities of the Town, I expect you may be able to renounce it for one week, and to make trial how you like My Tusculum because I can assure you it is no less yours, & hope you'l use it as your own Country Villa, the ensuing season. | I am faithfully yours | A: Pope.

*POPE *to* JACOB TONSON, JR.[1]   [1721 or 1722]
Add. 28275

Sunday night

Sir,—Whenever the Weather permits, & your Leisure joins with it, you will now find me at Twitnam. I hope you will quicken Fenton now & then by a letter: I have not had a word from him.

I must desire the favor of you to send me but for a day or two, a book calld, the Life of K. William the Third, printed in large Octavo about 12 years ago.[2] Im told ther is in it a Speech of the late Duke of Buck's: which I never heard of. In this you'l oblige | Your very affect. Servant | A. Pope.

POPE *to* JOHN DANCASTLE[3]   5 *Jan.* [1720/21]
The Gentleman's Magazine, ci[2] (1831), 291

Twitenham, Jan. 5.

I give you the trouble of this to recommend what needs no recommendation to you, an Act of Charity, in this holy time. It is in behalf of the poor Girl I formerly spoke to you of, and to whom you have been formerly charitable sometimes, Betty Fletcher. She is so deplorable an object, as well in regard of Sickness and Disability, as of Poverty, that if, out of Mrs. Moore's Beneficences[4] of this kind, which are many and great, she would please to allow her any small matter as a weekly salary, tho' never so little, it would help her necessities much more than any larger gifts at uncertain times. I know you'l make this your request, since I make it mine, and I almost hope you know me enough to be assured I would rather Do this, than Ask it. But I am

---

[1] Presumably the letter falls in the period when Pope is editing the *Works* of Buckingham and editing Shakespeare for Tonson, with help from Fenton, who is less at Twickenham since the death of Craggs.

[2] No such life has been accessible to the editor. Pope printed only two speeches of the Duke.

[3] The year is obviously impossible to fix; but Pope writes from Twickenham, and he was feeling more like 'one of the poor of my parish' after South Sea had disappointed him and his income from Homer had stopped, temporarily. But when charity is asked one can always feel poor.

[4] Mrs. Moore was Dancastle's sister. This letter may well be put alongside that written for Francis Bourne, here placed in the autumn of 1717 (i. 436).

become, like many other Too Covetuous people, one of the Poor of my Parish, who have learn'd very much on the sudden, and very much against my Will (which is just contrary at this time to the Lord's Will) that Charity begins at home. However, I'l promise you one thing, that is of consequence to any Friend at this season, that I'll not beg or borrow of you myself, provided you'l take some care of Betty Fletcher. I make you no Apology for this Letter, and so bluntly conclude, | Your Brother's and your faithfull | affect' Servant | A. Pope.

Address: To John Dancastle, Esq. att Binfield, | near Ockingham, Berks.

SWIFT *to* POPE[1]   10 *January* 1720/1

1741 Da

Dublin, Jan. 10, 1721.

A Thousand things have vex'd me of late years, upon which I am determined to lay open my mind to you. I had rather chuse to appeal to you than to my Lord Chief Justice Whitshed,[2] under the situation I am in. For, I take this cause properly to lie before you: You are a much fitter Judge of what concerns the credit of a Writer, the injuries that are done him, and the reparations he ought to receive. Besides I doubt, whether the Arguments I could suggest to prove my own innocence would be of much weight from the gentlemen of the Long-robe to those in Furs,[3] upon whose decision about the difference of Style or Sentiments, I should be very unwilling to leave the merits of my Cause.

---

[1] This 'letter' has a very special history. It seems not to have been in the clandestine volume that Pope sent to Ireland in 1740 for publication, but was added to that copy at Swift's instance and printed in Faulkner's Dublin octavo (1741 Da). Faulkner in Dec. 1740 sent the letter in type to Pope, together with the first sheets of his octavo so far as he had printed them at that time. (See the letters then passing between Pope and Lord Orrery, especially that of 27 Dec., now preserved in the Pierpont Morgan Library.) The Faulkner octavo was larger than the small octavo clandestine volume. In returning the dismembered clandestine volume to Faulkner Pope retained the early sheets, including this letter, which occupied something like a half-sheet and a quarter-sheet of the larger octavo. Pope included the letter in his quarto and folio editions, and reprinted and inserted it in the copies of the clandestine volume that he issued as vol. vii of his *Works* late in 1741.

To the heading of the letter Pope appended the footnote: 'This letter Mr. Pope never receiv'd.' The statement is in all probability true. Swift had, as Dr. Herbert Davis says in his edition of Swift's *Works*, ix, p. xii, probably written the letter as a pamphlet of self-defence rather than as a letter to Pope, but had not published it. He here seized an opportunity to publish it—as he also did, at the end of the Dublin octavo (1741 Da), *Some Free Thoughts on the Present State of Affairs, Written in the Year 1714*. The letter makes reference to *Some Free Thoughts*.

[2] In 1741 Da Faulkner printed here a footnote that seems superfluous: 'A Judge in Ireland.' Pope's quarto and folio omit the name of Whitshed; all his octavos include it. The fact suggests that possibly Pope had the letter reprinted in the small octavo format before he printed the quarto and folio.

[3] Lawyers and judges.

Give me leave then to put you in mind, (although you cannot easily forget it) that about ten weeks before the Queen's death, I left the town, upon occasion of that incurable breach among the great men at Court, and went down to Berkshire, where you may remember that you gave me the favour of a visit. While I was in that retirement, I writ a Discourse[1] which I thought might be useful in such a juncture of affairs, and sent it up to London; but upon some difference in opinion between me and a certain great Minister now abroad,[2] the publishing of it was deferred so long that the Queen died, and I recalled my copy, which hath been ever since in safe hands. In a few weeks after the loss of that excellent Princess, I came to my station here; where I have continued ever since in the greatest privacy, and utter ignorance of those events which are most commonly talked of in the world; I neither know the Names nor Number of the Family which now reigns,[3] further than the Prayer-book informs me. I cannot tell who is Chancellor, who are Secretaries, nor with what Nations we are in peace or war. And this manner of life was not taken up out of any sort of Affectation, but meerly to avoid giving offence, and for fear of provoking Party-zeal.

I had indeed written some Memorials of the four last years of the Queen's reign,[4] with some other informations which I receiv'd, as necessary materials to qualify me for doing something in an employment then design'd me:[5] But as it was at the disposal of a person,[6] who had not the smallest share of steddiness or sincerity, I disdained to accept it.

These papers, at my few hours of health and leisure, I have been digesting into order by one sheet at a time, for I dare not venture any further, lest the humour of searching and seizing papers should revive; not that I am in pain of any danger to my self, (for they contain nothing of present times or persons, upon which I shall never lose a thought while there is a Cat or a Spaniel in the house) but to preserve them from being lost among Messengers and Clerks.

I have written in this kingdom, a discourse[7] to persuade the wretched

---

[1] This 'Discourse' is *Some Free Thoughts* . . ., first published at the end of 1741 Da, with a separate title and separate pagination.

[2] Lord Bolingbroke.

[3] of the Family . . .] of the Royal Family *1741 Lab.*

[4] Parts of Swift's *History of the Last Four Years of the Queen* (published in 1758) had certainly been written before the summer of 1714.

[5] Historiographer.—Faulkner, 1741 : and all eds. 1741–2.

[6] D. of K—t.—Faulkner, 1741; D. of K.—1742 Labc; no identification in 1741 Labc. Later editors have identified the 'person' as the Duke of Shrewsbury, Lord Chamberlain, 1710–14; he succeeded the Duke of Kent in that office. As Swift's editors point out, he really showed no aversion to taking the office: it simply was not offered.

[7] *A Proposal for the universal Use of* Irish *Manufactures.* Vide Vol. IV of the Author's *Works* [1735].—Faulkner, 1741. This note does not appear in 1742 La, but does appear in 1742 Lbc.

people to wear their own Manufactures instead of those from England: This Treatise soon spread very fast, being agreeable to the sentiments of the whole nation, except of those gentlemen who had Employments, or were Expectants. Upon which a person in great office here[1] immediately took the alarm; he sent in hast for the Chief Justice, and inform'd him of a seditious, factious and virulent Pamphlet, lately publish'd with a design of setting the two kingdoms at variance, directing at the same time that the printer should be prosecuted with the utmost rigour of Law. The Chief Justice[2] had so quick an understanding, that he resolved if possible to out-do his orders. The Grand-Juries of the county and city were practised effectually with to represent[3] the said Pamphlet with all aggravating Epithets, for which they had thanks sent them from England, and their Presentments publish'd for several weeks in all the news-papers. The Printer was seized, and forced to give great bail: After his tryal the Jury brought him in Not Guilty, although they had been culled with the utmost industry; the Chief Justice sent them back nine times, and kept them eleven hours, until being perfectly tired out, they were forced to leave the matter to the mercy of the Judge, by what they call a special Verdict. During the tryal, the Chief Justice among other singularities, laid his hand on his breast, and protested solemnly that the Author's design was to bring in the Pretender; although there was not a single syllable of party in the whole Treatise, and although it was known that the most eminent of those who professed his own principles, publickly disallowed his proceedings. But the cause being so very odious and impopular, the tryal of the Verdict was deferred from one Term to another, until upon the Duke of G—ft—n the Lord Lieutenant's arrival[4] his Grace after mature advice, and permission from England, was pleased to grant a *noli prosequi*.[5]

This is the more remarkable, because it is said that the man[6] is no ill decider in common cases of property, where Party is out of the question; but when that intervenes, with ambition at heels to push it forward, it must needs confound any man of little spirit, and low birth, who hath no other endowment than that sort of Knowledge, which, however possessed in the highest degree, can possibly give no one good quality to the mind.

It is true, I have been much concerned for several years past, upon account of the publick as well as of myself, to see how ill a taste for wit

[1] The Lord Chancellor, Viscount Middleton.
[2] Lord Chief Justice Whitshed.—Faulkner, 1741 (omitted in Pope's editions).
[3] represent] present *1742 La.*
[4] G—ft—n . . . arrival] Grafton's arrival *1742 La.* The Duke arrived in Aug. 1721. Dr. Davis regards, plausibly, this sentence as an interpolation; hence the letter may be placed in 1720/1 rather than 1721/2.
[5] *Law Phrase signifying a* Stop to *further Proceedings.*—Dublin, 1741.
[6] This righteous Magistrate, at last, is dead.—Curll, 1741.

and sense prevails in the world, which politicks and South-sea, and Party, and Opera's and Masquerades have introduced. For, besides many insipid papers which the malice of some hath entitled me to, there are many persons appearing to wish me well, and pretending to be judges of my style and manner, who have yet ascribed some writings to me, of which any man of common sense and literature would be heartily ashamed. I cannot forbear instancing a Treatise called a Dedication upon Dedications,[1] which many would have to be mine, although it be as empty, dry, and servile a composition, as I remember at any time to have read. But above all, there is one Circumstance which maketh it impossible for me to have been Author of a Treatise, wherein there are several pages containing a Panegyrick on King George, of whose character and person I am utterly ignorant, nor ever had once the curiosity to enquire into either, living at so great a distance as I do, and having long done with whatever can relate to publick matters.

Indeed I have formerly delivered my thoughts very freely, whether I were asked or no, but never affected to be a Councellor, to which I had no manner of call. I was humbled enough to see myself so far out-done by the E. of Oxford in my own trade as a Scholar, and too good a Courtier not to discover his contempt of those who would be men of importance out of their sphere. Besides, to say the truth, although I have known many great Ministers ready enough to hear Opinions, yet I have hardly seen one that would ever descend to take Advice; and this pedantry ariseth from a maxim themselves do not believe at the same time they practice by it, that there is something profound in Politicks, which men of plain honest sense cannot arrive to.

I only wish my endeavours had succeeded better in the great point I had at heart, which was that of reconciling the Ministers to each other. This might have been done, if others who had more concern and more influence would have acted their parts; and if this had succeeded, the publick interest both of Church and State would not have been the worse, nor the Protestant Succession endangered.

But, whatever opportunities a constant attendance of four years might have given me for endeavouring to do good offices to particular persons, I deserve at least to find tolerable quarter from those of the other Party; for many of which I was a constant advocate with the Earl of Oxford, and for this I appeal to his Lordship: He knows how often I press'd him in favour of Mr. Addison, Mr. Congreve, Mr. Row, and Mr. Steel, although I freely confess that his Lordship's kindness to them was altogether owing to his generous notions, and

---

[1] A *Dedication* to a *Great Man*, concerning *Dedications*. This was written by *Thomas Gordon*, Esq.; Author of the *Independent Whig*.—Curll, 1741.

the esteem he had for their wit and parts, of which I could only pretend to be a remembrancer. For I can never forget the answer he
gave to the late Lord Hallifax, who upon the first change of the
Ministry interceded with him to spare Mr. Congreve: It was by repeating these two lines of Virgil,

> Non obtusa adeo gestamus pectora Pœni,
> Nec tam aversus equos Tyria Sol jungit ab urbe.[1]

Pursuant to which, he always treated Mr. Congreve with the greatest
personal civilities, assured[2] him of his constant favour and protection,[3]
adding that he would study to do something better for him.

I remember it was in those times a usual subject of raillery towards
me among the Ministers, that I never came to them without a Whig
in my sleeve; which I do not say with any view towards making my
Court: For, the new Principles fixed to those of that denomination, I
did then, and do now from my heart abhor, detest and abjure, as
wholly degenerate from their predecessors. I have conversed in some
freedom with more Ministers of State of all Parties than usually happens to men of my level, and I confess, in their capacity as Ministers,
I look upon them as a race of people whose acquaintance no man would
court, otherwise than upon the score of Vanity or Ambition. The first
quickly wears off (and is the Vice of low minds, for a man of spirit is
too proud to be vain) and the other was not my case. Besides, having
never receiv'd more than one small favour,[4] I was under no necessity
of being a slave to men in power, but chose my friends by their personal merit, without examining how far their notions agreed with the
politicks then in vogue. I frequently conversed with Mr. Addison,
and the others I named (except Mr. Steel) during all my Lord Oxford's
Ministry, and Mr. Addison's friendship to me continued inviolable,
with as much kindness as when we used to meet at my Lord Sommers
or Hallifax, who were leaders of the opposite Party.

I would infer from all this, that it is with great injustice I have these
many years been pelted by your Pamphleteers, merely upon account of
some regard which the Queen's last Ministers were pleased to have
for me: and yet in my conscience I think I am a partaker in every ill
design they had against the Protestant Succession, or the Liberties and
Religion of their Country; and can say with Cicero, that I should be

---

[1] In the text inserted in the clandestine volume these lines (*Aeneid*, i. 567–8) are badly
printed. The order of the lines is inverted (as also in 1742 La), and *cursus* is substituted for
aversus. In late proofs of 1741 Da the corrections were made.

[2] assured] assuring *1741 Labc*; *1742 Lc, Da*.

[3] protection, adding] protection, and adding *1741 Labc*; *1742 Lc, Da*.

[4] The *Deanery* of St. Patrick's being but 1000*l. per Annum*.—Curll, 1741. (Curll exag-
gerates. Professor Landa finds that the deanery income was slightly over £800. See *Pope
and His Contemporaries* (ed. by J. L. Clifford and L. A. Landa), pp. 159–70, for Landa's
detailed account of 'Swift's Deanery Income'.)

proud to be included with them in all their actions *tanquam in equo Trojano*.[1] But, if I have never discovered by my words, writings, or actions, any Party virulence, or dangerous designs against the present powers; if my friendship and conversation were equally shewn among those who liked or disapproved the proceedings then at Court, and that I was known to be a common friend of all deserving persons of the latter sort when they were in distress; I cannot but think it hard that I am not suffer'd to run quietly among the common herd of people, whose opinions unfortunately differ from those which lead to Favour and Preferment.

I ought to let you know, that the Thing we called a Whig in England is a creature altogether different from those of the same denomination here, at least it was so during the reign of Her late Majesty. Whether those on your side have changed or no, it hath not been my business to inquire. I remember my excellent friend Mr. Addison, when he first came over[2] hither Secretary to the Earl of Wharton, then Lord Lieutenant,[3] was extremely offended at the conduct and discourse of the Chief Managers here: He told me they were a sort of people who seemed to think, that the principles of a Whig consisted in nothing else but damning the Church, reviling the Clergy, abetting Dissenters, and speaking contemptibly of revealed Religion.

I was discoursing some years ago with a certain Minister about that whiggish or fanatical Genius so prevalent among the English of this kingdom: his Lordship accounted for it by that number of Cromwell's soldiers, adventurers establish'd here, who were all of the sourest Leven, and the meanest birth, and whose posterity are now in possession of their lands and their principles. However, it must be confessed that of late, some people in this country are grown weary of quarrelling, because interest, the great motive of quarrelling is at an end; for, it is hardly worth contending who shall be an Excise-man, a Country-Vicar, a Cryer in the Courts, or an Under-Clerk.

You will perhaps be inclined to think, that a person so ill treated as I have been, must at some time or other have discovered very dangerous opinions in government; in answer to which, I will tell you what my Political principles were in the time of her late glorious Majesty, which I never contradicted by any action, writing, or discourse.

First, I always declared my self against a Popish Successor to the Crown, whatever Title he might have by the proximity of blood: Neither did I ever regard the right line except upon two accounts, first as it was establish'd by law; and secondly, as it hath much weight in the opinions of the people. For necessity may abolish any Law, but

---

[1] As if in the *Trojan* Horse.—Faulkner, 1741. (The figure is derived from Cicero, *Pro Murena*, 37. 78.) [2] In the spring of 1709.
[3] to the Earl . . . Lieutenant] to the Lieutenant *1742 La.*

cannot alter the sentiments of the vulgar; Right of inheritance being perhaps the most popular of all topicks; and therefore in great Changes, when that is broke, there will remain much heart burning and discontent among the meaner people; which (under a weak Prince and corrupt Administration) may have the worst consequences upon the peace of any state.

As to what is called a Revolution-principle, my opinion was this; That whenever those evils which usually attend and follow a violent change of government, were not in probability so pernicious as the grievances we suffer under a present power, then the publick good will justify such a Revolution; and this I took to have been the Case in the Prince of Orange's expedition, although in the consequences it produced some very bad effects, which are likely to stick long enough by us.

I had likewise in those days a mortal antipathy against Standing Armies in times of Peace. Because I always took Standing Armies to be only servants hired by the master of the family, for keeping his own children in slavery: And because, I conceived that a Prince who could not think himself secure without Mercenary Troops, must needs have a separate interest from that of his subjects. Although I am not ignorant of those artificial Necessities which a corrupted Ministry can create, for keeping up forces to support a Faction against the publick Interest.

As to Parliaments, I adored the wisdom of that Gothic Institution, which made them Annual: and I was confident our Liberty could never be placed upon a firm foundation till that ancient law were restored among us. For, who sees not, that while such assemblies are permitted to have a longer duration, there grows up a commerce of corruption between the Ministry and the Deputies, wherein they both find their accounts to the manifest danger of Liberty, which traffick would neither answer the design nor expence, if Parliaments met once a year.

I ever abominated that scheme of politicks, (now about thirty years old) of setting up a mony'd Interest in opposition to the landed. For, I conceived, there could not be a truer maxim in our government than this, That the possessors of the soil are the best judges of what is for the advantage of the kingdom: If others had thought the same way, Funds of Credit and South-sea Projects would neither have been felt nor heard of.

I could never discover the necessity of suspending any Law upon which the Liberty of the most innocent persons depended: neither do I think this practice hath made the taste of arbitrary power[1] so agreeable as that we should desire to see it repeated. Every Rebellion subdued

---

[1] A probable allusion to the time of the Jacobite rebellion of 1715, when in July Parliament suspended the *habeas corpus* for six months.—Elwin.

and Plot discovered, contributes to the firmer establishment of the Prince. In the latter case, the knot of Conspirators is entirely broke, and they are to begin their work anew under a thousand disadvantages; so that those diligent enquiries into remote and problematical guilt, with a new power of enforcing them by chains and dungeons to every person whose face a Minister thinks fit to dislike, are not only opposite to that maxim, which declares it better that ten guilty men should escape, than one innocent suffer, but likewise leave a gate wide open to the whole Tribe of Informers, the most accursed, and prostitute, and abandoned race, that God ever permitted to plague mankind.

It is true, the Romans had a custom of chusing a Dictator, during whose administration, the Power of other Magistrates was suspended; but this was done upon the greatest emergencies; a War near their doors, or some civil Dissention: For Armies must be governed by arbitrary power: But when the Virtue of that Commonwealth gave place to luxury and ambition, this very office of Dictator became perpetual in the persons of the Caesars and their Successors, the most infamous tyrants that have any where appeared in story.

These are some of the sentiments I had relating to publick affairs while I was in the world; what they are at present, is of little importance either to that or my self; neither can I truly say I have any at all, or if I had, I dare not venture to publish them: For however orthodox they may be while I am now writing, they may become criminal enough to bring me into trouble before midsummer. And indeed I have often wish'd for some time past, that a Political Catechism might be published by authority four times a year, in order to instruct us how we are to speak and write, and act during the current quarter. I have by experience felt the want of such an instructor: For intending to make my court to some people on the prevailing side, by advancing certain old whiggish principles, which it seems had been exploded about a month before, I have passed for a disaffected person. I am not ignorant how idle a thing it is for a man in obscurity to attempt defending his reputation as a writer, while the spirit of Faction hath so universally possessed the minds of men, that they are not at leisure to attend to any thing else. They will just give themselves time to libel and accuse me, but cannot spare a minute to hear my defence. So in a plot-discovering age, I have known an innocent man seized and imprisoned, and forced to lie several months in chains, while the Ministers were not at leisure to hear his petition, till they had prosecuted and hanged the number they proposed.[1]

All I can reasonably hope for by this letter, is to convince my friends and others who are pleased to wish me well, that I have neither

---

[1] Presumably a reference to the imprisonment of the Earl of Oxford, who remained in the Tower from July 1715 to July 1717.

been so ill a Subject nor so stupid an Author, as I have been represented by the virulence of Libellers, whose malice hath taken the same
train in both, by fathering dangerous principles in government upon
me which I never maintained, and insipid productions which I am not
capable of writing. For, however I may have been sowred by personal
ill treatment, or by melancholy prospects for the publick, I am too
much a politician to expose my own safety by offensive words; and if
my genius and spirit be sunk by encreasing years, I have at least enough
discretion left, not to mistake the measure of my own abilities, by
attempting subjects where those talents are necessary, which perhaps
I may have lost with my youth.

CARYLL *to* WRIGHT[1]   28 *February* 1720/1

H. B. Vander Poel

28 Feb. 1720

Pray pay unto Mr Alex: Pope (or order) the Summe of Eleven pounds
and place itt to the Account of | Your freind | J Caryll

To Mr Wright Goldsmith | in Covent Garden.

POPE *to* CARYLL   30 [28?] *February* 1721

Add. 28618

[2]30 Feby. 1720/1

The favour of yours had sooner been acknowledged but for the many
distractions I have lately been in thro' the loss of some of my friends
and my own indispositions. I am sensible of the part you bear in any
loss I can sustain, of any sort; and such as this indeed I think of the
greatest sort. I must also acknowledge the justice, as well as good will,
of your reflection, and your wish that we may all be prepared to meet
the same fate, which inevitably we must undergo. However, even that
reflection does not mitigate what living we feel in the loss of others.
Nothing so natural occurs[3] upon these accidents as the desire that God
would prolong the date of the few deserving friends that remain to us,
in which number, I need not tell you the old title and long right you

---

[1] In his letter of 12 Dec. 1720 Pope had asked Caryll for immediate payment, because of
emergency, of interest not yet due. This order to pay indicates that Caryll did not pay as
promptly as Pope wished. Note also the letter of 2 Apr. here placed in 1722, but formerly
(by Elwin) placed in 1721. In it Caryll is said to have replied that he should keep the interest
until Pope came to Ladyholt in person to get it. This order, then, forces the letter of 2 Apr.
into the year 1722.

[2] Caryll's not too competent scribe may have given this fantastic date on the principle
of plenitude, that no type of error might be lacking.

[3] This is the text of the transcript. Elwin improves it to read, 'Nothing seems so natural
upon these accidents . . ,'.

have to claim in me. I heartily pray for your felicity, here and here-after.

There never lived a more worthy nature, a more disinterested mind, a more open and friendly temper, than Mr Craggs.[1] A little time I doubt not will clear up a character which the world will learn to value and admire, when it has none such remaining in it.

Several idle reports about the Duke of Buckingham's epitaph,[2] with very various and misrepresenting copies, are spread about the town. I remember only that what his Grace 2 years ago repeated to me as his intended inscription had nothing exceptionable in it, in any fair, or Christian construction.

I cannot express how disappointed I am in seeming again to have lost the hopes of seeing you here. My mother's uncertain state of health (which is like the last light of a Taper near going out, whose very brightest flashes but show it in more danger of expiring) obliges me to watch her, too closely to admit of any views of a longer journey than to London (whither by the way I very rarely go) or a longer absence than of a day or two at most. Pray assure Mrs Caryll, Lady Mary, and your whole family of the unalterable regard I must always bear to all [that] belongs to you. And as for your self, expect no words that can tell you with what esteem I am | your's most faithfully | A: P:

|| ATTERBURY *to* POPE[3]   26 *March* 1721

Longleat Portland Papers, xiii (Harleian transcripts)

Deanery Sat. Morn. | March 26 1721/2

You are not your Self glader you are well, than I am: especially, since I can please my Self with the thought, that when you had lost your health elsewhere, you Recover'd it here. May these Lodgings never treat you worse, nor you at any time have less reason to be fond of them!

---

[1] Secretary Craggs died of smallpox on 16 Feb., at a moment when he, as well as his father, the Postmaster-General, was deeply involved in South-Sea scandal. His father died under circumstances suggesting suicide, 16 Mar. 1720/1, and his South-Sea gains were confiscated.

[2] These idle reports were very prompt; for the Duke died on 24 Feb. His epitaph, even as published later in a conceivably softened form, might cause eyebrows to rise. It reads: 'Dubius, sed non Improbus, Vixi. | Incertus morior, non Perturbatus; | Humanum est Nescire et Errare. | Deo confido omnipotenti Benevolentissimo. | Ens Entium miserere mei. || Pro Rege saepe, pro Republica semper.'

Dr. Johnson characterized the Duke as one who 'sometimes glimmers but rarely shines'.

[3] In spite of the scribe the date must be 1721, since in March 1722 the bishop was at Bromley during the last illness of his wife. The Longleat text of the letter differs somewhat from that published by Pope 1737–42. Pope made three minor changes in phrasing (specified below); he omitted the brief postscript about Craggs and the Duke of Buckingham, and he added the long postscript about Huetius's MS. This last is not in the Harleian transcript at all, and is here added from the Roberts octavo of 1737.

I thank you for the sight of your Verses[1] and with the freedom of an honest, tho' perhaps injudicious Friend must tell you, that tho' I could like some of them, if they were any body's else but yours,[2] yet as they are yours and to be own'd as such, I can scarce like any of them. Not but that the four first Lines are good especially the second couplet, and might if follow'd by four others as good, give Reputation to a Writer of a less establish'd Fame, but from you I expected somewhat of a more perfect kind, and which the oftner it is read the more it will be admired. When you barely exceed other Writers, you fall much beneath your Self. 'Tis your Misfortune now to write without a Rival and to be tempted by that means to be more careless than you would otherwise be in your Composures.

Thus much I could not forbear saying, tho' I have a matter[3] of Consequence in the H. of Lords to day, and must prepare for it. I am even with you for your ill Paper, for, I write upon worse having no other at hand. I wish you the Continuance of your health most heartily and am ever | Affectionately Yours | F. R.

⌐Old Craggs you know took Opium on purpose to destroy himself tho' our Friend the D. of Bucks did not.⌐[4]

I have sent Dr. Arbuthnot the Latin M.S.[5] which I could not find when you left me; and am so angry at the writer for his design, and his manner of executing it, that I could hardly forbear sending him a line of Virgil along with it. The chief Reasoner of that philosophic farce is a *Gallo-Ligur*, as he is call'd—what that means in English or French, I can't say—but all he says is in so loose and slippery and trickish a way of reasoning, that I could not forbear applying the passage of Virgil to him.

> *Vane Ligur, frustraque animis elate superbis!*
> *Nequicquam patrias tentasti lubricus artes—*[6]

To be serious, I hate to see a book gravely written, and in all the forms of argumentation, which proves nothing, and which says nothing; and endeavours only to put us into a way of distrusting our own

---

[1] Epitaph on Mr. Harcourt.—Pope, 1737–42. Lord Harcourt's son, a close friend of Pope, died 1 July 1720. The epitaph was not perfected before the end of 1722.

[2] any body's else but yours] any body's but yours *1737b*.

[3] matter] motion *1737–42*. (Elwin says the motion concerned the building of a dormitory for Westminster School against which Dr. Friend, master of the school, had secured an injunction. Atterbury's motion was carried, but after he was exiled the designs by Lord Burlington were changed. See *Dunciad A*, iii. 323 (ed. Sutherland, p. 189)).

[4] This sentence, found in the Harleian transcript, was omitted from Pope's printed texts, and apparently has not hitherto been printed. 'Old' Craggs is the father of Pope's friend; he had died ten days before this letter was written.

[5] Of Huetius, left after his death.—Pope, 1737–42. (It seems as if Atterbury was unaware that Huet had died 26 Jan. 1721. The MS. is his *De Imbecillitate mentis humanae*, which was translated (by Ozell?) and printed in 1725.)

[6] *Aeneid*, xi. 715–16 (adapted).

faculties, and doubting whether the marks of truth and falshood can in any case be distinguish'd from each other? Could that blessed point be made out (as it is a contradiction in terms to say it can,) we should then be in the most uncomfortable and wretched state in the world; and I would in that case be glad to exchange my reason, with a dog for his instinct, to morrow.[1]

JOHN DENNIS *to* POPE[2]   29 *April* 1721

Dunciad, second edition octavo, 1729 (Griffith 224)

April 29, 1721.

Sir,—As you have subscrib'd for two of my Books,[3] I have order'd them to be left for you at Mr. *Congreve*'s Lodgings: As most of those Letters were writ during the Time that I was so unhappy as to be in a State of War with you, I was forced to maim and mangle at least ten of them, that no Footsteps might remain of that Quarrel. I particularly left out about half the Letter which was writ upon publishing the Paper call'd the *Guardian*.[4] | I am, | Sir, | Your most obedient, | Humble Servant, | John Dennis.

JOHN GAY *to* CHARLES LOCKYER[5]   1 *May* 1721

The Bodleian Library

May 1, 1721

Sir,—Please to place to the Account of Alexander Pope Esqr all such Stock as is due to me for one thousand pounds of the third Subscription paid in upon my Name for sale of South Sea Stock. | J. Gay.

POPE *to* JOHN DENNIS[6]   3 *May* 1721

1729 Dennis, *Remarks*

Sir,—I call'd to receive the Two Books of your Letters from Mr. *Congreve*, and have left with him the little Money I am in your Debt.

---

[1] These last two paragraphs, not found in the Harleian transcripts, are added from Pope's printed text in the Roberts octavo of 1737. Presumably Pope added them from another letter, not now preserved.

[2] This letter was printed by Pope in the second octavo edition of the *Dunciad* of 1729 at the end of 'Errata M. Scriblerus Lectori', from which it is reprinted.

[3] His *Original Letters*, 2 v. 1721.

[4] Dennis ended this letter (ii. 286) remarking that *The Guardian* was carried on 'by a Triple League' and promising 'an Account of the two other Confederates by the first Opportunity'. Doubtless the truncated letter had contained his opinion of Pope as one of the 'league'.

[5] The note exists in Gay's hand in Montagu MS. d. 1. It is here printed from W. H. Irving, *John Gay*, p. 186 n. The transaction, as Irving indicates, is somewhat obscure, but clearly either Pope or Gay, and perhaps both, had not done too badly in the South Sea.

[6] Published by Dennis in his *Remarks upon Mr. Pope's Dunciad* (1729), p. 40, from which it is here reprinted. It was also printed in Charles Wilson's *Memoirs* of Congreve (1730), ii. 136.

I look upon myself to be much more so, for the Omissions you have been pleas'd to make in those Letters in my Favour, and sincerely join with you in the Desire, that not the least Traces may remain of that Difference between us which indeed I am sorry for. You may therefore believe me, without either Ceremony or Falseness, | Sir, | Your most Obedient, | Humble Servant, | A. Pope.

May 3, | 1721

*ATTERBURY to POPE[1]   [27 May 1721]

E. H. W. Meyerstein

Deanery | Whitsund-Eve.

I have heard nothing from Mr Longville,[2] tho' I have calld there again in my Airings, & left my name, which implyd my busyness; He himself being abroad. I think there is now no restraint in point of Ceremony to your proceeding with what hast you please in your Epitaph—which I shall be ready to deliver to your Mason, when he calls for it. I hope you enjoy all that pleasure of the Season, which I want, & am forc'd to want; being detaind here in Town much against my will—cùm frondent Sylvae, cùm formosissimus Annus.[3] I am always—, | Affectionately yours, | F. Roffen.

Address: To | Mr Pope, at | Twitnam.

Frank: Fra. Roffen.

Annotation [in Pope's hand]: *on Butler's Tomb in Westminster Abby.

POPE to BROOME   16 July 1721

Elwin–Courthope, viii. 47

Twitnam, July, 16, 1721.

Your letter made me melancholy, to find that silence of yours, which I hoped the effect of diversion, or better amusements, to have pro-

---

[1] The text is from a transcript kindly furnished by the late Mr. Meyerstein. The date is derived from the fact that Whitsunday in 1721 fell on 28 May.

[2] William Longueville (d. 21 Mar. 1720/1) had been one of Samuel Butler's most valued friends. Presumably it was his son Charles (d. 1750) on whom Atterbury had called concerning Butler's monument in the Abbey, which Alderman Barber erected in 1721. In his *Impartial History of the Life . . . of Mr. John Barber*, Edmund Curll prints Pope's (?) epitaph, calling it 'equally mean and notoriously false as to his Circumstances in Life':

'SAMUELIS BUTLERI, Qui Strenshamiæ in Agro Vigorn. Nat. 1612. Obiit Lond. 1680. Vir doctus imprimis, acer, integer: Operibus ingenii, non item premiis felix: Satyrici apud nos Carminis Artifex egregius; quo simulatæ Religioni Larvam detraxit, et Perduellium scelera liberrime exagitavit: Scriptorum in suo genere, Primus et Postremus:

　　　　Ne, cui vivo deerant fere omnia,
　　　　Deesset etiam mortuo Tumulus,

Hoc tandem, posito Marmore, curavit | JOHANNES BARBER, Civis Londinensis 1721.'

[3] Cf. Virgil, *Eclogues*, iii. 57.

ceeded from indisposition and sickness. Indeed, I sincerely take part
in all that affects you, and shall ever preserve all the sensations of that
friendship for you, which not only your kind inclinations, but your
actual services have merited from me. I heartily rejoice at the thoughts
you express of coming into this part of the world, in which I am very
sure there is no man more yours than myself. I beg it in particular
that you will make this place your home, which is now more worthy
of being so than ever, as being quite finished, and greatly improved and
enlarged since you saw it.

I showed your very letter to my Lady Mary Wortley, who is not a
little pleased at the zeal[1] of Mr. Tr., and proud of the thoughts, you
seem not averse to entertain, of honouring her. It would be, I think,
one of the finest occasions, as well as the justest, of writing so well as
you are able; and immortality, if such a thing be in the gift of English
poets, would be but a due reward for an action which all posterity may
feel the advantage of. Your motto from Virgil, in relation to the world's
being freed from the future terrors of the small-pox,

> Irrita perpetua solvent formidine terras,[2]

is as good an one as ever I read. I must not conclude without doing
myself a small piece of justice in telling you I wrote to you about a
month ago a very long letter, and am forced to make this shorter rather
than defer it, for I have stolen from a great deal of company to write it.
I am ever, with all affection, and the sincerest wishes for your health,
dear sir, your faithful friend and servant.

POPE *to* CARYLL　　　　　　　　　　　　　16 *July* 1721

Add. 28618

July 16. 1721.

Tho' 'tis indeed no compliment to tell you your letters are always a
pleasure to me, your last was so in a more particular manner, as it
acquainted me that you improved in your health (you can improve in
nothing else you are so good already). I should delight myself extremely
to imagine those few Spa waters I sent were anyway instrumental to it,
and wish I had more left, which should have attended this letter. The
next thing to that is to tell you that the best of these waters now in
England are at Mr Pigott's, a druggist, at the Greyhound in Newgate
Street, whom I recommend to you (if you have any occasion in his
way of trade) as a very honest young man of the household of faith,

---

[1] The zeal of the unidentified 'Tr.' was probably in furtherance of inoculation for small-
pox. No verses on this subject by Broome are known.

[2] Virgil, *Eclogues*, iv. 14.

the son of Councellor[1] Pigott and one just set up. I'll take care to procure and send 'em to you on the least notice; for I think if you find
benefit by the waters, you ought to continue 'em, and I make it my
request that you would do so.

I take it kindly that you say you'll make me no other invitation to
Grinstead, but to assure me I shall be welcome whenever I come. In
sincerity I've long wished I could, and Sir John Evelyn's lying in the
way, tho' some motive, yet was no way needful to allure me to a place
I like so much more as your own. You pique me a good deal in mentioning it. I wish you knew me for what I really am in an ancient &
settled respect for you and yours.

I have hopes given me that you'll be soon in London, where so soon
as you give me notice I will come on purpose to wait on you, and hope
I may enjoy your company here, without any such interruptions as
when I saw you last here (which unfeignedly troubled me much). If
I were inclined to return evil for evil, and pique in return to what
you said of Sir J Evelyn's, I would say that Lady Seaforth lives still
at Twittenham. I am faithfully | Dear sir | Your affect. friend and |
obliged humble servant | A P.

ATTERBURY *to* POPE   2 *August* 1721

Longleat Portland Papers, xiii (Harleian transcripts)

Bromly Augt. 2: 1721.

I hear nothing of the Pictures yet; nor, I believe, shall hear any thing
of them, till you send new Messages to quicken the Frame makers. I
should be glad now to have them down here as soon as can be, & beg
you to give your Orders accordingly. As soon as I hear they are lodged
at the Deanery, they shall not be long without a proper Convayance
hither. The Parliament will, it seems be up next week, after which I
will begin to form the Rout of my Excursions towards your parts:
hoping not long after to thank you at Twickenham for the favour of
your Company here at Bromly; where my Lameness, I thank God,
weares off faster than I imagined it would, so that I shall be able in
a fortnight to walk out of my Coach into your house with Ease, &
perhaps take a Short turn in your Gardens. I have found time to read
some parts of Shakespear which I was least acquainted with. I protest
to you, in an hundred places I cannot construe him, I dont understand
him. The hardest part of Chaucer is more intillegible to me than some
of those Scenes, not merely thro the faults of the Edition, but the
Obscurity of the Writer: for Obscure he is, & a little (not a little)

---

[1] Elwin mistakenly printed *Cornelius* for *Councellor*. Councellor Nathaniel Pigott lived
not far from Pope at Whitton. At his house Pope received medical attention after his coach
accident in 1726. See letters of 16 Sept. 1726 and immediately thereafter.

enclin'd now & then to Bombast whatever Apology you may have con-
triv'd on that head for him. There are Allusions in him to an hundred
things, of which I knew nothing, & can guess nothing. And yet without some competent knowledge of those matters there's no understanding him. I protest Æschylus does not want a Comment to me,
more than he does: so that I begin to despair of doing you any considerable Service. I depend upon your destroying that part of Homer
which I margined with my scrawls, and am most affectionately yours.

ATTERBURY *to* POPE   20 *August* 1721

Longleat Portland Papers, xiii (Harleian transcripts)

This is the first time I have been able to use my right hand since this
new fit of the Gout, you see how scurvily. However, I was willing
to put my self & you to this trouble as soon as I could, in order to do
justice to a person, whom I have in some measure wrong'd. You
remember the Character I gave you of *Catrou*.[1] It was a just one, as
far as I had read him which was on the Eclogues only. His performance on that part no ways answers the Expectations he had rais'd,
nor did he at that time understand his Author. But my late illness has
given me an Opportunity of perusing him throughout upon the
Georgics & the *Aeneid*, & I find he mends upon his Reader, & having
study'd his Author well towards this Edition (which he had not done
when he wrote upon the *Eclogues*) has struck out Observations,
especially in the *Aeneid* which well deserve your perusall. You will
smile, when I tell you that one reason for my thus determining in his
favour is my finding 2 or 3 thoughts in him which I had lit upon before,
& was pleased with, & it is a piece of self flattery to begin now to think,
that he is not an inconsiderable Writer. for if he is, I who have been
already in the same strain of thinking, must be contented to share the
Reflection.

   In short, you will find him worth reading & therefore pray thank
Mr Fenton for the discovery he made of this book. There is a great
Character given in him of Maubrun's piece of Epic Poetry [that] I
know not[;] if you do, give me some account of it, whether it be in
French or Italian, & how long ago published; that I may make proper
Enquirys after it. And if you can tell me the Title of the Book, let me
have it in Terminis. I suppose, this finds you upon the wing for
Glocestershire whither Lord Bathurst by a Letter I reced this morn-
ing, tells me, he is going out of London. Wherever you are, let me
hear from you, and believe me | Most affectionatly yours | F. R.

   [1] Father (François) Catrou published a French version of Virgil (6 v.) in 1716. He had
published a translation of the *Eclogues* in 1708.

Bromley Augt 20. 1721.

I forgot to thank you for the Reflections on Pastoral Poetry. I never saw that part of them you doubled down. In good earnest, as to that wanton way of rediculing serious writers, you & I differ.

—ad cætera penè gemelli.[1]

*POPE *to*——[2] [*August* 1721?]

Christ Church (Oxford) (Evelyn Letters)

Fragment

Since I saw you, I found a Letter here, that obliges me upon an affair of the first concern to me to take a journey in four days to Oxfordshire for some time. I shall still imagine that Fate will prevent Our Meeting at Twitnam, unless you will Secure me that pleasure from all future accidents, by doing what we first designd, & laying hold of the Present Day which seems to be the Time Destind, & not to be over-past. You see the Brightness of the Morning, the shower is passed & the Sun appeareth in our land. There is no more Faith to be given to English Barometers, than to English Men, not indeed from any fault in their own Structure, but meerly from the Variability of our Climate. I earnestly desire you both to mount, I will get on horseback and attend you, and I will also return with you this afternoon. Do not deny me this day, I plainly see you belong to the Publick all other days. Or I shall say with Titus, to you both,

O Amici! Diem perdidimus.[3]

*POPE *to* JACOB TONSON, JR. 3 *September* [1721]

Add. 28275

Oxford. Sept. 3.

Sir,—I sent twice to speak with you, the day I left London, before my Journey. I was with the Bp of Rochester, but you forgot to send me your Waller,[4] in which I will do you what service I can. I have

---

[1] Horace, *Epistles*, i. x. 3.

[2] All one can say of this fragment is that its mention of Twitnam seems to indicate that its date is later than 1719 when Pope removed to that place. The addressee and date are impossible to fix. It may be written to a neighbour (Craggs and Fenton come to mind; but Pope did not go to Oxford, so far as we know, during Craggs's brief residence in Twitnam); it might be written to Fortescue at Richmond, and it might be written to some friend even so far away as London. It should be addressed to someone who (Sundays apart?) belongs to 'the Publick'. Since Pope was in Oxford on business connected with his edition of Shakespeare early in September, the letter is placed thereabouts: it might go almost anywhere.

[3] Cf. Suetonius, *De vita Caesarum*: Titus, viii.

[4] If this is an allusion to a projected edition of Waller, Tonson or Pope later passed the project on to Fenton, who published for Tonson his excellent edition in 1729.

also ingagd Mr Kent to draw the Outline of Mr Addison[1] upon the Copper plate itself. You must therfore get a Plate prepard to etch upon, that I may send it him for that purpose.

Pray let the Division[2] of the Scenes in Shakespear be finishd with all speed: it will else greatly retard the Index.

As to the D. of Bucks' works: I have resolvd upon further thoughts, to give up the business of the Impression intirely out of my hands, & have no concern in the profits at all. The Bishop & her Grace, I find, inclined to imploy Mr Barber[3] in the whole matter, so that I shall have nothing to do but with the Trouble, in which I'l have no View, but to oblige her Grace. In this I'm sure I can't be in the wrong, nor accountable, or lyable to any misconstruction, or Thought of any Interest in it. I know this will seem Romantic to a Bookseller, even to You that are least a Bookseller. But you must allow a little madness to Poets.

I have a favour to ask of you, that if (as I'm told) poor Mr Craggs's Library comes into your hands to be disposed of, you will lay your hands upon an odd Volume of Barrows Sermons, which I lent him a week before he dyed, the loss of which will spoil me a whole Sett. You'l easily know it, for he had no other; it is bound in a Cover with a Table in it, the leaves sprinkl'd with red & green.

I have got a Man or two here at Oxford to ease me of part of the drudgery of Shakespear, If you'l let me draw upon you (as you told me) by parcells, as far as sixty pounds as they shall have occasion. I shall be at my Lord Bathursts at Cirencester in three days where your Commands will find | Your humble Servant | A. Pope.

Lord Harcourt went yesterday | to London.

Address: To | Mr Tonson at Shakesper's | head neer Somerset house | in the Strand | London

Frank: Geo. Clarke[4]

Postmark: 5/SE

Endorsements (in Tonson's hand on the third, blank, page):

      35*l* paid To Mr Pope's ordr } both sums paid to
      25 D⁰   To E: Fentons ordr } Mr popes Waterman

The 2 Notes for these Sums I gave up to Mr pope as being no part of the 1st agreement but which I agreed to allow Mr pope further that he might not want help. | JT | answered.

[1] Addison's *Works* (4 v.) were published within a month of the time Pope was writing, and Kent did no engraving for it.
[2] Before the word *Division* Pope wrote and crossed through the word *Index*.
[3] On 18 Apr. 1722 Barber secured the licence to publish the *Works*. The two volumes were published in Jan. 1723—and promptly suppressed. Pope evidently took profits from his labours. See Sherburn, *Early Career*, p. 227.
[4] Fellow of All Souls and M.P. for the University of Oxford.

POPE *to* LADY MARY WORTLEY MONTAGU[1]

15 *September* 1721

The Pierpont Morgan Library

Madam,—I write this purely to confess myself ingenuously what I am, a Beast; first for writing to you without gilt paper, & secondly for what I said & did about the Harpsichord. For which (& many other Natural reasons) I am justly turn'd as a Beast to Grass & Parkes. I deserve no better Pillow than a mossie bank, for that Head which cou'd be guilty of so much Thoughtlessness, as to promise what was not in my power, without considering first whether it was or not. But the truth is, I imagind you would take it merely as an Excuse, had I told you I had the Instrument under such conditions: and I likewise Simply thought I could obtain leave to lend it; which failing on the Trial, I suffer now (I find) in your opinion of my Veracity, purely from my Over-forward desire to have gratifyd you.

The next thing I can do, is to intreat you, since you have not the Harpsichord, that you'd have That & the Gallery together, for your Consorts which I sincerely wish you would make Use of, & which I take to be mine to lend unless my Mother knows of some Conditions against it, to Mr Vernon.[2]

I very much envy you your Musical Company, which you have a sort of obligation to believe, in return to a Man, who singly asserts your fine Tast that way, in contradiction to the whole world.

It must be sure from that piece of Merit (for I have no other that I know of toward you) that you can think of flattering me at 100 miles distance, in the most affecting manner, by a mention of my Trees & Garden. What an honour is it to my Great Walk, that the finest Woman in this world, cou'd not stir from it? That Walk extremely well answerd the Intent of its Contriver, when it detaind her there. But for this accident, how had I despisd, & totally forgot my own little *Colifichies*, in the daily Views of the noble Scenes, Openings, & Avenues of this immense Design at Cicester? No words, nor painting, nor poetry, (not even your own) can give the least Image proportionable to it: And my Lord Bathurst bids me tell you, & the Young Lady with you, that the Description would cost me much more time than it woud cost You to come hither; Which if you have any regard either for my pains, or reputation, you will do to save me that trouble; as well as to take to your Self the glory of describing it.

For lodging, you need be under no manner of concern; for he invites hither every Woman he sees, & ev'ry Man: Those of a more

[1] This is the last letter preserved to us from Pope to Lady Mary.

[2] Pope's landlord, Thomas Vernon, Esq., of Twickenham Park, had been secretary to the Duke of Monmouth, was a Turkey merchant and, with Sir Godfrey Kneller, churchwarden. He died in 1726.

aerial or musical nature, may lodge [i]n the Trees with the Birds; and those of a more Earthly or gross temperature, with the Beasts of the field, upon the ground.

We exceedingly rejoyce that you are in the State of Nuripan; & in that Situation, can no more help wishing ourselves with you, than if you were my Lady God— on a Couch; Tho indeed its to be feard, few Men cou'd be perfectly in that State, with you.[1] I am very Sincerely | Madam | Your Ladyships most | faithfull humble Servant | A. Pope.

Cirencester, | Sept. 15. 1721.

*POPE *to* JOSEPH BOWLES[2]   26 *September* 1721

The Bodleian Library

Twitenham, Sept. 26. 1721.

Sir,—I have sent the two last Volumes of Homer directed to You, by one Godfry a Carrier, whose Inn is over against All Souls in High street. I hope you have receivd 'em, and I take this opportunity of thanking you for the honour you have done me, in not permitting My Books to be imperfect in Your Library, where it is always an Honour to be read. I am with all true wishes for the prosperity of Tho't & Learning, (which with a Man of Your turn I believe includes your owne) | Sir. | Your most obligd | humble Servant | A. Pope.

Address: To | Mr Bowles, Keeper of | the Bodley-Library, in | Oxford.
Postmark: 26/SE

||ATTERBURY *to* POPE[3]   27 *September* 1721

Longleat Portland Papers, xiii (Harleian transcripts)

Bromly Septr. 27. 1721.

⌈I have been ill almost ever since I saw you, and as soon as I thought my self free from one fit of the Gout, persecuted by another. However,

[1] Except Moy Thomas no editor hitherto seems to have printed the last paragraph of this letter. 'Lady God—' is probably Lady Godolphin, whose affair with Congreve Lady Mary mentions more than once. She was Henrietta, Duchess of Marlborough, upon the death of her father in 1722. 'Nuripan' is linguistically inexplicable.

[2] The text is from Rawlinson Letters 90, f. 47.

Bowles was Bodley's Librarian from 1719 to 1729. On earlier volumes of the *Iliad* sent to Oxford see Pope to Dr. Abel Evans [Aug. 1717]. The superscription, in Pope's hand apparently, seems impossible. Pope was in Oxford the 3rd of September and on the 27th Atterbury writes to him as if the poet were in Cirencester, where he remained until early October. It seems unlikely that he was in Twickenham on 26 Sept. but he may possibly have made a brief journey home. In his letter of 15 Oct. Atterbury implies that his letter of 27 Sept. had to be forwarded to Pope from Cirencester.

[3] Printed in Pope's editions 1737–42 with omission of the first and last paragraphs and certain other phrases, here placed in half-brackets.

without Legs, I made a Shift to wait on the Dutchess, as she pass'd thro' Westminster to the Bath; and, at my return, found your Letter, of the 15th here, which was so much the more welcome to me, because it was the first I had from you, after we parted. The other, you mention, never reach'd me.⌐

I am now confin'd to my Bedchamber, and to the matted Room, wherein I am writing; seldom venturing to be carry'd down even into the Parlour to Dinner; unless when Company to whom I cannot excuse my self, comes; which I am not ill pleas'd to find is now very seldome. This is my Case the Sunny part of the year; what must I expect when *inversum contristat Aquarius annum?*[1]

If these things be done in the Green-tree, what will be done in the dry?[2] Excuse me for employing a Sentence of Scripture on this occasion; I apply it very seriously. One thing relieves me a little under the ill prospect I have of spending my time at the Deanery this Winter; that I shall have the opportunity of seeing you oftner: tho' I am afraid you will have but little pleasure in seeing me there. So much for my ill State of health, which I had not touch'd on had not your friendly Letter been so full of it, ⌐which now lyes before me.⌐ One Civil thing you say in it, made me think you had been reading Mr Waller; and possess'd of the Image at the End of his Copy a la Malade, had bestow'd it on One, who has no right to the least part of the Character. If you have not read the Verses lately, I am sure you remember 'em, because you forget nothing.

> With such a grace you entertain
> And look with such Contempt on pain, &c.

I mention them on the account of the Couplet but one that follows,[3] which ends with the very same Rhimes and Words (Appear & Clear) that the Couplet but one after that does—and therefore in my Waller there is a various Reading of the first of these Couplets: for there thus runs it.

> So Lightnings in a Stormy Air,
> Scorch more than when the Sky is fair.

You will say that I am not very much in pain nor very busy, when I can relish these amusements, And you will say true: for at present, I am in both these respects very easy.

I had not strength enough to attend Mr Prior to his Grave:[4] else I would certainly have done it, to have shew'd his Friends that I had

---

[1] Horace, *Sermones*, i. i. 36. [2] Luke xxiii. 31.
[3] In his editions Pope clarified the sense here; he reads: 'I mention them not on account of that couplet, but one that follows; which ends with the very same rhimes and words [appear and clear] that the couplet but one after that does.'
[4] Prior was buried in the Abbey, 25 Sept. 1721.

forgot, and forgiven the Libel[1] he wrote on me. He is buried, as he desired, at the Feet of Spencer; and I will take care to make good in every respect what I said to him when living; particularly as to the Triplet,[2] he wrote for his own Epitaph; which while we were in good Terms, I promised him, should never appear on his Tomb, while I was Dean of Westminster.

I am pleas'd to find that you have so much pleasure and (which is the foundation of it) so much health at Lord Bathursts. May both continue, till I see you! May my Lord have as much satisfaction in building the House in the Wood and using it, when built, as you have in designing it! I cannot send a Wish after him that means him more Happiness; and yet I am sure I wish him as much, as he wishes himself. ⌜I will tell him so myself by this Post if the time permits; or if not, by the next.⌝

⌜Lady Dutches said nothing to me of the Dukes Papers.[3] Had she, my Answer would have been, what it always has been; the Trust cannot be lodg'd in more proper hands. I am really no judge of what's fit, or unfit in such a case: and tho' I would oblige her Grace in any way suitable to my Function, yet I would not step out of my Character, to do her a disservice. I honor'd the Duke while living, and I will not hurt his Memory, after his death; as I should probably do if I busyed myself in a matter to which I am no ways Equal. But I have fill'd my Paper, and must bid you good night, with assurances, that I am always and to all degrees | Yours F. R.⌝

†POPE *to* EDWARD BLOUNT[4]   *3 October* 1721

1735

Rentcomb in Gloucestershire, Oct. 3. 1721.
Your kind Letter has overtaken me here, for I have been in and about this Country ever since your departure. I am pleas'd to date this from a place so well known to Mrs. *Blount*, where I write as if I were dictated by her Ancestors, whose faces are all upon me. I fear none so much as Sir *Christopher Guise*, who being in his Shirt, seems as ready

---

[1] forgiven the Libel he] forgiven what he *1737–42*. (The libel was the annoying epigram 'On Bishop Atterbury's burying the Duke of Buckingham, MDCCXX.')

[2] Prior's triplet 'For my own Tombstone' (*Poetical Works*, ed. R. B. Johnson, ii. 9) is somewhat more cynical than his 'Epitaph Extempore' (ibid. ii. 202).

[3] This omitted paragraph is to be compared with Pope to Tonson, 3 Sept. 1721. The *impression* (printing?) is out of Pope's hands, but he is committed to the trouble of editing.

[4] Printed by Pope in all his editions except 1735 a2 and 1737 b. Rentcomb, not many miles from Cirencester, was the seat of Sir John Guise, brother of Mrs. Edward Blount. Sir Christopher was her grandfather. The first paragraph alludes to a quarrel between Sir John and Nicholas Lechmere, Chancellor of the Duchy of Lancaster. The circumstances of the quarrel are obscure, but a ballad on the occasion, 'Duke upon Duke' (published in 1720), was apparently in part the work of Pope. See Ault, *New Light*, pp. 186–94.

to combate me, as her own Sir *John* was to demolish Duke *Lancastere*. I dare say your Lady will recollect his Figure. I look'd upon the Mansion, Walls, and Terraces; the Plantations, and Slopes, which Nature has made to command a variety of Vallies and rising Woods; with a Veneration mixt with a Pleasure, that represented her to me in those puerile Amusements, which engaged her so many Years ago in this place: I fancy'd I saw her sober over a Sampler, or gay over a joynted Baby. I dare say she did one thing more, even in those early times; *remember'd her Creator in the Days of her Youth.*

You describe so well your Heremitical state of Life, that none of the antient Anchorites could go beyond you, for a Cave in a Rock, with a fine Spring, or any of the Accommodations that befit a Solitary. Only I don't remember to have read, that any of those venerable and holy Personages took with them a Lady, and begat Sons and Daughters. You must modestly be content to be accounted a Patriarch. But were you a little younger, I should rather rank you with Sir *Amadis*, and his fellows. If Piety be so Romantick, I shall turn Hermit in good earnest; for I see one may go so far as to be Poetical, and hope to save one's Soul at the same time. I really wish myself something more, that is, a Prophet; for I wish I were as *Habakkuk*, to be taken by the Hair of the Head, and visit *Daniel* in his Den. You are very obliging in saying, I have now a whole Family upon my hands, to whom to discharge the part of a Friend: I assure you I like 'em all so well, that I will never quit my Hereditary Right to them; you have made me yours, and consequently them mine. I still see them walking on my Green at *Twickenham*, and gratefully remember (not only their green Gowns) but the Instructions they gave me how to slide down, and trip up the steepest Slopes of my Mount.[1]

Pray think of me sometimes, as I shall often of you; and know me for what I am, that is, | Yours.

|| ATTERBURY *to* POPE[2]   15 *October* 1721

Longleat Portland Papers, xiii (Harleian Transcripts)

Bromly Octr 15. 1721.

Notwithstanding I write this here on Sund. Even: to acknowledge the Receipt of yours this morning, yet I forsee, it will not reach you at Twitnam, till Wedn. Morn. And before Set of Sun that day, I hope to reach my Winter Quarters at the Deanery. Hope did I say? I recall that word, for it implys desire and God knows that is far from being

---

[1] One judges that the two youngest daughters of Mr. Blount performed this feat. The second daughter (of four), who was later married to the Duke of Norfolk, was born in 1702.
[2] Printed by Pope, 1737–42, with some omissions here printed for the first time and placed in half-brackets. Other textual changes within Pope's texts are negligible.

the case. For I never part with this place but with Regret; tho' I generally keep here (what Mr Cowley calls) the worst Company in the world, my Own; and see either none beside or what is worse than none, some of the Arrij, or Sebosi of my Neighbourhood: Characters, which Tully paints so well in one of his Epistles,[1] and complains of the too Civil, but Impertinent Interruption they gave him in his Retirement.

Since I have nam'd those Gentlemen, and the Book is not far from me, I will turn to the place, and by pointing it out to you, give you the pleasure of perusing the Epistle, which is a very agreeable one, if my memory does not fail me—⌐It has cost me half an hour, to find out the place, to no purpose. however, without asking your excuse for so odd a manner of writing I proceed.⌐

I am surpriz'd to find that Lord Bathurst and you parted so soon. ⌐I thought I was sure of my Letters finding you there for a Month at least, after your Arrival, and by my Computation, you did not stay there much above a fortnight. You say not in yours whether he is come, or when he comes to Town.⌐ He has been sick, I know, of some late Transactions.[2] But should that Sickness continue still in some measure, I prophesy it will be quite off by the beginning of Novr. A Letter or two from his London Friends, and a Surfiet of Solitude, will soon make him change his Resolution and his Quarters. I vow to you, I could live here with pleasure all the Winter, and be contented with hearing no more news than the London Journal, or some such Trifling Paper, affords me, did not the Duty of my place require absolutely my attendance at Westminster where I hope the Prophet will now and then remember he has a Bed and a Candlestick. In short I long to see you, and hope you will come, if not a Day, yet at least an Hour sooner to Town than you intended, in order to afford me that satisfaction. I am now, I thank God, as well as ever I was in my life; except, that I can walk scarce at all, without ⌐the help of⌐ Crutches. And would willingly compound the matter with the Gout, to be no better, could I hope to be no worse. But that is a vain thought. I expect a new Attack long before Christmas. Let me see you therefore while I am in a Condition to rellish you; *before the Days* (and the Nights) *come, when I shall* (and must) *say, I have no pleasure in them.* I will bring your small 12° of Pastorals along with me, that you may not be discourag'd from lending me books, when you find me so punctual in restoring them. Shakespear shall bear it Company, and be put into your hands as clean and fair as it came out of them: tho' you,

---

[1] *Ad Atticum*, II. xiv and xv.

[2] Surely it is possible to surmise from this passage that Lord Bathurst and even Pope were not altogether unaware of the 'transactions' concerning the Pretender in which Atterbury was embarked. One can only surmise; but the tradition remains that Lord Bathurst's son, the Lord Chancellor, destroyed his father's papers as showing him involved in Jacobitism.

I think have been dabling here and there with the Text. I have had more Reverence for the Writer and the Printer, and left every thing standing just as I found it. However I thank you for the pleasure you have given me in putting me upon reading him once more before I dy. I believe I shall scarce repeat that pleasure any more, having other Work to do and other things to think of; but none that will interfere with the Offices of Friendship, in the Exchange of which with you, Sir, I hope to live and dye | Your affectionate faithful Servant | Fra Roffen.

Addison's Works[1] came to my hands yesterday. I cannot but think it a very odd set of Incidents that the Book should be dedicated by a Deadman[2] to a Deadman:[3] and even that the New[4] Patron to whom Tickell chose to inscribe his Verses should be dead also before they were publish'd. Had I been in the Editors place, I should have been a little apprehensive for my self, under a thought that every one, who had any hand in that work, was to dye before the publication of it. You see, when I am conversing with you, I know not how to give or'e, till the very bottome of the Paper admonishes me once more to bid you | Adieu.

†POPE *to* EDWARD BLOUNT[5]　　　　21 *October* 1721

¹735　　　　　　　　　　　　　　　Twickenham, Oct. 21. 1721.

Your very kind and obliging manner of enquiring after me, among the first Concerns of Life, at your Resuscitation, should have been sooner answer'd and acknowledg'd. I sincerely rejoice at your recovery from an Illness which gave me less pain than it did you, only from my Ignorance of it. I should have else been seriously and deeply affected,[6] in the thought of your danger by a Fever. I think it a fine and a natural thought, which I lately read in a private Letter of *Montaigne*,[7]

---

1 Addison's Works] Mr. Addison's Works *1737 b*. (Subscribers might have the four volumes at the end of September, but Atterbury did not subscribe.)

2 Mr. Addison.—Pope 1737-42.

3 Mr. Craggs.—Pope 1737-42.

4 Lord Warwick.—Pope 1737-42.

5 The date is as Pope always printed it. Elwin, without explanation, changed the year to 1723, perhaps because Coste's edition of Montaigne's letters is dated 1724. The letter appears in all of Pope's editions except 1735 a 2. Pope knew Coste and evidently saw a copy in advance of publication.　　　　　　　　　　　　5 affected] afflicted *1737-42*.

7 a private . . . giving] a letter of Montaigne's publish'd by P. Coste, giving *1737-42*.

P. Coste, who had been tutor to the Earl of Shaftesbury and was soon to be tutor to Edmund, Duke of Buckingham, in 1724 published in London his famous edition of Montaigne's *Essais*. The passage Pope translates is from a letter from Montaigne to his father concerning the death of La Boëtie, found in Coste, iii. 395-409. Since the mention of Coste appeared first in Pope's text of 1737, he may simply be mentioning 'the best edition', although he used in 1721 an earlier edition. Coste had evidently published a 'Specimen' of his edition

giving an account of the last words of an intimate Friend of his:
'Adieu my Friend! the pain I feel will soon be over, but I grieve for
that you are to feel, which is to last you for Life.'

I join with your Family in giving God thanks for lending us a
worthy Man somewhat longer. The Comforts you receive from their
Attendance put me in mind of what old *Fletcher* of *Saltoune*[1] said one
day to me: 'Alas, I have nothing to do but to die; I am a poor Individual; no Creature to wish, or to fear, for my life or death: 'Tis the
only reason I have to repent being a single Man; now I grow old, I
am like a Tree without a Prop, and without young Trees ⌐ of my own
shedding,⌐[2] to grow round me, for Company and Defence.'

I hope the Gout will soon go after the Fever, and all evil things
remove far from you. But pray tell me, when will you move towards
us? If you had an Interval to get hither, I care not what fixes you
afterwards, except the Gout. Pray come, and never stir from us again.
Do away your dirty Acres, cast 'em to dirty People, such as in the
Scripture Phrase *possess the land.* Shake off your Earth like the noble
Animal in *Milton.*

> The tawny Lyon, pawing to get free
> His hinder Parts, he springs as broke from Bonds,
> And rampant shakes his brinded Main: the Ounce,
> The Lizard, and the Tyger, as the Mole
> Rising, the crumbled Earth above them threw
> In Hillocks![3]

But I believe *Milton* never thought, these fine Verses of his should
be apply'd to a Man selling a parcel of dirty Acres; tho' in the main
I think it may have some resemblance; for God knows this little space
of Ground nourishes, buries, and confines us, as that of *Eden* did those
Creatures, till we can shake it loose, at least in our Affections and
Desires.

Believe me, dear Sir, I truly love and value you; let Mrs. *Blount*
know that she is in the list of my *Memento Domine's Famulorum
Famularumque's,*[4] &c. My poor Mother is far from well, declining;
and I am watching over her, as we watch an expiring Taper, that even
when it looks brightest, wastes fastest. I am (as you will see from the
whole Air of this Letter) not in the gayest nor easiest Humour, but
always with Sincerity, | Dear Sir, | Yours.

earlier. In a letter from Atterbury to the Duchess of Buckingham, 2 June 1723 (preserved in the Harvard College Library as MS. 218.2), we read concerning Coste: 'I do not
see but your Grace has chosen well; but I should better be able to judge upon a second Sight
of him, if that happens. What I do know of him, I like. He spoke to me about the Specimen of
Montagne, and lay'd it upon his Bookseller, and seem'd very sensible of the Indecency of it.'
   [1] Fletcher died in London in 1716. Pope's acquaintance with him is obscure.
   [2] Omitted 1737–42.   [3] *Paradise Lost,* vii. 464–9.
   [4] From the Memento for the Living in the Canon of the Mass.

||POPE *to* ROBERT, EARL OF OXFORD[1]   21 *October* 1721

Longleat Portland Papers, xiii

From my Lord Harley's in Dover Street
Octob. 21. 1721.

My Lord,—Your Lordship may be surpriz'd at the liberty I take in
writing to you; tho you will allow me always to remember, that You
once permitted me that honour, in conjunction with some others who
better deserv'd it.[2] Yet I hope, you will not wonder I am still desirous
to have you think me your gratefull & faithful Servant; but I own I
have an Ambition yet farther, to have Others think me so; which is
the occasion I give your Lordship the trouble of this. Poor Parnell,
before he dyed, left me the charge of publishing these few Remains of
his:[3] I have a strong Desire to make them, their Author, and their
Publisher, more considerable, by addressing & dedicating 'em All, to
You. There is a pleasure in bearing Testimony to Truth; and a
Vanity perhaps, which at least, is as excusable as any Vanity can be. I
beg you My Lord, to allow me to gratify it, in prefixing this paper of
honest Verses to the Book. I send the Book itself, which I dare say
you'l receive more Satisfaction in perusing, than you can from any
thing written upon the Subject of yourself. Therfore I am a good deal
in doubt, whether you will care for such an addition to it? I'll only
say for it, that tis the only Dedication I ever writ,[4] & shall be, whether
you permit it or not: For I will not bow the knee to a Less Man than
my Lord Oxford, & I expect to see no Greater in My Time.

After all, if your Lordship will tell my Lord Harley that I must not
do this, you may depend upon a total Suppression of these Verses (the
only Copy whereof I send you) But you never shall suppress that
Great, Sincere, & entire, Admiration & Respect, with which I am
always | My Lord, | Your most faithful, most | obedient, & most
humble Servant, | A. Pope.

Endorsement: From Alex: Pope Esqr | octo: 21: 1721 | with His verses.[5]

---

[1] Pope printed this letter, 1737–42, with only two or three negligible changes in phrasing.

[2] In conjunction with the members of the Scriblerus Club in 1713.

[3] Pope's edition of Parnell's *Poems on Several Occasions* was published by Lintot in
Dec. of 1721, but dated 1722. The epistle 'To the Right Honourable, Robert, Earl of
Oxford and Earl Mortimer' was printed on pp. [iii–vi], and was dated, somewhat curiously
in view of the present letter, 'Sept. 25, 1721'. Pope sent Oxford the verses with this letter,
and since the MS. text has been printed by Professor G. Tillotson in *Pope and His Contemporaries* (ed. J. L. Clifford and L. A. Landa, Oxford, 1949), pp. 65–67, they are not here printed.

[4] This statement is not literally true, since *The Rape of the Lock* had been dedicated to
Mrs. Arabella Fermor and Pope's *Iliad* (at the end of vol. vi) to Congreve, apart from casual
inscribing of poems by inclusion in the text of dedicatory phrases; e.g. *Windsor Forest* to
Lansdowne, *The Dunciad* (later) to Swift, the *Essay on Man* (also later) to Bolingbroke, &c.
But Pope did not write eulogistic dedications in the fashion practised by Dryden and others.

[5] This endorsement is in the hand of Lord Oxford, who also at the end of the poem wrote:
'Alexander Pope Esqr | His dedication | original. | 1721.'

*POPE *to* CHARLES LOCKYER¹   1 *November* 1721
The Bodleian Library

Novemb 1: 1721

Sir,—Pray Pay Mr Sam. Hasten or Order my Dividend on 2786: 13. 4 South Sea Stock due at Midsummer last 1721 & this shall be your Discharge. | Alr Pope

To Charles Lockyer Esqr | Accomptant to the South Sea Company | 1487.

‖ROBERT, EARL OF OXFORD *to* POPE²   6 *November* 1721
Longleat Portland Papers, xiii

Brampton-Castle, Nov. 6. 1721.

Sir,—I received your Packet by the Carrier, which could not but give me great Pleasure, to see you preserve an Old Friend in Memory: for it must needs be very agreeable to be Remembred by those we highly Value. But then, how much Shame did it cause me! When I read your fine Verses inclos'd, my Mind reproach'd me how far short I came of what your great Friendship & delicate Pen would partially describe me. You ask my Consent to Publish it; to what Streights doth This reduce me! I look back, indeed, to those Evenings I have usefully & pleasantly spent with Mr Pope, Mr Parnel, Dean Swift, the Doctor, &c. I should be glad the World knew you admitted me to your Friendship: and, since your Affection is too hard for your Judgement, I am contented to let the World see, how well Mr Pope can write upon a barren Subject. I return you an exact Copy of the Verses, that I may keep the Original, as a Testimony of the Only Error you have been guilty of. I hope very speedily to Embrace you in London, and to assure you of the particular Esteem & Friendship wherewith I am | Sir | Your most faithful | & most humble Servant | Oxford.

I keep the Printed Paper, because I think | you have more of them.

*POPE *to* ROBERT, EARL OF OXFORD³   12 *December* 1721
Portland MSS. Harley xxxiv

Dec. 12, 1721

My Lord,—I cannot, by any Words, express my obligation to you,

¹ The text is from Montagu MS. d. 1, f. 143.
² This is Oxford's reply to Pope's letter of 21 Oct. 1721. Preserved with the fair copy (elaborately done) is Oxford's rough draft of the letter. The 'Printed Paper' mentioned in the postscript was probably the volume of Parnell's *Poems*, very likely in folded sheets. The letter was printed by Pope, 1737–42, with no textual changes notable.
³ This letter was printed by the Hist. MSS. Comm. (*Portland MSS.* v. 630) as if addressed to Lord Harley. It seems surely to his father, and concerns the publication of Pope's Epistle to Lord Oxford, used as dedication in Parnell's *Poems*, which Pope published in December 1721 (dated 1722). The letter is here printed from the original, deposited in the British Museum.

for the permission your Lordship gives me to print these verses. I am thoroughly sensible how much Honour is done to any man, from whom, a Person of so much real Greatness of Mind, will Suffer Praise: & I am, with the truest Gratitude for this Distinction shown me, and with the utmost Faithfulness, | My Lord, | Your most sincere | Admirer, & most | affectionate Servant | A. Pope.

*POPE *to* VISCOUNT HARCOURT[1]   19 *December* 1721

Harcourt MSS.

Twitenham, Decr 19.

My Lord,—I know I need not give your Lordship any Thanks, or if I shou'd attempt it, before the thanks would reach you, I shoud find the Obligations doubled. I have sent Dr Parnel's book for the Duke,[2] & think it happy that I shall not go with it, since your Lordship will by that means be my Orator: an Advantage so great, that I think it would be my wisest way never once to come near you while you are doing me service, friendship, & honour.

Believe me my Lord, (what you cannot but believe me) with the sincerest respect & fidelity | Your most obligd, most obedient Servant | A. Pope.

Endorsement: 19 D:embr 1721 Mr Pope | to Lord Vicount | Harcourt.

1 This is the first of Pope's letters to Lord Harcourt that we have. It was printed in *Harcourt Papers*, ii. 87.
2 Parnell's *Poems* were published 7 Dec. 1721. The duke is unidentified.

As editor of the Duke of Buckingham's *Works* (to be published in 1723), of Shakespeare's *Works* (6v., 1725), and as translator, in part, of the *Odyssey*, Pope in 1722 was more than normally busy. The dominant figure in the correspondence of the year is Bishop Atterbury, who was charged with high treason and sent to the Tower in August. It is possible that Atterbury used Pope as a blind: i.e. his relations with the poet might serve to indicate complete engrossment in literature rather than in Jacobite plots. It is also possible that Pope served to keep the bishop in touch with such noble friends as Bathurst and Harcourt, who were not quite above suspicion in the plot of 1722–3. In June, other editors have thought, Pope made a very pleasant visit to the Digbys at Sherborne: it seems probable, however, that the letters dealing with that visit should be dated 1724, and in this edition they are placed there. On the whole Pope's health was as good as usual, but he had, as always, bad days at least.

---

*POPE *to* JONATHAN RICHARDSON[1] [1722?]

The St. James's Chronicle, 1–3 August 1776

I am to thank you for a Piece of Pleasure which I cannot abstract from a Piece of Vanity received in the Perusal of the young Lady's Verses upon me. But what Sort of Thanks I am to pay her, you can best inform me. She has made me too proud to say with the common Terms—I thank her humbly. This is saying all I can upon so delicate a Subject as one's own Commendation.

I can only wish I were as sure I writ well as I am sure the Lady does. | I am, Sir, | Your most humble Servant, | A. Pope.

ATTERBURY *to* POPE[2] 1 *January* [1721/2?]

Longleat Portland Papers, xiii (Harleian transcripts) Bromly
New Years day.

Sir,—My Son desires me to forward the enclos'd New-years-gift, but has not the Courage to write to you about it, himself. He has

[1] The heading of the letter in the *Chronicle* reads: 'Mr. Pope to Mr. Richardson, in answer to one of the Letters, with some Verses of Miss Cowper inclosed.' Miss Cowper's 90 lines commending Pope and beginning 'O Pope, by what commanding wond'rous Art' were written in 1720. It has been thought that they did not reach Pope until 1722, but this seems an improbable delay. After 1728 Miss Cowper wrote another set of verses (42 ll.) to Pope. See Falconer Madan, *The Madan Family*, pp. 265, 271.

[2] In the Harleian transcripts (ff. 209–14) this letter begins with the translation of Ode 9 of Book III; then the letter follows, and then Ode 3 of Book IV. Here it seems convenient

ventur'd to translate two Odes of Horace, that are every ones Favourites, and he now ventures to send those Translations to you: not out of any Opinion he has of their Value, but a desire of making you some little Present in Poetry, and an Inability to write anything from his own Invention. He hopes that if you see any thing in them of Horace's Spirit, and Turn, you will, for the sake of it, forgive whatever else is a miss, He wishes, you would touch them over with your Pen, and believes, that in a Quarter of an Hour you could make these Translations worth reading; which as they stand now, must be read by no other Eyes but your Own. He would fain have had me do something to them, before they went out of his hands, but I told him I was too Old, too Ill, and too Busy. However I found time enough to make several Objections, and will be Impertinent enough to give you his Answers.

In the Dialogue, I excepted against the last line of the first Stanza; where he has put *Phraates*, for *Persarum rege*, I thought it would not be understood. Why thats strange, says the Boy, sure every Body knows that to be the Name of the King of Persia, and there pertly quoted to me that line out of another Ode, *Redditum cyri solio Phraatem*[1]—However says he, 'tis easy to alter that Verse, and it may run if you please, *Not Eastern Kings were half so blest*. I did not like that neither, but not being able to suggest any thing better my self, pass'd on to the other Stanzas.

The Beginning of the 3d I told him was not exactly suited to Horace's Turn of Words.

> Me Chloe now possesses whole
> Her Voice and Lyre command my Soul

He confes'd it, and said, he had for that reason translated it, at first—

> Now Chloe reigns, my new Desire,
> Expert to sing, and touch the Lyre.

But he thought the other Verses had more Spirit in them than these, and were not very remote from the Poets manner of speaking—Don't you think so too Papa? says he. I was willing to humor him, and therefore quitted the Objection.

In the 5th Stanza, I for the same reason excepted against these two Verses.

> Should banish'd Chloe cease to reign
> And Lydia her lost power regain.

to place the two odes together after the letter. In Thomas Birch's Life of Atterbury in *The General Dictionary*, ii (1735), 414, the two odes are printed as by Atterbury himself 'when he was young'.   [1] *C*. ii. ii. 17.

and he was presently at me with two others—

> Should Chloe banish'd, leave the door
> Open to Lydia, as before.

This says he is close, but methinks 'tis Flat, the Metaphor of a Door will never do well, on this occasion in English.

By the same way he justify'd the Change of Cork into *Down* in the last Stanza, and there I agreed with him. But upon the last Verse of all, he told me one particular, which I confess, I was pleas'd with, that he had ballanc'd for half a Quarter of an Hour, whether it should run as it dos, or in this Manner.

> Would with thee Live, and with thee dye.

I thought this Verse the smoother of the two, and he own'd it was: but said, the Accent was there improperly plac'd on the word, *with* whereas the Word *Thee*, would much better support it. I encourag'd him, wherever he doubted, to try every thing by his Ear, with Equal Nicety; and assur'd him, however the doubt in most cases, might be of no great importance, yet that way of poysing words would bring him at last to write with some Exactness. Did I not venture too far out of my depth in saying so? if I did, yet there is no body but Us three that knows of it. I went back again from the last to the first Verse of the Ode.

> Whilst I was fond and you were kind.

I shew'd him, that he set out wrong, and that his English did not answer rightly to Horace's Words; but he insisted that it answer'd to his meaning, I could not deny that, and therefore let him enjoy his Turn, tho' I lookt upon it, as a Sin, against Simplicity:

As to the 2d Ode, he has got a Whim into his head, which I think not very Improbable, That it was written by Horace, upon the Honor that was done him, in placing his Bust among the heads of the other Poets, in the Palatine Library: and he has gotten together some scraps from Suetonius, the Old Commentator, and other parts of Horace, which he thinks, clears this point, as well as the Diction and turn of the Ode it self.

He observ'd, that the Verses—interamabiles—Vatum ponere me Choros, could no way so naturally be interpreted, and that the Word, *ponere* there was a Term of Art, relating to *Statues*, Nay the young Critic ventur'd to affirm, that unless this were the foundation of the Ode, the four last lines would not be intelligible: for what, says he, means Quod spiro &c. after he had allow'd himself to be pointed out by Passengers, when he walked the Street? But if the three first Verses relate to Notice taken of his Bust by those [who] walk'd in the Vatican

Gallery—the Quod spiro et placeo that follows, is an improvement, since it was not usual to place the Heads of living Poets there, especially by publick Order, as the Ode seems to insinuate that this was done—I found, upon reading this Translation, that it had an Eye to this Conjecture, all the way, and was turn'd accordingly; and so easily saw, why he was so fond of his new Criticism particularly, in the last[1] Stanza, he has left the Phrase of Horace, and express'd what he thinks his Sense upon this Supposition: for he tells me he can produce authoritys, to shew, that the Statue of Apollo was set up, on a Golden Base, at the Upper End of the Library, and that the Poets Heads were placed round him. But if that were the Case, I said, and the Digito prætereuntium did certainly relate to those who resorted to that Library, yet it was not allowable to depart so far from the Expression of his Author; and therefore advis'd him by all means to alter that Line—*Now see me near Apollo's Throne*, He did so, and put this other in the room of it, *My skill in Lyric numbers own*, or rather said he, *My new unrivall'd Honor own*, That, I allow'd was nearer to the Latin, but still not near enough. However, I could not perswade him to try again, for he said, the Digitus prætereuntium if strictly follow'd, would never appear graceful in English. But then I ask'd him, what became of that Parenthesis, si placeo? He said, he lookt upon it as improper and an ill tim'd piece of Modesty, and therefore had wholly omitted it. I frown'd upon him, but he justify'd himself, by observing, that after Horace had declar'd in the former part of the Ode, that he was acknowledg'd by the Romans to be the Prince of Lyric Poets, and pointed out as such by the Fingers of Passengers, it was too late for him to say, si placeo and inconsistent with what he had said before. I could not but allow him to have some reason in what he said, and yet I doubt not, but that the true Secret of the matter was, that he left out the Parenthesis because he had not Room for it.

You see, how free I make with you in relating this Chit Chat between me and my Son, with whose Prose as well as Verse I have now tir'd you, and am I own sufficiently tir'd my self. I add only, that, as you are the best Poet Living, so I wish you would be the best Friend to him too; and either burn his Verses, or make them worth preserving. | I am ever affectionately Yours | F. R.

When you come to London (any time after the 12th) be so good as to call at the Deanery.

Once more let me be so impertinent as to tell you, that, upon asking *Obby*, how he came to pitch upon these two particular Odes, his answer was, because they were of so different a kind: the one Sweet the other Noble: the One in Dialogue; the Other not. And therefore

---

[1] *last* is inserted in the second Lord Oxford's hand.

says he, I have translated them in a different sort of Verse (he meant Rhime) best suited, as I thought to each of them, But Papa says he, will you give me leave to ask you a Question? do you observe nothing particular in my Rhimes? I was at a loss—Why says he; I have heard you object against this sort of writing, because the same[1] Rhime return'd too often upon the Ear, sometimes more than once in short Copys written by great hands. Now says he, I have not repeated the same Rhime in all these Verses; except one in the Dialogue, where it was necessary to repeat the same Words in two different Stanzas.

I shall have trouble with this Boy, as He and I grow older I see, he will be an Errant Patron of Rhime, and Justify his Opinion of it to my Teeth. He has told me already, that it was no Constraint upon a good Pen, for Mr Dryden and Mr Pope write as easily with Rhime as others do without it.

But I'll fold up this long Letter, and plague you no farther.

Hor. L. iii. O. 9

Donec Gratus eram tibi, &c.

H.   Whilst I was fond, and you were kind,
Nor any Dearer youth reclin'd
On your soft Bosom, sunk to rest
Phraates was not half so blest.

L.   Whilst you ador'd no other Face
Nor Lov'd me in the Second place
My happy Celebrated Name
Out shone ev'n Ilia's envy'd fame.

H.   Me Chloe now possesses whole
Her voice and Lyre command my Soul;
Nor would I death it self decline,
Could her life ransom'd be with mine.

L.   For me young lovely Calais burns,
And warmth for warmth my heart returns
Twice I would Life with ease resign
Could his be ransom'd once with mine.

H.   What if Sweet Love, whose bands we broke,
Again should tame us to the Yoke!
Should banish'd Chloe cease to reign
And Lydia her lost power regain?

---

[1] *same* is inserted in the second Lord Oxford's hand.

L.   Tho' Hesperus be less fair than he,
Thou Wilder than the raging Sea,
Lighter than Down: yet glader I
With thee would live, with thee would dye.

Hor. L. iv. O. 3.
Quem tu Melpomene semel &c.
By the B. of R.[1]

I.   He, on whose Birth the Lyric Queen
Of Numbers smiles, shall never grace
The Isthmian Gauntlet nor be seen
First in the fam'd Olympic Race

He shall not after Toyls of War
And taming haughty Monarchs pride
With Lawrell'd Brows, conspicuous far
To Jove's Tarpeian Temple Ride.
But him the Streams that warbling Flow
Rich Tiburs flow'ry Vale along
And shady Groves (his Haunts) shall know
The Master of Æolian Song.

II.   The Sons of Rome, Majestick Rome
Have fix'd me in the Poets Quire
And envy now, or dead, or dumb
Forbears to blame what they admire.
Goddess of the sweet sounding Lute
Which thy harmonious touch Obeys,
Who can'st the Finny Race tho Mute
To Cygnets dying Accents raise.
Thy Gift it is, that all with ease
(Now see me near Apollo's Throne)
My new unrivall'd Honors own
That still I live, and living please
O Goddess, is thy gift alone!

---

[1] Obviously this ascription to the B[ishop] of R[ochester] has crept into the letter un-
authorized by the original as sent to Pope. Atterbury may have confessed authorship, or
may have had it thrust upon him.

†POPE *to* THE DUCHESS OF BUCKINGHAM¹

1735

27 *January* [1721/2?]

Twitnam, Jan. 27, 1720.

Madam,—I think myself obliged by your Grace's many Condescentions of Goodness to me, in particular your informing me by a Line of Dr. *Ch*—'s² State of Health. I am really impatient to hear further of him.

The Morning I left the Town, I went with Mr *Jervas* to *Belluchi*'s,³ but parting in Haste, I had not his Opinion at large; only he assures me, he thinks the Figures will not be too small, considering that those which are nearest the Eye, are, at least, as large as the Life. I can't but be of Opinion, that my Lord Duke's and your Grace's, ought to be made Portraits, and as like as possible; of which they have yet, no Resemblance. There being no Picture (as I believe) of the Duke in Profile, it might be well, I fancy, if *Belluchi* copied the Side-Face from that *Busto* that stands in the *Salon*.

I beg your Grace's Pardon for the Freedom with which I write to you: And I ought to ask it, (now I think on't) on another Occasion, in which I have used too much Freedom: Having a great Esteem for the famous *Bononcini*,⁴ not only from his great Fame, but from a Personal Knowledge of his Character; and this being increased by the ill Treatment he has met with here, I ventured, among other Persons of the first Distinction, who subscribed to me for his Composures,

¹ This letter was printed by Curll in vol. iii of *Mr. Pope's Literary Correspondence* (1735), but never included in Pope's editions of his letters. The text seems authentic, but the date is impossible, since the Duke of Buckingham did not die until Feb. 1720/1. Bellucci left England in July of 1722.

² Dr. Hugh Chamberlen (1664–1728), the friend and physician of the Duke and Duchess, had apartments in Buckingham House.

³ The Statuary who made the Duke's Monument, to which this alludes; whereon are represented the Portraiture of his Grace, habited like a *Roman* General; and at his Feet, that of her Grace weeping. On the Top of the Basis of the Column, is seen, in Relievo, *Time* bearing away the four deceased Children of the Duchess, whose Effigies are represented in Profile-Bustos, supported by Cupids Lamenting.—Curll, 1735.

⁴ Giovanni Battista Buononcini (1670–1755), a celebrated composer, spent the summer of 1721 in Twickenham, and evidently made a friend of Pope. His *Cantate* appeared in that year with both Pope and the Duchess listed among the subscribers. The fact that this very distinguished list of subscribers includes the names of many of Pope's friends suggests notable activity on his part in behalf of Buononcini. The list includes the Duke of Argyll, Dr. Arbuthnot, Lord Bathurst, Hugh Bethel, John Barber, the Duke of Chandos, Lord Cobham, Sir Clement Cottrell, William Congreve, the Duchess of Hamilton, Lady Henrietta C. H. Harley (5 books), Lord Harley (5 books), the Hon. Mrs. Hervey (*née* Molly Lepell), Mrs. Howard, Charles Jervas, Sir Godfrey Kneller, Mrs. Murray (6 books), William Pulteney (10 books), the Duke of Queensberry (25 books), the Duchess of Queensberry (25 books), Lord Radnor, the Countess of Sutherland (55 books), Mrs. Vernon, Lady Mary Wortley, the Hon. Edward Wortley (5 books).

Pope's mention of ill treatment possibly refers to the rivalry in the composite setting of *Muzio Scevola* (1721), which saw Handel's Act greatly preferred to the Act composed by Buononcini. It would not refer to the charges of plagiarism brought against the composer a decade later.

newly ingraved, to set down the Name of your Grace. When I did this, your Grace was at *Bath*, and I forgot ever since to tell you of it, 'till now, when the Book's coming out, put me in Mind of it.

If you can excuse this Fault, I sincerely think I shall not err this Way again, 'till such another great Man as *Bononcini* arises, (for whenever that happens, I doubt not the *English* will use him as scurvily) but that your Grace needs not apprehend, during our Lives. I am, with the sincerest Respect, | Madam, | Your Grace's most Obliged, | Most Obedient Servant, | A. Pope.

ATTERBURY *to* POPE[1] [1722?]

Longleat Portland Papers, xiii (Harleian transcripts)

Bromly Wedn. night

I can give no Judgment in the affair recommended to me by the inclos'd, having no clear remembrance of those Writings, tho' I once read them over with Attention enough. Onely in general I think, that if that which is entirely new be in it self Good, it should come on first,[2] because it will please most; and then the Credit of that will carry off the other—which perhaps has less to recommend it; the Dutchesses Judgment in that case being right, I think, that the Approbation given to it thus alter'd, will center in the Original Author, and will derive no Credit to what is to succeed it. But I speak at Random. I think of being in Town on Mund or Tuesd. Even. next—I hope, by Munday and to stay one or two days there. If it suits with your Convenience to come to Town, I should be glad to have the Affair of the Inscription over. | I am always yours | F. R.

POPE *to* JONATHAN RICHARDSON[3] 6 *February* [1721/2?]

Elwin–Courthope, ix. 492

Twitnam, Feb. 6.

I write this to desire a thing of you which I mentioned when last I saw you, but I believe may be forgot, that you will tell your friend

---

[1] More than one letter dating apparently in the first half of 1722—before Atterbury's arrest—concerns Pope's difficulties with the Duke of Buckingham's *Works*, published in Jan. 1722/3. This letter might fall in the latter part of 1721; see Pope to Tonson, 3 Sept. [1721].

[2] That which 'came on first' was not a new piece but the Duke's poem 'The Temple of Death', first printed in 1695.

[3] The original of this letter has not been traced. The letter contains perhaps Pope's first mention of the famous surgeon William Cheselden (1688–1752), who from about this time became a close, lifelong friend. He was especially helpful about the edition of Shakespeare, and attended Pope in his last illness, quoting, according to the earliest Spence MSS., the line from *Hamlet* and applying it to Pope's dying condition: 'sweet bells jangled and out of tune'. In the printed editions of Spence's *Anecdotes* the quotation is ascribed to Bolingbroke.

Mr. Chiseldon, I shall be obliged to him if he will put upon a paper those conjectures of some passages of Shakespeare which he mentioned to Dr. Arbuthnot, or any others that may have occurred to him. The edition of that author being reprinted, and from all hands (especially from a man of his good will and abilities) information or elucidation being welcome to me. Pray send me these as soon as you can, even before I see you, though I will do that as soon as I can. Your affectionate friend and faithful servant.

POPE *to* LORD HARLEY[1]   6 *February* 1721/2

Longleat Portland Papers, xii

Twitenham, Feb. 6. | 1721.

My Lord,—I was so entirely taken up with the honour you did me the last time, when I so abruptly broke upon your Lordship at dinner, that I quite forgot a Commission I have long had from the Duchess of Buckingham, & which your long Absence from the town has hinderd my obeying till now. She layd her commands upon me to put into your hands the Duke's Tragedyes, which she has kept from all eyes beside, & depends on your Lordship's honour you will not show to any one. I can't but think her Grace judges right, in keeping any thing from the common View, till it is publisht, having myself often known Instances of the best, as well as worst, pieces, suffering by it.

If your Lordship will pardon my not asking your leave to send them sooner, I shall reap the benefit of my neglect, in coming myself to bring them to you next week.

I beg leave to lay hold of the opportunity this gives me, of expressing, (tho in never so short a manner, yet in a very sincere one) how truly I am | My Lord | Your most obedient | & most faithfull hum- | ble Servant | A. Pope

I entreat your Lordship to give me your permission, as the only Title I have, to name my self my Lady Harriet Harley's most humble Servant.

†POPE *to* ATTERBURY[2]   8 *February* 1721/2

1737

Feb. 8, 1721–2.

My Lord,—It's so long since I had the pleasure of an hour with your Lordship, that I should begin to think myself no longer *Amicus*

---

[1] That the year date is given in Old Style is clear from the fact that the Duke of Buckingham did not die until 24 Feb. 1720/1. The tragedies were published in the *Works* (1723). Edward, Lord Harley, succeeded his father as 2nd Earl of Oxford in 1724.

[2] The text is from the first printing in the Roberts octavo (1737 a). The letter appeared in all Pope's octavos, 1737–42, but was omitted from the quarto and folio of 1737.

omnium horarum, but for finding myself so in my constant thoughts of you. In those I was with you many hours this very day, and had you (where I wish and hope one day to see you really) in my garden at Twitnam. When I went last to town, and was on wing for the Deanery, I heard your Lordship was gone the day before to Bromley, and there you continued till after my return hither. I sincerely wish you whatever you wish your self, and all you wish your friends or family. All I mean by this word or two, is just to tell you so, till in person I find you as I desire, that is, find you well; easy, resign'd, and happy, you will make your self, and (I believe) every body that converses with you; if I may judge of your power over other men's minds and affections, by that which you will ever have, over those of |
Your, &c.

LORD HARLEY *to* POPE¹   10 *February* 1721/2
Longleat Portland Papers, xii
                                   Dover Street. Feb: 10: 172½

Sir,—I am obliged to you for the favor of your letter, I am very sensible of the Honor the Dutchess of Bucks does me and I hope I shall not forfeit the ~~competence~~ trust she is pleased to ~~place~~ repose in me, I shall very religiously obey the injunction of not letting any person see the papers, they will be much more ~~wellcome~~ acceptable when brought by your self for I am ~~allways~~ extreamly glad of any opportunity ~~of~~ to enjoy~~ing~~ your company which when ever ~~you are pleased to be so good as to allow it me is~~ and you extreamly oblige me when ever you are pleased to afford me your conversation I am with a true esteem. | Sir |
Your most humble | servant | Harley
mr Pope.

POPE *to* BROOME   10 *February* [1721/2]
Elwin–Courthope, viii. 48
                                   Feb. 10 [1722].

I kindly thank you for your letter, and faithfully assure you, you would have many of mine, were I, in any tolerable degree, master of myself or my time. If I were to write to you as often as I think of you, you would be almost daily receiving them.

The play you mention will be of no use, nor any other whose date is not earlier than 1616. The oldest edition in folio is 1621, which I have,²

---

¹ Possibly a lord may send a slovenly letter like this to a poet, but one charitably supposes that this text is printed from a draft of a letter, not actually sent until copied.

² Either Pope's first folio antedated all known copies by two years or (what one had better assume) his date here is in error. The state of the bibliography of Shakespeare's plays and the seriousness of Pope's attempt to fix editions is seen by his advertisement in *The London Evening Post*, 5 May 1722: 'The new Edition of Shakespear being now in the Press; this is to give Notice that if any Person has any Editions of the Tempest, Mackbeth, Julius Caesar,

and it is from that almost all the errors of succeeding editions take rise.

I received your twelfth book from Fenton, who needs inspiriting, I fear. Pray animate him all you can. I could wish you prevailed on him to do as you desired, to be with you some time in Suffolk, for your example would urge on his slowness. I would have you proceed without delay, as I will take the first occasion, and all occasions, of doing myself. As you have hitherto been diverting yourself with parts of the book that were agreeable to you, so you must begin to think of bearing part of the burden and heat of the day with us. Therefore, take your choice, either of the second or third book.[1] Fenton or I will undertake the first and fourth, and the fifth I have made some progress in, which I will take upon myself. I think you had a mind to the sixth—so I leave it you: but, as they say in sermons, first to the first. Therefore pray plunge into the second or third. I must once more put you in mind, that the whole success of this affair will depend upon your secrecy. There is nothing, you may be assured, I will not do to make the whole as finished and spirited as I am able, by giving the last touches. You do not need any man to make you a good poet. You need no more than what every good poet needs, time and diligence, and doing something every day. *Nulla dies sine linea.* I very much like what I have yet seen of your version, without flattery; and have viewed and reviewed it.[2] It is like your friendship, and like that of all worthy men, the more pleasing the longer one is acquainted with it. Dear sir, adieu. May every happiness attend you; as I wish you well, and am ever yours most sincerely.

Pray do not be discouraged by my inconstant correspondence, but write whenever you have leisure, and know nothing hinders my answering, but unavoidable businesses, which I hope one day to live free from;

Vacare libris, mihi, et amicis.

Timon of Athens, King John, and Henry the 8th; printed before the Year 1620, and will communicate the same to J. Tonson in the Strand, he shall receive any Satisfaction required.' These six plays were, of course, among the eighteen first printed in the folio. One wonders why the other twelve were not advertised as well. One notes also the date 1620, which perhaps indicates that in May as well as in Feb. Pope clung to the date 1621 as that of the folio. At the very end of his edition (vol. vi) he lists the early texts that he has used, and there dates the first folio 1623.

[1] Broome ultimately translated eight books: II, VI, VIII, XI, XII (this, but not the others, finished by this time), XVI, XVIII, and XXIII. Fenton did four books: I, IV, XIX, and XX. Pope did the twelve remaining books, but in the Postscript to the *Odyssey* claimed eighteen.

[2] With Pope 'reviewing' would pretty certainly mean revising. The MSS. of Fenton's Books, now in the British Museum, may show relatively little revision by Pope, but in various letters there are several sentences like this one that indicate considerable revision by Pope, and Broome himself in the concluding note to the *Odyssey*, v (1726), 285, acknowledged such revision. The MSS. preserved evidently represent a later state of the work than the first copy by Fenton.

POPE *to* FORTESCUE   22 *February* [1721/2]

1797 (Polwhele, i. 323)
                                           Twitnam, Feb. 22.

I am very much pleased that poor Barclay's scruples are removed, and
will be gratefully and honestly your pay-master for what you expend
on his account. You know the scripture says, "he that giveth to the
poor lendeth to the Lord." I heartily thank you for remembering me
as to the escalops, which are in perfection, and will be responsible to
you for them when we meet next, which I beg may be as soon as
possible. I have seen our friend Dr. Arbuthnot spend some hours in
writing directions for us against the plague,[1] which, when finished,
I will take care to communicate to you. I am most faithfully and
affectionately, dear Sir, yours, | A. Pope.

Your purse is left with the doctor's man for you. My mother is better,
and your servant.

Address: To Wm. Fortescue, esq. at his chambers, in Harcourt-buildings, in
the Inner Temple.

||ATTERBURY *to* POPE[2]   26 *February* 1721/2

Longleat Portland Papers, xiii (Harleian transcripts)
                                           Feb: 26. 172½

Permit me, Dear Sir, to break into your retirement and to desire of
you a Compleat copy of those Verses on Mr Addison,[3] ⌜which you
wrote down in an imperfect manner for me. When you send it,⌝ send
me also your last Resolution, which shall punctually be observ'd, in
relation to my giving out any Copy of it: for I am again Sollicited by
another Lord; to whom I have given the same Answer, as formerly.
No small piece of your writing has been ever sought after so much;
it has pleas'd every man without Exception, to whom it has been read.
Since you now therefore know, where your real Strength lyes, I hope,

---

1 Dr. Arbuthnot seems to have been writing directions against the plague presumably
about the same time that Daniel Defoe was terrifying Londoners with his *Journal of the
Plague Year* (1722). In 1720 the great plague in Marseilles started the terror in England.
Dean Berkeley in a letter of 12 Oct. 1721 recommends 'a preservative against the plague . . .
it is no more than the Jesuits bark taken as against the ague. This I had from Dr. Arbuthnot
just before I left London.' Berkeley left London in the autumn of 1721. See B. Rand,
Berkeley and Percival, p. 179.
2 Printed by Pope, 1737–42. His text is reproduced by Nichols (1783), i. 85, and by
Elwin. Pope's omissions, here placed in half-brackets, illustrate various principles of his
editing. In the texts later than his first printing he made no changes.
3 It is perhaps imaginative to speculate on the fact that Atterbury is getting a copy of
the Atticus portrait and that it was first published in *The St. James's Journal*, 15 Dec.
1722, some months after Atterbury's arrest and the seizure (doubtless) of all his papers.

you will not suffer that Talent to ly unemploy'd. For my part, I should be glad to see you finish something of that kind, that I could be content to be a little sneer'd at in a Line, or so, for the sake of the pleasure I should have in reading the rest. I have talk'd my Sense of this matter to you, once, or twice, and now I put it under my hand, that you may see it is my deliberate Opinion. What weight that may have with you, I cannot say: but it pleases me to have an Opportunity of shewing you, how well I wish you, and how true a friend I am to your Fame; which I desire may grow every day, and in every kind of writing, to which you shall please to turn your Pen. Not but I have[1] some little interest in the Proposal, as I shall be known to have been acquainted with a man, that was capable of excelling in such different manners ⌜and did such honour to his country and language⌝[2] and yet was not unpleas'd sometimes to read what was written by his | Affectionate humble Servant | Fra Roffen.

⌜'Tis past Ten a Clock; however I hope my letter may find its way to the Post this night. If it does not, the Busyness of it will keep cold till another.⌝

FENTON *to* BROOME   *March* 1722

Elwin–Courthope, viii. 50

London, March, 1722.

I was some time since favoured with a letter from you, in which you give me a kind invitation to spend some part of the summer with you. This, sir, is too agreeable a motion to be rejected by me, but at present I cannot precisely fix the time of my coming, for I have an affair or two depending which I would willingly see the issue of before I leave these parts. Mr. Pope is now in very high spirits about Homer. I have begun the first book, but it is so long since I handled a quill that I proceed a little awkwardly, but I doubt not of having new metal infused when I have your example and conversation. I believe I shall hardly bring on Mariamne[3] before next winter. The history of my disappointments in that business, and whatever else of news the region of *belles lettres* affords, I will reserve to entertain you at Sturston. I will send you word when I have fixed the time of my setting out, and I desire your directions how I may order my journey, and let the

---

[1] Not but I have] Not but that I have *1737–42*.

[2] This phrase, appearing in the Harleian transcripts between lines written by the scribe, is in the hand of the 2nd Lord Oxford. Conceivably it is his own spontaneous addition; conceivably Pope (whose text later editors have followed) thought it modest not to print such commendation of himself.

[3] *Mariamne*, when first acted at Lincoln's Inn Fields, 22 Feb. 1722/3, had a notable success. After much delay Cibber, perhaps insultingly, had rejected it for Drury Lane.

letter come under cover directed to Mr. Robinson, at the Blue Periwig, at Charing Cross. I am sir, your most faithful humble servant.

Mr. Pope desires that the business of Homer may be carried on with all imaginable secrecy.

*POPE *to* JONATHAN RICHARDSON[1]   6 *March* [1721/2?]

Arthur A. Houghton, Jr.

Twickenham March 6.

I acknowledge your very kind Letter, I thank you Particularly for your Complaints of me. I wish with all my heart you had no other, or Juster. I wish you better health. I will be with you God willing, on Munday after Noone to pass the whole Evening. Let Friend Cheselden be of the party. I add no more, but that I am | Truly Yours.

A. Pope

Address: To Mr Richardson: in Queens Square, | Bloomsbury: | London.

†POPE *to* ATTERBURY[2]   14 *March* 1721/2

1737

March 14, 1721–2.

I was disappointed (much more than those who commonly use that phrase on such occasions) in missing you at the Deanery, where I lay solitary two nights. Indeed I truly partake in any degree of concern that affects you, and I wish every thing may succeed as you desire in your own family, and in that which I think you no less account your own, and is no less your family, the whole world: for I take you to be one of the true Friends of it, and to your pow'r its protector. Tho' the noise and daily bustle for the publick be now over,[3] I dare say a good man is still tendring its welfare; as the Sun in the winter, when seeming to retire from the world, is preparing benedictions and warmth for a better season. No man wishes your Lordship more quiet, more tranquillity than I, who know you shou'd understand the value of it: but I don't wish you a jot less concern'd or less active than you are, in all sincere, and therefore warm desires of publick good.

I beg the kindness (and 'tis for that chiefly I trouble you with this letter) to favour me with notice as soon as you return to London, that

---

1 The year is doubtful. The letter seems to concern one of the 'parties' arranged for collating the texts of Shakespeare's plays, in which the famous surgeon Cheselden took part. On the uncertain assumption that the text would be established before commenting began, the letter is placed early. It might fall in any year from 1721 to 1724.

2 Printed in Pope's editions of 1737–42, and reprinted from his text by Nichols in 1783. F. Williams (i. 369), printing from 'the Atterbury Papers', gives an identical text. Here the text is that of the Roberts octavo, 1737.

3 Alluding to the dissolution of the Parliament, four days before.—Nichols, 1783.

I may come and make you a proper visit of a day or two: for hitherto
I have not been your Visitor, but your Lodger, and I accuse my self
of it. I have now no earthly thing to oblige my being in town (a point
of no small satisfaction to me) but the best reason, the seeing a friend:
As long (my Lord) as you will let me call you so, (and I dare say you
will, till I forfeit what I think I never shall, my veracity and integrity)
I shall esteem my self fortunate, in spite of the Southsea, Poetry,
Popery, and Poverty.

I can't tell you how sorry I am, you shou'd be troubled a-new by
any sort of people. I heartily wish, *Quod superest, ut tibi vivas*[1]—that
you may teach me how to do the same: who, without any real impediment to acting and living rightly, do act and live as foolishly as if I
were a Great man. I am, &c.

||ATTERBURY *to* POPE[2]   16 *March* 1721/2

Longleat Portland Papers, xiii (Harleian transcripts)

Bromly March 16 172½.

As a Visitant, a Lodger, a Friend (or under what other Denomination
soever) you are always welcome to me, and will be more so, I hope,
every day that we live: for to tell you the truth, I like you, as I like
myself, best, when we have both of us least Buysness. It has been my
Fate to be engag'd in it, much; and often; by the Stations in which
I was plac'd: but God that knows my heart, knows, I never Lov'd it,
and am still less in Love with it than ever, as I find less Temptation
to Act with any hope of Success. If I am good for any thing, tis *in
angulo cum libello*: and yet a good part of my time has been spent, and
perhaps must still be spent, far otherwise. For I will never, while I
have health, be wanting to my Duty in any Post, or in any Respect,
how little soever I may like my Imployment and how hopeless soever
I may be in the discharge of it.

In the mean time the Judicious World is pleas'd to think, that I
delight in work, which I am oblig'd to undergo, and aim at things
which I from my heart despize. Let them think as they will, so I
might be at Liberty to act as I will, and spend my time in such a
manner as is most agreeable to me! I cannot say, I do so now; for I
am here without any Books, and if I had them, could not use them to
my Satisfaction, while my mind is taken up in a more Melancholly
manner:[3] and how long, or how little a while it may be so taken up,

[1] Adapted from Horace, *Epistles*, i. xviii. 107–8.
[2] The first two paragraphs were printed (without textual variation from the Harleian
transcript) in Pope's editions of 1737–42. The rest of the letter, which shows that the whole
is a reply to Pope's letter of 14 Mar., seems not to have been printed hitherto.
[3] In his Lady's last Sickness.—Pope, 1737–42.

God only knows and to his Will I implicitly resign my self in every thing.

⌐But I will endeavour to get out of this way of thinking for a Minute or two, and turn my Pen to a Subject, which tho' it may not give you more pleasure, will at least give me less uneasyness.

⌐I have not forgot my Promise of seeing you at Twitnam, and will Perform it, as soon as decency, and the present Circumstances I am in will allow me. In the meantime I cannot answer for myself, as to any Day, or Days I am likely to spend at the Deanery; not Intending to be there (unless Occasionally, upon some emergence and then for as little a while as is possible) till the Election for the School comes on, about five weeks hence.[1] And whether I shall be able to attend even that, I cannot say at this distance. Let me hear from you if I do not see you. I shall hear from you I reckon; on Wednesday next in answer to what I wrot to you from hence last Wednesday, or perhaps, you may Contrive to let me know your mind by the post that comes out from London to morrow night | I am yours always most Affectionately | F. R.

⌐I am not much dispos'd to smile at Present; but could Scarce forbear it, when Poetry, Popery, and Poverty came in my way, I could not help saying to myself What a pity twas that South Sea did not begin with the same letter for then the figure would have been compleat.

⌐There is a man that has out done you for he has written a Poem of about 30 or 40 lines, in praise of Hogs: every word of every Verse of Which begins with a P— I remember the end of the first Verse— *Porcorum pigra propago*—and with the end of that Verse I end my Letter.⌐

‖ATTERBURY *to* POPE[2]   [17 or 27] *March* 1722

Longleat Portland Papers, xiii (Harleian transcripts)

Bromly March 27th 1722.

I am here still attending on my Melancholly Work, which is not likely to last long, whenever the Event happens I shall immediately

[1] The Bishop probably refers to the 'Election' of scholars to be sent by Westminster School to the University, in which for this year he had a personal interest. 'Election Tuesday' came on 24 Apr., and Osborn Atterbury at that time headed the list of four scholars to be sent to Oxford. 'Obby' was the supposed translator of the two odes of Horace sent to Pope in the letter of 1 Jan. of this year. See Joseph Welch's *List of Scholars of St. Peter's College, Westminster* (1852), pp. 271–8.

[2] The date in the Harleian transcript is written with perfect clarity; but, as Elwin pointed out, the remark about the coach seems to make it certain that the scribe should have written 17, since Pope's letter of the 19th is an apparent answer to this letter, and the letter of 6 Apr. replies to that of 19 Mar.

exchange this place for the Deanery, and after staying there a few days shall be willing to go to some other place, where I may be more alone than I can be, either there or here. I know not how far it may be convenient for you to let me be with you on that Occasion. If it be not, let me know your mind frankly, If it be I will endeavour to be as little troublesome to you as I can for I will send my Coach back, and keep only One, or at most two Servants with me whom One Bed will hold. Your Mother must be consulted in this case, but I desire that neither She nor you would mention it to any other Person Living | I am yours always most affectionately | F. R.

†POPE *to* ATTERBURY¹   19 *March* 1721/2
¹⁷³⁷

March 19, 1721–2.
I am extreamly sensible of the repeated favour of your kind letters, and your thoughts of me in absence, even among thoughts of much nearer concern to your self on the one hand, and of much more importance to the world on the other, which cannot but engage you at this juncture. I am very certain of your good will, and of the warmth which is, in you, inseparable from it.

Your remembrance of Twitenham is a fresh instance of that partiality. I hope the advance of the fine season will set you upon your legs, enough to enable you to get into my garden, where I will carry you up a Mount, in a point of view² to shew you the glory of my little kingdom. If you approve it, I shall be in danger to boast like Nebuchadnezzar of the things I have made, and to be turn'd to converse, not with the beasts of the field, but with the birds of the grove, which I shall take to be no great punishment. For indeed I heartily despise the ways of the world, and most of the great ones of it.

*Oh keep me innocent, make others great!*³

And you may judge how comfortably I am strengthen'd in this opinion, when such as your Lordship bear testimony to its vanity and emptiness. *Tinnit, inane est*, with the picture of one ringing on the globe with his finger, is the best thing I have the luck to remember in that great Poet Quarles,⁴ (not that I forget the Devil at bowls; which I know to be your Lordship's favourite cut, as well as favourite diversion.)

The situation here is pleasant, and the view rural enough, to humour

¹ The text is from the Roberts octavo, 1737.
² The text of 1737 b reads, 'to shew you in a point of view'.
³ Dr. W. D. Ellis identifies the line as from 'An Imitation of the Second Chorus in the Second Act of Seneca's *Thyestes*', by George Granville. See *Examen Poeticum* (1693), p. 334.
⁴ Pope's favourite from Quarles is Emblem 10 in Book II; Atterbury's is 10 from Book I.

the most retir'd, and agree with the most contemplative. Good air, solitary groves, and sparing diet, sufficient to make you fancy your self (what you are in temperance, tho' elevated into a greater figure by your station) one of the Fathers of the Desert. Here you may think (to use an author's words, whom you so justly prefer to all his followers that you'll receive them kindly tho' taken from his worst work)

> That in Eliah's banquet you partake,
> Or sit a guest with Daniel, at his Pulse.[1]

I am sincerely free with you, as you desire I should, and approve of your not having your coach here, for if you would see Lord C*[2] or any body else, I have another chariot, besides that little one you laugh'd at when you compar'd me to Homer in a nut-shell. But if you would be entirely private, no body shall know any thing of the matter. Believe me (my Lord) no man is with more perfect acquiescence, nay with more willing acquiescence, (not even any of your own Sons of the Church) | Your obedient, &c.

POPE to ——   19 *March* 1721[2?]

[Sotheby's catalogue for a sale on 6 February 1865 lists as lot 871 an order from Pope for the payment of his dividend warrant. This has not been traced.]

POPE *and* FENTON *to* BROOME   *April* [1722]

Elwin–Courthope, viii. 51
                                        April[3] [1722]

POPE

Our friend Fenton tells me you speak of the old Greek, as one is apt to do of a companion one has had too much of.[4] The best company tires a man sometimes, if one is to travel long with it. But you that have gone already to Hell with him, and to Circe's island, and Scylla, and Charybdis,[5] methinks may pass a peaceable dull day or two in his house, eating and drinking by his fireside with his wife and children. And yet, it seems, the second book is a weariness of spirit to you. Well, be of good cheer, I will do the third, and save you the trouble of hearing old Nestor's long stories. Let us, like good christians, bear one another's burthens, that we may persevere to the end. Fenton intends

---

1 Adapted from *Paradise Regained*, ii. 277–8.

2 Lord C*] Lord Carteret—Nichols, i. 93. (Nichols gives no evidence, and Lord Carleton seems more likely; see the note to Atterbury's reply of 6 Apr.)

3 The month is from the postmark.—Elwin.

4 In this letter Mr. Pope laughs at me for complaining of weariness in translating the second book.—Broome [Elwin].

5 In the eleventh and twelfth books which are on those subjects.—Broome [Elwin].

to see you with a book in his hands, as a sample that he deserves his meat and drink at yours, and is not a mere vagabond, such as you find strolled about in Homer's days, and told everybody Jupiter was their particular friend. You will, I doubt not, receive him as cordially as good Eumæus himself could have done, and teach your very dogs good manners on his arrival at the vicarage.[1] Mrs. Broome will meet him, if you have any respect for Homerical rites, with a bason and ewer, to wash his head and feet; and if you slew a tithe pig by the force of your own arm, and broiled it with your own hands, you will do no more than becomes you, either as an hospitable friend or a sober priest. I do not absolutely require, that if you give him a calves' head, you should tip the horns with gold, in the manner of Laerceus,[2] but you must be void of all humanity if you do not provide one of your maids for his bedfellow.

There has been already a small omission, in my opinion, on your part towards him, which is, that having referred him for a safe passage to a certain modern vehicle called a stage coach; you never once have told him where that coach is to be found?

FENTON.

Mr. Pope was hurried away for London before he ended his letter, and, having given it me to send away, I take leave to conclude it with acquainting you that he intends to print proposals for subscriptions about Michaelmas,[3] in order to have the first volume, consisting of six books, published about March next. Pray, in your next, when you give directions about the coach, let me know what carrier I may send my trunk by; and where I may inquire for him. I hope to be at Sturston about the middle of May; in the meantime, and ever, I am, dear sir, your faithful humble servant.

POPE *to* CARYLL[4]　　　　　　　　　　　2 *April* [1722]

Add. 28618

London. April 2nd

I am very much pleased at all times with finding my self in your memory: I'm sure I shall never lose you from mine, where you'll ever

---

[1] The episode referred to is found in *Odyssey* xiv, not as yet translated by Pope presumably.

[2] For Laerceus see Pope's *Odyssey*, iii. 540–55. (This book Pope was at the moment translating).

[3] For various reasons the Proposals were deferred until Jan. 1725. Vols. i–iii of the translation were published in Apr. 1725.

[4] Elwin placed this letter in 1721, but the existence of an order to pay interest to Pope dated 28 Feb. 1720/1 makes impossible in 1721 Caryll's remark (here quoted by Pope) that he is keeping the interest until Pope comes in person to Ladyholt to get it. It might be possible for 1722, when, after this present protest by Pope, Caryll sends on the eleven pounds, and is thanked for it by Pope in his letter of May 1722. The remark about Sir John Evelyn's house irks Pope because it is at least the second time Caryll has used it. See Pope to Caryll, 16 July 1721.

possess the place of an old and valuable friend. I hope too I shall always live in such a manner and such a constant tenour, agreeable to my oldest professions (both of veracity and principle) as you shall never be ashamed of me, as you have been of some others of our acquaintances, whose miserable defection from their principles renders [them] so contemptible that they cannot, sure, vex or affect you any otherwise than in mere Christian compassion and pity.

Of late your letters pique me: they are writ in a style of suspicion and coldness, as if you doubted my inclinations to hear from you or see you. You remind me *that Sir John Evelyn's stands as much in my Way to your house as ever*, when in truth I never meant more by telling you of a visit to him than to make it the half-way house to yours, which was the whole end of the journey I intended. I know that gentleman but little and accidentally, from his relation to the Harcourt family; and that you have a much stronger and much older title to me and my projects is a truth you ought not to contest: indeed you ought not. I have had three or four successive misfortunes in regard to yourself and family whenever you happened to come this way. It was a real vexation that I missed since of Lady Mary, and since of Mr Rich: Caryll; and if I omitted to write on purpose to tell you so, it was because I doubted not but you would know I was sorry without being told so. Indeed of late a number of tiresome businesses of many kinds have taken me even from myself as well as from my friends in general. I am hoping still, but still disappointed, that I shall live composedly again and be as much my own as I was when first I was so happy as to know you. There wants only that, I assure you, to make me as much yours.

God knows when I can make such a journey as I wish I could to your house. My mother is grown too feeble to be left long alone, and too uneasy when I did leave her a month last year,[1] to let me think of doing [it] so long again; so that when you rally me about the little debt of interest, in saying you'll keep it till I come for it, you are a little inclined to a much greater piece of injustice than such trifles can be ever thought among friends; namely, in imagining that any motive of interest would sway me in regard to you. Dear sir, believe me truly yours, and think well of me; that is, as a Christian should, charitably, forgivingly and kindly. I've preached to you this holy time upon this one point: In all else I'm well assured you do your duty, and are everything that can be wished by one so much your friend as | Dear sir | Your most faithful | affect. servant | A. P.

[1] In the early autumn of 1721 Pope had visited Oxford, Cirencester, and Rentcomb. We have no record of any month's absence from Twickenham in 1720: hence this letter is placed preferably in 1722.

‖ATTERBURY *to* POPE[1]   6 *April* 1722

Longleat Portland Papers, xiii (Harleian transcripts)

Bromly Apr. 6. 1722.

Under all the Leysure in the world, I have no Leysure, no Stomach to write to you. The Gradual approaches of death are before my eyes.[2] I am convinc'd, that it must be so; and yet make a shift to flatter my self sometimes with the thought, that it may possibly be otherwise.

And that very thought, tho' it is directly contrary to my reason, dos for a few moments make me easy, however not easy enough, in good earnest to think of any thing but the melancholly Object that employs them. Therefore wonder not, that I do not answer your kind letter. I shall answer it too soon, I fear by accepting your friendly invitation. When I do so, no Conveniencys will be wanting; for I'll see no body but You and your Mother, and the Servants. Visits to Statesmen always were to me (and are now more than ever) insiped things. Let the men that expect, that wish to thrive by them, pay them that Homage: I am free. When I want them, they shall hear of me at their doors, and when they want me, I shall be sure to hear of them at mine. But probably they will despise me so much, and I shall court them so little, that we shall both of us keep our distance.

When I come to you, 'tis in order to be with You only. A President of the Council[3] or a Starr and Garter will make no more impression upon my mind, at such a time, than the hearing of a Bagpipe, or the sight of a Poppet shew. I have said to Greatness some time ago: Tuas ⟨tibi⟩ res habeto Egomet curabo meas. The Time is not farr off, when we shall all be upon the Levell: and I am resolv'd, for my own part to anticipate that Time, and be upon the Levell now: for he is so that neither seeks, nor wants them.

Let them have more Virtue and less Pride; and then I'll court them as much as any body: ⌈but⌉ till they resolve to distinguish themselves some way else than by their outward Trappings, I am determin'd (and, I think I have a right) to be as proud as they are: tho' I trust in God, my Pride is neither of so Odious a nature as theirs, nor of so mischievous a Consequence.

I know not how I have fallen into this Train of thinking, when I sat down to write I intended only to excuse myself for not writing, and

---

[1] Printed in Pope's editions, 1737–42. Here (for the first time?) the letter is printed from the Harleian transcripts. Two transcripts of the letter occur in Portland Papers, vol. xiii. The text here given is that from ff. 220–1, which is somewhat more orthodox in spelling, &c. That occurring on f. 233 is perhaps earlier and has been corrected in the hand of Lord Oxford. The two transcripts have the same text, and Pope printed his editions without verbal changes, though he omitted the first sentence of the last paragraph.

[2] Atterbury's wife died on 26 Apr. 1722.

[3] Henry Boyle, Lord Carleton, was Lord President from 1721 to 1725. Here Atterbury seems to be replying to Pope's remark in the letter of 19 Mar. about seeing 'Lord C*'.

to tell you that the Time drew nearer and nearer, when I must dis-
lodge. I am preparing for it, for I am at this moment building a Vault
in the Abby for me and mine. Twas to be in the Abby, because of my
Relation to the Place: but 'tis at the West door of it, as far from Kings
and Kaisars, as the space will admit of.

I know not but I may step to Town to morrow, to see how the
work goes forward, but if I do, I shall return hither in the Evening.
⌜However I give this to One that is going to Town that he might
put it into the Post tomorrow.⌝ I would not have given you the trouble
of it, but that they tell me it will cost you nothing, and that our Privi-
ledge of Franking (one of the most valuable we have left) is again
allow'd us. | Yours ever | F. R.

POPE to VISCOUNT HARCOURT   7 *April* 1722

Harcourt MSS.

My Lord,—You will too naturally allow the misfortune of Want of
Sight to be a very great one, but I assure your Lordship I never more
found it so, than when I met your Coach & family on the Road to
the Country, without knowing who you were, till you was past call.
I was going to London, with the very design of claiming a most
obliging Promise, that yourself & Family would lose one Day upon
me at Twitnam. How dissapointed I returnd, to my Mother (whom
I had filld with the same hope) at night. I am uncertain whether your
Lordship sees the town again this Season. If you do, I wish you would
reflect, among the many kind, and the many good things you do, how
greatly you might please & reward a man who desires no greater
Satisfaction than the honour of your Company, & no greater Bribe
than the Continuance of your Friendly Opinion. Be pleased to accept
my most sincere wishes for Your happiness, which includes that of
a whole Race that I am obliged to. I am with the truest respect and
acknowledgement | My Lord | Your most obliged most | faithfull
humble Servant | A. Pope.

Twit'nam, Apr. 7th | 1722.

Address: To the Rt Honble the | Lord Viscount Harcourt, | at Cockthorp,
near | Witney, | Oxon.
Postmark: 14/AP
Endorsement: 22 Apr 1722 | Mr Pope | to Lord Vicount | Harcourt

VISCOUNT HARCOURT *to* POPE[1]   *27 April* 1722

Homer MSS. Add. 4809

27. Ap: 1722: Cockthrop

I have received Your very obliging letter & can with great truth
assure you, that it was with much uneasienesse that we submitted to
the appearance of a necessity to leave the town, without taking leave
of Mrs Pope and yourself, the Badness of the ways & weather for
some time prevented us from giving you that trouble, & the weather
no sooner changed than Dr Mead press'd us to get in to the Country
for the Recovery of my Grandsons cough, He is much better since he
came hither, & I hope in a few days will be perfectly well. I have some
thoughts of coming to Town with my wife about the Middle of
August. Whenever any Objection throws itself in our way, the pleasing thoughts of waiting on Mrs Pope weighs down the Scale. If any
thing should lead you into these Parts, You will allways here meet
with a most sincere & hearty wellcome. I am | Sir Your most Affec-
tionate | & faithfull humble | Servant | Harcourt

Pray Assure Nurse I have not forgott her

†POPE *to* ROBERT DIGBY[2]   [*May*] 1722

1735

Your making a sort of Apology for your not writing, is a very genteel
reproof to me. I know I was to blame, but I know I did not intend to
be so, and (what is the happiest Knowledge in the World) I know you
will forgive me: For sure nothing is more satisfactory than to be certain
of such a Friend as will overlook one's failings, since every such instance is a Conviction of his Kindness.

If I am all my life to dwell in Intentions, and never rise to Actions,
I have but too much need of that gentle disposition which I experience
in you. But I hope better things of my self, and fully purpose to make
you a visit this summer at *Sherbourn.* I'm told you are all upon removal
very speedily, and that Mrs. *Mary Digby* talks in a Letter to Lady
Scudamore, of seeing my Lord *Bathurst*'s Wood in her way. How
much I wish to be her Guide thro' that enchanted Forest, is not to be
exprest: I look upon myself as the Magician appropriated to the place,

---

[1] Dictated, but signed by Harcourt. The postscript is in his lordship's autograph.
[2] Printed in all Pope's editions, except 1735 a2. The year is added by Pope in editions
of 1737–42. The month is inferred from the fact that Pope writes during the visit of Atterbury after the death of his wife on 26 Apr. In the Orrery Papers in the Harvard College
Library there is a copy of a letter from Atterbury to Lord Orrery dated from Bromley May 4.
Since Atterbury wrote to Pope from Bromley on May 25, the supposition is that the visit
to Twickenham took place between those two days.
The variants in Pope's texts of the letter are negligible.

without whom no mortal can penetrate into the Recesses of those sacred Shades. I could pass whole Days, in only describing to her the future, and as yet visionary Beauties, that are to rise in those Scenes: The Palace that is to be built, the Pavillions that are to glitter, the Colonnades that are to adorn them: Nay more, the meeting of the *Thames* and the *Severn*, which (when the noble Owner has finer Dreams than ordinary) are to be led into each other's Embraces thro' secret Caverns of not above twelve or fifteen Miles, till they rise and openly[1] celebrate their Marriage in the midst of an immense Amphitheatre, which is to be the Admiration of Posterity a hundred Years hence. But till the destin'd time shall arrive that is to manifest these Wonders, Mrs. *Digby* must content herself with seeing what is at present no more than the finest wood in *England*.

The Objects that attract this part of the world, are of a quite different Nature. Women of Quality are all turn'd Followers of the Camp in *Hyde-Park* this Year, whither all the Town resort to magnificent Entertainments given by the Officers, &c. The *Scythian* Ladies that dwelt in the Waggons of War, were not more closely attached to the Luggage. The Matrons, like those of *Sparta*, attend their Sons to the Field, to be the Witnesses of their glorious Deeds; and the Maidens with all their Charms display'd, provoke the Spirit of the Soldiers: Tea and Coffee supply the place of *Lacedemonian* black Broth. This camp seems crowned with perpetual Victory, for every Sun that rises in the Thunder of Cannon, sets in the Musick of Violins. Nothing is yet wanting but the constant presence of the *Princess*, to represent the *Mater Exercitûs*.[2]

At *Twickenham* the World goes otherwise. There are certain old People who take up all my time, and will hardly allow me to keep any other Company. They were introduced here by a Man of their own sort, who has made me perfectly rude to all my Contemporaries, and won't so much as suffer me to look upon 'em. The Person I complain of is the Bishop of *Rochester*. Yet he allows me (from something he has heard of your Character and that of your Family, as if you were of the old Sect of Moralists) to write three or four sides of Paper to you, and to tell you (what these sort of People never tell but with Truth, and religious Sincerity) that I am, and ever will be, | Dear Sir, | Yours, &c.

---

[1] *openly* is omitted in Pope's texts, 1737–42.

[2] The camp in Hyde Park was formed about 8 May (see *The Whitehall Evening Post* of that day). On 3 June when the Prince and Princess of Wales removed to Richmond they were attended part of the way by a detachment from the camp (*Political State*, xxiii. 648–9). *Mater Exercitûs* is very likely invented by Pope on analogy to *Mater Castrorum*, commonly applied to Roman empresses after the time of Faustina (wife of Marcus Aurelius). Pope's title has been found but in inscriptions probably unknown in his day. This information is due to the kindness and learning of Professor Mason Hammond.

POPE *to* CARYLL[1]   [? *May* 1722]

Add. 28618

I should have not so long delayed sending the enclosed receipt, but was
absent from home when yours arrived; for which I thank you, but
will not excuse you from a longer epistle (since I am always sincerely
rejoiced to hear from you) when you next have leisure to gratify me
so far. Tho' 'twould please one much better, if you did what I have
been made to hope you would, come, and make a visit to Twitnam
with Lady Mary. I've told you in my last how much my mother is
obliged to Lady Seaforth,[2] who is the best neighbour she has, and the
only one she cares to visit, since poor Mrs Stonor's death.[3] Tho' I can
give you no good account of myself as to any [things] of my own,
yet I am very busy in doing justice to a far greater poet,[4] of whose
works I am giving a new edition. Besides this, I have the care of
overlooking the Duke of Buckingham's papers, and correcting the
press. That will be a very beautiful book, and has many things in it
you will be particularly glad to see in relation to some former reigns.
You'll see by this I am quite idle, tho' not so much a poet as formerly.   *? not*
Tho' I live here (at this time of the year) in a glut of company, yet I
can keep some thinking hours to myself, which I ought to employ
(since they are not many) in thoughts of more serious importance than
versifying deserves. I hope they'll turn to that which one may justly
call, one's best advantage, and I know your own way of thinking so
well, that I'm sure you'll approve of this method of employing my
time, much more, than if it were spent in poetry.

I am unfeignedly | Dear sir | ever yours. | A: P:

---

*POPE *to* JACOB TONSON, JR.   [? *May* 1722]

Add. 28275

From St. James's Square[5]

Sir,—I coud be very glad if you had a Day & a Night's leisure to
spend your time with me at Twitnam, upon some necessary affairs in
relation to our undertaking. I wish to morrow would agree with your
conveniency. I'm going with Lord Burlington to Chiswick, from

---

[1] The year, but not the time of year, for this letter seems sure. The 'glut of company'
may refer to Atterbury's visit. The 'absence from home' mentioned in the first sentence may
mean only a short unidentified visit.

[2] The Countess of Seaforth was Lady Mary Caryll's mother.

[3] Presumably the wife of Pope's 'very easy, humane, and gentlemanly neighbour', Mr.
Thomas Stonor. He himself died in Aug. 1724; his wife had died on 28 Jan. 1721/2 (Burke's
Commoners, ii. 442).

[4] Shakespeare.

[5] Pope is probably writing from Lord Bathurst's house in town. The letter seems related
to that next following.

whence I take a Chaise to night, home; & shall stay there till Friday morning. I'd be glad to fix a party with Mr Carpenter & yourself, but of this when we meet.

I am | Your humble Servant | A. Pope.
Saturday

I desire a word by the | bearer.

Address: To | Mr Tonson.

---

*POPE *to* JACOB TONSON, JR.[1]   [16 or 23 *May* 1722?]

Add. 28275

Twitenham, Wednesday

Sir,—My ill fortune so orderd it, that I had three people who came and took possession of all the Beds in my house last week. I sent to acquaint you with it, depending otherwise upon your promise of passing a night or so here. Since that time, my affairs have hurryd me to & from London, interchangeably every day; the last part of the Planting Season taking me up here, & business which I think less agreeable, there. I'm resolvd to pass the next whole week in London, purposely to get together Parties of my acquaintance ev'ry night, to collate the several Editions of Shakespear's single Plays, 5 of which I have ingaged to this design. You shall then hear of me. Till when too, I'm forced (much against my inclination) to put off our meeting at Mr Carpenter's. I wish you'd inform Sir Godfry how busy I have been. I think it three Ages since I saw him and if my Features are altred, in proportion to the length of Time which it has seemd to me since I saw him, my Picture at next sitting, will be as old as Nestor.[2] So tell him, & tell yourself that I am | Sir | Your very humble | Servant | A. Pope.

Address: To Mr Tonson, at Shakes-|pear's head over against Catha-|rine street in the | Strand | London.

[1] This seems to be written under strain of the 'glut of company' mentioned in Pope's recent letter to Caryll; in other words during the time when Atterbury and his two servants —or elderly friends (see the preceding letter to Digby)—occupied all Pope's beds. The time fits also Fenton's reports concerning Pope's fluttering from Twickenham to London and back again. The possible Wednesdays are determined by Atterbury's account of his adventurous arrival at Bromley (letter of 25 May). Since he may have paused in London, the 16th is possible as well as the 23rd.

[2] In 1722 Sir Godfrey painted the portrait of Pope called in the Grolier Club *Catalogue of First Editions and Portraits of Pope* (1911) 'the second Kneller type'. Professor Wimsatt informs the editor that chronologically this is the third and last portrait by Kneller of Pope. The others were done in 1716 and 1721.

FENTON *to* BROOME   23 *May* 1722
Elwin–Courthope, viii. 52

Twickenham, May 23, 1722.

I have been favoured with two letters from you which I have delayed
to answer till I saw the issue of an affair which I doubt will disappoint
me of the pleasure of seeing you at Sturston, unless it suits with your
convenience to receive me on the following condition, which, in short,
is this. A gentleman of Sir Clement Cottrell's acquaintance, has a son
who is lately come from Oxford, whom he would recommend to my
care for five or six months. They would, indeed, have prevailed with
me to travel with him into Italy the next spring, but I think you know
I am pre-engaged.[1] Sir Clement having heard of my design of seeing
you this summer, desires extremely to have his young friend to be a
sojourner with me at your house. His father will agree to your own
terms of boarding us and one footman, and I am assured the young
gentleman is addicted to no irregularities to make either your family or
myself uneasy. His greatest crimes, *entre nous*, are sins of omission,
which I think we at Cambridge call lounging, and his friends judge
rightly that they may too soon grow into habits, where plays, assemblies, and tea-tables are continually tempting him. I should be extremely glad to hear by the very first post (for the matter will admit of
no delay) that this proposal is not disagreeable to Mrs. Broome and
yourself; and at the same time let me know the terms on which we are
to be received. Mr. Pope is well, but I have not seen him since I received your last. I finished the first book about a fortnight since, and
shall now begin upon the fourth. Pray fail not to write speedily, and
believe me to be ever, dear sir, your most faithful humble servant.

Direct for me at Mr. Hutchins', in Twickenham, Middlesex.

‡ATTERBURY *to* POPE[2]   25 *May* 1722
1737

Bromley, May 25, 1722.

I had much ado to get hither last night, the water being so rough that
the ferry-men were unwilling to venture. The first thing I saw this

---

[1] Apparently Fenton continued to live in Twickenham after the death of Craggs. He is
now to serve temporarily as tutor to Henry Pope Blount, son of Sir Thomas Pope Blount,
a resident of Twickenham. Fenton was pre-engaged to become tutor to the son of
Lady Trumbull, widow of Sir William, in Binfield days Pope's neighbour and preceptor.
Sir Clement Cottrell's aunt had been the first Lady Trumbull, and Sir Clement (also a
resident of Twickenham) was adviser to the second Lady.

[2] The second and a large portion of the third paragraph here are apparently 'lifted' from
a letter preserved in the Harleian transcripts and dated 'Augt 1722'. The duplicated passages
are printed in the two places as specimens of Pope's habits of revision and amalgamation.
With these two paragraphs omitted, this letter becomes a 'thank-you' note written after
the bishop's return from a visit to Twickenham in May. See ii. 132.

The letter appears in all Pope's editions, 1737–42, without notable verbal changes.

morning after my eyes were open, was your letter, for the freedom and
kindness of which I thank you. Let all compliments be laid aside between us for the future; and depend upon me as your faithful friend in
all things within my pow'r, as one that truly values you, and wishes
you all manner of happiness. I thank you and Mrs. Pope for my kind
reception, which has left a pleasing impression upon me that will not
soon be effac'd.

Lord * has press'd me terribly to see him at *[1] and told me in a
manner betwixt kindness and resentment, that it is but a few miles
beyond Twitenham.

I have but a little time left, and a great deal to do in it; and must
expect that ill health will render a good share of it useless: and therefore what is likely to be left at the foot of the account, ought by me to
be cherish'd, and not thrown away in compliments. You know the
motto of my sun-dial, *Vivite, ait, fugio.* I will as far as I am able,
follow its advice, and cut off all unnecessary avocations and amusements. There are those that intend to employ me this winter in a way
I do not like: If they persist in their intentions, I must apply my self
to the work they cut out for me, as well as I can. But withal, that
shall not hinder me from employing myself also in a way which they
do not like. The givers of trouble one way shall have their share of it
another; that at last they may be induc'd to let me be quiet, and live
to myself, with the few (the very few) friends I like: For that is the
point, the single point, I now aim at; tho' I know, the generality of
the world who are unacquainted with my intentions and views, think
the very reverse of this character belongs to me. I don't know how I
have rambled into this account of myself, when I sat down to write
I had no thought of making that any part of my letter.

You might have been sure without my telling you, that my right
hand is at ease; else I should not have overflow'd at this rate. And yet
I have not done, for there is a kind intimation in the end of yours,
which I understood, because it seems to tend towards employing me
in something that is agreeable to you. Pray explain your self, and believe
that you have not an acquaintance in the world that would be more in
earnest on such an occasion than I; for I love you, as well as esteem you.

All the while I have been writing, Pain, and a fine Thrush have
been severally endeavouring to call off my attention; but both in vain,

---

¹ This sentence Nichols (i. 101–4) printed as 'Lord Bolingbroke has pressed me terribly
to see him at Dawley'; and later editors have copied that text. Unfortunately Bolingbroke
in 1722 was in exile, and had no connexion with Dawley for two or three years thereafter.
On the other hand, the Harleian transcript in the letter dated 'Augt 1722' offers the reading:
'Ld B. has press'd me terribly to see him at Riskins.' This reading makes sense, since Lord
Bathurst's estate at Riskins was 'but a few miles beyond Twitnam'. The Nichols text prob-
ably comes from footnotes in Curll's *Mr. Pope's Literary Correspondence,* v (1737), 111.
Curll gave the wrong proper names in footnotes, and Nichols inserted them in the text.

nor should I yet part with you, but that the turning over a new leaf frights me a little, and makes me resolve to break thro' a new temptation, before it has taken too fast hold on me. I am, &c.[1]

BROOME *to* FENTON   29 *May* 1722
Elwin–Courthope, viii. 53

May 29, 1722.

I choose this happy day to answer your letter. The parish bells are all ringing, and I will imagine it to be for the joyful news of your restoration to Sturston,[2] where you will be happier than a king. I will imagine you and the young Oxonian to be celestial visitants. Your gravity shall be Jupiter, and your companion the gay Mercury. Upon your arrival at my cottage, I will, like the hospitable Philemon, take down the bacon from my chimney, and my good house-wife, Baucis, shall fry it for your entertainment. But to be serious, you shall find a most sincere welcome at Sturston. Never talk of terms of boarding. If the gentleman's parents will pay, let the payment be as low as possible.

Te meis
Immunem meditor tingere poculis.[3]

I am glad you have translated the first of the Odyssey. You stand in the front of the battle, and the array of critics will naturally fall first upon you. I have translated the second, and shall therefore, like Teucer, be sheltered behind the shield of an Ajax.[4] I am pretty much unconcerned about the issue of the war. We are but auxiliars, yet I hope we shall behave so valiantly as to secure Mr. Pope on his throne on Parnassus. The weapons of most critics are weak; they may scratch, but seldom wound.

Pray consider what a weight lies upon my shoulders who, besides eight books of translation, am to write twenty-four of annotations. You only travel hand in hand with old Homer through flowery walks; I labour through dirt and rubbish with dull commentators.[5] It is

---

[1] The Hist. MSS. Comm. (*Portland MSS.* vii. 325–6) prints a letter from Dr. William Stratford, Canon of Christ Church, Oxford, to Lord Harley (soon to be the 2nd Earl of Oxford), dated 2 June 1722, which gossips about Atterbury's making advances to the Duchess of Buckingham. He says: 'She dined with him last Monday at Bromley. The young Duke . . . Pope & Chamberlain came along with her.' If these statements are true, the dinner took place on 28 May, and it is somewhat strange that the correspondence shows no trace of it.

[2] The parish bells rang for the anniversary of the restoration of King Charles II. Broome affects to believe that they ring because Fenton has definitively decided to come, with his pupil, to Sturston.

[3] Horace, *Carmina*, IV. xii. 22–23.

[4] Teucer's fighting protected by Ajax was doubtless proverbial. It was used of Pope fighting behind Gay in the attack called *A Compleat Key to . . . the What' D'ye Call It* (1715).

[5] Broome remembers Pope's phrases on the notes to the *Iliad*, and echoes them. See Pope to Broome, 24 Mar. 1720.

almost impossible for you to conceive how tiresome the task is of consulting fifty annotators every day, and finding them generally saying everything but just the thing they ought to say. It was happy for me that I had translated the eleventh and twelfth books some years ago for my diversion, otherwise I must have been too hasty either in the notes or the verse; but now I hope to execute both with some degree of reputation. I have finished three books—2, 11, 12—and if either you or Mr. Pope presume to touch 16, 18, and 23, I will punish you, and desire you to write your own notes upon them. Take notice, I give you fair warning, and as soon as I have fixed upon two more to complete my dividend, I expect to be humoured with full resignation. Remember the horror of the notes hangs over your heads, like the sword of Damocles, by a single hair. If you rebel I shall break it with a touch, and let it drop upon you. Be wise therefore, and obedient.

Pray bring your first book with you. There are some lines repeated in the second, and if your translation be better than mine, as I am certain it is, I shall transplant them as flowers to adorn my own garden. I hope to see you in a few days, and be assured I will make your habitation easy if not happy, being most faithfully yours.

FENTON *to* BROOME   7 *June* 1722

Elwin–Courthope, viii. 55

Twickenham, June 7, 1722.

Sir Clement gives his service to you, and thanks you for the kind reception you promise his friend; but both he and I wish you had expressed yourself more particularly on the terms on which we are to sojourn, which you and I must settle as soon as I arrive at Sturston, which I hope will be at the latter end of next week. I intend to come in the coach to Bury, and there take horses. In that affair I hope to be assisted by mine host of the Bushel. The young gentleman who comes along with me, is Sir Thomas Pope Blount's eldest son. I think I told you in my last that he would bring a footman, but they being a sort of cattle who are generally more troublesome in a family than their masters, I believe we shall come un-manned, and trust our throats to the barbers of Norfolk. I have quite forgot the directions you gave me to send my trunk, and therefore beg the favour of a line from you immediately, directed to Mr. Robinson, at the Blue Periwig at Charing Cross, for, dear sir, your most faithful humble servant.

I saw Mr. Pope yesterday. He was very well, and I am sure would have sent his service to you, had he known of my writing. Do not you owe him a letter?

ATTERBURY *to* POPE[1]   [1722]

Longleat Portland Papers, xiii (Harleian transcripts)

Bromly Frid. Even 1722

After you left me this morning Lord Bathurst came in, and he being in very good humour, I took the Opportunity of recommending my Gardiner to him, who was then in the house, and has accepted him upon the same Terms that he serv'd me. So I hope you did not see Lord B. to day, nor will see him before this reaches you, on Sund. morn. If unluckily that shall have prov'd the case, let me know the particulars that pass'd, that I may make amends for my mistake as far, and as soon as is possible.

I found, at my coming hither, a Riddle of the Dutchesses, what you only can explain. I send it you in her own Words and Hand, and expect the Solution. You must seriously think of that matter of the Dedication, and give her an explicit answer. It must be delay'd no longer than till we meet at the Deanery. In order to it, you shall know (if I my self have due notice) at what time I next come to Town.

And pray get me the Sheets of both Volumes,[2] stich'd up, that I may cast my Eye over them.

You are the first man, I sent to, and saw this morning, and the last man I desire to converse with this Evening, tho' at 20 Miles distance from you.

Te veniente die, Te decedente, requiro.[3]

Mrs Robn[4] haunts Bononcini, you follow her, and I plague you, which with the Liberty he sometimes took, Virgil has thus translated.

Torva Leæna Lupum sequitur Lupus ipse Capellum;
Te Corydon, o Alexi.[5]

So much to shew you, that both in English and Latin, in Verse and in Prose, I am ever yours.

---

[1] Written on a day when Pope and Atterbury had both been in town, and when Atterbury had returned to Bromley, probably during Pope's frequent visits to town early in June. The operatic personages mentioned at the end of the letter spent the summer of 1722 in Twickenham. By the end of July Atterbury had a new gardener (Atterbury to Pope, 30 July or 3 Aug.). 'Lord B' may be Burlington, to whom Pope was to offer the gardener.

[2] The Duke of Buckingham's *Works* appeared in two quarto volumes. The riddle just mentioned evidently concerned the Dedication.

[3] Adapted from *Georgics*, iv. 466.

[4] Mrs. Anastasia Robinson was about this time secretly married to the Earl of Peterborow. She had long been a friend of Pope's. Buononcini's new opera *Griselda* was frequently performed during the early months of 1722.

[5] *Eclogues*, ii. 63, 65.

‖ATTERBURY *to* POPE[1]   15 *June* 1722

Longleat Portland Papers, xiii (Harleian transcripts)

June 15th 1722.

You have generally written first, after our parting; I will now be before you in my Enquiries, how you got home and how you do, & whether you met with Lord ——, and deliver'd my civil reproach to him, in the manner I desir'd. I suppose you did not, because I have heard nothing either from You, or from him on that head; as I suppose I might have done if you had found him. I am sick of these Men of Quality; and the more so the oftner I have any Business to transact with them. They look upon it as one of their distinguishing Priviledges not to be punctual in any business, of how great importance so ever, nor to set other People at Ease, with the loss of the least part of their own. This conduct of his vexes me; but to what purpose? or how can I alter it.

I long to see the Original M.S. of Milton; but dont know how to come at it, without your repeated assistance, ⌈I shall have superstition enough to Collate it with my printed Book if Tonson will allow me the use of it for a few days. There was a time when his Uncle would have leap'd at such an opportunity of Obliging me, but then I was a Retainer to the Muses, and he did not know but he might have got something by me.⌉[2]

I hope you won't utterly forget what pass'd in the Coach about *Sampson Agonistes*. I shan't press you as to time: but sometime or other, I wish you would review, and polish that Piece, if upon a new Perusal[3] of it (which I desire You to make) you think as I do, that it is Written in the very Spirit of the Ancients, it deserves your care and is capable of being improv'd,[4] with little trouble, into a perfect Model and Standard of Tragic Poetry, always allowing for its being a Story taken out of the Bible which is an Objection that at this time of day, I know is not to be got over.

⌈You left your rough Draught of the Inscription intended for the

---

[1] Printed with omissions by Pope, 1737–42, with printed texts unchanged. Here first printed (?) from the Harleian transcripts, The transcript of this letter stops in the middle of the last line, and seems perhaps incomplete. Two extensive omissions by Pope are here placed in half-brackets.

[2] The Jacob Tonsons (uncle and nephew) had pretended to perpetual copyrights in both Shakespeare and Milton: at this time they possessed Milton manuscripts.

[3] Pope's texts begin a new sentence with 'If upon a new perusal'. The clause seems to go with that preceding it. One would like to begin a sentence after 'Ancients', where Pope placed a semicolon.

[4] Atterbury's desire to have *Samson* polished has been justly scorned. It is difficult to tell how far Pope accepted the bishop's judgement in matters of taste. He did not polish *Samson*; he did not revise the epitaph on John Hewet and Sarah Drew according to Atterbury's suggestions, and the 'Inscription' for the Duke of Buckingham's *Works* as printed seems moderately grandiloquent—a fact that may be due to the influence of the Duchess.

D's¹ Works behind you. Me thinks it should be turn'd in a manner some what more Simple and Natural. If I am not interrupted this Evening by some Accident besides that of writing Letters (several of which I have upon my hands) I will put down some what that comes near to what I mean⁷²

POPE *to* BROOME

9 *July* [1722]

Elwin–Courthope, viii. 56

Twitenham, July 9 [1722].

I had sooner thanked you for yours of the 25th of last month, but have been almost always ill, and am so yet. Let this too excuse me, for indeed it is not laziness or Fentonism, from transcribing the verses you mention. If you leave a blank of competent size for them when you write out your book, I will put them in there, though I cannot but remark that there seems some touch of the said Fentonism to be communicated to you by infection; for those verses are not absolutely the same with those in the second book, and will necessarily require to be turned in some measure differently.³ I hope I shall not hear that when Fenton has had his nap, you succeed to his elbow chair, and that the same may not befall you in conjunction with him, which is usual in two horses, where the higher-mettled is apter to be brought to the pace of the slower, than the slower to keep up with the other. But to say truth, *Fungar vice cotis*,⁴ &c., is at present applicable to me, for I am good for nothing just now but to whet others.

The grotto you have heard so poetical an account of, is what I very much want you to see. I hope when the season of study and retirement is over, about the time when both harvests are gathered—that of your head as well as of your field—you and Mr. Fenton will come hither, laden with the complete and ripe fruits of this year, which will be an earnest of what we are to expect in years to come. I have so good an opinion of the soils, that I am sure they can produce the very best, if proper sun, and air, and due pruning be not wanting—I mean the encouragement and care necessary.

I am very sick while I am writing this, and can scarce see the lines I write: therefore I desire you both to allow me at present to be short, not only in words but in sense. I faithfully assure you both, not ill health itself, which renders men indifferent to most things of the world, makes me at all the less warmly, or the less entirely, dear sir, your most affectionate friend and humble servant.

¹ Duke of Buckingham's.—Note in the Harleian transcript.
² It might have been injudicious to print this last paragraph in 1737 when the Duchess, still alive, was hostile to Pope.
³ He tells me I am lazy for not filling up those chasms I did not translate in my second book, being the same with those in the first book translated by Mr. Fenton, and I then filled them up.—Broome [Elwin]. ⁴ Horace, *Ars Poetica*, l. 304.

*POPE to VISCOUNT HARCOURT[1]   [17 *July* 1722]

Harcourt MSS.

                                                     Tuesday.

My Lord,—Hearing by Mr Vernon of your Lordships return to
town, and of the favourable mention your Lordship made of me, &
my little Workes at Twickenham, I earnestly beg you will now be so
good to Compleat my Vanities, by giving us the honour of your Company one day, whichsoever can best be spared from your better
affaires. A word to me from Mr Rock will secure your Lordship from
being starv'd that day, while there are chickens at Brentford, &
Mutton at Twitnam. I am with the sincerest respect | Your Lord-
ships most faithful obligd Servant | A. Pope.

Address: To the Rt Hon. the | Lord Viscount Harcourt.

Endorsement: 17 July 1722
                    Mr Pope | to Lord Vicount | Harcourt

*POPE to MRS. CÆSAR[2]   22 *July* [1722 or 1723]

Rousham

Madam,—It is no new thing for us Poets, to be oblig'd to Mrs
Cæsar: I therefore do as you order me. I beg you to accept a vile Print
which I promis'd you at Lord Harley's. I will soon have the honour
of sending you a better. I am Mr Cæsar's, & | Madam, | Your most
faithfull & | obedient Servant: | A. Pope.

Twitenham: | July the 22d

POPE to LORD BATHURST[3]   [25 *July* 1722?]

Cirencester

My Lord,—It's sincerely a great Disappointment to one who loves
you as I do, (that is, at a greater rate than any Busy, Ambitious, or

---

[1] Printed in *Harcourt Papers*, ii. 90–91. The bracketed date is from Harcourt's endorsement. 17 July 1722 was a Tuesday.
[2] In few of Pope's correspondences are the superscriptions and subscriptions spaced so
formally as in the letters to Mrs. Cæsar. One suspects that the lady affected a noble Roman
quality. The year is uncertain, but Pope's portrait by Kneller was engraved in 1722, and very
likely was promptly given to Mrs. Cæsar, who in 1723 was very active in getting subscribers
to Pope's *Odyssey*. The year 1723 is perfectly possible for the letter. Before July 1724 Lord
Harley was Earl of Oxford.
  Mrs. Cæsar, daughter of Ralph Freeman of Aspenden Hall, was, as her letters (now
preserved at Rousham) show, something of a literary lion-hunter. Her husband, Charles
Cæsar of Bennington, was an active Jacobite and was arrested as such in 1717. The Cæsars
were friends of Lord Harley, Judith Cowper, *et al.*, and Mrs. Cæsar's brother, William
Freeman, married Katharine Blount, sister of Sir Henry Pope Blount of Twickenham.
Through these or other connexions Pope's acquaintance with Mrs. Cæsar began.
[3] About twice in any year 'Wensday' falls upon the 25th of a month. Consequently the
date chosen for this letter is completely hypothetical. It seems a fairly early letter so far as

even any man that has any Thought of the world, can love another)
That I am unable to get to town this day to meet you, which was my
whole design. Every body here is as willing to leave me, & this place,
as I am to continue by myself, and in it, (were not You in Towne).
This has occasiond all our Coaches to be full, which hinders my
coming till another day. I hope to find your Lordship to morrow, but if
not, I very much wish you could call here at your return.

One Desire I must communicate to you, for a particular reason,
That my Friend Patty may not be mortifyd with the thought, you
only took notice of her at my Instigation; therefore I beg you will
call upon her during your stay in towne. I wish Her so well, as to wish
you knew her well; & when I dye, I'll leave her to you for a Legacy.

I have been very ill, ever since I saw your Lordship, which is apt
to give one melancholy thoughts; and puts me upon wishing to those
I esteem, the same thing that made me happy myself, namely, such a
Friendship as yours.

I have no more too add, but what, while I live I must always say,
and what, when I am dead I beg you will sometimes think of; That I
am truly, & with sincere Esteem & obligation, | My Lord | Your most
faithfull, | most affectionate, & obliged | Servant, | A. Pope.

Wensday the 25.

Address: To the Right Honourable, the | Lord Bathurst, in | St. James's
Square

†POPE *to* ATTERBURY[1]   27 *July* [1722]
1737
                                                    July 27.
I have been as constantly at Twitenham, as your Lordship has at
Bromley, ever since you saw Lord Bathurst. At the time of the Duke
of Marlborough's funeral,[2] I intend to lye at the Deanery, and moralize one evening with you on the vanity of human Glory.—

The Dutchesses[3] letter concerns me nearly, and you know ⌈it, who
know⌉ all my thoughts without disguise: I must keep clear of Flattery;
I will: and as this is an honest resolution, I dare hope your Lordship
will not be so unconcern'd for my keeping it, as not to assist me in so

an acquaintance between Lord Bathurst and Martha Blount is concerned. On several other
possible Wednesdays Lord Bathurst would not be in London. In this case he apparently was;
Pope had been ill, and the summer traffic from Twickenham was doubtless heavier than at
other times of the year.
   [1] Printed with practically no revision of text in all Pope's editions, 1737–42. In 1783
Nichols reprinted Pope's text from the quarto of 1737 and (by accident?) omitted three
words, here in half-brackets, in the third sentence.
   [2] The Duke's funeral took place on 9 Aug. 1722.
   [3] The Duchess of Buckingham.

doing. I beg therefore you would represent thus much at least to her
Grace, that as to the fear she seems touch'd with, [That the Duke's
memory should have no advantage but what he must give himself,
without being beholden to any one friend.][1] Your Lordship may
certainly, and agreeably to your character, both of rigid honour and
christian plainness, tell her that no man can have any other advantage:
and that all offerings of friends in such a case pass for nothing. Be but
so good as to confirm what I've represented to her, that an inscription
in the antient way, plain, pompous, yet modest, will be the most uncommon, and therefore the most distinguishing manner of doing it:[2]
And so I hope she will be satisfied, the Duke's Honour be preserv'd,
and my integrity also: which is too sacred a thing to be forfeited, in
consideration of any little (or what people of quality may call great)
Honour or distinction whatever, which those of their rank can bestow
on one of mine; and which indeed they are apt to over-rate, but never
so much as when they imagine us under any obligation to say one
untrue word in their favour.

I can only thank you, my Lord, for the kind transition you make,
from common business to that which is the only real business of every
reasonable creature. Indeed I think more of it than you imagine, tho'
not so much as I ought. I am pleas'd with those latin verses extreamly,
which are so very good that I thought 'em yours, till you call'd 'em
an Horatian Cento, and then I recollected the *disjecti membra poetæ*.[3]
I won't pretend I am so totally in those sentiments which you compliment me with, as I yet hope to be: You tell me I have them, as the
civillest method to put me in mind how much it fits me to have 'em.
I ought, first, to prepare my mind by a better knowledge even of good
prophane writers, especially the Moralists, &c. before I can be worthy
of tasting that supreme, of books, and sublime of all writings. In which,
as in all the intermediate ones, you may (if your friendship and charity
toward me continue so far) be the best guide to | Yours, &c.

||ATTERBURY *to* POPE[4]   [30 *July* or 3 *August* 1722]

Longleat Portland Papers, xiii (Harleian transcripts)

Bromly Friday Even 1722.

I have written to the Dutchess just as you desir'd, and referr'd her to
our meeting in Town for a farther account of it. I have done it the

---

[1] Pope's own brackets.

[2] The inscription was printed opposite the frontispiece in 1723.

[3] Horace, *Sermones*, I. iv. 62.

[4] Printed without textual revision in Pope's editions 1737–42. The date is doubtful. In
Pope's printed texts it is dated 'July 30, 1722', but the Harleian transcript, here printed, has
only 'Friday Even' and Pope's printed date was probably his guess—a better guess than he
ordinarily made for undated letters. In 1722, 30 July was Monday. The last Friday before
Marlborough's funeral was 3 Aug.

rather, because your Opinion in the case is sincerely mine. And if it had not been so, you your self should not have induced me to give it. Whether, and how far she will acquiesce in it, I cannot say: for quicquid vult, valde vult; and in no case so remarkably, as where She thinks the Dukes Honor concern'd. But should she seem to persist a little at present, Her good Sense (which I depend upon) will afterwards satisfy her, that we are in the right.

The Gardiner has been here these two days, but I have scarce had Leysure to speak to him much less to discover, whether he is likely to answer the Ends for which I took him.[1] However, I give you my hearty Thanks for the Trouble you have had in this affair. I go to morrow to the Deanery, and believe I shall stay there, till I have said, Dust to Dust, and shut up the last Scene of Pompous Vanity. Tis a great while for me to stay there at this time of the Year; and I know I shall often say to my self, while I am expecting the Funeral,

> O Rus, quando ego te aspiciam! quandoque licebit
> Ducere sollicitæ jucunda oblivia vitæ![2]

In that case, I shall fancy I hear the Ghost of the Defunct, thus intreating me.

> At Tu sacratæ ne parce malignus Arenæ
>   Ossibus et capiti inhumato
> Particulam dare—[3]
> Quanquam festinas, non est mora longa; licebit,
>   Injecto ter pulvere, curras.

There is an answer for me some where in Hamlet to this Request, which You remember tho' I don't—Poor Ghost thou shalt be satisfy'd—or some thing like it. However that be, take care you do not fail in your appointment, that the Company of the living may make me some amends for my attendance on the Dead.

I know, you will be glad to hear, that I am well. I should always be so, could I always be here.

Sed me
> Imperiosa trahit Proserpina; Vive, valeque;[4]

---

¹ Atterbury has passed on his gardener to Lord Bathurst earlier (see Atterbury to Pope, 'Frid. Even', ii. 123), and Pope has helped the bishop to another, who apparently does not answer Atterbury's ends, since in the bishop's next letter to Pope still another gardener is in question.   ² Horace, *Sermones*, ii. vi. 60, 62.
³ Hor. Lib. I, Od. 28.—Harleian transcript note. Atterbury adapts the passage (ll. 23–25; 35–36).
⁴ Horace, *Sermones*, ii. v. 110.
After this last quotation from Horace, Pope added in his printed texts a sentence from Atterbury's June (?) letter dated, like this one, 'Frid. Even'—a letter which Pope did not print, except for this one abstracted sentence. It read: 'You are the first man I sent to this morning, and the last man I desire to converse with this evening, tho' at twenty miles distance from you, | Te veniente die, Te decedente, requiro.' Cf. *supra*, ii. 123.

*POPE *to* JACOB TONSON, JR.¹   [6 *August* 1722?]

Add. 28275

Sir,—The Indisposition that continues much upon me hinders my
coming to town as yet. I dare say you'l not find the Volumes too thick,
dividing the whole into five, as I sent a direction, Pray let me have
That copyd out. Unless we settle this, Fenton must stop in the Index,
& much time will be lost I fear.

Address: To Mr Tonson, at Shakespears | head over against Catharine
street, | in the Strand, | London
Postmark: 6/AV

POPE *to* BROOME²   12 *August* [1722]

Elwin–Courthope, vii. 57
                                                           August 12 [1722].

I was just sitting down to write when I received yours. You shall
have a short answer as to your prologue: I will do all I can to it.

I am pleased to hear of your progress in the grand work. But you
say nothing of Mr. Fenton, and he will say nothing for himself. However, tell him that I have sent to Mr. Barber about the note he speaks
of.³ He answered, that he was in such a hurry when he left London,
and had besides so many unforeseen odd accounts to pay and settle,
that he could not answer it as he ought; but assured me that he had
destroyed Mr. Fenton's note.

Be pleased also to inform Mr. Fenton, that he may refer all the
historical plays of Shakespeare to volume three, into which division we
have contrived to bring them.⁴ I hope he sometimes writes to Lady
Blount, and does not forget Sir Clement Cottrell, who wondered some
time since he never heard from him. I hope, nay, I depend upon, your
finishing the book you are upon, before your guests leave you. I must
desire you too to animate our friend to dispatch his. The next winter
will be the crisis of that affair, and we should be prepared. It is the
more needful you two should, because the unavoidable avocations that

¹ The year of this letter is somewhat uncertain, but work on the Indexes of the edition
of Shakespeare began early. The letter is written upon the cover of a letter from Temple
Stanyan to Pope, addressed 'To Alexander Pope Esqr at | his house in | Twickenham |
Middlesex. | Free | Tem: Stanyan.'
    Comments on the work on Shakespeare in the letter to Broome, 12 Aug., make the date
of this letter fairly certain.
² Broome has written a Prologue for Fenton's *Mariamne*, which evidently he has asked
Pope to revise.
³ Elwin interprets this paragraph as referring to Alderman Barber, a Jacobite, to whom
Fenton, a Non-juror, may have written an indiscreet note. Already some of the lesser agents
of the Pretender were under arrest, and Atterbury was seized within a fortnight after this
letter was written. But one doubts if Fenton had any connexion with disloyal elements.
⁴ Fenton assisted Pope considerably in editing Shakespeare.

hinder me from what is my part, will not cease till that time, when I will overtake you, I promise, ride as hard as you will. Would to heaven I enjoyed that tranquillity you both can and do; that I were as much my own lord and master; as much retired to my beloved studies, the only things I am made for and born to. But, alas! every man almost is in this condition—envying other men's lives and losing his own. Even at this moment I scarce have time to read what I have writ; and when I have read it, none to mend the many imperfections I see so plainly. It is all I can do, to tell you in this strange rambling manner, how little I am myself, and how much yours.

Do not talk of franking letters; write to me without scruple; the oftener the better. Adieu. I heartily wish myself with you.

*ATTERBURY *to* POPE[1]   *August* 1722
Longleat Portland Papers, xiii (Harleian transcripts)

Bromly, Sund. Even. Augt 1722

I was glad to see any thing under your hand this morning, tho' I don't like the account you give of this last Fitt, both as to its Length, and Violence. Indeed you must be content for the future not to go by water, but when the Weather is so good, that you are sure of not catching Cold. All your Headachs, I believe proceed from thence: and therefore that is what you are chiefly to fence against, and to neglect any Pleasure, any Busyness, that comes in competition with your health in this particular. I am of a Stronger constitution than you (at present at least, I am; for I never was better in all my Life): and yet, when ever I catch an hearty Cold, I am sure of a Fitt of the Gout, tho' I should have been but just recover'd out of one. Let you and I therefore, resolve to guard against our Common Enemy: and hearken to my Advice the rather, because you are sure I am in earnest in it, since tis what I my self follow.

I thank you for your enquirys about a Gardiner,[2] and should be glad to see the man you mention if he be a Single man, and Sober. I think, I shall be at the Deanery to morrow, or Tuesday, and perhaps stay there all Wednesday: but this Letter, I fear, will not reach you soon enough, to give the man notice; and you do not tell me, where I may find him. And after all, my going to London depends upon so many Accidents, that, if you could send him to me either on Tuesd. or Wedn. I am not sure, he would find me there. So much for the important Affair of my Gardiner. I have another of as great moment

---

[1] In his editions, 1737–42, Pope added paragraphs 3 and 4 of this letter (with omissions) to Atterbury's letter of 25 May 1722 (q.v.). The date is probably 12 or 19 Aug. Pope had planned to be in London for Marlborough's funeral (9 Aug.), and may have caught cold returning home on the Thames. Atterbury was arrested on Friday, 24 Aug.

[2] On the gardener see Atterbury to Pope, 30 July or 3 Aug.

now to impart to you. The enclos'd Letter contains it: which being
of a very Singular Turn, and mentioning your name, I have thought
my self oblig'd to transmit it to You. When you have smil'd over it
for a moment, pray return it to me carefully by the same Method of
conveyance. I cannot imagine, who has put the Man upon Comple-
menting me, at this distance from the Time, when I serv'd him. It
must be either the Dutchess, or You. I dare not resent any thing that
is done by a fair Lady: but if you put him upon it, I shall not be easy
till I am even with you and found out such another Correspondent to
entertain You.

Lord B. has press'd me terribly to see him at Riskins,[1] and told me
in a manner betwixt kindness and resentment, that it is but a few miles
beyond Twitnam, ⌐and that I have much better health now than I had
two Months ago. It is true I have: but I am less dispos'd to motion
than I was then, and shall be less and less so every day that I live. If
I would go twenty, or thirty Miles to see any one of his Rank, he is
the Man: but I question whether I shall ever again be guilty of such
a Frolick.⌐ I have but a little time left, and a great deal to do in it, and
must expect that ill health will render a good share of it useless: and
therefore what is likely to be left at the foot of the account ought by
me to be cherish'd, and not thrown away in Complements. You know
the Motto of my Sundyal, Vivite, ait, fugio: I will as far as I am able,
follow its advice, and cut off all unnecessary Recreations[2] and Amusements, there are those that intend to employ me this Winter, in a
way I do not like.

If they persist in their Intentions, I must apply my self to the Work
they cutt out for me, as well as I can. But with all that shall not hinder
me from employing myself also in a way they do not like: the givers
of Trouble one way shall have their share of it, another; that at last
they may be induc'd to let me be quiet, and live to my self, and with
the few (the very few) Friends I like. For that is the point the Single
point I now aim at: tho' I know the generality of the world, who are
unacquainted with my Intentions and Views, think the very reverse
of this Character belongs to me. I don't know how I have rambl'd
into this account of myself: when I sat down to write, I had no
thoughts of making that ⌐the Subject of⌐ any part of my Letter. ⌐You
complain'd of the shortness of my last; and will now perhaps complain
of the Length of this. That I may not add to it, Adieu, and believe me
always | Yours most heartily | Fra: Roffen.

You have Leysure—pray send me the Draught of such an Answer,
as you think I should return to Mr Morley.⌐[3]

---

[1] For annotation of this passage see Atterbury to Pope, 25 May 1722.

[2] Recreations] Avocations *1737–42*.

[3] Pope's printed text (dated 25 May 1722) uses a different ending for the letter.

†POPE *to* JOHN GAY[1]   11 *September* 1722

1735

London,[2] Sept. 11, 1722.

Dear Gay,—I thank you for remembring me. I would do my best to forget my self, but that I find your Idea is so closely connected to me, that I must forget both together, or neither. I'm sorry, I could not have a glympse either of you, or of the Sun (your Father) before you went for *Bath*. But now it pleases me to see him, and hear of you. Pray put Mr. *Congreve* in mind that he has one on this side of the World who loves him; and that there are more Men and Women in the Universe, than Mr. *Gay* and my Lady Dutchess of *M*.[3] There are Ladies in and about *Richmond* that pretend to value him and yourself; and one of 'em at least may be thought to do it without Affectation, namely Mrs. *Howard*. [4]⌈As for Mrs. *Blounts* (whom you mercifully make mention of) they are gone, or going to *Sussex*.[5] I hope Mrs. *Pulteney*[6] is the better for the *Bath*, tho' I have little Charity and few good Wishes for the Ladies, the Destroyers of their best friends the Men. Pray tell her she has forgot the first Commission I ever troubled her with, and therefore it shall be the last (the very thing I fear she desires.) Dr. *Arbuthnot* is a strange creature; he goes out of town, and leaves his Bastards at other folks doors. I have long been so far mistaken in him as to think him a Man of Morals as well as of Politicks. Pray let him know I made a very unfashionable inquiry t'other day of the welfare of his Wife and family: Things that (I presume) are below the consideration of a Wit and an *Ombre*-player.[7] They are in perfect health. Tho' Mrs. *A*—'s Navel has been burnt, I hope the Doctor's own Belly is in absolute ease and contentment. Now I speak of those Regions about the *Abdomen*,⌉[8] pray ⌈dear *Gay*⌉ consult with him and Dr. *Chene*, to what exact pitch yours may be suffer'd to swell, not to outgrow theirs, who are, yet, your Betters. ⌈Pray⌉ tell Dr. *Arbuthnot* that even Pigeon-pyes and Hogs-puddings are thought dangerous by our Governors; for those that have been sent to the Bishop of *Rochester*, are open'd and prophanely[9] pry'd into at the *Tower*: 'Tis the first time dead Pigeons have been suspected of carrying

---

[1] Printed in all Pope's editions. Most of the textual revisions are noted below.
[2] *London* is omitted 1737–42.
[3] Dutchess of M.] Dutchess. *1737–42*. (i.e. Henrietta, Duchess of Marlborough).
[4] This long passage in half-brackets was omitted 1737–42.
[5] To visit Caryll probably.
[6] Born Anna Maria Gumley, this lady brought Pulteney a fortune. She was beautiful, but otherwise not amiable.
[7] Dr. Arbuthnot was highly skilled at ombre.
[8] The passage omitted in 1737–42 ends here and the sentence following begins: 'Pray consult with Dr. Arbuthnot and Dr. Chene, to what exact pitch your belly may . . .' The words hereafter in half-brackets were omitted in the 1737–42 editions.
[9] This word was omitted in the quarto and folio of 1737.

Intelligence. To be serious, you, and Mr. *Congreve* (nay and the Doctor if he has not dined)[1] will be sensible of my concern and surprize at the commitment of that Gentleman,[2] whose welfare is as much my concern as any Friend's I have. I think my self a most unfortunate wretch; I no sooner love, and, upon knowledge, fix my esteem to any man; but he either dies like Mr. *Craggs* or is sent to Imprisonment like the Bishop. God send him as well as I wish him, manifest him to be as Innocent as I believe him, and make all his Enemies know him as well as I do, that they may love him and think[3] of him as well!

If you apprehend this Period to be of any danger in being address'd to you; tell Mr. *Congreve* or the Doctor, it is writ to them. I am | Your, &c.

POPE *to* BROOME   18 *September* 1722

Elwin–Courthope, viii. 58
                                                      Sept. 18, 1722.

I think I ought not to delay this letter, for fear of leading my friend into a false expectation and disappointing him. He knows, from what I formerly told him, my reasons and inability from some circumstances, of writing anything like a prologue, and you must have mistaken me strangely to fancy I meant any such thing. I only promised to look over yours, and do the very best I could to it. As to my writing one, were it to be engaged for as the greatest of secrets, I have learnt by experience nothing of that kind is ever kept a secret; and therefore I must not delude Fenton, though at the same time I faithfully assure him, I would most gladly make the prologue, to-morrow, could it be done without any man's knowing it. I have actually refused doing it for the Duke of Buckingham's play.[4]

Your report of my quitting, or being in the least inclined to quit, the easy, single state I now enjoy, is altogether groundless; as idle, as the news which people invent, merely because they are idle.[5]

I am very much pleased with the progress made in the old bard, and the more so, as I have been able to do little. Several matters of extreme concern to me, both as a friend, and as a creature dissipated

---

[1] Congreve . . . will] Congreve and the Doctor will *1737–42.*

[2] at the commitment . . . whose] at his commitment, whose *1737–42.*

[3] may love him and think] may think *1737–42.*

[4] *The British Journal*, 22 Sept. 1722, announced that 'Two Plays, alter'd by the late Duke of Buckinghamshire from Shakespear's Julius Caesar, have been offer'd to the House; but whether they are to be acted, we cannot as yet say'. The Duchess probably had asked Pope for a prologue in event of performance. There was a private performance of at least portions of the plays at Buckingham House, 10 Jan. 1722/3, at which Pope's two choruses (already printed in his *Works*, 1717) were sung. See *Book Prices Current* for 1919, pp. 552–3.

[5] On the rumours concerning Pope's marriage see Pope to Caryll, 25 Dec. 1725 and 18 Feb. 1734/5. There were also reports of a secret marriage. See Sherburn, *Early Career*, pp. 291–4.

with many businesses, having wholly taken me off from any thought of study.

Pray tell Mr. Fenton Sir Clement Cottrell has received his letter. I cannot but envy the manner in which your time is spent, and wish myself with you. Believe me always to both of you a most faithful affectionate servant.

*POPE *to* LORD PERCIVAL¹   22 *September* [1722]

Add. 47029 (p. 260)

Twitenham 22 Sept.

My Lord,—I fear your Lordship will think a letter from me very impertinent, just a day or two after I Saw you, & saw you in so odd a manner, that I cannot but apologize for giving you so inhospitable a reception. but the occasion of my troubling you now is to ask a favour of you, which I believe of that nature which one may ask of any gentleman. I did not know till after you were gone that the person who was with you, Coll. Hunter is one of the Directors of the Opera. The Dutchess of Buckingham has a request to that board that the late Dukes Play may be perform'd at the Theatre in Drury lane with Several pieces of musick written in the manner of the ancient Chorus's, partly by himself, & partly by me, & that in case any voice, or part of the Instrumental Musick shou'd be wanted, they wou'd permit them to perform in it for a few nights, supposing those nights not to interfere with the Operas. Your Lordships interest with Mr Hunter in this affair will be a double obligation to her & to | My Lord | Your most obedient & most faithfull Servant | A. Pope.

*LORD PERCIVAL *to* POPE²   25 *September* 1722

Add. 47029 (p. 266)

Charlton 25 Sept. 1722

Sir,—I beg your pardon that I did not thank you for the favour of your letter as I might have done the next day after I received it, but

¹ Printed from the letterbooks of Lord Percival. The letter was partially printed in the Seventh Report of the Hist. MSS. Comm.

² The text is from the Percival letterbooks. Apparently the Duke's musical version of *Julius Caesar* never had public performance. The choruses were sung at a ball and concert in Buckingham House in the following January. On a copy of the texts then printed Katherine, Duchess of Buckingham, wrote: 'These choruses were performed at Buckingham House in the great Salon on the Birthday of Edmond Duke of Buckingham, Jan. the 10th, 1723. The musick was performed by Mrs. Robinson, Mrs. Barbier and another singer Mrs. Clark. All the Opera Instruments performed their severall parts, and the Chapell Singers. The management of which was under the care of Signor Bononcinni, who sett the choruses with great skill and love.' On the Chorus of the Romans the Duchess wrote: 'These two last choruses were made by the Duke of Buckingham; the two first at Lord Duke's desire by Mr. Pope.' See the Sotheby Sale Catalogue for 7 Nov. 1918, lot 528.

I was desirous first to know what Success your application to the Directors met with. This morning Brigadier Hunter return'd from London, & told me that the chief Singers engaged, wou'd not be permitted to perform at Drury Lane, but he was Sure you might have Bosci, & any of the instrumental musick on Such nights as did not interfere with the Operas. He was very ready to serve you, and desired I would let you know that Sagioni formerly known here by the name of Maria Gallia is lately return'd, & sings to his judgment extreamly well. She is not engaged to the Hay market, & probably will perform at Drury lane upon moderate encouragement, for she is come with a view of maintaining her Self by Schollars. I am | Sir | Your humble & obedient Servant | Percival.

POPE *to* JUDITH COWPER[1]   30 *September* 1722

Arthur A. Houghton, Jr.

Twitenham, Sept. 30th 1722

Madam,—No Confidence is so great, as that one receives from persons one knows *may be* believd, and in things one is *willing* to believe. I have (at last) acquir'd this; by Mrs H***[2] repeated assurances of a thing I am unfeignedly so desirous of, as Your Allowing me to correspond with you. In good earnest there is sometimes, in Men as well as in Women, a great deal of Unaffected Modesty: and I was Sincere all along, when I told her personally, & told you by my Silence, that I fear'd only to seem impertinent, while perhaps I seem'd negligent, to you. To tell Mrs ****[3] any thing like what I really thought of her, would have lookd so like the Common Traffick of Compliment, that

---

[1] First printed in *Letters to a Lady* (1769), this letter was there placed as number 7 among the dozen Pope addressed to Miss Cowper. In the Elwin–Courthope edition, as here, it is regarded as Pope's earliest letter to the lady. For the first time since 1769 this correspondence is here printed from the originals.

[2] It is improbable that Bowles was correct in assuming that the Mrs. H. mentioned in almost every letter Pope wrote to Miss Cowper is Mrs. Howard. Bowles, however, had not seen the originals, in which the name is heavily blotted out and replaced, normally, by three or four crosses. The spacing of the name leaves room for not more than four or five letters, and a name like Howe is more plausible than Howard. Whereas there is no evidence of friendship between Miss Cowper and Mrs. Howard, there is evidence of a considerable friendship between Miss Cowper and Miss Mary Howe, a Maid of Honour, who in 1725 became the third countess of the 8th Earl of Pembroke. In verses written on her own birthday in 1723 Miss Cowper (like Pope in this letter) couples Pope and Miss Howe as friends. She wrote:

> Yet to this Merit may the Wretch pretend,
> That *Howe* and *Pope* vouchsafe to call her Friend.

See F. Madan, *The Madan Family*, p. 268. See also Pope to. Mrs. Cowper, 29 Aug. 1723, and Mrs. Caesar to Pope, 10 Sept. 1723. Mrs. Cowper was niece of a lord chancellor, and aunt to the poet William Cowper. In Dec. 1723 she married Captain Martin Madan. Since she died in 1781 one may assume that she supervised the publication of Pope's letters to her in 1769.

[3] Mrs. Cowper herself.

pays only to receive; & to have told it her in distant or bashful terms, would have appeard so like Coldness in my sence of good Qualities, (which I cannot find out in any one without feeling, from my nature, at the same time a great Warmth for them), that I was quite at a loss what to write, or in what stile, to you? But I am resolvd, plainly to get over all objections, and faithfully to assure you, if you will help a bashful man to be past all Preliminaries, & Forms, I am ready to Treat with you for your Friendship. I know (without more ado) you have a valuable Soul; & Wit, Sense & Worth enough, to make me reckon it (provided you will permit it) one of the happinesses of my life to have been made acquainted with you.

I don't know, on the other hand, what you can think of me? But this, for a beginning, I'll venture to ingage, that whoever takes me for a Poet, or a Wit (as they call it) takes me for a creature of less value than I am: and that where-ever I profess it, you shall find me a Much better Man, that is, a much better friend, or at least a much less faulty one, than I am a Poet. That whatever Zeal I may have, or whatever regard I may shew, for things I truly am so pleasd with as Your entertaining writings; yet I shall still have more for your person, and for your Health, and for your happiness. I would, with as much readiness, play the Apothecary or the Nurse, to mend your Headakes, as I would play the Critick to improve your verses. I have seriously lookd over & over those you intrusted me with, and assure you, Madam, I would as soon Cheat in any other Trust, as in this. I sincerely tell you I can mend 'em very little, & only in Triffles, not worth writing about, but will tell you every tittle when I have the happiness to see you. I am more concern'd than you can reasonably believe, for the ill state of health you are at present under: but I will Appeal to Time to shew you how sincerely I am (if I live long enough to prove myself what I truly am) | Madam | Your most faithfull Servant | A: Pope

I am very sick all the while I write this letter, which I hope will be an excuse for its being so scribbled.

†POPE *to* JOHN GAY[1]   *[September–October* 1722]

1735

I think it obliging in you to desire an account of my health. The truth is, I have never been in worse state in my life, and find whatever I

---

[1] Printed in all Pope's editions. In 1737 and thereafter Pope added the date 'Sept. 11, 1722'. This seems a probable error, for in the editions of 1737–42 the next letter but one preceding this was also so dated. After this first letter of 11 Sept. Gay seems to have replied inquiring for Pope's health, and this present letter is Pope's answer. Apart from the date textual variations are negligible.

have try'd as a remedy so ineffectual, that I give myself entirely over.
I wish your health may be set perfectly right by the Waters, and be
assur'd I not only wish that, and every thing else for you, as common
friends wish, but with a Zeal not usual among those we call so. I am
always glad to hear of, and from you; always glad to see you, whatever
accidents or amusements have interven'd to make me do either less
than usual. I not only frequently think of you, but constantly do my
best to make others do it, by mentioning you to all your acquaintance.
I desire you to do the same for me to those you are now with: do me
what you think Justice in regard to those who are my friends; and if
there are any, whom I have unwillingly deserv'd so little of, as to be
my Enemies, I don't desire you to forfeit their opinion or your own
judgment in any case. Let Time convince those who know me not,
that I am an inoffensive person; tho' (to say truth) I don't care how
little I am indebted to Time, for the World is hardly worth living in,
at least to one that is never to have health a week together. I have been
made to expect Dr. *Arbuthnot* in town this fortnight, or else I had
written to him. If he, by never writing to me, seems to forget me,
I consider I do the same seemingly to him, and yet I don't believe he
has a more sincere friend in the world than I am; therefore I will
think him mine. I am His, Mr. *Congreve*'s, and | Your, &c.

POPE *to* JUDITH COWPER[1]   18 *October* [1722]

Arthur A. Houghton, Jr.

Twitenham, Oct. 18.

Madam,—We are indebted to Heaven for all things, & above all for
our Sense & Genius (in whatever degree we have it) but to fancy
yourself indebted to any thing else, moves my anger at your modesty.
The regard I must bear you, seriously proceeds from yourself alone;
& I will not suffer even one I like so much as Mrs H.[2] to have a share
in causing it. I challenge a kind of Relation to you on the *Soul*'s side,
which I take to be better than either on a Father's or Mothers; and if
you can Overlook an ugly *Body* (that stands much in the way of any
Friendship, when it is between different Sexes) I shall hope to find you
a True & constant Kinswoman in Apollo. Not that I woud place all
my Pretensions upon That Poetical foot, much less confine 'em to it;
I am far more desirous to be admitted as yours on the more meritorious
title of Friendship. I have ever believd this as a sacred maxime, that
the most Ingenious Natures were the most Sincere, & the most Knowing & Sensible Minds made the Best Friends. Of all those that I have

---

[1] The Dodsley edition of 1769 placed this letter first among the letters to Miss Cowper,
but it seems rather to follow that of 30 Sept. 1722.
[2] Mrs. Howe or Mrs. Howard. See note 2 to the letter of 30 Sept. 1722.

thought it the felicity of my life to know, I have ever found the most distinguishd in Capacity, the most distinguishd in Morality: and those the most to be depended on, whom one esteemd so much as to desire they shoud be so. I beg you to make me no more complements. I coud make you a great many, but I know you neither need 'em, nor can Like 'em: Be so good as to think I don't. In one word, your writings are very good, & very entertaining, but not so good, nor so entertaining as your Life & Conversation. One is but the Effect & Emanation of the other. It will always be a greater pleasure to me, to know you Are well, than that you write well, tho every time you tell me the one, I must know the other. I am willing to spare your modesty, & therfore, as to your writing may perhaps never say more (directly to yourself) than the few verses I send here; which (as a proof of my own modesty too) I made so long ago as the day you sate for your picture,[1] & yet never till now durst confess to you.

> Tho sprightly Sappho force our Love & Praise,)
> A softer Wonder my pleasd soul surveys,   }
> The mild Erinna, blushing in her Bays.   )
> So while the Sun's broad beam yet strikes the sight,
> All mild appears the moon's more sober Light,
> Serene, in Virgin Majesty, she shines;
> And un-observd, the glaring Sun declines.[2]

The brightest Wit in the world, without the better qualities of the heart, must meet with this fate; and tends only to endear such a character as I take yours to be. In the better discovery, and fuller con-viction of which, I have a strong opinion I shall grow more and more happy, the longer I live your acquaintance, and (if you will indulge me in so much pleasure) | Your faithfull Friend, & most | obligd Servant. | A. Pope.

POPE *to* CARYLL   26 *October* [1722]
Add. 28618

Oct. 26.

I am ashamed as well as pleased to receive a most obliging letter from your hands, at the time I should not only by inclination but by pro-mise have written one to you. I never was in a greater hurry and dis-traction in my life and faithfully I assure you I intended every day,

[1] Jervas did a crayon portrait of Miss Cowper designed for 'Lady P.' but Pope 'stole' the picture; see his letter to Miss Cowper here placed in Nov. 1722. After Pope's death Martha Blount returned the portrait to Mrs. Madan (formerly Miss Cowper). Pope here recalls first seeing Miss Cowper as she sat for the portrait. There is no reason to think the acquaintance began in 1722, though the correspondence may have. On the Jervas crayon see F. Madan, *The Madan Family*, p. 97.

[2] Pope omitted the triplet, improved the remaining four lines, and placed them in 1735 in his *Epistle on the Characters of Women* (To Martha Blount) ,ll. 253–6.

nay, thrice sat down to write, but I find I'm concerned for so many
people and love my friends so well that every thing that befalls them
interests me so farr in it as to make me seem to forget the rest. Indeed,
dear sir, when I'm seeming so to do, I forget none so much as I do
myself and attend [no] one's concerns so little. I may not pass such a
life, as to have that sentence of Seneca the tragedian applied to me,

> Infelix ille!
> Qui notus nimis omnibus,
> Ignotus moritur sibi.[1]

I know I have your good wishes, as against all misfortunes, so against
this greatest one above all. And I am truly sensible of your friendship,
and truly ready to make the due returns to it on any occasion. I very
much condole with my friend[2] whose confinement you mention, and
very much applaud your obliging desire of paying him a compliment
at this time of some venison, the method of which I've been bold to
prescribe to Lady Mary.[3] I must not omit telling you how much I,
and all of us, are obliged to that Lady; for her kind notice and obliging
visits while at Twitenham. She is every way of a piece with the rest
of your family, and brings all Ladyholt into my mind wherever I converse with her.

The news about our friend Gay must be a mistake occasioned by
another of the same name, who is qualified for a member of Parliament.

I must again sincerely protest to you, that I have wholly given over
scribbling, at least any thing of my own, but am become, by due gradation of dulness, from a poet a translator, and from a translator, a mere
editor. Were I really capable at this time of producing any thing, I
should be incapable of concealing it from you, who have been so many
years one of my best critics, as well as one of my best friends. I can't
express how much I wish we were nearer together to enjoy the fruits
and pleasures, as well as I feel the warmth and reality, of friendship.
Let Lady Mary express it for me, from whom it will both convince
and please you more, than any cold words at this distance can do from |
Dear sir | Your most affectionate faithful | Servant. A: P:

POPE *to* JONATHAN RICHARDSON[4]   4 *November* [1722]

Elwin–Courthope, ix. 493

Twitenham, Nov. 4.

I thank you for the agreeable present of your book,[5] of which I can

---

[1] *Thyestes*, ll. 402–3.   [2] Bishop Atterbury.   [3] Lady Mary Caryll.
[4] Elwin took the text from 'Richardson's transcript'. The letter was printed in *The
St. James's Chronicle*, 20 July 1776. The original letter, offered for sale by Thomas Thorpe
in 1833, has not been traced.
[5] *The St. James's Chronicle* in printing the letter identifies this book as *An Account of*

say no better than that it is worthy Mr. R. and his son,—worthy two such lovers of one another, and two such lovers of the fine arts. It will certainly be a most useful book to all such, and to me in particular a most delightful one, who think the saying of the Psalmist yet stronger if applied to parents and children: *Behold how good and how pleasant it is for them to dwell in unity.*[1] I am ever your obliged affectionate humble servant.

POPE *to* JUDITH COWPER[2]   5 *November* [1722]

Arthur A. Houghton, Jr.

Tho I am extremely oblig'd by your agreable Letter, I'll avoid all mention of the pleasure you give me, that we may have no more words about Complements; which I've often observd people talk themselves into, while they endeavour to talk themselves out of. Tis no more the Diet of Friendship & Esteem, than a few thin Wafers & marmalade were of so hearty a stomach as Sancho's. In a word I am very proud of my new Relation, & like Parnassus much the better, since I found I had so good a Neighbour there. Mrs H****, who lives at court, shall teach two Countryfolks sincerity; and when I am so happy as to meet you, she shall settle the proportions of that Regard, or Goodnature, which she can allow you to spare me, from a heart, which is so much her own as yours is.

That Lady is the most trusty of Friends, if the Imitation of Shakespear be yours;[3] for she made me give my opinion of it with assurance it was none of Mrs ****.[4] I honestly lik'd & praisd it, whose-soever it was: There is in it a sensible melancholy, & too true a picture of human life; so true an one, that I can scarce wish the verses yours at the expense of your thinking that way, so early. I rather wish you may love the Town (which the author of those lines cannot *immoderately* do) these many years. Tis time enough to like, or affect to like, the Country; when one is out of love with all but ones-self, & therfore studies to become agreable or easy to oneself. Retiring into oneself is generally the *Pis-aller* of mankind. Wou'd you have me describe my

some of the Statues, Bas-reliefs, Drawings, and Pictures in Italy . . . (1722), the joint work of Richardson and his son. The *Chronicle* thought the book appeared 'about the year 1730', but its date, and so the date of the letter, is 1722.

[1] Psalm 133.

[2] When Pope's letters to Miss Cowper were sent to press in 1769 addresses and mentions of Miss Cowper's name in the texts had all, as here, been either erased or obliterated. Even in 1806, when Bowles printed the letters from the edition of 1769, he did not know the name of the lady recipient.

[3] The line quoted later in this letter indicates that the verses shown to Pope were from Dr. Benjamin Ibbot's 'Fit of the Spleen; in Imitation of Shakespeare', and not by Miss Cowper.

[4] The name (doubtless *Cowper*) has been heavily blotted out.

Solitude & Grotto to you? What if after a long and painted Description of 'em in verse, (which the writer I've just been speaking of could better make, if I can guess by that line

> No noise but water, Ever friend to Thought)[1]

what if I ended it thus?

> What are the falling rills, the pendant Shades,
> The morning Bow'rs, the Evening Colonnades?
> But soft Recesses for th' uneasy mind,
> To sigh un-heard in, to the passing Wind.
> So the struck Deer, in some sequestred part
> Lies down to dye (the arrow in his heart)
> There hid in shades, & wasting day by day,
> Inly he bleeds, & pants his soul away.

If these lines want poetry, they don't want Sence. God almighty long preserve you from a feeling of 'em! The book you mention, Bruyere's Characters, will make any one know the world, & I believe at the same time despise it, (which is a sign it will make one know it thoroughly.) Tis certainly the proof of a Master-Hand, that can give such striking Likenesses in such slight Sketches, & in so few strokes on each subject. In answer to your question about Shakespear, the book is about a quarter printed, & the number of Emendations very great. I have never indulged my own Conjectures, but kept meerly to such amendments as are authorized by the old Editions in the authors life time: But I think twill be a year at least before the whole work can be finished.[2] In reply to your very handsome (I wish it were a very true) Compliment upon this head, I only desire you to observe, by what natural, gentle degrees I have sunk to the humble thing I now am: First from a pretending Poet to a Critick, then to a low Translator, lastly to a meer Publisher. I am apprehensive I shall be nothing that's of any value, long, except | Madam | Your most obligd, and | most faithfull humble | Servant, | A. Pope.

Twitenham. | Nov. 5.

I long for your return to town, a place I am unfit for, but shall not be long out of, as soon as I know I may be permitted to wait on you there.

---

[1] A misquotation of some lines by Dr. Ibbot: 'A Fit of the Spleen':

> 'No noise be there
> But that of falling water, friend to thought.'—Elwin.

[2] The edition of Shakespeare was published finally in Mar. 1724/5, but earlier talk of index-making may indicate that Pope had some warrant for expecting an earlier publication date.

POPE *to* JUDITH COWPER[1]   [1722]

Arthur A. Houghton, Jr.

Madam,—I cou'd not play the Impertinent so far as to write to you, till I was encouraged to it by a piece of news Mrs H**** tells me, which ought to be the most agreeable in the world to Any Author, That you are determin'd to write no more— It is now the time then, not for me only, but for every body, to write without fear, or wit: and I shall give you the first Example here. But for this Assurance, it wou'd be ev'ry way too dangerous to correspond with a Lady, whose very first Sight & very first Writings had such an effect, upon a man us'd to what they call fine sights, & what they call fine writings. Yet he has been dull enough to sleep quietly, after all he has seen, & all he has read; till yours broke in upon his Stupidity & Indolence, & totally destroyed it. But God be thanked you'l write no more, so I'm in no danger of encreasing my Admiration of you one way; & as to the other, you'l never, (I've too much reason to fear) open these eyes again with one glympse of you.

I'm told, you nam'd lately in a letter a Place calld Twitenham, with particular distinction. That you may not be mis-constru'd & have your meaning mistaken for the future, I must acquaint you, Madam, that the name of the place where Mrs H**** is, is not Twitenham but Richmond;[2] which your Ignorance in the Geography of these parts has made you confound together. You will unthinkingly do honour to a paltry Hermitage (while you speak of Twitenham) where lives a Creature altogether unworthy your memory or notice, because he really wishes he had never beheld you, nor yours. You have spoild him for a Solitaire, and a Book, all the days of his life, and put him into such a condition, that he thinks of nothing, & enquires of nothing but after a Person who has nothing to say to him, & has left him for ever, without hope of ever again regarding, or pleasing, or entertaining him, much less of seeing him. He has been so mad with the Idæa of her, as to steal her Picture,[3] & passes whole days in sitting before it, talking to himself & (as some people imagine) making Verses: But 'tis no such matter, for as long as he can get any of hers, he can never turn his head to his own, it is so much better entertained.

[1] The year is doubtful, but the placing in the edition of 1769 makes 1722 probable. Miss Cowper's threat never to write again was evidently playful: she kept on writing verses for some years.

[2] Miss Howe, like Mrs. Howard, was in the service of Princess Caroline. The Prince and Princess of Wales went to Richmond during the first week in June 1722, intending to remain for the summer, and both Miss Howe and Mrs. Howard might also be there. Mrs. Howard's projected residence in Twickenham (Marble Hill) was not 'in the air' in 1722.

[3] On this stolen picture (apparently done originally for Lady P[embroke]) see the letter of 18 Oct. 1722 and its notes.

POPE *to* JUDITH COWPER[1]   [1722]

Arthur A. Houghton, Jr.

Thursday night

Madam,—It was an agreeable Surprise to me, to hear of your Settlement in Town. I lye at my Lord Peterborow's in Bolton street, where any Commands of yours will reach me to morrow, only on Saterday Evening I am pre-ingag'd. If Mrs. H— be to be ingaged, (and if she is by any Creature, it is by you) I hope she will joyn us. I am with great truth | Madam | Your most faithfull | Friend & obligd Servant | A. Pope

TOWNLY *to* ——   12 *November* 1722

[This letter, printed in *The St. James's Journal*, 15 November 1722, is the first of a series of four reprinted in *PMLA*, xxix (1914), 236 ff. and there unwarrantably ascribed to Pope. They concern in general the quarrel raging between Sir Richard Steele and John Dennis over the management of the theatre and the rival claims of Etherege's gentleman in *The Man of Mode* and Steele's in *The Conscious Lovers* (not yet staged) to the title of true gentleman. Pope had no interest in this quarrel, and the fact that the last of the letters included the first printing of his lines about Addison (*Epistle to Arbuthnot*, ll. 151–214) does not mean that Pope sent it to the press. Pope at this moment was hardly looking for trouble! For the other letters see 18 November, 3 and 12 December. The other three letters are signed 'Dorimant'.]

DORIMANT *to* ——   18 *November* 1722

[*The St. James's Journal*, 22 November 1722, published this letter, which is reprinted in *PMLA*, xxix (1914), 239–43, and there unwarrantably ascribed to Pope. See the 'Townly' letter immediately preceding this.]

POPE *to* BROOME   22 *November* [1722]

Elwin–Courthope, viii. 59

Twitnam, Nov. 22 [1722].

You very sensibly please me when you form prospects of seeing Twitenham. Let them be ever so remote, they please, but the sooner all projects are executed the better, or they are apt to cool. I would, for my own interest, wish that you kept our friend Fenton till after Christmas, since you say you would on that condition come up here with him. But whether it is better or not for his interest as to the play,

---

[1] Dodsley (1769) placed this letter among those of 1722, but the Elwin–Courthope edition places it in 1723. It is here returned to the Dodsley placing on the assumption that the next letter to Miss Cowper (here placed in December 1722) is not a letter welcoming the lady to London, but a letter indicating that illness has kept Pope and Miss Cowper from seeing each other.

I cannot determine. No man knows less of anything relating to the seasons propitious, or aspects favourable to the stage. The winter is like to prove an unquiet one, and the world much heated by politics and plots. Yet on the other side, the harvest for a poet is the season when most people are gathered together, and probably the town will grow thin early, by a more quick rising of the Parliament than usual. Most are of opinion the sessions will break up in February or March. I have a good while expected Fenton's demand for his play to * * *[1] thinking that if he declines it, Jacob Tonson might not improperly be employed in that transaction, and I dare say would do his best. But if, upon the whole, Mr. Fenton is indifferent whether it be played this year or not, of which he only is judge—not that I think he can mend it any more, for sure it is correct enough—if so, indeed I wish he would stay with you, where I am sure he is so happy and in so good a way both as to health, quiet, and content, that I sincerely envy him.

I have nothing particularly to recommend to you both, but the prosecution of the translation. It cannot be in too much forwardness, and I will watch the critical season to publish the project, which is not yet ripe, and depends on many contingencies.[2] Pray send me, when you have done with it, the second book. I would rather see it with all your blots and interlineations, than fair written: for perhaps I may sometimes choose betwixt both, or at least have hints from what you may have blotted out, for corrections of my own or improvements. It is a thing that has often happened to me. Nothing can be more right than your particular care to avoid any mention of the * * *.[3]

I have nothing to add, but the repetition of the many good wishes I feel, and the many hopes I entertain of seeing you, with all that contentment and satisfaction which I dare say will accrue to us all from such a meeting. Believe me ever, to you both, an affectionate friend and faithful servant.

My mother has her health very well, and is much yours and Mr. Fenton's servant.

---

[1] A line of the MS. is worn away. The lost name was probably that of Lintot, who had previously published for Fenton. Pope's suggestion was adopted, and the play came forth from the shop of Tonson.—Elwin.

[2] Probably the fact that religion as well as friendship for Atterbury (now in the Tower) caused Pope to be regarded as politically disloyal was at this time a leading 'contingency'. In 1723 the suppression of his edition of the Duke of Buckingham's *Works* was an added deterrent.

[3] A part of a line is here worn away. Broome had no doubt spoken of the secrecy he preserved respecting his share in the translation, and Pope commended his silence.—Elwin.

*POPE *to* VISCOUNT HARCOURT¹   [24 *November* 1722]
Harcourt MSS.

Saturday 8 a clock

My Lord,—I was to see the Bishop at his Grate to day, where I had
a proof of what I before knew & once took the liberty to mention to
your Lordship, His dependance on your personal Friendship for him.
He desired me to acquaint your Lordship, that he designs to trouble
you with a line or two, by the hands of my Lord Carlile,² which he
hopes no accident will hinder your receiving to morrow. I know your
Lordship's Humanity so well, that I'm sure you'l be Pleas'd if you can
do any Good-natur'd office: and were I myself in misfortune, I
shou'd think I could feel but half its weight while I had the happiness
to have you a Friend to me in it.—I hope I need not tell you I cannot
Sleep till I have mended the Epitaph,³ the Subject of which I shall
never forget: tho I ought not to put you in mind of a point so tender,
but that tis necessary you shou'd think of His Partiality to me, to
make you continue yours, to him who is with the greatest respect &
obligation | My Lord | Your most faithfull | most obedient, | humble
Servant, | A. Pope.

On Munday I shall in person come to beg your pardon for this
Scroll.

Endorsement: 24 Novr 1722 | Mr Pope | to Lord Vicount Harcourt.

DORIMANT *to* ——   3 *December* 1722

[*The St. James's Journal*, 8 December 1722, printed this letter, which in *PMLA*,
xxix (1914), 243–6, was reprinted and most improbably ascribed to Pope. See the
'Townly' letter of 12 November.]

---

†VISCOUNT HARCOURT *to* POPE   6 *December* 1722
1737

Decemb. 6, 1722.

I cannot but suspect my self of being very unreasonable in begging you
once more to review the inclos'd.⁴ Your friendship draws this trouble
on you. I may freely own to you that my tenderness makes me exceed-
ing hard to be satisfied with any thing which can be said on such an
unhappy subject. I caus'd the Latin Epitaph to be as often alter'd before
I could approve it.

When once your Epitaph is set up, there can be no alteration of it;

---

¹ The date is from the endorsement. 24 Nov. was in 1722 a Saturday. The letter is printed
from the original, which was printed in *Harcourt Papers*, ii. 91–92.
² Charles, Earl of Carlisle, was Constable of the Tower at this time.
³ The epitaph for Lord Harcourt's son, who had died in 1720.
⁴ The epitaph for Lord Harcourt's son, much revised already.

it will remain a perpetual monument of your friendship, and I assure my self you will so settle it, that it shall be worthy of you. I doubt whether the word, *deny'd*, in the third line, will justly admit of that construction which it ought to bear (viz.) renounced, deserted, &c. *deny'd* is capable in my opinion of having an ill sense put upon it, as too great easiness, or more good nature than a wise man ought to have. I very well remember you told me, you could scarce mend those two lines, and therefore I can scarce expect your forgiveness for my desiring you to reconsider them.

> Harcourt stands dumb, and Pope is forc'd to speak.[1]

I can't perfectly, at least without further discoursing you, reconcile my self to the first part of that line; and the word *forc'd* (which was my own, and I persuade my self for that reason only submitted to by you) seems to carry too doubtful a construction for an Epitaph, which as I apprehend, ought as easily to be understood as read. I shall acknowledge it as a very particular favour, if at your best leisure you will peruse the inclosed and vary it, if you think it capable of being amended, and let me see you any morning next week. I am, &c.

DORIMANT *to* ——   12 *December* 1722

[*The St. James's Journal*, 15 December 1722, printed a letter from Dorimant dated 12 December from Button's which appended as postscript the first printed version of the Atticus portrait. In *PMLA*, xxix (1914), 247, this letter is ascribed to Pope. The first printing of the Atticus lines is important, but there is no reason whatever to think Pope was the author of the letter or was the publisher of his lines on Addison. See the 'Townly' letter of 12 November 1722.]

FENTON *to* BROOME   13 *December* 1722

Elwin–Courthope, viii. 61

December 13, 1722.

Dear Mr. Broome,—I omitted writing to you by the last post because I was in hopes of seeing Mr. Pope before this, but he will not be in town before Saturday. However, I can inform you from Sir Clement [Cottrell], with whom I dined to-day, and who desires your acquaintance, that the little man has declared he will push on the translation of Homer with the utmost vigour and expedition. But more of this in my next. In the meantime pray do not fail to send me the prologue next week, that I may carry it with me to Twickenham. Mr. Blount went thither on Monday in high good humour after visiting Mrs. Bovy, who came to town about a fortnight since. Lady Blount is so

---

[1] The line ultimately became:

> If Pope must tell what Harcourt cannot speak.

well pleased with the last campaign, that I believe she will use her utmost endeavours that he may make another with us the next year. Excuse this hasty scrawl. I will make amends in my next. My humble service to Mrs. Broome, pretty Miss and Mr. Burlington,[1] and to all I know. I am ever, dear sir, your most affectionate humble servant.

Pray remember my prologue, and direct it to Mr. Robinson's, at the General Post-office, Charing Cross.

POPE *to* JOHN MORLEY[2]   13 *December* 1722

Longleat Portland Papers, xii

Twitenham, Decr 13. 1722

I owe you two letters, to acknowledge the receit of Two very kind Presents from you, of Oysters & Eringo-roots. I don't know what you design, by repeating them so soon, unless you have some young Woman in your Eye, whom you would marry me to, & therfore send me (what indeed I need very much, as to Marriage) Provocatives of all sorts. You know Papists cannot with any Encouragement in these days, purchase Lands, and I have none to sell:[3] So 'twill not be easy for me to make any Settlements that may be Satisfactory to the Lady, and My Personalitys I fear will not please her much, tho I shoud add Body & Moveables into the bargain. Therfore, good Mr Morley, none of your Provocatives, but as much of your good will as you please: here's enough for the present. I shall always be glad to hear from you, tho without these attendant Bribes, for I am always | Yours faithfully | A. Pope

My Mother thanks you for her Feast of Oisters, & is much your Servant.

Address: To Mr Morley, at | Halsted, | in | Essex.

POPE *to* JUDITH COWPER[4]   [1722]

1769

Five o'clock.

Madam,—I think it a full proof of that unlucky star, which upon too many occasions I have experienced; that this first, this only day that

---

[1] Mr. Burlington was a gentleman who resided at Diss, near Sturston.—Elwin.

[2] On Morley's career and services to the Harley family see *DNB*. When the Harley fortunes were definitely declining, Swift wrote to Alderman Barber (8 Aug. 1738): 'I remember a rascally butcher, one Morley, a great land-jobber and knave, who was his Lordship's [Oxford's] manager, and has been the principal cause of my Lord's wrong conduct, in which you agree with me in blaming his weakness and credulity' (Ball, vi. 92).

[3] Pope jokes about Morley's appetite for 'land-jobbing'.

[4] In the edition of 1769 this letter is placed at the very end of 1722—as it is here. Other letters of Dec. give no evidence of ill health; but the supposition is that Pope writes while

I should have owned happy beyond expectation (for I did not till yesterday hope to have seen you so soon) I must be forced not to do it. I am too sick (indeed very ill) to go out so far, and lie on a bed at my doctor's house, as a kind of force upon him to get me better with all haste.

I am scarce able to see these few lines I write; to wish you health and pleasure enough not to miss me to-day, and myself patience to bear being absent from you as well as I can being ill. | I am truly, | Your faithful servant, | A. Pope.

GAY *to* SWIFT[1]　　　　　　　　　　　　　22 *December* 1722

Add. 4805

After every post-day for these 8 or 9 years I have been troubled with an uneasiness of Spirit, and at last I have resolv'd to get rid of it and write to you; I don't deserve that you should think so well of me as I really deserve, for I have not profest to you that I love you as much as ever I did, but you are the only person of my acquaintance almost that does not know it. Whoever I see that comes from Ireland, the first Question I ask is after your health, of which I had the pleasure to hear very lately from Mr Berkeley.[2] I think of you very often, nobody wishes you better, or longs more to see you. Duke Disney[3] who knows more news than any man alive, told me I should certainly meet you at the Bath the last Season, but I had one comfort in being disappointed that you did not want it for your health; I was there for near eleven weeks for a Cholick that I have been troubled with of late, but have not found all the benefit I expected. I lodge at present in Burlington house, and have received many Civilitys from many great men, but very few real benefits. They wonder at each other for not providing for me, and I wonder at em all.[4] Experience has given me some knowledge of them, so that I can say that tis not in their power to disappoint me.

You find I talk to you of myself, I wish you would reply in the same manner. I hope though you have not heard from me so long I

suffering from one of the violent, transitory headaches entailed by his chronic Pott's disease. It is interesting to note that writing to Broome, 9 July 1722, he phrases in similar words his inability to see what he is writing.

[1] Printed by Hawkesworth in 1767; not printed by Pope, who did, however, print Swift's reply (8 Jan. 1722/3). From the first sentence one judges that Gay had not written to Swift since the dean had left England in 1714.

[2] George Berkeley, the philosopher.

[3] On 'Duke' Disney see Pope's letter to Martha Blount of 19 Aug. 1715.

[4] Passages like this have developed exaggerated ideas as to the 'neglect' from which Gay suffered. In view of what was done for others, Gay had fewer sinecures than he deserved; but in spite of anecdotes about his going hungry, he seems in general to have been well provided for if never quite independent of casual patronage.

have not lost my Credit with you, but that you will think of me in the same manner as when you espous'd my cause so warmly which my gratitude never can forget. I am | Dear Sir | Your most obliged & Sincere humble Servant | J. Gay.

London. Decembr 22. 1722.

Mr Pope upon reading over this Letter desir'd me to tell you that he has been just in the same Sentiments with me in regard to you, and shall never forget his obligations to you.

Address: To | The Revd Dr Swift Dean of | St Patrick's in | Dublin. | Ireland

Endorsements: (in Swift's hand) Mr. Gay | Rx Decr 28th 1722

Mr. Gay Decr 22d 1722

Postmarks blurred.

BROOME *to* FENTON   23 *December* 1722

Elwin–Courthope, viii. 61

Dec. 23, 1722.

Dear Fenton,—I find you insist upon me to be gentleman-usher to your tragedy. I can deny you nothing, but I fear this prologue will prove a greater instance of my friendship than poetry. I have frequently had it in my thoughts, but have produced nothing that pleases me. What is the meaning that it is hardest to begin a poem, and why is the beginning often the worst part of it? I have really begun at the end, as in reading Hebrew, and next week I hope I shall end at the beginning, as in climbing we begin at the root of the tree in order to reach the top of it. Pray carry the prologue with you, as you promise, to Mr. Pope. He turns everything he touches into gold.

Sir Clement Cottrell does me great honour by the offer of his friendship, but is he sensible of what he is doing? I shall trouble him with long letters, and wicked rhyme, and perhaps with visits. Put him in mind of the Spaniard who travelled from the remotest corner of Spain barely to see Livy, and let him know that the same curiosity will bring me to Twickenham. If under all these disadvantages he will grant his friendship, I embrace it with earnestness.

Lady Blount cannot be better pleased with the last campaign than I am, and you and Mr. Blount shall always have a room in the house and heart of him who is affectionately yours.

By the end of 1723 Pope was still much involved in work on his edition of Shakespeare, and he had, in his other main project, translated by then about half the books of the *Odyssey* to be 'undertaken' by him. No public proposals for subscription to the *Odyssey* were issued until January 1725, but throughout 1723 Pope's friends were actively securing subscribers. In January 1723 appeared his edition of the Duke of Buckingham's *Works*, which caused him anguish when the government promptly, but temporarily, suppressed the handsome volumes.

The year is perhaps more interesting on the side of personal relations than on that of literary activity. Atterbury had been in the Tower since the preceding summer, and his trial began on 6 May. Pope was a 'character' witness at the trial, and he was very nervous at the prospect of testifying. Among his friends practically no one voted against Atterbury. About the time of the bishop's departure into exile Bolingbroke was pardoned and briefly returned. This fact may have awakened Swift out of 'a scurvy sleep' of ten years, and encouraged him to renew correspondence with Gay, Pope, and Bolingbroke. During frequent visits to London in this year Pope seems to have lodged with Lord Peterborow, with whom from about this time until the death of his lordship in 1735 Pope was intimate. It is regrettable that so few of their letters have come down to us.

FENTON *to* BROOME   1 *January* 1722/3

Elwin–Courthope, viii. 62

Jan. 1, 1723.

Dear Mr. Broome,—I hope this will find you perfectly recovered of your indisposition, and full of spirits to conclude the prologue you have so happily begun.[1] Pray do not fail to send it complete by Saturday sev'night at furthest, or I shall be miserably disappointed. I think I am at present one of the busiest bees in this great hive—the city. I have very much to entertain you with, but have not time to pen it. When the hurry is over I will write nothing but folios to you. In the meantime I wish you, yours, and all our friends a happy new year, and am ever, dear sir, your most affectionate humble servant.

Remember Thursday sev'night.

---

1 Fenton's *Mariamne* was finally acted on 22 Feb., and the Prologue by Broome was naturally in demand. The letter immediately following explains that this present letter, which must have enclosed the Prologue with Pope's comments on it, went astray. It was evidently retrieved.

FENTON *to* BROOME   1 *January* [1722/3]

Elwin–Courthope, viii. 63

New Year's Day [1723].

Dear Mr. Broome,—I enclosed the prologue in a letter to you by this post, and left it for Mr. Robinson to frank, but by mistake it was sent away to the General Post-office without any direction, but I will endeavour to retrieve it, that you may have it by Saturday. You will then find that Mr. Pope likes it much, but would have the eight last lines left out, and advises you to turn all the rest on Mariamne, and beauty and virtue in distress. And pray do not fail to let me have it by Saturday sev'night at the very furthest, or I shall be miserably disappointed. The post stays for this. I am ever, dear sir, your most faithful humble servant.

My service to your family and all friends.

‖SWIFT *to* GAY[1]   8 *January* 1722/3

Longleat Portland Papers, xiii (Harleian transcripts)

Dublin Jan. 8th 1722-3

Coming home after a Short Christmas Ramble, I found a Letter upon my Table, and little expected when I opened it to read your Name at the Bottom. The best and greatest part of my Life till these[2] last eight years I Spent in England, there I made my Friendships and there I left my Desires; I am condemned for ever to another Country, what is in Prudence to be done? I think to be *oblitusque meorum obliviscendus et illis*;[3] what can be the Design of your Letter but Malice, to wake me out of a Scurvy Sleep, which however is better than none, I am towards nine years older Since I left you Yet that is the least of my Alterations: My Business, my Diversions my Conversations are all entirely changed for the Worse, and So are my Studyes and my Amusements in writing; Yet after all, this humdrum way of Life might be passable enough if you would let me alone, I shall not be able to relish my Wine, my Parsons, my Horses nor my Garden for three Months, till the Spirit you have raised Shall be dispossessed. I have Sometimes wondred that I have not visited you; but I have been Stopt by too many Reasons besides years & Lazyness, and yet these are my good ones; Upon my Return after half a year amongst you there would be to me *Desiderio nec pudor nec modus*.[4] I was three years reconciling my

---

[1] Printed by Pope in 1741 with the omission of passages here placed in half-brackets. The verbal changes in the printed texts of 1741 and 1742 are negligible. The Longleat text, though less readable than Pope's printed text, is here given as (in very small details) closer to Swift's original holograph. The scribe in transcribing Swift's difficult hand made obvious errors, one or two of which have been silently corrected.

[2] these] those (*error of scribe*) *Longleat*.   [3] Horace, *Epistles*, i. xi. 9.

[4] Horace, *Carmina*, i. xxiv. i. (Swift, like Pope, adapts frequently in quoting.)

Self to the Scene and the Business to which fortune hath condemned me, and Stupidity was what I had recourse to. Besides, what a Figure Should I make in London while my Friends are in Poverty, Exile, Distress, or Imprisonment, and my Enemyes with Rods of Iron. Yet I often threaten my self with the Journy, and am every Summer practicing to ride and get health to bear it, The onely Inconvenience is, that I grow old in the Experiment. Tho I care not to talk to you as a Divine Yet I hope you have not been Author of your Cholick, Do you drink bad Wine? or keep bad Company, Are you not as many years older as I? It will not be alwayes *et tibi quos mihi dempserit apponet annos*.[1] I am heartily Sorry you have any Dealings with that ugly Distemper, and I believe our Friend Arburthnott will recommend you to Temperance and Exercise I wish they would have as good an Effect upon the Giddyness I am Subject to and which this Moment I am not free from. I would have been glad if you had lengthened your Letter by telling me the present Condition of many of my old Acquaintance, Congreve Arbuthnott Lewis[2] &c, but you mention onely Mr Pope, who I believe is lazy or else he might have added three Lines of his own. I am extremely glad he is not in your Case of Needing great Mens favor, and could heartily wish that you were in his. I have been considering, why, Poets have such ill Success in Making their Courts Since they are allowed to be the greatest and best of all Flatterers; The Defect is that they flatter onely in Print or in writing, but not by word of Mouth. They will give Things under their Hand which they make a Conscience of Speaking, besides they are too libertine to haunt Antichambers, too poor to bribe Porters and Footmen, and too proud to cringe to Second hand Favorites in a Great Family. Tell me, are you not under originall Sin by the Dedication to your Eclogues,[3] I am an ill Judge at this distance, and besides, am for my Ease utterly ignorant of the commonest things that pass in the World, but if all Courts have a Sameness in them (as the Parsons phrase it) Things may be as they were in my Time, when all Employments went to Parliament mens Friends who had been usefull in Elections, and there was always a huge List of Names in Arrears at the Treasury, which would take up, at least take up, your Seven years expedient to discharge even one half; I am of Opinion, if you will not be offended, that the Surest Course would be to get your Friend who lodges in your House[4] to recommend you to the next Chief Governor who comes over here for a good Civil Employment or to be one of his

---

[1] Horace, *Carmina*, II. v. 14–15 (adapted).
[2] Erasmus Lewis, Under-Secretary of State in the Oxford Ministry.
[3] *The Shepherd's Week* had been dedicated to Bolingbroke three or four months before his downfall at the death of Queen Anne.
[4] Swift is playful. Gay lodged in Burlington House, and his friend ('landlord' below) is the Earl.

Secretaryes which your Parliament men are fond enough of when there is no room at home, The Wine is good and reasonable you may dine twice a week at the Deanry house. There is a Sett of Company in this Town Sufficient for one man, Folks will admire you, because they have read you, and read of you, and a good Employmt. will make you live tolorably in London, or Sumptuously here or if you divide between both Places it will be for your Health. ⌜The D. of Wharton Sattled a Pension on Dr Young[1] your Landlord is much richer. These are my best Thoughts after three days Reflections Mr Budgill got a very good office here, and lost it by great want of common Politicks.[2] If a Recommendation be hearty and the Governor who comes here be already enclined to favour you, nothing but fortuna Trojana can hinder the Success. If I write to you once a Quarter will you promise to Send me a long Answer in a week, and then I will leave you at rest till the next Quarter day, and I desire you will leave part of a blanck Side for Mr Pope. Has he Some quel[que] chose of his own upon the anvil I expect it from him Since poor Homer helpt to make him rich, why have not I your works? and with a Civil Inscription before it, as Mr Pope ought to have done to his for So I had from your Pridecessors of the 2 last Reigns. I hear yours were Sent to Ben Took[3] but I never had them. You See I wanted nothing but Provocation to Send you a long Letter, which I am not weary of writing because I do not hear my Self talk and yet I have the Pleasure of talking to you and if you are not good at reading ill hands, it will cost you as much Time as it has done me⌝ I wish I could do more than Say I love you. I left you in a good way both for the late Court, and the Successors, and by the Force of too much Honesty or too little Sublunary Wisdom you fell between two Stools, Take Care of your Health and Money be less modest and more active, or else turn Parson and get a Bishoprick here, would to God they would Send us so good ones from your Side. | I am ever ⌜with all Friend Ship and Esteem Yours | J.S.⌝

⌜Mr Ford[4] presents his Service to Mr Pope & you. We keep him here as long as we can.⌝

[1] Young's financial successes led Swift ten years after this in his *On Poetry: a Rhapsody* to write:

> Where Young must torture his invention,
> To flatter knaves, or lose his pension.

[2] Budgell had somewhat madly detailed his quarrel with E. Webster, secretary to the Lord Lieutenant (the Duke of Bolton), in his pamphlet *A Letter to the Lord **** from Eustace Budgell* (1718).

[3] A London publisher frequently employed by Swift.

[4] Charles Ford was at this time in Ireland.

POPE *to* JUDITH COWPER   17 *January* 1722/3

Arthur A. Houghton, Jr.

Madam,—After a very long Expectation and daily Hopes of the satisfaction of seeing & conversing with you, I am still depriv'd of it in a
manner that is the most afflicting, because it is occasiond by Your Illness & Your Misfortune. I can bear my own, I assure you much better:
and thus to find you Lost to me, at the time that I hop'd to have re-
gaind you, doubles the Concern I shou'd naturally feel in being depriv'd
of any pleasure whatever. Mrs H*** can best express to you the Concern of a Friend, who esteems & pities: for she has the liberty to express
it in her Actions, & the satisfaction of attending on you in your
Indisposition. I wish sincerely Your Condition were not such as to
debar me from telling you in person how truly I am yours. I wish I
cou'd do you any little offices of friendship or give you any Amusements, or help you to what people in the present state most want,
Better Spirits. If Reading to you or writing for you, could contribute
to entertain your hours, or to raise you to a livelier relish of life,
how well shoud I think my time imployed! Indeed I shou'd, &
think it a much better End of my poor Studies, than all the Vanitys
of Fame or Views of a character that way, which ingage most men of
my Fraternity.

If you thoroughly knew the Zeal with which I am your Servant,
you would take some notice of the Advice I would give you, & suffer
it to have a weight with you proportionable to the sincerity with which
it is given. I beg you to do your utmost to call to you all the Succours,
which your own Good Sense & natural Reflection can suggest, to
avoid a melancholy way of thinking, & to throw up your Spirits by
Intervals of moderate Company; not to let your distemper fix itself
upon your Mind at least, tho it will not entirely quit your body. Do
not indulge too much Solitariness. Tho most company be not proper
or supportable during your illness, force yourself to enter into such as
is good & reasonable, where you may have your Liberty & be under
no restraint. Why will you not come to your Friend Mrs H****, since
you are able to go out, & since Motion is certainly good for your
health? Why will you not make any little Sets of such as you are
Easiest with, to sit with you sometimes? Do not think I have any
interested aim in this Advice: tho I long to see you & to try to amuse
you. I would not for the world be considerd as one that would ever
require for my own Gratification any thing that might either be improper or hurtful to you. Pray let me know by our Friend Mrs H. if
there can be any thing in my power to serve, or to amuse you. But
use me so kindly, as not to think ever of writing to me till you are
so well as that I may see you, & then it will be needless. Don't even

read this, if it be the least Trouble to your eyes or head. believe me with great respect & the warmest good wishes for your speedy recovery | Madam | Your most faithfull | & most humble Servant | A. Pope

Jan. 17th 1722/3.

POPE *to* JOHN MORLEY[1]   [24 *January* 1722/3]
Longleat Portland Papers, xii

I am in a great hurry, but would not defer performing my promise in sending you the inclosed. I heartily thank you for the Oysters, which I am grown very fond of. My Mother & myself are | Your very affect. Servants.

Address: To | Mr Morley, at his house | in Halstead, in | Essex.
Postmark: 24| IA

*POPE *to* VISCOUNT HARCOURT[2]   [27 *January* 1722/3]
Harcourt MSS.

Sunday night

My Lord,—If your Lordship shall be at leisure to night, I beg leave to wait on you. I always take the liberty you have by long and friendly Precedent indulgd me, to apply to y[ou] on all my occasions, and I have one at present which gives me great concern, very Innocently. I am just arrivd in Town, & with the Sincerest heart, | Your Lordships most grate-|ful obligd humble Servant | A. Pope.

Endorsements: 27 Jan 1722 | Mr Pope | to Lord Vicount | Harcourt

POPE *to* LORD HARLEY[3]   [1723?]
Longleat Portland Papers xii

My Lord,—I am of a sudden made to determine, forthwith to push the affair of my Subscription. And therefore I Set your Lordship at full liberty to do me all the good you can, which I know you will, with the Town, particularly to take the inclos'd paper with you to the

---

[1] The day and month are from the postmark; the year is perhaps a guess; but Morley had at this time just sent the Popes delicious oysters, and it seems likely that the enclosure would be the Proposals for the *Odyssey* which were being circulated at this moment. Morley subscribed in any case.

[2] The endorsement furnishes the date. In 1723, 27 Jan. was a Sunday.

[3] This undated letter might seem plausibly to fall in Jan. 1725, when the formal Proposals for the *Odyssey* were advertised. But the suggestion that the enclosed paper be taken to the House of *Commons*, where Harley was a member 1722–4 for Cambridgeshire, suggests early 1723, when Pope intended to announce his project and was suddenly dissuaded by the outcries concerning the Duke of Buckingham's *Works*, &c.

House of Commons. I will add nothing but what I think I need not assure you of, for tis what I cannot but be. | Your Lordships most | obligd, most faithful | Servant, | A. Pope.

*POPE *to* BUCKLEY*[1]   12 *February* [1722/3]

Lord Rothschild

Twitenham Feb. 12

Sir,—I ought before this to have thankd you for your Present, & to have desird you to convey my acknowledgments to Sir Luke Schaub. Madam Dacier has not done me the honour I expected as a Critick, in answering any observations I had made; but has attackd me as a Poet only in two or three of my Simile's, which is a tender part, (for every body knows nothing is so dear to a Poet as his Simile's.) Her two greatest objections to my Preface, the curious who would be willing to search for 'em will not be so happy as to find there; being only in that French Translation of it which she saw. So that if I shou'd be ambitious of recanting my errors, I could only make satisfaction to my French Readers, which I apprehend to be very few, if any. What indeed most concerns me is her last period, in which she seems both angry & merry (so far I like it very well) but she concludes, that because I sometimes own Homer not to be the Pope, that is not to be infallible; therfore I must think myself wiser, & so correct him. And consequently that I must be qualifyd to Reform all mankind, and be at the Head of the Government. Upon which she cries out,

Voilà une grande Ressource pour l'Etat![2]

This truly Sir I do not like, & think proper (to you, who are a sort of a Minister, and to all my Friends of the Office) to enter my Protest against such suggestions; especially at this time, when I am told

[1] The year is assumed from Pope's reference to the outcry over his connexion with the Duke of Buckingham's *Works* (1723). The present from Sir Luke Schaub (at this time ambassador to the French court) was presumably the second edition of Mme Dacier's translation of the *Iliad* (1719), in which the Preface to Pope's *Iliad* was attacked. One might have expected the attack to reach Pope earlier, but second editions get less attention than firsts. Pope had published in Jan. Buckingham's *Works*, in which appeared a letter by the Duke 'on the Late Dispute about Homer' (between Mme Dacier and Houdard de la Motte), and this probably aroused interest in Mme Dacier's attack on Pope. In 1724 Curll published a translation of Mme Dacier's attack under the title, *Remarks upon Mr. Pope's Account of Homer, Prefixed to his Translation of the Iliad, Made English . . . By Mr. Parnell.* This Parnell (a creation by Curll?) was not Pope's friend the archdeacon (d. 1718).

This letter was printed in *The Athenaeum*, 17 May 1884. It was sold at Sotheby's in 1935, at which time the transcript from the original was made for the editor by the late R. Eustace Tickell. Samuel Buckley, printer and skilled linguist, had a post in the Foreign Office.

[2] In ironic (?) compliment Madame Dacier says of Pope: 'Un homme si habile ne se bornera pas à perfectionner l'art du poëme Epique; ce seroit peu de chose, il perfectionnera l'art de la politique . . . un homme capable de corriger Homère, sera capable de former des hommes. . . . Voilà une grande ressource pour un Etat!' With his intimate friend Atterbury in the Tower Pope would not relish remarks connecting him with politics.

People blame me for having Seen a Book.[1] And such a Book (God knows) as I had no more thoughts of Correcting, than of Homer himself—But I'll say no more of that Book, only surely you flatter us Poets, when you say tis we that give Immortality: Alas! tis you Secretaries are the men, to make Books Immortal!

I believe you have heard I had thoughts of translating the Odyssey. I won't tell you whether tis my mortification at Madam Dacier's, or at any others Displeasure, that has made me put a sudden stop to my Friends eagerness in that affair. But I desire you to tell Mr Tickel,[2] I was three times to wait on him, to ask if he had no view of that design himself, before I would actually ingage in it. And I yet will certainly desist from it, if he will Faithfully promise for himself, or if his Superiors will but ingage for him, that he will do Homer this justice? I wish you could exhort him hereto, for the honour & safety of the Protestant Religion & Establishment, which otherwise (according to M. Dacier) a Papist may do much damage to. I did not think I had such Talents in Politicks, but I will now begin to look about me, since I am thought so capable of great affairs, by the consent of two nations.

Pray assure all our Friends of the Office, of my Services & good intentions toward them all, when I am Premiere Ministre.[3] Particularly remember me to Mr Stanyan,[4] & desire him *not to forget his Servant Jacob*,[5] who seems to me in tribulation, & not mindful of the text which admonishes Booksellers *patiently to Bear one anothers Burdens*. I wish He & you could spare a Sabbath-day to see my Plantations & Edifices. I wish you both all success in your own, & am very much | Sir, | Your affectionate humble Servant | A. Pope.

POPE *to* LORD HARLEY   13 *February* 1722/3

Longleat Portland Papers, xii

Twitenham. Feb. 13. 1722/3

My Lord,—I think myself obligd, after the permission you gave me (& even made it your Request) that I shoud send you a Paper of Pro-

---

[1] The Duke of Buckingham's *Works*, suppressed upon publication in Jan.

[2] When he published in 1715 his translation of the first book of the *Iliad* Tickell had announced somewhat equivocally, 'I would not therefore be thought to have any other View in publishing this small Specimen . . . than to bespeak, if possible, the Favour of the Public to a Translation of Homer's Odysseis, wherein I have already made some Progress.' Regarded at the time as disingenuous, the statement was partly responsible for Pope's three calls in 1723.

[3] From the English point of view a 'Premier Ministre' was the tool of a tyrant. The title, though still unpopular, was gaining ground in England.

[4] Abraham Stanyan was a friend of Pope's.

[5] Jacob Tonson may have been in some tribulation as publisher of Buckingham's *Works*. Barber was the printer. Tonson's name does not appear on the title-page among the booksellers, but he presently paid Pope the profits of the edition. See ii. 211.

posals, to tell your Lordship the reason I did not. I find such a Cry upon me, however unreasonable, about the Duke's Books: (& from persons, from whose Education & Quality one might expect a more sensible proceeding.) that I am advis'd by Lord Harcourt, to defer pushing this Subscription till a more seasonable time. I know your Lordships Temper so well, that it will be a Pain to You, to delay doing Good, to one you honour with a Share of your Friendship: & I am sure the mortification will be greater to You, than to Me. Indeed I am pretty indifferent, as to having any more Stakes, or giving any more Hostages, to the Publick: who seldome use a man well, so long as they have done me, & one must expect a Bad Run, after any continuance of a good one, in the common Reputation, as well as in the common Fortune, of the world. If our Governors are displeas'd at me, Im not fond of being the Slave of the Publick against its will, for three years more. Let the Odyssey remain untranslated, or let them employ Mr Tickell upon it.

My Mothers Illness not only gave me the concern I ought to feel for her, but another for myself, in depriving me of the Satisfaction of being among so many more of those, who wish, with me, the welfare & long life of all your Lordships Family. I thought of you all yesterday, & drank the young Lady's health with my sick Mother.[1] I beg Lady Harriet's acceptance of my sincere Services, & your Lordships belief of my being always my Lord Oxford's & | My Lord, Your most faithful Servant | A. Pope.

POPE *to* LORD CARTERET   16 *February* 1722/3

Longleat Portland Papers, xiii (Harleian transcripts)

To the Right Honourable the Lord Carteret, one of his Majesty's Principal Secretary's of State

Twickenham Feb. 16. 172$\frac{2}{3}$

I beg your Lordship will look upon this letter less as a presumption, than as an effect of the real respect I owe You. I have long known how to bear my share in such false Reports and Misconstructions as no Man is Exempt from; but there is one that touches me more nearly, I am told (and in Print too by some of the Party Scriblers) that I've been suspected of putting that vile thing a Trick upon you, in being the procurer of your Licence to the Duke of Buckingham's Book.[2]

---

[1] The Hon. Margaret Cavendish-Holles-Harley was evidently having a party in honour of her eighth birthday, 11 Feb. In 1734 she was married to the Duke of Portland. She had been celebrated as a child in Prior's lines beginning 'My noble, lovely, little Peggy'. In later years she disliked Pope. Pope's 'yesterday' makes the date (13th) of the letter doubtful.

[2] In Apr. 1722 Alderman Barber had applied to Lord Carteret for a licence to print the Duke of Buckingham's *Works*, and it had apparently been too hastily given. It may be true that when Barber got the licence Pope had not examined in detail the contents of the two

When I had the honour of waiting on your Lordship, I did not dream there was any need of speaking on this Article: But I now think my self oblig'd to assure you that I never look'd into those Papers, or was privy to the Contents of 'em, when that Licence was procured by Mr Barber, to secure his own property.

Give me leave my Lord to pay you my thanks for your Intentions to promote my design on Homer;[1] but allow me to add, that if I am, (however innocently) under the least displeasure of the Government: I desire not to be oblig'd by those that dislike or think me unworthy. Indeed my Lord I love my Country, better than any Personal friend I have; but I love my Personal Friend so well, as not to abandon, or rail at him, tho' my whole Country fell upon him. And I assure your Lordship, tho' the King has many Subjects much more valuable than my self, he has not one more Quiet; no Man is more Sensible of the Indulgence I enjoy from my Rulers, I mean that which is common to every Subject from the Protection of a Free Government. But as to any particularly I take my self to be the only Scribler of my Time, of any degree of distinction, who never receiv'd any Places from the Establishment, any Pension from a Court, or any Presents from a Ministry. I desire to preserve this Honour untainted to my Grave; and to have the pleasure of saying; I am as much obliged to my Lord Carteret (this way) as to any Man living, ev'n to your Predecessor dead,[2] whom I lov'd above all Men. I thought my self particularly favour'd by your late Treatment of me, and in the Sense of it endeavour'd in this small Affair to do you all the Justice I could, not only with truth but with warmth. I am with all respect | My Lord | Your &c.

POPE *to* VISCOUNT HARCOURT   20 *February* [1722/3]

Harcourt MSS.

Twitenham. Feb. 20th

My Lord,—It is really the height of Respect to you, that I do not write oft'ner: for every day since I saw your Lordship, I have had much difficulty to refrain, from telling you what you need not be told:

volumes. It is more probable, however, that he strains the truth when telling Carteret that he had 'never look'd into those papers'. His enemies, notably in *Pasquin*, accused him of submitting only a selection of the papers to Carteret's office with the application for a licence, but this would have been a highly dangerous and improbable procedure. It is certain that Barber, not Pope, secured the licence, and consequently the charges of *Pasquin* (13 and 20 Feb. 1723) are false.

[1] Carteret's goodwill with regard to the *Odyssey* was shown on 29 Apr. 1725, when out of the Civil List Pope received £200 'as his Matys Encouragement to the Work . . . of Translating the Odysses of Homer into English Verse'.

[2] The younger Craggs had been the immediate predecessor of Lord Carteret as Secretary of State.

the warm sense I ever must have of the Obligations of every kind you have layd & daily are laying upon me. I could almost forget all Respect & distance, & use the Phrase to you which I us'd to Mr Harcourt, [Friendship]¹ & never say [Obligations]¹ more.

The Advice your Lordship gave me,² has not been the single reason of my stay here in the Country, for God and Nature have given me another, in my poor Mothers Illness; which has been dangerous, tho she now seems to recover. I think my melancholy office of attending her in this last Decline of Life, is much like that of watching over a Taper that is expiring; & even when it burns a little while brighter than ordinary, is but the nearer going out. And such indeed, are the very best Intervals of Life, when so nigh its end.

I have lately been struck with a Thought, upon which, as upon all others, I would be determind by your Lordships advice. In case I am under any displeasure of my Governours, (however innocently) I shou'd be uneasy to be obligd, in the affair of Homer, by any who dislike me: Neither do I believe you would have me. Your Lordship, I very well know, has defended me to many, with that Weight & Success which attends whatever Defence is made by you. With My Lord Carteret I have had myself an opportunity of Eclaircissment: but I have a particular inclination (if you judge it not unfitting) to write a word in the most respectful terms to my Lord Chancellor,³ proposing to resign my Design on the Odysses to Tickell, in deference to his judgment & at the same [time] take occasion to vindicate myself from the notion of being a Party man, to Him who is more absolutely a Stranger to me, than any Man (I believe) in the Government. I've drawn up such a letter, which I'll consult you upon, when I've the pleasure to see your Lordship next: It will at least make you smile, if it be good for nothing else. I fancy in general, my Appearing cool in this matter, & taking upon me a kind of dignity while I am abus'd & slanderd, will have no ill effect in promoting it.

My Mother is not so ill, but she will always remember her services to your family. I am ever | My Lord, your most faithfull Servant | A. Pope.

Endorsement: 20 Feb 1722 | Mr Popes letter | Answered | 21 Feb | To Lord Vicount | Harcourt.

†POPE *to* ROBERT DIGBY   [*Winter of* 1723]
1735

The same reason that hinder'd your writing, hinder'd mine, the pleasing Expectation to see you in Town. Indeed since the willing Confine-

---

¹ These brackets are Pope's—to indicate the 'phrases' as such.
² Lord Harcourt has evidently advised Pope to stay at home, and perhaps to say little about politics.   ³ Thomas Parker, Earl of Macclesfield.

ment I have lain under here with my Mother, (whom it is natural and reasonable I should rejoice with as well as grieve) I could the better bear your Absence from *London*, for I could hardly have seen you there; and it would not have been quite reasonable to have drawn you to a sick Room hither from the first Embraces of your Friends. My Mother is now (I thank God) wonderfully recovered, tho' not so much as yet to venture out of her Chamber, yet enough to enjoy a few particular Friends, when they have the good Nature to look upon her. I may recommend to you the Room we sit in, upon one (and that a favourite) Account, that it is the very *warmest* in the House: We and our Fires will equally smile upon your Face. There is a *Persian* Proverb that says, I think very prettily, *The Conversation of a Friend brightens the Eyes.* This I take to be a Splendor still more agreeable than the Fires you so delightfully describe.

That you may long enjoy your own Fire-side, in the metaphorical Sense, that is, all those of your Family who make it pleasing to sit and spend whole wintry Months together, (a far more rational Delight, and better felt by an honest Heart than all the glaring Entertainments, numerous Lights and false Splendors, of an *Assembly* of empty Heads, aking Hearts, and false Faces) This is my sincere Wish to you and yours.

You say you propose much Pleasure in seeing some few *Faces* about Town of my Acquaintance, I guess you mean Mrs. *Howard*'s and Mrs. *Blount*'s. And I assure you, you ought to take as much Pleasure in their *Hearts*, if they are what they sometimes express with regard to you.

Believe me, dear Sir, to you all, a very faithful Servant.

BROOME *to* FENTON[1]   6 *March* 1722/3

Elwin–Courthope, viii. 63

March 6, 1722-3

Dear Fenton,—I am certain I feel a greater satisfaction than you in the happy success of your tragedy. You hold the balance so even that you are scarce ever depressed or exalted. Your sedate countenance resembles a calm, deep stream, that flows along with a sullen silence,

---

1 (Mist's) *Weekly Journal*, 2 Mar. 1723, comments on the great success of *Mariamne*. At Fenton's first benefit (25 Feb.) 'there was the greatest Audience that was ever seen in any Theatre in England; and it is thought there will be as full a House to-night, it being also for the Author's Benefit'. The tragedy was acted 17 times before the end of the season—a most unusual number—and Fenton's four benefit nights (the fourth being an extraordinary favour) were said by Johnson to have brought him a thousand pounds. The poet Young thought Fenton's profits were about fifteen hundred pounds. In any case, Fenton and Broome were not penniless hacks expecting large financial returns from Pope and Homer. They were successful writers who expected to have their merits recognized because of their translation; but Pope seemed unwilling to share properly with them in reputation.

and never obliges us with more than a few dimples. I love a little more sensibility. It is true this sometimes lays the heart too open,—but where is the misfortune, though the very bottom be discoverable, if it be uncorrupted and clear. To be always upon the reserve is to wear always an intellectual vizor, and as absurd as for a fine lady to go always masked on purpose to hide her beauties from admiration. This conduct is inexcusable in a person who has no deformities to conceal.

I have seen a little slandering paper against your play. I dare say you despise it. The poor author writes out of hunger, not malice; he eats by abusing you. A man you know feeds a louse that bites and disgraces him, but still he feeds him. Let the censorious rail! A person of real merit will build himself a monument with the very stones that are thrown at him by the hands of the malicious or envious.

I am glad the prologue came in time, and since you would compel me to write it, that it did not discredit you. I was contented to hang out my miserable sign-post daubings before your play, as vintners do theirs before their houses, only to let people know there was good entertainment within. I was a kind of dwarf in romance, and served as a precursor to inform the audience that the giant approached. If you go on with the tragedy of Dion, pray build the porch before the house, that is, write the prologue before the play. I beg you would raise up no more ghosts of old stern heroes from their graves to torment me. Mariamne indeed was a fine lady, and a great beauty, and therefore not so apt to affright one.

Dear Fenton, continue to love me, continue to write. I need not labour for words to assure you that I love you. It is easy to be sincere, and no one is more so when he gives you that assurance than yours affectionately.

POPE *to* BROOME   6 *April* [1723]

Elwin–Courthope, viii. 64

April 6 [1723].

I had sooner congratulated you upon the success of our friend Fenton, but that I have been too busy, partly in that affair, and partly in the prosecution of our common business, in which I hope to put a finishing stroke to all his moderate desires. The pleasure it would be to me to be capacitated, in serving myself, to serve my friend also, would be greater than I could express to you, and I dare say your own good-natured way of thinking can tell you all I could say on that head. Therefore, be assured, I should see nothing in this world with more concern and uneasy sensation, than the sacrifice you talk of,—that of burning and suppressing your part, to give up the whole to me. Abraham, sacrificing his own offspring, could not have felt more

trouble. No, let us sacrifice only that animal, who coming, unfortunately for himself, too near our altars, stuck in the brambles, and
still sticks there.[1] I have, within these three days only, given a loose to
a few of my commissioned friends, which I judge better than to make
any proposal yet to the public,—first to try my own personal interest,
which I hope will answer my own personal views, and then to see at
once what the town will do for us all.[2] I am very certain it is judging
right to think that the public will enter much more heartily and
readily into any project after the most considerable men in the nation
have exalted it into a fashion and reputation to be of the list. Alas!
almost every creature has vanity; but few, very few, have either judgment, taste, or generosity.

I very much please myself in the prospect of seeing you here at
Twitnam,—you must live nowhere else,—with Fenton, and one,
who is no less yours, though less in his own power, and therefore, only,
seemingly less yours. We shall pass many philosophical days and nights,
many a studious morning, cheerful noon, and contemplative evening
together, as I hope, if we continue long on this side the grave. No
ambition but that of writing well,—an ambition which gratifies, not
[injures][3] mankind,—shall enter into our hearts, [and disturb] the
quiet course of our days.

I must recommend to you the closest application, which I assure
you I now practice myself. *Nulla dies sine lineâ*, makes short and easy
the longest and hardest tasks. I wish you forwarded the sixth and
second books, if not already quite finished, and transmit them to me
by the first safe opportunity. This is necessary in the first place. I
could say a thousand things to you, but time will not be granted me,
and I am outrageously called upon. Pray keep the utmost secrecy in
this matter; nothing else can be done as I would have it, who am ever
sincerely yours.

[1] Elwin thought this scapegoat was Tickell, who in 1715 had proposed to translate the
Odyssey. Letters to Lord Harley (13 Feb. 1723) and to Lord Harcourt (20 Feb. 1723) somewhat bear out this suggestion, which nevertheless is not altogether probable. Some totally
unknown translator may have tried to intervene.

[2] The public campaign for subscribers was exasperatingly postponed. *The British Journal*,
9 Mar. 1723, had printed an item to the effect that 'Mr. Pope is translating the *Odyssey*
of Homer, which will be printed in the same Manner, and upon the same Terms as his
Translation of the *Iliads*'. But the public advertisements of the Proposals came only at the
end of Jan. 1725, when *The Daily Courant* (25 Jan.) and a fair number of other papers
began a series of announcements. A letter from the Archbishop of York (Sir William Dawes),
dated 24 Apr. 1723 and preserved at Rousham, indicates that Mrs. Cæsar was busily collecting subscribers in 1723.

[3] The edge of the original is here worn away.—Elwin.

‖ATTERBURY *to* POPE[1]

10 *April* 1723.

Longleat Portland Papers, xiii (Harleian transcripts)

Tower April 10. 1723.

I thank you for all the Instances of your Friendship, both before, and since my Misfortunes. A little Time will compleat them, and seperate You, and Me for ever. But in what part of the World soever I am, I will live mindful of your sincere Kindness to me, and will please my self with the thought, that I still live in your Esteem and Affection, as much as ever I did; and that no Accidents of Life, no distance of Time, or Place, will alter You in that respect, any more than it can Me,[2] who have loved[3] and valu'd you, ever since I knew you; and shall not fail to do it, when I am not allow'd to tell you so; as the Case will soon be. Give my faithful services to Dr Arbuthnot and Thanks for what he sent me, which was much to the purpose ⌐if any thing can be said to be to the purpose⌐[4] in a Case that is already determin'd. Let him know my Defence will be such, that neither my Friends need blush for me, nor will my Enemys have great Occasion of Triumph, tho sure of the Victory, I shall want his Advice, before I go abroad, in many things. But I question whether I shall be permitted to see Him, or any body, but such as are absolutely necessary towards the dispatch of my private affairs. If so, God bless you both! and may no part of the Ill fortune that attends me, ever pursue either of You! I know not but I may call upon you at my Hearing, to say some what about my way of Spending my Time at the Deanery, which did not seem calculated towards managing Plots and Conspiracys. But of that I shall consider—You and I have spent many Hours together upon much pleasanter Subjects; and, that I may preserve the old Custom, I shall not part with you now, till I have clos'd this Letter, with three Lines of Milton, which you will I know, readily, and not without some degree of concern apply to | Your ever affectionate Friend | and faithful Servant | Fra. Roffen.

> Some natural Tears he dropt, but wip'd them soon:
> The World was all before him, where to choose
> His place of rest; and Providence, his Guide.

[1] The text is from the Longleat Papers, xiii, ff. 225–6, which is a transcript proof-read and corrected by Lord Oxford. A second copy of the letter, exactly similar to that here printed, is found in the same volume on folio 236. There is also a transcript at Mapledurham, and doubtless others elsewhere. Copies of the remaining letters in the Pope–Atterbury correspondence were in demand in the early eighteenth century. Printed by Pope, 1737–42.

[2] respect, any more than it can me] respect. It never can me; *1737–42*.

[3] The Harleian scribe wrote *lived*; all printed editions have *loved* or *lov'd*.

[4] The clause in half-brackets is inserted between the lines in the hand of Lord Oxford.

⌐I need not tell you that I must not be known to have written to you.
. My Respects to your Mother, when proper.⌐¹

‖POPE *to* ATTERBURY²   [20 *April* 1723]

Longleat Portland Papers, xiii (Harleian transcripts)
                                                                April 20 1723

It is not possible to express what I think, and what I feel, only this;
that I have thought and felt for nothing but you, for some time past,
and shall think of nothing so long for the time to come. The greatest
comfort I had was an intention which I would have made practicable
to have attended you in your journey, to which I had brought that
Person to consent, who only could have hindered me by a Tye, which
tho' it may be more tender, I do not think ⌐can be⌐ more strong than
that of friendship. But ⌐now I find that Malice, which could be no
more foreseen than, one would think, it could be contrived by any
humane creature, has rendered every friendly, nay every grateful
thought towards you impracticable.⌐ I fear there will be no way left
me to tell you this great truth, that I remember you, that I love you,
that I am grateful to you, that I intirely esteem and value you, but that
one ⌐which I will find, even though it were death to correspond with
you. A way⌐ which³ needs no open warrant to authorize it, or secret
conveyance to secure it; which no Bills can preclude, nor any Kings
prevent: a way which may⁴ reach to any part of the world where you
may be, where the very whisper, or even the wish of a friend must not

---

¹ This postscript, which Pope did not print, indicates that this was a secret letter,—
a fact which perhaps adds rather sinister implications to the prayer 'May no part of the ill
fortune that attends me, ever pursue either of you'; i.e. Arbuthnot or Pope.

² The text is printed from the Harleian transcript in Portland Papers, xiii. 227–9, where
the date is added in a modern hand. It was probably taken from Pope's printed texts (1737–42)
where this date is always found. In the same volume of Portland Papers occurs another
transcript (ff. 238–42), which is undated.

The first printed text of this letter seems to be that discovered by Professor Maynard
Mack in a pamphlet called *Select and Authentick Pieces Written by the Late Duke of Wharton*
(Boulogne, 1731). Professor Mack's explanation of this first publication is here heavily
relied upon.

Other early transcripts in addition to the one here printed are known as follows: Add.
MS. 5822, ff. 107–9 (by William Cole); Harleian MS. 7053, ff. 74–75; Watson Bequest (Nat.
Lib. of Scotland) MS. 582, item 621; Woolley Park (Yorkshire) MS. (printed by John
Gough Nichols, *Letters of Pope to Atterbury when in the Tower* [Camden Society], 1859,
pp. 7–11). Professor Mack has given the text with variant readings in *RES*, xxi (1945),
117–25. He gives the variant readings so carefully that there seems to be no need of reprinting all the smaller ones, especially since they are purely rhetorical. The Boulogne text
is practically identical with that found at Longleat. Pope's printed texts have interesting
omissions (here placed in half-brackets) and one or two additions, indicated in footnotes.

Other transcripts (Cole's, for example) are copies of copies and omit several phrases found
in the Longleat MS., which seems preferable to any of the others.

³ value you . . . A way which] value you: no way but that one which *1737–42*.

⁴ which may] that can *1737–42*.

be heard, or even suspected. By this way I dare tell my esteem and affection for[1] you to your enemies in the Gates, and you, and they, and their Sons shall[2] hear it.

You prove your self, my Lord, to know me for the ⌜zealous⌝ friend I am, in judging that the manner of your defence, and your Glory[3] in it, is a point of the highest concern to me, assureing me,[4] that it will be, it shall be such, That none of your Friends shall blush for you. Let me further prompt you to do your self the best and most lasting justice; the instruments of your fame to Posterity will be in your own hands. May[5] it not be that Providence has appointed you to some great and useful work, and calls you to it this Severe way. You may more eminently and more effectually serve the Publick, even now, than in the Stations you have so honourably fill'd. Think of Tully, Bacon, and Clarendon; is not the latter, the most disgraced part of their lives, what you must[6] envy, and which you would choose to have lived?

I am tenderly sensible of the wish you express, that no part of misfortune may pursue me; But God knows ⌜how short a time we may be suffered, or we may desire to be suffered, to live in this Country.⌝ I am every day less and less fond of it,[7] and begin ⌜seriously⌝ to consider a friend in exile,[8] a friend in death, one gone before, where I am not unwilling, nor unprepared to follow after; and where (however various and uncertain the Roads and voyages of another world may be) I cannot but entertain a pleasing hope that we may meet again. ⌜This⌝ I faithfully assure you, that in the mean time, there is no one living or dead, of whom I shall think oftener, or better than of you. I shall look upon you as in a State between both, in which you will have for[9] me, all the passions, all the warm wishes that can attend the living, and all the respect and tender sense of loss, that we feel for the dead: and I shall always[10] depend upon your friendship,[11] kind memory, and good offices, as though[12] I never were to hear, or see[13] the effects of them. Like the trust we have in benevolent Spirits, who, though we never see or hear them, we think to be constantly serving us, and praying for us.

Whenever I am wishing[14] to write to you, I shall conclude that you

---

[1] for] of *1737–42.*   [2] shall] may *1737–42.*
[3] Glory in it] Reputation by it *1737–42.*
[4] to me, assureing me] to me: and assuring me *1737–42.*
[5] The Harleian scribe wrote *My* for *May.* All Pope's texts have *May.*
[6] must] most *1737–42.*
[7] fond of it, and] fond of my native country (so torn as it is by Party-rage, and *1737–42.*
[8] exile, a] exile, as a *1737–42.*
[9] for] from *1737–42.* (*From* also occurs in Cole and Wooley Park.)
[10] always] ever *1737–42.*   [11] your friendship] your constant friendship *1737–42.*
[12] as though] tho' *1737–42.*   [13] hear, or see] see or hear *1737–42.*
[14] wishing *1737–42*] willing *in all transcripts seen.* (The text of the transcript is here amended by Pope's printed text, as giving a more plausible reading. If *willing* is retained, it must be understood as meaning *desirous.*)

are intentionally doing so to me; and every time I¹ think of you I will believe ⌈that⌉ you are thinking of me. I shall never suffer to be forgotten (nay to be but faintly remembered) the honour, the pleasure, the pride, I must ever have in reflecting how frequently you have delighted me, how kindly you have distinguish'd me, how cordially you have advised me, in conversation and in study; ⌈in which⌉ I shall² always want you, and wish for you. In my most lively, in my most thoughtful hours, I shall equally bear about me the impressions of you: and perhaps it will not be in this life only, that I shall have cause to remember and acknowledge the friendship of the Bishop of Rochester.

⌈Be assured that I wish for any occasion of publickly bearing testimony of the truth in your behalf, and shall be glad to be called upon, and so will the friend you mention. Would to God we could act for you, but if not that, at least let us appear for you.⌉³

POPE *to* ATTERBURY⁴　　　　　　　　　　　　　　　　　　*May* 1723

Longleat Portland Papers, xiii (Harleian transcripts)

May 1723.

My Lord,—While yet I can write to you, I must and will correspond with you, till the very moment that it is Felony; and when I can no longer write to you, I will write of you.

To tell you that my heart is full of your Defense, is no more than I believe the worst enemy you have must own of his. You have really, without a figure, had all the triumph that antient eloquence boasts of. Their Passions and Consciences have done you right, though their Votes will not. You have met with the fate frequent to great and good men, to gain applause where you are denied justice. Let me take the only occasion I have had in the whole Series of your misfortunes, to

---

¹ time I] time that I *1737–42.*

² me, in conversation . . . I shall] me! In conversation, in study, I shall *1737–42.*

³ Though omitted from Pope's printed texts, this last paragraph is found in all the transcripts seen.

⁴ The text is printed from Portland Papers, xiii. 229–30. Other transcripts exist; notably in Portland Papers, xiii. 240–2 (verbally identical with the text here given); in Add. MS. 5822, f. 108 (William Cole's transcript); in Harleian MS. 7053, f. 76, and at Woolley Park (Yorkshire), which last is printed by John Gough Nichols in *The Letters of Pope to Atterbury when in the Tower* [Camden Society], 1859, pp. 14–15. This is the second of the two letters printed in 1731 as by the Duke of Wharton in *Select and Authentick Pieces Written by the Late Duke of Wharton,* discussed by Professor Mack in *RES,* xxi (1945), 117–25. Since Professor Mack has recorded the variant readings thoroughly, and since they are small rhetorical variations rather than factual, they are not given here. The Boulogne text and that at Longleat are almost identical, and present the best texts we have. The worst is that printed by Nichols in 1783 (ii. 79–89).

The letter is clearly an outburst of congratulation over Atterbury's speech in his own defence. The trial had filled the whole week of 6–11 May, and since the House voted (83–43) against the bishop on 16 May (Pope here prophesies an unfavourable vote), this letter was probably written 12–15 May. Only the Longleat transcript and the Boulogne text include the date, both lacking the day of the month.

congratulate you; not you only, but Posterity, on this Noble Defense. I already see in what Lustre that Innocence is to appear to other Ages, which this has overborn and oppressed. I know perfectly well what a share of credit it will be, for [me] to have appeared on your side, or being called your Friend. I am far prouder of that word you publickly spoke of me, than of any thing I have yet heard of my self in my whole life. Thanks be to God, that I a Private man, concerned in no Judicature, and employed in no Publick cause, have had the honour, in this great and shining incident, (which will make the first figure in the history of this time) to enter, as it were, my Protest to your Innocence, and my Declaration of your Friendship.

Be assured, my Dear Lord, no time shall ever efface the memory of that from my heart, should I be denied the power of expressing it ever more with my Pen, in this manner. But could that permission be obtained, which you had once the extream goodness to think of asking (even of those from whom you would ask nothing, I believe, but what lyes very near your heart) could the permission of corresponding be obtained, I do assure you, I would leave off all other writing, and apply it wholly to you, where it would please me best, and to the amusement, or, if I could be so happy as to say, Comfort of your Exile; till God and your Innocence, which will support you in it, restore you from it; than which there is not a Sincerer, or warmer Prayer, my Lord, in the breast of your ever obliged and affectionate Friend.

†POPE *to* ATTERBURY[1]   *May 1723*
1737

                                                            May 1723.
Once more I write to you as I promis'd, and this once I fear will be the last! the Curtain will soon be drawn between my friend and me, and nothing left but to wish you a long good night. May you enjoy a state of repose in this life, not unlike that sleep of the soul which some have believ'd is to succeed it, where we lye utterly forgetful of that world from which we are gone, and ripening for that to which we are to go. If you retain any memory of the past, let it only image to you what has pleas'd you best; sometimes present a dream of an absent

---

[1] The Roberts octavo text of 1737 (and all Pope's later octavos) gave the date for this letter without day. The folio and quarto of 1737 added the day as 'May 2'. This is doubtless too early, and probably indicates either a faulty memory on Pope's part when editing the letters in 1737 or an intention to indicate an early cessation of the correspondence. It was forbidden to correspond with the bishop after 25 June except through channels, one of which was his son-in-law, William Morice. Presumably Pope had a final interview with Atterbury on 17 June, the date inscribed in the Bible which the bishop then presented to Pope, and which in 1739 Pope gave to Ralph Allen for use in the chapel at Prior Park. This letter, unlike the two preceding it to Atterbury, seems not to have invited transcription.

On 19 June Atterbury boarded a man-of-war at the Tower steps, and so passed into France and exile.

friend, or bring you back an agreeable conversation. But upon the whole, I hope you will think less of the time past than of the future; as the former has been less kind to you than the latter infallibly will be. Do not envy the world your Studies; they will tend to the benefit of men against whom you can have no complaint, I mean of all Posterity: and perhaps at your time of life, nothing else is worth your care. What is every year of a wise man's life but a censure or critique on the past? Those whose date is the shortest, live long enough to laugh at one half of it: the boy despises the infant, the man the boy, the philosopher both, and the christian all. You may now begin to think your manhood was too much a puerility; and you'll never suffer your age to be but a second infancy. The toys and baubles of your childhood are hardly now more below you, than those toys of our riper and of our declining years, the drums and rattles of Ambition, and the dirt and bubbles of Avarice. At this time, when you are cut off from a little society and made a citizen of the world at large, you should bend your talents not to serve a Party, or a few, but all Mankind. Your Genius should mount above that mist in which its participation and neighbourhood with earth long involv'd it: To shine abroad and to heav'n, ought to be the business and the glory of your present situation. Remember it was at such a time, that the greatest lights of antiquity dazled and blazed the most; in their retreat, in their exile, or in their death: but why do I talk of dazling or blazing? it was then that they did good, and they gave light, and that they became Guides to mankind.

Those aims alone are worthy of spirits truly great, and such I therefore hope will be yours. Resentment indeed may remain, perhaps cannot be quite extinguished, in the noblest minds; but Revenge never will harbour there: higher principles than those of the first, and better principles than those of the latter, will infallibly influence men whose thoughts and whose hearts are enlarged, and cause them to prefer the Whole to any part of mankind, especially to so small a part as one's single self.

Believe me, my Lord, I look upon you as a spirit enter'd into another life, as one just upon the edge of Immortality, where the passions and affections must be much more exalted, and where you ought to despise all little views, and all mean retrospects. Nothing is worth your looking back; therefore look forward, and make (as you can) the world look after you: But take care, that it be not with pity, but with esteem and admiration.

I am with the greatest sincerity, and passion for your fame as well as happiness, Yours, &c.[1]

---

[1] At the end of this letter Pope added when printing the letter the footnote: 'The Bishop of Rochester went into Exile the month following, and continued in it till his death, which happen'd at Paris on the fifteenth day of February, in the year 1732.'

EDWARD YOUNG *to* POPE[1]   2 *May* [1723]

Homer MSS. Add. 4809

May 2d

Having been often from home I know not if You have done me the
favour of calling on me, but be that as it will, I much want that
instance of Your Friendship I mentiond in my last, a Friend Ship I'm
very sensible I can receive from no One but Your self. I should not
urge this thing so much, but for very particular reasons; nor can You
be at a loss to conceive how a *Trifle of this Nature* may be of serious
moment to me. & while Im in hope of your great Advantage of Your
advice about it, I shall not be so absurd as to make any farther Step
without it. I know You are much engagd, & only hope to hear of
You at Your entire leisure | I am Sir | Your most faithfull | & Obedient
Servant | E Youn[g]

Address: To | Mr Pope | at Twitnam
Postmark: 2/MY

POPE *to* VISCOUNT HARCOURT[2]   [6 *May* 1723]

Harcourt MSS.

Munday 9 a clock

My Lord,—Your Lordship gave me a Hint, in relation to what I was
to say before the Lords, & to the proper manner of answering, which
I thought would be of great service to me, as well as extreamly obliging
in your Lordship. I shall certainly to the best of my memory observe
it. But I have chanc't to drop a paper in which I had sett it down, &
where I had enterd another memorandum to ask you about. Which
makes me wish I had found an opportunity this day, or early to morrow,
to talk further to your Lordship hereon. I resolve to take any opportunity of declaring (even upon Oath) how different I am from what
a reputed Papist is. I could almost wish, I were askd if I am not a
Papist? Would it be proper, in such case, to reply, That I dont perfectly know the Import of the word, & would not answer any thing
that might for ought I know, be prejudicial to me, during the Bill
against such, which is depending. But that *if to be a Papist be to profess
& hold many such Tenets of faith as are ascribd to Papists, I am not a*

---

[1] On this letter Pope translated a part of Bk. III of the *Odyssey*, and consequently the
letter cannot be dated later than 1723. It is possible, but not probable, that the letter was written
before 1723. Conceivably it relates to some detail about Young's tragedy *The Brothers*, on
which he may have been working in 1723.

[2] The text is from the original, which was printed in *Harcourt Papers*, ii. 92–93, and in
Elwin–Courthope, x. 199. The date is inferred from the faulty endorsement by Lord Harcourt. 5 May was Sunday, and Pope's remark 'I may not be calld upon this day' fits with his
superscription of Monday [the 6th]. Atterbury's trial before the House of Lords began 6 May.

*Papist. And if to be a Papist, be to hold any that are averse to, or destruc-
tive of, the present Government, King, or Constitution; I am no Papist.*
I very much wish I had your Lordships opinion a little more at large,
since probably I may not be calld upon this day or to morrow. I know
your humanity & particular Kindness to me, & therfore will add no
more, but that I am, what it is Impossible for me not to be, highly
sensible of it, & entirely | Your Lordships | Most obligd | faithful
Servant | A. Pope.

Endorsement: 5 May 1723 | Mr Pope | to | Lord Vicount Harcourt

POPE *to* HIS MOTHER[1]   [14 *May* 1723]

Homer MSS. Add. 4809

Dear Mother,—I hope you continue as I do pretty well. To morrow
I believe will conclude the Trial,[2] but twill be late first. On Thursday
at soonest, if not Friday I hope to see you. If any body comes with me,
you shall be informd. I have not been able to see Lord Harley. All
here are your Servants, & particularly Mr Fortescue, who is at supper
with me. It is late & the Post stays so that I can only add that I am
ever | Your most affectionate | dutiful Son | A. Pope

Tuesday

Address: To Mrs Pope, at Twitenham | near Hampton court | Middlesex.
Postmark: 14/ MA

POPE *to* CARYLL   [*c.* 17 *May* 1723]

Add. 28618
                                                          Twittenham.

I sent you a few words to your lodgings in London, but (as I since
understood) you had been gone a week before. I fancied my letter
might have been forwarded to you from thence and hoped to hear of
you. There was indeed no business in it, but only a kind of incitive
to your writing and a renewal of a correspondance I ever delighted in.
I now accost you again; and had this been dated yesterday, as I intended, it had been as free from business as my last, whereas a thing
has passed to day[3] that makes me acquaint you with a private design

    [1] Before translating the end of Bk. III of the *Odyssey* on the back of this letter Pope
heavily overscored the text, which, however, is still legible.
    [2] The trial had ended on 11 May, but the vote against the bishop was not taken until
Thursday the 16th.
    [3] Unfortunately the date bracketed for this letter must depend on a corrupt text. The
editor assumes that Pope wrote in the third sentence, 'whereas a thing has passed today'.
Caryll's scribe, however, wrote 'has posted'—which makes no sense and no grammar. A bill

of mine, which I now hear of a probability of executing. It is indeed
a friend's right to tell you anything that relates to my affairs, as knowing the kind interest you take in 'em, tho' you were not concerned
in 'em in any other regard. But this will require my drawing together
what money I can in order to purchase an advantageous annuity. I
could be glad of the principal 200ll. which you have in your hands,
for this End as soon as 'tis convenient for you to pay it, but if it will
be any way troublesome, let me know by the first opportunity that I
may procure it elsewhere, and be pleased to tell me what time you will
choose to repay it in: and I'll order my matters according to your
conveniency. As for the year's interest due at Christmas last, I should
be glad of it now, unless you choose to send the whole in a shorter
time than I would press you to do it.

The worthy gentleman our friend, whom we went together to
visit,[1] gives you his most hearty services, and has given them you
several times since (as one of my letters told you). I see nothing but
melancholy prospects for my friends, and shall be a common sufferer
with you; yet I assure you, much more from my concern for the
sufferings of a great number of honest and conscientious men, than
from my own little part in 'em: yet if this Bill passes[2] I shall lose a
good part of my income and in this expectation I am providing the
annuity I told you of, to enable me to keep myself that man of honour
which I trust in God ever to be. I believe firmly you and I shall
never be ashamed of, or for, one another. I know I wish my country
well and if it undoes me, it shall not make me wish it otherwise. You
see I go on acquainting you with my grievances, as I did upon another
occasion when you was last in town. I know I need not put you in
mind of doing that or any other sort of justice or kindness to one who
is so sincerely and by so long established a title | Dear sir | Your most
faithful | affect. friend | & servant | A. P.

My Mother is extremely your servant. Lady Seafort has not been
here a good while, or I should have given you some account of her.
My faithful service to Mrs C., Lady Mary, and your whole family
with all wishes for all your felicity.

for added taxes on Catholics was introduced ('posted'?) in the House of Commons on 26 Apr.
It passed the House on 17 May. Since Pope says here, 'if this bill passes', one may assume
that he writes before its final passage by the Lords on 22 May.
  [1] Elwin suggested Atterbury as the friend visited, but this may be unlikely, since only on
18 May did Lord Townshend issue a warrant allowing the bishop's relations and 'such other
persons as may have business with his Lordship' to visit Atterbury. For eight months or
more his daughter had not been allowed to see him. See Atterbury's *Correspondence* (ed.
John Nichols, 1783–90), iv. 20–22. But Pope had earlier seen him. See ii. 146.
  [2] The Bill for raising money from Papists received the royal assent on 27 May.

POPE *to* JUDITH COWPER   2 *June* 1723

Arthur A. Houghton, Jr.

Twitenham, June 2d 1723.

Madam,—It was an inexpressible pleasure to me to see your Letter, as I assure you it had long been a great Trouble, to reflect on the melancholy reason of your Silence & absence. It was That only which hinderd my writing, not only again, but often, to you; for fear your good-nature shoud have been prompted to oblige me too much at your own expence, by answering. Indeed I never express'd, (& never shall be able to express) more Concern & good wishes for you, than I shall ever feel for one of your merit.

I am sorry, the moment you grow better, to have you snatcht from those, who I may say Deserve the pleasure of seeing you in health, for having so long lamented & felt your Illness. Mrs. H**** I hope, will find it not impossible to draw you to Richmond, and if not, I dare say will not be long out of Hertfordshire. I want nothing but the same Happy Pretence she has, of a title thro' your Friendship, & the privilege of her Sex, to be there immediately. I cannot but wonder You have not heard from her, tho I shoud wonder if any body else had; for I am told by her family she has had much of the Headake at Bath, besides the Excuse of a great Giddiness occasiond naturally by the Waters. I writ to her at the first going, & have not had a word from her: and now you tell me the same thing, I conclude she has been worse than I imagined. I hear she returns on Wednesday, when I shall have the Satisfaction (I doubt not) to talk & hear a great deal of Mrs ****.[1]

I wish I could say any thing, either to comfort you when ill, or entertain you when well. Tho nothing could, in the proper proportion of Friendship, more affect me than Your Condition; I have not wanted other Occasions of great melancholy, (of which the least is the Loss of part of my Fortune by a late Act of Parliament).[2] I am at present in the afflicting Circumstance of taking my last leave of one of the truest Friends[3] I ever had, & one of the greatest men in all polite learning, as well as the most agreeable Companion, this Nation ever had. I really do not love life so dearly, or so weakly, as to value it on any other score, than for that portion of happiness which a Friend only can bestow upon it: or if I must want That myself, for the pleasure which is next it, of seeing Deserving & virtuous people happy. So that indeed I want Comfort; & the greatest I can receive from You (at least unless I were so happy as to deserve what I never can) will be to

---

[1] Here as elsewhere Mrs. Madan in 1769 erased her maiden name of Cowper before sending the letter to press.

[2] See Pope to Caryll, 17 May 1723.   [3] Bishop Atterbury.

hear you grow better till you grow perfectly well, perfectly easy, & perfectly happy, which no one more sincerely wishes than | Madam | Your faithfull & obligd Friend & Servant | A. Pope

POPE *to* VISCOUNT HARCOURT   21 *June* 1723
Harcourt MSS.

Twitenham, June 21st 1723.

My Lord,—I write this to your Lordship in the zeal and fulness of my heart, which has scarce permitted me to stay till your return from Oxfordshire (of which I had the news but to day). You have done me many & great favours, and I have a vast deal to thank you for. But I shall now go near to forget all that is past, & perhaps be so ungrateful as never to mention it more; since ev'ry thing you could hitherto do for me is quite swallowd up & lost in what you have now done, for me & for the whole Nation, in restoring to us my Lord Bolingbroke.[1] Allow me my Lord, in a private letter to phrase it thus plainly, & not to seek other terms, to seem to lessen my own particular obligation, in ascribing any Great part of it to any other than yourself. Allow me farther to say, (with a freedom which your Lordships constant Openness, & may I presume to think, Friendship? has encouraged me to use, with all possible respect, to you:) that nothing which could have been a mortification to me this year, either as to the loss of any of my Fortune, or any of my Friends, could have been so well recompens'd, as by this Action of our Government. My personal Esteem for & Obligation to, my Lord Bolingbroke, are such, that I could hardly complain of any Afflictions, if I saw him at the End of His. I know no real merit I have, but in a sincere & lasting Sense of Gratitude to every Friend I have found; I can deeply grieve in Their Grief, and rejoice in Their Joy. I have had my Share, very lately, in one; and it is owing to your Lordship that I shall now have my Turn in the other. That I may ever be happy in Subjects of Congratulation, & never know an Occasion of Condoleance with your Lordship (after that Great one which I shall never forget, on the Loss of That Friend,[2] to whose recommendations I owe the honour I have to call your Lordship so) this, my Lord, is the sincerest wish of him who shall ever be, with all Truth, | Your most faithfull & | ever obliged Servant, | A. Pope.

Address: To | The Right Honourable, the | Lord Viscount Harcourt, | in Red lyon street | Bloomsbury. | London
Postmark: 22/IV
Endorsement: 21 June 17 | Mr Pope | to | Lord Vicount | Harcourt

[1] Bolingbroke's pardon had been granted in May. He arrived in England on 23 June. How far Harcourt had been instrumental in securing the pardon is uncertain; he had evidently aided Bolingbroke's financial interests during the exile.   [2] Lord Harcourt's son, Simon.

†POPE *to* EDWARD BLOUNT   27 *June* 1723

1735
                                                        June 27, 1723.

You may truly do me the Justice to think no Man is more your
sincere Well-wisher than myself, or more the sincere well-wisher of
your whole Family; with all which, I cannot deny but I have a
mixture of Envy to you all, for loving one another so well; and for
enjoying the sweets of that life, which can only be tasted by people of
good will.

> They from all Shades the Darkness can exclude,
> And from a Desart banish Solitude.

Torbay[1] is a Paradise, and a Storm is but an Amusement to such
people. If you drink Tea upon a Promontory that overhangs the Sea,
it is preferable to an Assembly; and the whistling of the Wind better
Music to contented and loving Minds, than the Opera to the Spleenful,
Ambitious, Diseas'd, Distasted, and Distracted Souls, which this
World affords; nay, this World affords no other. Happy they! who are
banish'd from us: but happier they, who can banish themselves; or
more properly, banish the World from them!

> Alas! I live at *Twickenham*!

I take that Period to be very sublime, and to include more than a
hundred Sentences that might be writ to express Distraction, Hurry,
Multiplication of Nothings, and all the fatiguing perpetual Business
of having no Business to do. You'll wonder I reckon translating the
Odyssey as nothing?[2] But whenever I think seriously (and of late I
have met with so many occasions of thinking seriously, that I begin
never to think otherwise) I cannot but think these things very idle;
as idle, as if a Beast of Burden shou'd go on jingling his Bells, without
bearing any thing valuable about him, or ever serving his Master.

> Life's vain Amusements, amidst which we dwell;
> Not weigh'd, or understood by the grim God of Hell!

Said a Heathen Poet; as he is translated by a Christian Bishop,[3] who
has, first by his Exhortations, and since by his Example, taught me to
think as becomes a Reasonable Creature.—But he is gone! ⌐He carry'd

---

[1] Of Blount's residence John Kirk (*Biographies of English Catholics* [1909], p. 27) says:
'The mansion was situated at the foot of the hill, which obstructed all prospect of the sea,
but on the top of it stood a summer house that commanded the whole expanse of the Bay.'
It was doubtless in the summer-house that one on occasion took tea.

[2] Evidently Pope had inadvertently shown that this task was not to be so heavy as one
might think: probably he had not confessed that he was to have collaborators.

[3] Elwin says vaguely: 'The couplet is from Atterbury's translation of an ode of Horace.'
The present editor has not discovered the translation.

away more Learning than is left in this Nation behind him: but he left us more in the noble Example of bearing Calamity well. 'Tis true, we want Literature very much; but pray God we don't want Patience more! if these Precedents are to prevail.¹¹

I remember I promis'd to write to you, as soon as I should hear you were got home. You must look on this as the first Day I've been myself, and pass over the Mad Interval un-imputed to me. How punctual a Correspondent I shall hence-forward be able, or not able, to be, God knows: but he knows I shall ever be a punctual and grateful Friend, and all the good Wishes of such an one will ever attend you.

---

*POPE *to* JONATHAN RICHARDSON²   1 *July* [1723?]

The National Library of Scotland

Why do you use me so? Have you not born my Infirmities in the Headake & Languors that attend it? And am I so much a worse & more Inconsiderate man than You?³ Homo sum, humani nihil alienum puto. But I thank you for telling me your Indisposition went off the next morning: and I know it will be equally agreable to you to hear that mine did. Pray give Mr Cheselden my heartyest Service, & let me see you & him, when you can. I am always truly | Your affectionate | Friend & faithfull | Servant | A. Pope.

Twitenham: | July 1st at night.

Address: To Mr Richardson, at his | house in Queen-Square | Bloomsbury. | London.

Postmark: 3/IY

---

*POPE *to* THE EARL OF PETERBOROW⁴   12 *July* [1723]

Add. 22625

Twitenham. July 12.

My Lord,—My Indisposition has continued to this day, in such a degree; that I think, for my Resignation in it, I deserve to go strait out of it to Paradise, If a good Guardian Angel be pleas'd to introduce

¹ This passage Pope omitted in his editions of 1737–42.
² The year is assumed on the hypothesis that since the Richardsons and Cheselden helped in collating texts of the plays of Shakespeare in 1723, that may be the year of the letter.
³ That is, Am I likely to be less considerate of your headaches than you have been of mine?
⁴ The year is made fairly certain by the reference to the retarding of the Congress of Cambrai. Lord Polwarth, as the English plenipotentiary, made a state entry into Cambrai 25 Mar. N.S. 1722, and yet as late as 4 Jan. 1723/4 *The British Journal* noted that, thanks to the Emperor, the Congress was not yet officially opened. Peterborow was on the Continent in Aug. of 1723, and possibly had some interest in the Congress.

me. I will therfore hope to find at Mrs Howards door,[1] next Sunday morning about 12 The Appearance of that Benevolent Being, without whom I had never been blest with such a Celestial Conference. A Lady of her acquaintance inform'd me, She was to be Approachd at that canonical hour; & as tis the piece of Devotion & Adoration which I shall pay with the most Zeal & Spirit, I wish your Lordship were a Witness, how Pious a Poet may be, on a proper occasion.

I will nevertheless comission you, (if you design unfeignedly that This Congress may not be retarded so long as that of Cambray) to be the sole-acting-Plenipotentiary in the meantime since to be a Man of Business in this sense, is what a Man of Wit would desire, tho in no other—I am, with all due sense of your Lordships Goodness to me, most faithfully | My Lord | your most obligd obedient Servant | A. Pope.

†POPE *to* HUGH BETHEL[2]   12 *July* 1723

1737

July 12, 1723.

I assure you unfeignedly, any memorial of your good-nature and friendliness is most welcome to me, who know those tenders of affection from you, are not like the common traffick of complements and professions, which most people only give that they may receive; and is at best a commerce of Vanity, if not of Falsehood. I am happy in not immediately wanting the sort of good offices you offer: but if I did want 'em, I shou'd not think my self unhappy in receiving 'em at your hands: this really is some complement, for I would rather most men did me a small injury, than a kindness. I know your humanity, and allow me to say, I love and value you for it: 'Tis a much better

---

[1] At Richmond Lodge probably; Marble Hill was not yet built. Although attached (perhaps secretly married) to Mrs. Anastasia Robinson in 1722, Lord Peterborow was making ardent, if possibly political, love to Mrs. Howard in 1723. His well-known song addressed to her ('I said to my heart, between sleeping and waking') was printed, without the author's name but with Mrs. Howard's name fully given in the last line, in *The British Journal*, 28 Dec. 1723. In Add. MS. 22625, f. 81, is preserved a letter from Peterborow to Mrs. Howard which indicates that Pope had about this time (?) written a song concerning her. The letter begins in phraseology related to this letter by Pope: 'Mr Popes angell and woeman being both imaginary, and att his own disposall, he were to blame had he not made her kind, if it were in my power to continue itt, my Angell & my Lady should be so too. However the little gentleman has brought Angell, woeman, man, and Love together in a song, there was no expedient but that which he has taken, to justifye the persuit of a She Angell by a humane Lover, or to save an Angellick passion from your raillery', &c. Peterborow's letter is undated.

[2] This, the earliest of Pope's surviving letters to Bethel, was printed by him in his editions of 1737–42, without verbal change. The original letter is not preserved. Pope's dating is followed, with reservations. Bethel is evidently travelling on the Continent, and one does not know how long he intended to remain there. Pope talks of sending him the *Odyssey*, and there is some evidence that he had hoped to publish that work before 1725. The books mentioned at the end of the letter were doubtfully available in 1723.

ground of love and value, than all the qualities I see the world so
fond of: They generally admire in the wrong place, and generally
most admire the things they don't comprehend, or the things they can
never be the better for. Very few can receive pleasure or advantage
from wit which they seldom taste, or learning which they seldom
understand: much less from the quality, high birth, or shining circumstances of those to whom they profess esteem, and who will
always remember how much they are their Inferiors. But Humanity
and sociable virtues are what every creature wants every day, and still
wants more the longer he lives, and most the very moment he dies. It
is ill travelling either in a ditch or on a terras; we should walk in the
common way, where others are continually passing on the same level,
to make the journey of life supportable by bearing one another company in the same circumstances.—Let me know how I may convey
over the Odysses for your amusement in your journey, that you may
compare your own travels with those of Ulysses: I am sure yours are
undertaken upon a more disinterested, and therefore a more heroic
motive. Far be the omen from you, of returning as he did, alone,
without saving a friend.

There is lately printed a book wherein all human virtue is reduced
to one test, that of Truth, and branch'd out in every instance of our
duty to God and man.[1] If you have not seen it, you must, and I will
send it together with the Odyssey. The very women read it, and pretend to be charm'd with that beauty which they generally think the
least of. They make as much ado about truth, since this book appear'd
as they did about health when Dr. Cheyne's came out; and will doubtless be as constant in the pursuit of one, as of the other. Adieu.

POPE *to* JUDITH COWPER[2]   [13 *July* 1723]

Arthur A. Houghton, Jr.

Madam,—I am touchd with Shame when I look on the date of your
letter. I have answerd it a hundred times in my own mind, which I
assure you has few thoughts, either so frequent or so lively, as those
relating to you. I am sensibly obliged by you in the Comfort you
endeavor to give me upon the loss of a Friend.[3] It is like the Shower
we have had this morning, that just makes the drooping Trees hold up
their heads, but they remain checkd & witherd at the Root: the Bene-
diction is but a short relief, tho it comes from Heaven itself. The Loss

---

[1] William Wollaston's *Religion of Nature Delineated* had been privately printed in 1722;
it is normally dated 1724. Dr. George Cheyne's *Essay of Health and Long Life* (1724) seems
to make Pope's date of 1723 for this letter improbable. Warburton identified Wollaston's
book as the one here mentioned. See his edition of Pope's *Works* (1751), viii. 202 n.

[2] The postmark indicates the date of the letter, hitherto unnoted.

[3] Doubtless Atterbury.

of a Friend is the Loss of Life; after that is gone from us, 'tis all but a
Gentler Decay, & wasting & lingring a little longer. I was tother day
forming a Wish for a Lady's happiness, upon her Birthday:[1] and thinking of the Greatest Climax of felicity I could raise, step by step, to end
in This—a Friend. I fancy I have succeeded in the Gradation, &
send you the whole copy to ask your opinion, or (which is much the
better reason) to desire you to alter it to your own Wish: for I believe
you are a Woman that can wish for yourself more Reasonably, than
I can for you. Mrs. H**** made me promise her a Copy: & to the
End she may value it, I beg it may be transcribd & sent her by You.

To a Lady on her Birthday
1723.

Oh be thou blest with All that Heav'n can send:
Long Life, long Youth, long Pleasure—and a Friend!
Not with those Toys the Woman-World admire,
Riches that vex, and Vanities that tire:
Let Joy, or Ease; let Affluence, or Content;
And the gay Conscience of a Life well-spent,
Calm ev'ry Thought; inspirit ev'ry Grace;
Glow in thy Heart; and smile upon thy Face!
Let Day improve on Day, and Year on Year;
Without a Pain, a Trouble, or a Fear!
And ah! (since Death must that dear frame destroy),
Dye, by some sudden Extacy of Joy:
In some soft Dream may thy mild Soul remove,
And be thy latest Gasp, a Sigh of Love!

Pray, Madam, let me see this mended in your Copy to Mrs H****
& let it be an exact Scheme of Happiness drawn; & I hope enjoyd, by
Yourself. To whom I assure you I wish it all, as much as you wish
it Her.

I am always with true respect | Madam | Your most faithfull
Friend | & most humble Servant | A. Pope.

Address: (completely obliterated).

Postmark: 13/IY

---

[1] The 'wish' that follows had been prepared for the birthday of Martha Blount (15 June),
but this letter unfortunately led Miss Cowper to think the verses were addressed to her.
See Pope to Caryll, 16 Feb. [1729]. If Mrs. H**** were really Mrs. Howard, as has been
supposed, Mrs. Howard, who knew Miss Blount well, would have undeceived Miss Cowper.
Norman Ault, *New Light on Pope*, pp. 195–206, gives a history of the poem. Miss
Cowper's birthday was 26 Aug.

POPE *to* CHARLES RACKETT[1]   13 *July* [1723]
Homer MSS. Add. 4809

Twitenham. July 13.

Dear Brother,—Every day past, we had a designe to see yourself &
my Sister, at Hallgrove; and every day I have been prevented. My
Mother is now not so well, as she was; and quite afrayd of the Dust,
which this Excessive dry weather has made Insupportable to her,
especially attended with such a Shortness of breath as she is troubled
with. We do yet resolve to be with you after the first Good Rain:
(Except it should happen at the end of this week, for then I am obligd
to be at home upon business.) If any of you can come this way, we
hope to see you, & very much desire it, in the mean time. Pray be
assured of our hearty Loves & Services. I am ever Yours | [A. Pope.][2]

Address: To Mr Rackett, at | Hallgrove, near | Bagshot: | in Surrey.

†POPE *to* JOHN GAY[3]   13 *July* 1723
1735

July 13, 1723.

I was very much pleas'd, not to say oblig'd, by your kind letter, which
sufficiently warm'd my heart to have answer'd it sooner, had I not
been deceiv'd (a way one often is deceiv'd) by hearkening to Women;
who told me that both Lady *Burlington* and yourself were immediately
to return from *Tunbridge*, and that my Lord was gone to bring you
back. The world furnishes us with too many examples of what you
complain of in yours, and I assure you, none of 'em touch and grieve
me so much as what relates to you. I think your Sentiments upon it
are the very same I should entertain: I wish those we call Great Men
had the same Notions, but they are really the most Little Creatures
in the world; and the most interested, in all but one Point; which is,
that they want judgment to know their greatest Interest, to encourage
and chuse Honest men for their Friends.

I have not once seen the Person you complain of, whom I have of
late thought to be, as the Apostle admonisheth, *one Flesh with his Wife*.

Pray make my sincere compliments to Lord *Burlington*,[4] whom I
have long known to have more Mind to be a Good and honourable
man,[5] than almost any one of his rank.

[1] On the back of this letter Pope translated a part of *Odyssey*, Bk. V. The letter, consequently, cannot be dated later than 1723; it might be earlier. July in 1723 (as well as in other
years?) was very dry. See Pope to Broome, 14 July [1723], on the state of Pope's garden in
drought.   [2] The signature is badly blotted out.
[3] Found in all Pope's editions, this letter was in 1737–42 dated 1722—a year impossible
because Bolingbroke was not then in England.
[4] At this time Gay was living in Burlington House.
[5] to have more Mind . . . than] to have a stronger bent of mind to be all that is good and
honourable than *1737–42*.

I have not forgot yours to Lord *Bolingbroke,* (tho' I hope to have speedily a fuller opportunity) he returns[1] for *Flanders* and *France,* next month.

Mrs. *Howard* has writ you something or other in a letter which she says she repents. She has as much Good nature as if she had never seen any Ill nature, and had been bred among Lambs and Turtle-doves, instead of Princes and Court-Ladies.

By the end of this week, *Fortescue* will pass a few days with me. We shall remember you in our Potations, and wish you a Fisher with us, on my Grass-plat. In the mean time we wish you Success as a Fisher of Women, at the Wells, a Rejoycer of the Comfortless and Widow, ⌜an Impregnator of the Barren,⌝[2] and a Playfellow of the Maiden. I am | Your, &c.

POPE *to* BROOME

14 *July* [1723]

Elwin–Courthope, viii. 66

July 14, [1723].

Yours of the 25th I have not had time to answer more speedily. Your commission of altering a verse in the poem you sent me shall be obeyed, and some others altered in that and the rest, whether you will or no; for I use you as I would myself, that is, severely and friendlily. I am glad yourself and Mr. Fenton proceed like two fat men, leisurely and safely. You will be at your journey's end by that means sooner than some Hotspurs. Would you imagine that I have finished two books of Homer, when I have not had, at that time, two entire hours to myself! Yet so it is, and I am beginning the ninth. You forgot a promise you made me, of going upon the eighth first, and of standing excused on that score from one of the remaining. It will be wanted else, and I beg you to undertake it. The tale of Mars and Venus will suit your gay genius, and be such a comfort to you, that I would not have it any other man's property for the world. I hope our friend Fenton has done the fourth, which will be very soon necessary. I desire it by the first opportunity.

I wish I could tell you any agreeable news, either of the polite or learned world; I will not add, of the gallant or amorous. Every valuable, every pleasant thing is sunk in an ocean of avarice and corruption. The son of a first minister is a proper match for a daughter of a late South Sea director,[3]—so money upon money increases, copulates, and multiplies, and guineas beget guineas in *sæcula sæculorum.*

---

[1] returns] returning *1737–42.*   [2] Omitted *1737–42.*

[3] Elwin thought the marriage alluded to was that of Lord Lynn, son of Viscount Townshend, which had been celebrated on 29 May. He married the daughter of Edward Harrison of Balls Park (Herts.). Harrison seems not to have been a director in the South Sea Company, but he was in other companies. It seems possible that Pope alludes to gossip concerning the

O cives, cives! quaerenda pecunia primum est
Virtus post nummos.[1]

My body is sick, my soul is troubled, my pockets are empty, my time is lost, my trees are withered, my grass is burned! So ends my history. I hope you can give a better account of yourself and yours. I am always, with great truth, your well wisher, and honest Fenton's faithful servant.

My mother sometimes toasts you. So does Sir Clement Cottrell. Have you any particular interest with Dr. Snape?[2] Adieu.

POPE *to* MEAD & CO. 25 *July* 1723

Homer MSS. Add. 4809

July the 25. 1723.

Sir,—Pray pay to Mr Harvest, or Bearer, the Sum of twelve pounds & place it to the account of | Sir | Your most humble Servant | A. Pope

Address: To Mr Mead & Co: | in Fleetstreet.

THE EARL OF PETERBOROW *to* POPE[3] [1723]

Homer MSS. Add. 4809

Sir,—if I can make a party with Lord Bolingbroke & Lord Harcourt to dine att Parsons gren, you will give me leave to send my Coach for you   pray doe me the favour to send me the breadth, & depth of the marble Field, you may have itt measured by moon light by a Ten foot Rod, or any body used to grounds will make a neer guesse by pushing itt over. | Your most humble & affectionate | Servant | Peterborow

||POPE *to* SWIFT[4] [*August* 1723]

Transcript at Cirencester

I find a rebuke in a late Letter of yours that both stings & pleases me extreamly. Your saying that I ought to have writt a Postscript to my

---

search of Sir Robert Walpole's eldest son for a bride. The son had recently been created Baron Walpole, and in 1724 he married an heiress, a daughter of Samuel Rolle—who, again, had no directorship in the South Sea Company.   [1] Horace, *Epistles*, i. i. 53–54.
   [2] Dr. Andrew Snape was at this time Vice-Chancellor at Cambridge, and Pope is frequently worried about that university's lack of subscribing interest in his translations. Oxford was another matter.
   [3] On the back of this letter Pope translated a part of Book V of the *Odyssey*, in the summer of 1723. See his letters to Broome, 14 July [1723] and 3 Apr. 1724. The mention of Bolingbroke makes the letter fall after 23 June, when Bolingbroke landed at Dover, returning from exile, and before 14 Aug., when he left England again.
   [4] This letter (clandestinely furnished by Pope?) first appeared in Curll's *New Letters of Mr. Pope* (1736) and in his volume v of *Mr. Pope's Literary Correspondence* (1737). Pope

friend Gay's, makes me not content to write less than a whole Letter, & your seeming to receive His kindly gives me hopes you'll look upon this as a sincere effect of friendship. Indeed as I cannot but owne, the laziness with which you tax me, & with which I may equally charge you (for both of Us I beleive have had & one of Us has both had & given[1] a surfeit of writing) so I really thought you would know yourself to be so certainly entitld to my Friendship, that twas a possession, you cou'd not imagine[2] needed any further Deeds or Writings to assure you of it. ⌜It is an honest Truth, there's no one living or dead of whom I think oft'ner, or better than yourself. I look upon You to be, (as to me) in a State between both: you have from me all the passions, & good wishes, that can attend the Living; & all that Respect & tender Sense of Loss, that we feel for the Dead.⌝[3] Whatever you seem to think of your withdrawn & separate State, at this distance, & in this absence, Dr Swift lives still in England, in ev'ry place & company where he woud chuse to live; & I find him in all the conversations I keep, & in all the Hearts in which I wou'd have[4] any Share. We have never met these many Years without mention of you. Besides my old Acquaintances I have found that all my Friends of a later date, were[5] such as were yours before. Lord Oxford, Lord Harcourt, & Lord Harley, may look upon me as one immediately entail'd upon them by You. Lord Bolingbroke is now return'd (as I hope) to take me, with all his other Hereditary Rights; & indeed he seems grown so much a Philosopher as to set his heart upon some of 'em as little as upon the Poet you gave him. Tis sure my particular ill fate, that all those I have most lov'd & with whom I have most liv'd, must be banish'd. After both of You left England, my constant Host was the Bishop of Rochester. Sure this is a Nation that is cursedly afraid of being overrun with too much politeness, & cannot regain one Great Genius but at the expense of another. I tremble for my Lord Peterborow (whom I

---

used the publication as ground for urging Swift to return all his letters. On extra sheets added at the end of the volume Pope immediately reprinted this letter and the letter of Bolingbroke joined with it, in the Roberts octavo of 1737 and in his quarto and folio (1737 ab). He prefixed to the letters the following note: 'P.S. The following Letters having been lately published without the Consent of their Writers, we have added them, tho' not in the order of time.' Later, in the Cooper octavos (1737 e, 1739 ab), the letters were placed with other Swift letters just after the letters to Atterbury and before those to Gay.

 Curll dated the letter in a footnote, 'Written in the Year 1723'. In Pope's editions 1737–9 the letter is dated 'August 1723'; in both the Dublin and London editions of 1741–2 the date is changed to 'Jan. 12, 1723'. This last date is impossible, since Bolingbroke was not then in England. The transcript (made by a contemporary of Pope's) is textually close to Curll's printing, but is independent of it—as of other printed texts. Some variant readings are here noted. [1] Alluding to his large work on Homer.—Warburton, 1751.

 [2] imagine . . . Deeds] imagine stood in need of any further Deeds *1737–42 in Pope's editions.* (Curll agrees with the Bathurst MS.)

 [3] The bracketed passage is omitted in all Pope's texts; Curll printed it.

 [4] would have] desire *1737–42 in all Pope's texts.* (Curll agrees with the Bathurst reading.)

 [5] were] are *1737–42.*

now lodge with) he has too much wit, as well as Courage to make a solid General,[1] & if he escapes being banish'd by others, I fear he will banish himself. This leads me to give You some account of my manner of Life & Conversation which has been infinitely more various & dissipated than when You knew me, among all Sexes, Parties & Professions. A Glutt of Study & Retirement in the first part of my Life cast me into this, & this I begin to see will throw me again into Study & Retirement. The Civilities I have met with from Opposite Sets of People have hinder'd me from being either violent or sowre to any Party: but at the same time the observations & experiences I cannot but have collected, have made me less fond of, & less surpriz'd at any. I am therefore the more afflicted & the more angry, at the violences & Hardships I see practis'd by either. The merry vein you knew me in, is sunk into a Turn of Reflexion, that has made the world pretty indifferent to me, & yet I have acquir'd a Quietness of mind which by Fitts improves into a certain degree of chearfullness, enough to make me just so good humourd as to wish that world well. My Friendships are increas'd by new ones, yet no part of the warmth I felt for the old is diminish'd. Aversions I have none but to Knaves, (f[or] Fools I have learn'd to bear with) & those[2] I cannot be commonly Civil to: For I think those are next of knaves[3] who converse with them. The greatest Man in Power of this sort, shall hardly make me bow to him, unless I had a personal obligation ⌜to him⌝[4] & that I will take care not to have. The Top-pleasure of my Life is one I learnd from you both how to gain, & how to use the Freedomes[5] of Friendship with Men much my Superiors. To have pleasd Great men according to Horace is a Praise; but not to have flatterd them & yet not to[6] have displeasd them is a greater. I have carefully avoided all intercourse with Poets & Scriblers, unless where by great[7] Chance I find a modest one. By these means I have had no quarrels with any personally, & none have been Enemies, but who were also strangers to me. And as there is no great need of Eclaircissements with such, Whatever they writ or said

---

[1] Pope here echoes a phrase used in his letter to Peterborow placed immediately after this present letter and that of Bolingbroke to Swift. In replying, Swift (20 Sept. 1723) assumes that Peterborow was suspected of involvement in Atterbury's plot; but Peterborow (with whom Pope lodged during Atterbury's trial) voted in favour of banishing the bishop.

The letter must be written during the brief period (23 June to 14 Aug.) when Bolingbroke was in England. Pope's phrase about lodging with Peterborow might well place the letter earlier than Aug., since presently his lordship went to France and returned (*The British Journal*, 14 Sept. 1723) on 7 Sept.

[2] those] such *1737–42 all printed texts except Curll's.*

[3] those are next of knaves] those men are next to knaves *1737–42 in all Pope's texts except the 1737 quarto and folio. (These last follow Curll in reading* those next.)

[4] Omitted in all texts except Curll's vol. v and the quarto and folio of 1737.

[5] The plural is printed only in Curll's vol. v; in all Pope's printed texts we find *Freedom.*

[6] *to* is omitted in all Pope's texts. Curll has it.

[7] *great* is omitted in all texts except Curll's.

I never retaliated;[1] not only never seeming to know, but often really never knowing any thing of the matter. There are very few things that give me the anxiety of a wish: the strongest I have wou'd be to pass my days with you, & a few such as you. But Fate has dispers'd them all about the world. & I find to wish it is as vain as to wish to live to see[2] the millennium, & the Kingdom of the Just upon Earth.

If I have sinned in my long silence Consider there is One, to whom You yourself have[3] been as great a Sinner. As soon as you see his Hand you'll learn to do me justice, & feel in your own heart how long a man may be silent to those he truly loves & respects. | I am Dear Sir | Your everfaithfull Servant | A: Pope

BOLINGBROKE *to* SWIFT[4]   [*August,* 1723]

1736 (Curll)

I am not so lazy as Pope, and therefore you must not expect from me the same indulgence to Laziness; in defending his own Cause he pleads yours; and becomes your Advocate while he appeals to you as his Judge; you will do the same on your Part; and I, and the rest of your common Friends, shall have great Justice to expect from two such righteous Tribunals: You resemble perfectly the two Alehouse-Keepers in *Holland*, who were at the same time Burgomasters of the Town, and taxed one another's Bills alternately. I declare before hand I will not stand to the Award; my Title to your Friendship is good, and wants neither Deeds nor Writings to confirm it; but Annual-Acknowledgments at least are necessary to preserve it; and I begin to suspect by your defrauding me of them, that you hope in time to dispute it, and to urge Prescription against me. I would not say one Word to you about myself (since it is a Subject on which you appear to have no Curiosity) was it not to try, how far the Contrast between Pope's Fortune and Manner of Life, and Mine may be carried.

I have been then infinitely more uniform and less dissipated, than when you knew me and cared for me; that Love which I used to scatter with some Profusion, among the whole Female[5] Kind, has

---

[1] retaliated] related *Curll, 1737.*

[2] to wish to live to see] to wish to see *Cooper octavos of 1737 and Pope's texts thereafter.*

[3] have] has *Pope's octavo eds. 1737–42.*

[4] First published by Curll in his *New Letters* (1736) with the footnote 'This seems to be written by way of *Postscript* to Mr. Pope's Letter.' That is, to Pope's letter here immediately preceding this. Curll included the sheets of his *New Letters* in his *Mr. Pope's Literary Correspondence,* vol. v (June 1737). Bolingbroke, writing from London, speaks of leaving 'this town . . . in a few days'. He sailed for the Continent on 14 Aug. Among the Shaftesbury MSS. of Lord Harcourt is a copy of a document in which Bolingbroke authorizes the banker John Drummond to settle the matter of a disputed £50,000 with Sir Matthew Decker. It is dated 12 Aug. 1723.

[5] the whole Female Kind] the female kind *1741 Lab.*

been these many Years devoted to One Object;[1] a great many Misfortunes (for so they are called, though sometimes very improperly) and a Retirement from the World, have made that just and nice Discrimination between my Acquaintance and my Friends, which we have seldom Sagacity enough to make for Ourselves; those Insects of various Hues, which used to hum and buz about me while I stood in the Sunshine, have disappeared since I lived in the Shade. No Man comes to a Hermitage but for the Sake of the Hermit; a few Philosophical Friends come often to mine, and they are such as you would be glad to live with, if a dull Climate and duller Company have not altered you extreamly from what you was[2] nine Years ago.

The hoarse Voice of Party was never heard in this quiet Place;[3] Gazettes and Pamphlets are banished from it, and if the Lucubrations of Isaac Bickerstaff are admitted, this Distinction is owing to some Strokes by which it is judged that this illustrious Philosopher, had (like the *Indian* Fohu, the *Grecian* Pythagoras, the *Persian* Zoroaster, and others his Precursors among the *Arabians*,[4] *Magians*, and the *Egyptian* Seres[5]) both his Outward and his Inward Doctrine, and that he was of no Side at the Bottom—When I am there, I forget I was ever of any Party myself; nay, I am often so happily absorbed by the abstracted Reason of Things, that I am ready to imagine there never was any such Monster as Party. Alas, I am soon awakened from that pleasing Dream by the *Greek* and *Roman* Historians, by Guicciardin, by Machiavel, and by Thuanus; for I have vowed to read no History of Our own Country, till that Body of it which you promise to finish appears.[6]

I am under no apprehensions that a Glut of Study and Retirement should cast me back into the Hurry of the World; on the contrary, the single Regret which I ever feel, is that I fell so late into this Course of Life: My Philosophy grows confirmed by Habit, and if you and I meet again I will extort this Approbation from you, I am[7] *consilio bonus, sed more eo productus, ut non tantum recte facere possim, sed nil non recte*

[1] The Marquise de la Villette, whom he married in 1720.

[2] was] were *1741 Dab.*

[3] Curll (1737) ineptly identified this quiet place with Dawley; but in 1723 Bolingbroke had no connexion with Dawley. It seems clear that when in the sentences just preceding Bolingbroke spoke of his hermitage he meant La Source, his place in France near Orleans. He contemplates a return to that hermitage. Below this passage he remarks, 'When I am *there*', a phrase indicating that he is not writing from what he calls 'this quiet place'. *This* refers to *hermitage*.

[4] Arabians] Zabians *1737 e, 1739–42.* (See Curll's defensive note at the end of this letter.)

[5] Seres] Seers *1737 e, 1739–42.*

[6] Swift had presumably by this time completed not only his 'History of England from the Death of William the Conqueror to the Accession of Henry II' but also his 'Last Four Years of the Queen'. Probably this last is what interests Bolingbroke. Neither was published in Swift's lifetime.

[7] I am *consilio*] *Iam non consilio 1737 e, 1739–42.*

facere non possim.[1] The little Incivilities I have met with from opposite Sets of People, have been so far from rendring me violent or sour to any, that I think myself obliged to them all; some have cured me of my Fears, by shewing me how impotent the Malice of the World is; others have cured me of my Hopes, by shewing how precarious popular Friendships are; all have cured me of Surprize; in driving me out of Party, they have driven me out of cursed Company; and in stripping me of Titles, and Rank, and Estate, and such Trinkets, which every Man that will may spare, they have given me that which no Man can be happy without.

Reflection and Habit have rendred the World so indifferent to me, that I am neither afflicted nor rejoiced, angry nor pleased at what happens in it, any farther than personal Friendships interest[2] me in the Affairs of it, and this Principle extends my Cares but a little Way: Perfect Tranquillity is the general Tenour of my Life; good Digestions, serene Weather, and some other mechanic Springs, wind me above it now and then, but I never fall below it; I am sometimes gay, but I am never sad; I have gained New Friends, and have lost some Old ones; my Acquisitions of this kind give me a good deal of Pleasure because they have not been made lightly: I know no Vows so solemn as those of Friendship, and therefore a pretty long noviciate of Acquaintance should methinks precede them; my Losses of this kind give me but little Trouble, I contributed[3] nothing to them, and a Friend who breaks with me unjustly is not worth preserving. As soon as I leave this Town (which will be in a few Days) I shall fall back into that Course of Life, which keeps Knaves and Fools at a great distance from me; I have an aversion to them Both, but in the ordinary Course of Life I think I can bear the sensible Knave better than the Fool: One must indeed with the former be in some, or other, of the Attitudes of those Wooden Men whom I have seen before a Sword-Cutler's Shop in *Germany*, but even in these constrained Postures the witty Rascal will divert me; and he that diverts me does me a great deal of good, and lays me under an Obligation to him, which I am not obliged to pay him[4] in another Coin: The Fool obliges me to be almost as much upon my Guard as the Knave, and he makes me no amends; he numbs me like the Torpor, or he teizes me like the Fly. This is the Picture of an old Friend, and more like him than that will be which you once asked, and which he will send you, if you continue

---

[1] Seneca, *Epistles*, cxx. 10, reads: 'Iam non consilio bonus, sed more eo perductus, ut non tantum recte facere posset, sed nisi recte facere non posset.' Bolingbroke was, of course, capable of adapting a text, but since Curll was printing from a transcript and not from the original, probably Bolingbroke's difficult hand in part misled the transcriber.

[2] interest] interested *1741 Dab.*

[3] contributed] contribute *1741 Dab.*

[4] pay him in] pay in *1741 La, Lb.*

still to desire it—Adieu, dear Swift with all thy Faults I love Thee intirely, make an Effort, and love me on with all mine. | Boling-broke.[1]

POPE *to* THE EARL OF PETERBOROW[2]   *[August* 1723?]

Arthur A. Houghton, Jr.

My Lord,—I am very much pleasd and satisfyd to have it now at last in my power to make your Lordship a Return, for so many Favors from you as I thought un-repayable. You'l scarce think I mean by writing this Letter, and yet I do, and you yourself will own it a peculiar mark of Esteem and Gratitude, when I tell you I lose an hour of Mrs Howard's Conversation, to converse in this manner with You. She sits by my side, I look not on her, but on these lines; I give no attention to her, but indulge the remembrance of you. These are my Merits as a Man, but as a Woman (for you know I am abhominably Epicœne) what merits have I not, that can remember & preserve my duty to my Husband after a Whole Fortnight's absence? I will now begin in the tender Strain, and ask you pathetically, My dear Lord, is it my unhappy fate in particular, that I can no sooner learn to love, but I must be *banishd* from what I love? Even when the mercy of the Government has excused you from that Sentence of Exile, (notwith-standing you have more Wit, & Courage, than can be consistent with a Solid General) will you impose it on yourself? only to make your poor Wife unhappy? Others indeed of this nation can spare you, for you have dwelt among us here but like a sort of Noah, preaching Sense & Honour many years, to a Generation who are doomd to be swallowd up & drownd in their own Dulness & Dirtiness. What alas

---

[1] At the end of the letter from Swift to Gay, 8 Jan. 1722/3, which Curll in *Dean Swift's Literary Correspondence* (1741) professed to reprint from the Dublin octavo of the Swift–Pope letters, but which actually reproduces the London text of the quarto and folio, is a note concerning the joint Pope–Bolingbroke letters to Swift here printed. In part it reads:

> The *Irish* Editor owns, That Mr. Curll first obliged the Public with Dr. Swift's and Lord Bolingbroke's *Letters* above-mentioned, but with an equal *Impudence* and *Ignorance* calls them *Stolen Copies.* This is so far from True, that we know they were given to Mr. Curll by a Person of the *first Rank.*
>
> By having been many times copied, it seems, *Two* literal Faults have been committed, *viz. Arabians* for *Zabians,* and the Transposition of a *Letter* in the Word *Seres,* which should be *Seers.*—*Risum teneatis Amici?* | *Verum est.* E. C.

Possibly the transcript of Pope's letter now preserved at Cirencester was among those that were 'many times copied'. One would hesitate to associate Lord Bathurst with the 'Person of the first Rank' who passed the two letters on to Curll.

[2] There seems little possibility of a sure date for this letter. Peterborow's qualifications as a general were probably called in question by critics in May 1722 when he was given the larger title of 'General of all the Marine Forces of Great Britain'. Pope repeats this comment jokingly here and again in the year; see his letter to Swift dated [Aug. 1723], which interest-ingly anticipates (ii. 185) this curious remark. Lord Peterborow went briefly to the Continent in Aug. 1723.

to me are your Houses that you leave me, your Gardens, your Groves, your Ponds, & the full Command of all but your Carps & Grandsons?

> Tityrus hinc aberat, ipsæ te Tityre pinus
> Ipsi te fontes, ipsa & hæc ar[busta vocabant][1]

Having now writ a whole page, I begin to see I have said nothing. But I comfort myself with this reflection, that I have the example of numberless great Authors, deep Divines, profound Casuists, grave Philosophers, who have written not Letters only, but vast Tomes & voluminous treatises about Nothing. Why shou'd a man who all his life does nothing, be asham'd to write of nothing? and that to one who (thanks to the present, firm, & self-sufficient flourishing State of Great Britain) after having conquerd Spain in 3 weeks, has now nothing to do? But perhaps your Lordship, not to be thought quite idle, will alledge that you have something to do; that instead of subduing Mexico & bringing us the Mines of Potosi, you spend the same time in Piquett; & enjoy the same Unconcern & tranquillity as if you were in the Day of Battel? Or that, instead of confirming & strengthning our Alliances with forein Princes, you really take the same pains (tho not quite so successfully) in reconciling & healing the wounds of the various & discordant Potentates & Parties of the Opera? But let me seriously represent to you My Lord, in answer to this; that whatever you, or the whole world besides you are employd about, whether what we call great, or little; all the Somethings that they have to do, to talk of, to wish for; let them all make ever so large a figure, Yet do but cast up the whole Account, put all those Somethings together, and what for God's sake is the Sum Total, but just Nothing?

I would infer from hence, that one can't do a better thing than live, and write, and act to please oneself; which is the same (with all people that are good for any thing,) as to please ones Friends. If this Epistle, empty as it is, please your Lordship for half an hour, tis the best half hour I've spent since I saw you. And could I ever have the least ground to fancy, it can be half the Satisfaction to you to be put in mind of me, that it is to me, to remember, & to wish for, you; I would not change That Single Sensation of mind, for all that flatters the Souls of the Vain, or glads the hearts of the Wealthy. This is true, as I am truly | My Lord, Your faithfull obliged humble | Servant. | A. Pope[2]

---

[1] Virgil, *Eclogues*, i. 38–39.
[2] Two lines of postscript are mainly torn away. All that remains is: 'that are rambling abroad.'

*MARTHA BLOUNT *to* POPE¹   [*August* 1723?]

Homer MSS. Add. 4809

I was in hopes of seeing you last night. I sent word by Bowry, and by
the Messenger that came from your Mother, that I should be very
glad to see you in the evening. this morn, I've expected you, and I
begin to take it a little ill that you come so seldom to me. To day I
dine at Lady Worsleys. and can't tell where I shall be in the evening
prehaps with her. Your letter to the Doctor is perfectly well. I thank
you. adieu.

Address (in a different hand): To | Mrs Martha Blount

†DIGBY *to* POPE²   14 *August* 1723

¹737
                                      Sherburne, Aug. 14, 1723.

I can't return from so agreeable an entertainment as yours in the
country without acknowledging it. I thank you heartily for the new
agreeable idea of life you there gave me; it will remain long with me,
for it is very strongly impressed upon my imagination. I repeat the
memory of it often, and shall value that faculty of the mind now more
than ever, for the power it gives me of being entertained in your villa,
when absent from it. As you are possessed of all the pleasures of the
country, and as I think of a right mind, what can I wish you but
health to enjoy them? This I so heartily do, that I should be even
glad to hear your good old mother might lose all her present pleasures
in her unwearied care of you, by your better health convincing them
it is unnecessary.

I am troubled and shall be so, till I hear you have received this
letter: for you gave me the greatest pleasure imaginable in yours, and
I am impatient to acknowledge it. If I any ways deserve that friendly
warmth and affection with which you write, it is, that I have a heart
full of love and esteem for you. So truly, that I should lose the greatest
pleasure of my life if I lost your good opinion. It rejoices me very
much to be reckoned by you in the class of honest men; for tho' I am
not troubled overmuch about the opinion most may have of me,
yet I own it would grieve me not to be thought well of, by you and
some few others. I will not doubt my own strength, yet I have this

---

¹ The note is written on the blank side of a letter addressed to Miss Blount. Pope's letter
to the 'Doctor' is not known, but Arbuthnot's reply seems to be that dated 'September 1723'.
The place of the letter in the Homer MSS. as part of Book X helps in the dating.
² The text is from 1737 a, where it was first printed. The textual changes (chiefly in
1737 b) are negligible. The letter is possibly a conflation.

further security to maintain my integrity, that I cannot part with that, without forfeiting your esteem with it.

Perpetual disorder and ill health have for some years so disguised me, that I sometimes fear I do not to my best friends enough appear what I really am. Sickness is a great oppressor; it does great injury to a zealous heart, stifling its warmth, and not suffering it to break out in action. But I hope I shall not make this complaint much longer. I have other hopes that please me too, tho' not so well grounded; these are, that you may yet make a journey westward with Lord Bathurst; but of the probability of this I do not venture to reason, because I would not part with the pleasure of that belief. It grieves me to think how far I am removed from you, and from that excellent Lord, whom I love! indeed I remember him as one that has made sickness easy to me, by bearing with my infirmities in the same manner that you have always done. I often too consider him in other lights that make him valuable to me. With him, I know not by what connection, you never fail to come into my mind, as if you were inseparable. I have as you guess, many philosophical reveries in the shades of Sir Walter Raleigh, of which you are a great part.[1] You generally enter there with me, and like a good Genius applaud and strengthen all my sentiments that have honour in them. This good office which you have often done me unknowingly, I must acknowledge now, that my own breast may not reproach me with ingratitude, and disquiet me when I would muse again in that solemn scene. I have not room now left to ask you many questions I intended about the Odyssey. I beg I may know how far you have carried Ulysses on his journey, and how you have been entertained with him on the way? I desire I may hear of your health, of Mrs. Pope's, and of every thing else that belongs to you.

How thrive your garden-plants? how look the trees? how spring the Brocoli and the Fenochio?[2] hard names to spell! how did the poppies bloom? and how is the great room approved? what parties have you had of pleasure? what in the grotto? what upon the Thames? I would know how all your hours pass, all you say, and all you do; of which I should question you yet farther, but my paper is full and spares you. My brother Ned is wholly yours, so my father desires to be, and every soul here whose name is Digby. My sister will be yours in particular. What can I add more? | I am, &c.

----

[1] Lord Digby's residence near Sherborne was originally built by Sir Walter Raleigh. Digby's remark might imply that Pope has already (1722) visited Sherborne; but just above he hopes Pope may *yet* come. Pope came probably in 1724.

[2] On Pope's role as introducer of broccoli see his letter to Stopford, 17 Feb. 1726/7 (ii. 425, note 4).

POPE *to* VISCOUNT HARCOURT¹   22 *August* [1723]

Harcourt MSS.

Twitnam August 22d

My Lord,— It is a Satisfaction to me to tell your Lordship, that I shall not be any way disappointed of the Honour you intend me, of filling a place in your Library with my Picture. I came to Town yesterday, & got admission to Sir Godfrey Kneller, who assur'd me the Original was done for Your Lordship, & that You, & no man but You, shoud have it. I saw the picture there afterwards, & was told then by his Man, that you had sent & put a Seal upon it. So I am certain this affair is settled. Give me leave, my Lord, with great Sincerity, to thank you for so obliging a Thought, as thus to make me a Sharer in the Memory, as well as I was in the Love of a Person, who was justly the dearest object to you in the world: and thus to be Authorized by You to be calld his Friend, after both of us shall be Dust—I am ever with all good wishes to your Lordship & your Family (in which too I must do my Mother the justice to join her) | My Lord | Your most obligd & most faithfull Servant: | A. Pope.

Whether this will find you in the town or at Cockthrop, I am ignorant: but hope, when you return to wait on your Lordship.

Address: To the Right Honourable, the | Lord Viscount Harcourt, to | be left in Downing Street, | Westminster.

Postmark: 24/AV

Endorsement: 22 August 1723 | Mr Pope | to Lord Vicount | Harcourt.

POPE *to* LORD HARLEY²   24 *August* [1723]

Longleat Portland Papers xii

Twitenham, August 24. | 1723.

My Lord,—At my return home, I find you are not content with doing me all favours, & shewing me all kind distinctions, but you extend them to my Mother in my absence, whose health she tells me you sent purposely to enquire of. I now not only desire, but want, & long, to read the Remains of Mr Prior. My Respect for him living extends to his memory; & give me leave to say, In this I resemble your Lordship, that it dies not with his person. I will honestly tell you my

---

¹ Here printed from the MS. It was printed in the Newnham Guide (1797), so Elwin says.
² On the original letter the year is added to the date in the unmistakable hand of Lord Harley. Pope evidently has been away from home, lodging with Lord Peterborow and spending some time with Lord Bolingbroke. Prior had died in Sept. 1721, leaving his papers to the care of his friends Adrian Drift and Lord Harley.

fair opinion of each particular, & be as Severe as I would to my best living Friend, or as I would have my best Friend be to me.

I've been so long from home, that I must retire into myself a while, to recover a disposition to Study or thinking: Nothing will be more serviceable to me in this, than the Book I expect from You, & for which I send the bearer. I beg my services to Lady Harriet Harley, & am with all sincerity | My Lord | Your most oblig'd obedient Servant | A. Pope.

Address: To | the Right Honble the | Lord Harley, in | Doverstreet.

*[LADY MARY WORTLEY MONTAGU] to POPE[1]

Homer MSS. Add. 4809

As I carefully return'd your Arcadia without damage, I hope you will trust me with a volume of Shakespears plays, which I shall take the same care to restore.

POPE *to* JUDITH COWPER   29 *August* [1723]

Arthur A. Houghton, Jr.

Twitenham, Augst 29.

Madam,—Your last letter tells me, that if I don't write in less than a month, you will fancy the Length of yours frighted me. A Consciousness that I had upon me of omitting too long to answer it, made me look (not without some fear & trembling) for the Date of it: but there happend to be none; & I hope, either that you have forgot how long it is, or at least that you can't think it so long as I do, since I writ to you. Indeed a multitude of things (which singly seem Triffles, & yet altogether make a vast deal of Business, & wholly take up that Time which we ought to value above all such things) have from day to day made me wanting, as well to my own greatest pleasure in this, as to my own greatest Concerns in other points. If I seem to neglect any Friend I have, I do more than seem to neglect myself, as I find daily by the Encreasing ill Construction of my Body & mind. I still resolve this Course shall not, nay I see it Cannot, be long; & I determine to retreat within myself to the Only business I was born for, & which I am only good for (if I am entitled to use that phrase for any thing.) Tis great folly to sacrifice one's self, one's time, one's quiet, (the very Life of Life itself) to Forms, Complaisances, & amusements, which do

---

[1] This note has been identified by Professor Robert Halsband as the autograph of Lady Mary Wortley Montagu. See *Philol. Quart.* xxix (1950), 349–52. The placing in the Homer MSS. as part of Book IX suggests 1723 as year, and the nearby letters are dated July or August. Lady Mary was a great reader.

not inwardly please me, & only please a sort of people who regard me
no farther than a meer Instrument of their present Idleness, or Vanity.
To say truth, the Lives of those we call Great & Happy are divided
between those two States; & in each of them, we Poetical Fidlers
make but part of their Pleasure, or of their Equipage. And the misery
is, we, in our turns are so vain (at least I have been so) as to chuse to
pipe without being payd, & so silly to be pleasd with piping to those
who understand musick less than ourselves. They have put me of late
upon a Task before I was aware, which I am sick and sore of: &
yet ingaged in honour to some persons whom I must neither dis-obey
nor disappoint (I mean 2 or 3 in the world only) to go on with it.
They make me do as mean a thing as the greatest man of 'em could
do; Seem to depend, & to sollicite, when I dont want, & make a kind
of Court to those above my rank, just as they do to those above theirs,
when we might much more wisely & agreably live of ourselves, & to
ourselves. You'l easily find I am talking of my Translating the Odyssey
by Subscription: which looks, it must needs look, to all the world as a
Design of mine both upon Fame & Mony, when in truth I believe I
shall get neither; for one I go about without any Stomach, & the other
I shall not go about at all.

This freedom of opening my mind upon my own situation will be
a proof of Trust, & of an opinion your goodness of nature has made me
entertain, that you never profess any degree of Goodwill without being
pretty warm in it. So I tell you my grevances; I hope in God you have
none, wherewith to make me any return of this kind. I hope that was
the only one which you communicated in your last, about Mrs H****
silence; For which she wanted not reproaches from me; & has since,
she says, amply attond for. I saw a few lines of yours to her, which are
more obliging to me than I could have imagind:[1] If you put *My
Welfare* into the small number of things which you heartily wish, (for
a sensible person, of either sex, will never wish for many) I ought to
be a happier man than I ever yet deservd to be.

Upon a review of your papers, I have repented of some of the trivial
alterations I had thought of, which were very few. I would rather
keep 'em till I have the satisfaction to meet you in the winter, which
I must beg earnestly to do, for hitherto methinks you are to me like
a spirit of another world, a Being I admire, but have no Commerce

---

[1] Mr. Falconer Madan in *The Madan Family*, p. 268, item 19, thinks these lines were
two from Mrs. Cowper's lines written on her own birthday, 26 Aug. 1723. This may possibly
be so, but the communication must have been very prompt. Mrs. Cowper more than once
complimented Pope in her verses. It was perhaps about this date that Pope wrote to Jonathan
Richardson concerning verses about him written by Miss Cowper. That letter is at present
unknown; but it was offered for sale in 1833 by Thos. Thorpe as item 809 of his catalogue
of that year. Thorpe summarizes Pope's remarks to the effect that 'the subject of one's own
commendation is so delicate, that, to say the truth, he has very lamely acquitted himself in
thanking her'.

with: I can't tell but I am writing to a Fairy, who has left me some
favours, which I secretly injoy, & shall think it unlucky, if not fatal,
to part with. So pray don't Expect your verses till farther acquaintance.

DR. ARBUTHNOT *to* POPE[1]   [*September* 1723]

Homer MSS. Add. 4809

FRAGMENT

I have yours, and thank you for the Care of my picture; I will not be
usd like an old good for nothing by Mrs Patty. The Handsome thing
would have been, to have taken away my picture & sent me her own;
now to return the compliment I must pay for hers. I hope she is well,
& if I can make her so, It will be a sensible pleasure to me. I know
no body has a better Right to a Ladys good looks in a picture than her
physician if he can procure them.

I was with My Lord Peterborow when I receaved yours. he was
spick & span new just come ffrom ffrance   you was the first man he
askd for. I din'd with him & the Mrs Robinsons[2] on Tuesday & suppd
with him last night with the same company: he had been employd all
that day in Running the Robinsons' [Goods][3] for them which he
executed with great Conduct. I cannot tell how much I am obligd to
him   he deliverd a Memorial from me to the Regent with his own
hand   he is mightily enamourd of my Brother Robert   he is indeed
a Knight errant like him Self.[4] I am just now going to Langly not that
Master is in any danger but to order some things after the small pox.
I am heartily glad Mrs Pope keeps her health this summer   she has
been better then any body   I wish the [   ]ent at your home

THE EARL OF PETERBOROW *to* POPE[5]   [1723]

Homer MSS. Add. 4809

Sir,—I intended to waite on Mrs Howard to day att Richmond, but
going in the night to Lady Mohun,[6] I have gott such a cold & pain

---

[1] The letter is dated by its position in the Homer MSS., which is reinforced by the
remark that Lord Peterborow is 'just come from France'. He landed at Dover on 7 Sept.
The bottom of the letter was torn away perhaps by Pope himself.

[2] The Mrs. Robinsons included the mother and the two daughters, Anastasia, the operatic
singer now secretly married to Peterborow, and Margaret, who by 1728 was married to Dr.
Arbuthnot's half-brother George (see Gay to Swift, 15 Feb. 1727/8). The Robinsons were
removing from Twickenham to Fulham, so as to be nearer Lord Peterborow, who had a
place in Parson's Green.

[3] The words *Running* and *Goods* are practically undecipherable. Arbuthnot's hand is no joy.

[4] Compare Pope's character of Robert Arbuthnot in his letter to Digby, 1 Sept. 1724.

[5] On the back of this letter Pope translated part of Book X of the *Odyssey*—evidently
before 3 Apr. 1724 when he wrote to Broome that the first thirteen books were translated.
Since neighbouring letters in Add. 4809 are all from 1723, this is placed in that period. It
could hardly come in the autumn of 1722 because of the talk about Marble Hill.

[6] Lady Mohun was at this time married to Peterborow's nephew, Col. Charles Mordaunt.
She died in 1725.

in my breast that I am Forcd to Sweat to endeavour to remove itt in the beginning.

I was impatient to know the issue of the affaire, and what she intended for this autumn for no time is to be Lost either if she intends to build out houses or prepare for planting, I will send to morrow to know if you can give me any account, & will call upon you as soon as I am able that we may goe together to Mrs Howards

pray tell her I was charged with compliments to her from Lady Mohun, who was despaird of the day before Yesterday but I left her happily out of pain & out of danger | Sir | Your most affectionate Servant | Peterborow.

*THE EARL OF PETERBOROW *to* POPE[1]   [1723]

Homer MSS. Add. 4809

Mr Pope,—I could not disengage my self time enough to be with you as I intended to night, but will be with you betimes to morrow morning. | your affectionate Servant | Peterborow

Sunday night

Address: For Mr Pope att Twickenham

MRS. CÆSAR *to* POPE[2]   10 *September* 1723

Homer MSS. Add. 4809

Bennington Septr 10 1723

Sir,— I Should not have the vanity to Send this Beautifull Description of Bennington had I not a farther view then Even to Please You with this fine Ladys Lines, who has so beautifully Describd this Place that Mr Cæsar and I cant but hope it will tempt Mr Pope to Honor our roof with his Presance | Sir | Your Most Obledgd | Homble Servant | M Cæsar

I bedg You to | make my Compliments | to Mrs Pope | and send me twelve | Acquittances[3]

Address: To | Mr Pope | at Twicknam.

[1] Part of Book X of the *Odyssey* is translated on the back of this note. Neighbouring letters suggest by their dates that this may have been written shortly after Peterborow's return from France in 1723.

[2] The fine lady who wrote the lines on Bennington was Judith Cowper. The lines are printed by 'George Paston' in *Mr. Pope and His Times*, i. 287. See Pope's reply of 12 Sept.

[3] i.e. for twelve subscribers to the *Odyssey*.

*POPE *to* MRS. CÆSAR   12 *September* [1723]

Rousham

Sept. 12th

For Gods sake Madam, do not worry my Soul out of this miserable
body, with making it too Proud to stay in it. The Verses you sent me
will certainly send me to Phœbus & the Gods:[1] And then, for ever
adieu to ye!

Tell Mrs Cowper she does very ill by me to send me so many Tokens
of heav'nly favour & never afford me One beatifical Vision.

Her friends here are well. so Madam are Yours, I mean my Mother
& myself, whom you honour too much by mentioning.

I obey you twelve times more, & am always Mr Cæsar's & | Madam |
Your most obliged Servant | A. Pope

Address (on detached cover): To | Mrs Cæsar, | Present

||SWIFT *to* POPE[2]   20 *September* 1723

Longleat Portland Papers xiii (Harleian transcripts)

Dublin Septemb. 20th 1723

Returning from a Summer Expedition of four Months on Account of
health, I found a Letter from you with an Appendix longer than yours,
from Ld B.[3] I believe there is not a more universall[4] Malady than an
unwillingness to write Letters to our best Friends and a Man might be
philosopher enough in finding out Reasons for it. One thing is clear
that it shews a mighty difference betwixt Friendship and love; for a
Lover (as I have heard) is allways Scribling to his Mistress, if I could
permit my self to beleive what your civility makes you say, that I am
still rememberd by my Friends in England, I am in the right to keep
my self here *Non Sum qualis eram*;[5] I left you in a period of life where
one year does more Execution than three at yours, to which if you
add the dullness of the Air and of the People it will make a terrible
Summ: ⌐I have often made the same remark with you of my Infelicity
in being so Strongly attached to Traytors (as they call them) and Exiles,
and State Criminalls, I hope Lord Peter with whom you live at present
is in no danger of any among those Characters I allways loved him
well but of late years the few I converse with have not well known how

---

[1] Mrs. Cowper's lines on Bennington began:

> In Tempe's shades the living lyre was strung,
> And the first Pope (immortal Phœbus) sung.

[2] Printed in all the editions of 1737–42. Here printed from the Longleat transcript,
which at various points has been corrected in the hand of the 2nd Lord Oxford himself in such
fashion as to make one believe it transcribed directly from the original letter. The punctuation
is probably not Swift's.   [3] B.] Bolingbroke *1737–42*.

[4] universall] miserable *1737–42*.   [5] Horace, *Carmina*, iv. i. 3.

to describe him⌐¹—I have no very strong Faith in you pretenders to retirement, you are not of an age for it, nor have you gone through either good or bad Fortune enough to go into a Corner and form Conclusions de contemptu mundi et fuga Seculi, unless a Poet grows weary of too much applause as Ministers do with too much Weight of Business—Your happiness is greater than your Merit in chusing your Favorites so Indifferently among either party, this you owe partly to your Education and partly to your Genius, employing you in an Art where² Faction has nothing to do. For I suppose Virgil and Horace are equally read by Whigs and Toryes you have no more to do with the Constitution of Church and State than a Christian at Constantinople, and you are so much the wiser, and the happier because both partyes will approve your Poetry as long as you are known to be of neither. ⌐But I who am sunk under the prejudices of another Education, and am every day perswading my self that a Dagger is at my Throat, a halter about my Neck, or Chains at my Feet, all prepared by those in Power, can never arrive at the Security of Mind you possess.⌐³ Your Notions of Friendship are new to me; I believe every man is born with his quantum, and he can not give to one without Robbing another I very well know to whom I would give the first place in my Friendship, but they are not in the way, I am condemned to another Scene, and therefore I distribute it in pennyworths to those about me, and who displease me least and should do the same to my fellow Prisoners if I were Condemned to a Jayl. I can likewise tolerate knaves much better than Fools because their knavery does me no hurt in the Commerce I have with them which however I own is more dangerous, tho' [not]⁴ so troublesome as that of Fools, I have often endeavoured to establish a Friendship among all Men of Genius, and would fain have it done. they are seldom above three or four Cotemporaries and if they could be united would drive the world before them; I think it was so among the Poets in the time of Augustus, but Envy and party and pride have hindred it among us I do not include the subalterns of which you are Seldom without a large Tribe under the Name of Poets and Scriblers; I suppose you mean the Fools you are content to see sometimes when they happen to be modest, which was not frequent among them while I was in the world. I would describe you⁵ my way of Living if any Method could be called so in this Country, I chuse my Companions among those of least Consequence and most Complyance I Read the most trifling books I can find, and when ever I write it is upon the most Trifling Subjects:⁶

---

¹ Omitted in all Pope's own texts.   ² where] in which *1737–42.*
³ Omitted in editions of *1737–42.*   ⁴ This word occurs in all Pope's printed texts.
⁵ describe you] describe to you *1737–42.*
⁶ Dovelike innocence was one of Swift's best poses. In Jan. 1724 he wrote to Ford, 'I

But Reading[1] Walking and Sleeping take up 18 of the 24 hours. I procrastinate more than I did twenty years ago and have severall things to finish which I put off to twenty years hence Hæc est vita Solutorum[2] &c, I send you the Compliments of a Friend[3] of yours who have[4] passed four Months this Summer with two grave Acquaintances at his Country house without ever once going to Dublin which is but 8 Miles distant, yet when he returns to London, I will engage you shall find him as deep in the Court of Request, the Park, the Operas, and the Coffee house as any man there; I am now with him for a few days.

⌐I am going to write to the Person who joyned in your Letter, we are made to fear that he may not Succeed in what will be Attempted for him in Parliament which would leave him in a worse Scituation then he was before.⌐[5]

You must remember me with great Affection to Dr Arburthnet, Mr Congreve, and Gay I think there are no more eodem tertio's between you and me except Mr Jervas[6] to whose house I address this for want of knowing where you live for it is not Clear from your Letter whether you Lodge with Lord P——[7] or he with you

I am ever ⌐Your Most faithfull humble Servant | J. S.⌐

⌐I never Subscribe my Name et pour cause⌐[8]

Address: To Mr Pope at Mr Jervas's | House in cleveland court | St James's London.

Endorsement: Dean Swifts Letter to mr Pope Sepr 20: 1723——[9]

*THOMAS MOORE to POPE[10]   [1723]

Homer MSS. Add. 4809

Chislehurst.
Saturday afternoon.

Sir,—The two enclos'd Letters are just now come to my hands, & I am desir'd to transmit 'em assoon as I can. I know not where Lord

have left the Country of Horses, and am in the flying Island.' Yahooism was evidently one of his trifling subjects, and soon he was to appear as M. B. Drapier.

[1] Reading] riding *1737–42* (The scribe erred here.)
[2] Horace, *Satires*, i. vi. 128–9.   [3] Charles Ford, Esq.—1741 Dab.
[4] *have* is corrected to *hath* between the lines of the transcript.
[5] Omitted 1737–42.   [6] Jervas] J— *1737–42*.   [7] P—] Peterborow *1737–42*.
[8] The conclusion and postscript were not printed by Pope.
[9] The address and the endorsement are both copied on separate sheets in the hand of Lord Oxford.
[10] Thomas Moore (1662?–1733) had long been attached to Westminster Abbey as Librarian, &c. He was also Registrar of the diocese of Rochester. See J. L. Chester, *The Marriage, Baptismal, and Burial Registers of Westminster Abbey*, p. 340. He had also been Atterbury's chaplain, and the two letters presumably come from Atterbury, possibly after he reached Brussels. The summer of 1723 is indicated by the place of the letter in the Homer MSS. See also the next letter from Moore.

Bathurst is, & therefore beg the favour of you to take the charge of his Letter, & send it to him the first convenient opportunity you have.

I am in haste (the Messenger staying for this) | Your most obedient | humble Servant[1]

---

*THOMAS MOORE *to* POPE   23 *September* 1723

Homer MSS. Add. 4809

                                        Westmr Cloysters.
                                         Sept: 23. 1723.

Sir,—I am extremely oblig'd to you for the Bp's Picture,[2] which I receiv'd this morning, & desire to know, how much I am indebted to the Person who Copyed it, & to whose hands the mony shall be lodg'd for him. I heard from Brussels two days ago, Mr Morice & his family[3] are well and desire to be heartily remember'd to you. He does not intend to return home till the middle of October, but Mr Hughes is expected every day. If you favour me with a line be pleas'd to direct it hither, & it will be sent after me to Chislehurst. I am Sir, | Your faithfull humble Servant | Tho: Moore.

Address (on a detached leaf): For Alexander Pope Esqr | at Twitnam in Middsx.

Postmark: [2]4/SE

POPE *to* JUDITH COWPER   26 *September* 1723

Arthur A. Houghton, Jr.

                                        Twitenham. Sept. 26. 1723

Madam,—It would be a Vanity in me to tell you why I trouble you so soon again: I can't imagine my self of the number of those correspondents whom you call Favorite ones; yet I know tis thought, that Industry may make a man what Merit cannot: and if an old Maxime of my Lord Oxford's be true, that in England if a man Resolve to be any thing, & constantly stick to it, he may: (Even a Lord Treasurer) if so, I say, it shall not be want of Resolution that shall hinder me from being a Favorite. In good earnest, I am more Ambitious of being so to You, Madam, than I ever was or shall be, of being one to Any Prince or (which is more) any Prince's Minister, in Christendome. I wish I could tell you any agreable news of what your heart is concern'd in; but I have a sort of Quarrel to Mrs. H**** for not loving

---

[1] The signature is torn away, though the bare tops of the T and the M remain. The hand is identifiable from the next (signed) letter from Moore, 23 Sept. 1723.

[2] Atterbury's?

[3] William Morice, the High Bailiff of Westminster, was son-in-law to Atterbury and (with his wife) had accompanied the bishop to the Continent. Morice wrote to Pope upon his return to England; see letter of 19 Oct. 1723.

Herself so well as she does her Friends: For those she makes happy, but not Herself. There is an Air of sadness about her which grieves me, & which I have learnt by experience, will increase upon an indolent (I won't say an affected) Resignation to it. It will do so in Men, & much more in Women, who have a natural softness that sinks them even when Reason does not. This I tell you in confidence, and pray give our friend such Hints as may put her out of humour with Melancholy:[1] Your Censure, or even your Raillery, may have more weight with her, than mine: A Man cannot either so decently, or so delicately, take upon him to be a physitian in these Conceald Distempers. You see Madam I proceed in trusting you with things that nearly concern me. In my last letter I spoke but of a Triffle, myself: In this I advance farther, & speak of what touches me more, a Friend.

This beautiful season will raise up so many Rural Images & Descriptions in a Poetical Mind that I expect You & all such as you (if there be any such), at least all who are not Downright dull Translators like your Servant, must necessarily be productive of Verses. I lately saw a sketch this way on the Bower of BEDINGTON.[2] I could wish you tryd something in the descriptive way on any Subject you please, mixd with Vision & Moral; like the Pieces of the old Provençal Poets, which abound with Fancy & are the most amusing scenes in nature. There are 3 or 4 of this kind in Chaucer admirable: The Flower & the Leaf every body has been delighted with. I have long had an inclination to tell a Fairy tale; the more wild & exotic the better, therfore a *Vision*, which is confined to no rules of probability, will take in all the Variety & luxuriancy of Description you will. Provided there be an apparent moral to it. I think one or 2 of the Persian Tales would give one Hints for such an Invention: And perhaps if the Scenes were taken from Real places that are known, in order to compliment

[1] In earlier letters of 1723 to Miss Cowper, Pope shows that she herself was hypochondriac. It seems possible, therefore, that much of this present letter has a therapeutic purpose. It will do Miss Cowper good to rally Miss Howe on melancholy, and the elaborate suggestions for occupying Miss Cowper's mind with poetic fantasies might also serve purposes of health.

[2] Before 1769 someone wrote on the cover of this letter the following footnote, which Dodsley printed in his edition:

'The Lines here alluded to are as follows—

> 'In Tempe's Shades the living Lyre was strung,
> And the First Pope (Immortal Phœbus) sung—
> These happy Shades, where equal beauty reigns,
> Bold rising Hills, slant Vales, & far-stretch'd Plains,
> The Gratefull Verdure of the waving Woods,
> The soothing Murmur of the falling Floods,
> A Nobler Boast, a higher Glory yield
> Than that which Phœbus taught on Tempe's Field:
> All that can charm the eye, or please the ear,
> Says, *Harmony* Itself inhabits Here.'

Bedington is the same as Bennington, where lived Mrs. Cæsar, who had sent Pope these lines earlier in this month. See Mrs. Cæsar to Pope, 10 Sept. (ii. 197).

particular Gardens & Buildings of a fine Taste, (as I believe several of Chaucer's descriptions do, tho tis what nobody has observd) it would add great beauty to the whole.—I wish you found such an amusement pleasing to you; If you did but, at leisure, form descriptions from Objects in nature itself which struck you most livelily, I would undertake to find a Tale that shoud bring em all together: which you'l think an odd undertaking, but in a Piece of this fanciful & Imaginary nature I am sure is practicable. Excuse this long letter, & think no man is more | Your faithfull & obligd Servant. —A. Pope.

POPE *to* LORD HARLEY   29 *September* 1723

Longleat Portland Papers xii

Sunday | Sept 29: 1723

My Lord,—It was really an additional trouble to me when I was so ill, not to be able to wait on You either at morning or Noon. I came fasting home to Twitenham, where I always recover soonest, & have had a pretty good night, but my Head & eyes are yet extremely disorderd by the straining & Vomiting for 9 or 10 hours yesterday. Your Lordship therfore will excuse me for expressing myself ill, but I could no longer delay giving you some account of my Trust, in relation to Mr Priors papers. The greater part I think are very good (& correct for the most part) but some of the very best written, I believe your Lordship will judge with me, ought not to be publishd. I mean some Satyrs on the French King, & some that touch people yet living, or their fathers. Some others Mr Prior himself thought it prudent to dis-own, when surreptitiously printed by Curll, & methinks it would make a wrong figure to ascribe 'em to him after such a publick denial, tho really his. But of this your Lordship, (who have doubtless considerd all this) will, & ought to be, the Determinate Judge, who shew the same Goodness & tenderness to the memory, that you did to the Person, of the Friend. I cannot but say with a Secret Sigh, few Poets have this good fortune! tho there be One more of that class, greatly honourd by you, besides Mr Prior: I wish he deserv'd it as well!

I have markd with a D. the beginning of every Poem which I think shoud be omitted, both such as I mentiond just now; & any which seem'd to me inferior to the rest, or not so fit for the publick. As to alterations here & there of particular lines, or the like, those will easily be made as the sheets are at the press. If your Lordship would have the Manuscript again before you leave the town, I will send it, but I could be glad it lay in my hands till your Return, if there's no objection to it.

My Lord, I beg yours & Lady Harriet's acceptance of my sincerest Respects & best wishes. No man I assure you is more faithful in the

first, or more warm in the last, than | My Lord | Your most obligd
obedient | & humble Servant | A. Pope.

I would fain wait sometimes on my Lord Oxford, during your Stay
in the Country, if I knew the Times of the day that would be least
improper.

I should be very glad of a better Copy than I have of Mr Priors
Picture from Rigault. And an acquaintance of mine has a particular
liking to my Copy. If your Lordship cares to lend yours to my house
to be copied, I will be very careful of it. Or else the Painter may do
it where you please. If you please to give your Servants any order, I'll
send & enquire in Dover street.

Address: To the Right Honourable the | Lord Harley, in | Dover street, |
Piccadilly.

[LADY MARY WORTLEY MONTAGU] *to* POPE[1]

[*October* 1723?]

Homer MSS. Add. 4809

Friday night

If you are not well enough to come hither, I will be with you to
morrow morning, having something particular to say to You.

POPE *to* BROOME

3 *October* [1723][2]

Elwin–Courthope, viii. 67

October 3 [1723].

I have not been at home a good while, and received yours long after
the date of it. I had a mind however to accost you once more before
Mr. Fenton's return hither, who I hope will bring with him all that
I expect, not only his books, but his health and good humour. I foresee long peace and indolence coming upon him, as soon as he settles in
Windsor Forest.[3] I have formerly experienced how amusing, and solitary, and studious a scene that is. I have done my part, and I now begin
to want his. But I assure you I want both your persons more. It will
be necessary we should all meet before winter; absolutely necessary
that you and I should be a month at least together (let that be what
month you best can spare), for a thousand reasons not to be given, or
but very imperfectly, by writing, for all our mutal advantage and satisfaction; and, I hope, for our honour and credit.

---

1 The date is guessed at from the position of the letter among the leaves of Book X of the
Odyssey. The letter was printed in the *Supplemental Volume to the Works of Pope* (1825),
p. 42, as from Lord Peterborow to Pope. It is certainly not in Peterborow's hand. Professor
Robert Halsband identifies the hand, convincingly, as that of Lady Mary.

2 The day and month are from the postmark.—Elwin.

3 In the family of Lady Trumbull.

The reasons I gave you long since as to our conduct in the whole matter, and the injunctions I then laid, I daily find more and more necessary. All men have enemies, though they so little deserve them sometimes that they know them not. I can tell you, you are not without them, and sometimes under the appearance of friends.[1] Most men, if not dishonest, or even if not ill-natured, are yet careless enough of the fame or quiet of others, though those others never envied their fame or disturbed their quiet. I cannot but smile, to think how envy and prejudice will be disappointed, if they find things which they have been willing, or forced, to applaud as belonging to one man, to be the just praise of another whom they have a malignity to. I would, I protest to God, at any time gladly part with anything that was my own due, to see this confusion in those fellows.

I have had very ill health, but guess I am on the mending hand at last. What I have done in my present task of Homer, I think is not quite so spirited as I could wish. It is close and fluent enough, and I hope in the narrative style much resembling my author; but far from any thought of improving either his thoughts, or expression, I try to be as exactly like him as I can.

My mother always remembers you both. Sir Clement Cottrell and I frequently make mention of you. I always wish you well, and desire to serve you in all I can. Adieu, dear sir, yours faithfully.

I must desire you to look over the second book. There is a chasm at verse 140, &c., and at verse 188 to 300, and again at 215.

*POPE to VISCOUNT HARCOURT[2]   16 *October* 1723
Harcourt MSS.

Twitenham, Oct. 16. 1723.

My Lord,—If your Lordship did not know how much your Welfare is my Interest, in very many respects, I yet hope you could not but think it extreamly & warmly my wish, from many better reasons than Interest. I can scarce use so cold a word to you as Gratitude, Your Lordship & your family have a stronger title to me, begun from your Son, & not to end with your Grandson, if ever I live to see your Great Grandson. I beg to know that your Lordship is fully recover'd. I am easy enough in every other article, for we are so well at home (my Mother & I) that I want little or no news from abroad but that of the Equal health & Ease of those I am to esteem & wish well.

I have lately receiv'd a long letter from Dean Swift,[3] in which a very affectionate mention is made of your Lordship & a Friend of

---

[1] Pope's attempt here to scare Broome into discretion naturally provoked inquiry as to the identity of these enemies. See Pope to Broome, 24 Oct.

[2] The letter has been printed in *Harcourt Papers*, ii. 96–98. It is here printed from the original.   [3] The letter of 20 Sept. 1723 does not mention Harcourt.

yours. The rest of it is spleenatic & too philosophical for this world; I hope the Dean is fitter for the next, or he is good for neither. But there is so much wit, & surly good Sense in all he writes, that one can hardly wish him in any point more of one's own opinion, he sustains the contrary so well.

Speaking of Letters, puts me in mind of a Complaint I forgot when I last waited on you to trouble you with—(for your Lordship knows I have a sort of right by Precedent, to trouble you with all my Complaints; To other great men I am silent & patient, to you only a Grumbler) They have whisperd about the town[1] a Story of a strange Letter writ by me to the Bishop during his Confinement: & I have met with one or two who have seen Copies of such a pretended Letter, which I never writ. I wonder at these things, & am in the dark to find for what end, or by what persons they can be propagated?

I will not longer take up your Lordships time, I believe you know my Sentiments of private respect & friendship, not to be Inconsistent with publick Quiet & Allegiance. But even the most Inconsiderable man must be content thus far to share Censure & Slander with the most Eminent. All that either You (my Lord) or I can do, is to stand acquitted in the Judgment of the Best & most Knowing Persons. If I am so in yours, & a few more such persons' (which I believe I must owe to you too) I am satisfyed, & so must [be] the greatest man in the Nation.

I am ever with sincerity & respect | My Lord | Your most obliged & most faith-|full h. Servant, | A. Pope

Endorsement: 16 Oct 1723 | Mr Pope | to Lord Vicount | Harcourt.

WILLIAM MORICE to POPE   19 *October* 1723

Homer MSS. Add. 4809

I cant be long in Town without letting you know it. I arriv'd late last night,[2] & when your other Affairs call you to Town, I shall hope for the pleasure of seeing you, who am with great truth | Dear Sir | Your very faithfull humble | Servant | Wm Morice

Sat night | Octr 19. 1723.

Address: To Alexander Pope Esq; | at Twittenham in | Middlesex
Postmark: 19/OC

[1] No such whisperings have now been traced, but there were later stories, and doubtless stories at this time, about Pope's correspondence with Atterbury. The reference might be to the letter of Pope to Atterbury, 20 Apr. 1723, which when Pope printed it in 1737 omitted his proud announcement of communicating with Atterbury in a way 'which no Bills can preclude, nor any Kings prevent'. Contemporary transcripts of this letter circulated, and it is strange that not more than 'whispers' resulted.

[2] He and his family had been in Brussels with Bishop Atterbury. See the letter from Thomas Moore, 23 Sept. 1723.

LORD BATHURST *to* POPE[1]　　　　　21 *October* 1723

Elwin–Courthope, viii. 329–31

Cirencester, Oct. 21, 1723

I am heartily sorry to find by yours that you have been troubled with a new complaint, but I hope by this time you are free from it, and all its consequences. I have not been tainted with this general looseness which has spread itself so much about the metropolis. My disorder has been a particular giddiness, which though perhaps you that have been for a long time acquainted with me may fancy you have often seen symptoms of, yet I do assure you I never had it, in this manner at least, to my knowledge before. I have been blooded, vomited, and purged one day after another, and every one of those days visited my plantations either on foot or horseback, which I took to be the most effectual remedy of all, and it has succeeded accordingly; for I am now got well again. I set out this week to visit Sir William Wyndham in the lower end of Somersetshire, and as soon as I can return from thence I shall be moving southwards, so that I hope to see you at Riskins according to your promise, about the 4th or 5th of November. You shall be sure to hear from me as soon as I come there, and for an encouragement to you, I must let you know that the scheme I am at present upon is what you will like, for I am resolved to begin the alteration of my wood house,[2] and some little baubling works about it, which you shall direct as you will. I have tired myself with computations and designs of things which cannot be completed in my own time, and I am now resolved to follow the rules of Horace, who in one place says,

Vitæ summa brevis spem nos vetat inchoare longam;[3]

and in another,

Carpe diem, quam minimum credula postero.[4]

This, or something like it, he says, though some allowance must be made for the times in which he lived, which were not so settled and composed as ours at present are, and therefore there is not the same occasion now for a rapidity in executing of projects. Adieu. We shall have more time at Riskins I hope.

[1] Printed by Elwin as 'From the Oxford Papers'. This seems to mean the Portland Papers at Longleat; but the present editor has not found the letter there.

[2] Mrs. Pendarves, writing to Swift on 24 Oct. 1733, gives an account of Cirencester Park and of the improvements made in promoting the wood house ("a cottage not a bit better than an Irish cabin") to be "a venerable castle".—Ball, v. 34–35.

[3] *Carmina*, i. iv. 15.

[4] *Carmina*, i. xi. 8.

POPE *to* BROOME   24 *October* [1723]

Elwin–Courthope, viii. 69

Oct. 24 [1723].

Whatever real concern a friend can feel, or whatever heavy wound one bears either for oneself or for another, it is certain no reason, no religion can go so far towards quieting the mind and reducing it to its own state, as time alone. It is to that hand of time we must owe the healing what the hand of God has inflicted. I do not therefore make you any apology for not immediately writing to you upon the news of your loss.[1] It was the juncture at which any arguments could do you least good. I trusted you awhile to that only physician, time, to make you capable of hearing any, or forming any to yourself. And as I very well know that none can be suggested from abroad to you, which you have not already at home, so indeed no man can give another a disposition of resignation unless he has it from himself. That is a gift, not of man, but of God. I hope, and believe, you have it. As a friend, I feel for you heartily. That is all I am able.

I am sensible it is very unreasonable for me to press to see you at this time. I rather wish I could visit you. I am sure I gladly would. I fear Fenton will be sent for hither; the lady is coming,[2] or come already, to town. Sir Clement, the last time I saw him, spoke of writing for him if he did not come forthwith. I have delayed showing him yours in a view that it might prolong time, in your regard; for when he does write, then a letter of request from you to detain him awhile on this occasion, may spin out a few days more.

You seem too much touched with the little hint I gave you of some trifling ill-natured turns with relation to you. They were really of no consequence, therefore let nothing of the kind add to the trouble you are under. I shall myself have the pleasure to be instrumental in setting your character far above such small enemies, if we live a year to the end. Believe me, dear Broome, always faithfully and affectionately yours.

My heartiest services to Mr. Fenton are always of course included. Why will he never write to me? My mother sincerely condoles with you, and is truly yours.

---

1 Broome had lately lost his daughter Anne, who was born on October 1, 1718.—Elwin. Broome's 'Melancholy' was written, he tells us, as 'an Ode, occasioned by the death of a beloved daughter, 1723'.

2 Lady Trumbull. It was time for Fenton to begin his duties in her family, and Sir Clement was expected to summon him from Sturston.

POPE *to* JUDITH COWPER¹

9 *November* [1723]

Arthur A. Houghton, Jr.

Twitenham, Novr 9th

Madam,—It happend that when I determin'd to answer yours, by the Post that followd my receipt of it, I was prevented from the first proof I have had the happiness to give you of my Warmth & readiness, in returning The Epitaph [on Ld Cowper]² with my sincere Condolements with you on that melancholy Subject. But nevertheless I resolvd to send you the one, tho unattended by the other: I beg'd Mrs. H**** to enclose it, that you might at least see I had not the power to delay a moment the doing what you bid me; especially when the Occasion of obeying your Commands was such, as must affect every admirer & wellwisher of Honour & Virtue in the Nation. You had it in the very blotts, the better to compare the places; & I can only say it was done to the best of my judgment, & to the Extent of my sincerity.

I do not wonder that you decline the poetical amusement I propos'd to you, at this time. I know (from what Little I know of your Heart) Enough at least to convince me, it must be too deeply concern'd at the Loss, not only of so Great, & so near a Relation; but of a Good Man: (a Loss this Age can hardly ever afford to bear, and not often can sustain.) Yet perhaps tis one of the best things that can be said of Poetry, that it helps us to pass over the Toils & Troubles of this tiresome journey, our Life; as Horses are encouraged & spirited up, the better to bear their Labour, by the Jingling of Bells about their heads. Indeed as to myself, I have been used to this Odd Cordial, so long that it has no effect upon me: but You (Madam) are in your Hony-Moon of Poetry; you have seen only the smiles & enjoyd the Caresses of Apollo. Nothing is so pleasant to a Muse as the First Children of the Imagination; but when once she comes to find it meer Conjugal duty, & the Care of her numerous Progeny daily grows upon her, tis all a sower Tax for past Pleasure. (As the Psalmist says on another occasion) The Age of a Muse is scarce above five & twenty: all the rest is labor & Sorrow.³ I find by Experience that his own Fiddle is no great pleasure to a common Fidler, after once the first good Conceit of himself is lost.

¹ This seems the latest letter preserved to us in the correspondence with Miss Cowper. Some editors have assumed that the correspondence ceased after Miss Cowper's marriage to Captain (later Colonel) Martin Madan (1700–56). Evidently the shifting residences of an army officer might make meetings more difficult, and certainly the preservation of letters received would be so. On 23 Jan. 1733 Mrs. Madan wrote to Mrs. Cæsar a letter (preserved at Rousham) which in part says: 'I own it a sensible mortification to be forgotten by Mr. Pope, for so I must interpret his not knowing if such a one lives. I am however just to the valuable friendship he once express'd for me, & shall to the last moment of my life preserve the most gratefull idea of it. He constantly contributes to enliven my retirement, and 'tis to reading him I owe that I have tast enough to be pleas'd with the verses you sent me.'

² The words in brackets are illegibly scored over. William, Earl Cowper, Lord Chancellor, and uncle of Judith, had died on 10 Oct. 1723.
³ Psalm xc. 10.

I long at last to be acquainted with you, & Mrs H**** tells me you shall soon be in towne, & I blest with the Vision I have so long desired. Pray believe I worship you as much, & send my Addresses to you as often, as to any Female Saint in Heaven: It is certain I see you as little, unless it be in my sleep; & that way too, Holy Hermits are visited by the saints themselves.[1]

I am without figures & metaphors, Yours: & hope you'l think, I have spent all my Fiction in my poetry; so that I have nothing but plain Truth left for my Prose. With which I am ever, Madam, | Your faithful humble Servant.

POPE *to* BROOME   24 *December* 1723

Elwin–Courthope, viii. 70   Dec. 24,[2] 1723.

I must write you a few words, though in haste, to acknowledge the receipt of the sixth book. Fenton and I designed to have joined in a letter to you, to say many things we both think ought to be said by your friends, and believed and considered by you, in relation to the present state of your mind. That we wish you with us, is certain; but whether you can yet leave Mrs. Broome I cannot judge. But Fenton tells me she bears it much more like a man of the two, and that you may learn resignation from her. If amusements would be agreeable or serviceable to you, I would endeavour here to contrive them: but I am in some doubt whether those, or the avocation you now pursue of reading and writing, would be the better. That too, nevertheless, you might have here with me, and be as private at Twitnam as at Sturston. In short, you can only judge for yourself; but for God's sake, if I can any way help to comfort you, make me be of use to you, or of pleasure.

We now much want the extracts on the first books.[3] I have not yet fixed the bookseller's affair, nor made a public proposal. However, one way or other, I will put the beginning to the press in a few weeks, having fully corrected and put the last hand to it. But there is still more and more need of that conduct, which at first I saw necessary.

I am sorry to tell you our friend Fenton has been a long time confined to his chamber, but I hope he is now recovered, and will forthwith be settled in the lady's family, or else I fear he will miss of the properest place in the world for him, and what I dare say will be the most suitable to his temper. Believe me, dear Broome, ever faithfully yours.

---

[1] This seems a poetically indirect way of saying that Pope hasn't seen Miss Cowper for a long time. Is it possible that he has never 'met' her?

[2] The day and the month Elwin took from the postmark.

[3] That is, the 'Observations' or notes appended to each book.

POPE *to* BROOME   28 *December* [1723]

Elwin–Courthope, viii. 71

Dec. 28 [1723].

Your letter gives me as much concern and trouble, as you can express
at the occasion of it. I told you sincerely I had not given the least
credence to such reports; nay, I know them to be impossible to be true.
Therefore be quite out of pain and take an honest man and a friend's
word they had not the least effect or slightest impression upon me. Idle
people always multiply and exaggerate every trifle. I have since I writ
to you told Sir Thomas Hanmer[1] everything, and fully vindicated you.
I will do the same to Ford,[2] and to all the world, and declare myself
your friend, *Deo, Angelis, et Hominibus.* So never talk of dedicating
your poem[3] to me, in this most needless view. I would rather you did
not send the packets to Lintot,[4] who is such a fool. I will send to look
for it. The haste I am in must excuse my short letter, but I would not
omit writing the very same day I received yours to give you full
assurance how truly and unalterably I am, dear sir, your most affectionate faithful friend and servant.

A hundred happinesses attend you every new year! That is better
than a hundred new years.

JACOB TONSON, JR. *to* POPE[5]   [1723–4]

Homer MSS. Add. 4809

Satturday.

Sir,—You have Inclosed the account of the D. of Bucks Works: for
the Books sold I have allowed you all the mony I have rec'd, & the
binding &c I have charged at the price it cost me. The Balance
197᪵ 9s is ready when you will please to call & bring with you the
agreement between Us which may be cancelled as I will do mine. & I

---

[1] One may assume that Sir Thomas, who lived in the same county with Broome but was
not acquainted with him, had perhaps heard gossip unfavourable to Broome. Pope's intervention would seem to have done no harm, since in 1725 Broome and Hanmer became
acquainted at the latter's desire.

[2] Cornelius Ford had been an acquaintance of Broome's at Cambridge. Ford was a cousin
of Dr. Johnson's and is mentioned in Johnson's lives of Fenton and Broome.

[3] *On the Seat of the War in Flanders*, written in 1710.—Elwin.

[4] Lintot was normally Broome's publisher, but he had not yet agreed to publish the *Odyssey*.

[5] On the back of this letter Pope translated the beginning of Book X of the *Odyssey*.
Writing to Broome, 3 Apr. 1724, he says the first thirteen books are done, except some of
Broome's. Most of the adjacent letters in the Homer MSS. date late in 1723, though one
occurring 30 leaves before this letter dates Feb. 1723/4. The returns on the Duke of Buckingham's *Works*, which were published in Jan. 1723 and promptly, if temporarily, suppressed,
might well be given here as an annual statement.

Practically all of the letter has been overscored by Pope.

will give you my Note to deliver the Books left when required. I wish
you would send me the Merchant of Venice by your Waterman. I
am Sir | Your most obliged | humble Servant | J. Tonson

*HENRY BAKER *to* POPE[1]   [1723-4]

Victoria and Albert Museum

To Mr Pope,—The meanest Follower of the Muses, intreats You,
their cheifest Favourite, to accept this humble performance: and the
better to secure your pardon for his presumption, begs leave to urge
your own just & generous Sentiment,

> To err, is human, to forgive, divine.[2]

which he hopes You will apply to his Case in particular, who is, with
the highest Respect, | Sir, | Your most devoted Servant

1 Baker's autograph transcript of this letter appears in Forster MS. 23, after some 'Auto-
biographical Memoranda' and in a section headed 'Letters sent with the Invocation of
Health', a poem which appeared in 1723. In 1725 Baker tried (apparently in vain) to secure
an expression of Pope's opinion as to Baker's *Original Poems*, published in February of that
year. Baker (1698–1774) was Defoe's son-in-law, a Fellow of the Royal Society, and until
19 May 1733 chief writer for *The Universal Spectator*, a periodical of some distinction,
uniformly favourable to Pope.

2 *An Essay on Criticism*, l. 585.

This year is marred by ill health for Pope himself in the spring and for his mother, now 82, in the late autumn. It is also characterized by tedious work both on the edition of Shakespeare and on the translation of Homer. The first fourteen books of the *Odyssey* (to be published in April 1725 as the first unit in the translation) were translated by October. Several letters to Broome concern the 'observations' or notes, for which Broome was largely responsible. Fenton saw little of Pope this year, and wrote to him not at all; yet Fenton was at work on the edition of Shakespeare, presumably for Tonson rather than for Pope, and for Tonson Fenton this year began work on his large quarto edition of Waller (1729). Pope did little or no original writing, but he was, as usual, ready with the most miscellaneous kind deeds for others. Lord Bathurst, Bridgeman, and he were in the autumn designing the gardens for his new neighbour, Mrs. Howard, at Marble Hill.

Pope's rambles for the year consisted only of the brief visit to Lord Digby's family at Sherborne in late June. A visit to Lord Oxford at Wimpole was projected in September, but was at once cancelled when Mrs. Pope fell seriously ill.

---

*POPE *to* JACOB TONSON[1]   [1724?]

Arthur A. Houghton, Jr.

Sir,—I send you as many of the Shakespears as I have Setled the Scenary of, in order; that you may have them copyd & divided accordingly in some book of your own, for these are every day of use to me; so return them soon.

Whoever you set upon the Index, may proceed upon the Plan of mine to Homer, & whoever has Sense & Judgment enough to draw up this Index, will find that a Sufficient direction.

He must begin in order as the Plays lye, ranging whatever occurs under those heads; (but not upon One particular Play in an Index by itself) referring each Character, Speech, Simile, Description, &c. to such a play, such an Act, such a Scene, such a Speaker. As for example, all being to be placd alphabetically.

[1] As early as 3 Sept. [1721] Pope was writing to Tonson about the index to Shakespeare, and as late as 19 July 1724 Fenton expressed to Broome his hope of finishing the index that summer. Here Pope speaks of 'your first index-maker', who had evidently passed out of the picture. If Fenton was the second (as he seems to be the last), the letter probably dates in the first half of 1724. In print the index fills about 30 pages and is disposed in seven sections. It must have been done after the 'scenary' (i.e. the division into acts and scenes) was settled.

Characters	Descriptions
A	A
An ambitious man; characterizd in Caesar.	An Army describd
Act—Sc.—. in Hotspur, Hen. 4. act—sc—	Armour, a suit of armour.
An Avaricious character, in Shylock, Merch.	
of Ven. act—sc— &c.	B
	A Ball describd
B	Burning of a Town
Boldness, in such an one, such a play, such an	C
act, &c.	Cliff of Dover. K. Lear, act.
Again, in such another, such a play &c.	sc. Edgar

My own few Hints of this kind at the end and beginning of some
of the Vols. I send you, will show it clearly to him.

I can no where find the 3 parts of Hen. 6. interleavd.[1] perhaps your
first Index-maker had it; I want that volume next.

I am (in great haste) Your Humble Servant | Sir, | A. Pope.

FENTON *to* BROOME   9 *January* 1723/4

Elwin–Courthope, viii. 73

January 9, 1723–4

I thank you for the favour of your two letters, which I should have
done much sooner had they not found me very ill of a fever, which I
have scarce yet conquered. However, I have been for some days fixed
in my new station in Leicester Fields,[2] very much to my satisfaction.
Mr. Pope visited me here last Sunday, and told me that you intended
to come into these parts this month, which we both, as well as Sir
Clement Cottrell, are of opinion will be very unseasonable, and will
in all probability renew the suspicions that are already in town about
the triple alliance; and the affairs of Greece are already so perplexed
and uncertain, that they will not need any additional circumstance to
sink their proceeding. Tonson does not care to contract for the copy,
and application has been made to Lintot, upon which he exerts the
true spirit of a scoundrel,[3] believing that he has Pope entirely at his
mercy. I believe Mr. Pope will hardly be as free in delivering his
sentiments on your coming to town as I am, for fear you should doubt
of being welcome at Twickenham. Poor Lady Blount is strangely

---

[1] The three parts of *Henry VI* fall in vol. iv of Pope's edition, 'Consisting of Historical
Plays'. The interleaved copy was probably made from the second edition (12mo) of Nicholas
Rowe (1714), which was Pope's basic text.

[2] The London residence of Lady Trumbull.—Elwin.

[3] Negotiations with Lintot were apparently prolonged. The agreement was signed on 18
Feb. For various reasons Pope got much less from Lintot for the *Odyssey* than he had for the
Iliad. See Sherburn, *Early Career*, pp. 313–16 for the indenture, and pp. 253–7 for the profits
taken.

alarmed at the news, not knowing how at present to dispose of Mr. Blount.¹ The small-pox has driven her from her own house, and has prevented her from preparing for his travels. Pray give my humble service to Mrs. Broome, Mr. Blount, Mr. Burlington, &c., to whom with yourself I wish many happy new years, and am ever, dear sir, your affectionate humble servant.

To-morrow Gay has a tragedy to come on at Drury Lane, called The Captives.² The story is of his own invention.

---

*POPE *to* JACOB TONSON, JR.³   [21 *January* 1723/4?]

Add. 28275

Tuesday night.

Sir,—Mr Gay & myself think it absolutely necessary that you should cancel that Leaf in which the Epilogue is printed, or if it falls out wrong, Cancell both leaves rather than fail; It must necessarily be inserted, after the Title *EPILOGUE* [*Sent by an unknown Hand.*] Whatever charge this Cancelling will cost, shall be paid. It is yet time, I am very sure, to do it, before the general publication on Thursday. This must be done to oblige him, & | Your most humble Servant | A. Pope.

I must go out before ten & shall be glad to see you (upon the other affair) before nine.

Address: To | Mr Tonson over against | Catharine street in the | Strand.

POPE *and* FENTON *to* BROOME   30 *January* [1723/4]

Elwin–Courthope, viii. 74

Jan. 30 [1724].

[POPE.]

Dear Broome,—I think it necessary to advertise you that I have received the notes on the first book, in which I see your pains, and pity them. At the same time how much am I obliged then to thank and love you for them.

You say infinitely too much of the little justice I did you on a late

---

¹ He was then an inmate of Broome's house.—Elwin.
² First acted, rather, on the 15th.
³ The date is based on the argument by Ault, *New Light*, pp. 207–14, to the effect that this letter concerns the epilogue of Gay's *Captives*. Gay's play was published on Thursday, 23 Jan., and this is consequently as 'Tuesday' made the 21st. Ault's argument is not altogether convincing, but it is the best theoretical dating now available. The first edition of *The Captives* shows no sign of any cancellation.

occasion.[1] I would have done the same to any man; I only felt more joy in doing it to you. You may set your heart fully at ease as to that piece of ill nature, which I can confidently assure you has not hurt, but served you, and enhanced your character with many, who otherwise had not known or heard so many good things of it. I wish, dear sir, nothing may ever touch or affect your heart more than this has touched or affected your character. You would be the easiest man in the world.

I delivered your letter to Sir Clement Cottrell, who always speaks kindly of you, and wishes always to see you: but I cannot say at present he wishes it so much as I, for I found he was a little afraid of your parting with Mr. Blount too soon, on my desiring your coming.[2] Yet I hope as the spring advances you will come with it, and add to the pleasures it always brings me. My health has been this winter, and generally is all winters, scarce good enough to relish any pleasure, even that of a friend, in perfection. But, however, if you *will* come sooner, I *will* be well, or die for it.

I have never seen the Latin version you mention, but you say it is done by a German.

[FENTON.]

You will see by the beginning of this letter that I received and forwarded the notes to Mr. Pope, who gives me the use of his paper to acquaint you that you shall have Bossu by the next carrier. Yours entirely.

Gay's play had no success. I am told he gave thirty guineas to have it acted the fifth night.[3]

POPE *to* FORTESCUE[4]   [*February* 1723/4]

Arthur A. Houghton, Jr.

I am renewing my old habit of employing you one way or other to your trouble, the moment you are got to town. I sent yesterday all

---

[1] The late occasion was the defence of Broome from discreditable reports; see Pope's letter to him, 28 Dec. 1723. Elwin quotes a letter from Sir Clement Cottrell to Broome, also on the occasion : 'The affair you hint at was crudely told me, and though neither Pope nor I could give it credit, we judged it not amiss to be prepared at all adventures. It is much better there was no ground for any such precautions; but had the affair really happened as told to us, I am very sure all the candid would entirely have excused you.'

[2] During the period of negotiation with Lintot Pope had *not* desired the presence of Broome in town. Earlier he had urged the necessity of a meeting of the collaborators.

[3] Fenton is living in the household of Lady Trumbull in London. Pope has called and asked him to add the news that Bossu will reach Broome speedily. There is no evidence that Pope and Fenton discussed Gay's tragedy—as of course they might have. Fenton's information concerning the first performance in his letter to Broome of 9 Jan. was faulty, and he is here pretty certainly wrong in suggesting that Gay paid for the performance of the fifth night. The tragedy was acted at least seven times, and was for Gay apparently a financial success. See W. H. Irving, *John Gay*, pp. 201–3.

[4] Pope and Lintot signed the agreement drawn for them and the witnesses were Fortescue

about after you in hopes to fix an hour for us to meet and chatt, not upon business, but joy & society. To day I believe I must go to Twitnam, to get [rid] of a violent Cold. In the meantime I beg you to [draw] up a draught of an article on the enclosed heads between Mr L. & me, & to speak to him to give you his former agreement for the Iliad, which will help the wording of some part, better than this Scroll. The purport however of this is clear. I am ever | Dear Sir | Your most faithfull | affect. Servant | A. Pope.

Address: To | Wm Fortescue, Esq; in | Tom's Coffeehouse in Deve-|reux court | Temple

Endorsement: Mr Pope; Pt Term. Hillar. 10 Geor.

*POPE to JACOB TONSON, JR.¹ [February 1723/4]

Add. 28275

Sir,—I had writ to Mr Lintot just as I left the town, but at my coming hither I find yours. Pray give my Services to Mr Lintot, & acquaint him that I shall make him the Compliment which you desire, of accepting one Royal for the other, so that the work need not to be retarded. Since you assure me that is as good, tho somewhat less Expensive.

I must desire a favor of you, in return to this, which is also to redound to the credit of Mr Lintot. I mean in regard to the beauty of the Impression, that you will use your interest with Mr Watts,² to cause them to work off the Sheets more carefully than they usually do: & to preserve the blackness of the Letter, by good working, as well as by the best Ink. The sheets I've seen since the first Proof, are not so well in this respect as the first. I beg your Recommendation as to this particular, There's nothing so mu[ch] contributes to the Beauty & credit of a Book, which would be Equally a reputation to Mr Lintot & to me.

Knight³ has writ to me for Prints of the Duke's Monument. I have no such thing, & suppose you have them: so be pleasd to acquaint

and Edmund Bickford, on 18 Feb. 1723/4. Hence this letter should be dated shortly before the event. In 1724 Hilary Term began on 23 Jan.

¹ A vague dating is arrived at from the fact that Lintot signed an indenture for publishing the *Odyssey* on 18 Feb. 1723/4 (BM Egerton Chart. 130) and thus became again Pope's bookseller. The *Odyssey* is now in press, and it was so in Feb. 1724; for on the 25th of that month Sir Clement Cottrell wrote to Broome, 'Pope has, I hear, begun to print. With much ado I brought him and Bernard [Lintot] together, and reckon I shall still be consulted frequently as occasions may arise, which I doubt not will be many from such a suspicious, wrongheaded fellow as my friend Lintot.' (Quoted by Elwin, Pope's *Works*, viii. 73 n.)

² John Watts, the printer.

³ John Knight was a friend of Craggs and of Craggs's sister, Mrs. Newsham, whom he later married. In planning for her brother's monument she evidently wished to see a print of the Duke of Buckingham's tomb.

him. Pray (as you know I am ignorant of the whole matter) tell me
what Booksellers are concernd in the Shares of the Duke's Book,[1] now
Re-publishd, besides yourself, Mr Taylor & Innys? Why should not
Lintot be admitted among 'em if there's any thing to be gott? You
know I must be concernd in his interests, now he is again My Book-
seller. | Yours | A. Pope.

Address:[2] To Mr Tonson, over against | Catherine street in the | Strand

BOLINGBROKE *to* POPE   18 *February* 1723/4

Longleat Portland Papers, xiii (Harleian transcripts)

Feb. 18th 1724.

I forgot you as little during an absence of several Years, as I have
done during another which has now lasted some Months.[3] During
both you have be[en] so constantly present to my mind, and the
impressions I took of your Character long ago are there so fresh and
so strong, that I never did and I think I never shall suspect You of
forgetting me. Follow this Example and be equitable in your Friendship.

I read your letter of the 14th of Jan. with a great deal of pleasure,
and yet there wanted something to make my satisfaction compleat.
You writ to me but you did not Answer me. I was in hopes that I had
provok'd you to say something about your Studys, in which I Interest
my self, and have a right to do so; the right of a friend and the right
of an Englishman. If you imagine the matter dropp'd you are mistaken, I shall attack you once more upon the same Subject. Are you
composing? or are you wholly taken up with the Translation which
you meditated when I saw you at London?[4] Monsieur de Sacy one of
the best Writers this Country affords, has often assured me that his
translation of Pliny the Younger cost him more than all his other
Writings.[5] The translation of Greek Verse into English Verse is
perhaps easier than that of Latin Prose into French Prose. The Rich-
ness of our Language improv'd by those libertys which Custom, (on
whose despotick power the *Jus et Norma loquendi* entirely depends)
allows our Authors, compar'd with the poverty of the others, and with
the cruel Restraints which the same despotick power has impos'd on

---

1 Buckingham's *Works* were advertised as republished on 29 Feb. (*Evening Post*). The
booksellers named were Taylor, Wm. and John Innys, and J. Bowyer.
2 On the cover Tonson wrote certain names, as follows: 'Hoopers | Stickleys book | Popes
Mrs. Hough' [Howe?]. None of these appears as a subscriber to the *Odyssey*.
3 Bolingbroke had left England in the middle of August 1723.
4 Bolingbroke perhaps already is urging Pope away from translation towards original,
philosophical poetry.
5 This translation by Louis de Sacy (1654–1727) had since its appearance in 1699–1700
(3 v.) gone through at least half a dozen editions.

the French Writers, makes this appear to my apprehension not at all improbable. But however it be, sure I am, that you must not look on your translations of Homer as the great Work of your Life. You owe a great deal more to your self, to your Country, to the present Age, and to Posterity: Prelude with translations if you please, but after translating what was writ three Thousand Years ago, it is incumbent upon you that you write, because you are able to Write, what will deserve to be translated three Thousand years hence into Languages as yet perhaps unform'd. I hear all your Objections at this distance. What write for Fame in a living Language which changes every year, and which is hardly known beyond the bounds of our Island, continue to Write, and you'll contribute to fix it. Claudian, nay Lucan who was so much elder, had not certainly the Diction of Virgil; but if Virgil had not Writ, both these, and Silius Italicus and several others, who came between them, or after them, would have writ worse; and we should find the Latin tongue degenerate in the course of so many Centurys much more than it improv'd in that short space between the Age of Lucilius or of Ennius, and that of the Mantuan (the very contrary of which is the Truth.) You have said I am sure to your self at least, *tentanda via est quâ me quoque possim tollere humo,*[1] and if you add that you have succeeded you are not in the wrong, but there remains half a Verse and half your task behind—*Victorque virum volitare per ora.* This perhaps you despair of atchieving, and it is that despair I would recover you from. Virgil indeed wrote when the Roman Arms had carry'd the Roman Language from the Euphrates to the Western Ocean, and from the Deserts of Lybia to the Danube and the Rhine: but your friend Homer wrote for a parcel of little States who compos'd in his days a Nation much inferior every way to what our Nation is in yours. Recall to your mind the image of Ancient Greece which Thucidides gives in the Introduction to his History, and which may be form'd out of Herodotus, Pausanias, Strabo, Plutarch &c. You will soon agree that your Theatre is vastly more considerable than that of Hesiod and Homer, and you will conceive much more reasonable hopes than they could entertain of immortality. Luxury & Learning made the Greeks famous in process of time, and brought their Language into use, as well as their Vices, even among their Conquerors, for Greek like Christianity has spread by Persecution, and Latin like Mahometanism by Victory. The French and the Italians have more lessons of Luxury to give than we, but we have been these several Years their Masters in Learning. Methinks we should improve this advantage. The Philosophers of the Continent learn English, and the Mathematicians might have been under the

---

[1] *Georgics,* iii. 8–9, with a possible reference to the epitaph of Ennius, which Virgil had in mind, from Cicero, *Tusculan Disputations,* I. xv. 34.

same necessity if Sir Isaac Newton had pleased.[1] But there are few Philosophers and Mathematicians any where. A Language which is design'd to spread, must recommend it self by Poetry, by Eloquence, by History. I believe England has produced as much Genius first as any Country. Why then is our Poetry so little in request among Strangers? several Reasons may be given, and this certainly as the most considerable, that we have not one Original great Work of that kind wrote near enough to perfection to pique the Curiosity of other Nations, as the Epick Poetry of the Italians, and the Dramatick Poetry of the French pique ours. Eloquence and History are God knows, at the lowest ebb imaginable among us. The different Stiles are not fix'd, the Bar and the Pulpit have no Standard, and our Historys are Gazettes ill digested, & worse writ. The case is far otherwise in France and in Italy. Eloquence has been extreamly cultivated in both Countrys, and I know not whether the Italians have not equall'd the Greeks and the Romans in writing History. Guicciardine[2] seems to me superior to Thusidides on a Subject still more complicated than that of the Peloponesian war, and perhaps the vastness of the undertaking is the principal advantage which Livy has over Davila.[3] In short excellent original writings can alone recommend a Language, and contribute to the spreading of it. No man will learn English to read Homer or Virgil. Whilst you translate therefore you neglect to propagate the English Tongue; and whilst you do so, you neglect to extend your own reputation, for depend upon it your writings will live as long and go as far as the Language, longer or further they cannot.

After saying so much to you about your self, I must say a word or two in Answer to a Paragraph of your letter which concerns me. First then I'd assure you, that I profess no System of Philosophy whatever, for I know none which has not been push'd beyond [the bounds] of Nature and of Truth. Secondly far from despising the world I admire the work, and I adore the Author, *ille opifex Rerum* (you Greeks call him Δημιουργὸς.) At Physical evils I confess that I tremble but as long as I preserve the use of my Reason I shall not murmur. Moral evils, the effects of that *Mala Ratio,* as Cotta[4] methinks with great impropriety calls error, we may avoid, or we may bear. That Stock of them to which I was Predestinated, is I hope pretty near Spent, and I am willing to think that I have neither bore them unworthily, nor neglected to draw some advantage from them. ⌜Me Ratio vitæ receptui canere permittit, nec Veteranum usque adeo certamina partium delectant ut Miles evocatus sim futurus. Pass me this Latin, the expression of my

----

[1] That is, if Newton had written his *Principia* in English instead of in Latin.—Elwin.

[2] Francesco Guicciardini (1483–1540) wrote in twenty books his widely known *Storia d'Italia* (1561–4).

[3] Arrigo Caterino Davila (1576–1631), author of *Historia delle guerre civili di Francia* (Venice, 1630; Paris, 1642).   [4] Cicero, *De natura deorum,* III. xxviii. 71.

thought presented it self more readily to me in that Language than in English[1]

Give me leave in the third and last place to assure you that I have Study'd neither the Fathers nor the Councils, I began late to read, & later to think. It behooved me therefore to husband my time. I have a friend in this Country who has been devoted these five and twenty Years to judicial Astrology. I begin to believe, for I know not whether I should wish it or no, that he will have the mortification before He dyes of finding out that a quarter of an hour well employ'd in examining Principles would have saved him a quarter of a Century spent about Consequences.

Having done with you and my self, there remain to be spoken of, an Irish Parson and a French Saint,[2] of your making, and I would as lieve take her of your making for such, as of any Man's who ever bore the name. I am extreamly well pleased with Dr. Arbuthnot's comparison which is very happily apply'd. The poor Dean has not disipation enough where he is to divert his Spleen, and I know not whether he has Spirit enough left to get the better of it any where else. Those black corrosive Vapours which he exhal'd so profusely formerly in the open Air, have been long pent up in a Cloyster, and he is become the Martyr of that humour which was given him for the punishment of others. He dreams to be sure of Gibbets and halters, and I fancy if he met two of his old acquaintance in the Street, he might very possibly after Ten Years absence take them for Constables or Messengers, since there seems to be no proportion between the impressions of fear and those of Friendship which he carry'd out of England with him.

I thought to have several Revelations to have communicated to you from our Lady of Lasource, but she says that She neither sends nor receives any more Messages for reasons best known to herself. She vows by her immaculate conception that She will very shortly appear to you in a Vision under the form of an old Frenchwoman, or else you shall hear from her as the Council of Trent did from the holy Ghost. Tir'd [of] the Town, and with the hurry of a Marriage,[3] I am at a little house on the banks of the Seine where I intend to see no body these seven or Eight days, except the company I have carry'd with me, which are my Judgment and my Imagination. My Judgment resides in the head of an excellent young Man[4] whom I hope some time or other to bring you acquainted with, & my Imagination in that of

---

[1] Omitted by Elwin. Bolingbroke's ready Latin obviously owes something to Pliny's *Letters*, III. i, at the end: 'Hanc ego vitam voto et cogitatione praesumo, ingressurus avidissime, ut primum ratio aetatis receptui canere permiserit. . . .'

[2] Lady Bolingbroke, spoken of below as Our Lady of La Source.

[3] Possibly the marriage of a son of Lady Bolingbroke by her first husband.

[4] Levesque de Pouilly (1691–1750) was one of Bolingbroke's closest philosophical friends. He was known for his *Théorie des sentimens agréables* (1736) and for his discipleship of Newton.

Voltaire, who says that he will introduce himself to you, and that the Muses shall answer for him. I am read[ing] in a Tragedy which he has just finish'd and which will be play'd this Lent. The Subject is the Death of Meriamne,[1] you will I believe find in it that Art which Racine put into the Conduct of his Pieces, and that delicacy which appears in his diction, with a Spirit of Poetry which he never had, and which flags often in the best of Corneilles Tragedys, But I will say no more of it since he intends to send it You. | Adieu.

*POPE *to* JACOB TONSON, JR. [1724]

Add. 28275

Twitnam, Wensday

I calld twice & mist of you. I have prevaild upon Mr Fenton to correct the Sheets of one volume, the first of which is Timon of Athens which I send you to begin the Fifth Volume. Let the Sixth be under my care, & continue to send the Sheets of Cymbeline[2] to me. I shall be at Bolton street[3] agen on Friday.

By what Mr Wright tells me,[4] I don't find you have got in any Bookseller (besides yourself) to ingage in the affair of his Master the night you met with him & Innys, I conclude you have, or will, tho you did not bring any body else to that meeting. I remember you mentiond Taylor & some others to me as whom you had a personal influence upon. I need not repeat how much I depend upon your assistance in this point. In any thing in my power you shall ever command & in commanding oblige | Your faithfull affect. Servant | A. Pope

Pray shew Mr Fenton this letter. I've chose these plays for him, because they will be infinitely less troublesome than the other volume, When he is weary, he shall be discharg'd.

Address: To Mr Tonson

JACOB TONSON, JR. *to* POPE[5] [1724]

Homer MSS. Add. 4809

Thursday 11 at Night

I have just now received yrs, & Indeed it is not my fault I have not seen you, having been hindred by business I could not help minding;

---

[1] *Mariamne* was acted on 6 Mar. [2] *Cymbeline* is found in vol. vi.
[3] At Lord Peterborow's.
[4] See the letter to Tonson here placed earlier in Feb. 1724 (and its notes). Wright's Master was very likely Alderman Barber, who was deeply concerned in Buckingham's *Works*.
[5] From its position among the Homer MSS. this letter should fall in the autumn of 1723, but it seems to fit as a reply to Pope's letter that immediately precedes it. The placing is obviously guess-work.

but I will not faile seeing you on Sunday morning early, but must return to Barns to dinner, having a little Company to dine with me that day; Do but Excuse me till I see you, & I will satisfie you then I have not Neglected you: as for Shakespear, Watts[1] Brother die'd lately, which has hindred his business a little, but now things will go on better. | Ever Faithfully yours | J: Tonson

*A. CORBIÈRE[2] *to* POPE   28 *February* 1723/4

Homer MSS. Add. 4809

Whitehall 28. Febry 1723/4

I was with Mrs Newsham[3] this morning who desired me to send you word that she is very desireous to see you, and should be glad if, when your leisure will permit, and you are in Town, you would be so kind as to breakfast with her.

I am extremely sorry I was not in the way when you were pleased to call at our house; pray do not let such disappointments deprive me of the hope of seeing you there when you can do me that favour, for I am, | Sir Your most obedient | humble Servant | Ant Corbiere

Mr Tickell[4] presents his humble Service to you.

*A. CORBIÈRE *to* POPE[5]   [29 *February* 1723/4]

Homer MSS. Add. 4809

Saturday.

Sir,—Mrs Newsham will be glad to see you tomorrow morning at 11. If you will be pleased to call upon me by that time, I shall wait on you thither, being always | Sir | Your most obedient | humble Servant | Ant Corbiere

POPE *to* BROOME   6 *March* [1723/4]

Elwin–Courthope, viii. 76

March 6 [1724].

Dear Broome,—I wrote to you since I received any line from you, and both Fenton and I are in some fear you may not be well. We sent

---

[1] John Watts, the printer (1700?–63), is apparently referred to.

[2] Corbière was employed in the Foreign Office, where at this time Tickell was Under-secretary of State. Corbière doubtless knew Craggs when he was Secretary of State.

[3] Mrs. Newsham, later Mrs. Knight, and still later Mrs. Nugent, was a sister of Pope's friend Craggs. Pope had perhaps become acquainted with her while Craggs lived at Twickenham.

[4] Tickell's acceptance of Pope's verses for inclusion in the edition of Addison's *Works* (1721) indicates a reconciliation, for which there is other evidence. See Sherburn, *Early Career*, p. 127 n. In Apr. 1724 Tickell became secretary to the Lord Lieutenant of Ireland, and thereafter lived chiefly in Ireland.

[5] The position of this letter immediately following that of 28 Feb. in the Homer MSS. (Add. 4809, f. 64) leads one to date it the following day, especially since in 1724 the 29th fell on a Saturday. It might well come a week later perhaps.

to Lady Blount's for some news of you, but heard no satisfactory
account. This makes me give you the trouble of a word or two, just
to inquire of your health, as well as to tell you we still hope the spring
will restore us two things which we want not a little,—our spirits and
you. For my own part, I have been much out of order, and yet continue so. Fenton has been on the mending hand ever since he came
to Lady Trumbull's, but we seldom meet or stay long together. His
affairs keep him in town, mine detain me in the country. If you come
among us, I guess you will prove a cement to unite us better, *in aliquo
tertio.* I writ long since to tell you I had received the abstracts of
Eustathius on the first book. I must now press you to send those for
the second, which will be wanted as soon as they can arrive, in order
to our adding others to them, and the press, I fear, will stay. But let
me have previous notice a post or two before. I write this in haste, but
not in so much as to omit wishing you all felicity, or, in lieu of all
felicity, all resignation, being truly and faithfully at all times, with all
affection, dear sir, your most sincere servant.

*JOHN CROOKSHANKS *to* [POPE][1]   20 *March* 1723/4

Homer MSS. Add. 4809

London 20 March 1723/4

Sir,—I can never make a suitable Return for my obligations.—nor a
sufficient acknowledgment of them.

This Morning our Parish officers answered my Letters, & this
Evening I have Spoke to a Justice of Peace & he sent for the Church
Warden of Covent Garden, & they have promised that the Idiot shall
be removed, if they fail I shall pass him away, which before could not
be done so securely, because they have acknowledged him to be their
Parishioner, which we could not have descover'd, the Idiot being Incapable of Examination.

To morrow I shall have the honour to kiss your hands & acquaint
you with the Event of my appeal in the mean time pray beleive me
to be with Sentiments of Gratitude | Sir | Your obliged & faithful
Servant | Jon Crookshanks

POPE *to* LORD HARLEY   23 *March* 1723/4

Longleat Portland Papers, xii

Twitnam Munday | march, 23. 1723/4.

My Lord,—I ever find myself heartily obliged by You; Your Lordships kind Letter was a sincere pleasure to me. Indeed my head was

---

[1] The letter is printed simply to illustrate another and curious aspect of Pope's frequent
and varied kindnesses. Crookshanks had business in the City (Add. 4809, f. 65) and a house
in Twickenham.

too giddy of the fever I have had, to write even a few words, when I sent my Messenger. May this (with faithfulness) assure You, that tho I think myself at present out of danger: Yet in no circumstance that can happen to my own health or life, I shall forget to wish for that of yourself & whole family, to which I am as firmly attached, as if by a longer possession, theirs & | Your Lordships ever | sincere Servant | A. Pope.

Address: to the Rt Honorable | the Lord Harley.

*POPE to THE DUCHESS OF [BUCKINGHAM][1]

Homer MSS. Add. 4809   30 or 31 *March* [1724]

FRAGMENT

Twitenham, March 31

Madam,—In one word, Your Grace is always too obliging, for me to pretend to take notice of it. You always think so much for others, that they hardly need to think for themselves: which really makes it very fitt for me, to be of the number of those you honour with the name of your Friends. I have done little for myself, and yet I begin to think I am a man pretty deserving as the world goes, (especially from my self)~~I am a little asham'd to see One so disregarded at Court who~~ & ~~sufferd to live without a considerable pension, who~~

POPE to BROOME   3 *April* 1724

Elwin–Courthope, viii. 76

April 3, 1724.

I assure you I want no encouragement to write to you, which I am always ready and inclined to do. But what now hindered me was a severe illness and a fever of some danger, of which I am just recovered. I thought Fenton had advertised you of it, for I sent to desire him to write to you, when I could not, of the receipt of the notes to lib. 2. Those to the third will not come too soon on the 11th of this month; for the second are printed. If you think the fourth too tedious, skip it, and proceed to the notes on the fifth book, which I have finished, and will probably be in the press before the fourth. The verse of the whole thirteen first books is now done, except the eighth book in your hands, and part of the fourth.

I am infinitely obliged to you for the dispatch you make, and long for the time to tell you at large what I think myself in your debt. The

---

[1] This seems to be a draft of a letter probably not sent. On the back of it is translated a part of *Odyssey*, vii. For this book letters dating from 1722 to 1724 are used. One guesses—and it is only a guess—that Pope started this complaisant letter early in 1724 when Tonson had sent him just under £200 as profits on the Duke of Buckingham's *Works*. But both the date (apart from the month) and the addressee are uncertain.

end of this month I shall expect you impatiently. Some additional criticisms on your verse relating to the character of the Phæacians[1] have occurred to me, which confirm Bossu's opinion out of Homer himself. I will be very careful in that passage, and as to all the other parts which need any correction. I must, in your turn, ask your assistance to correct what I have been employed upon. When we meet all this may be done at once, and with pleasure. Many parts of the second book I have altered since you saw it,[2] &c.

I am extremely and unfeignedly rejoiced, dear sir, at what you tell me at last, of the recovery of your mind, as well as body, to its state of tranquillity and resignation. May God increase all your reasonable satisfactions, and by degrees lead you to the greatest which human nature is capable of. No man wishes you solid contentment, mixed with innocent and useful amusement, more truly than your faithful friend and servant.

POPE *to* BOLINGBROKE   9 *April* 1724

Longleat Portland Papers, xiii (Harleian transcripts)

April 9. 1724.

You will think me very Indolent till I tell you I have been very Sick, the only reason that has left your Letter unacknowledged so long by Words which has every day been acknowledg'd in my heart. A severe fit of illness (a sort of intermitting Fever) has made me unfit for all sorts of Writing and application. You will see (I fear) the effects of it in this Letter, which will be almost enough to convince you that all those mighty hopes of the Improvement of the English Language, and the glory of its Poetry, must rest upon some abler Prop than your Servant. To answer first to your Lordship's Charge against me as a translator Convict; I do confess I don't translate Homer as a great Work, but as an easy one, which I really find less difficult than it seems Mr de Sacy does to write Pliny into French Prose. Whatever expectations my own Vanity, or your Partiality, might give me of a better fate than my predecessors in Poetry; I own I am already arriv'd to an Age which more awakens my diligence to live Satisfactorily, than to write unsatisfactorily, to my self: more to consult my happiness, than my Fame; or (in defect of happiness) my Quiet. (Methinks quiet serves instead of happiness to Philosophers, as vanity serves instead of Fame to Authors, for in either case the *Art of Contentment is all.*) But

---

[1] Note 30 of Book VI contains the final views of the translators on the manners of the Phæacians. The views stimulated some later controversy, conditioned largely by the century's belief in the primitive life.

[2] These remarks support the view that Pope revised Broome's work with some thoroughness. Whether Broome accepted the invitation to reciprocate is doubtful. In the Postscript to the *Odyssey* Pope says his collaborators did not revise his work.

when Men grow too Nice and too knowing, the Succidaneum will not do to such delicate constitutions, and the Author becomes miserable to himself in the degree that he grows acceptable to others. What you call a happy Author is the unhappiest Man; and from the same cause, that Men are generally miserable from aiming at a State more perfect than Man is capable of. *Victor virum Volitare per ora*[1] may indeed sound nobly in the Ears of the Ambitious, whether in the Field, the State, or the Study; But sure that Consideration (to a Man's self) is not of such weight, as to sacrifice to that alone all the more the more attainable and the more reasonable aims of our Being. To write well, lastingly well, Immortally well, must not one leave Father and Mother and cleave unto the Muse? Must not one be prepared to endure the reproaches of Men, want and much Fasting, nay Martyrdom in its Cause. 'Tis such a Task as scarce leaves a Man time to be a good Neighbour, an useful friend, nay to plant a Tree, much less to save his Soul. Pray my Lord may not one ask this question, of so just, so grateful, and so deserving a thing, as the present Age?

Tanti est, ut placeam tibi perire? That present Age which you charge me as so much in debt to and which you rank with my two other great Creditors, Posterity and my Country—To the two first, truly I think I'm indebted just equally; for one of 'em has done exactly as much for me as the other. But to my Country sure (My Lord) I owe nothing, for it has driven away my best friends; I shall owe it something when it calls them back again.

The general Reflection makes me shake my head at all the Encouragements you muster up, to induce me to Write. I own your observations, (as to the possibility of fixing a Language, and as to your necessity of good Original works to perpetuate it) to be just, and of a much greater strength & solidity than the usual Arguments on that head: I admire your remark that it is not always a consequence that Languages must decay as Governments fall; and it is very truly as well as finely said, that Greek like Christianity spread by persecution, as much as Latin like Mahometanism by Victory: But allow me to say, that for an Englishman to ground an opinion of the Immortality of his Language from that of Homer, because the States of Greece were then Inferior to what our Nation is at present; wou'd be just such a way of Reasoning as if five or six hundred Rapparees getting together to plunder a few Villages should hope to lay the foundations of an Empire; because that of the Ottoman's began much in the same manner. Neither do I think the Examples of the best Writers in our time, and Nation, wou'd have that Prevalance over the bad ones, which your Lordship observes them to have had in the Roman times. A State constantly divided into various Factions and Interests

---

[1] Virgil, *Georgics*, iii. 9. This echoes Bolingbroke's letter to Pope of 18 Feb. 1724.

Occasions an eternal swarm of bad Writers. Some of these will be Encourag'd by the Government equally if not Superiorly to the good ones, because the latter will rarely, if ever dip their Pens for such ends: And these are sure to be cry'd up, and follow'd by one half of the Kingdom, and consequently possest of no small degree of Reputation. Our English Stile is more corrupted by the Party Writers, than by any other cause whatever; they are universally read, and approv'd (in proportion to their degree of Merit) much more than any other set of Authors in any Science, as Mens passions and Interests are Stronger and surer than their Tastes and Judgments.

It is but this Week that I have been well enough in my head to read the Poem of the *League*[1] with the attention it deserves. Next to my obligation to Mr de Voltaire for writing it, is that I owe to you for sending it. I cannot pretend to judge with any exactness of the beauties of a foreign Language, which I understand but Imperfectly: I can only tell my thoughts in Relation to the design and conduct of the Poem, or the sentiments. I think the forming the Machines upon the Allegorical persons of Virtues and vices very reasonable; it being equally proper to Ancient and Modern subjects, and to all Religions and times: Nor do we look upon them so much as Heathen Divinities as Natural passions. This is not the Case when Jupiter, Juno &c. are introduc'd who tho' sometimes consider'd as Physical powers yet that sort of Allegory lies not open enough to the apprehension. We care not to Study, or Anatomize a Poem, but only to read it for our entertainment. It should certainly be a sort of Machinery, for the meaning of which one is not at a loss for a Moment, without something of this Nature, his Poem wou'd too much resemble Lucan or Silius: and indeed the Subject being so modern, a more violent or remote kind of Fable or Fiction wou'd not suit it: if I have any thing to wish on this head, it were to have a little more of the *Fictitious* (I dare not say the *Wonderful*, for the reason just now given) yet that would give it a greater resemblance to the Ancient Epick Poem. He has help'd it much in my opinion by throwing so much of the Story into Narration, and entering at once into the middle of the Subject; as well as by making the Action single namely only the Siege of Paris. This brings it nearer the Model of Homer and Virgil; yet I can't help fancying if the fabulous part were a little more extended into descriptions and Speeches &c. it wou'd be of service: And from this very cause methinks that Book which Treats of the King's Love to Madam Gabrielle appears more of a Poem than the rest. Discord and Policy might certainly do and say something more, and so I judge of some other occasions for Invention and description which methinks are dropt too suddenly.

[1] *La Ligue* was first published in 1723. This letter of Pope's seems to have led to some correspondence with Voltaire. See Pope to Caryll, 25 Dec. 1725.

As to all the parts of the Work which relate to the actions or Sentiments of Men, or to Characters and Manners, they are undoubtedly excellent, and the *Fort* of the Poem. His Characters and Sentences are not like Lucans, too profess'd or formal and particularized, but full short and Judicious, and seem naturally to rise from an occasion either of telling what the Man *was*, or what he thought. It seems to me that his Judgment of Mankind, and his Observation of human Actions in a lofty and Philosophical view, is one of the principal Characteristicks of the Writer; who however is not less a Poet for being a Man of Sense, (as Seneca and his Nephew were.) Do not smile when I add, that I esteem him for that honest principled Spirit of true Religion which shines thro' the whole; and from whence (unknown as I am to Mr de Voltaire) I conclude him at once a Free thinker and a Lover of Quiet; no Bigot, but yet no Heretick: one who honours Authority and National Sanctions without prejudice to Truth or Charity; One who has Study'd Controversy less than Reason, and the Fathers less than Mankind; in a word, one worthy from his rational temper of that share of Friendship & Intimacy with which you honour him.[1] Notwithstanding you tell me of[2] the Oracles of our Lady of Lasource are ceas'd and that She returns no more answers, I shall expect the favour She promises to a poor Hermit on the banks of the Thames. In the mean time I see Visions of her and of Lasource.

> —An me ludit amabilis
> Insania, Audire et videor pios
> Errare per lucos, amœnæ
> Quos et aquæ subeunt et auræ.
> What pleasing Phrensy steals away my Soul?
> Thro' thy blest Shades (La Source) I seem to rove
> I see thy fountains full, thy waters roll
> And breath the Zephyrs that refresh thy Grove
> I hear what ever can delight inspire
> Villete's soft Voice and St John's silver Lyre.
> —Seu voce nunc mavis acuta
> Seu fidibus, cytharave Phœbi.

I cannot subscribe my self better than as Horace did.

> Vestris Amicum Fontibus et choris.[3]

---

[1] The scribe wrote *him notwithstanding* with no pause, punctuation, capital, or new paragraph. The change is the editor's.
[2] Elwin improves the text by changing *of* to *that*. *Of* is in the transcript.
[3] The Latin lines all come from Horace, *Carmina*, III. iv.

*JAMES PEARSE¹ to POPE   19 *April* 1724

Homer MSS. Add. 4809
                                              April 19th 1724

Mr Lant shewd me your Letter which by his Order I Have the
pleasure of answering The misffortune of all men of Business is that
they are never their own Masters at least very rarely, Wednesday in
the next week is the first day of our Term & by consequence wee
cannot Have the pleasure of waiting on you next tuesday but If your
Affairs give you Leave to be at your pretty place at Twitnam on this
day fortnight vizt the 2d of May & you will lett us wee shall depend
on the pleasure of waiting on you there in the mean time as always
I am | Sir | Your most obedient | Humble servant | James Pearse

Mr Lant is much your Humble servant. whenever you are pleased
to answer this direct for me the last House in Arundell street in the
strand

*MATHEW LANT² to POPE   20 *April* 1724

Homer MSS. Add. 4809

Sir,—I had return'd an answer to your letter I received ffriday if Mr
Pearse had not undertaken to doe it I shew'd him your letter and he
said Tuesday was the day before the Term and he could not possibly
wait on you but that if Saturday sennight would be convenient to you
he would desire it might be then and said he would write to you to that
purpose I am very sorry he did not and I hope it has not prevented
your doeing any thing else you intended I am | Sir | Your most
obedient servant | Mat Lant

Ap. the 20. | 1724

*POPE to MRS. CÆSAR   23 *April* [1724]

Rousham

Madam,—I obey you in sending 5 more of my Receipts;³ few people
obey so readily, as those who are rewarded for their Obedience; which

---

¹ Mr. Pearse was a member of the Inner Temple, possibly a partner or employee of Mathew
Lant. In 1729, if not earlier, Pearse was employed in the office of the Deputy Remembrancer.
See the letter of Mathew Lant, 20 Apr. 1724. The 19th was Sunday; hence possibly Mr.
Pearse misdated his letter. He seems to be writing on a Saturday.
² Mathew Lant was called to the Bench in the Inner Temple in 1717. Neither he nor his
fellow Templar James Pearse is normally Pope's attorney, and the letters seem to indicate
a social rather than a business connexion.
³ The indefatigable lady has by now secured seventeen subscribers for the *Odyssey*. See
also her letter to Pope, 10 Sept. 1723.

I find I am by You much above my merits. I am | Madam | Your most Obedient | humble Servant | A. Pope.

Twitnam, | Apr. 23d.

Address: To | Mrs Cæsar, in | Poland street | Present.

POPE *to* BROOME   24 *April* 1724

Elwin–Courthope, viii. 77

Twitnam, April 24, 1724.

The indolence of our friend obliges me to write at his request, though I have no time, and he a great deal. It is just to tell you, first from my-self, that I have received the eighth book, though I think it a great providence that I did so, for it came half-opened by the penny post. I beg you for the future to give better directions, or send by surer hands. The consequences would be very bad, if any accident should happen. Our friend has not yet done the fourth, and the work will stop for want of it, which vexes me. Your punctuality is commendable beyond all the power of my expression. The notes on the fifth are next wanted, for the verse goes to the press in a week or little more. I want you here to help to correct me. The sooner you come the better, but I agree with you, that it is necessary the fourth and fifth should be extracted first from Eustathius. Why should you not bring him up with you, and proceed here along with me? I will every day translate from the first of May. We may pass the morning together in study, the rest of the day in amusements, roving the fields, sailing on the waters, and, as you Cantabrigians call it, lounging in the shades. Twitnam is now in the highest beauty, How beautiful are those lines of Persius, and there are not many so, though there are many very sensible and philosophical.

> Tecum etenim longos memini consumere soles,
> Et tecum primas epulis decerpere noctes;
> Unum opus, et requiem, pariter disponimus ambo,
> Atque verecunda laxamus seria mensa.[1]

You have good luck if you can read this letter; I never was in more hurry, yet never more, dear sir, yours.

FENTON *to* BROOME   30 *April* 1724

Elwin–Courthope, viii. 78

April 30, 1724.

I am extremely sorry that your coming to town happens to be just when I shall leave it, for on Tuesday morning we set out for Windsor

---

[1] Persius, *Satires*, v. 41–44.

Forest. Mr. Robinson's lodgings are full, but I have writ to Lady Blount to let her servant be ready to wait your arrival at Lintot's on Wednesday. Order matters so that our friend[1] may go to Twickenham that day, for a masquerade is on the night following. Pray give my humble service to Mrs. Broome and all friends, and believe me to be ever most affectionately yours.

*POPE *to* JAMES PEARSE [2 *May* 1724]

Homer MSS. Add. 4809

Sir,—I was yesterday to wait on you and put you in mind of yours & Mr Lants kind engagement. It happening that I am in town, if you go in a Coach, I would have your company so much the longer, if you call at my lodgings at Mr Digby's next door to the Golden ball on the second Terras in St. James Street. Be pleasd to give the bearer a word in answer, or otherwise I will be before you at Twitnam ready with pleasure to receive you. I am with much esteem | Your most oblig'd | humble Servant | A. Pope.

Saturday morning 7 a clock.

Address (on detached leaf): To | James Pearse, Esqr.

*SIR PETER VANDEPUT *to* POPE[2] [1724]

Homer MSS. Add. 4809

Least there should be any mistake by Massages, this is to desire, that you, & Mrs Pope, would dine with us to morrow, there will be only Sir Clement & Dr Burscough. from | Sir | Your most affectionate & | humble Servant | Peter Vandeput

friday Evening

Address: To Mr Pope

*POPE *to* EDWARD, EARL OF OXFORD 22 *May* [1724]

Portland MSS. Harley xxxiv

Friday, May 22d

My Lord,—I came this day to town to wait on your Lordship with the pleasure I always have done; when I was met with the News[3] that

---

[1] 'Our friend' is young Blount, for whom masquerades and other amusements of the town were deemed dangerous.

[2] Neighbouring letters in the *Odyssey* MSS. indicate that probably this letter falls in the first half of 1724. Dr. Burscough was appointed chaplain to Lord Carteret, Lord Lieutenant of Ireland, on 4 Apr. 1724. Later in the year he became Dean of Lismore; but this letter may antedate that honour. Sir Peter lived in Twickenham, as did Sir Clement Cottrell. Lady Vandeput has been suggested as the lady whose death Pope (according to Welsted's 'lie') occasioned by compelling her to read repeatedly his *Iliad*! See D. A. Fineman, 'The Case of the Lady "Killed" by Alexander Pope', in *Modern Language Quarterly*, xii (1951), 137–47.

[3] Robert, Earl of Oxford, died on 21 May 1724.

turns it into an unfeigned Concern, I will venture to say As Sincere, tho in a less degree, as what I know you feel on this melancholy occasion. Tho indeed it is the End of Such a Life, as every one (but a son or a Friend) must much more admire, & venerate, than lament. For your Great Father is, without flattery, not *Now* more Above All Fears, Passions, & Interests, than he was when Living.

My Lord, I could not content the warmth of my heart with barely sending to your doors, to leave a Common Compliment. Pray excuse this breach of Decorum, which I am sensible I commit in writing to you. No man honourd the last Earl of Oxford more; no man loves the present better, than, | My Lord, | Your most faithfull, ever obligd Servant | A. Pope.

FENTON *to* BROOME

31 *May* 1724

Elwin–Courthope, viii. 79

Easthampstead, May 31, 1724.

Dear Mr. Broome,—Your London journey was very unfortunately timed. If it had suited with your affairs to have come but one week sooner, I had proposed to have spent two or three days in my hermitage at Twickenham[1] to have enjoyed your company. It was unkind in you not to recompense the disappointment with a visit into Windsor Forest, where you would have found me in a delicious retirement, man and horse in full health, and ready to have waited on you to Mr. Pope's old grove, which is about two miles distant, to catch the Muse soft whispering through the trees, as Homer says. That old gentleman's name brings another subject to consideration.

I was encouraged by your letter to expect Sir Clement here last week, but I believe the birthday prevented his coming;[2] so I sent a footman this morning to Mr. Pope with the fourth book complete, being sensible that I had trespassed too long on his patience. I sent him word that I had fixed on the nineteenth and twentieth books, which I hope I shall not be long in conquering. I have finished almost a third part of the former. The latter I take in pure compliance with your aversion to it. How I shall get over the bitch and her puppies, the roasting of the black puddings, as Brault translated it, and the cowheel that was thrown at Ulysses' head, I know not.[3] But, though I have Sussex ways to walk in, I thank my stars they are not measured by the Yorkshire scale, which I think is a very proper allusion when (I know you love a pun) I am talking of journey work.

[1] He means a lodging which he sometimes took at the house of one Mr. Hutchins.—Elwin.

[2] As Master of Ceremonies Sir Clement would be at Court for the royal birthday on 28 May.

[3] The comment is a good example of the fear timid poets had of 'lowness' in Fenton's day.

I am sorry to hear you give up yourself so much to retirement. Believe me, dear Broome, it will impair your health and good-humour sooner than you imagine. I often wish that providence had made us nearer neighbors, that I might now and then raise your envy and admiration with my quibbles. I really think my own constitution is not so good since I have put a violence upon it by suppressing them. That tyrant custom should make free-born man subject to such an unnatural and painful restraint!

Old Southerne[1] was extremely pleased with your compliment, and would have spent this summer with you if he had not been previously engaged to Lady Scudamore. He promised Lady Judith to pass some weeks here before he went into Herefordshire, but I have heard nothing of him since I left London. The last packet I received from thence surprised me with a sad account of poor landlord Robinson's sudden death,—merry and dead in two hours. I desire you to direct your letters for the future to be left for me with Mr. Moore, at Mr. Taylor's, a chandler in Frith Street, near St. Ann's Church, Soho, and they will come with my lady's letters.

In your last, you gave me no account what was become of Mr. Blount. I bid the footman wait upon the family to-day with my compliments, but he is not yet returned. You never give me any memoirs of Norfolk and Suffolk, where I hope I have, to speak in your own language, a sort of friends, to whom I desire you to neglect no opportunity of making my services acceptable, especially to your own family and Mr. Stebbing.[2] Pray, thank him for his book, which I had read with great satisfaction before I received his present by Mr. Tonson's money-catching hand. And if these topics are not sufficient to furnish out a long epistle, take me down the map of Berkshire and having traced out the very nearest way from hence to Mr. Marriott's, send me a geographical draft thereof, that when I have nothing else to do I may find him out. Well, dear Broome, good night,—not that it is bed-time, but a fine hot gloomy sky, and a swarm of bees that have just settled under my window, conspire with my own dulness to lull me asleep.

Molli languore solutum
Deposuitque caput, stratoque recondidit alto.[3]

Yours most sincerely.

---

[1] Thomas Southerne (1660–1746), the prosperous dramatist, had many friends in Pope's circle.

[2] Henry Stebbing (1687–1763), a Cambridge friend of Broome's, published in 1724 *An Essay concerning Civil Government, considered as it stands related to Religion*.

[3] Ovid, *Metamorphoses*, xi. 648–9.

*POPE *to* MRS. CÆSAR   1 *June* [1724]

Rousham MSS.

Madam,—I know You to be sincere in your concern for the Loss of this Great Man,¹ & therfore you will believe me so. The Degree of friendship with which he honourd me, tho I will not call it a great one, is one I shall never forget. I believe we shall always concurr in our Concerns, & in our Satisfactions; as well as in our Esteem or Disesteem of Men & Manners. The World is not worth living in, if all that are good in it, leave it for a better. Pray think me | Your very much obligd & | faithfull Servant | A. Pope.

Twitnam | June 1st

I beg my most humble services to Mr Cæsar; and pray tell Mrs Madan,² that I sit down by the River, & weep, till she returns; & when they bid me sing, I reply, How can I sing a Song, when She is in a strange Land?

Address: For | Mrs Cæsar.

†**POPE *to* MARTHA BLOUNT**   [15 *June* 1724]³

1737

This is a day of wishes for you, and I hope you have long known, there is not one good one which I do not form in your behalf. Every year that passes, I wish some things more for my friends, and some things less for myself. Yet were I to tell you what I wish for you in particular, it wou'd be only to repeat in prose, what I told you last year in rhyme;³ (so sincere is my poetry:) I can only add, that as I then wish'd you a friend, I now wish that friend were Mrs. ——⁴

Absence is a short kind of death; and in either, one can only wish, that the friends we are separated from, may be happy with those that are left them. I am therefore very sollicitous that you may pass much agreeable time together: I am sorry to say I envy you no other companion; tho' I hope you have others that you like; and I am always pleas'd in that hope, when it is not attended with any fears on your own account.

¹ Robert, Earl of Oxford. Mr. Cæsar had been Treasurer of the Navy, and there was a considerable intimacy between the two families.

² Judith Cowper had been married to Captain Martin Madan late in 1723. Pope's tone in speaking of her seems unchanged, and he probably continued to write to her occasionally, though no letters postdating the marriage are known.

³ The day is determined by the fact that Pope writes on Miss Blount's birthday; the year by his mention of 'what I told you *last year* in rhyme'. At Mapledurham, among Pope's letters to Teresa and Martha, is preserved the page of verse, 'Written, June the 15th. On Your Birth-Day. 1723.' On the history of the lines see N. Ault, *New Light*, pp. 195–206.

⁴ Mrs. —— is presumably Mrs. Howard.

I was troubled to leave you both,[1] just as I fancy'd we should begin to live together in the country. 'Twas a little like dying the moment one had got all one desir'd in this world. Yet I go away with one generous sort of satisfaction, that what I part with, you are to inherit.

I know you wou'd both be pleas'd to hear some certain news of a friend departed; to have the adventures of his passage, and the new regions thro' which he travell'd, describ'd; and upon the whole, to know, that he is as happy where he now is, as while he liv'd among you. But indeed I (like many a poor unprepar'd soul) have seen nothing I like so well as what I left: No scenes of paradise, no happy bowers, equal to those on the banks of the Thames. Wherever I wander, one reflection strikes me: I wish you were as free as I; or at least had a tye as tender, and as reasonable as mine, to a relation that as well deserv'd your constant thought, and to whom you wou'd always be pull'd back (in such a manner as I am) by the heart-string. I have never been well since I set out; but don't tell my Mother so; it will trouble her too much: And as probably the same reason may prevent her sending a true account of her health to me, I must desire you to acquaint me. I wou'd gladly hear the country air improves your own; but don't flatter me when you are ill, that I may be the better satisfy'd when you say you are well: for these are things in which one may be sincerer to a reasonable friend, than to a fond and partial parent. Adieu.

POPE *to* [MARTHA] BLOUNT[2]　　　　　　22 *June* [1724?]

Mapledurham

June 22'd

Madam,—I promis'd you an account of Sherborne, before I had seen it, or knew what I undertook. I imagin'd it to be one of those fine old Seats of which there are Numbers scatter'd over England. But this is so peculiar and its Situation of so uncommon a kind, that it merits a more particular description.

The House is in the form of an H. The body of it, which was built by Sir Walter Rawleigh, consists of four Stories, with four six-angled Towers at the ends. These have since been join'd to four Wings, with a regular Stone Balustrade at the top & four towers more that finish the building. The Windows & Gates are of a yellow Stone throughout, and one of the flatt Sides toward the Garden has the wings of a newer Architecture with beautiful Italian Window-frames done by the first

---

[1] While Pope rambles off to Sherborne to see the Digbys, Miss Blount is staying with his mother. Pope returned about the beginning of July. See Pope to Broome, 4 July.

[2] The year of Pope's visit to Lord Digby's family at Sherborne is difficult to determine. The few letters concerning it have by other editors been placed in 1722. The present placing of them in 1724 seems definitely preferable, but perhaps not absolutely sure.

Earl of Bristol, which, if they were joind in the middle by a Portico covering the Old Building, would be a noble Front. The design of such an one I have been amusing myself with drawing, but tis a question whether my Lord Digby will not be better amus'd than to execute it. The finest room is a Salon 50 ft. long, & a Parlor hung with very excellent Tapistry of Rubens, which was a present from the King of Spain to the E. of Bristol in his Ambassy there.

This stands in a Park, finely crownd with very high Woods, on all the tops of the Hills, which form a great Amfitheatre sloping down to the house. On the Garden Sides the Woods approach close, so that it appears there with a thick Line & Depth of Groves on each hand, & so it shows from most parts of the Park. The Gardens are so Irregular, that tis very hard to give an exact idea of 'em but by a Plan. Their beauty rises from this Irregularity, for not only the Several parts of the Garden itself make the better Contraste by these sudden Rises, Falls, and Turns of ground; but the Views about it are lett in, & hang over the Walls, in very different figures and aspects. You come first out of the house into a green Walk of Standard Lymes with a hedge behind them that makes a Colonnade, thence into a little triangular wilderness, from whose Centre you see the town of Sherborne in a valley, interspersd with trees. From the corner of this you issue at once upon a high green Terras the whole breadth of the Garden, which has five more green Terras's hanging under each other, without hedges, only a few pyramid yews & large round Honisuckles between them. The Honisuckles hereabouts are the largest & finest I ever saw. You'l be pleasd when I tell you the Quarters of the above mentiond little Wilderness are filld with these & with Cherry trees of the best kinds all within reach of the hand. At the ends of these Terras's run two long Walks under the Side walls of the Garden which communicate with the other Terras's that front these opposite. Between, the Vally is layd level and divided into two regular Groves of Horse chestnuts, and a Bowling-green in the middle of about 180 foot. This is bounded behind with a Canall, that runs quite across the Groves & also along one Side, in the form of a T. Behind this, is a Semicircular Berceau, and a Thicket of mixd trees that compleats the Crown of the Amfitheatre which is of equal extent with the Bowling-green. Beyond that runs a natural River thro green banks of turf, over which rises another Row of Terras's, the first supported by a slope Wall planted with Vines (So is also the Wall that bounds the channel of the river.) A second & third appeard above this, but they are to be turnd into a Line of Wilderness with wild winding walks for the convenience of passing from one side to the other in Shade, the heads of whose trees will lye below the uppermost Terras of all, which compleats the Garden and overlooks both that & the Country. Even above the wall of this the natural Ground rises, & is crownd with several venerable Ruins of an Old Castle, with Arches & broken views, of which I must say more hereafter.

When you are at the left corner of the Canal and the Chesnut groves in the bottome, you turn of a sudden under very old trees into the deepest Shade. One walk winds you up a Hill of venerable Wood over-archd by nature, & of a vast height, into a circular Grove, on one side of which is a close high Arbour, on the other a sudden open Seat that overlooks the Meadows & river with a large distant prospect. Another walk under this hill winds by the River side quite coverd with high Trees on both banks, over hung with Ivy, where falls a natural Cascade with never-ceasing murmurs. On the opposite hanging of the Bank (which is a Steep of 50 ft) is plac'd, with a very fine fancy, a Rustick Seat of Stone, flaggd and rough, with two Urns in the same rude taste upon pedestals, on each side: from whence you lose your eyes upon the glimmering of the Waters under the wood, & your ears in the constant dashing of the waves. In view of this, is a Bridge that crosses this Stream, built in the same ruinous taste: the Wall of the Garden hanging over it, is humourd so as to appear the Ruin of another Arch or two above the bridge. Hence you mount the Hill over the Hermits Seat (as they call it) describd before, & so to the highest Terras, again.

On the left, full behind these old Trees, which make this whole Part inexpressibly awful & solemn, runs a little, old, low wall, beside a Trench, coverd with Elder trees & Ivyes; which being crost by another bridge, brings you to the Ruins, to compleat the Solemnity of the Scene. You first see an old Tower penetrated by a large Arch, and others above it thro which the whole Country appears in prospect, even when you are at the top of the other ruins, for they stand very high, & the Ground slopes down on all sides. These venerable broken Walls, some Arches almost entire of 30 or 40 ft deep, some open like Portico's with fragments of pillars, some circular or inclosd on three sides, but exposd at top, with Steps which Time has made of disjointed Stones to climb to the highest points of the Ruin: These I say might have a prodigious Beauty, mixd with Greens & Parterres from part to part, and the whole Heap standing as it does on a round hill, kept smooth in green turf, which makes a bold Basement to show it. The open Courts from building to building might be thrown into Circles or Octagons of Grass or flowers, and even in the gaming Rooms you have fine trees grown, that might be made a natural Tapistry to the walls, & arch you over-head where time has uncoverd them to the Sky. Little paths of earth, or sand, might be made, up the half-tumbled walls; to guide from one View to another on the higher parts; & Seats placd here and there, to enjoy those views, which are more romantick than Imagination can form them. I could very much wish this were done, as well as a little Temple built on a neighboring round Hill that is seen from all points of the Garden & is extremely pretty. It would finish some Walks, & particularly be a fine Termination to the River to be seen from the Entrance into that Deep Scene I have describd by the Cascade where it would appear as in the clouds, between the tops of some very lofty Trees that form an Arch before it, with a great Slope downward to the end of the said river.

What should induce my Lord D. the rather to cultivate these ruins and do honour to them, is that they do no small honour to his Family; that Castle, which was very ancient, being demolishd in the Civil wars after it was nobly defended by one of his Ancestors in the cause of the King. I would sett up at the Entrance of 'em an Obelisk, with an inscription of the Fact: which would be a Monument erected to the very Ruins; as the adorning & beautifying them in the manner I have been imagining, would not be unlike the Ægyptian Finery of bestowing Ornament and curiosity on dead bodies. The Present Master of this place (and I verily believe I can ingage the same for the next Successors) needs not to fear the Record,[1] or shun the Remembrance of the actions of his Forefathers. He will not disgrace them, as most Modern Progeny do, by an unworthy Degeneracy, of principle, or of Practise. When I have been describing his agreable Seat, I cannot make the reflection I've often done upon contemplating the beautiful Villa's of Other Noblemen, raisd upon the Spoils of plunderd nations, or aggrandiz'd by the wealth of the Publick. I cannot ask myself the question, 'What Else has this man to be lik'd? what else has he cultivated or improv'd? What good, or what desireable thing appears of him, without these walls? I dare say his Goodness and Benevolence extend as far as his territories; that his Tenants live almost as happy & contented as himself; & that not one of his Children wishes to see this Seat his owne. I have not lookd much about, since I was here: All I can tell you of my own knowledge is, that going to see the Cathedral in the town hard by, I took notice as the finest things, of a noble Monument and a beautiful Altar-piece of Architecture; but if I had not inquird in particular, he nor his, had ever told me that both the one & the other was erected by Himself: The next pretty thing that catchd my eye was a neat Chappel for the use of the Towns-people, (who are too numerous for the Cathedral) My Lord modestly told me, he was glad I lik't it, because it was of his own architecture.

[1] This seems to refer to the 'strange curse belonging to Shireburne Castle'. St. Osmund, Bishop of Sarum, gave the castle and other lands to the bishopric, 'to which Gift he annexed this Curse, "That whosoever should take those Lands from the Bishoprick, or diminish them in great or in small, should be accursed, not only in this World, but also in the World to come; unless, in his Life-Time he made Restitution thereof." '—Elwin, and Francis Peck, *Desiderata Curiosa*, ii, lib. xiv, pp. 5, 6.

I hope this long letter will be some Entertainment to you, I was pleased not a little in writing it; but don't let any Lady from hence imagine that my head is so full of any Gardens as to forget hers.[1] The greatest proof I could give her to the contrary is, that I have spent many hours here in studying for hers, & in drawing new plans for her. I shall soon come home, & have nothing to say when we meet, having here told you all that has pleas'd me: But Wilton is in my way, & I depend upon that for new matter. Believe me ever yours, with a sincerity as old-fashiond, and as different from Modern Sincerity, as This house, this family, & these ruins, are from the Court, & all its Neighbourhood. | Dear Madam, Adieu.

†POPE *to* ROBERT DIGBY[2]   [*27 June* 1724?]

1735
                                                            Saturday night.

I have belief enough in the goodness of your whole family, to think you will all be pleas'd that I am arriv'd in safety at *Twickenham*; tho' 'tis a sort of Earnest, that you will be troubled again with me at *Sherborne*, or *Coleshill*; for however I may like One of your places, it may be in that as in liking One of your family; when one sees the rest, one likes them all. Pray make my services acceptable to them; I wish them all the happiness they may want, and the continuance of all the happiness they have; and I take the latter to comprize a great deal more than the former. I must separate Lady *Scudamore* from you, as I fear she will do herself, before this letter reaches you: So I wish her a good journey, and I hope one day to try if she lives as well as you do; tho' I much question if she can live as quietly:[3] I suspect the Bells will be ringing at her arrival, and on her own and Miss *Scudamore's* birthdays, and that all the Clergy in the County come to pay respects; both the Clergy and their Bells expecting from her, and from the young lady, further business, and further employment. Besides all this, there dwells on the one side of her the Lord *Coningsby*, and on the other Mr. *W*— Yet I shall, when the Days and the Years come about, adventure upon all this for her sake.

I beg my Lord *Digby* to think me a better Man than to content myself with the thanking him in the common way. I am in as sincere a sense of the word, His Servant, as you are his Son, or he your Father.

---

[1] Referring to Mrs. Howard and Marble Hill.

[2] On 4 July (a Saturday) Pope writes to Broome that he has returned 'but two days since'. Since he is here writing on an antecedent Saturday, one assumes it is 27 June, and that his 'two days' is a loosely false statement, excusing a delay in writing.

[3] Pope was accompanied as far as Clarendon (?) by young ladies of the Digby family. Lady Scudamore is apparently expected to return soon to Holm Lacy. Lord Coningsby lived not far from Holm Lacy at Hampton Court, Herefordshire. Mr. *W*— is unidentified.

I must in my turn insist upon hearing how my last fellow-travellers got home from *Clarendon*, and desire Mr *Philips* to remember me in his Cyder, and to tell Mr. W— that I am dead and buried.

I wish the young Ladies, whom I almost robb'd of their good Name, a better Name in return (even that very name to each of them, which they like best for the sake of the Man that bears it.) | Your ever faithful | and affectionate Servant.

POPE *to* BROOME¹   4 *July* [1724]

Elwin–Courthope, viii. 81

Twitnam, July 4 [1724].

I am well got home, but two days since, from my Dorsetshire journey, and have only a moment's time to thank you for yours, and to tell you I have obeyed your orders in buying three lottery tickets. The price was at 11*l*. 7*s*. each. I believe it will be just the same thing if I send you only the numbers of them, and keep the receipts for you till you can have the receipts themselves by a safe hand. Or if you would have them sent, I will. I am with all affection, sir, your faithful affectionate friend and servant.

I have seen Fenton. He is better than ever I knew him.

POPE *to* FORTESCUE²   [*July* 1724?]

Harvard University

I have been twice or thrice at your door, but found it lockd, and was told since you were gone into the Country, which (till I met your man this morning) I took to be Devonshire. I rejoyce at your being still among us, as at a Friend's being alive, whom one had thought departed. I very earnestly desire you to spend a day or two at Twitnam, I shall be there to night, for some days. Pray don't deny that favour to | Your faithfull | obligd affectionate | Servant | A. Pope.

Saturday.
Gay is, and | will be, at | Chiswick

Address: To Wm Fortescue Esq.

¹ Succeeding letters to Broome mentioning the lottery tickets make the year certain. If the year is 1724, the visit to Sherborne must also have taken place in 1724 (as the present editor thinks) and not in 1722, as Elwin thought.
² Not surely datable, this letter *may* have been written in the summer of 1724 before Fortescue started on his 'circuiteering'. For various reasons, chiefly connected with Gay and Chiswick, it could hardly come in a later summer. Gay was with Lord Burlington.

POPE *to* FORTESCUE[1]   [*July* 1724?]

Harvard University

Mrs Howard will be glad to see you either Thursday or Friday, which suits your Conveniency, but it must be at the hour of eleven, (as I fancyd before) & not sooner. I shall be glad to have you in your Whole Self, i.e. your family & posterity, dine here that day, and will not meet therfore at Richmond where you would be alone with her, but attend the Ladies here, at any hour you'l direct. I thank you for your last kind visit, & am sincerely Dear Sir | Your affect. Friend and | obligd Servant | A. Pope.

Address: To Wm Fortescue Esqr at | his house in Bell-yard | near | Lincolns-inn. | London.

POPE *to* MRS. NEWSHAM[2]   9 *July* [1724]

Bowles (1806), x. 93

Twitenham, July 9th.

Madam,—You would have had a very free companion and correspondent of me, and have inherited that open and unreserved behaviour, which I both learned from your brother, and practised to him: But the day that you passed at Twitnam, you did a thing that took away all my liberty, and made me a much less easy acquaintance than I hoped to have been to you. Methinks this period looks like a love-letter, to tell a lady she has taken away my liberty: But you'll understand it in a more serious sense: and I assure you, I am, instead of your friend, so much your enemy for this, that I will live to be revenged of you. And in the mean time (like one that is very much intent upon revenge), I will say not a word more about it, but seem entirely to forget it.

The Italian sculptor has not yet finished his clay model.[3] Indeed, it is a vast disadvantage as to the likeness, not to be able to see the life.

---

1 This undatable letter must fall at a time when Fortescue was in London and Mrs. Howard (i.e. the Court) was at Richmond. July 1724 is such a time. Obviously there were many others.

2 The three letters of Pope to Mrs. Newsham which Elwin placed in 1727 (those of 9 July, 8 Aug., and 13 Oct.) can hardly be later than 1724. They cannot, on the other hand, antedate the death of Secretary Craggs, Mrs. Newsham's brother, whose monument in the Abbey they concern. *The Daily Journal*, 12 June 1727, speaks of the monument as about to be 'opened', and in the three letters under consideration the monument is still in the stage of design only. Mr. Newsham died 21 Nov. 1724, and Elwin was compelled to assume that the reiterated concern over 'Mr. Newsham's' health referred to the lady's son—who was in 1727 about 12 years old. It seems probable that the monument was designed in 1724, slowly executed, and unveiled in June 1727. It is possible that the three letters should fall in 1723; the year 1722 is improbable.

3 This statement is impossible for a date of 1727. The sculptor was Giovanni Battista Guelfi, who worked in England as a protégé of Lord Burlington, 1714–34. Towards the end of his stay his reputation declined. See the Vertue *Diaries* (Walpole Society), v. 115–17.

What would not you and I give that that were possible? But at last, by comparing the two other pictures and the print, (together with my own memory of the features of that friend who had often looked so kindly upon me,) he has brought it to a greater degree of resemblance than I could have thought. If you happened to come to town, I could wish you saw the model yet, before the marble be begun: for if you were not satisfied, I would have another sculptor make a model in clay after the pictures, for a further chance of likeness: If the artist were a worse carver than this man, yet it might be a help to improve his Statue in this respect (since all the rest he cannot fail to perform excellently). I am really in pain to have you pleased, in a point that I am sure is a tender one, since it is all you can do for the best of brothers, and I for the best of friends!

What can I write to you about? Of him, we think alike, and (I dare say) we shall think always. His very memory more engages my mind, than the present enjoyment of almost all that remains in the world to strike my senses. These things appear but as a dream, and that as a reality. A friend gone, is like youth gone, never to be recalled, and leaves all that follows insipid and spiritless.

I'll add no more upon this subject, though I know we shall never meet, or perhaps never write, without repetition of this kind. I heartily wish well to all that he would have wished well to, had he been yet among us. The wound is eternal, but it is some ease to us to give it air, by shewing it to one another, and pitying one another. I hope to hear from you at your leisure, and be assured, as the only reasonable motive you can have for your favour to me, that you cannot correspond with one more his admirer, his lover, and deplorer, than, | Madam, etc.

My humble services[1] to Mr. Newsham. My Mother begs your acceptance of hers.

EDWARD[2] DIGBY *to* POPE   18 *July* 1724

Homer MSS. Add. 4809

Sherborne July 18 1724

I am sure this will want no Excuse to you; for it carries good News of a friend. My Brother has not had any fit of his Ague, since Sunday last: he has slept a little every night, but with some interruptions by the Cramp

---

[1] It is hard to believe that Pope was sending 'humble services' to a lad of twelve years—as he must have been if the letter dates from 1727. The boy's father is more probable.
[2] Published in the *Supplemental Volume to the Works of Pope* (1825) and by Elwin as from Miss E[lizabeth] Digby, the second daughter of Lord Digby; but since she had in 1720 been married (see *The Weekly Packet*, 6 Aug. 1720) to Dr. John Dolben (in 1722 *Sir* John), the writer seems more probably to have been Robert's brother Edward.

Last night he began to drink Asses Milk, which had it's usual Effect, in giving him a good night's rest, & free from Pain. I am, Dear Sir, in great haste but with great Truth | Your Friend & Servant | E Digby

All here are your Servants

FENTON *to* BROOME   19 *July* 1724

Elwin–Courthope, viii. 82

Easthampstead Park, July 19, 1724.

Dear Mr. Broome,—I have finished the nineteenth Odyssey, and after I have completed the index for Shakespeare,[1] I intend to proceed to the next, and if that does not break my heart, I have marked the twenty-second for another.[2] I must beg the favour of you to send me an abstract of what Eustathius says on the 573 verse, etc. of the twentieth book. Our old friend Joshua[3] leaves me in the lurch with a κ.τ.λ., and refers to the 714th p. line 17 of the same edition that I think you have.

Another small affair comes into my thoughts, which I must take the liberty to recommend to your care, and that is to procure Lady Rich's Life for me from Mr. John Briars.[4] I employed Mr. Brown all last winter to procure it for some service it will be of to me if I undertake a new edition of Waller,[5] which Tonson mentioned again to me before I left London, and I did not refuse his proposal. I know Mr. Briars is an uncertain man, but when you happen to see him, do not forget me.

I am encouraged to turn over the leaf of the laudable account you gave of the length of my last in your letter to Mr. Pope, which he showed me here in his way from Devonshire[6] to Twickenham, about three weeks since. Our friend Sir Clement has likewise paid Lady Judith a visit since I wrote last, and wonders that you have not sent him the verses you promised. Mr. Blount, he told me, continued still at his father's, he believed very much to his own satisfaction, but by the account he gave of a sword, which might measure blades with the longest Spanish espada in Madrid, I fancy he has some direful apprehension, but I hope more asleep than awake.

[1] Obviously Fenton did a considerable amount of work on Pope's edition of Shakespeare. In his *Lit. Anec.* v. 597, Nichols (quoting from *The Gentleman's Magazine*) indicates that Fenton was paid £30. 14s. for his work. On Pope's letter to Tonson of 3 Sept. [1721] the publisher indicated an *additional* payment to Fenton of £25, a fact which somewhat undermines confidence in the figures given in *The Gentleman's Magazine*.

[2] Fenton's heart failed him, and Pope did Book XXII.

[3] Joshua Barnes's edition of Homer (1711) was much used at this time in spite of adverse comments on it by Bentley and others.

[4] Mr. Briars was rector of Diss, in Norfolk.—Elwin. He evidently furnished data on Lady Rich for Fenton's edition of Waller.   [5] Fenton's edition of Waller appeared in 1729.

[6] A slip of the pen for Dorsetshire.—Elwin.

I am very sensible of my old friend Mr. Newcome's kindness,[1] and of the great honour the Duke of Wharton did me in inquiring after my welfare, but why did you not make that part of your letter still more agreeable by informing me of Mr. Holt's good health,[2] for whom you know I have both by inclination and gratitude the sincerest esteem imaginable. Not a word of Lady Jane neither. I have as much devotion for her ladyship as you, Mr. Broome, but I cannot conceive that her name, like the Jews' Tetragrammaton, ought not to be mentioned.

The latter end of September is, I think, fixed for our return to Leicester Fields, where I hope I shall not be disappointed of seeing you. In the meantime, let me hear often from you, and depend on my maintaining a punctual correspondence. I am grown an extravagant letter-writer. This is the fourth I have penned to day, and I think some years have passed with a less number. *Tempora mutantur*, says my almanac very truly, but nothing can be falser than the other half of the verse, when applied to the sincerity with which I am ever your affectionate humble servant.

My service as usual.

FORTESCUE *to* POPE

25 *July* 1724

Homer MSS. Add. 4809

FRAGMENT

to Mrs Blounts let me Know it: let me Know[   ] or
Gay shall be in Town to day or to morrow [   ]
    I am in great Hast, Dear Sir, | Your most sincere [   ] | Friend
& servant.

Inner Temple | July 25th 1724.

    P.S. My sister & Miss Fortescue join [   ] best thanks & services
to Mrs Pope & [   ]mendations likewise to Gay, & desire [   ]
~~the Great~~ Barnstaple & the Great B[   ]

POPE to JOHN DRUMMOND

1 *August* 1724

1885 *Hist. MSS. Comm., Report X*, App. 1, p. 153

Twitnam, August 1st 1724.

Sir,—I ought to acknowledge the obliging disposition which Dr Arbuthnot tells me you were pleas'd to show of favoring a request of

---

[1] John Newcome (1683–1765), fellow of St. John's, later Master of the College and Dean of Rochester.—Elwin.

[2] Mr. Holt was the nephew and heir of Lord Chief Justice Holt. He resided at Redgrave, in the neighbourhood of Sturston, . . . [he] was married in the preceding year to Lady Jane Wharton, sister to the Duke of Wharton.—Elwin.

mine in behalf of a nephew[1] who has been bred a sailor and made four
or five voyages. His desire is to be recommended as a second or third
mate in an East India Merchantman. I know him to be a very industrious sober and well dispos'd lad; and hope when you do me the
favour to examine him he will not be found wanting in the knowledge
of his profession any more than I am sure I shall in the sense of your
intended obligation to him, who is (with respect and sincerity), Sir, |
Your most obedient and most humble servant | A. Pope.

Address: To John Drummond Esq. Director of the East India Company at
Norfolk Street in the Strand.

POPE *to* MRS. NEWSHAM[2]　　　　　　　　　8 *August* [1724]

Bowles (1806), X, 95　　　　　　　　　　　　　　Twitenham, Aug. 8.

Madam,—I should not tell you I have been so disagreeably employed
as in taking care of my own health, (which too much sickness makes
me value more than otherwise I would,) if I did not really believe you
intend to have some concern about me, and that therefore I owe you
some apology for writing no sooner, to one who wishes me so well. I
have no answer to make to one part of yours, but that your manner
of doing things does not (nor did in the instance I mentioned) displease
me, it is so like your own brother's manners, and nothing like him
can ever displease me. But, you will yet more oblige me, if you will
let me use you as I did him, and transfer a part of the favours you
designed me, to the benefit of some objects I may recommend to you:
whom one sort of favours may make happier; though the other, of
friendliness and good-will, I covet from you, and would not give a
grain of as much as you allow me from myself. I have met with an
object of extreme charity, to whom I will venture to give some of the
money you have left in my hands: whose story I will take another
time to tell you, and only now say, that if your brother had lived, she
would not have wanted relief. I have paid but as far yet as 60*l*. to the
Statuary: the model I begin to be satisfied with, and he is to proceed[3]
upon the Statue forthwith. You are very just to me in your thoughts
of that affection that will prompt me in every thing relating to him.
But I must also think you are very kind in them: In this age, Justice is
Kindness. Yet I doubt not your mind is of a better sort, as his was,

---

　¹ John Rackett was Pope's sailor nephew.
　² This letter is transferred from 1727, where Elwin placed it, chiefly as part of a sequence.
See Pope to Mrs. Newsham, 9 July and 13 Oct. of this year. Evidently at Twickenham
before 9 July the lady had bound Pope, by an excessive sum of money, to procure her brother's
monument.
　³ Proceed, that is, to model the statue. The marble is not yet procured. See Pope to Mrs.
Newsham, 13 Oct. 1724.

and forward to judge favourably of such, as on any account deserve regard or belief. I shall use no ceremonial with you, on no occasion, but take you for what you are pleased to profess yourself toward me: and only assure you I shall think, (if ever I found myself tempted to be too complaisant, or in the least degree insincere to you,) that I am offending the remains of the sincerest man I ever knew in the world, and growing ungrateful to him after his death.

Believe me therefore, Madam, sensible of the obligation of being thought well of, and yet more sensible of that which occasioned your good opinion, your tenderness for him, and your acquiescence in his judgment, which was so favourable (indeed so partial) to me. In a word, I esteem you more for loving him, than for liking me; nay, I not only esteem, but love you the more for that very reason: and I will be always, dear Madam,

Yours, etc.

Pray desire Mr. Newsham to accept my services. I hope the young gentleman is well.[1]

WILLIAM PULTENEY *to* POPE[2]　　　13 *August* 1724

Homer MSS. Add. 4809

I cannot call upon you as I promised in my way to Ashley, My Lord Berkeley having sent to me to come to Cranford to him, upon some business; after a day or two there, I shall go to Causham, & then return to Ashley about the 25th, when I shall be extremely obliged to you, ~~to~~ if you will lett me have the honour of your Company for a week; & I will send my Coach for you or come & fetch you my self | I am Sir | Your most Obedient humble | Servant | Wm Pulteney

Arlington street | Augt 13th 1724

POPE *to* BROOME　　　16 *August* [1724]

Elwin–Courthope, viii. 84

Aug. 16 [1724].

Dear Broome,—You charge me, in the appearance very justly, of being a bad correspondent, but in reality, I am not so. Put your leisure hours, and mine, into the balance, and I employ as much of them to write to my friends as I can possibly—only you have more of

---

[1] The two sentences of the postscript refer respectively to Mrs. Newsham's husband and her nine-year-old son.

[2] Pulteney, later Earl of Bath, was early a friend of John Gay, and is now seen as friendly to Pope. His dubious alliance with Bolingbroke in opposition to Sir Robert Walpole was yet to come.

them. Ill-health has been of late added to the account and almost put a stop at present to my writing of all sorts. Let this misfortune of mine be a spur to your diligence, and may you never have the same excuse for being inactive as I have; for I sincerely wish you, dear sir, long health and life. I have never had one word from Fenton.

Be in no pain about any debt you fancy you have, or any commission of money affairs relating to me. You have a right to the lottery tickets, which I set on account as your own; and I before told you that whatever subscriptions your own interest can procure, I look upon as your own money. Therefore enrich yourself as fast as you can that way, as I will do on my part by my particular interest with others.[1] The notes you cannot do too soon for me. Those for the eighth will be wanted,—those of the fourth and sixth being just done. I will send them printed to you very speedily.[2] Pray did you not take the second volume of Dacier[3] along with you from hence, for I can nowhere find it? But I will not fail to consult the passage. Maximus Tyrius[4] I can nowhere procure.

I must send you the good wishes of a friend to your family, not forgetting your very poultry, and hogs, for Eumæus[5] puts me horribly in mind of them. I never laboured through anything so heavily, and have undertaken I know not what. If your notes do not make amends for my translation of that book, the reader may sleep as I am just now ready to do; for it is late at night, and I am as tired of the day as any labourer ever was. Believe me in all circumstances, dear sir, yours affectionately.

POPE *to* LINTOT[6]   [1724]

Homer MSS. Add. 4809

Sir,—Pray send Mr Broom the Sheets of all the notes from the first, that are printed. that he may avoid the repetitions &c. but I would not have the Poetry sent, knowing the consequences of its being shown about to every body, before it's publishd; which I will not have done: nor (I suppose) would You. | I am always | Yours | A. Pope

[*Address*:] To Mr Lintot.

---

[1] There is little evidence that Pope treated his collaborators parsimoniously; but Broome and Fenton evidently might find it difficult to secure subscribers if prohibited from explaining their real connexion with the project. They seem to have made little effort to get subscribers.

[2] See Pope's letter to Lintot (also on this page).

[3] Mme Dacier's translation of the *Odyssey* (1716) was in three volumes.

[4] Maximus Tyrius wrote a Dissertation on Homer, which, as Elwin suggests, is doubtless what Broome wished to read.

[5] The reference to Eumæus suggests that Pope is working on Book XIV.

[6] The placing of this letter in the Homer MSS. indicates that it was written in the summer of 1724. On the back of it part of *Odyssey* ix is translated.

BOLINGBROKE *to* POPE[1]   18 *August* 1724

Longleat Portland Papers, xiii (Harleian transcripts)

Augt 18th 1724.

You have delay'd Writing to me in Expectation of one Person's departure from London, and I have put off Answering your letter several
Posts in expectation of the same persons Arrival here. I wanted to
know whether She understood you as little as you say that you understood her,[2] if She did so Sir W. Wyndham is an excellent interpreter,
and none of the Spirit of your Conversation has been lost in the trans-
fusion from one Language to another. For the impressions which you
have made on her are exactly those which I have been so long acquainted with, et qui sont Marquees à votre coin.

You are likely I find, as much as her presence vexes You, to be
troubled with it again towards the beginning of the Winter. Against
that time let me desire you to take up another Sentiment, and instead
of feeling a more lively Sense of my Absence, imagine me present, the
best part of me really is so, wherever She is; when the rest of me will
be with You, I know not possibly, nay probably never; unless your
Zeal to partake of the Spiritual Benefits which I am assured will not
come dear at the next Jubilee, should carry you to cross the Sea.

In the mean while I shall take the liberty of Writing to you a little
oftener than the three or four times a Year which you tell me are all
you can allow your self to Write to those you like best, and yet I
declare to you with great Truth, that you never knew me so busy in
your life as I am at present. You must not imagine from hence that
I am writing Memoires of my Self, the Subject is too slight to deserve
to descend to Posterity in any other manner than by that occasional
Mention which will be made in the History of our Age. Sylla, Cæsar,
and others of that rank were whilst they liv'd at the head of Mankind.
Their Story was in some sort the Story of the World, and as such
might very properly be transmitted under their Names to future
Generations. But for those who have acted much inferior parts, if they
Publish the piece, and call it after their own Names they are impertinent, if they publish only their own Share in it, they inform Mankind
by halves, and neither give much instruction nor create much Attention. France abounds with Writers of this sort, and I think we fall
into the other extream. Let me tell You on this occasion what has
sometimes come into my thoughts.

There is hardly any Century in History which began by opening so

---

[1] This letter, without the first two paragraphs, the next to the last paragraph, and some
minor bits, was printed as Bolingbroke's 'Plan for a General History of Europe'. See his
Works, ii (4to, 1754), 501–8, or *Works*, iv (1809), 155–61.
[2] Bolingbroke's wife, the Marquise de Villette, had been in England. Pope's command of
spoken French might well be doubted.

great a Scene, as the Century wherein we live, and shall I suppose dye.
Compare it with others, even the most famous and you will think so.
I'll sketch the two last to help your Memory.

The loss of that Ballance which Laurrent of Medicis had preserv'd
during his time, in Italy, the Expedition of Charles the 8th to Naples,
the intrigues of the Duke of Milan, who spun with all the refinements
of Art that Net wherein he was taken at last himself, the successful
dexterity of Ferdinand the Catholick, who built one Pillar of the
Austrian greatness in Spain, in Italy, and in the Indies, as the Succession of the House of Burgundy joyn'd to the Imperial dignity, and
the Hereditary Countrys, establish'd another in the upper and lower
Germany, these causes, and many others combin'd to form a very
extraordinary conjuncture, and by their consequences to render the
16th Century fruitful of great Events, and of Astonishing Revolutions.

The beginning of the 17th open'd still a greater, and more important
Scene. The Spanish Yoke was well nigh impos'd on Italy, by the
famous Triumvirate, Toledo at Milan, Ossuna at Naples, and La
Cueva at Venice. The distraction of France, as well as the State Policy
of the Queen Mother, seduc'd by Rome, and amus'd by Spain, the
despicable Character of our James the first, the rashness of the Elector
Palatine, the bad intelligence of the Princes and States of the League
in Germany, the Mercenary temper of John George of Saxony, and
the great qualities of Maximilian of Bavaria, rais'd Ferdinand the 2d
to the Imperial Throne, when the Males of the Elder Branch of the
Austrian Family in Germany being extinguish'd at the death of
Matthias, Nothing was more desireable, nor perhaps more practicable
than to throw the Empire into another House. Germany run the same
risque as Italy had done. Ferdinand seem'd more likely even than
Charles the 5th had been to become absolute Master, and if France
had not furnish'd the greatest Minister and the North the greatest
Captain of that Age in the same point of time, Vienna and Madrid
would have given the Law to the Western World. As the Austrian
Scale sunk, that of Burbon rose. The true date of the rise of that
power which has made the Kings of France so considerable in Europe
goes up as high as Charles the 7th and Lewis the 11th. The weakness
of our Henry the 6th, the loose Conduct of Edward the 4th as well as
the Corruption of his Court, & perhaps the oversights of Henry the
7th help'd very much to knit that Monarchy together as well as to
enlarge it. Advantage might have been taken of the Divisions which
Religion occasion'd, and supporting the Protestant party in France,
would have kept that Crown under restraints and under inabilitys in
some measure equal to those which were occasion'd anciently by the
vast alienations of its demesnes, and by the exorbitant power of its
Vassals. But James the first was incapable of thinking with Sense or

Acting with Spirit. Charles the 1st had an imperfect Glimpse of his true Interest, but his Uxorious temper, and the extravagancy of that Madman Buckingham gave Richlieu time to finish a great part of this project, and the Miseries that follow'd in England gave Mazarine time and opportunity to compleat the System. The last great Act of this Cardinal's Administration was the Pyrenean Treaty.

Here I would begin, by representing the face of Europe such as it was at that Epocha, the interests and Conduct of England, France, Spain, Holland and the Empire. A summary Recapitulation should follow of all the Steps taken by France during more than Twenty Years to arrive at the great object She had propos'd to her Self in making this Treaty, the most solemn Article of which the Minister who Negociated it, design'd should be violated, as appears by his Letters writ from the Island of Pheasants, if I mistake not. After this another draught of Europe should have its place, according to the Relations which the several Powers stood in one towards another in 1688, and the alterations which the Revolution in England made in the Politicks of Europe. A summary Account of the events of the War ended in 1697, the different views of K. William the 3d and Lewis the 14th in making the Peace of Ryswick, which matter has been much canvass'd, and is little understood, might follow; and then the dispositions made by the Partition Treatys, the Influences and Consequences of these Treatys, and a third draught of the State of Europe at the death of Charles the 2d of Spain. All this would make the Subject of one or two Books, and would be the most proper introduction imaginable to an History of that War with which our Century began, and of the Peace which follow'd.

This War foreseen for above half a Century had been during all that time the great and constant object of the Councils of Europe. The prize to be contended for was the richest that ever had been Stak'd since those of the Persian and Roman Empires. The Union of two Powers which seperately and in opposition had aim'd at Universal Monarchy was apprehended. The Confederates therefore engag'd in it to maintain a Ballance between the two Houses of Austria and Bourbon in order to preserve their Security, and to Assert their Independance. But with the Success of War they chang'd their Views, and if Ambition began it on the side of France, ambition continu'd it on the other. The Battles, the Sieges, the surprizing Revolutions which happen'd in the Course of this War, are not to be parallel'd in any period of the same compass. The Motives and the Measures by which it was protracted, the true Reasons why it ended, in a manner not proportionable to its Success, and the new Political State into which Europe was thrown by the Treatys of Utrecht and Baden, are Subjects, on which few persons have the necessary Informations, and yet every one speaks with assurance and even with passion. I think I could speak on them with some knowledge, and with as much indifference, as Polybius does of the Negociations of his Father Lycortas, even in those points where I was my self an Actor.

I will even confess to you that I should not despair of performing this part, better than the former. There is nothing in my opinion so hard to execute as those Political Maps, if you will allow me such an Expression, and those Systems of hints rather than Relations of Events, which are necessary to connect and explain in them and which must be so concise and yet so full, so complicate & yet so clear. It is Natures Master-piece in the most difficult kind of Writing; for, with your leave my good friend, to say her chief Master-piece, is to speak with great impropriety, I know nothing of this sort well done by the Ancients. Salust's Introduction as we[ll] as that of Thucidides might serve almost for any other piece of the Roman or Greek Story as well as for those pieces which those two great Authors chose. Polybius does not come up in his introduction to this Idea neither. Among the Moderns the first Book of Machiavels History of Florence is a noble Original of this kind, and perhaps father Paul's History of Benefices is in the same kind of composition inimitable.

These are some of those thoughts which come into my Mind when I consider how incumbent it is on every Man, that he should be able to give an Account even of his leisure, and in the midst of Solitude be of some use to Society.

Hic sitrus est vatius[1] was a Motto in the Stile of an Epitaph which Seneca had a mind to write over the door of a Slothful Wretch, who liv'd in his Villa like a Drone in some remote Cell of an Hive.

I know not whether I shall have courage enough to undertake the task I have Chalk'd out: I distrust my Abilitys with reason, & I shall want several Informations from England, not easy I doubt for me to obtain. But in all Events it will not be possible for me to go about it this Year, the reasons of which would be long enough to fill another Letter, and I doubt that you will think this grown too bulky already. | Adieu.

---

[1] This whole brief paragraph, not printed in Bolingbroke's *Works* or in Elwin, is an interesting comment on the mood of Bolingbroke's retirement. The Latin has been, either by Bolingbroke or by the Harleian scribe, somewhat mangled. Professor Mason Hammond has suggested that it should be related to Seneca's 55th Epistle to Lucilius (Bk. VI, Ep. 3). Seneca has visited the villa of the obscure Servilius Vatia south of Cumae; he recalls the reputation of Vatia: 'ille prætorius dives, nulla alia re quam otio notus.' During the troubled years of Sejanus, Vatia's retirement was so lucky that men cried out 'O Vatia, solus scis vivere!' Bolingbroke agrees with Seneca's serious comment: 'At ille latere sciebat, non vivere. Multum autem interest, utrum vita tua otiosa sit an ignava. Nunquam aliter hanc villam Vatia vivo præteribam, quam ut dicerem: "Vatia hic situs est".' Bolingbroke's projected history would have made his life *otiosa* and have rescued him from the stigma of Vatia's living death. See here iii. 413.

†POPE *to* ROBERT DIGBY[1]   1 *September* [1724]
1735

Twickenham, Sept. 1.

Your Doctor[2] is going to the *Bath,* and stays a Fortnight or more:
Perhaps you would be comforted to have a Sight of him, whether you
need him or not. I think him as good a Doctor as any for one that is
ill, and a better Doctor than any[3] for one that is well. He would do
admirably for Mrs. *Mary Digby:* She needed only to follow his Hints,
to be in eternal business and amusement of Mind, and even as active
as she could desire. But indeed I fear she would out-walk him: For
(as Dean *Swift* observ'd to me the very first time I saw the Doctor)
He is a Man that can do every thing but walk. His Brother,[4] who is
lately come into *England,* goes also to the *Bath;* and is a more extraordinary Man than he, worth your going thither on purpose to know
him. The Spirit of *Philanthropy,* so long dead to our World, is reviv'd
in him: He is a Philosopher all of[5] Fire; so warmly, nay so wildly in
the Right, that he forces all others about him to be so too, and draws
them into his own *Vortex.* He is a Star that looks as if it were all Fire,
but is all Benignity, all gentle and beneficial Influence. If there be
other men in the world that would serve a Friend, yet he is the only
one I believe that could make even an Enemy serve a Friend.

As all human Life is chequer'd and mix'd with Acquisitions and
Losses (though the latter are more certain and irremediable, than the
former lasting or satisfactory) so at the time I have gain'd the Acquaintance of one worthy Man I have lost another, a very easy, human, and
gentlemanly Neighbour, Mr. *Stonor.*[6] It's certain the Loss of one of
this Character puts us naturally upon setting a greater Value on the
few that are left, though the Degree of our Esteem may be different.
Nothing, says *Seneca,* is so melancholy a circumstance in human Life,
or so soon reconciles us to the thought of our own death, as the reflection and prospect of one Friend after another dropping round us! Who
would stand alone, the sole remaining Ruin, the last tottering Column
of all the Fabrick of Friendship; once so large, seemingly so strong,
and yet so suddenly sunk and buried? | I am, &c.

[1] Printed in all of Pope's editions except 1735a2. In editions of 1737–42 Pope added the
year 1722 to the date, but the mention of Mr. Stonor's death (which, according to Burke,
occurred on 10 Aug. 1724) makes 1724 the proper year. Arbuthnot was at Bath in both
1722 and 1724. The numerous textual revisions are negligible, but a few are given below.
[2] Your Doctor] Doctor Arbuthnot *1737–42.*
[3] Doctor than . . . for] Doctor than any one for *1735d.*
[4] Robert Arbuthnot, a banker in Paris, where he was of considerable service to English
travellers, especially, perhaps, to Jacobites.
[5] all of Fire] all on fire *1735n.*
[6] Thomas Stonor of Stonor (Watlington Park) in Oxfordshire evidently lived at times in
Twickenham.

WILLIAM PULTENEY *to* POPE   4 *September* 1724

Homer MSS. Add. 4809

Ashley Septr 4th 1724

Sir,—I have ever since my return, had my House full of such Company as I very little expected, and you would very little have liked, which was the reason I did not send to you sooner, But at present, if you have nothing better to do, & will spend a few days with Mrs Pulteney & me we shall be obliged to you, and will send the Coach for you when you please.

I am Sir | Your most humble Servant | William Pulteney.

JOHN KNIGHT *to* POPE   4 *September* 1724

Homer MSS. Add. 4809

4 Sepbr 1724

Sir,—According to my promise this is to [a]cquaint you that Last night Mrs Newsham came to Town, & having been to wait on her today she tells me that having but a week to stay & many things to do she would be glad you would send her word what day you intend her the favour of a visit that you may be sure of finding her at home. I am | Sir | Your most humble | Servant | J. Knight

*POPE *to* JOHN KNIGHT[1]   [5 *September* 1724]

The Earl Stanhope, K.G.

Sir,—I am very much obliged to you for yours & will wait on you & Mrs Newsham on Monday morning. In case, by any accident, any Business shou'd intervene to make that time inconvenient to her, I determine to stay all night, & be at her service whatever hours she pleases. I am unfeignedly hers, & | Sir | Your most faithfull | humble Servant | A. Pope

Address: To | Mr Knight, at his house in | Dover street.

‡POPE *to* ROBERT DIGBY   10 *September* 1724

1735

[Under this date Pope's editions of 1735 all contained a letter to Digby, which in the editions of 1737–42 was printed as if sent to Dr. Arbuthnot rather than Digby.

----

1 This seems perhaps a reply to the note from Knight of 4 Sept. Pope's letter is printed from a transcript of the original made by Dr. R. W. Chapman. Monday would be the 7th.

In either case the letter was fabricated from two letters written to Caryll on 23 November and 25 December 1725. In the editions of 1737–42 the letter has no year date, but is not textually changed except by the omission of two phrases and the year date and the change in the addressee. In view of the fact that the letter mentions attacks on the *Odyssey* it is strange that Pope ever dated it so early as 1724. See Pope to Arbuthnot, 10 September 1725.]

POPE *to* FORTESCUE   10 *September* 1724

Arthur A. Houghton, Jr.

Sept. 10th 1724[1]

I heartily thank you for yours, and the rather, because you are so kind as to employ me, tho but in little matters: I take it as an Earnest you would do so in greater. As to the House of Preparation for the Small pox why shou'd it not be my own? It is entirely at your Service, & I fancy 2 Beds or 3 upon necessity, (besides your Servants may be disposd of in the next house to me) will amply furnish your family. It is true the Small pox has been in Twitnam, but it is pretty well gone off. I can't find any Village freer from it so near London, except that of Petersham, where I hear it has not been, but I'll further inform myself upon your next notice.

As to the Receit of Sir Stephen Foxe's Eye-water, which I have found benefit from, it is very simple, & only this

Take a Pint of Camphorated Spirit of Wine, & infuse thereinto 2 Scruples of Elder-Flowers: Let them remain in it, & wash your temples & the nape of your neck, but do not put it into your Eyes, for it will smart abominably.

When you have taken breath a week or two, & had the full possession of that blessed Indolence which you justly value, after your long Labours & Peregrinations, I hope to see you here again first exercising the Paternal care, & exemplary in the tender offices of a Pater-familias; and then conspicuous in the active Scenes of business, eloquent at the Bar, & wise in the Chamber of Council. The future Honour of your native Devon, & to fill as great a part in the History of that County for your Sagacity & Gravity in the Laws, as Esquire Bickford is likely to do for his many Experiments in Natural Philosophy on the bodies of Maids, Wives, & Widows, & the whole extensive Circle of Generation.

I am forcd to dispatch this by the post, which is going, or else I could not have forborn to expatiate upon what I last mentiond. I must now only give Mr Bickford my services, & join 'em to those I shall

---

[1] The year date has been added in a later hand. The year 1724 is not impossibly early but is most unfashionably early for inoculation against smallpox.

ever offer to your own family. Believe me | Dear Sir | Your faith-fullest affectionate Servant, | A. Pope

Gay was well five days ago at Chiswick.

Address [on f. 2v]: To | Wm Fortescue, Esqr at | Fallapit near Kingsbridge | Devonshire.

Postmark: 10/SE

Endorsement (in Fortescue's hand?): Pope 10. Sept 1724.

POPE *to* BROOME   .   12 *September* 1724

Elwin–Courthope, viii. 85

Sept. 12, 1724.

I received yours, and it pleases me that you take some diversion, amidst those righteous and I hope useful labours which friendship has made you undertake. It would be hard and unjust, indeed, if I did not desire you should take some pleasure with a friend when I know you take so much pains for one. I wish I could salute you with congratulations for the 10,000*l*. in the lottery, but, what every sanguine person takes for the next happiness to it, I can tell you it is not yet come up and may be waiting for you. Nay, more, that none of your numbers are yet drawn,—so all your hopes are yet alive. I had given orders to a broker in the city to send me information as fast as any of yours or mine came up: and out of six, two are drawn blanks; but, as I told you, none yet of yours—at least not on Thursday last, and I write this on Saturday morning. I received the notes on the ninth. You are most laudably punctual, that is honest, in all your ways. I have but one thing to complain of you, and that I will tell you when we meet, and not before.[1] I hope, if you are impatient to know it—you will the sooner make me a visit. I now begin to want the eleventh and twelfth books, for it is scarcely credible how fast the press plies me. I will not neglect to send you the ninth as soon as finished, &c. In the meantime, it is necessary you send me the initial letters, or first words, of the eleventh and twelfth for the graver to proceed upon.

I am much recovered from the ill state of health I have lately laboured under, very busy in laying out of a garden,[2] shall be busier next month in planting, but with all avocations, will proceed cheerfully through the version of the fourteenth book, which is heavy and laborious to me more than all the rest. What to do with the seventeenth I know not, and my soul sickens to think of it, next winter,— a season when I must expect worse health and worse spirits. Adieu,

---

[1] The complaint may have been, as Elwin thought, Broome's lack of concealment with regard to his part in the *Odyssey*. The remark, however, sounds rather like a good-natured friendly bit of facetiousness.

[2] Very likely for Mrs. Howard at Marble Hill, which was nearing completion.

dear sir. My mother and I wish you and yours all felicity. Believe me, with sincerity and affection, ever yours.

I never hear one word from Fenton.

POPE *to* FORTESCUE   17 *September* 1724
1797 (Polwhele, i. 323)

                            Twitnam, Sept. 17, 1724.

Your friendly and kind letter I received with real joy and gladness, to hear, after a long silence, of the welfare of a whole family, which I shall ever unfeignedly wish well to in all regards. I knew not in what part of the land to level a letter at you, or else you had heard first from me. My mother, indeed, is very ill, but as it seems only the effect of a cold, which always handles her severely, I hope not in any danger. I am in the old way,—this day well however, and the past and future are not in my power, so not much in my care. Gay is at the bath with Dr. Arbuthnot. Mrs. Howard returns your services, and Marblehill waits only for its roof,—the rest finished. The little prince William[1] wants Miss Fortescue, or to say truth, any body else that will play with him. You say nothing at what time we may expect you here; I wish it soon, and thought you talked of Michaelmas. I am grieved to tell you, that there is one Devonshire man not honest, for my man Robert proves a vile fellow, and I have discarded him; *auri sacra fames* is his crime, a crime common to the greatest and meanest if any way in power, or too much in trust! I am going upon a short ramble to my lord Oxford's, and lord Cobham's, for a fortnight, this Michaelmas, and the hurry I am at present in, with preparing to be idle, (a common case) makes it difficult for me to continue this letter, tho' I truly desire to say many things to you. Homer is advanced to the eighth book, I mean printed so far. My gardens improve more than my writings; my head is still more upon Mrs. Hd.[2] and her works, than upon my own. Adieu! God bless you; an ancient and Christian, therefore, an unmodish and unusual salutation. I am ever, sincerely and affectionately, yours, A. Pope.

Address: To Wm. Fortescue, esq. at Fallapit, near Totnes, Devon.

*POPE *to* LORD BATHURST[3]   17 *September* 1724
Wellesley College

                            Twitenham, Sept. 17. 1724.

My Lord,—Nothing flatters me so much or (to give it a much more agreeable word) nothing pleases me so much as a thought, that we

---

[1] The Duke of Cumberland.   [2] Mrs. Howard and her gardens.
[3] This letter was printed with explanations by Professor Helen Sard Hughes in *Studies in Philology*, xxv (1928), 462–7.

exactly keep pace in thinking of each other. I remember a few weeks ago, when in Zeal of heart I was running over Hounslow-heath to see you, I met you just half-way, (as one would always wish to meet a Friend.) And the very moment, as near as I can guess, that I was writing to you the Impatiences of my heart, your Lordship was imploying your pen the same way to me: for the same post that carryd out my Impetuosities, brought hither yours. Tho 'tis but 2 days since I filld 4 sides of paper, in the thoughts of you; yet I must write this day again to thank you for yours: & to tell you that you are rememberd, in the very manner you would be, by the two Prose-Ladies you mention.[1] As to the Verse-Lady, I can say little, but will endeavour (for Your sake) to know more of her, than perhaps I might otherwise do. I don't know what further fiction, than that which is necessary to Poetry, may be in her? but I can assure you that in me there is no Degree of Fiction sufficient to qualify me for a Decypherer. God forbid there ever should!

It is true that I writ to Digby,[2] to give two of the few people I esteem the mutual pleasure of seeing each other. A dis-interested Design! I wish with all my heart it had not been so; For I sincerely wish to be at that meeting, could I but have the Wishing Cap of Fortunatus, & wish my self one day with you at Ciceter, the next day at Twitnam with the Ladies you wot of, and an old woman to whom I owe much, because to her I owe that ever I knew the world, and (what is vastly more) that ever I knew a few like yourself.

That I may do more good offices, I tell you that the Dr[3] is yet at Bath; if ever you intend to consult your health this is the time, therfore. I will add no more to the long Scroll I sent your Lordship so lately, but that Mrs Howard by name, & Miss Patty Blount, return you most sincere Services, & that they take kindly your Distinction of them as Prose Friends. In the same class pray for ever rank My Lord Your faithfull Servant A. Pope.

You rejoice me in what you have thought for poor Dart.[4] It is every way worthy of you, & I esteem it kind to me, as it proceeds partly thence: You will not be the less pleased also, for knowing, that

---

[1] The prose-ladies (see below) were Mrs. Howard and Martha Blount. The verse-lady (mentioned in terms that show some change of attitude) was Lady Mary Wortley Montagu. Pope told Spence (*Anecdotes*, p. 175) that 'Lord Bathurst used to call Prior his verse-man and Lewis his prose-man'. The terminology turns up in letters that mention Erasmus Lewis or others.

[2] Probably Robert Digby, who may simply have been told of an opportunity of seeing Lord Bathurst at Cirencester. They had certainly met before Digby visited Riskins in 1725. See his letter of 2 July 1725. See also ii. 58, 132.

[3] Dr. Arbuthnot.

[4] The Rev. John Dart (d. 1730) was an historian of Canterbury Cathedral and of Westminster Abbey. Two of his poems were dedicated to Bishop Atterbury.

a Departed Friend of ours[1] will place it to his own account, (I am sure
of it.) Bonum, quo communius, eo melius.

Address: To | the Right Honorable the | Lord Bathurst, at | Cirencester, |
Glocestershire.

Postmark: 19/SE

POPE *to* [THE HON. GEORGE BERKELEY][2]   [1724]

Add. 22626

I received this Paper on Saturday, but we were abroad all yesterday.
The Purport of it, as to altering the Road, is true, & that I went &
obtaind their Consent, provided the New Road were kept up. But as
to the further particulars of my assuring them Mrs H. *had* agreed with
Mr Vernon, I could only say I understood so, or that Mr V. had told
me so. &c.[3] The Fact of the Keys is true—If you can call on us to day,
we need not say you will be heartily welcome, & sure of finding my
Lord,[4] and | Sir | Your most faithfull | humble Servant | A. Pope

Endorsement: Mr Pope to Mr B

POPE *to* EDWARD, EARL OF OXFORD[5]   22 *September* 1724

Longleat Portland Papers, xii

My Lord,—I should really think myself no way worthy the honour
of a part in your regard, if I was not perfectly sincere in all my professions to your Lordship, even to small things. Therfore I hope you
believd the Intention I exprest of waiting on you at Wimpole, which
unfeignedly would be a great pleasure to me & one I have long, &
much desired, in my heart. The Duchess of Buckingham has challengd
a prior promise of attending her to Leighs, from whence I design to
travel on to your Lordship by the way of Ware. What I apprehend is,

---

[1] Bishop Atterbury, departed in exile now for over a year.
[2] On the assumption that this letter has to do with the arrangement of Mrs. Howard's
grounds at Marble Hill, it is placed in this chronological sequence. More than the date must
be doubtful. There is no address, and the endorsement (though the only evidence as to the
addressee) is far from conclusive. The letter belongs to the period before Mrs. Howard became
a countess, and she did not marry Mr. Berkeley until 1735. Mr. B might be any business
agent, Charles Bridgeman, for example. The letter, here misplaced, belongs in v. 5.
[3] Thomas Vernon, Esq., of Twickenham Park, died in Aug. 1726: hence the letter must
have been written before that time.
[4] Possibly Lord Peterborow or Lord Bathurst, both of whom were concerned in helping
design Mrs. Howard's gardens.
[5] The autograph text of this, the first letter to Edward Harley after he became Earl of
Oxford, if one excepts the brief note of condolence written on the death of the 1st Earl, is
preserved in vol. xii of the Portland Papers. The cover of the letter, from which are taken
the address, postmark, and endorsement, is bound up as f. 28 in vol. xiii.

that she will not go out of London till the middle of next week, & I fear that may be so late as to come full upon your Journey to Bath. I therfore beg the favor of a line to know precisely what will be the latest time that you shall be to be found at Wimpole that I may manage accordingly, or (if possible) hasten my way to You. Next Saturday I shall be in London (which I have never once seen since your Lordships removal) & a Letter directed to Lord Bathurst's will reach me.

I would fain some way or other express what I really am in regard to your Lordship, & the Sense I shall ever have of so many Instances of obliging favour to me. I can only say I ~~truly honour~~ from my soul esteem, those uncommon Qualities of True Honour, true Greatness, & true Virtue. This made me your great Fathers Admirer: I could not help it, & have no merit therfore in it; And yet I think that was all that recommended me to yourself. I wish my future life may be such as to manifest something that might be a more peculiar claim to the distinction you shew me, in proving with what truth, & to what degree, I am your whole family's, & particularly your own | Most faithfull | Most obligd & | most sincere Servant | A. Pope.

Twitnam | Sept. 22d | 1724.

Address: To | The Right Honble the | Earl of Oxford, at | Wimpole: | near Cambridge. | Free

Postmark: 22/SE

Endorsement (in Oxford's hand): Mr Pope. Sepr 22 1724 | R at Wimpole Sepr 23 1724

EDWARD, EARL OF OXFORD *to* POPE   25 *September* 1724

Longleat Portland Papers, xii

Wimpole. Sepr 25. 1724.

Sir,—I am very much obliged to you for the favor of yours I received last post I do not know any letter has given me so much pleasure and satisfaction because you tell me you are resolved to see this place this year. I shall not move from hence above these three Weeks; I do not pretend to alter your resolution of waiting upon the Dutchess of Buckingham at her House in Essex but I would only suggest this, as this place is much the farthest from London, why should you not come here first and go from hence to her Graces, my fear is least the Rains should come and the ways from Leighs to London are much better then from me to Ware, I shall be glad to know what you resolve to do & when you design to move, pray let me know when you will be at Ware because I will send a servant to meet you that you might not be misled. The Bearer of this will call on munday morning to know if you have any commands. you make me ashamed when you set so high a value upon my poor endeavors to serve you, I will allow nobody to esteem, to value, or love you more then I do, and I do so from the conviction that you are the Best Poet, the truest Friend, and the Best natured man, these are characters that are extreamly amiable but very seldom fall to the share of one man to possess in such a degree as you do—I shall wait with great impatience to know when I shall be so happy as to see you under this Roof. I am | Sir your most | affectionate humble Servant | Oxford.

CHARLES BRIDGEMAN *to* POPE[1]   28 *September* 1724

Homer MSS. Add. 4809

Broadstreet Sepr 28th 1724

Sir,—Since I waited on Mrs Howard & You at Twickenham, I have been continually abroad on business that I then knew not of; but of great Moment, & of which You shall know more when I have the Honour to see You I came home on Fryday night & had Your kind Letter [O]n Saturday morning I begun on the plann, & have not [lef]t from that time to this so long as I could see, nor shall [I] leave it till 'tis finish'd which I hope will be about tomorrow Noon, but the affair I mention to You above will not let me move from Home this fortnight, so shall be glad if Your affairs call you to Towne on Tuesday or any other day this week that I may a little explain it to you, or if not I will Send it to You by my man on Wednesday morning. I am | Sir Your most obliged humble Servant | Charles Bridgeman

Address: To Mr Pope at | his house in | Twittenham | Middlesex
Postmark: 28/SE

POPE *to* EDWARD, EARL OF OXFORD   29 *September* 1724

Longleat Portland Papers, xii

My Lord,—I had no sooner manifested my Intentions to your Lordship, but that Ill fortune, which generally has made me unable to put into act, or render any of my Intentions toward my friends effectual, has stopt me here, much against my will. For my Mother was taken ill the day I writ to you, & yet continues so. The Duchess I hear does not go to Leighs as yet, & if She recovers, I will not Stay for her,[2] but

---

[1] A doubtful digit has led earlier editors to date this letter 26 Sept. The credit for the gardens of Marble Hill has frequently been given to Lord Bathurst and Pope. Bridgeman seems to be the only professional called in to advise. There is an account of Bridgeman in *DNB*, vol. xxii (Supplement).

[2] He means, 'If my mother recovers, I will not stay for the Duchess.'

fly directly to Wimpole, by the way of Ware, or call & lye one night
at Mr Cæsars; and so return by way of Leighs. Of this your Lordship
shall be certifyd; (since I see you are so good as really to desire to be
troubled with me; for I shall always do you the Compliment (and, as
the world goes, a great one it is) to believe every thing you say, literally.
I would not defer writing this very first post, tho in the utmost hurry,
occasiond by Her Illness & the discharge of two Servants (which are a
great Revolution & change of Ministry in a small family) But I must
take more time to assure you with what true sense of your favour &
with what solid satisfaction ~~from~~ in it, I am ever | My Lord | Your
most obliged | most faithfull Servant | A. Pope.

Twitenham: | Sept. 29th | 1724.

Address: To | The Right Honble the Earl | of Oxford & Earl Mortimer, | at
Wimpole, near | Cambridge. | Free

Postmark: 29/SE

Endorsement (in Oxford's hand): Mr. Pope. Sepr 29 | 1724

*POPE *to* MRS. CÆSAR¹   [1724?]

Rousham

Madam,—I can only Admire at your Ambition, & pay that Devotion
which meaner Souls are apt, to such great & Exalted Spirits: & with
which I always am, | Madam | Your most obedient | very much obligd
Servant | A. Pope

My humble Services to Mr Cæsar, & to Mrs Madan when you see
her. I was very near waiting on you & her last week. But Fate denyd!
My Mother is your obedient Servant

Address: For | Mrs Cæsar | at | Bennington.

LORD BATHURST *to* POPE²   [*October* 1724?]

Elwin–Courthope, viii. 361–2

My dear Sir,—Having missed two posts already I am determined by
this to send you my thanks for your last kind letter, though I am at

---

¹ The letter seems to fit well into Pope's plans for a visit to the eastern counties; see the
immediately preceding letter to Lord Oxford. Mrs. Cæsar's 'ambition' is probably connected
with a request for more acquittances for the *Odyssey*.

² Obviously impossible to date, this letter is placed here because the period 1723–6 was
the major period for early improvements in Pope's garden, and 1724 was the time when
Pope, Lord Bathurst, and Bridgeman were helping arrange the grounds of Marble Hill for
Mrs. Howard. The fact that a number of lime-trees is desired leads one to suspect Marble
Hill is the garden considered, but the fact that the trees are to be delivered to Pope makes his

present in so ill a disposition to write that I could hardly talk to you if you were here. I went out in the morning to take my usual exercise which lasted till dinner-time. I was forced to entertain at that time two or three odd people, who were not fools enough to be laughed at and yet were far from having sense enough to make a conversation; a most accursed mediocrity. After this I was obliged to make a visit to a country neighbour. I found him in his hall. I may properly say I found him, for I looked sometime before I could discover him, being enveloped in thick clouds of tobacco. So much civility was paid to me that I was obliged to remove out of the great hall into a little parlour, which by misfortune had just been washed. The honest friends who had been entertaining him before were to follow us into this parlour, and the agreeable smoke which had filled a larger hall was to be transferred to the little room, with the addition of a good deal of other smoke which proceeded from a chimney that had not been incommoded with fire since last Christmas, and consequently the soot helped to the delightfulness of the smell. Not to trouble you further with this description, our drink was as bad as our conversation, and I have had too much of each. What I write will smell of it. Therefore I will defer the rest which I have to say till I am purified by walking round Oakley wood, and conversing with the hamadryads which you have lodged there. Adieu.

I had like to have forgot what was principally in my thoughts when I sat down to write. I have left orders with my gardener at Riskins to deliver to you or your order all the limes which can possibly be spared, but if you are not in too much haste I think you had better stay till I come back, and then I shall have horses to bring them over to Twitname, and Burton will be there to see them transplanted with care.

POPE *to* EDWARD, EARL OF OXFORD   8 *October* 1724

Longleat Portland Papers, xii
Octr 8th 1724.

My Lord,—I should be unworthy of that which I above all things desire to deserve, your Lordship's good Opinion, if I was not thoroughly vext, & thoroughly Disappointed at this accident which has hinderd my absolute Resolutions of waiting upon you; Notwithstanding the accident itself be one, which (to a man of your humanity) will seem rather Melancholy, than Piquing or vexatious. My poor Mothers Illness, & that Dispiritedness which attends Illness in Old people,

---

four acres probable. If we are to accept the remark that Curll (*Mr. Pope's Literary Correspondence*, ii. 79 [last series in pagination]) puts into the mouth of Pope's gardener, John Searle, trees were a necessary addition to the place. Searle, so Curll says, 'has lived with Mr. *Pope* above Eleven Years, and in the Hortulan Dialect told us, that, *there were not Ten Sticks in the Ground when his Master took the House*'. Searle's long service began about 1724.

makes me afraid, as well as troubled, to leave her. Besides, (having watchd every day for a fortnight past, till she might be enough on the mending hand) I find the time of your Lordships departure for Bath drawn too nigh, to satisfy me in so short a Stay with you. As to the Dutchess, I had put it off till my return from Wimpole; but now too I find, She is not gone yet: so that I had my full liberty to have travelld directly first to you. The Other Objections are too strong, and you had heard of 'em sooner, but that I daily was in some hopes of getting to You. I am heartily disappointed, and so is another man, of the Virtuoso-Class as well as I; (and in My notions, of the higher kind of class, since Gardening is more Antique & nearer God's own Work, than Poetry) I mean Bridgman,[1] whom I had tempted to accompany me to you.

My Lord, pray think well of me, that is, think me Your true Honourer, and | Your faithfull, obliged | and obedient Servant, | A. Pope.

I had the satisfaction to hear from Dr Arbuthnot, that my Lady Oxford was pretty well.

Address: To | The Right Honourable, the | Earl of Oxford, at | Wimpole: | near | Cambridge. | Free

Postmark: 8/OC

Endorsement (in Oxford's hand): Mr. Pope. Octr 8. 1724.

POPE *to* BROOME   8 *October* [1724]

Elwin–Courthope, viii. 86

Oct. 8, [1724]

I deferred writing to you till I had sent a reprimand to my correspondent in the city about not notifying your 50*l.* prize. He said that ticket was drawn so early that it was before he had received any commission from me. I congratulate you on fortune's readiness and forwardness to serve you. To me, she always was a jade, and neither now, nor formerly, would show me the least of these favours. But let her give me friends, and give them money: I have the better of it. Yours was drawn on the second day of drawing. It is in the twenty-third course of payment, which is all that is needful to inform you about it.

I shall send for the notes and verse to Mr. Tonson. I hope you have taken care of their being sent from the carrier thither; for, as to the mushrooms, I have not received nor otherwise heard of them but in your letter. I am extremely obliged to you for remembering me in everything, and in every way. Pray, if I can accommodate you with any matters from this part, freely command me.

---

[1] Charles Bridgeman, who had been helping design the gardens at Marble Hill.

The labour of Eustathius, or rather of Mr. Broome, would lessen, if you did not take in quite so many of those notes which are, I think sometimes, too studiously vindicative of Homer upon objections which he seems to start, only to answer. I hope when that work is at an end, the modern Eustathius will repose in some good bishopric as did the ancient one.

I heard not, this whole year, one syllable of or from Fenton. I will inquire when he comes to settle in London. As to the catalogue of subscribers, send it as soon as you can, and increase it as much as you can, particularly at Cambridge, where I want a proper agent. But let me advise you not to deliver receipts but where the money is paid, for I know by experience so much will be your loss, as is your trust.

My mother has been extremely ill, but has not forgotten you. I hope she will recover and live another spring to entertain you. I have at last ended the fourteenth book, *multo cum sudore*.[1] In all my labours, I think of yours, and am, dear sir, with sincere affection, yours faithfully.

POPE *to* MRS. NEWSHAM[2] [13 *October* 1724]

Bowles (1806), x. 90

Madam,—I hope you are so good a relation as to think it a reasonable impediment to my writing to you, (which I purposed as soon as you got into Warwickshire,[3]) that my mother was very ill. She is now so much better,[4] that I begin to look with more cheerfulness on the coming part of my life: contrary to most sons, I think, of all friends, a friend of one's family is the best; they are generally the surest, for merit seldom gets the better of blood. The world of late has been so bad, that it has seemed unwilling to attribute much merit to those who love us naturally, as kindred (and above all, parents) do: The true reason of which I fear is, that we are too ready to depreciate the kindnesses we receive, to excuse our own careless, if not ungrateful, returns to them. But though our relations *be obliged* to be kind to us, are we therefore *not obliged* to be grateful to them? For my part I am so unfashionable as to think my Mother the best friend I have, for she is

---

[1] Pope has been working on Book XIV at least since about 16 Aug.; see his letter to Broome of that date. Book XIV was the last in the third volume of Pope's *Odyssey*. Vols. i–iii were published in Apr. 1725. The rest of the translation (Books XV–XXIV) was published about the middle of June 1726.

[2] The date 'Oct. 13' appears in Elwin, from a transcript made by Cunningham for him. Elwin supplied the year as 1727. For the reasons for transferring it to 1724 see the letters to Mrs. Newsham of 9 July and 8 Aug. of this year. Elwin substitutes for *hope* (the second word in the letter) the bracketed word *know*.

[3] Mrs. Newsham has just returned from a visit to town to Chadshunt, the Newsham estate.

[4] Mrs. Pope's recovery was apparently cut short by a relapse.

certainly the most partial one. Therefore as she thinks the best of me, she must be the kindest to me. And I am morally certain she does that without any difficulty, or art, which it would cost the devil and all of pains for any body else to do.

In this domestic way of thinking, you will not take me too much for a complimental person, if I, seriously and heartily, wish to know from you that Mr. Newsham is in a better state of health. I am truly sorry that you can't pass the winter here,[1] especially when it is occasioned by such an obstacle: but I know from myself (who am like on the same[2] account to see very little of the town this winter), that there is more true satisfaction in doing right, and in acting tenderly, than in all the vain, empty things, which the lovers of the town (the Cornishes of the world) can call pleasures. They hate the very thoughts of paradise, because it is described as a garden: and have no opinion of heaven, but as they fancy it like an Opera.

I would not say this before Mr. Elliot,[3] who has bought (at my instigation) the marble for the Statue, upon which the Italian is now at work. I will not forget those cautions about the forehead, hair, etc. which we observed when we met on that occasion. You know that I have enough of yours in my hands, to answer the Statuary's demands for the future. I have made the Latin Inscription as full, and yet as short, as I possibly could. It vexes me to reflect how little I must say, and how far short all I can say is, of what I believe, and feel, on that subject; like true lovers' expressions, that vex the heart from whence they come, to find how cold and faint they must seem to others, in comparison of what inspires them inwardly in themselves: The heart glows, while the tongue faulters.

I shall try my interest with Mr. Nichols,[4] in behalf of the young gentleman, who is so much a part of you. I had once an interest with him: and (because he is a good man) I will believe I have it still, for the same[5] cause that I have some with you: One whom he loved and respected, happened to love me, though now removed from us for ever! That will be a reason with grateful and reflecting minds, to devolve benevolencies, and continue good wishes, from generation to generation. | I am, etc.

---

[1] Mrs. Newsham will be kept in Warwickshire by the ill health of her husband. He died on 21 Nov. 1724.

[2] That is, on account of illness, but not of the same person.

[3] Not Mrs. Newsham's brother-in-law Edward Eliot, as Elwin thought; for Edward died in 1722. Probably Richard (Edward's brother), who later married Harriot, natural daughter of the late Secretary Craggs.

[4] Presumably John Nicoll, who is frequently called Nicholls. He was second master at Westminster School and had been a close friend of Atterbury. Young James Newsham had been admitted to Westminster in Apr. 1723.

[5] Mrs. Newsham and Pope have lost Craggs; Pope and Nicoll have had Atterbury 'removed from us for ever'.

*LORD PERCIVAL *to* POPE[1]   22 *October* 1724

Add. 47030 (p. 206)

London 22d Oct 1724

Sir,—I have a favour to beg which I promise my self you will not refuse me being sensible of your inclination to oblige and confident that you believe me desirous to serve you on all occasions.

Dr. Langford[2] late preacher to the Charter House is dead and my Chaplain Mr Philip Bearcroft Fellow of Merton Colledge in Oxen, and bred at that School makes interest to Succeed him. He has I think assurances from the greater number of the Governors; nevertheless as a wise man will never make too Sure of any thing he does not actually possess, he begs that you will mention his affair to my Lord Harcourt in as hearty a manner as your intimacy with that Lord will permit. I had not troubled you on his Account, if his living in my house were the only motive for my interesting my Self in his behalf, but his good learning and regular life known to me for severall years, oblige me not only to serve him my self but to make him all the friends I can.

I ask your pardon for taking this liberty, and only add that I shall embrace all opportunitys of obeying your commands | being | Sir | Your Faithfull and obedient humble servant | Percival.

*POPE *to* LORD PERCIVAL   26 *October* 1724

Add. 47030 (p. 207)

Twitenham Oct 26 1724

My Lord,—I assure your Lordship I take it as an obligation, that you think so rightly of me as to Judge the pleasure I should receive in obeying any commands of yours. There are some people in the world for whom one's esteem can never be extinct, tho it may be dormant, by distance or accident: and I beg you to apply this where I mean it, not to transfer it where your Modesty otherwise might, to any other of my acquaintance.

I went as soon as I received yours to my Lord Harcourt, whose answer was, that he was not Pre-ingaged, and would give the Gentleman his vote, but was unwilling to *throw it away*; as he must, unless there were a Majority made by it. He order'd me to inquire of your Lordship what persons of the Governors they were who had engag'd for Mr Bearcroft, and if the addition of his own Voice to theirs, will do the business, he shall have it.

I forget who are the Governors; it is not unlikely but I may know

---

[1] Printed from the Percival letterbooks.

[2] Dr. Emanuel Langford had been both chaplain of Chelsea Hospital and preacher to the Charterhouse. On Bearcroft (1697–1761) see *DNB*. His successful candidacy as preacher to the Charterhouse is treated here in letters dated 26 and 31 Oct. and 20 and 21 Nov.

one or two others of them: if I had a list of those you are not yet sure of, It would be sincerely a pleasure to me to do my best with any such.

My Lord I earnestly desire you to think me with all respect (tho the hurry of my Life is such that I have few opportunities of expressing it as I would in person) | Your most faithfull | and most obedient | Servant | A: Pope.

I desire your Lordship to put my old friend, Young Mrs Minshul[1] in mind that I am always hers: My Services attend your whole Family.

EDWARD, EARL OF OXFORD *to* POPE   26 *October* 1724
Longleat Portland Papers, xii

Wimpole. Octr 26. 1724

Sir,—It is not possible for me to be more pleased then I was with the hopes you gave me of seeing you here this year except the real enjoyment of your company, and consequently when I found I was not to expect you the disappointment made the greater impression, and the reason of your not being able to come the Illness of your mother which I know from your own tenderness and good nature gives you great trouble, so it is an adition to my greif, I could almost talk like a fond woman upon this occasion but I will not give my self to Dispair, but hope that next year will be more fortunate to me.

I remember you are a Lover of Brawn I shall next week send you a coller. I am with true respect | Sir | your most humble | Servant. | Oxford

I hope mrs. pope is well pray present my humble service to her. you have forgot to send me the copy of Verses upon Durfey. pray how goes Homer on under Lintot

Address:[2] For | Alexander Pope esqr | at Twickenham in | Middlesex | by way of London
Frank: Oxford
Postmark: 28/OC

*LORD PERCIVAL *to* POPE   31 *October* 1724
Add. 47030 (p. 209)

London 31 Octr, 1724

Sir,—I know not how to express my obligations to you for the service you have done Mr Bearcroft with my Lord Harcourt, but by assuring

---

[1] Mrs. (i.e. Miss) Minshul was apparently a daughter of Richard Minshul, who was (like Lord Percival) active in prison reform. The daughter lived frequently with the Percivals, and was very likely a relative.

[2] On another side of the cover is written in a strange hand the name: Royston. This presumably means that the letter passed through that town.

you that the sense I have of it, is beyond expression. To obey your commands, for I shall always esteem your desires as such, I have enclosed a list of the present Governors, but I entreat you not to think of giving your self any further trouble on this Account for except in cases of necessity we should not desire the utmost services of our friends, and I Judge ours dos not require it.

The Governors Mr Bearcroft is not sure of are the A:B: of Cant, Duke of Somerset, Earl of Dartmouth and Sr Peter King. but he has reason to be confident that the rest will declare for him, tho some having fixed themselves a Rule not to engage before hand would not give an absolute promise. Nevertheless they assure us they are not engaged to any other, and by the manner of their answers let us understand they will be his friend. Others have promised to go with Lord Townshend or the B: of London who are both heartily for him, as are likewise the Duke of Newcastle and Chandois, and Bishop of Durham his Godfather.

I shall stay six weeks in town in which time I hope for an opportunity of acknowledging your friendship in person. In the meantime I am | &c. | Percival.

POPE *to* BROOME   31 *October* [1724]

Elwin–Courthope, viii. 87

Twitenham, Oct. 31 [1724].

Since my last I received your acceptable present of mushrooms. You are twice as good as your word, for I had some pickled, as well as powdered. I had both the ashes and the mummy, which to those who love mushrooms is as curious and delightful as to those who love antiquities.

I will carefully do as you desire in relation to the eleventh book.[1] As to my Miscellany, I hear of nothing like it at present,[2] but a miscellany of villanies and follies and corruptions with which this nation abounds, and which makes the entertainment, horrid as it is, of each winter.[3] But whenever times and seasons are so composed as to relish the old and polite arts, no opportunity shall be missed to place your verse in the best lustre I can.

I am much obliged to you for your good wishes to my mother, but

---

[1] That is, he will correct Broome's translation of it.—Elwin. Broome had finished the book two years back (29 May 1722).
[2] Pope's Miscellany was Lintot's *Miscellaneous Poems and Translations,* first published in 1712. A fifth edition was evidently projected, which ultimately appeared in 1726 or 1727. New pieces by Broome were to be (and were) substituted for his other earlier verse. Two lines of his Epistle to Fenton on *Mariamne* found their way into Pope's *Bathos* (ch. vii), and Broome was naturally very greatly annoyed by such treatment. See Fenton to Broome, 7 Apr. [1728] and Broome to Fenton, 15 June [1728].
[3] An expression of disillusionment concerning Parliament.

she is now very ill—so ill that I can hardly write this: but would not omit the first post to acknowledge your kindness. As soon as the notes on lib. 9 are printed I will send them,[1] remembering your former desire; but tell me how far you have had them already.

Shakespeare is finished. I have just written the preface, and in less than three weeks it will be public.[2] Fenton is just come to Leicester Fields. Dear Broome, believe me ever your faithful friend and servant.

POPE *to* EDWARD, EARL OF OXFORD   6 *November* 1724

Longleat Portland Papers, xii

Twitenham Novr 6th 1724.

My Lord,—I faithfully assure you, I never was so unwilling to fear what has since happend, and never so sorry to give way to any Obstacle to my desires, as when the Apprehension of my poor Mother's Illness put a stop to my resolution of waiting on your Lordship. And nothing in nature could have hinderd my Repenting that I did not see you, but what has unfortunately Authorized my Stay, namely, my poor Mother's ensuing Fever, in which she now lies in the last danger of Life. I am sure if your Lordship could (as you obligingly say) talk like a fond woman upon this occasion, I have doubly a cause now to do so. And I am confident, Your own heart will bear me testimony that no Woman's Tenderness can exceed that of a Reasonable & Grateful man, who loses a kind Parent, which I am every hour now expecting.

At this season, really My Lord, any one to whom I can sit down to write a part of what fills my heart, must have no small share in it. Tis a natural Effort of my mind to communicate itself thus to you, whom I know to have so true a feeling of This melancholy circumstance.

I received the present you sent me,[3] & want to have You come to Town, as one of the Props I am to lean upon (pardon the familiarity of such an expression) when My Best Friend is gone: Yet God knows how long it may be before I can go thither, whether She lives or dies. I am with great Sense of all your favor & a sincere esteem & Respect | My Lord | Your most faithful Servant, | A: Pope:

I hope all that belongs to you are well, & heartily pray for the Continuance of all that is, by any Tye, dear to your Lordship.

Endorsement (by Oxford): Mr Pope. Nov. 6. 1724. Twickenham

---

[1] For correction.   [2] The work was not published until 12 Mar. 1725.
[3] The collar of brawn.—Elwin.

POPE *to* BROOME   [*November* 1724][1]

Elwin–Courthope, viii. 88

Saturday, [Nov., 1724].

I was heartily sorry to hear of your illness, and really more so, on account of its being occasioned, according to your description, by a lowness of spirit, which is too apt to grow upon people past the first vigour of youth. My poor mother was at the point of death, and I think it a miracle that she is yet among the living, though weak to the last degree, and doubtless confined to her bed and chamber for many months to come. If it had been my melancholy fortune to have lost her, I had given you a particular, though perhaps unseasonable, evidence of my friendship, and of the opinion I have of yours, in going directly from hence to your house, there to have passed the first weeks of my affliction, and depended on the consolation of a friend who has too well been acquainted with sufferings of that tender kind.

I beg to hear in particular how you do, when you send the notes on lib. 11, which indeed are very much wanted, for the verse of it is half printed. The twelfth and notes will be wanted in a week or more, at least the verse. I am concerned to press you at a time when perhaps you want rest; but the fate of the work depends on punctuality at this crisis. I received the names of your subscribers, and wish you could have procured more of the colleges in Cambridge, for the honour of the matter, since those of Oxford are much forwarder in this affair. I shall forthwith publish the proposal to the town;[2] and, as I before told you, if you make it your choice, you shall fairly divide what profit shall arise from the future subscribers; for I have done with those procured by my personal interest, and will push my particular friends no farther. Therefore you are to divide whatever comes above my present list; and for any that your own interest can make, or already has made, you are to look upon them as wholly your own, unless you prefer a certain though small gratuity, as I first proposed by Mr. Fenton to you two years ago. Take your choice. I think I need not recommend to you further the necessity of keeping this whole matter to yourself, as I am very sure Fenton has done, lest the least air of it prejudice it with the town. But if you judge otherwise, I do not prohibit you taking to yourself your due share of fame. Take your choice also in that.

I desire you to send with speed what is wanting for the eleventh and twelfth. I have taken care in what you desired; and I do not, upon the whole, make any doubt but I shall have some merit in advancing your fame to its just pitch. The public is both an unfair and a silly judge, unless it be led or trepanned into justice. The *case is altered* was

[1] This letter must antedate that from Pope to Broome dated 4 Dec. 1724.
[2] The Proposals were dated 10 Jan. 1724/5.

not more a maxim of Plowden,[1] when the Court was concerned, than it is of the public, when any favourite, how undeservedly soever they have raised him, comes into consideration with them. Believe me, dear sir, I am heartily and sincerely your affectionate friend and servant.

Advertise me by a letter beforehand when you send the notes, &c.

POPE *to* JONATHAN RICHARDSON[2]   [1724]

Roscoe, 1824, i. 364

I think you were directed by Providence, which took care both to show your kindness in a full light, and to prevent the uneasiness you would have had, to have found me lamenting by the side of a sick mother, and our whole family in confusion. Besides this, it was lucky that your friendship was not *a light shining in darkness*, as it must have been if you resolved to return home that evening. Your reasons both for going out, and for going home, were equally good, and agreeable to a good friend, and good husband, father, &c. I can add no more. I am confined, and likely to be so for some time. Whenever I can be a day in Town, a part of it shall be spent with you. I was once there since I saw you, but it was only to confer with Dr. Arbuthnot upon my Mother. Adieu.

*LORD PERCIVAL *to* POPE   20 *November* 1724

Add. 47030 (p. 217)

London 20 Nov: 1724

Sir,—My Lord Harcourt honourably performed his promise in appearing the day of Election for a Preacher to the Charterhouse and [has] given his vote for Mr Bearcroft my Chaplain,

I ought not to miss the first opportunity of acquainting you therewith and returning you thanks for the service you have done in this affair by prevailing on his Lordship to attend; and I beg when you have next occasion to write to him that you will express the sense I have of this obligation.

Mr Bearcroft carry'd his point with much honour, and desires me to let you know that he shall always acknowledge your kindness to him. I am | &c. | Percival.

---

[1] Edmund Plowden (1518–85) originated the proverbial expression here attributed to him. See *DNB*.

[2] This letter cannot be surely dated. It fits, however, the period in the autumn of 1724 when Mrs. Pope was very ill. It is clearly written before Mrs. Richardson died in Jan. 1725.

*POPE *to* LORD PERCIVAL   21 *November* 1724

Add. 47030 (p. 218)

Twitenham 21 Nov: 1724

My Lord,—I received the honour of yours, and am sincerely pleased
at the success of your Lordships friend. I shall express to my Lord
Harcourt what you command me, but as to my own small part; I'me
sorry your Lordship took any further notice of it than Just to order
me to do as you desired. which be assured at all times I shall most
readily do; being (with much more respect than my ways of Living
give me occasion to manifest towards you) | My Lord | your most
obedient | and faithfull | Servant | A: Pope

My Mothers very dangerous Illness has all this while prevented my
waiting on you, which I very much wished to have done.

I beg my Ladys acceptance of my Services.

POPE *to* BROOME   4 *December* 1724

Elwin–Courthope, viii. 90

Twitenham, Dec. 4, 1724.

Dear Broome,—I received yours, with the notes on lib. XI. I shall
want the twelfth by the first opportunity. The sincerity which you
really have from me, so that I will not take what you say upon that
head as a compliment, is what one friend ought to expect and to bear
from another. I will, therefore, give you a farther proof of it, both to
you who are my friend, and to the world, which I take to be my foe
thus far, that it will be ready, and for the majority, glad to take any
opportunity to blame a man it has too long praised or, at least, been
forced not to dispraise,—it being with the public, as with women, who
are cruel till they are conquered, and the moment they can defeat
themselves of him who has got the better of them, by their setting up
a new character, or gaining a new and more vigorous or responsible
gallant, they show how little for his own sake it was, that ever they
loved him. Upon a due consideration of this, as well as from an aversion against taking to myself what is not my due, it is impossible I
should do what you desire me, namely to proceed in the affair of Homer,
as if there were no person concerned in it but myself. Had our design,[1]
which I will call ours, since it was intended to promote your reputation

[1] The 'design' refers clearly not to the project of translation but to the design to deceive
the public into thinking the work of translation entirely Pope's own. Pope's reasoning in this
letter shows him in a most disingenuous light: there would have been no harm, he thinks,
in deceiving the public if the deception were complete; but now that Broome has talked of
the collaboration, attempts at deception would be futile and embarrassing. So 'honesty'
demands a confession.

in one respect more than my own, and to do what you express a great desire of, to let the public at first mistake your work for mine,—had, I say, our design been made a secret as to the particular parts we were each engaged in, as much by you, as it really was by Fenton and me, there had been no harm in it, nor any ill consequence from it, which I could have reclaimed against or scrupled, as long as I did not to my private friends make any secret of it, further than you yourselves enjoined. But, to be honest with you, you have betrayed your own secret to so many people, that it would be dishonourable and unjust for me to seem, though it were no more than by connivance or silence in the point, to take to myself what does not belong to me. If, there-fore, the fortune or fame of the work receive any prejudice from the partial opinion of the town on my side, preferably to what it ought to have on yours, I am not to blame. But when I am to propose to the public the undertaking, it would be dishonest to do it as purely my own.[1] To common acquaintance indeed there was no necessity or obligation upon me to give a particular account. But it is you yourself who have altered the case. I must therefore give the world the hint, that it is not obliged to me only for this undertaking, *coute qui coute*. All I can do in honour is not to let them into the particulars, what parts of it are, or are not mine. That I leave to you, at your own time, to do; but, to deal plainly with you, I think, for your own interest, you have chosen a wrong one, in being so early in it.

To open my mind to you freely as a christian, and talk as to a divine I protest, in the sight of Him to whom I owe any talents I have, I am as far above the folly of being vain of those I have, as I should be above the baseness of arrogating to myself those I have not. These are arts that I ever looked upon but as embellishments, not as essentials, to any estimable character. One goodnatured action or one charitable intention is of more merit than all the rhyming, jingling faculties in the world. Nay, I should think it more valuable to gratify a private friend in his desire of a character this way, than to advance my own, which I can never be proud of, when I reflect to the suffrage of what sort of creatures it is owed, and how vast a share of popular admiration proceeds from ignorance. I am, dear sir, with great sin-cerity and true good wishes, your faithful affectionate friend and servant.

I will, by the first opportunity of more leisure, give you my sincere

---

[1] Pope weakened, and when he published his Proposals in the *Daily Courant* (25 Jan. 1724/5) and other newspapers, there was no mention of collaborators. Elwin, however, in a note on this passage (ed. cit. viii. 92) quotes Pope as announcing, 'The benefit of this proposal is not solely for my own use, but for that of two of my friends, who have assisted me in this work. One of them enjoins me to conceal his name; the other is the Rev. Mr. Broome, whose assistance I have formerly acknowledged in many of the notes and extracts annexed to my translation of the Iliad.' Presumably this passage comes from the separate Proposals dated 10 Jan. 1724/5. No copy of these Proposals is now known.

opinion of the poem you sent me,[1] &c. I am now in very great haste, and express myself ill; but take it as it is meant, honestly. If you do, you will have a merit I know few capable of, but I believe you one of those few. Dear sir, adieu.

*POPE *to* EDWARD, EARL OF OXFORD

[c. 7 December 1724]

[In vol. xiii of the Portland Papers at Longleat is preserved the cover of a letter addressed 'To the Right Honourable | the Earl of Oxford | in London'. The post-mark is 7/DE, and Lord Oxford's endorsement reads, 'Mr Pope R. at Wimpole. | Dec. 8. 1724.' The letter itself is not forthcoming, and one doubts if Pope wrote to Lord Oxford between 6 November and 12 December. Those letters give no indication of a third coming between them. There is the possibility that this cover really goes with the letter of 6 November, which may have had the wrong month written into the date by accident, or Pope may have delayed posting the letter for a month. In any case no letter is known for early December.]

POPE *to* EDWARD, EARL OF OXFORD   12 *December* 1724

Longleat Portland Papers, xii

My Lord,—I troubled your Lordship with a few lines at a time, when I just expected to lose the most valuable thing I had in the world, a tender Parent, and nothing but the Certainty of your Lordships humanity in general, as well as Friendlyness to me in particular, could excuse my taking upon me to interest you so far, in what was purely a concern of my owne. Since that time, I have been so happy as to see her still alive, tho in a weak languishing condition, which at so advanced an age as hers we are yet obliged to call a Recovery. God knows for how little a time he lends her to me! long it cannot be; and I am still in constant attendance upon her in the country; excepting one day that I stole to town, more I assure you in hope of finding you there with one or two of those I most value, than for any other motive. Tho if ever I attend my Subscription, I must do it now; the time of publication drawing so nigh, & I not having (thro this unfortunate accident) yet publish'd the Proposals to the Town. I am at last determined to do it, & to take no further care about it than to publish it: since I really cannot leave my poor Mother on any account whatever. I must desire to know in what manner to treat your Lordship & Lady Oxford in the printed List, which I am to annex to this Proposal?[2] If I were to set you down for as many Subscriptions as You have procurd me, half my List

---

[1] Possibly the Epistle to Pope inserted in the concluding note to Book XXIV of the *Odyssey.* See Pope to Broome, 25 May [1725].

[2] The projected proposals were doubtless those dated 10 Jan. 1724/5, which seem to have contained a preliminary list of subscribers.

would lye at your door, & I might fairly make you a Benefactor of the greatest number. Yet as I am sensible you care not to be known for the Good you do, I am afraid to put you down in any distinguishing manner; & Yet again, I cannot bear but the world should know, that you do distinguish me. I have set down the Duchess & Duke of Buckingham for five Setts; will you allow me to do the same to your self & Lady Oxford? Mr Walpole & Lord Townshend[1] are sett down for Ten, each: I would not deny my obligations; & tis all I owe Them. But to the Duchess & to your Lordship I would keep some measures; I am so much, & ever like to be so much, in hers & your debt, that I will never tell how much, without your absolute command or leave. Let but the whole world know you favor me, & let me enjoy to myself the satisfaction of knowing to what degree? I have kept back my Proposal from the press till I have the honour of your Commands on this subject.

In the melancholy & hurry I have been, I had forgot to send the Verses on Durfey:[2] Here they are, as much corrected as they deserve, that is, but little. It would be a sincere satisfaction to me to hear that your Lordship, Lady Oxford, & Lady Margaret,[3] enjoy all the health I wish them; and that you are moving toward the place where I may tell them how truly, & with what unfeign'd respect, I am | My Lord | Your most obliged & | most obedient faithfull Servant | A. Pope.

Twitenham. | Decr 12th 1724.

Address: To | The Right Honourable, the | Earl of Oxford [Pope's hand to here]. Att | Wimpole | Cambridgeshire | By Royston Bagg [another's hand].

Frank: Free.

Postmark: 15/DE

EDWARD, EARL OF OXFORD *to* POPE   17 *December* 1724

Longleat Portland Papers, xii

Wimpole. Dec 17 1724

Sir,—I had acknowledged the favor of your letter of the 6th of November which gave me a melancholy account of your Mothers Health, not hearing she was dead I expected that every post I should have heard of her being recovered that I might have had the pleasure of congratulating you upon it, yesterday I received your letter of the

---

[1] Is it possible that the subscriptions of these two ministers of state may have been credited to them because of the grant of £200 which they secured for Pope from the royal treasury? For a facsimile of the treasury warrant, executed 26 Apr. 1724, see Maggs Bros., Catalogue 301, plate xxiii.

[2] First printed in Curll's *Miscellanea* in 1726.

[3] Lord Oxford's ten-year-old daughter, the future Duchess of Portland.

12th I am very glad to hear Mrs Pope is still alive, but though according to the course of nature it cannot be expected she should continue long here, yet when the stroke does come it will not be so surprising; since you must be sensible of the gradual approach of it. I cannot express what I feel for you upon this occasion. I leave it to you to imagine it; I thank God I am of that frame that I can and do feel very sensibly for my Friends in such circumstances. I will leave this subject. I must first thank you for sending me the Verses upon Durfey corrected: I value them as being yours.

as to the affair of your subscription I wish you had met with more success, I do not think it is at an end yet. pray why do you print the names of your subscribers with your proposals? I thought the names of your subscribers had been printed with the book that was first delivered, I think you are in the right to print proposals. as to my being set down I did forget to mention it to you when I was in town and saw you last, I would be for ten setts my Wife for five setts and peggy for one.[1]

I have some few names to give you and some few guineas. I should think my self very happy if I could at any time do you any real Service in this or any other occasion. reading over the notes upon the first book of your translation I find two lines of Horace quoted and the printer has left out a word in the first line

Seditione, dolis scelere, atque libidine & Ira,[2]

the Word *atque* is left out, there are likewise several mistakes in the pointing, I beg pardon for being so impertinent but I hope you will forgive it since friendship is the motive.

My Wife writes me word she finds great benefit by the use of the Bath Waters, I am sure she is much your Servant.

I am with true respect and esteem | Sir | Your most humble | Servant | Oxford.

I see this paper so blotted I am ashamed to send it but I have not time now to transcribe it fair. My Humble Service to mrs pope she has my Wishes for her Health.—I shall be glad to hear this comes to your hand.

---

[1] Among the subscribers named in the first volume of the *Odyssey* Robert, Earl of Oxford (d. 1724), is put down for a set; Edward, Earl of Oxford, for ten sets; the Countess of Oxford for five sets, and Lady Margaret Harley ('Peggy') for one set. It is possible that the missing letter of [c. 7 Dec.] also dealt with this matter of subscribing, and that this paragraph answers that letter, unmentioned by date.

[2] Pope printed the line with *atque* still omitted; see *Odyssey*, i (quarto 1725), 36. The line s from *Epistles*, i. ii. 15.

FENTON *to* BROOME   19 *December* 1724

Elwin–Courthope, viii. 93

Leicester Fields, Dec. 19, 1724.

Dear Mr. Broome,—I have been sitting down twenty times to give
you thanks for the favour of your last, but one trifle or other, as this
town has variety, has disturbed me, and, indeed, I have but just time
enough now to promise a closer correspondence for the future. I have
seen Pope but twice, in passing, since I came to town. How the great
affair goes on I know not, nor am inquisitive; only he told me he every
day expected the notes for I think he said the twelfth book, from whence
I conclude it advances fast. I have at last undertaken the new edition of
Waller. Mr. Briars promised to supply me with Lady Rich's life, which
will be of service to me, and I beg you to procure it for me as soon as
possible. I am very sorry to hear that you have anything to damp your
health and good-humour. To a divine and philosopher it becomes me
only to say, *modice curate ipsum*; but I am sure my best wishes ever
attend you and yours. Pray let me hear from you speedily, and do me
justice in ever believing me your affectionate humble servant.

POPE *to* MRS. NEWSHAM   21 *December* [1724]

Bowles (1806), x. 89

Twit'nam, Dec. 21.

Madam,—Having been long and closely confined at home in attending
a most dangerous illness of my mother, (whose life was wholly des-
paired of, and, through several relapses since, very precarious,) I never
heard till last week what I sincerely condole with you upon. I cannot
help breaking through the ceremony of the world, and writing as if I
had the title of a relation to you. I thank God I am of that frame, that
I can and do feel very sensibly for my friends in such circumstances.[1] I
cannot express how much; nor will words lessen whatever you feel. I
will leave this subject. When you care to hear more from me, I shall
wish to write to you; and am, indeed, with all the good wishes of a
friend, sincerely.

POPE *to* EDWARD, EARL OF OXFORD   22 *December* 1724

Longleat Portland Papers, xii

Decr 22d 1724

My Lord,—I receivd a satisfaction from your letter which nothing
was wanting to make compleat, but some news of your return to town

---

[1] Mrs. Newsham's husband had died 21 Nov. Note Pope's appropriation of sentence
from Lord Oxford's letter, *ante*, p. 277.

I very much long for it, & you will judge from hence I am in circumstances to relish the joys of life, & consequently that the Cause of my fears & griefs is removd: My Mother is beyond all degrees of Expectation, recoverd. I do not indeed ground any great prospect upon what may betray my hopes so soon; yet I can't but owne, I look upon the world with better spirits, & am more capable of enjoying its Sunshine.

I assure you my Lord I think the greatest Comfort of life, next to a good Conscience, is the Good Opinion of Good Men. If I rank you among the first of those, in whose Breasts a great part of my private felicity consists, you must pardon me for making what approaches I can towards it, in endeavoring to keep (& to deserve the first moment I am able) your *friendship*: for Upon my faith, my *Vanity* in that Word is less than my *Satisfaction* in it.

There is something of the former I must confess, in my desiring to print your Lordships name so early, with those of some others but there is also a worse thing than Vanity, some Interest too, concernd in printing the names of the Subscribers with the Proposalls. They are Incitements to Other men's vanity of being joyned with them.—Your Lordship obliges me in telling the Errata in the Notes, I wish you would do the same as to any in the Verse, which I would cancell yet, if material, both for my own sake & my friends, to whom the greater part of the notes belong. I verily think by not having loaded myself so heavily with the whole weight, I have made this Translation more exact than that of the Iliad. And indeed I was sensible it would be a much more difficult task to make the Odyssey appear in any Splendor. I hope you think it reads well upon the whole. I have printed Eleven books, & have fourteen finishd; which I hope soon to show you in London. Believe me my Lord with a full sense of your many favors | Your most faithfull | & ever obliged Servant | A. Pope.

I write to your Lordship upon the last piece of paper I have in my house, but I could not Stay so long as to get more. My Impatience must excuse my Incivility.

Address: To the Right Honorable, the | Earl of Oxford, at | Wimpole, | near | Cambridge.
Frank: Free
Postmark: /DE.

JACOB TONSON, JR. *to* POPE   23 *December* 1724

Homer MSS. Add. 4809

23d Decbr 1724.

Sir,—I cannot possably see you at Twitnam my self, I have therefur sent you the Preface from Lord Cobham, and a proof of the

Monument,[1] with the Draft; I request the favour of you to settle the Inscription as you would it, & return it to me; that the plate may be work'd: I do assure you I shall allways be very glad to oblige & serve you all in my power & am | Your obliged Faith-|full Servant | J: Tonson

I was with the Speaker[2] yesterday   he told me that you had promised to dine with him at Chiswick in the Holydays & bring your Preface (with some alteration) with you. after that I beg to have it for I am Impatient to Publish | Yours &c

‡POPE *to* ROBERT DIGBY[3]   28 *December* 1724

1735

Decemb. 28.

It is now the Season to wish you a good End of one Year, and a happy Beginning of another: but both these you know how to make yourself, by only continuing such a Life as you have been long accustomed to lead. As for Good Works, they are things I dare not name, either to those that do them, or to those that do them not; the first are too modest, and the latter too selfish, to bear the mention of what are become either too old fashion'd or too private, to constitute any Part of the Vanity or Reputation of the present Age. However, it were to be wish'd People would now and then look upon Good Works as they do upon old Wardrobes, meerly in case any of 'em should by chance come into Fashion again; as ancient Fardingales revive in modern Hoop'd Petticoats (which may be properly compar'd to Charities, as they cover a Multitude of Sins).

They tell me that at ——[4] certain antiquated[5] Charities, and obsolete Devotions are yet subsisting: That a thing called *Christian* Chearfulness (not incompatible with *Christmas* Pyes and Plumb-broth) whereof frequent is the mention in old Sermons and Almanacks, is really kept alive and in Practice: That feeding the Hungry, and giving Alms to the Poor, do yet make a Part[6] of good House-keeping, in a

---

[1] Pope's Preface to the edition of Shakespeare was making the rounds of noble critics. Tonson also encloses a proof of George Vertue's engraving of the monument in Stratford Church—which appears opposite p. xxxi of the first volume of the edition.

[2] The Hon. Spencer Compton, later Earl of Wilmington.

[3] This letter, entirely fabricated by combining two letters written to Caryll, 28 Dec. [1717] and 29 Mar. [1718], is here printed as an example of Pope's methods of adaptation. The small factual changes necessary, together with the rhetorical improvements made, can be seen in the footnotes to the two Caryll letters. Below are noted some of Pope's revisions in successive editions of the 'Digby' letter.

[4] at ——] at Coleshill *1737-42*. (The original had *Ladyholt*, and after Caryll's death Pope inserted the name of Lord Digby's estate.)

[5] certain antiquated] certain of these antiquated *quarto and folio of 1737*.

[6] yet make a Part] yet continue a part *1737 quarto and folio*.

Latitude not more remote from *London* than fourscore Miles: And lastly, that Prayers and Roast-beef actually make some People as happy, as a Whore and a Bottle.[1] But here in Town I assure you, Men, Women, and Children, have done with these things. Charity not only begins, but ends, at home. Instead of the four Cardinal Virtues, now reign four Princely[2] ones: We have Cunning for Prudence, Rapine for Justice, Time-serving for Fortitude, and Luxury for Temperance. Whatever you may fancy where you live in a State of Ignorance, and see nothing but Quiet, Religion, and Good Humour, the Case is just as I tell you where People understand the World, and know how to live with Credit and Glory.

I wish that Heaven would open the Eyes of Men, and make 'em sensible *which* of these is right: Whether upon a due Conviction, we are to quit Faction, and Gaming, and High-feeding and Whoring, and take[3] to your Country Way? or you to leave Prayers, and Alms-giving, and Reading and Exercise, and come into our Measures? I wish (I say) that this Matter were as clear to all Men, as it is to | Your affectionate, &c.

---

[1] After *Bottle* Pope switches to the second Caryll letter here used, and it is the source of the rest of the letter. See 29 Mar. [1718].

[2] Princely] courtly *1737–42*. (In the early thirties politics grew complicated. The *court* party was that of Walpole, and the Prince of Wales was in some sort allied with the Opposition, and was before 1737 a friend of Pope's: hence the shift in adjectives.)

[3] High-feeding . . . and take] High-feeding, and all manner of luxury, and take *1737–42*.

The publication of fourteen books of the *Odyssey* (vols. i–iii) and the publication of the edition of Shakespeare are the chief events of Pope's career in 1725. It is notable that letters to Aikman, Buckley, and Caryll indicate that the appearance of a name in vol. i of the *Odyssey* as a subscriber does not mean that he paid for his copy or that he paid for only one copy. One cannot estimate Pope's profits surely from the list of subscribers, but it is certain that his contemporaries thought him avaricious to bring out by subscription two lucrative works at the same time.

In his personal relations Pope's year was made pleasant by the second return of Bolingbroke, and his settlement near by at Dawley. This return, or perhaps Swift's natural elation over the completion of *Gulliver*, increased Swift's interest in his English friends, and he renewed notably his correspondence with Pope and Gay. In other quarters Pope as well as Lord Harcourt and Lord Bathurst assisted the Duchess of Buckingham in her suits against John Ward, M.P., and Pope visited her at Leighs in June briefly. The summer was marked by a disagreeable controversy with Lady Kneller over her project for removing the Pope monument from Twickenham Church to make room for a monument for Sir Godfrey. During the summer, however, Pope had pleasant rambles about Buckinghamshire with Stowe as a 'base'.

In September Dr. Arbuthnot was seriously ill, and later in the year Mrs. Pope was dangerously afflicted with jaundice. Pope himself suffered from a fever briefly in October, and on 5 November his *nutrix fidelissima*, Mercy Beech, died, aged 77.

The drudgery of completing the *Odyssey* continued throughout the year.

POPE to JACOB TONSON, JR.[1] [1725]

Add. 28275

Sunday night

Sir,—You are so perfectly in the right in your Correction of *Containing* to *Consisting of*, that I think when I print any thing of my own I must get you to do for me, what you make me do for Shakespear, and Correct in my behalf. I think now the Title is very well. I could have been very glad (not only now, but at any time) to see you; being really, with a sense of your many civilities to me, Ever | Your affect. humble Servant | A. Pope.

I thank you for the paper.

[1] Individual title-pages of the six volumes of Pope's *Shakespeare* indicate the contents in Tonson's phrase; i.e. 'Volume the First. Consisting of Comedies.' For some unknown reason these individual title-pages are all dated 'MD CC XXIII'; but the general title-pages, *The Works of Shakespear*, are dated 1725. Since title-pages are determined late, this letter falls after Pope's letter to Broome 31 Oct. 1724 and before 12 Mar. 1724/5, when finally the edition was published.

*POPE *to* CHARLES FORD[1]　　　　　[1725?]

Lord Rothschild

I find it impossible to be with you this Evening, and Gay is gone out of towne (to whom I would else have sent to go) my short stays in town, & plagu'd with business which leaves me no Hours of my own, makes me seem, much less than I am | Dear Sir | Your affectionate | humble Servant, | A. Pope.

Address: To Mr Ford at Mr Hoyes's | at the blue periwig over against the | Coco tree's in | Pall mall.

*POPE *to* CHARLES FORD　　　　　[1725?]

Harvard University

I am not only ashamed, but disapointed & uneasy, to be so long, from day to day, prevented from waiting on you; to challenge a promise you so kindly made me a fortnight ago, of passing a day here whenever I would fix it. You would give me the best and most friendly proof, that you know me so well, as not to take it ill; if you would the moment you receive this, come away & meet a Friend of yours & mine, Mr Robert Digby, here at dinner. If Mr Lewis can be induc'd by your Interest to move so quick as to attend you, I shall be very glad, I'll stay in hopes till half an hour past 2, but hope to see you as much earlier as you can. If this be not possible, I wish you would come single: Or if that be not possible, on Thursday next nothing shall prevent my waiting here for you, if you will favor me with a line by the bearer.

Believe me sincerely | Dear Sir, | Your most obli-|ged, affectionate | Servant, | A. Pope.

Tuesday, | 7 a clock in | the morning.

Address: To | Charles Ford Esqr | next door to the Greyhound | in | Berry street. | St. James's.

[1] The three 'Ford' letters that follow are undatable. The one from the Homer MSS. (Add. 4809, f. 194) is a part of Book XXI of the *Odyssey*, and naturally falls in early 1725 or thereabouts. Just preceding this (Add. 4809, f. 193*v*) is the fragment of a letter from Ford, only the first two or three words on the left margin of the page being visible. This fragment possibly declines an invitation; it mentions Thur[sday], dining with (possibly) the Duke of Wharton, and it also mentions Mr. Digb[y]. And so, by a most hypothetical inference, the letters are placed here together. During the summer and autumn of 1725 Ford was in Ireland.

*CHARLES FORD *to* POPE¹   [1725?]

Homer MSS. Add. 4809

Saterday

I sent yesterday to Mr Lewis, who accepts of your kind invitation on
monday, & I hope then I shall have the pleasure of seeing you, & of
assuring you how much I am | Dear Sir | your most obedient, & |
faithful servant | Cha: Ford.

I beg my humble respects to Mrs Pope, & pardon for the haste in
which I am oblig'd to write

BERNARD LINTOT *to* POPE   7 *January* 1724/5

Elwin–Courthope, ix. 543

London, 7th Jany., 1724.

Sir,—I have transcrib'd your 14th book of the Odyssey myself,² not
caring to trust it out of my House. Many places seem not to be
finish'd, and there are several omissions which you'll supply.

I wrote on one side only, that you might not want room for corrections. I am, sir, your most humble servant.

POPE *to* JONATHAN RICHARDSON³   20 *January* [1724/5]

Elwin–Courthope, ix. 494–5.

Twitenham, Jan. 20.

I had written you a letter by my waterman before I received that
melancholy one from your son, to which there can be no answer in
words, but I assure you my heart is sorrowful for you. I cannot but
break through all the forms of the world so far as to tell you just thus
much. For the rest you will remember the words of Job, which include
all, on these sad submissive subjects. "God has given and God has
taken." I am confined by a severe illness to take physic every day; I
would not have told you that I am so bad, but that I am troubled to be
kept from you at a time when friendship is most felt. God send you
and preserve to you other comforts to extenuate the bitter sense of
your present loss. It is the hearty prayer of, dear sir, your faithful
affectionate friend and servant.

---

¹ The position of this letter as part of *Odyssey* xxi makes it probable that the letter was
written late in 1724 or early in 1725.
² The MS. of Book XIV as preserved in Add. 4809 is in Pope's hand. The fair copy,
made in one column by Lintot, assumed that further revisions would be made—according
to Pope's almost invariable custom.
³ Nichols (*Lit. Anec.* iv. 615n.) says Richardson's wife died in 1725 on her birthday, aged
51. The letter may of course belong in Jan. 1725/6.

*POPE *to* BUCKLEY   20 *January* 1724/5

1923 William Harris Arnold[1]

Twitnam, Jan. 20th.

Sir,—I shall take it as a favour of you to insert the inclosed advertisement both in the Gazette & Daily Courant, three times. What I particularly recommend to your care is to cause it to be distinguishd with proper dignity, & the title in Capitals, as here drawn. Also to stand at the head of the more vulgar advertisements at least rankd before Eloped wives, if not before Lost Spaniels & Strayd Geldings. Do not, I beseech you, grudge to bestow One Line at large in honour of my name, who wd bestow many to celebrate yours, who am sincerely Mr Buckleys | Affectionate & hearty | Servant | A. Pope

Pray give Mr Stanyan[2] my Sincere Services. I will shortly endeavor to see you together; for, (contrary to other Poets), I will not shun you when I am in your Debt.

*POPE *to* JACOB TONSON[3]   [*January* 1724/5]

Add. 28275

I assure you I have considerd & reconsider'd this matter, & would give you all the Proofs possible that I would please you, which are consistent

---

[1] Printed from the text given (from the original) by Mr. Arnold in his *Ventures in Book Collecting* (1923), p. 183. The year is determined by Mr. Arnold from the resulting advertisements: e.g. in the *Gazette*, 23 Jan. 1724[5], headed 'Proposals by Mr. Pope, | For a Translation of Homer's Odyssey'. Mr. Arnold gives a facsimile of the advertisement, which was placed above others, as Pope requested.

[2] *Stanyar* (Mr. Arnold's reading) is corrected to *Stanyan*. Abraham Stanyan and Samuel Buckley were both employed in the office of Lord Townshend, then Secretary of State. Buckley was publisher of both the *Gazette* and the *Courant*.

[3] This letter is difficult to date unless we assume that it concerns the advertisements for subscriptions to both the *Odyssey* and the edition of Shakespeare. The proposals for both works were formally presented to the public in newspaper advertisements late in Jan. 1724/5, although subscriptions for both had been received much earlier. The proposals for the Shakespeare appeared (*Daily Courant*, 18 Jan. 1725) under the heading 'Proposals by Jacob Tonson for Mr. Pope's Edition of Shakespear'. Those for the *Odyssey* appeared exactly a week later in the same newspaper. It was unusual for a bookseller to announce a subscription for his own benefit; hence Pope wished to say that the edition of Shakespeare was not, so far as the subscription went, for his benefit. Tonson might get more subscribers if the impression that Pope was benefiting was allowed to get abroad. That Lintot (who seems to have been extremely jealous of Tonson) was annoyed is seen by the fact that the day after *The Daily Courant* (25 Jan.) published 'Proposals by Mr. Pope, For a Translation of Homer's Odyssey', the same paper published 'Proposals by Bernard Lintot for his own Benefit, for Printing a translation of Homer's Odyssey by Mr. Pope'. Lintot's advertisement practically told the public that if it did not subscribe through Pope it could save a guinea on a folio set by buying from Lintot directly. Pope had not at this stage made it clear that the Shakespeare subscription was not for his benefit, and consequently Tonson may not have been in a rage on the 26th: pretty certainly both Pope and Lintot were! See *Early Career*, pp. 240, 256, &c.

The letter is written on the blank back of a cover addressed to 'Mr Pope at the [Ear]l of Peterboroughs | Piccadilly.'

with my reason & honour. I am absolutely obligd to mention the business of Shakespear, (& it is Requird directly of me, besides, by those
whom I cannot dis-obey). But you see I comply to the utmost with
you, in leaving out all your Three Objections. The saying before that
I could not *deny it at your Request* was meant meerly to express our
Friendship, which you seemd, as well as myself to desire. Tho indeed
the putting you down as a Receiver of the Subscriptions for me, was
enough to demonstrate upon what good terms we stood. You'l see, by
this wondrous Letter inclosed, how highly Lintot takes it, in that very
light. I should be glad you could call at Lord Peterborows as soon as
you go out this morning. As to the other particular I thank you for
your advice, which I'm sure is well meant, & I believe partly Right,
but I don't think it so honourable a part to conceal the least branch
of a Truth till an Interest is servd: tis fairer to do it at first, & that's
all my reason. You may depend on my taking every thing right of you,
& upon my being sincerely, (without any views, for you'l find I have
none) | your affect. humble Servant, | A. Pope

*POPE *to* BUCKLEY¹   2 *February* [1724/5]

The Athenaeum, 17 May 1884, p. 631

Twitenham, Feb. 2d.

I am very much obligd to you for yours of the 30th. How to thank my
Lord Townshend in a proper way, I know not; but my way of thanking You, must be to beg your View of my Gardens, & to take a view
of yours, that we may put each other upon new projects, which I take
to be the True Felicity of all Planters: The Season now advancing, I
shall soon call upon you to fix a time for this—Tho you have made me
a Compliment (and still a greater, in joining my Lord Townshend to
it), yet I don't intend to give you your Full Swing that way: you must
allow me in my turn, Some pleasure of the same kind, by your accepting the Book you talk of subscribing to. I hope in a few days to find
you, & assure you how much I am, Sir | Your most faithfull Servant |
A. Pope

THE DUCHESS OF BUCKINGHAM *to* POPE²   [1725]

Homer MSS. Add. 4809

Sir,—I am much oblig'd to Lord Harcourt for his friendly assistance
in helping my Son against the variety of Injustices which we meet with

¹ Pope here thanks Buckley for giving the Proposals for the *Odyssey* good space in the
Gazette. Lord Townshend seems to have sent word by Buckley that he will subscribe for the
translation. He subscribed for ten sets, and Pope tells Buckley here that Buckley must accept
a present of a set rather than subscribe for one. Buckley's name appears among the subscribers.
² The date is based on the position of the letter in the Homer MSS. and on the mention of
the case against John Ward, M.P. for Weymouth, who had been an agent for the young Duke

HILL AND LADY SUFFOLK

Lady Suffolk is a riddle. How can one reconcile her reputation
for truth and honesty, ~~kindness and sweetness~~, *and intelligence* with the facts of her
liaison with George II? Could anything but ~~or~~ greed ~~for gain~~ or~~a~~
~~fear of~~ *have* poverty, made her tolerate the rude bullying to which he sub-
jected her? The only decent thing he did, as far as one can discover,
was to ~~build this particularly lovely house for her by the banks of~~
the Thames.

Nothing is more illuminating about the house, and its indisputably
charming occupant, that her old friend Horace Walpole's description

from Ward, there is no Body who can be oblig'd Whose Gratitude, is soe useless as a Woemans & a childs, but Ile answer for the first having a great Share of it, & I hope the other will always shew the same disposition, I am always Sir | Your faithfull humble Servant | K B

I have wrote to Lord Trevor who has appointd a meeting at our house & hopes to have the Bussines heard this sessions—I expect you to morrow

POPE *to* BROOME   13 *February* [1724/5]

Elwin–Courthope, viii. 93

London, Feb. 13, [1725].

The extreme application I am forced to at this time about the completing and publishing the book[1] is more than can be imagined by one so unacquainted with cases of this kind as yourself, besides a thousand other plagues. The only pleasure I have had was in my mother's recovery, which I thought I writ you word of. I am much obliged for the impatience you show in her regard. She is wonderfully picked up, except a great cold which still confines her. I sent lately the notes upon lib. 10, 11. Those that remain you shall have in a week or thereabouts, that the errata may be completed. You cannot imagine what a scoundrel Lintot is in all respects;[2] pray send not to him for anything, or on any account correspond with or answer him. I will take care to convey the books to you for your subscribers. I can add no more, for the post is going; but I would not omit giving you the satisfaction of a word forthwith. Believe me, dear sir, ever yours.

POPE *to* BROOME   5 *March* [1725]

Elwin–Courthope, viii. 94

March 5, [1725].

I am really concerned not to have been able, through multiplicity of business, as well as many domestic employments, joined to a very ill

of Buckingham. The Duke's trustees (he was only nine years old) included Lords Bathurst and Trevor, and they with others on 5 Feb. 1724/5 presented a petition to the House of Lords designed to clarify the title to certain estates in which there were alum works. *The British Journal*, 27 Mar. 1725, reports that the mother of the Duke has arrived at Whitby in Yorkshire and taken possession of her son's estate and alum works there pursuant to a decree in Chancery against John Ward, Esq. Presently, if not already, Ward was being accused of forgery in regard to these properties. He defended himself in *The Daily Journal* for 10 Feb. 1725/6, but was found guilty in the King's Bench Court. He was expelled from Parliament on 16 May 1726, and later stood in the pillory. See *The Historical Register* for 1725, pp. 74–76, and Cobbett, viii. 521–2. In more than one poem Pope satirized Ward.

[1] *The Odyssey.*—Broome-Elwin.

[2] It is conceivable that Lintot was refusing to furnish free subscription copies to anyone but Pope; i.e. refusing to give them to Broome. Certainly Pope might regard him as a scoundrel for his advertisements competing with Pope's for subscribers. See Sherburn, *Early Career*, p. 256.

state of health, to answer yours more fully, or to express more amply my desires of being a better correspondent to you. In a few weeks this hurry will be over, or I in a condition past requiring an excuse. My mother returns you her hearty acknowledgments, and I mine for the concern you show for us both in her. She is much better. Lintot, I perceive, will give me what silly uneasiness he can, and if I were as great a fool as he, he might. I once more desire, for very good reasons, that whatever he may write to you, you will return him no sort of word in answer. I am sorry you ever writ to him, for I know he has ill designs.¹ I hope you said nothing as to your part in the work. Upon no account write a syllable to him. It will be five or six days at least before I can send you the notes on lib. 13, 14. Return your errata with speed after you receive those.²

I have taken all care to dignify your aldermen exactly as you desired. The books shall be sent you by me. Send me a punctual direction of the carrier and his days to that end. I hope, and shall make it my particular request, soon after the books are delivered, to see you here. You shall then hear of iniquities you can have no idea of, of that fellow. Adieu till I have more leisure. If you have nothing else to do, proceed upon Eustathius. God keep you, dear Broome, and all that is yours, in which I make a prayer for your faithful affectionate servant.

Your verses on the war in Flanders³ the fool will not hear of. But I have a better project about them.

*POPE to JACOB TONSON⁴   [March 1725?]

The British Museum

Munday.

Sir,—I ought to beg your pardon for dissapointing you one morning. I thought I'd sayd I would call on you *Early*, (in order not to detain

¹ The ill designs are obscure; but already Lintot had paralleled Pope's advertisements of his Proposals with 'Proposals by Bernard Lintott for his own Benefit, for Printing a translation of Homer's Odyssey by Mr. Pope'; and Lintot's Proposals were for a large folio edition at four guineas and a small folio at fifty shillings the set. Pope's quartos only for subscribers cost five guineas. With significant emphasis Pope advertised in the *Evening Post*, 15 Apr. 1725, that 'No other Edition of this Work is printed on the same Paper, or in the same Size, or with Ornaments on Copper, which are fifty in Number, designed by Mr. Kent: Nor will any ever be exposed to Sale, or to be procured by any but the Subscribers.' He reprinted this statement at least three times later. On 18 Mar. Pope writes complaining to Fortescue (q.v.) that Lintot was trying to evade the articles concerning the distribution of the volumes. There were many chances for ill designs. See Pope's later (1743?) jottings on his letter to Henry Lintot, 29 Jan. 1739/40 (iv. 223–4), for evidence of his suspicions concerning the elder Lintot's fair dealing.

² Book XIV concluded the third volume. Vols. i–iii were published on 23 Apr. 1725.

³ Broome's 'Seat of the War in Flanders' appeared in his *Poems* (1727).

⁴ The original of this letter is bound into the British Museum copy of T. Moore's edition of Byron's *Works* (1844), xxv. 272. The pressmark of the book is C. 44. f. The present editor acknowledges transcripts furnished by Professors Knox Chandler and R. C. Bald.

The letter seems to date from 1725. One guesses that Pope wished to get from Sir Godfrey's

you long within) but your man told me you stayd the whole morning.
It so happend that I was oblig'd to go to my Lord President, who kept
me so long that I concluded you gone out. I shall be in Town on
Wensday & Thursday. On Thursday morning I'll try to find you,
Early, unless I can call sooner on you. I have a particular request to
you to send Jemmy that livd with Sr. Godfrey, to me. It requires haste,
& I wish he could be at your house by nine on Thursday morn. I am
afraid the thing cannot be done soon enough, unless you help me. I
will tell you the whole when I see you, & am Ever | Dear Sir Your
faithful hum. Servant | A. Pope

Address [verso]: To | Mr Tonson.

*POPE to FORTESCUE   18 *March* [1724/5]

The Pierpont Morgan Library

March 18th

I am extremely obliged by your kind letter; nothing gives one so much
Satisfaction, not even one's Recovery from an Illness, as to find the
very people one wishes, concernd for us. I am but barely well again, &
yet under certain regulations & restrictions not at all welcome to a
man of my temper.

Your dismal journey (the circumstances whereof you paint with a
grievous Vivacity) makes me apply to you what Catullus says, very
a propos to your Sentiments of Home & Ease.

> O quid solutis est beatius Curis!
> Cum mens onus reponit, & Peregrino
> Labore fessi, venimus Larem ad nostrum,
> Desideratoque acquiescimus Lecto![1]

One sees the Ancients are often content with saying a very plain
thing, if it be but very natural. The last of these lines has a lazy indolent Flow of languishing Numbers, that perfectly corresponds with
the Weariness and Sense of Repose describd in it.

It is really a piece of Consideration & kindness, that you express, in
excusing me from writing a long letter, or showing my Witt at such
a distance as Devonshire. Tho could I do Devonshire or you any

Jemmy the servant's story concerning a conversation possibly overheard between Sir Godfrey
and Pope concerning the painter's monument. Pope would like to hear it before Lady Kneller
had the story biased in her favour; hence the haste. (See letters to the Earl of Strafford and
Lord Harcourt in July and thereafter.) But the Lord President must pretty certainly be
Lord Carleton (the only Lord President with whom Pope is known to have been intimate),
and Lord Carleton died on 14 Mar. 1724/5. Lady Kneller's first legal *démarches* began late in
June, but she had doubtless alarmed Pope by personal approaches considerably earlier, and
when legal action became possible, he would rush for Jemmy's evidence.

[1] Catullus, xxxi. 7–10.

pleasure, it is but what I honestly owe, for the fine Scollops which that happy Clime produces. Those you favor me with are very safe arrived & have done me no little credit with the Dutchess of Hamilton. Alas! with any Female they will do me little credit, if I eat them myself: I have no way so good to please 'em, as by presenting 'em with any thing rather than with my self.

Dr Arbuthnot is highly mindful of you. He has (with my Consent) put a Joke upon Gay & me, out of pure disposition to give him joy & gladness. Gay is made to believe that I had a Clap, of which I fancy you'l hear his Sentiments in that ludicrous way, which God has given him to excell all others in.

Lintot has manifested great Desire, but attended with great Impotence, to play the Scoundrell. I could not but smile when he told me, you took him by the hand at parting, & advisd him, Mr Lintot, whatever you do, don't go to Law! You are to [be] a judge whether by the articles he is obligd to deliver the books at his Shop to the Subscribers who send for 'em. The words are— *& to deliver the same books at his House or Shop fr[om ti]me to time to whatever person or persons Mr Pope shall appoint.*[1] But of this (in which are many things that will make you laugh) you will hear when we meet, which I hope will be soon. I am with all fidelity & affection | Dear Sir. Your most obligd | humble Servant | A. Pope.

Address (in part perished): To | William Fortescue [Esq.] | [at] Fallapit | Kingsbridge | Devon
Postmark: 18/MR

BOLINGBROKE to HARCOURT[2]   22 March 1725

Harcourt MSS.

Dawley Farm March the 22d | 1725

My Lord,— Whilst I am here troubling myself very little about any thing beyond the extent of my farm, I am the subject of some conversations in town which one would not have expected. Ile mention one of these to your Lordship. Arthur Moore has in two several

1 The indenture signed 18 Feb. 1724/5 does not contain the words here reported by Pope. It simply says copies shall be delivered 'unto the said Alexander Pope his Executors Administrators or Assignes'. When the copies were ready for delivery, Pope advertised in the *Gazette* of 13, 17, and 20 Apr. (and in other newspapers), 'That the first 3 Volumes are ready to be deliver'd to the Subscribers, at Mr. Jervas's Principal Painter to his Majesty, next Door to the Right Hon. the Lord Viscount Tounshend's, in Cleveland-Court, St. James's.' (The *Iliads* also had been delivered from Jervas's house.)

2 This letter so intimately concerns the closest friend of Pope for the rest of his life that it seems worth printing. One judges that Bolingbroke is newly settled at Dawley. His case was decided (not to his satisfaction) in May 1725, and he took the oaths of allegiance in June. It is conceivable that the letter was designed to suggest that whereas he had not caballed with Pulteney, such an alliance might under certain circumstances be made—as indeed it presently was.

companys answer'd persons, who were inquisitive whether my at-
tainder would be repeal'd in this session, by saying that it could not
be imagin'd the government would do any thing in my favour whilst
I was caballing against it with Mr Pulteney. if this report was to be
thrown into the world, Arthur Moore might with a better grace have
left it to be propagated by some other Emissary;[1] and if it be design'd
as an excuse for leaving me in my present condition, than which none
more cruel can be invented, I do assure your Lordship that the Excuse
shall not stand good. I have very much esteem for Mr Pulteney, I
have met with great civillity from him, and shall on all occasions behave myself towards him like a man who is oblig'd to him. but my
Lord I have had no private correspondence, or even conversation with
him, and whenever I appeal to the King & beg leave to plead my
cause before him, I will take care that his Ministers shall not have the
least pretence of objection to make to me in any part of my conduct.
I will only say upon this occasion that if I had caball'd against them,
there would have been other things said than were said, and another
turn of opposition given. I dare say your Lordship acquits me upon
this head, but I do not know Whether you will so easily forgive me
the length of this letter upon so trifling a subject. do in the matter what
you think proper. perhaps you will mention it to my Lord privy Seal,[2]
as I shall do when I have the honour of seeing him. my return to
London will depend on the arguing my pleas in chancery, & that
cannot be long delay'd. I am faithfully your Lordships most obedient
humble | Servant | Bolingbroke

Endorsement: 22 March 1725 | Lord Bolingbroke | to | the Lord Vicount |
Harcourt

POPE *to* BROOME   30 *March* [1725]

Elwin–Courthope, viii. 95

March 30, [1725].

Dear Broome,—I would not omit writing to you this very day I
received yours, though I have a great parcel of company, who hinder
me from saying more than just this—that I would not have you come
to town, for a very good reason relating to the fool you write about,
till the books are safely delivered to your people. It will be ready, I
hope, within seven days; but the days of your carrier falling out cross,
it must be Saturday se'ennight before they can be sent.[3] I will before

---

[1] Although Arthur Moore was at this time a devoted follower of Walpole, he had before
1714 been more than once aided and protected by Bolingbroke: hence his lack of 'grace' in
propagating gossip about Bolingbroke. See *DNB*.   [2] The Duke of Kingston.
[3] 'Saturday se'ennight' would be 10 Apr. On 8 Apr. Pope again wrote to Broome and promised the books on the 10th. According to the *Gazette* copies were available for subscribers
at Jervas's house on the 13th.

that write largely to you, and I hope to see you before Whitsuntide,—the sooner after the delivery the better. However, if you can procure a longer recess, I wish it, that I may keep you the longer here, Dear sir, adieu.

POPE *to* LORD BATHURST[1]   [1725?]

Cirencester

Twitnam. Saturday

My Lord,—There was a Man in the Land of Twitnam, called Pope. He was a Servant of the Lord Bathurst of those days, a Patriarch of great Eminence, for getting children, at home & abroad. But his Care for his Family, and his Love for strange women, caused the said Lord to forget all his Friends of the Male-Sex; insomuch that he knew not, nor once rememberd, there was such a man in the Land of Twitnam as aforesaid. It were to be wisht, he would come & see; or if nothing else will move him, there are certain Handmaids belonging to the said Pope which are comely in their goings, yea which go comelily. If he will not vouchsafe to visit either his Servant, or his handmaids, let him (as the Patriarchs anciently did) send flocks of Sheep & Presents in his stead: For the grass of Marble hill springeth, yea it springeth exceedingly & waits for the Lambs of the *Mountains*, (meaning Riskins) to crop the same

Till then, all Mrs Howard's Swains
Must feed—*no* flocks, upon—*no* plains.[2]

My dear Lord, adieu, (if *Adieu* be not too impertinent, pretending, a word, where one has never once *met*.) I am faithfully Your most Real Servant | A. Pope.

My hearty Service to all your Wives & Daughters.

[On verso, near the edge, appears:] Patty is yours extremely.

Address: To the Rt. Hon. the | Lord Bathurst. | St. James Square |

POPE *to* BROOME   8 *April* 1725

Elwin–Courthope, viii. 96

April 8, 1725.

On Saturday next, according to your desire, I will send by your carrier,

---

[1] Since Lord Bathurst had been concerned in laying out the grounds of Marble Hill, he probably would be interested in the springing of the grass in the lawns there for the first time n 1725. Early spring seems the proper moment for the letter.

[2] In 1714 members of the Scriblerus Club had invited Robert, Earl of Oxford, to meet with them, addressing him each in an original couplet. Gay's couplet was:

Leave Courts, and hye to Simple Swains,
Who feed *no* Flocks upon *no* Plains. (See i. 217.)

in a wooden box, fourteen sets of Homer for your subscribers.¹ Some of their names came from you too late to be inserted, but shall in the last volume, together with the errata, which the bookseller desired to have postponed to the end of the book. I shall rejoice to see you the moment the delivery is over here, which will be about the twentieth of this month. Before, I shall not have leisure to enjoy any pleasure, and would not lose one that will be unfeignedly so great as the seeing and living with you. Pray let me have a line of your receipt of the books. My mother is much better. I wish you as myself all domestic happiness, and increase of all sorts of happiness. Dear Broome, adieu. Fenton is well. So am I. Your own books I keep till we meet. Yours ever.

---

*POPE *to* MRS. CÆSAR²   [*April* 1725?]

Rousham

Madam,—You will see by the inclosed I have obeyd You in some Articles, as to Lord Stafford Lady Sarah, &c. I took another liberty with Your own Name, which you knew nothing of, nor I dare say could have Suspected; & have made a Star of Mrs Cæsar,³ as well as of Mrs Fermor. If any body asks you the reason of this, quote to 'em this verse of Virgil,

—Processit Cæsaris astrum. | Ecl. 5.

I am daily in hopes of waiting on you when I hear you are in town, Your most oblig'd Servant | A. Pope.

Address: To | Mrs Cæsar | Present

¹ This remark fixes the number of subscribers Broome had at this time secured. In a note to the quarto *Dunciad* of 1729, Bk. III, l. 328, Pope answered critics by announcing that 'in the undertaking of the *Odyssey* . . . Mr. *Broome* having ingaged without any previous agreement, discharged his part so much to Mr. *Pope's* satisfaction, that he gratified him with the full sum of *Five hundred pounds*, and a present of all those books for which his own interest could procure him Subscribers, to the value of *One hundred more*.' Fourteen subscribers would mean seventy guineas rather than 'the value of one hundred more'. It is possible that before June 1726, when the last volumes were published, Broome secured an additional half-dozen subscribers. He certainly read Pope's note in *The Dunciad* before making his formal statement verifying Pope's footnote in his letter to Pope of 29 Oct. 1735. Broome was never better paid for poetry than by Pope, and his complaints normally were that he was robbed of reputation by the concealment of his full share in the work, not that he was financially robbed.

² This letter is bound into the copy of the *Odyssey* presented by Pope to Mrs. Cæsar. At Rousham also is preserved a receipt in Pope's hand, dated 20 Feb. 1724/5, for 210 guineas received from Mrs. Cæsar for 70 subscriptions secured by her.

³ Among the printed names of subscribers are the Earl of Stafford and Lady Sarah Cowper. Mrs. Cæsar's name is printed in capitals (as no others are) with an asterisk or 'star' prefixed. This was in reward for her notable efforts in getting subscribers. Mrs. Fermor (or her 'lock') became a star at the end of *The Rape of the Lock*. The phrase from Virgil is not from Eclogue V but from Eclogue IX. 47. Line 51 of Eclogue V *might* have been adapted to the occasion.

*W. AIKMAN *to* POPE¹   [1725]

Homer MSS. Add. 4809

Sir,—I receiv'd your Valuable Present by the hands of Mr Clerk, as
much unexpected as it is unmerited, the obligation putts me out of
countenance but I owne it with Gratitud, which is all that is in the
power of | Sir | Your most obliged | humble Servant | W. Aikman

Suffolk Street | Freyday 11. a clock.

POPE *to* FORTESCUE²   10 *May* [1725?]

Add. 32567 (Mitford's transcript)
                                          Twitnam May 10th.

I thank you for the Constant Memory of me which upon every occasion you show, when (God knows) my daily infirmities make me
hardly capable of showing, tho very much so, of feeling the concerns
of a friend. I am glad your family are well arrived, & your taking care
first to tell me so, before I enquired, is a proof you know, how glad
I am of yours & their Welfare. I intended to tell *you* first, how kind
Sir R. Walpole has been to me, for you must know he *did* the thing,
with more dispatch, than I could use in *acknowledging* or *telling* the
News of it. Pray thank him for obliging you, (that is *me*) so readily: and
do it in strong terms, for I was awkward in it, when I just mentioned
it to him. He may think me a worse Man than I am, tho' he thinks
me a better Poet perhaps: and he may not know that I am much more
his Servant, than those who would flatter him in their Verses. I have
more esteem for him, & will stay till he is out of Power (according to
my Custome) before I say what I think of him. It puts me in Mind
of what was said to him once before by a Poet,

        In Power, your Servant, out of Power, your friend.

which a Critick (who knew that Poet's mind) said should be alterd
thus,
        In Pow'r your friend; but out of Power—your Servant.

Such most Poets are! but if Sir R. ever finds me the first low Character,

¹ Aikman's name is found among those of the subscribers to the *Odyssey*, but from this
letter one suspects that his set was a gift. If Aikman is the portrait-painter, his connexion
with Pope is not too clear, but he painted various of Pope's friends, including John Gay.
Aikman is said to have lived in Leicester Fields. A portrait of Pope still in Chiswick House
has been ascribed both to Aikman and (more plausibly) to Kent. It is badly reproduced in
Elizabeth Balch's *Glimpses of Old English Houses*, 1890, p. 137.

² The indeterminate year has been thought by Roscoe and Elwin to mark the favour
Walpole did in securing an abbey for Pope's early benefactor Father Southcote. Possibly
Pope here refers to the treasury order for £200 which Walpole had signed in Apr. 1725 to
further the translation of the *Odyssey*. The abbey was not secured 'with dispatch'. See
G. D. Henderson, *Chevalier Ramsay*, p. 90.

let him expect me to become the second. In the Meantime I hope he will believe me his, in the same Sincere disinterested Manner that I am | Dear Sir | Yours | A. Pope.

Next Sunday I expect some Company here, but that needs not hinder you from a Night's lodging in the Country, if you like it.

Address: To Wm Fortescue Esqr. at his House in | Bell-yard near Lincolns-Inn, | London.

POPE *to* BROOME   25 *May* [1725]

Elwin–Courthope, viii. 96

May 25, [1725].

I am very glad of your safe return,[1] but wanted a good while to hear of it. The shade and solitude you so much delight in is indeed a truer and more rational situation to a good mind, than all the glitter and vanity of that part of the world which we sillily call the great world, which glitter is only fit, as Milton expresses it somewhere, to

Dazzle the crowd, and set them all agape.[2]

It is but a pleasure for the mob; and those we call the great are the meanest creatures of all, since they are most in the cognizance and most under the judgment of the populace; whereas the retired and contentedly unambitious person is above all their opinions and censures, and appeals only to the highest of all powers, God, for his actions and life.

I hope, at intervals from Eustathius, you will seriously overlook those pieces of poetry you told me of; and by all means make an entire volume of them, not dispersed and scattered into nothing in Miscellanies, where a few good things among a crowd of bad fare like a few good men in the same circumstance, and are put out of countenance, if not corrupted. I only could be glad one copy of yours, that which you design to me, as a memorial of our friendship, may appear not only among your own, but attend also upon mine, in the new edition of my things which Lintot is printing, together with the testimonies of some other of my friends.[3] Therefore, when you have finished your additions to it, send them to me, with the sixteenth and eighteenth books. After you have done the notes to those books in

---

[1] Broome (with Mrs. Broome?) has evidently paid a visit to Twickenham, and returned to Sturston.

[2] *Paradise Lost*, v. 357.

[3] Under varying titles Broome's verses 'To Mr. Pope, On his Works, 1726' appeared in the fifth edition of Lintot's (and Pope's) *Miscellaneous Poems and Translations*, 1726 and 1727; in the fifth volume of the *Odyssey* (1726) in Broome's final note; in Broome's *Poems* (1727, 1739, &c.), and in vol. i of Pope's *Works*, 1736 ff.

their order, proceed to the twenty-first, omitting the nineteenth and twentieth, if you please, at present.

My mother always remembers you, and wishes we were near enough to be neighbours to Mrs. Broome. Sir Clement Cottrell and the rest of your friends here drink your health and inquire of you. Fenton only is silent. His body is buried in Windsor Forest; his εἴδωλον glides over those lawns, and his soul flies up to Homer and heaven. Dear sir, adieu.

Sit tibi cura mei, sit tibi cura tui.

Yours faithfully.

†POPE *to* EDWARD BLOUNT[1]   2 *June* 1725

1735

June 2, 1725.

You shew your self a just Man and a Friend in those Guesses and Suppositions you make at the possible reasons of my Silence; every one of which is a true one. As to forgetfulness of you or yours, I assure you, the promiscuous Conversations of the Town serve only to put me in mind of better, and more quiet, to be had in a Corner of the World (undisturb'd, innocent, serene, and sensible) with such as you. Let no Access of any Distrust make you think of me differently in a cloudy day from what you do in the most sunshiny Weather. Let the young Ladies[2] be assured I make nothing new in my Gardens without wishing to see the print of their Fairy Steps in every part of 'em. I have put the last Hand to my works of this kind,[3] in happily finishing the subterraneous Way and Grotto; I there found a Spring of the clearest Water, which falls in a perpetual Rill, that echoes thro' the Cavern day and night. From the River *Thames*, you see thro' my Arch up a Walk of the Wilderness to a kind of open Temple, wholly compos'd of Shells in the Rustic Manner; and from that distance under the Temple you look down thro' a sloping Arcade of Trees, and see the Sails on the River passing suddenly and vanishing, as thro' a Perspective Glass. When you shut the Doors of this Grotto, it becomes on the instant, from a luminous Room, a *Camera obscura*; on the Walls of which all the objects of the River, Hills, Woods, and Boats, are forming a moving Picture in their visible Radiations: And when you have a mind to light it up, it affords you a very different Scene: it is

---

[1] This letter appeared in all Pope's editions except 1735 a2. The more important of Pope's textual revisions, given below, indicate that in revising he brought up to date certain small details concerning the development of his gardens. In his octavo editions of 1737–42 Pope added 'Twick'nam' to the superscribed date.

[2] Blount's daughters.

[3] To the end of his life Pope was always just completing 'final' improvements in his garden.

finished with Shells interspersed with Pieces of Looking-glass in angular forms; and in the Cieling is a Star of the same Material, at which when a Lamp (of an orbicular Figure of thin Alabaster) is hung in the Middle, a thousand pointed Rays glitter and are reflected over the Place. There are connected to this Grotto by a narrower Passage two Porches⌐, with Niches and Seats⌐;[1] one toward the River, of smooth Stones, full of light and open; the other toward the Arch of Trees,[2] rough with Shells, Flints, and Iron Ore. The Bottom is paved with simple Pebble, as the[3] adjoining Walk up the Wilderness to the Temple, ⌐is to be Cockle-shells,⌐[4] in the natural Taste, agreeing not ill with the little dripping Murmur, and the Aquatic Idea of the whole Place. It wants nothing to compleat it but a good Statue with an Inscription, like that beautiful antique one which you know I am so fond of,

> *Hujus Nympha loci, sacri, custodia fontis,*
> *Dormio, dum blandæ sentio murmur aquæ.*
> *Parce meum, quisquis tangis cava marmora somnum*
> *Rumpere, seu bibas, sive lavere, tace.*

> Nymph of the Grot, these sacred Springs I keep,
> And to the Murmur of these Waters sleep;
> Whoe'er thou art, ah gently tread the Cave,
> Ah Bathe in silence, or in silence lave.[5]

You'll think I have been very Poetical in this Description, but it is pretty near the Truth. I wish you were here to bear Testimony how little it owes to Art, either the Place itself, or the Image I give of it. | I am, &c.

POPE *to* JONATHAN RICHARDSON[6]   10 *June* 1725

The Pierpont Morgan Library

I was much pleas'd at the receiving your kind letter, after an Involuntary absence of above a Month (for I was thrice at your door) I'm just return'd from the Duchess of Buckingham's in Essex, & shall

---

[1] The seats and niches are omitted in editions after *1735.*
[2] toward the Arch of Trees] toward the Garden shadow'd with trees *1737–42.*
[3] as the] as is also the *1737–42.*
[4] Omitted *1737–42.*
[5] The second couplet in editions of *1737–42* reads:

> Ah spare my slumbers, gently tread the cave!
> And drink in silence, or in silence lave!

The quarto and folio of *1737* have *Ah drink* in the last line.
[6] The punctuation and meaning of the first sentence are confusing. The comma after *letter* might well have been omitted, and a period after the parenthesis would help. The involuntary absence is from Richardson's society: Pope has called in vain thrice, and being now just returned from Leighs, invites Richardson to Twickenham.

be heartily glad you will take a Bed at my house when you come to Bushy. Homer (whom I hope you will read, for that is the best way of thanking me) will tell you, that Hospitality is the Glory of Friendship, & that, in His days, no man visited a Friend, without passing the Night as well as Day, with him, & making a Libation to Mercury, A bon repos. If nothing else calls you out of town, why not Make the Sunday Holy to Friendship? Let me know first. You seem to me a Poet, no less than a Painter, in forgetting to tell me what new house you have taken. However I'll try to find you the next (and I believe only time) I shall see London this summer, in Lincolns inn fields. Dear Sir adieu | Yours faithfully | A. Pope

June 10th | 1725.

Address: To Mr Richardson, | at the Golden ball in | Holborne row | Lincolns inn fields

Postmark: PENY [POST PAYD]

JAMES GIBBS *to* POPE[1]   [1725?]

Homer MSS. Add. 4809

Gerard street 4 acloke

Sir,—Mr Rysbracks[2] house is in the further end of Bond street Just cross Tyburn Rode in Lord Oxfords ground upon the right hand, going to his Chaple—but I will wait on you att Williames coffie house near St Jameses about five on thursday who am Sr | your most humble servant | Ja Gibbs

I beg my most detutyfull respect to My Lord Bathurst

Address: For Alexr Pope Esqr | at the Right Honble the | Lord Bathursts House | in St James Sqr |

LORD BATHURST *to* POPE[3]   [*June*, 1725?]

Homer MSS. Add. 4809

Sir,—I will not fail to attend Mrs Howard upon Marble Hill next

[1] The position of the letter in the Homer MSS. indicates that it was written in the summer of 1725. Rysbrack, so Mrs. M. I. Webb informs the editor, began paying rates for his premises in Vere Street in August of 1725.
[2] Vertue in 1732 reports seeing various carvings of Michael Rysbrack, among them 'Mr. Alex Pope ... a Marble'. *Walpole Society*, xxii (1934), 56. Michael came to England in 1720. By 1730 Lord Oxford had in his library at Wimpole a bust or head of Pope (see Pope to Oxford, 1 Oct. 1730). On 2 Apr. of a year undetermined but here guessed at as 1726 Pope addressed an epigrammatic quatrain to Oxford about a busto that was not too satisfactory.
[3] The position of this letter near the end of Book XXII of the *Odyssey* suggests the approximate date. Pope had made a visit to Leighs (Essex) earlier in the month, and was doubtless at home for the vestry hearing about the Kneller monument on the 30th. From Bath Lady Hervey wrote to Mrs. Howard on 7 June 1725 saying 'here it is as cold as in winter'. Lord Bathurst probably writes from Riskins.

tuesday, but Lady Bathurst is not able to come at this time, which is no small mortification to her. I hope I shall perswade John Gay & you to come hither to me, for I really think such a wintry summer as this shou'd be past altogether in society by a Chimney-corner. but I believe I shou'd not lie if I assur'd you that I wou'd quit the finest Walk on the finest day in the finest Garden to have your Company at any time. this is saying a great deal more than is commonly understood by an¹ I am | Yr most faithfull humble servant | Bat[hurst]

Address: To | Alexander Pope Esq

POPE *to* CARYLL   [*Mid-June* 1725]

Add. 28618

I was not a little vexed at such a series of ill luck and of mistakes as happened to me last week. First, I missed of being at home, which I would not have done had I known in the least of your calling. Then I was obliged the next day but one to go into Essex with the Duchess of Bucks.² The only four hours I was able to be in town I could not learn where you lodged, and your letter met me at my return, which told me you were gone.

I ordered my agent expressly to leave your book³ without payment. All I meant was to send you one to read till you ordered the remainder. I also fancied that since 'twas possible you might not have got off the 4 subscriptions I sent you, you might prefer to have but 2 Sets, and so I would have taken the payment you made to Mrs Cope for the whole in full. Indeed, I can't imagine how Lady Mary's name was omitted in the list. I sent it myself to the printer; but many such mistakes have been committed, (which I'll take effectual care to set right in the last volume)⁴ to the number of 30, or 40. I did purposely omit to set you down for four sets, for the reason I just now mentioned to excuse you from being taxed too high, which I least of all Care my friends should be. Pray assure Lady Mary (for whom I have a just value) of my concern at this. I know you yourself will excuse everything in | Dear sir | Your aff. friend and servant | A. P.

¹ The article shows the conclusion treated as a substantive.
² This letter must have been written after the publication of the *Odyssey* (vols. i–iii) late in April. It is here assumed, perhaps wrongly, that Pope's visit to Leighs took place between 2 June, when he wrote to Edward Blount from Twickenham, and 10 June, when he wrote to Richardson that he had just returned from the visit. In Pope's idiom 'just returned' is an indefinite expression.
³ The *Odyssey*.
⁴ Lady Mary Caryll's name, however, does not appear in vol. v, where names of subscribers unhappily omitted from vol. i were set down. In vol. i Caryll's name appears, but without indication that he subscribed for extra sets. The case indicates how unreliable the list of subscribers is as a basis for determining Pope's monetary rewards for the 'undertaking'.

SIR JAMES ASHE to POPE[1] [1725?]

Homer MSS. Add. 4809

Sir,—I beg I may waite on you before you [go] from Twick this day, or to send me the paper you brought yesterday Just to see it, by the bearer, to be Returned againe, I hope you will excuse the Early hower and oblige in this without faile | Yoor Humble | Servant Ja Ashe

Munday

POPE *to* THE EARL OF STRAFFORD[2] *June* [1725]

The Hyde Collection

My Lord,— Your Lordship will be surprized at my impudence in troubling you in your repose & elegant retirement at Boughton: You may think I could only do so at Twitnam. And much less could you expect Disturbance from any but a Living bad Neighbour. Yet such my Lord is now your Case, that you are to be molested at once by a Living, & a Dead one. To explain this riddle, you may find it very inconvenient, on a Sunday (your usual day of Rest here) not only to be prest in upon, in an Evening by me, but Shoulder'd in a morning at Church by Sir Godfrey Kneller, & his huge Lady into the bargain. A *Monition* (I think they call it) from the Doctors Commons was publishd here last Sunday, wherein That Pious widow desires their Leave to pull down the Tablet I set up at the head of your Lordships Pew, to fix there a Large one to Sir G. & herself, with both their Figures. If your Lordship should really chance to take no great pleasure in beholding My Name full before your eyes, (which I should not wonder at,) Yet at least, (Dangerous as that Name is, & dreadful to all true Protestant ears,) It cannot Incommode you so much, as a vast three-hundred-pound-Pyle, projecting out upon you, overshadowing my Lady Strafford with the Immense Draperies & Stone Petticoats of Lady Kneller, & perhaps crushing to pieces your Lordships Posterity! This period sounds very poetical; and yet Reeves

---

[1] It is a possible assumption that this neighbour of Pope's is interested in Pope's trouble with Lady Kneller over the monument for Sir Godfrey. Writing to Lord Harcourt (3 July) Pope remarks that 'some of the chief Gentlemen of this Parish have enter'd their Dissent & signd a Certificate to object to the removal of the Tomb' of Pope's father. In 1713 Sir James was one of the trustees appointed to consider rebuilding the parish church, 'it having fallen down on the night of Thursday, April 9th, 1713' (Cobbett, *Memorials of Twickenham* [1872], p. 198). We shall presently find Pope suggesting to the Earl of Strafford that the monument designed for Sir Godfrey will be so heavy as to endanger the wall of the church.

[2] This letter and later ones concerning the desire of Lady Kneller to have the Pope monument removed so as to give space for a monument to Sir Godfrey are largely self-explanatory. The monition was evidently first read on 27 June, and Pope started a counter-offensive at once. For the early stages of the affair the best account is found in his letter to Lord Harcourt, 3 July.

seriously tells me, & allows me to tell your Lordship as seriously, that the main Wall at your Pew will be greatly in danger of falling, by the addition of such a Tomb. What I have to beg of your Lordship as a favor is, that you will please to declare your Dissent & Objection, directing a few lines only in general to That effect as your Commands to Mr Pearson, Proctor in the Doctors Commons, & inclose it to me at Twitnam.[1] They have appointed the *thirtieth of this month* for such of the Parish as have Any Objections, to shew them in Court, otherwise the License will be given her. I thought fit, first of all, to apply to you, My Lord, who (I would fain persuade myself) will be concernd against it, next to me; not only as the neerest Neighbor to it, but as the person I would hope would most favour me. The Innovations upon all sorts of Property, & the Dangers of ill Precedents of all kinds, are what your Lordship is a well-known Opposer of: I hope you will not be so the less tho' it is but the particular Cause of one, who so justly, & so sincerely, respects & honours you.

I am | My Lord, | Your Lordships most Obedient | & most obligd humble Servant | A. Pope.

My Mother joins in her faithful humble Services, & in my petition for Your PROTEST (a word, your Lordship is of late well acquainted with).

Endorsement: Mr Pope about Lady | Knellers pew in July 1725[2]

*ROBERT PEIRSON to POPE[3]   29 June 1725

Homer MSS. Add. 4809

Sir,—I was favour'd with yours with the Certificate inclosed and shall according to your directions attend Dr Phipps therewith and in due time wait on Mr Pigott, all possible Care shall be taken by | Sir | Your most humble servant | Robt Peirson.

Doctors Commons | 29: Junii 1725

[1] See 29 June for Peirson's letter acknowledging the receipt of documents from Pope.

[2] The month named in the endorsement is the month of most of this affair, but obviously not of this letter.

[3] Peirson is mentioned in Pope's earlier letter to Lord Strafford as his proctor in Doctors' Commons. Mr. Pigott is evidently Pope's neighbour at Whitton, an eminent Catholic man of law, who could ably present the rights of a Catholic under circumstances such as Pope faced. Dr. Phipps is perhaps the officer to hear Lady Kneller's petition. The certificate is evidently that signed by 'some of the chief Gentlemen of this Parish' protesting against Lady Kneller's proposal.

POPE *to* BROOME   29 *June* [1725]

Elwin–Courthope, viii. 98

June 29, [1725].

I received yours, and ought to express my sense of the favour you so
zealously show me many ways, particularly in the verses you design to
me. I want to see them, for it is sure something a better principle than
vanity that renders such testimonials valuable to me from valuable
men. All incense from other hands, stinks. Honesty only can make
fiction itself pleasing; and fiction itself has no grace but from honesty.

I cannot learn whether Tonson yet prints a small edition of Shakespear. Your conjecture of "cloves in my cap," instead of "gloves," in
King Lear, is certainly a right one.[1]

Fenton is at the Lady Judith Trumbull's at Easthampstead Park,
near Ockingham, by Bagshot Bag, Berks. I condole with you upon
his deep taciturnity, not a word having, that I hear of, escaped him
to anybody.

I am concerned that you seem to feel your labour increase, as your
task grows lighter, and nearer your journey's end. *Dabit Deus his
quoque finem*, &c.[2] *O passi graviora!* I believe Bayle's Dictionary on
the article of Penelope will relieve you. I desire a packet; the sooner
now the better. I have got through two books of verse.[3] The sixteenth
ought to be furnished without delay for the press. I have gone backwards and been at the wrong end till now. Be sure let me have notice
before you send, and send by a safe hand.

My cares are grown upon me, and I want relaxation. But when
shall I have it? Hurry, noise, and the observances of the world, take
away the power of just thinking or natural acting. A man that lives so
much in the world does but translate other men; he is nothing of his
own. Our customs, our tempers, our enjoyments, our distastes are not
so properly effects of our natural constitution, as distempers catched by
contagion. Many would live happily without any ill ones, if they lived
by themselves.

Infelix!
Qui notus nimis omnibus,
Ignotus moritur sibi.[4]

For a few weeks I shall be obliged to go into Buckinghamshire,[5]

---

[1] For his duodecimo edition of Shakespeare (1728) Pope did not use Broome's emendation
in spite of this momentary approval. 'Cloves in my cap' would not seem absurd in Pope's
day, when a remedy for head colds was the wearing of pads enclosing savoury herbs under
the wig.   [2] *Aeneid*, i. 199.   [3] Presumably xv and xvii?

[4] Seneca, *Thyestes*, 402–3 (without 'Infelix!').

[5] Presumably to Lord Cobham at Stowe. See his letter to Digby here placed 12 Aug.
[1725]. Visits to Riskins, which was not far from Twickenham, normally were frequent
and brief, and such a visit seems to be the one mentioned by Digby in his letter to Pope of
2 July.

where I hope for more leisure than at home; so I could wish to hear from you as soon as possible. I may stay here yet these seven or eight days. Believe me most sincerely and affectionately yours.

My mother is moderately well, and very truly your servant.

*THE EARL OF STRAFFORD *to* POPE[1]   [*June* 1725]

Homer MSS. Add. 4809

FRAGMENT

. . . the difference will be very conspicuous between a man favour with many advantageous Court imployments & one turnd out of all

one valluable thing I hope I shall preserve which is the hapiness of your friendship & esteem the continuation of which is much desired | by sir | Your most sincere | humble servant | Strafford

THE DUCHESS OF BUCKINGHAM *to* POPE   [1725?]

Homer MSS. Add. 4809

This is first to tell You that I hope You found Your Mother in very good Health & made your peace with the old woman for staying abroad soe long[2] she will probably describe You by the Gadder as she did Mr Compton[3] by the Prater—I know tis unnecessary but I desire Youl say nothing of what you know about [Mr. Sheff]eilds[4] being at present not well in my favour Except to my Lord Bathurst in Case he mentions it because I have many Reasons to have the perticuler Circomstances as little spoke on as possible & not the Man at all at least for some time

I am ever | Sir | Your most humble | Servant | K B

[1] This fragment (of Strafford's reply to Pope's letter to his lordship) seems worth printing as showing friendship but diffidence as to his lordship's 'interest' with the ecclesiastical authorities. One judges that he sent something in the way of protest for Pope to forward to Doctors' Commons.

[2] Pope had visited Leighs (Essex) with the Duchess early in June.

[3] Presumably Spencer Compton (1673?–1743), Speaker of the House from 1722 to 1727. In May of 1725 he had become Sir Spencer Compton; but either Her Grace did not choose to recognize that fact or was ignorant of it. 'Speaker' might be translated 'prater' if one wished to be critical. While living at Chiswick the Popes may have had some acquaintance with 'Mr.' Compton, who was M.P. for East Grinstead. See Tonson to Pope, 23 Dec. 1724.

[4] Duke John had bequeathed his alum works to his nearest relative, Robert Sheffield, who seems to have died in March of this year. The present 'Mr. Sheffield' is probably the natural son of Duke John, mentioned in the will as Charles Herbert, but there enjoined to take the name of Sheffield. It was only in 1736 (after the death of Duke Edmund) that Charles Herbert, 'now called Charles Sheffield', secured by Act of Parliament the right 'to take and use the surname of Sheffield, pursuant to the will of John, late Duke of Bucks and Normanby'.

POPE *to* HUMPHREY WANLEY[1]   1 *July* 1725

Harleian 3780

from Twickenham, this | fyrste of Julie, 1725.

Worthy Sir,—I shall take it as a signal mark of your freindly Love
& kindnesse unto mee, if you will recommend to my palate from the
experiensed Taste of yours, goode Mr Wanley, a Douzaine of quartes
of goode & wholesome Port Wine, such as yee drinke at the Genoa
Armes, forr the which, I will in honourable sort be indebted, & well &
kindlie pay to the Owner thereof, Your saide Merchant of Wines at
the saide Genoa-Armes. As witness this myne hand, which also wit-
nesseth its master to bee in sooth & sincerity of harte, | Goode Syr, |
Yours ever bounden | A. Pope.

Address: This to my worthy & special ffriend | Maister Wanley, dwelling at
my | singular goode Lord's, my Lorde of | Oxford's | Kindly Present
Endorsement: Mr Pope. | Re the penult day[2] of July 1725

ROBERT DIGBY *to* POPE   2 *July* 1725

Mapledurham

Hom Lacy near Hereford. July 2d | 1725

Whilst we were reflecting last night on our late entertainment with
yourself & John Gay at Riskins I received your double letter. Your
unexpected coming-in upon us & making part of the Company[3] when
we thought you a hundred miles off, made the rest of the night very
joyfull to us. I must do an odd thing for once, & give you an account
of your own reception; for tho' we knew our selvs to be in company
with you, yet you knew not the same of us. There was as general
a joy & your names were ecchoed in the same manner as is usual at
the first entrance of a Candidate for Member of Parliament into a
Borough. We drank your healths often & heartily; & commended
much your not forgetting us who so often remembered you, & have

---

[1] Wanley had at this time been for some years librarian to the Earls of Oxford. He died
in 1726.

[2] The endorsement seems not to agree with Pope's superscribed date. The letter may not
have been posted promptly, or Wanley may have been away from Lord Oxford's house for a
month. On 31 July Pope again writes to Wanley and thanks him for his *promptness* in performing this commission.

[3] i.e. in the form of a letter. Unfortunately this joint letter has not been traced. In a sale
on 16 Mar. 1852 at Sotheby's a letter was sold that might be this of which Digby writes.
It was 'among the letters of Lord Bathurst's correspondence', and the catalogue of the sale
described it as follows: 'The two concluding pages of a joint letter, detailing, with some
poetic licence, the particulars of a visit to the mansion of a noble friend. The first page is
believed to be in the very rare autograph of Gay, the concluding paragraph commencing with
the last line of that page, and continuing on the other side in the hand of Pope. Both poets
sign the letter.'

made you part, tho' an invisible one, of our society. Observing in your
letter that you have joyned hands, I will not separate you, but write
to you as One Person; & shall think myself obliged to do so, till I see
you divorced from the same pen & paper. Tho' you say you shall think
of us at Riskins, yet we know the company, whoever they are that
you shall wait on thither, will wipe out of your memory that of which
we were part. New pleasures in the Temple, in the Greenhouse & the
Grotto will only hereafter be remembered by you, with those fair
faces that accompanyed them. How rural we are! is an exclamation
should have come hence to you, for from you to us it sounds not
serious. if you are really fond of all which that word signifys, you must
come away with the Innocence you rejoyce-in hither a hundred miles
into the country, where I am authorised from the Lady of the place[1]
to tell you you will be more welcome, & where I will say you are both
more wished-for than a Gondola by Lord Bathurst. Had I been with
you & John Gay when the Ducks lately invaded you, my Stomach
would have been more up (I find) at such an ennemy than his; &
I think I should have given-in to the Kitchen an Account of some
Prisoners. The Salmon he expected Old Thames should bring into the
Kitchen, I should have expected from him who calls himself a Fisherman. How indolent does he picture himself to us Active Spirits here.
Rouse him, dear Sir, bring him hither to the banks of Wye, where his
Art may take (if fortune cross him not) some huge Salmon of dimensions worthy to be recorded by his own pencil on the Kitchen-wall,
& where it may remain a Trophy of his Skill in Fishery. So shall his
name be as great among the Cooks & Fishermen as Caesar's among the
Men of War. He knows not how in this sphere of life such Works as
these immortalise a Man. I hope Lord Bathurst whose intentions are
soon to survey & criticise these parts will seduce you both to come with
him. Yet I would not wish Gay so far from Richmond to the ruine of
any interest he may have begun to make there by a close attendance.
You must expect when you come here profound tranquillity; there is
no noise of Coaches, Horses or Chariots; the Silence of the Fields &
Woods surpasses imagination. Pray when you next see Mrs Howard
give my humble Service to her, & ask her whether she knows that a
Scene like this is properly the Country; when she wishes to live in it.
Or whether she loves the Country only as you do & would exclaim
with you—How Rural we are! at Twittenham. I send you no news
hence for tho' the Fooleries of the Town are good entertainment,
those of the Country are not. I hope Mrs Blounts are in possession of
their Richmond house & find all imaginable pleasure there. I shall
ever remember *your good Mother Mrs Pope* & have you in my heart,
whose health I wish & prosperity in all things.   the same hearty wishes

---

[1] Holm Lacy was the seat of Viscountess Scudamore, Digby's cousin.

to John Gay shall conclude this that already is too long with a sincere Adieu to both of you from your sure Friend & Servant Rt. D:—

My Brother is well at Paris.

POPE *to* VISCOUNT HARCOURT[1]   3 *July* 1725

Harcourt MSS.

Twickenham July 3d

My Lord,—It was my intention to put your Lordship in mind of me, not as an importunate, but as a Grateful follower of you; for Gratitude is the only thing I know that may Eternally pursue, without being impertinent.

I heartily hope your Lordship finds every advantage both of mind & body, Health & Quiet in perfection & all that either the Fair Weather of the Season, or (which is better) the Fair weather of the Soul, can afford you of content & satisfaction.

I should not omit acknowledging my receit of the D. of Newcastle's Subscription[2] by the hands of my Agent: but those are things I may forget to acknowledge to you, & yet remain brim full of acknowledgments, I have so very many of a higher nature.

Tho, as I was saying, 'twas my resolution, Once at least to break in upon your Retirement & make your Lordship & my Lady a Country Visit upon paper, in a Letter something longer than I ought, Yet it now befalls, (as it often does in Country Gentlemens Visits of Civility to Men in power,) that the Compliment is attended with some Petition.

A very Extraordinary instance of this will appear in this letter. My Lord, I am in Law, & in the worst Law, Spiritual Law: And my Lord, You are a party in it, in a very unexpected manner. My Lady Kneller has petitioned the Doctors Commons to pull down my Fathers Monument (in which also my Mother is to lye) to make room for Sir Godfry's; on pretence that there is no other place in the church large enough. This only reason was alledgd in the Monition which was read in the church a week since. And I have proof given that The said Monument is not so much as Begun, so may be made of any size: But she further alledges since, that I Promised Sir Godfry so to do, which is false. I formerly told your Lordship the whole truth, that he did ask me 2 things, that I would write his Epitaph which I granted, but as to the other of removing the Tomb, I told him I apprehended it was Indecent, & that my Mother's consent was requisite, after which

---

[1] In printing this letter from a transcript Elwin somehow omitted the first four paragraphs and the first sentence of the fifth.

[2] The Duke of Newcastle was named in vol. i of the *Odyssey* as subscribing for ten sets. It is not clear why he is mentioned in this letter.

I never saw him more. The utmost I said which he might mistake for a Consent, was meerly not to disturb a dying man, in these very words which I can swear to; *That I beggd him to be easy, & I would do for him whatever I coud with Decency.* My Lady was by me informd to the contrary, first the day after his funeral by her Servant Byng, & a few weeks after by myself. And this request was never made to me till a few days before his death when he was almost in his Agony, hardly (if at all) Compos mentis, & very unfit to be contradicted peremptorily.

To strengthen this pretence, she affirms, that I received from Sir Godfry some pictures on this consideration. The fact of which is that one was given me *above a year before,* (tho never to this day finished) and sent indeed about that time she mentions. And another was sent by him *Before I knew any thing of this request of his.* She has annex'd this circumstance very falsely.

Your Lordship will wonder how You can be any way concernd in all this: One of these pictures is that of myself which hangs in your Library, which your Lordship well knows was an Exchange of Sir Godfry's with you for another picture which you had long before, from Him & not from me, & of which he took the honour. But I have no proof of this.

I could be very glad of your Lordships advice upon the whole: some of the chief Gentlemen of this Parish have enter'd their Dissent & signd a Certificate to object to the removal of the Tomb. My Lord Strafford, whose Pew butts upon the place, in strong terms has writ to the Proctor to declare it will be dangerous to him, to have so large a Monument as she proposes fixd in that Wall & in general the President of such removals is apprehended by them, as well as the power of the Spiritual Court to cause them. Mr Pigot tells me, I may have a Prohibition at Common Law, even if the other Court do Order a removal. He advised me to write to your Lordship & wishes your Autority & Influence were employd any way to represent this matter fairly, & intercede by any proper person, with the Bishop of London, to put a stop hereto. What has been hitherto done in it is this. The Monition was read, & I cited to appear in 7 days time. Mr Pigot imployd a Proctor, who appear[d]. Lady Kneller was orderd to give an Allegation next Court day which is this day sennight. If your Lordship can be the means to rid me of this trouble, or to shorten it, I am pretty sure you will have pity on a man who has half Homer on his shoulders [&] a Lawsuit. I am in full pursuit of my Work, & tis the very Time I shoud have been least interrupted. Pray my Lord excuse this trouble, and the most grateful wish I can make you in return is May you never know a greater than I shall give you.

I am My Lord, with the sincerest respect | Your most obliged & most | faithfull Servant, | A. Pope.

My Mother is in good heart & sincerely your Servant, Poor old Nurse is very ill.

Saturday night

Endorsement: 3 July 1725 | Mr Pope | to | the Lord Vicount | Harcourt

POPE *to* THE EARL OF STRAFFORD   6 *July* [1725]

The Hyde Collection

Twitnam, July the 6.

My Lord,—I deferr'd acquainting your Lordship with the process of the affair about the Tomb, till I could receive from my Proctor & from Mr Pigot some particulars of the first Court-day, which is but just over. I find my Lady has a mind to make the Point as *Personal* as she can, with *me*, therby to disengage herself from any opposition from the Parish and to pass over (if possible) the Merit of Pretensions in general to Property in Monuments, (the Injustice of which your Lordship very reasonably animadverts upon in the letter you favord me with; for it ruins at once all the design of dying men, or their Survivors, to perpetuate their memories by the Certain Fixing of Inscriptions as a Property) My Lady, I say, has therfore pretended in her New Allegation, (which is to be exhibited next Saturday) that besides there being no other Place (that she likes) for her Monument but that over your Lordships Pew; She claims it by *a promise pretended to be made by Me to Sir Godfry on his deathbed*. Now if the Doctors Commons, upon such evidence as she shall bring, shall order Hers to be erected; the Injury, as well as Impertinence, would still remain the same towards your Lordship, (whose Consent ought doubtless to have been askd as well as mine.) And the Injury to Property too, and the Ill Precedent is the same. So whatever she may bring her Butler to say (which Mr Pigot tells me is her design,) of Sir Godfry's understanding that I consented to it) it would only amount to make it seem that I had done foolishly, but no way obviate the General or particular Objections of any other, who shall enter his Caveat against it. But The only Ground of this silly Pretence of hers is what follows: I will tell your Lordship the Story as shortly as I can: The particulars would make you smile (which I hope to tell you at Boughton.) Sir Godfry sent to me just before he dy'd. He began by telling me, he was now convincd he could not live, & fell into a passion of tears. I said I hopd he might; but that if not, he knew it was the Will of God & therfore shou'd do his best to Resign himself to it. He answerd with great Emotion *No, no no. It is the Evil Spirit*.—The next word he said was this—*By God, I will not be buried in Westminster*. I askd him Why? he answer'd—

They do bury Fools there. Then he said to me, My good friend, where will You be buried? I said, Where-ever I drop, very likely in Twitnam. He replyd, So will I. Then proceeded to desire I would write his Epitaph, which I promisd him. It would be endless to tell your Lordship the strange things he suggested on that head: It must be in Latin, that all foreigners may read it: it must be in English too &c. I desird him to be Easy in all that matter, I would certainly do the best I could. Then he desird me that I would take down my Father's Monument. *For it was the best Place in the Church to be seen at a distance.* This (as your Lordship may well imagine) surprized me quite. I hestitated, & said I feard it would be Indecent, & that my Mother must be askd as well as I. He fell a crying again, & seem'd so violently moved, that In pure humanity to a dying man (as well as to one I thought *non Compos*) I would not directly persist in Denying it strongly but beggd him to be Easy upon the whole, & said *I* would do for him all that I could *with Decency.* Those words, & that reserve, I can swear to: But your Lordship sees the Whole Fact (represented, upon my word, with the strictest Truth,) upon which this idle woman would ground her Answer, of which I was accidentally informd by Mr Pigot.

I have scarce room left, my Lord, to express what my mind is full of, the Sense of your favour in general, & of the unmerited honour you do me in your Letter, in particular. I hope it may be in my power to come personally to thank you at Boughton to which place, it is probable you will find as few words sufficient to invite me, as servd for Lord Bedford.[1] I have long been convinced that neither Acres, nor Wife; nor any publick Professors of Gardening, (any more than any publick Professors of Virtue) are equal to the Private Practisers of it. And I will as soon travel to contemplate your Lordships works, as the Queen of Sheba did to contemplate those of Solomon.[2]

Since I am got into another page, I will fill it with an Epitaph, which over & above my promise to Sir G. may serve for my Lady's: & justly celebrates her pious Design of making as Large a figure on the Tomb as Sir G. himself.

> One day I mean to Fill Sir Godfry's tomb,
> If for my body all this Church has room.
> Down with more Monuments! More room! (she cryd)
> For I am very large, & very wide.

My Lord, I beg yours & my Lady Straffords acceptance of my Mothers & my humble Services: and am, with Sincere respect &

---

[1] The Duke of Bedford invited Pope at this time to visit him at Woburn with Lord Strafford. See *Wentworth Papers*, pp. 454–5. Pope wrote to His Grace regretfully declining the invitation, before 5 Aug.

[2] This whole paragraph is omitted by Elwin.

obligation, My Lord, | Your most obedient & faithfull Servant | A. Pope.

Address: To the Rt. Honorable, the | Earl of Strafford, at | Boughton, near | Northampton.

Postmark: 8/IY

Endorsement:[1] Mr Pope. July the 3d | 1725

POPE *to* THE EARL OF OXFORD[2]   [*July* 1725?]

Longleat Portland Papers, xii

Tuesday morning. July

My Lord,— I am sorry you cannot lye here on Wensday night, where your Broth should be prepard by your own Instructions. I will be ready by seven on Thursday morning if your Lordship would have me sooner, you'l please to send a line by to nights post. As to the Guide, I will take care. I congratulate my self upon this pleasure, which I shall give my Lord Cobham, & take myself, in seeing You pleas'd. I am ever | My Lord | Your most sincerely | obliged, faithful Servant | A. Pope

I find I must not think of going farther, & Lord C's Memorandum of my crazy Condition is too true.

Address: To the Rt. Hon. the | Earl of Oxford.

SWIFT *to* POPE   19 *July* 1725

Longleat Portland Papers, xiii (Harleian transcripts)

July 19th 1725

Sir,—The Young Gentleman Mr Stopford[3] who delivers you this you will use with all goodness, if you love me; Si me amas ut ames, et ut ego te amo et amabo (Vide Tull. Epist. nescio ubi).[4] He has had his Tour of Traveles, and yet out of egerness to Travell again, he goes Governor to a Rich lad in such a manner as to grow rich enough himself to put his Estate out of Debt, yet after all he is no better nor worse then an Irish Parson born in London, without any Preferment, only Fellow of the University here, and a little foolish Land, but

---

1 The impossible date in the endorsement seems due to the blurring of the postmark which looks like a 3. The superscribed date is clear.

2 There is no very plausible July for this projected jaunt with Lord Oxford. If they went to Stowe this year, the visit was brief. The postscript indicates that Oxford was going farther than Pope, and at the end of August he writes to Pope that he is going into Herefordshire. Would a guide be necessary to get them to Stowe?

3 The Rev. James Stopford (d. 1759) was one of Swift's closest friends; he served as an executor of Swift's will, and in 1753 became Bishop of Cloyne.

4 Swift possibly has vaguely in mind such passages as the beginning of Cicero to Atticus, XVI. XVI. 10.

excepting these abatements he is such a Youth as you could wish, with abundance of Greek and other Learning, and modesty and good nature, and an humble admirer of Poetry and you, without any pretensions to the muses at least as he asserts. You will do him all the good offices you can because (tho an Englishman) he well deserves them, and I would not have him leave London without the Privilidge of boasting that he is known to you. I must require you likewise to introduce him to Dr Arbuthnett Mr Gay, and others whom you will think fit.

I am so full (quod ad me attinet) of grand designs that I believe I shall never bring them to pass but to your Comfort (grandia loquimur) they are all in prose. I would have seen you many times if a Cursed Deafness did not Sease me every 2 or 3 Months, and then I am frighted to think what I should do in London while my Friends are all either banished or attained[1] or beggars, or retired But I will venture all if I live and you must in that Case get me two or three Harridan Ladys that will be content to nurse and talk loud to me while I am deaf. Say nothing of my being eleven years older then when we parted, Lord Oxford the young writ me word that you were again embarqued to Homers land (as he called it) Are you Rich and Healthy Det vitam det opes &c.[2] Reputation you will take care to encrease though you have too much in Conscience for any Neighbor of yours to thrive while he lives by you.

Our Lord Oxford used to curse the Occasions that put you on Translations, and if he and the Qu— had lived you should have entirely followed your own Genius built and planted much, and writ only when you had a mind, pray come and show your self in Ireland and live some Months in the Deanry. you say right and yet I have heard as wild propositions. I have empowered Mr Stopford to tell you all my Story how I live; how I do nothing, how I grow old, what a Sorry life I lead, how I have not the Spleen &c. &c. &c.

I am ever | Your obedient Servant | J. Swift.

POPE *to* THE EARL OF OXFORD   30 *July* 1725
Longleat Portland Papers, xii

July 30th | 1725.

My Lord,—It was a concern to me to be obligd to leave the town without waiting once more on your Lordship as you obligingly invited me. I beg to remind you my Lord, & my Lady Oxford of a promise, to lose a day at Twitenham before you go to Downhall. This Evening the water looks so finely, & my house stands so very near it, that I hope my Lady would hardly think herself upon the Land, here, but

---

[1] Doubtless for *attainted*.

[2] Horace, *Epistles*, i. xviii. 112. On f. 103 of the Portland Papers transcript of this letter a modern hand has inserted the full Latin passage together with Francis's translation.

in her own favorite Element. I hope it is an Omen of an agreeable week to come; What will make it particularly such to me, is the honour & favour of seeing you any day in the beginning of it. Pray pardon my Self Love, which I faithfully assure you is mixd with a very Just (that is a very high) Esteem of, & Respect for your Lordship, to whom I am by many tyes, a | Most sincere | Most obligd & | Most humble Servant, | A. Pope.

Endorsement: Mr Pope | July 30. 1725

POPE *to* HUMPHREY WANLEY   31 *July* 1725

Harleian 3780

Worthy Sir,—I am greatly contented with your kind Token of affection; although I meant not, in any wise, to have put you to so sudden a discharge of the Trust I reposed in you: nor to have caused you a Journey to a distant part of the Towne; nor to have obliged you to renew an acquaintance with Signior Alberto after an intermission of divers yeares. Signor Alberto may thanke me, but not you.[1] I did verily thinke you had seen him daily, & do really beg your pardon. Notwithstanding, the Zeal, as well as Punctuality[2] you have kindly shewn herein, doth, & ought, much to oblige me. As an assurance whereof, I will again, as you admonish, renew your care & trouble, when these same bottles are on the Rack to refill them, & me, with such wholesom liquor of the like sort as to your judgment shall seem good: I paying the just price for the same. I desire very truly to have some occasion of serving you, & that you will require it whenever opportunity shall offer, being sincerely | Sir | Your very affectionate | faithfull Servant | & wellwisher | A: Pope.

Twickenham | July 31. | 1725.

Address: To | Mr Wanley, at the | Rt Hon. the Earl of Ox-|ford's, in Dover-street, | Piccadilly.

Endorsement: Mr Alexander Pope 31 July 1725.

*POPE *to* MRS. CÆSAR[3]   4 *August* [1725?]

Rousham

Twitenham Aug. 4th

Madam,—Had I known of your Trip to London, I would have met you there; and endeavourd, by my presence & exhortations, to have

---

[1] Alberto Croce was Wanley's wine merchant.—Elwin.

[2] Note this remark in connexion with the date of Pope's commissioning letter (1 July) and its strange endorsement.

[3] The year is most difficult to determine. For Aug. 1732 we have no information as to

Animated the Images & Likenesses at Mr Jervas's. I saw my Lord & Lady Oxford yesterday, first there, & after at their own house where you were commemorated. He resents (as he ought) your Slander, in representing him as a Man of Uncertainty: & insists that I shall not go to Benington but in his company. I shall rejoyce to do so, & in the meantime, pray acquaint Mrs Madan that I'm sorry to find all her Laurels are turnd into myrtles. I am faithfully Mr Cæsars & | Madam | Your own, obligd affect. Servant | A. Pope

Address: To Mrs Cæsar at Bening-|ton | Hertfordshire

POPE *to* THE EARL OF STRAFFORD   12 *August* [1725]

The Hyde Collection

Twitnam, Augst 12th

My Lord,—I think myself obliged to acquaint your Lordship with what past upon the Chancellor of London's Visiting our Church on the 9th of this instant. Dr Henchman[1] lookd upon the place of the Monument, & enquird the dimensions: Which, upon measuring, he found to be so large as to fill the whole wall from the very Cieling above the Cornice, to the wainscote below, which is within 3 or 4 foot of the ground. He questiond of the thickness of the Wall, into which it was to be lett by cutting, (as my Lady Kn.'s mason there present informed him.) Tho. Reeves assurd him it would be of danger, & the Wall was but 2 ft odd inches. He askd of the Projection? which her mason answerd was, beneath, of 18 inches, & above, to 3 foot gradually: The whole, 8 ft wide, by near 14 high. He then askd, Whose Pew that was before it? Edw. Reeves answerd, Your Lordships; & declard you had orderd him, in your name, to protest against the Removal of the Monument. The Chancellor replyd, that undoubtedly your Lordships Reasons & Objections should have the due weight, when the Time came of the Hearing. Upon this a very silly thing happend, which I ought not to conceal from you: The Minister Dr Booth,[2] with a good deal of ridiculous warmth, told Dr Henchman, *That of all men, my Lord Strafford's Objections ought to have No weight, for he never came to Church.* And added, That you had never given *him* any thing, since he was Parson: with more to that idle purpose.

the whereabouts of all concerned, but for practically all other probable years there are details that perplex. The year 1725 may do, especially in view of Lord Oxford's letter to Pope, 30 Aug. 1725. But Nichols, *Lit. Anec.*, i. 92, quotes Wanley's Diary as saying that Pope visited the Harleian Library late in the day of 4 August, and that makes the poet's movements complex for the 3rd and 4th. Perhaps Pope dated this letter one day too early?

  [1] Humphrey Henchman (1669–1739) had been Chancellor of London since 1715. His close friendship with Atterbury might influence his attitude towards Pope.

  [2] The Rev. Pennyston Booth was vicar of the parish 1723–30. He was later Canon and subsequently Dean of Windsor.—Cobbett, p. 113.

Two that were present said My Lord Strafford had given 50¹ to the Church; & I observd you had scarce been in the Country since this Parson came, & that He himself had been but once a month, or not so often, here. You will smile at Dr Henchmans grave Answer, which was, *Is my Lord Strafford a Roman Catholick, or a Dissenter? If he were either, that would not lessen his right of objecting, or Any other man's.* This was all that past.

I hope your Lordship & my Lady are in perfect health & happiness, without any accident from the Late water-Expedition, (not even of a sore Eye) arrived att Another of your Seats, and that you find pleasures there not inferior to those of Boughton. I believe you'l Improve Every thing that belongs to you, as well as every thing that is near you: Witness the young Duke, & myself. My Mother is faithfully yours, & looks upon you as the Defender of her Husband, Son, & Family, nay the Protector of Her Ashes. Believe me (my Lord) with reall respect & sincerity | Your Lordships | Most obliged & most | [obed]ient faithful Servant | [A. Pope]

The Lady Kneller has set about a report, that I would compromize the matter with her, Which I assure you is quite false, & the Suit continues gloriously.

Address: To The Right Honble the Earle | of Strafford.

Endorsement: Mr Pope augt the 12th | 1725

---

†POPE *to* ROBERT DIGBY¹   12 *August* [1725?]

1735
                                                                Aug. 12.

I have been above a Month strolling about in *Buckinghamshire* and *Oxfordshire*, from Garden to Garden, but still returning to Lord *Cobham*'s with fresh Satisfaction. I should be sorry to see my Lady *Scudamore*'s, till it has had the full Advantage of Lord *Bathurst*'s² Improvements; and then I will expect something like the waters of *Riskins*, and the Woods of *Oakley* together, which (without Flattery) would be at least as good as any thing in our World: For as to the hanging Gardens of *Babylon*, the Paradise of *Cyrus*, and the Shara-waggi's of *China*, I have little or no Ideas of 'em, but I dare say Lord

---

¹ It is impossible to find a clear case of Pope's 'strolling about in Buckinghamshire' for a month in any plausible July and August. In 1725 it is possible if one does not take Pope's statement too literally—and his statements about the lapsing of time can seldom be taken so. The letter is written at a time when Lord Bathurst is entertaining Robert and Mary Digby at Cirencester or when he is with them as guest of Lady Scudamore at Holm Lacy. It seems also, from the talk of the vice and folly of the town, to have political implications. The Hon. Robert Digby was M.P. for Co. Warwick, 1722–6. Textual revisions suggest that Lord Bathurst did not altogether relish this letter.

² *Bathurst*'s] *B*'s *1737–42*.

B—t[1] has, because they were certainly both very *Great*, and very *Wild*. I hope Mrs. *Mary Digby* is quite tired of his Lordship's *Extravagante Bergerie*; and that she is just now sitting, or rather inclining, on a Bank, fatigu'd with over much Dancing and Singing at his unwearied Request and Instigation. I know your love of Ease so well, that you might be in danger of being too Quiet to enjoy Quiet, and too Philosophical to be a Philosopher; were it not for the Ferment Lord *B.* will put you into. One of his Lordship's Maxims is, that a total Abstinence from Intemperance or Business, is no more *Philosophy*, than a total Consopition[2] of the Senses is *Repose*; one must Feel enough of its Contrary to have a Relish of either. But after all, let your Temper work, and be as sedate and contemplative as you will, I'll engage you shall be fit for his Lordship[3] when you come to Town in the Winter. Folly will laugh you into all the Customs of the Company, here; nothing will be able to prevent your Conversion to her, but Indisposition, which I hope will be far from you. I am telling the worst that can come of you; for as to Vice, you are safe, but Folly is many an honest Man's, nay every good-humour'd Man's Lot: Nay it is the Seasoning of Life; and Fools (in one Sense) are the Salt of the Earth; a little is excellent, tho' indeed a whole Mouthful is justly call'd the *Devil.*

So much for your Diversions next Winter, and for mine. I envy you much more at present, than I shall then; for if there be on Earth an Image of Paradise, it is in such perfect Union and Society as you all possess. I wou'd have my innocent Envies and Wishes of your State known to you all; which is far better than making you Compliments, for it is inward Approbation and Esteem. My Lord *Digby* has in me a sincere Servant, or would have, were there any occasion for me to manifest it.

THE EARL OF OXFORD *to* POPE   30 *August* 1725

Homer MSS. Add. 4809

Aug. 30: 1725. | Dover Street.

Sir,—I write this to enquire how you do   I am just going into my coach for Oxford and thence I belive I shall go further as far as Herefordshire, Mrs caesar tells me I have got such a habit of Rambling that she supposes I shall be like Teague never stand still; she told me of your kind design of coming to Wimpole   I hope I shall return soon enough to have that pleasure before the Winter comes on. I had a

[1] *B—t*] B* *1737–42.*
[2] This word was emended to *Composition* by the error of Curll's compositor in *Mr. Pope's Literary Correspondence* (i. 144) in 1735.
[3] for his Lordship when] for any of us, when *1737–42.*

letter lately from Dean Swift he complains of his being very Deaf
which makes him retire from company   he is else well. I hope Mrs
Pope is well   please to make my compliments to her.

I am Sir Your most | humble Servant | Oxford

If you direct your letter to me in Dover street it will come to me
where ever I shall be and it will be a great pleasure to me to hear from
you

GAY *to* POPE[1]   [*2 September* 1725]

Homer MSS. Add. 4809

I can neglect no opportunity that can give you Satisfaction or pleasure.
I this instant came from Dr Arbuthnot, & I hope found him reliev'd
from all the danger of his distemper; about an hour or two ago, he
made water & had a Stool, and is quite free from pain. He is weak, &
very much reduc'd, but Amiens whom I found with him thinks him
out of danger. I shall dine at Petersum[2] on Sunday, & intend to see
Mrs Howard; From Petersum we set out for Wiltshire on Monday.
Pray give my sincere service to Mrs Pope, & Mrs Blount.

I am | Dear Sir | Yours most affectionately | J. G.

Thursday | 10 at night.

Postmark: 2/SE

POPE *to* THE EARL OF OXFORD   7 *September* 1725

Longleat Portland Papers, xii

Sept. 7th 1725

My Lord,—Your Lordships being pleasd to tell me that it will be
some pleasure to You to hear from me, is (I assure you) a very great
one to Me. I went to the town the day after you left it, purposely to
wait on you, not imagining you would so soon again have been on the
ramble. But I have long known you willing to oblige all that have a
regard for you, & therfore should not wonder if you visited the four
quarters of the Universe. Remember only, my Lord, that you have
broke your promise with One man in the world, & that you have as
little heeded one Pope of Twitnam, as if he had been one Maister
Johnston of Twitnam. I believe I must for the future trust myself to
my Lady Oxfords memory, because her Barge will be a help to it,

---

[1] The date comes from the postmark, and is reinforced by the account of Arbuthnot's
illness in Pope's letter to Swift, 14 Sept. 1725.

[2] With the Duke and Duchess of Queensberry, and from thence he was to go with them
to Amesbury.—Elwin. ('Petersum' is of course Petersham.)

& may put her in mind of our Water-side. Mrs Cæsar is a good woman, & would not have forgot me so, (unless I had quitted this side of the water for the other, & been a visiting with Lord Bat[hurst]) I take it a little ill that you mention my design upon Wimpole as a thing *told your Lordship by Mrs Cæsar*, when it has been known to yourself to have been the very Point my heart is piqu'd upon, the place for to which I'm to leap, at an hours warning, from any other part of the land, the Neplus-ultra of this year, & in a word the next Sign of my Zodiack. Some Phaëton must drive me quite out of my regular course; if I see any place before I see Wimpole, be it winter or summer, or spring, or autumn.

> With you conversing, I forget all change
> Of Seasons and of Times, All please alike.

There is also some Impropriety in your Lordships expression, as if my said design was to *Go to Wimpole*, I say it was rather to go *with* You. Make Wimpole as good as you will, improve it as much as you can, you can't make so good a thing as your Father made before. I leave you to explain this Riddle,[1] and I don't doubt you will all your life, (whether you know it or not.)

In sincere truth, my Lord, I have more desire to be with you, on any occasion, than I dare (for your Quiet) express; and I really have some Modesty, tho I am a Poet.

I know it will be more pleasing to your Temper than what I have been saying last, to tell you, that I have quite recoverd that Fever I labourd under just before you left London: In which, tho you may seem to have little interest yet thus much you really have gaind by it; Your old Lease a faithful Servant is renew'd to you; abundance of good wishes and grateful thanks will be added to those you have already. and my Lord Oxford will be spoken of with respect & affection some time longer, by one man more.

I am, with the truest esteem, | My Lord | Your most faithfull | and most obedient | Servant | A. Pope.

My Mothers most humble Services wait on your Lordship She is pretty well. I hope this Letter will not fright your Lordship from favoring me with another.

Address: To the Rt Hon. the Earl | of Oxford.

Endorsement: Mr Pope R. Sepr at Egwood [?] 1725

---

[1] Possibly this passage is an attempt at facetiousness over the fact that Lord and Lady Oxford were at the moment hoping for a son. One was born to them on 18 Oct., but lived only four days. See Ball, iii. 285.

‡POPE *to* DR. ARBUTHNOT¹   10 *September* [1725]

1737

Sept. 10.

I am glad your Travels delighted you, improve you I am sure they could not; you are not so much a youth as that, tho' you run about with a King of sixteen, and (what makes him still more a child) a King of Frenchmen. My own time has been more melancholy, spent in an attendance upon death, which has seized one of our family;² my mother is something better, though at her advanced age every day is a climacteric. There was joined to this an indisposition of my own, which I ought to look upon as a slight one compared with my mother's, because my life is not half the consequence to any body, that her's is to me. All these incidents have hinder'd my more speedy reply to your obliging letter.

The article you enquire of, is of as little concern to me as you desire it should; namely the railing papers about the Odyssey. If the book has merit, it will extinguish all such nasty scandal, as the Sun puts an end to stinks, meerly by coming out.

I wish I had nothing to trouble me more; an honest mind is not in the power of any dishonest one. To break its peace, there must be some guilt or consciousness, which is inconsistent with its own principles. Not but malice and injustice have their day, like some poor short-lived vermine that die in shooting their own stings. Falshood is Folly (says Homer) and liars and calumniators at last hurt none but themselves, even in this world: in the next, 'tis charity to say, God have mercy on them! they were the devil's vice-gerents upon earth, who is the father of lies, and I fear has a right to dispose of his children.

I've had an occasion to make these reflexions of late, more justly than from any thing that concerns my writings, for it is one that concerns my morals, and (which I ought to be as tender of as my own) the good character of another very innocent person, who I'm sure shares your friendship no less than I do.³ No creature has better natural dis-

---

¹ This obviously spurious letter is fabricated from two letters to Caryll dated 23 Nov. 1725 and 25 Dec. 1725. It appears in all Pope's editions (except the 'afternoon' issue of 12 May 1735); but in the editions of 1735 it was printed as to Robert Digby and dated 'Sept. 10, 1724'. In the editions of 1737–42 it is addressed to Dr. Arbuthnot and the impossible year date is dropped. The text as printed was reprinted substantially without revision. It varies slightly from the two fragments combined from the Caryll letters. If readers of the 1735 text expressed surprise that the *Odyssey* should be attacked months before its publication, Pope could have pointed out that the editions of 1735 were piratical and unreliable. He had arranged for that, intentionally or through carelessness. For variations from the Caryll letters, see their texts given later.

² His nurse, specifically mentioned in the Caryll letter (23 Nov.), died 5 Nov. 1725— making Pope's final dating of his fabrication impossible at this point.

³ In his text of 1735 Pope here inserted four asterisks, to indicate an omission. For the matter omitted see his genuine letter to Caryll, 25 Dec. 1725.

positions, or would act more rightly or reasonably in every duty, did she act by herself, or from herself; but you know it is the misfortune of that family to be governed like a ship, I mean the Head guided by the Tail, and that by every wind that blows in it.

†POPE *to* EDWARD BLOUNT[1]   13 *September* 1725

1735
                                                        Sept. 13, 1725.
I should be asham'd to own the receipt of a very kind Letter from you, two whole Months from the date of this; if I were not more asham'd to tell a Lye, or to make an Excuse, which is worse than a Lye (for being built upon some probable Circumstance, it makes use of a degree of Truth to falsify with: It is a Lye *Guarded*). Your Letter has been in my Pocket in constant wearing, till that, and the Pocket, and the Suit, are worn out; by which means I have read it forty times, and I find by so doing, that I have not enough consider'd, and reflected upon many others you have obliged me with; for true Friendship, as they say of good Writing, will bear reviewing a thousand times, and still discover new beauties.

I have had a Fever, a short one, but a violent: I am now well. So it shall take up no more of this Paper.

I begin now to expect you in Town, to make the Winter to come more tolerable to us both. The Summer is a kind of Heaven, when we wander in a Paradisaical Scene ⌜of Nature⌝ among Groves and Gardens; but at this Season, we are like our poor first Parents turn'd out of that agreeable tho' solitary life, and forc'd to look about for more people to help to bear our labours, to get into warmer Houses, and hive together in Cities.

I hope you are long since perfectly restor'd, and risen from your Gout, happy in the delights of a contented Family, smiling at Storms, laughing at Greatness, and merry over a Christmas-fire, exercising all the Functions of an old Patriarch in Charity and Hospitality. I will not tell Mrs. *B.* what I think she is doing; for I conclude it is her opinion, that he only ought to know it for whom it is done: and she will allow herself to be far enough advanc'd above a fine Lady, not to desire to shine before Men.

Your Daughters perhaps may have some other thoughts, which even

---

[1] Printed, with no important revisions of text, in all Pope's editions except 1735 a2. Some omissions in editions of 1737–42 are placed here in half-brackets. This is the last letter to or from Mr. Blount that Pope printed, and at the end of it in 1737–42 he added the note, 'Mr. Blount dyed in London the following Year, 1726.' It is perhaps true, as letters to Caryll (Dec. 1726) and to Swift (28 Nov. 1729) indicate, that Pope secured the return of his letters to Blount from Blount's widow. The fact remains that more than one of the letters printed as to Blount is fabricated.

their Mother must excuse them for, because she is a Mother. I will not however suppose those thoughts get the better of their Devotions, but rather excite 'em, and assist the warmth of them; while their Prayer may be, that they may raise up and breed as irreproachable a young Family as their Parents have done. In a Word, I fancy you all well, easy, and happy, just as I wish you; and next to that I wish you all with me.

Next to God, is a good Man: Next in dignity, and next in value. *Minuisti eum paullo minus ab Angelis.* If therefore I wish well to the good and the deserving, and desire They only shou'd be my Companions and Correspondents; I must very soon, and very much think of you. I want your Company, and your Example. Pray make haste to Town, so as not again to leave us: Discharge the Load of Earth that lies on you, like one of the Mountains under which the Poets say the Giants (⌈that is,⌉ the *Men of the Earth*) are whelmed: Leave Earth to the Sons of Earth; your Conversation is in Heaven. Which that it may be accomplish'd in us all, is the Prayer of him who maketh this short Sermon. Value (to you) Three pence. Adieu.

POPE *to* BROOME   14 *September* [1725]

Elwin–Courthope, viii. 99

Sept. 14. [1725].

I deferred writing till I had received the parcel which you promised long ago; and if I have been too long, you must lay the blame on your misreckoning, for you told me Sir Edmund Bacon[1] was to come on Monday, the end of last month; instead whereof your packet came not till yesterday to my hands. I thank you for your dispatch, and I believe you thank yourself for it. I will put both volumes together to the press, having myself done all the rest already.[2] I correct daily, and make them seem less corrected, that is, more easy, more fluent, more natural, which, give me leave to say, is the style of Homer, in this work especially. The narrative is perspicuous to the last degree. I would not discourage you; but, since you seem to be a little in triumph upon your last book,[3] I will just so far take you down, as to say, you are sometimes too figurative and constrained, not quite easy or clear enough. But as I am to act, not only to my best judgment, but to one of my best friends, not only for my own, but for your reputation, I will never spare you, but alter so freely whatever I do not quite approve, that possibly you may like it the worse, if your sentiments of Homer's

---

[1] Sir Edmund, the premier baronet of England, had Sturston connexions, and evidently conveyed Broome's packet from there to Pope—more slowly than was desired.
[2] Later letters indicate that there was much still to do.
[3] Lib. 16.—Broome (Elwin).

style differs from my idea of it. But I believe it does not, and if ever
you appear with any different air from the author, it proceeded from
a well-meant endeavour to raise him.[1] Indeed, these five or six books,
after the thirteenth, are more languid, less active, more conversation-
like, than all the remainder, and than all that went before; and the
reader will inevitably find them more tiresome, as well as the translator. Send me the other as soon as you can: perhaps it is better you
should not be too laborious in correcting, and, to say truth, another
man always corrects more easily than one's self,—an advantage, by
the way, which I have all along wanted to my own. I approve of your
resolution to divert yourself a good while after this task. I beg part of
the vacation may be spent with me. It is not possible to tell you many
necessary things that I would, and it is no flattery to tell you many kind
ones, for I am sincerely, dear Broome, your affectionate friend.

Fenton says you never writ to him. I have had a fever. Adieu.

†POPE *to* SWIFT   14 *September* 1725

1740

Sept. 14, 1725.

I need not tell you, with what real delight I shou'd have done any
thing you desired, and in particular any good offices in my power
towards the bearer of your Letter,[2] who is this day gone for France.
Perhaps 'tis with Poets as with Prophets, they are so much better lik'd
in another country than their own, that your Gentleman, upon arriving in England, lost his curiosity concerning me. However, had he
try'd, he had found me his friend; I mean he had found me yours. I am
disappointed at not knowing better a man whom you esteem, and
comfort my self only with having got a Letter from you, with which
(after all) I sit down a gainer; since to my great pleasure it confirms
my hope of once more seeing you. After so many dispersions, and so
many divisions, two or three of us may yet be gather'd together; not
to plot, not to contrive silly schemes of ambition, or to vex our own
or others hearts with busy vanities (such as perhaps at one time of life
or other take their Tour in every man) but to divert ourselves, and the
world too if it pleases; or at worst, to laugh at others as innocently and
as unhurtfully as at ourselves. Your Travels I hear much of;[3] my own
I promise you shall never more be in a strange land, but a diligent, I
hope useful, investigation of my own Territories.[4] I mean no more

---

[1] Pope himself was not guiltless of this 'raising'. He forgave Spence (*Essay on Mr. Pope's
Odyssey*, 1725–6) for charging him with it.
[2] Mr. Stopford. See Swift to Pope 19 July 1725.
[3] *Gulliver's Travels*—probably reported on by Ford.
[4] The *Essay on Man*.—Warburton, 1751. If Warburton is right, this is the earliest
mention of Pope's philosophical project.

Translations, but something domestic, fit for my own country, and for my own time.

If you come to us I'll find you elderly Ladies enough that can hallow, and two that can nurse, and they are too old and feeble to make too much noise; as you will guess when I tell you they are my own mother, and my own nurse. I can also help you to a Lady who is as deaf, tho' not so old as your self;[1] you'll be pleas'd with one another, I'll engage, tho' you don't hear one another: you'll converse like spirits by intuition. What you'll most wonder at is, she is considerable at Court, yet no Party-woman, and lives in Court, yet wou'd be easy and make you easy.

One of those you mention (and I dare say always will remember) Dr. Arbuthnot, is at this time ill of a very dangerous distemper, an imposthume in the bowels; which is broke, but the event is very uncertain.[2] Whatever that be (he bids me tell you, and I write this by him) he lives or dies your faithful friend; and one reason he has to desire a little longer life, is the wish to see you once more.

He is gay enough in this circumstance to tell you, he wou'd give you (if he cou'd) such advice as might cure your deafness, but he would not advise you, if you were cur'd, to quit the pretence of it; because you may by that means hear as much as you will, and answer as little as you please. Believe me | Yours &c.

GAY *and* POPE *to* FORTESCUE   23 *September* 1725
1817 (Warner)

Sept. 23, 1725.

I am again returned to Twickenham, upon the news of the person's death you wrote to me about.[3] I cannot say I have any great prospect of success; but the affair remains yet undetermined, and I cannot tell who will be his successor. I know I have sincerely your good wishes upon all occasions. One would think that my friends use me to disappointments, to try how many I could bear; if they do so, they are mistaken; for as I do not expect much, I can never be much disappointed. I am in hopes of seeing you in town the beginning of October, by what you writ to Mr. Pope; and sure your father[4] will think it reasonable that Miss Fortescue should not forget her French and dancing. Dr. Arbuthnot has been at the point of death by a severe fit of illness, an imposthumation in the bowels; it hath broke, and he

---

[1] Mrs. Howard, now a neighbour at Marble Hill.

[2] See Gay to Pope [2 Sept. 1725].

[3] The person whose death has stimulated Gay's hope of getting 'a place' is unidentified. At Twickenham Gay would be near Richmond or Windsor, the fountain-head of rewards. See W. H. Irving, *John Gay*, pp. 209–13, on Gay's futile attempts during this summer to get preferment.

[4] Possibly his father-in-law; or Fortescue himself, *your* being an error; i.e. 'ye' read as 'yr'.

is now pretty well recovered. I have not seem him since my return from Wiltshire, but intend to go to town the latter end of the week.

I have made your compliments to Mrs. Howard this morning: she indeed put me in mind of it, by enquiring after you. Pray make my compliments to your sisters and Mrs. Fortescue; Mr. Pope desires the same.

Your's, most affectionately, | J. G.

"Blessed is the man who expects nothing, for he shall never be disappointed," was the ninth beatitude which a man of wit (who, like a man of wit, was a long time in gaol) added to the eighth; I have long ago preached this to our friend; I have *preached* it, but the world and his other friends *held it forth*, and exemplified it. They say, Mr. Walpole[1] has friendship, and keeps his word; I wish he were our friend's friend, or had ever promised him any thing.

You seem inquisitive of what passed when Lord Peterborow spirited him thither, without any suspicion of mine. Nothing extraordinary, for the most extraordinary men are nothing before their masters; and nothing, but that Mr. Walpole swore by G—d, Mrs. Howard should have the grounds she wanted from V—n.[2] Nothing would be more extraordinary, except a statesman made good his promise or oath, (as very probably he will.) If I have any other very extraordinary thing to tell you, it is this, that I have never since returned Sir R. W.'s visit. The truth is, I have nothing to ask of him; and I believe he knows that nobody follows him *for nothing*. Besides, I have been very sick, and sickness (let me tell you) makes one above a minister, who cannot cure a fit of fever or ague. Let me also tell you, that no man who is lame, and cannot stir, will wait upon the greatest man upon earth; and lame I was, and still am, by an accident which it will be time enough to tell you when we meet, for I hope it will be suddenly. Adieu, dear Sir, and believe me a true well-wisher to all your's, and ever your faithful, affectionate servant, | A. Pope.

Twitenham, Sept. 23, 1725.

Address: To Wm. Fortescue, esq; at Fallapit, near Totnes, Devon.

GAY *to* POPE[3]   [*September* 1725]

Homer MSS. Add. 4809

Saturday night

I really intended to have been with you to day, but having been dis-

---

[1] *Mr.* Walpole is perhaps Sir Robert's brother Horatio; Sir Robert is mentioned below as Sir R. W. Did both brothers visit Pope? Or did Mrs. Howard's affairs engage them?

[2] Sir Thomas Vernon of Twickenham Park, churchwarden and Pope's landlord, evidently possessed land that Mrs. Howard wanted.

[3] This letter is placed chronologically because of its position in the Homer MSS. and because, if Gay's salary was paid quarterly, Michaelmas would be a natural time for him to be getting a payment.

appointed yesterday of meeting Mr Selwyn;[1] & going to the Exchequer about my Salary to day, & to Mrs Howard's to meet him made it too late, so that I made a visit this morning to Mr Congreve, where I found Lord Cobham they both enquir'd kindly for you & wish'd to see you soon, Mr Fortescue could not have come with me but intends the latter end of next week to see you at Twickenham. I have seen our Friend Dean Berkeley[2] who was very solicitous about your health and welfare. He is now so full of his Bermuda's project that he hath printed his Proposal, and hath been with the Bishop of London about it. Mrs Howard desir'd me to tell you that she had a present of Beech Mast, which this year hath been particularly good. When tis wanted she would have you send to her. I writ to you yesterday; and am in hopes that Mrs Pope will soon be so well that you may be able to come to town for a day or so about your business. I really am this evening very much out of order with the Cholick but I hope a night's rest will relieve me. I wish Mrs Pope & you all health & happiness, pray give my service to her.

‖SWIFT *to* POPE[3]   29 *September* 1725

Longleat Portland Papers, xiii (Harleian transcripts)

                                                           Sep. 29. 1725

⌐Sir,—I cannot guess the Reason of Mr Stopfords management but impute it at a venture either to hast or bashfullness, in the latter of which he is excessive to a fault, although he had already gone the Tour of Italy and France, to harden him: perhaps this second Journey and for a longer time may amend him. He treated[3] you just as he did Lord Carteret, to whom I recommended him. My letter you saw to Lord Bolingb[4] has shewn you the Situation I am in, and the Company I keep: If I do not forget some of the Contents. But⌐ I am now returning to the noble Scene of Dublin in to the Grande Monde, for fearing

---

    1 He was a groom of the bedchamber to the Prince of Wales.—Elwin.
    2 On 3 Sept. 1724 Swift wrote a letter of introduction for Berkeley to take to Lord Carteret (see Ball, iii. 212–13), and he supposed Berkeley ready to start for Bath and London. But Berkeley's Proposal seems not to have been published before July 1725, and hence this letter is placed after that month.
    3 Printed by Pope, 1740–42, with omissions here placed in half-brackets.
    Here the Harleian transcript is textually important. The scribe (who writes *guest* for *guess*, *tracked* for *treated*, and *fearing* for *fear* in the first part of the letter) is not too competent. His instructions evidently were to leave blank spaces wherever Swift's difficult hand was illegible, and the whole letter was proof-read by Lord Oxford himself, in whose hand more than a score of words are corrected or added. Important also is the address, which is added in his hand, since the presence of an address almost certainly shows that his lordship was proof-reading against the original letter and not from any 'copy' prepared by Pope, who discarded addresses. These facts, so clear in this letter, apply presumably to most or all of the Harleian transcripts.
    This Longleat text seems closer to the original letter than the printed texts of Pope's day, which are based on another transcript now lost.   4 This letter is not now known.

of burying my parts to Signalise my self among Curates and Vicars, and correct all Corruption crept in relating to the weight of Bread and Butter through those Dominions where I govern.[1] I have employd my time (besides ditching) in finishing correcting, amending, and Transcribing my Travells,[2] in four parts Compleat newly Augmented, and intended for the press when the world shall deserve them, or rather when a Printer shall be found brave enough to venture his Eares, I like your Schemes[3] of our meeting after Distresses and dispertions but the chief end I propose to my self in all my labors is to vex the world rather then divert it, and if I could compass that designe without hurting my own person or Fortune I would be the most Indefatigable writer you have ever seen without reading I am exceedingly pleased that you have done with Translations Lord Treasurer Oxford often lamented that a rascaly World should lay you under a Necessity of Misemploying your Genius for so long a time. But since you will now be so much better employd when you think of the World give it one lash the more at my Request. I have ever hated all Nations professions and Communityes and all my love is towards individualls for instance I hate the tribe of Lawyers, but I love Councellor such a one, Judge such a one for so with Physicians (I will not Speak of my own Trade) Soldiers, English, Scotch, French; and the rest but principally I hate and detest that animal called man, although I hartily love John, Peter, Thomas and so forth. this is the system upon which I have governed my self many years (but do not tell) and so I shall go on till I have done with them I have got Materials Towards a Treatis proving the falsity of that Definition *animal rationale*; and to show it should be only *rationis capax*. Upon this great foundation of Misanthropy (though not Timons manner) The whole building of my Travells is erected: And I never will have peace of mind till all honest men are of my Opinion: by Consequence you are to embrace it immediatly and procure that all who deserve my Esteem may do so too The matter is so clear that it will admit little dispute.[4] nay I will hold a hundred pounds that you and I agree in the Point.

I did not know your Odyssey was finished being yet in the Country, which I shall leave in three days I shall thank you kindly for the Present but shall like it three fourths the less from the mixture you mention of another hand,[5] however I am glad you saved yourself so much drudgery—I have been long told by Mr Ford of your great Atchivements in building and planting and especially of your Sub-

---

[1] The liberties of St. Patrick's cathedral.—Nichols (Elwin).
[2] *Gulliver's Travels.*—Pope, 1740–42.
[3] your Schemes] the schemes *1740–42.*
[4] admit little dispute] admit of little dispute *1741 Dab*; admit of no dispute *1741 Labc*; *1742 Lbc.* (The clandestine [1740] text and 1742 La agree with Longleat.)
[5] of another hand] of other hands *1740–42.*

terranean Passage to your Garden whereby you turned a blunder into a beauty which is a Piece of Ars Poetica

I have almost done with Harridans and shall soon become old enough to fall in love with Girls of Fourteen, The Lady whom you describe to live at Court, to be deaf and no party Woman, I take to be Mythology but know not how to moralize it. She cannot be Mercy, for mercy is neither deaf nor lives at Court Justice is blind and perhaps deaf but neither is she a Court Lady. Fortune is both blind and deaf and a Court Lady, but then she is a most Damnable party Woman, and will never make me easy as you promise. It must be riches which Answers all your description; I am glad she visites you but my voice is so weak that I doubt she will never hear me.

Mr Lewis sent me an Account of Dr Arbuthnett's Illness which is a very sensible Affliction to me, who by living so long out of the World have lost that hardness of Heart contracted by years and generall Conversation. I am daily loosing Friends, and neither seeking nor getting others. O, if the World had but a dozen Arbuthnetts in it I would burn my Travells but however he is not without Fault. There is a passage in Bede highly commending the Piety and learning of the Irish in that Age, where after abundance of praises he overthrows them all by lamenting that, Alas, they kept Easter at a wrong time of the Year. So our Doctor has every Quality and virtue that can make a man amiable or usefull, but alas he hath[1] a sort of Slouch in his Walk. I pray god protect him for he is an excellant Christian tho not a Catholick and as fit a man either to dy or Live as ever I knew.

I hear nothing of our Friend Gay, but I find the Court keeps him at hard Meat I advised him to come over here with a[2] Lord Lieutenant. ⌐Mr Tickell is in a very good Office[3] I have not seen Philips, tho' formerly we were so intimate He has got nothing, and by what I can find will get nothing though⌐ he[4] writes little Flams (as Lord Leicester call'd those sort of Verses) on Miss Carteret[5] and others. it is remarkable and deserves recording that a Dublin Blacksmith a great poet hath imitimated his manner in a Poem to the same Miss. Philips is a Complainer, and on this Occasion I told Lord Carteret that Complainers never Succeed[6] at Court though Railers do.

---

[1] The inconsistent use of *has* and *hath* in this sentence is of interest. Longleat and the clandestine text agree, as here. The Dublin texts have *hath* in both places; Pope's London texts allow the inconsistent readings, but Curll (1741 Lc) corrected to *has* in both cases. Normally Swift and Dublin throughout the correspondence prefer *hath* in places where the London texts have *has*.   [2] a] the *1741 Dab.*

[3] In 1724 he was appointed secretary to the lords justices. He now lived permanently in Ireland, with visits to England—where he died in 1740.

[4] he] Philips *1740 and all London texts.* (Dublin texts replaced the name with three asterisks.)

[5] The infantile trochaics of Philips were what gave rise to the expression 'namby-pamby', invented about this time. The 'flam' called 'A Poem to the Hon. Miss Carteret' was on sale in London before the middle of June of this year.   [6] Succeed] succeeded *1741 Dab.*

Are you altogether a Country Gentleman that I must Address to you out of London to the Hazard of your losing this pretious Letter, which I will now Conclude although so much Paper is left. I have an ill name and therefore shall not Subscribe it. but you will guess it comes from one who esteems and loves you about half as much as you deserve. I mean as much as he can

I am in great concern at which I am just told is in some News Paper[1] that Lord Bolingbroke is much hurt by a fall in Hunting I am glad he has so much youth and Viger left of which he hath not been thrifty but I wonder he has no more Discretion.

Address [added in Oxford's hand]: For mr pope at his | House at Twickenham near | Hampton Court | by London.

Endorsement: Dean Swift's Letter to | Mr Pope. Sepr 29. 1725.

POPE *to* CHARLES BRIDGEMAN[2]   [1725]

Elwin–Courthope, ix. 517

Dawley, Thursday [1724].

I am sorry it is not possible for me to go to Lord Oxford's with you, so soon: for a hundred objections lye in my way just now. But pray assure my lord faithfully of my truest respects, and earnest desires to see him. I wish you a good journey, and total recovery of your health, being faithfully, dear sir, yours.

I hope you will fix that matter with Mrs. Howard. My Lord Bolingbroke received yours, and shall be glad to see you at your conveniency.

POPE *to* THE EARL OF STRAFFORD[3]   5 *October* [1725]

The Hyde Collection

My Lord,—I will not deny but what you mean for a sort of reproach is really true, (& I hope, in modesty, a Commendation) That I should not have had the confidence to trouble you, my Lord, in the manner I have, but for the Controversy with Lady Kneller. But if I lose my Suit, I shall be a Gainer; I mean, of what I value much above any

---

[1] some News Paper] some of the news papers *1740–42*.

[2] This letter Elwin found in 'the Harley Papers' presumably at Longleat, among which papers the present editor has not found it—though very likely it is there. Elwin dated it 1724, but that year is impossible since the letter is written at Dawley, first occupied by Bolingbroke in the summer of 1725. Pope had planned a visit to Wimpole in the summer of 1725 (see Lord Oxford to Pope, 30 Aug.), which did not take place. In the Christmas season of 1725/6 Pope and Bridgeman were both at Down Hall (Pope to Lord Oxford, 22 Jan. 1725/6). Bridgeman had worked at Wimpole as early as 1721 (*Hist. MSS. Comm. Bath MSS*. iii. 498), and he and Pope had in 1725 worked on the landscaping of Marble Hill.

[3] See Pope's letter of 12 Aug. 1725, of which this is a sort of continuation.

thing else I can gain, of Your Favour & approbation in some sort, at least of your Letters. For I am really not so self-conceited, as to take literally some obliging things you do me the honor to say to me. Your Lordship, I fear however, will think I do so, when I write this without the least pretence of business, or indeed without having any thing to say for myself, but the only good thing perhaps I can say for my self, that I am sincerely Your humble Servant.

There ends my Letter. What follows is a kind of Epitaph after the death of my Subject: (a thing not unfrequent both in writers & Speakers.) I did not doubt but the account I gave you of the Fulminations of the Parson against you, would have no better Effect, than what usually Church-Thunder has upon Sons of the Court, & Men of the world. It does but clear the Air of your Faces (is not that a Pun?) and leave a greater Serenity than before, it makes You smile in short, as the other makes Nature smile. Well my Lord, we submissive Sons of the Mother Church, the Papists, are otherwise affected by these Denunciations. We bend the knee; & kiss the Toe, of the Priest, upon these occasions. Lady Kn. I am told, is resolved I shall go to Church (tho I should be ever so willing) no more than your Lordship; for she threatens to have me Excommunicated. And so I shall no more go to Church, dead than alive. Is not this horrible to Christian ears? Very horrible, and yet after all, not half so horrible to Christian ears as a Sermon of Our Parson's.

I shall know nothing more of my Cause till the middle or end of this month. If I then cry out for help of your Lordship, I hope my Help *which is in the Lord*, will not be *far* from me, because you may probably be returning to London & I would give a good deal you had half an hours conference with Dr. Henchman. It is but necessary to support your Character, after such an *Ecclesiastical*, I need not add to that, *Furious* attack. The truth is, the black puppy provokd me, which was more than all the fat woman could do. with all her other dirty Gownmen. A dull Blockhead sometimes galls me more than a Smart cunning rogue; as a blunt Knife cuts & mangles worse than a keen one. I wonder the man shoud be angry at your Lordship of all men, who (by his own account) are the only one of his parish that does not know him to be a Dunce, by never having heard him hold forth.

I am as busy in three inches of Gardening, as any man can be in threescore acres. I fancy my self like the fellow that spent his life in cutting the twelve apostles in one cherry-stone. I have a Theatre, an Arcade, a Bowling green, a Grove, & what not? in a bitt of ground that would have been but a plate of Sallet to Nebuchadnezzar, the first day he was turn'd to graze. My chief comfort is, that its too little to afford Tythe to the aforesaid Parson.

I must not omit my Mothers humblest Services to your Lordship

& my Lady Strafford, my own Wishes for Lord Wentworths[1] better health & the young Lady's who was so obliging as not to think me an Old man. I am with all unfeigned respect and with that Esteem which I can't help, & so is no degree of merit in me, but the meer conse-quence of yours, | My Lord, | Your most Obliged | & obedient humble | Servant, | A. Pope.

Twitenham: | Oct. 5th

*MRS. D. ROBINSON *to* POPE[2]   9 *October* 1725

Homer MSS. Add. 4809

I am extreamly Concarn'd to hear of Mrs Popes illness; as I am, to trouble you at this time, for those goods, I wrote to Mrs Pope for, which are the same you mention'd in yours, to my daughter Anastasia Viz: three Sconcess. two Landskips. five black & white Prints, which goods I beg the favour, may be deliver'd; Monday or Tuesday to the same person I sent before, if the Weather prove tollerable he shall waite on you for them, with my most humble Service to Mrs Pope. I am | Sir | your | Most humble | Sarvant | D. Robinson.

Fullham | Octobr the 9th: 1725

   My family are | your most humble | Sarvants
Postmark: 9/OC

†POPE *to* ROBERT DIGBY[3]   10 *October* [1725]

1735
                                                    Octob. 10.

I was upon the point of taking a much greater Journey than to *Ber-mudas*, even to That undiscover'd Country, from whose Bourn no Traveller returns!

⌜A Fever carry'd me on the high Gallop towards it for six or seven days⌝[4]—But here you have me now, ⌜and that's all I shall say of it: Since which time an impertinent Lameness kept me at home twice as long; as if Fate should say (after the other dangerous Illness) "You shall neither go into the other World, nor any where you like in this." Else who knows but I had been in *Hom-lacy?*⌝[4]

[1] Lord Strafford's three-year-old son. The 'young lady' might be a small daughter.
[2] The Robinsons had moved from Twickenham to Fulham in 1723, but apparently had left certain things in the care of the Popes.
[3] This letter, like other letters to Digby, appears in all Pope's editions 1735–42, except 1735 a2. Pope never gave it a year date, but Elwin dated it [1723]. That year seems impossible; for Pope was not then confined by a fever, as he was in 1725. The letter is aglow with the thought of the Bermudas and Berkeley's project. In 1723 Berkeley was in Ireland, but he came over to London in 1724, and published his Proposals for his Bermuda project in July 1725.
[4] The passages in half-brackets were omitted in the quarto and folio of 1737.

I conspire in your Sentiments, emulate your Pleasures, wish for your Company. You are all of one Heart and one Soul, as was said of the Primitive Christians: 'Tis like the Kingdom of the Just upon Earth; not a wicked Wretch to interrupt you; but a Set of try'd, experienc'd Friends, and fellow Comforters, who have seen Evil Men and Evil Days, and have by a superior Rectitude of Heart set yourselves above them, and reap your Reward. Why will you ever, of your own accord, end such a Millenary[1] Year in *London*?[2] transmigrate (if I may so call it) into other Creatures, in that Scene of Folly Militant, when you may reign for ever at *Hom-lacy* in Sense and Reason Triumphant? I appeal to a Third Lady in your Family, whom I take to be the most Innocent, and the least warp'd by idle Fashion and Custom, of you all; I appeal to Her, if you are not every Soul of you better People, better Companions, and happier, where you are? I desire her Opinion under her Hand in your next Letter, I mean Miss *Scudamore*'s[3]—I'm confident if she would, or durst speak her Sense, and employ that Reasoning which God has given her, to infuse more thoughtfulness into you all; those Arguments could not fail to put you to the blush, and keep you out of Town, like People sensible of your own Felicities. I am not without hopes, if She can detain a Parliament Man and a Lady of Quality from the World one Winter, that I may come upon you with such irresistable Arguments another Year, as may carry you all with me to *Bermudas*,[4] the Seat of all Earthly Happiness, and the new *Jerusalem* of the Righteous.

Don't talk of the decay of the Year, the Season is good where the People are so: 'Tis the best Time of the Year for a Painter; there is more Variety of Colours in the Leaves, the Prospects begin to open, thro' the thinner Woods, over the Vallies; and thro' the high Canopies of Trees to the higher Arch of Heaven: The Dews of the Morning impearl every Thorn, and scatter Diamonds on the verdant Mantle of the Earth: The Frosts are fresh and wholesome: What wou'd ye have? The Moon shines too, tho' not for Lovers these cold Nights, but for Astronomers.

Have ye not *Reflecting Telescopes*[5] whereby ye may innocently magnify her Spots and Blemishes? Content yourselves with them, and do not come to a Place where your own Eyes become Reflecting

---

[1] Pope frequently shows an interest in the millennial thought of his day.

[2] London? transmigrate] London? and transmigrate *1737b*.

[3] Afterwards Duchess of Beaufort, at this time about twelve years old.—Pope, 1735.] at this time very young *1737–42*. (Miss Scudamore was married to the Duke of Beaufort in 1729, and divorced by Act of Parliament in 1744. She was born in 1711, and in 1723 [Elwin's date for the letter] she would be 12 years old.)

[4] About this time the Rev. Dean Berkley conceiv'd his Project of erecting a Settlement in Bermuda for the Propagation of the Christian Faith, and of Sciences in America.—Pope, 1735.

[5] These Instruments were just then brought to perfection.—Pope, 1735.

Telescopes, and where those of all others are equally such upon their Neighbours. Stay You at least (for what I've said before relates only to the Ladies, don't imagine I'll write about any *Eyes* but theirs) Stay, I say, from that idle, busy-looking *Sanhedrin*, where *Wisdom* or *No Wisdom* is the Eternal Debate, not (as it lately was in *Ireland*) an Accidental one.

If after all, you will despise good Advice, and resolve to come to *London*; here you will find me, doing just the things I should not, living where I should not, and as worldly, as idle, in a Word as much an *Anti-Bermudanist* as any body. Dear Sir, make the Ladies know I am their Servant, You know I am | Yours, &c.

POPE *to* THE EARL OF OXFORD   *c.* 11 *October* 1725

[At Longleat, in the Portland Papers, vol. xiii, f. 30, is preserved the cover of a letter addressed in Pope's hand to Lord Oxford and endorsed by his lordship, 'R. Octr 11. 1725.' The postmark bears the same day and month. The letter has not been found.]

‖POPE *to* SWIFT[1]   15 *October* 1725

Longleat Portland Papers, xiii (Harleian transcripts)

Twitenham, near Hampton Court | Octr 15: 1725.

I am wonderfully pleas'd with the suddenness of your kind answer. It makes me hope you are coming towards us, and that you incline ⌜more and more⌝ toward your old friends in proportion as you draw nearer to them; in short, that you are getting[2] into Our Vortex. Here is one, who was once a powerful Planet. ⌜Lord Bol.⌝[3] who has now (after long experience of all that comes of shining) learn'd to be content with returning to his First point, without the thought or ambition of shining at all. Here is another,[4] who thinks one of the greatest Glories of his Father was to have distinguish'd and Lov'd you, and who loves you hereditarily. Here is Arbuthnot, ⌜yet living,⌝ recover'd from the jaws of death, and more pleas'd with the hope of seeing you again, than of reviving a world he has long despis'd every part of, but[5] what is made up of a few men like yourself. He goes abroad again, and is more chearful than even Health can make a man, for he has a good Conscience into the bargain (which is the most *Catholick* of all Remedies, tho not

---

[1] Published in 1741 and found in all Pope's editions thereafter. The omissions in the printed texts are here placed in half-brackets.
[2] to them . . . are getting] to them; and are getting *1740–42*.
[3] Pope's texts omitted the name, but Curll (1741Lc) added it in a footnote.
[4] Lord Oxford.—Curll, 1741Lc.
[5] reviving . . . but] reviewing a world, every part of which he has long despis'd, but *1740–42*.

the most *Universal*) I knew it would be a pleasure to you to hear this; and in truth, that made me write so soon to you.

I'm sorry poor Philips[1] is not promoted in this age; for certainly if his reward be of the next, he is of all Poets the most miserable. I'm also sorry for another reason; if they don't promote him they'l spoil a very good conclusion[2] of one of my Satyrs,[3] where having endeavour'd to correct the Taste of the town in wit and Criticisme, I end thus.

> But what avails to lay down rules for Sense?
> In ——'s[4] Reign these fruitless lines were writ,
> When Ambrose Philips[5] was preferr'd for wit!

Our friend Gay is used, as the friends of Tories are by Whigs, (and generally by Tories too) Because he had Humour, he was suppos'd to have dealt with Dr Swift; in like manner as when any one had Learning formerly, he was thought to have dealt with the Devil. He puts his whole trust at Court, in that Lady whom I describ'd to you, and whom you take to be an allegorical Creature of fancy. I wish she really were *Riches* for His sake; tho as for yours, I question whether (if you knew her) you would change her for the other?

Lord Bol.[6] had not the least harm by his fall, I wish he had no more[7] by his other Fall[8]—⌐Our⌐ Lord Oxford had none by his—But Lord B.[9] is the most *Improv'd Mind* since you saw him, that ever was without[10] shifting into a new body or being Paullo minus ab angelis.[11] I have often imagined to myself, that if ever All of us met[12] again, after so many Varieties and Changes, after so much of the Old world, and of the Old man in each of us, had been alter'd; ⌐after there has been a New Heaven, and a New Earth, in our Minds, and bodies,⌐ that Scarce a single thought of the one any more than a single atome of the other, remains just the same: I've fancy'd, I say, that we shou'd meet like the Righteous in the Millennium, quite in peace, divested of all our former passions, smiling at all our own designs,[13] and content to enjoy the Kingdome of the Just in Tranquillity. But I find you would rather be employ'd as an Avenging Angel of wrath, to break

---

[1] Philips] *** *1741 Dab*;] P. *1741 Lab*; *1742 Lc, Da.*

[2] they'l . . . conclusion] they'll spoil the conclusion *1741 Labc*; *1742 Lb, Da.*

[3] Presumably the 'Progress of Dulness', destined to become *The Dunciad*. The line about Philips came in 1728 near the end of the poem (iii. 274), and in the text of 1743 became iii. 326.   [4] Curll filled in the blank (*1741 Lc*) with *Brunswick's.*

[5] Ambrose Philips] —— —— *1741 Dab* (i.e. the Dublin texts omit the name).

[6] Lord Bol.] Lord Bolingbroke *1740–42.*

[7] had no more] had receiv'd no more *1740–42.*

[8] Removal.—Curll (*1741 Lc*).   [9] B.] Bolingbroke *1740–42.*

[10] was without] was improved without *1740–42.*

[11] A little lower than the Angels.—Footnote in *1741 Dab, Lc.*

[12] met] meet *1740–42.*

[13] at . . . designs] at our past designs *1740, 1741 Dab*] at our past follies *1741 Labc*; *1742 Lc, Da.*

your Vial of Indignation over the heads of the wretched pityful[1]
creatures of this World; nay would make them *Eat your Book*, which
you have made as bitter a pill[2] for them as possible.

I won't tell you what designes I have in my head (besides writing a
Set of Maximes in opposition to all Rochefoucaults Principles)[3] till
I see you here, face to face. Then you shall have no reason to complain
of me, for want of a Generous disdain of this World, or of the loss of
my ears,[4] in yours and Their service.

Lord Oxford[5] (whom I have now the third time mentioned in this
letter, and he deserves to be always mention'd, in every thing that is
addrest to you, or comes from you) Expects you. That ought to be
enough to bring you hither; tis vastly a better[6] reason, than if the
Nation Expected you. For I really enter as fully as you can desire, into
your Principle, of Love of Individuals: And I think the way to have
a Publick Spirit, is first to have a Private one: For who the devil can[7]
believe any[8] man can care for a hundred thousand people, who never
cared for One? No ill humoured man can ever be a Patriot, any more
than a Friend.

I designed to have left the following page for Dr. Arbuthnot to fill,
but he is so touch'd with the period in yours to me concerning him,
that he intends to answer it by a whole letter. He too is busy about a
book,[9] which I guess he'll tell you of. So adieu—what remains worth
telling you? Dean Berkley is well, and happy in the prosecution of his
Scheme.[10] Lords Oxford and Bol. in health. Arbuthnot's recover'd,
Duke Disney so also from the gates of death; Sir W. Wyndham better.[11]
Lord Bathurst well, and a Preserver of ancient[12] Honour and ancient
Friendship. The rest, if they were d—d,[13] what is it to a Protestant[14]
Priest, who has nothing to do with the Dead? I answer for my own
part as a Papist, I would not pray them out of Purgatory.

1 wretched pityful creatures] wretched creatures *1741 Dab.*

2 made . . . a pill] made (I doubt not) as bitter a pill *1740–42.*

3 Swift in reply to this (Swift to Pope, 26 Nov. 1725) claims Rochefoucauld as his
favourite author, 'because I found my whole character in him'.

4 World . . . ears] World, tho' I have not lost my ears *1740–42.*

5 Oxford (whom] Oxford too, whom *1740–42.*

6 tis vastly a better] tis a better *1741 Labc; 1742 Lc, Da.*

7 who the devil can] who can *1741 Labc; 1742 La, Da.*

8 believe any] believe (said a friend of mine) that any *1740–42.*

9 Curll (*1741 Lc*) glossed this remark with the title of *A Treatise of Aliments*, but since
this work appeared in 1731, it is more likely Arbuthnot's *Table of Ancient Coins, Weights,
and Measures* (1727) that is in question.

10 Curll again goes wrong (*1741 Lc*) in his footnote '*The Minute Philosopher*'. Berkeley's
'scheme' was doubtless his college in the Bermudas.

11 health . . . better] health, Arbuthnot recover'd, Duke Disney so also; Sir William
Wyndham better *1740–42.* (But *Arbuthnot recover'd* is omitted in *1741 Labc; 1742 Lc, Da.*)

12 better . . . Friendship.] better, Lord Bathurst well. These and some others, preserve their
ancient honour and friendship. *1740–42.*

13 Friendship . . . d—d] Friendship. Those who do neither if they were d—d *1740–42.*

14 to a Protestant] to Protestant (*misprint in 1741 La1, corrected in La2*).

My name is as bad an one as yours, and hated by all bad Poets from Hopkins and Sternhold to Gildon and Cibber. The first pray'd against me ⌜join'd⌝ with the *Turk*; and a Modern Imitatour of theirs (whom I leave you to find out) has added the *Christian* to 'em with proper definitions of each, in this manner,

> The Pope's the Whore of Babylon,
>   The Turk he is a Jew
> The Christian is *an Infidel*
>   *That sitteth in a Pew.*[1]

⌜My paper is without the Doctors help.⌝

Endorsement (in Oxford's hand): Mr Pope. to Dr Swift | Oct. 15. 1725.

POPE *to* THE EARL OF OXFORD   17 *October* [1725]

Longleat Portland Papers, xii

Twitenham, Oct. 17th

My Lord,—The Humanity your Lordship has upon all occasions shown me (& I know it to be natural to you; when you think another sincere in his concerns & affections, to partake 'em) gives me the assurance of telling you that my Mother is something better, or at least we hope so, for the first time. She is sensible of yours & My Lady Oxfords favours every way; & begs, while she lives, to be thought your Servant. I don't know why I trouble you with the inclosed to Dean Swift, unless in a kind of hope of rewarding his kind letter to me, with something better than my own, in a line of your Lordship's, if you have leisure. You'l be so good as to forward it; & to believe no man is with more Esteem, truth, & obligation,

Your Lordships most faithfull | humble Servant | A. Pope.

Inclosed.

Address: To the Rt. Honble the | Earl of Oxford, in | Dover street. | London.
Postmark: 18/OC

THE EARL OF OXFORD *to* POPE   19 *October* 1725

Longleat Portland Papers, xii

Dover street. Octr 19. 1725.

Sir,—I am very glad to hear that good mrs Pope is better   I have taken care of your letter to the Dean   I have the pleasure and happiness I

---

[1] The stanza comes from 'The Monster of Ragusa', printed in *Poems on Several Occasions* (1717) and later in the 5th ed. of Lintot's *Miscellany Poems* (1726). See Norman Ault, *Pope's Own Miscellany*, pp. xlvi and 92.

thank god to tell You that yesterday morning my Wife was safly brought to bed of a Son[1]   I thank god both are as well as can be expected,   I am hindred from writing a longer letter to you Now   I hope I shall See you Soon   I desire you will make my compliments to mrs Pope I heartily wish her, the recovery of her Health

I am Sir with great esteem | your most affectionate | humble Servant | Oxford.

Address: For | Alexander Pope Esq at | Twitenham | Middlesex
Frank | Oxford
Postmark illegible; probably: 20/OC

POPE *to* FORTESCUE[2]   [*October–November*, 1725?]

1797 (Polwhele, i. 322)

If this reaches you, I beg we may meet at the doctor's about six to night. I must run again out of town, for my mother is very ill of a jaundice, and I come to speak to the doctor chiefly; I am afraid she will be too ill to let me have the pleasure of seeing you on Sunday, but the first day I can, I will send to beg it of you; being, with great truth and esteem, dear Sir, ever yours, | A. Pope.

Two oclock. I've been every where about to find you about your lodgings, Chambers, Dutton's, Merin's, Tom's, Lintot's. Pray try if you can find Gay.

Address: To Wm. Fortescue, esq.

POPE *to* THE EARL OF OXFORD[3]   [? *November* 1725]

Longleat Portland Papers, xii

My Lord,—I send to know of the State of Lady Oxfords health, for which I have a true concern. I cannot but thank your Lordship for the great Indulgence and Liberty you gave me, in my variety of Negotiations at your house, in my irregular Entrances & Exits, in my unseasonable Suppers & Seperate Breakfasts, & in all my Ways. I hope a Day will come when I may be allowed, meerly as a Curiosity, to show you, my Lord that I can be five or six hours in one place: This will be, when ever you can pass a day here, or whenever next

---

[1] This, the only son born to Lord Oxford, lived only until 22 Oct.
[2] Mrs. Pope's jaundice dates this letter. See Pope to Broome, 2 Nov. [1725].
[3] The letter is obviously not surely datable. In November of this year Lady Oxford was recovering from a recent confinement (18 Oct.) and Mrs. Pope was again in need of saffron for her jaundice. Pope's use of Oxford's house at such a time would be intermittent.

you will command me to go to Town for a better cause than business, namely for your company.

I am with the Sincerest Esteem, | and most pleasing obligation, | My Lord. Yours. | A. Pope.

You'l be so good as to Send my Mother a little Saffron.

Address: To the | Right Hon. the | Earl of Oxford.
Endorsement: Mr Pope

POPE *to* BROOME   2 *November* [1725]

Elwin–Courthope, viii. 101

Nov. 2, [1725].

You may conclude I am in no small agitation and trouble, when I cannot be calm enough to write above three lines to you. My family is in the utmost confusion, and melancholy of circumstances; my mother in a dangerous jaundice, at her great age, dispirited and plied with hourly medicines; my old nurse on her death-bed,[1] in all the last pains of a dropsy. In a word, no hour of day or night but presents to me some image of death and suffering. I was very lately in hopes of seeing you; now they are turned to fears. I could not receive you with any comfort, therefore beg you to defer your journey till I am, one way or other, fit, if not desirous to see you and to welcome you. If the worst misfortune happens to me, when it is over your sight will be a comfort to me.

I had almost forgot to tell you I paid your brother what you desired a fortnight ago: but probably he acquainted you of it. Dear Broome, I am faithful yours.

The eighteenth book will soon be wanted.

POPE *to* THE EARL OF OXFORD   7 *November* 1725

Longleat Portland Papers, xii

Twitenham, Novr 7th | 1725.

My Lord,—I did not leave your Lordship without a painful desire of returning to wait on you again; I say a painful one, because I knew the condition of my sick family would not allow me, so soon as I apprehended you would be going out of town. Accordingly, my poor old Nurse, who has lived in constant attendance & care of me, ever since I was an Infant at her breast, dyed the other day.[2] I think it a fine verse, that of your friend Mr Prior.

---

[1] In his Elzevir Virgil, in which Pope entered the deaths of friends, is the entry: 'Nutrix mea fidelissima M. Beech, obiit 5 Novem. 1725, aet. 77.' (Elwin–Courthope, *Works*, i. p. ix.)
[2] 5 Nov. 1725.

> —and by his side,
> A Good man's greatest loss, a faithful Servant, dy'd!
> and I dont think one of my own an ill one, speaking of a Nurse,
> The tender Second to a Mother's cares.
>
> Hom. Odyss. 7.

Surely this Sort of Friend is not the least, and this sort of Relation, when continued thro life, Superior to most that we call so. She having been tryd, & found, kind & officious so long, thro so many accidents and needs of life, is surely Equal to a meer Natural Tye. Indeed tis Nature that makes us Love, but tis Experience that makes us Grateful: and I believe, to thinking minds, Gratitude presents as many Objects & Circumstances to render us melancholy, as even Hope itself (that great Painter of Ideas) can do. But in truth, both what good-natur'd minds have experienced, & what they Expect to experience, fills them to the brimm: The better a man is, the more he expects & hopes from his Friend, his Child, his fellow creature; the more he reflects backward & aggrandizes every Good he has receiv'd; His own Capacity of being Good & kind & grateful, makes him think others have been, or would be so.—The only satisfaction this world can afford us under such losses, is to see those whom we believe to have a mutual feeling with us, participate & talk to us. This buoys us up from day to day, till somebody loves us, and buryes us, and grieves for us, and there's an end of it. Our Comfort is certainly Beyond this world, because the Best of men have none here, under those very misfortunes which most affect them.

My Lord, forgive me: A more General & Common Style would better suit the distance between us: But Humanity renders men as equal, as Death does. I know you to have So very much of it, that I honour you the more, the more I pity you, in any thing you can suffer; I sincerely pray, that all you wish may be added to you. I could not speak any thing like what I thought, when I saw you; but this melancholy of my own has been like a Vernish, to bring out a little more of the real colour of my mind in relation to my Sensibility toward you.[1] It is however a most certain truth, that *one can never Express Any thing that one really feels.*

If it happens that your Lordship does not go away in four or five days, I will hope to wait on you, the moment I can get my Mother another to supply my absence for a day. Believe me, with true esteem & the most hearty wishes, my Lady Oxfords, and | Your Lordships most obliged obedient faithful | Servant, | A. Pope.

Address: To | The Right Honble the | Earl of Oxford, in | Dover-street. | London.

Postmark: 8/NO

[1] Lord Oxford's new-born (and only) son had died on 22 Oct.

POPE *to* THE EARL OF OXFORD[1]   [*November* 1725 ?]
Longleat Portland Papers, xii

Twit'nam. Wensday.

My Lord,—I may just once more bid you adieu, & wish you every felicity where you are going. I found my Mother in want of Saffron, & I know you would not leave us in want of any thing. She is truly your Lordships & my Lady Oxfords Servant: If Her Prayers will do you good, you have 'em; My Wishes of You, & for you, will be as lasting as my Life.

My Lord, | Your ever obligd faith-|full Servant | A. Pope.

Address: To the Rt. Honble the Earl of Oxford.
Endorsement (by a secretary): Mr Pope

POPE *to* BROOME   10 *November* 1725
Elwin–Courthope, viii. 101

Nov. 10, 1725.

Though my family continues in the same dejecting posture, my mother still ill, and my poor old nurse gone to her long home, I must acknowledge the receipt of the two books,[2] and of a very kind letter from you. I assure you your advice and your company would at all times be comfortable to me under affliction; it was for your sake I mentioned what I did, in the fear of that confusion which has since happened in so long sicknesses. Yet I now have hopes given me that my mother may outlive this present illness—a short reprieve! but very dear, very desirable to me, though not much to herself at these years. I mistook something you said in a former letter, so much in my own favour, and am disappointed at your saying you never thought of it.[3] I hope you will in spring at least. I am sorry you have had your share of filial concerns,[4] probably in another way than mine; but whatever trouble you may undergo will be recompensed by the good intention that makes you undertake it, and I hope also by the success of everything you desire. I wonder your brother never writ to you. He told me he would in a post or two, by the same token that I bespoke a periwig of him, in which I expect to make such a figure as better to become that of bays, wherein his brother has dressed me so gaily in a like little fine paper of verses.[5]

---

[1] The letter is placed here because it fits a moment of farewell to Oxford and because of the request for saffron, which was medicinal for jaundice. Mrs. Pope was afflicted with jaundice in this part of 1725.   [2] Books XVI and XVIII.
[3] Never thought, that is, of visiting Twickenham then.
[4] Concerns probably for the financial support of his father. See Broome to Pope, 29 Oct. 1735. Broome's relatives were financially less secure than Broome himself. His brother, as we see by the end of this paragraph, made wigs.
[5] The verses 'To Mr. Pope, on his Works, 1725'.

I congratulate with you, beyond all words, on the closing of Eustathius. What will next be wanted are the notes on lib. 22, 23, 24, for I have deferred the 17th, 18th, and 19th till the last. I have been as sick of the translation as you can be of the notes, and indeed, as you know, have had many things to make me quite sour about it. I know myself to be an honest man, and, I will add, a friendly one; nor do I in my conscience think I have acted an unfair or disreputable part with the public, if my friends will do me justice. This indeed is my sore place; for I care not what they say of my poetry, but a man's morals are of a tenderer nature, and higher consequence.[1]

Believe me very sincerely yours. The people whose friendship I have wished, and endeavoured all the ways I could to deserve, have generally allowed it me, and that is all the solid pleasure I ever received from the partiality the world has shown my character. If, from thinking I did not want sense, they have come to know I do not want honour and tenderness, it is enough. It is all I desire to be esteemed for. In the rank of these I have ever held you, and I know ever shall, being sure of your integrity, friendship, and all good offices; and I am gratefully, dear Broome, yours.

FENTON *to* BROOME   20 *November* [1725]

Elwin–Courthope, viii. 103

Leicester Fields, Nov. 20, [1725]

I heartily congratulate you on your concluding your laborious task, and am glad to hear you have spirits enough remaining to undertake Apollonius, who, in the main, I am afraid, will be found a heavy writer. In my notes on Waller, I shall have occasion to quote a passage concerning Talus, which is in the fourth book, and begins at the 1636th verse, which if you think proper to translate now I will insert it, and give notice to the world that you intend a translation of the whole.[2] I think it is now high time for you to come to town, that we may settle affairs with Mr. Pope. The last time I saw him at Sir Clement's he would have had me declare what I expected to receive, which I absolutely refused without your participation, and, therefore the sooner we concert our demands the better. We have been but coarsely used this last summer, both in print and conversation, which, in truth, was

---

[1] Jealous of Pope's fame and prosperity, his numerous enemies were attacking him this summer for his use of 'hackney-hands for the sake of Idleness'. *The London Journal*, 17 July 1725, had a violent attack signed 'Homerides', and doubtless there were others. Publication of the edition of Shakespeare and of the *Odyssey* in the same year made Pope look particularly avaricious.

[2] In his *Poems* (1727) Broome prints (pp. 168–72) the desired translation; but in his quarto edition of Waller (1729) Fenton did not mention Broome in the note on Talus ('Battel of the Summer Islands', iii. 11).

no more than I always expected. But this will serve us to chat over when we meet, which I hope will be before Christmas.

We have at present a very dull, empty town. I hear of no new plays, but a comedy by our old friend Tom Southerne,[1] who desired me to send his service to you, and begs you to write him a prologue, and hopes to receive a favourable answer by the next post. Gay is busy in writing fables for Prince William. Your old acquaintance Jack Marriot is curate at Easthampstead, and behaves himself very well out of the pulpit. I have had two short visits from Mr. Pope since I came to town. He tells me that he has buried old nurse, and poor Mrs. Pope is not likely to survive her long. I am ever, dear sir, your affectionate humble servant.

POPE *to* BROOME   22 *November* [1725]

Elwin–Courthope, viii. 104

Nov. 22, [1725].

The confused state I have been in, both of head and heart, will excuse my mistaking the seventeenth and twenty-second book of notes for the eighteenth and twenty-third, which will be wanted when you conveniently can send them to Lintot's. I have a further kindness to beg of you, being myself employed in so melancholy a way that it's impossible to turn my head to anything. I wish to God you would translate, instead of me, the small part now wanted of the seventeenth book at the press, namely from verse, of the original, 505 to the end, beginning at 'Ἡ μὲν ἄρ' ὣς ἀγόρευε, etc.[2] We are put to a stop for this at present in one volume. I just saw Fenton and a letter from you to him. I am going to print your verses in a Miscellany. I wish you altered the strength of that extravagant compliment, "what Heav'n created, and what you have wrote."[3] Excuse my haste, and believe, all that is fit for a friend to believe, I do of you, and doubt not you do of me, and would do any reasonable thing in my justification. I am ever truly yours.

My mother continues ill.

---

[1] Southerne's *Money the Mistress* was finally acted at the theatre in Lincoln's Inn Fields in Feb. 1725/6. He had long been a friend of Fenton's, who in 1711 published an *Epistle to Mr. Southerne*. Southerne's friendly offices with regard to *Mariamne* are acknowledged in the Dedication to that play.

[2] This I did.—Broome (Elwin).

[3] As printed, this line became: 'What Heav'n created, and what Heav'n inspires.'

POPE *to* CARYLL[1]   23 *November* [1725]

Add. 28618

Novr 23

I was obliged to you for a kind letter before you took your journey,[2] to ask if you could do me any service in your travels; but as I have little or no correspondences abroad, I needed not to give you the trouble you so obligingly offered. I am glad your travels delighted you; improve you I'm sure they could not. You are not so much a youth as that, tho' you run about with a king of sixteen,[3] and (what makes him more a child) a king of Frenchmen. My own time has been more melancholy, spent in ⌈a trembling⌉ attendance upon death, which has ⌈at last⌉ seized one of our family, my poor old nurse. My mother is something better, tho' at her advanced age, every day is a climacterique. I'm glad you received the second set of the *Odyssey*. I will shortly send you the whole work complete, between the cares of myself and my two friends. I believe not only the future but the present age will soon allow it to be an exacter version than that of the *Iliad* where all the drudgery was my own. When I translate again I will be hanged; nay I will do something to deserve to be hanged, which is worse, rather than drudge for such a world as is no judge of your labour. I'll sooner write something to anger it, than to please it.

I would not repeat a matter of interest to you, which I mentioned above a year since; namely, that when it is convenient to you I would be glad to receive the 200ll.; but I must again repeat, that if it is not, I'm very easy while it is in your keeping. I hope you left Lady Mary well, if you have left her in Paris (for you never nam'd her in your letter). Pray, in what condition of life is Mrs Cope? She told me of your intention of charity towards her, and I suppose by this time she is in the convent. I am (with all esteem and memory of the long acquaintance with which you have honoured me) | Sir | Your most affectionate obliged | Servant A: P.

My sincere wishes to all your family.

[1] In his editions of 1735 Pope used the second and third sentences of this letter as part of a letter printed as if to Robert Digby under date of 10 Sept. 1724. In his editions of 1737–42 Pope printed the fabricated letter as if to Dr. Arbuthnot and dropped the year from the date. Since his nurse died in Nov. 1725, the September date is impossible; but the fabrication is here printed as to Arbuthnot, 10 Sept. [1725]. Omissions in the printed texts to Digby or Arbuthnot are indicated in half-brackets. In and after 1737 Pope made few textual changes in his printed text.

[2] In July 1725 Mr. Caryll escorted Lady Mary Caryll and her young family to Paris, where she remained until 1736.—Elwin.

[3] Louis XV.

||SWIFT *to* POPE 26 *November* 1725

Longleat Portland Papers, xiii (Harleian transcript)

⸢Dublin⸣ Novr 26, 1725

Sir,—I should sooner have acknoledged yours if a Feaverish Disorder and the Relick[1] of it, had not disabled me for a fortnight, I now begin to make excuses, because I hope I am pretty near seeing you, and therefore I would cultivate an Acquaintance, because if you do not know me when we meet you need only keep one of my Letters, and compare it with my Face, for my Face and Letters are Counterparts of my heart, I fear I have not expressed that right, but I mean well, and I hate blotts; I look in your Letter, and in my Conscience you say the same thing, but in a better manner. Pray tell my Lord Bolingbroke that I wish he were banished again, for then I should hear from him, when he was full of Philosophy, and Talked de contemptu mundi.[2] My Lord Oxford was so extremely kind as to write to me immediatly an Account of his Sons Birth, which I immediatly acknowledged, but before my Letter could reach him I wished it in the Sea[3] I hope I was more afflicted then his Lordship—Hard[4] that Parsons and Beggars should be overrun with Bratts while so great and good a Family wants an Heir to continue it. I have received his Fathers Picture but I lament (Sub Sigillo confessionis)[5] that it is not so true a Resemblance as I could wish⸢; I had a very kind Letter from Dr. Arbuthnot; but I will not trouble him with an Answer. this is no Excuse for I would rather write then not. I will answer him when I see him; in the mean time you shall do it for me. Tis enough that I know he is in health and loves me;—⸣ Drown the World, I am not content with despising it, but I would anger it if I could with safety. I wish there were an Hospital built for it's despisers, where one might act with safety and it need not be a large Building, only I would have it well endowed. —Mr Philips[6] is fort chancellant[7] whether he shall turn Parson or no. But all employments here are engaged or in Reversion. Cast Wits, and cast Beaux have a proper Sanctuary in the Church. Yet we think it a Severe Judgment that a fine Gentleman, and so much a finer[8] for hating Eclesiasticks should be a domestick humble Retainer to an Irish Prelate. He is neither Secretary nor Gentleman usher yet serves

[1] Relick] relicks *1740–42*.

[2] Contemning the World.—Footnote in 1741 Dab. (Curll, who pretended to reprint the Dublin text, has, like 1741 Lc, the footnote 'Of Despising the World'.)

[3] Because of the news that the infant son had died.

[4] Lordship—Hard] Lordship. 'Tis hard *1740; 1741 Lab; 1742 Lc, Da.* (In 1741 Dab and Lc *'Tis* becomes *It is*.)

[5] Under the Seal of Confession.—Footnote in 1741 Dab, Lc.

[6] Mr Philips] P** *1740–42* (Except in 1741 Lc, where Curll prints *Philips*.)

[7] Very wavering.—Footnote in 1741 Dab.

[8] much a finer] much the finer *1742 Lbc.*

in both Capacities. He hath published several reasons why he never came to see me, but the best is that I have not waited on his Lord.[1] We have had a Poem sent from London in Imitation of his[2] on Miss Carteret.[3] It is on Miss Harvey of a day old, and we say and think it is yours. I wish it were not, because I am against Monopolyes.— You might have spared me a few more lines of your Satyr but I hope in a few Months to see it all. ⌐I would have the Preferment Just enough to save your lines, let it be ever so low, for your sake we will allow it to be Preferment—Mr Ford hath explained to me your Allegoricall Lady. She is our Friend Gays Steward.[4] He would better find his account in dealing with the Devil then with me, who have not one Friend at Court—⌐ To hear Boys like you talk of Milleniums and Tranquility. I am older by thirty years, Lord Bol— by Twenty and you but by Ten then when we last were together and we should differ more then ever. You coquetting a Maid of Honour, My Lord looking on to see how the Gamesters play and I railing at you both. I desire you and all my Friends will take a special care that my Affection[5] to the World may not be imputed to my Age, for I have Credible witnesses ready to depose that it hath never varyed from the Twenty First to the f—ty[6] eighth year of my Life, (pray fill that Blank Charitably) I tell you after all that I do not hate Mankind, it is vous autres[7] who hate them because you would have them reasonable Animals, and are Angry for[8] being disappointed. I have always rejected that Definition and made another of my own. I am no more angry with ———[9] Then I was with the Kite that last week flew away with one of my Chickins and yet I was pleas'd when one of my Servants Shot him two days after, This I say, because you are so hardy as to tell me of your Intentions to write Maxims in Opposition to Rochfoucault who is my Favorite because I found my whole character in him, however I will read him again because it is possible I may have since undergone some alterations—Take care the bad poets do not outwit you, as they have served the good ones in every Age, whom they have provoked to transmit their Names to posterity Mævius is as well known as Virgil, and Gildon will be as well known as you if his name gets into your Verses; and as to the difference between good

---

[1] Lord] Lordship *1740–42*.   [2] his] that *1741 Labc, 1742 Labc, Da*.

[3] The rumour that it was Pope's would not be likely to endear him to Lord Hervey.

[4] Ball seems to have thought (iii. 292 n. 2 and 296 n. 1) that this reference to Gay's steward, omitted when Pope printed the letter, was to the Duchess of Queensberry. It seems rather to be Mrs. Howard.

[5] Affection] disaffection *1740–42*. (In the MS. someone has written in the prefix *dis* in pencil between the lines.)

[6] f—ty] forty *1741 Lc*. (Curll here erred: Swift was approaching his fifty-eighth birthday as he wrote.)

[7] People of your way of thinking.—Footnote in 1741 Dab.

[8] for] at *1740–42*.

[9] Curll (*1741 Lc*) fills in the blank with *Philips*; Elwin suggests *Walpole*.

and bad Fame is a perfect Trifle⌐—I guess your Modern Imitator, and desire to be a Sub-imitator tho' I must bestow 4 lines upon one Sect

> The Heathen doth believe in Christ
> And doth all Christians hate
> For never was Informer he
> Nor Minister of State.

But this on Second thought is not of a Piece with yours, because it is a Commendation; for which⌐ I ask a Thousand pardons, and so I leave you for this time, and will write again without concerning my self whither you write or no—I am ever——

⌐My Service to the Dr our Friend Gay & Mr Lewis &c.⌐

BROOME *to* FENTON   1 *December* 1725

Elwin–Courthope, viii. 105

Dec. 1, 1725.

Dear Mr. Fenton,—I am now to return you thanks for your obliging stay at Sturston, where you had all the welcome that one friend can give another, and consequently such a visit could not be made without some satisfaction. You lived in your own way, and Sturston was but another home; and, indeed, without such a liberty a visit is but a civil kind of imprisonment, and the master of the house but a more obliging gaoler. I will therefore make no excuses for the dulness of Suffolk. Your reception was honest, was sincere, and pleasure you knew how to find or to create. You are so happy as to carry your own entertainment along with you, and a person of such a disposition can never be without a tolerable accommodation. He resembles a man who carries his own provisions along with him when he travels. He is certain to find sufficient entertainment in the very worst inns.

I do not intend to see London till the spring. I often resemble myself to a full-grown tree; it will not admit of a transplantation. At best it but barely lives, or rather languishes, though placed in a better soil. You tell me it is necessary to make my appearance in town to account with Mr. Pope about the Odyssey. I leave, my dear friend, that part to you; at least let these accounts sleep till spring. I fancy Mr. Pope will forgive us for letting the money rest in his hands. But to deal plainly, I expect a breach rather than peace from that treaty. I fear we have hunted with the lion, who, like his predecessor in Phaedrus,[1] will take the first share merely because he is a lion, the second because he is more brave; the third because he is of most importance; and if either of us shall presume to touch the fourth, woe be to us. This perhaps may not be the case with respect to the lucrative part, but I

---

[1] *Fables,* I. v.

have strong apprehensions it will happen with regard to our reputations. Be assured Mr. Pope will not let us divide—I fear not give us our due share of honour. He is a Caesar in poetry, and will bear no equal. But to pass from suspicions of faults to a real one of my own. In the conclusion of the fourteenth book, I have unnecessarily played the hypercritical upon Cowley and Addison.[1] They speak of a tigress thus:

> She swells with angry pride
> And calls forth all her spots on ev'ry side

Here I arrogantly affirm, in the true spirit of a critic, that it is impossible for the hair of any creature to change into spots, and that the assertion is absolutely contrary to nature. True, but may not those spots appear more visible when the tigress roughens her hair in anger, and, when she raises her hair, may not the spots rise with it? And is not this a sufficient foundation for poetry to say she calls forth her spots? A passage in Claudian which I lately read, full loath to believe my own eyes, convinced me of my error. He agrees with Statius, Lib. 2. De Raptu Proserpinæ:

> Arduus Hyrcana quatitur sic matre Niphates,
> Cujus Achæmenio regi ludibria natos
> Avexit tremendus eques. Fremit illa marito
> Mobilior Zephyro, totamque virentibus iram
> Dispergit maculis, jamjamque hausura profundo
> Ore virum, vitreæ tardatur imagine formæ.[2]

Claudian is always fanciful, and often obscure, and here scarce intelligible, but I think I have not mistaken his meaning in the following translation. That poet intends to express how a tigress is robbed of her whelps (if I were fond to show my learning, I would here quote Ælian and Pliny, etc.), which is done by this method. The huntsman watches till she goes abroad to prey; then he steals the young. The savage pursues, and the huntsman drops a ball of glass, in which the tigress seeing her own resemblance, and mistaking it for one of her whelps, stops her pursuit, and the huntsman escapes. Ælian, I know, speaks of the greenish colour of the spots, and Claudian here calls them *maculæ virentes*; but to observe such little exactnesses in translation is pedantry, not poetry.

> So shakes Niphates when, with vengeance stung,
> The mother tigress mourns her ravished young.

[1] In his note to *Odyssey*, xiv. 510 (iii [1725], 360–1) Broome wanders into this vapid argument. As Elwin points out, the context of the passage from Statius (*Thebaid*, ii. 129) should have shown Broome how wrong he was. For Addison see *Spectator*, No. 81.

[2] *De Raptu Proserpinæ*, iii. 263–8.

To Persia's court the hunter bears the prey,
To please her monarch in his dreadful play.
Fleeter than winds away the savage skims,
Her spots enkindling glow o'er all her limbs.
Now, now she stretches her wide jaws, and now
She only not devours the trembling foe.
Then from his hand th' affrighted youth lets fall,
Sudden to stay her flight, a crystal ball;
At once she stops, astonished to survey
The mimic tigress shining in her way.[1]

Pray your opinion of the whole? I have now troubled you with a long letter, but, in your absence, I deem writing to you is discoursing with you upon paper, as when present talking to you was only speaking to myself aloud. True friendship is a marriage of minds; you are my *alter ego*, and the hour that ravished you from me, as Horace expresses it, *me surripuit mihi*. Yours, dear Fenton, affectionately.

FORTESCUE *to* POPE[2]   [1725]

Homer MSS. Add. 4809

The Account Bowery left at my House [y]esterday of Mrs Pope's continuing ill, and [y]our being out of order likewise, gives me [t]he greatest Uneasiness in the world. I would [h]ave waited upon you my self, but that [I] fear any Company may be troublesom; [b]~~ut~~ I have sent John to Know how you [b]oth doe, & hope He will bring me a better [a]ccount than I had yesterday.

Pray consider how much your Friends are [i]nterested in your health & how much their hap[p]iness depends upon it; for all our sakes therefor [as] well as your own, let me beg you to take all [ ] possible care of it.

FORTESCUE *to* POPE[3]   [1725]

Homer MSS. Add. 4809

I am very much obliged to you for your Kind letter, and am glad to hear that Mrs Pope is something better; considering how ill she is, you can't Expect her to Recover but by degrees, & therefore you ought to hope the best; but above all, let me renew my request to you to be carefull of your own health. I have sent John for the lead, &

---

[1] This translation from Claudian, if by Broome, is not found in his *Poems*.
[2] The position in the Homer MSS. (as part of Book XXI) indicates that this letter dates during the period of Mrs. Pope's illness late in 1725. Pope's indisposition was brief.
[3] This letter is a part of Book XXII of the *Odyssey*.

hope He will be able [to] procure some to send with this. I am in the greatest Hast Dear Sir Munday morning. | Yours, WF.

Remember me Kindly to Gay.

FORTESCUE *to* POPE[1] [1725]

Homer MSS. Add. 4809

Be so good as to deliver the Inclosed to Gay as soon as you [see] him. I am | Your most affect | W. F.

Fryday.

POPE *to* THE EARL OF OXFORD 14 *December* 1725

Longleat Portland Papers, xii

Decr 14th 1725.

My Lord,—When I write to you, I foresee a long letter and so must intreat your patience beforehand. Not that I intend to reckon up any obligations to you, for at that rate, no letter would be long enough; I know you will wonder what Obligations I mean, because (not to flatter you) your memory is none of the best, nay tis a very bad one, if that be such which forgets great things and remembers only small ones: for you always remember the smallest devoirs which others pay to you, and forget the kind offices you do to others. I have often applyd to you what somebody says of a French Nobleman, that he never forgot to do his friend a favor, & never remember'd it when 'twas done. Your Lordship cannot imagine how pleasd I am that you shoud be so mindful of me, & I doubt not you remember me to my advantage, because I can't believe myself so unhappy as to be the only *ill* thing you ever rememberd.

Tho you oblige always in so Unambitious a manner, that one would think the best Gratitude to you were the forgetting your favours; yet there is nothing wherein a reasonable man may so justly boast his good memory, as in remembring the obligations a good man has laid upon him. To boast it in what we have learned, or read is but to be proud of the Alms we have receivd from others: But there can be sure, no Pride so satisfactory, as that which one honest man takes in being obliged to another, since to be distinguishd by a person of merit gives us the pleasure of imagining that we have some ourselves. Indeed I am now Above Gratitude, and can return your Lordship nothing less than Affection: the Only thing in which I am sure to be your equal. I have often been pleasd with a thought of Montagne's, who says, that the

[1] This letter forms a part of Book XXII of the *Odyssey*.

person who receives a Benefit, obliges the Giver, because as the chief Endeavor of one friendly man is to do good to another, He who gives both the matter, and the Occasion, properly speaking, is the man who is Liberal. So my Lord, it is impossible You should ever be out of My debt, and you may daily expect all the obligations in nature from me— When last you was in the Country, you desird me to write to you, and my doing it now, is an instance how little I think it possible your mind shoud change, (which as the world goes, is no small complement in one's opinion of a Man of quality) otherwise, in decency, I should have stayd for your permission before I had ventured to do it. But I consider, you are to be a Month absent, and if you would forget me, I won't let you. I have also something that I can please you with, if I am not mistaken, from Dr Swift, (whose letter I wou'd have here inclos'd, but Lord Bolingbroke got it to answer a period of it, & never sent it me again). But it will please you, I know, sufficiently, only to tell you he is coming to town; and I add my answer to it, to show you how glad I am of it, that your Lordship may make my words good, and let him know I don't lye, when I tell him how much you press for his coming: (which a word or two from you, at this Crisis, when he plainly harkens towards us, will certainly determine him to do) Your being now alone in the country, intitles one to send you *any thing*: even dull Newspapers are legible in the Country, & dull Letters, even in print, are look'd over, there.

I earnestly wish you, my Lord, the continuance of all the happiness you have, & the addition of any part of it that you want! May every loss be made up to you! And depend upon it, it will, if the prayers of a sinful papist can avail, namely of | My Lord | Your most faithfull & | most obedient Servant, | A. Pope.

I have many apologies to make to my Lady Oxford for a Visit that I fear was a very unseasonable one, just as I saw her Chaise at the door for her journey. I receivd an account at Chiswick, that she had sent after me, & returnd purposely to Town, imagining her journey was deferred till next day: but upon sight of the chaise I retreated, & went home again. I humbly beg her Ladyships pardon, & find it was some Blunder of my Waterman.

||POPE *and* BOLINGBROKE *to* SWIFT   14 *December* 1725

Longleat Portland Papers, xiii (Harleian transcripts)

┌Decr the 14th 1725

┌You say you don't much care whether I write to you or not, and therefore I don't much care if I do. But whereas you tell me You'l

---

[1] All Pope's texts (1737–42) date this letter 10 Dec. 1725. This is one of the four letters to or from Swift first published in 1736 or 1737—possibly to encourage Swift to return letters

write whether I do or not; I take it as kindly as I do many an other favour you have had the kindness to do for me, whether I deserv'd it or not. I shall however begin to fancy I do deserve it, because I find my own heart so prodigiously pleas'd with it. . . . Let me tell you[1] I am the better acquainted with you for a long Absence, as men are with themselves for a long affliction: Absence does but hold off a Friend, to make one see him the truer. I am infinitely more pleas'd to hear you are coming near us, than at anything you seem to think in my favour, (an opinion which perhaps has been aggrandized by the distance, or dulness of Ireland, as objects look larger thro' a Medium of Foggs.) And yet I am infinitely pleas'd with that too: For Praise is like Ambergrize; a little unexpected Whiff of it (such as I meet with in your letter) is the most agreeable thing in the world; but when a whole lump of it is thrust to your nose, it is a Stink, and strikes you down. However, like the verses on Miss Harvey as well as you will, I'm never the better for it, for they are none of mine. But I am much the happier for finding (a better thing than our *Witts*) our *Judgments* jump, in the notion of entirely passing all Scriblers by in silence: To vindicate ones self against such nasty Slanders, is much as wise, as it was in your[2] Countryman when people said he was besh— to show the contrary by showing his A—[3] so let Gildon and Philips[4] rest in peace. What Virgil had to do with Mævius, that he shou'd wear him upon his Sleeve to all eternity, I don't know? but I think a bright author should put an end to Slanders only as the Sun does to Stinks; by shining out,[5] exhale 'em to nothing. I've been the longer upon this, that I might prepare you for the Reception both you and your works might possibly meet in England. We your true acquaintance, will look upon you as a good man, and love you; Others will look upon you as a Witt, and hate you: so you know the worst, unless you are as vindicative as Virgil or the foresaid Hibernian.

I wish as warmly as you, for the Hospital to lodge the *Despisers of the world* in, only I fear it would be fill'd wholly like Chelsea with Maim'd Soldiers, and such as had been dis-abled in *its* Service. And I wou'd rather have those that out of such generous principles as you and I, despise it, Fly in its face, than Retire from it. Not that I have much Anger against the Great, my Spleen is at the little rogues of it:

---

to Pope. Curll in his *New Letters* (Nov. 1736) seems first to have printed the letters of Aug. 1723 from Pope and Bolingbroke to Swift; but the letters of 20 Sept. 1725 and this present letter apparently appeared first in Pope's official edition (1737b), from which they were transferred to the Roberts octavo (1737a). The postscript to the letter first appeared in 1741 (all texts).

[1] As printed in 1737-42 the letter begins 'I find myself better acquainted', &c.
[2] your] our *1741 Db*
[3] people . . . so let] people imputed a stink to him, to prove the contrary by showing his backside. So let *1737-42*.   [4] Philips] P—s *1741 Dab*.
[5] Pope uses the same elegant metaphor to Caryll, 25 Dec. See ii. 352.

It would vexe one more to be knockt o' the Head by a Pisspot, than by a Thunderbolt. As to great Oppressors (as you say) they are like Kites or Eagles, one expects mischief from them: But to be Squirted to death (as poor Wycherley[1] said to me on his deathbed) by *Potecaries Prentices*, by the under Strappers of Under Secretaries, to Secretaries, who were no Secretaries—this would provoke as dull a dog as Ph—s[2] himself.

But I beg your pardon, I'm tame agen, at your advice. I was but like the Madman, who on a sudden clapt his hand to his Sword of Lath, and cry'd, *Death to all my Enemies!* when another came behind him and stopt his wrath, by saying, *Hold! I can tell you a way worth twenty on't: Let your Enemies alone, and they will dye of themselves.*

So much for Enemies, now for friends. Lewis thinks all this very Indiscreet: the Dr not so; he loves mischief the best of any Good natured man in England. Lord B. is above triffling, he is grown a great Divine. Jervas and his Don Quixot are both finish'd.[3] Gay is writing Tales for Prince William:[4] I suppose Philips[5] will take this very ill, for two reasons; one, that he thinks all childish things belong to him; and the other, because he'l take it ill to be taught, that one may write things to a Child, without being childish.—What have I more to add? but that Lord Oxford, the best man in the world, desires earnestly to see you: and that many others who you do not think the worst, will be gratify'd by it: none more be assured, than | Your very affectionate faithfull Servant | A. Pope.

⌐What is become of Mr Ford. I'm glad to hear of his name: but tell him from me, he does not know a *Maid* of Honour from a *Woman* of Honour (by what you write of Gay's Steward) I am much his Servant.⌐

⌐Lord Bo—[6] I am so far from being above triffling that I wish with all my heart I had nothing else to do. But I need not take any pains to convince you that Pope advances a meer Slander; his manner of proving is like that of an Irish man whose life and death were lately Transmitted to Posterity by that great Historiographer Paul Lorraine.[7] I did not rob the witness, said your Countryman, for by my Shawl I did put my hand into his left pocket, and seize him by the left arm, not

---

[1] This casual remark suggests that the friendship between Pope and Wycherley continued, with interrupting coolnesses perhaps, to the end of Wycherley's life.
[2] Ph—s] Philips *1737c* [Curll!].
[3] Jervas's translation was not published until 1742, after his death. Pope evidently means by 'both finished' that the translation is done, and Jervas tired out.
[4] Gay's *Fables* were published in 1727.   [5] Philips] P— *1741 Dab.*
[6] Lord Bo— is added in the margin by Oxford to indicate that this part of the letter is by Bolingbroke. It is usually printed as a postscript—first published in the texts of 1741.
[7] Paul Lorraine was ordinary of Newgate Prison from 1698 to his death in 1719. He published (perhaps wrote?) the lives and dying speeches of criminals after their executions.

by the right.⁷ Pope and you are very great wits, and I think very indifferent Philosophers; if you dispise the world as much as you pretend,
and perhaps believe you would not be so angry with it. The founder of
your Sect,¹ that noble original whom you think it so great an Honour to
resemble was a Slave to the worst part of the world, to the Court, and
all his big words were the Language of a Slighted Lover who desired
nothing so much as a reconciliation, and fear'd nothing so much as a
rupture. I believe the world has us'd me as scurvily as most people,
and yet I could never find in my heart to be throly² angry with the
Simple false capricious thing. I should blush alike to be discover'd fond
of the world or piqu'd at it. Your Definition of Animal ⌐capax⌐
Rationis instead of the Common one Animal Rationale, will not bear
examination.   define but Reason, and you will see why your distinction
is no better than that of the Pontiffe Cotta³ between mala Ratio and
bona Ratio.⁴ But enough of this. make us a visit and I'le subscribe to
any side of these important Questions which you please. We differ less
than you imagine perhaps when you wish me banish'd again. But I am
not less true to you and to Philosophy in England than I was in
France.⁵

To the Reverend Dr Swift

Endorsement (in Oxford's hand): Mr Pope to Dean Swift Dec. 14. 1725

FENTON *to* BROOME   21 *December* 1725

Elwin–Courthope, viii. 108

Dec. 21, 1725.

Dear Mr. Broome,—From the date of this present epistle I hope you
will never have the assurance, not to give it a stronger term, to call or
even to think me lazy. I am now, and have for some time past been,
crippled with the gout, and yet Pope, who is as brisk as a wren, called
upon me to write to you for the remainder of the notes, which he
desires may be sent to Lintot immediately, because the press is at a
stand for want of them.

   I am sorry to hear that you have taken a resolution not to come to
town before spring. I think you should have had a better reason to have
grounded it on than what you give me. Neither can I understand what
you mean by leaving that part to me, when I have so small a proportion in the performance. Since I came hither I have refused his offer

---

¹ Seneca.—MS. note in transcripts (in Oxford's hand); footnote by Pope, 1741–2.
² In the margin of the transcript Lord Oxford has inserted as a note on this word a derisive
sic.
³ See Cicero, *De Natura Deorum*, III. xxviii. 71.
⁴ The Dublin editions translate all these Latin phrases in footnotes.
⁵ At the end of this letter Curll (*1741 Lc*) adds a footnote explaining that he prints only
Lord Bolingbroke's 'postscript' since he had printed Pope's part of the letter in *1737c*.

of drawing for money, as I told you I did last year, till we all met to clear accounts, and, as my stay in London may be as uncertain as your coming, the affair may be adjourned to be considered by our executors, if any one at his peril shall undertake to be mine. Besides, in my opinion, your presence would have been absolutely necessary to see what is to be said at the end of the last volume with relation to the coadjutors in the work; but you think otherwise, and I am satisfied.

As to what you mention about Claudian, I have never a one by me, but I believe it is an error, and the greater because you went out of your way to fall into it.

Southerne's play has been rejected at Drury Lane, and is now in the other house. Welsted gives him a prologue, but an epilogue is much wanted. I believe he intends to try your neighbour Pack.[1] I heartily wish you, Mrs. Broome, and all friends many happy new years, and am ever your affectionate humble servant.

POPE *to* CARYLL[2]   25 *December* 1725

Add. 28618

Decr 25. 1725.

⌜Both an indisposition of my own, which I ought to look upon as a slight one compared with my mother's (because my life is not half the consequence to anybody that hers is to me) have hindered my more speedy reply to your very obliging letter of the beginning of this month. First, to get rid of all the business of it, be assured as to money I'm well satisfied it is in your hands, if you care to keep it. It was no more than a doubt, remaining from a former mention of your parting with it, that made me question in my own mind, whether you had not a mind to pay it in.⌝ The ⌜next⌝ article you inquire of, is as little concern to me, as you desire it should; namely, the railing papers about the *Odyssey*,[3] ⌜which I venture to say will be fully answered the moment the work is finished. If I take any notice of such fellows, it must be a wretched work of supererogation.⌝ If the book has merit (and since you like it, it must) it will extinguish all such sh——n[4] scandal, as the sun puts an end to stinks, by *shining*[5] *out*.

 [1] Major Richardson Pack (1682–1728) of Stoke Ash (Suffolk) had furnished an admired epilogue for Southerne's *Spartan Dame*. The epilogue for *Money the Mistress* was by George Jeffreys, Esq.

 [2] Parts of this letter form most of the text printed in 1735 as a letter to Robert Digby (10 Sept. 1724) and in 1737–42 as to Dr. Arbuthnot (with no year in the date). Omissions made for printing are here placed in half-brackets, and some textual changes for printing are noted. After 1735 no significant textual changes were made. The printed Digby–Arbuthnot letter has a first paragraph from another source and its second paragraph begins with the fourth sentence of the Caryll letter, 'The next article . . . .'

 [3] See Sherburn. *Early Career*, pp. 262–9.

 [4] sh——n scandal] nasty scandal *1735–42*.

 [5] shining out] coming out *1735–42*. (Pope uses this same metaphor to Swift, 14 Dec. 1725.)

I wish I had nothing to trouble me more: an honest mind is not in the power of any dishonest one. To break its peace, there must be some guilt or consciousness, which is inconsistent with its own principles. Not but malice and injustice have their day, like some poor part-lived[1] vermin that die of shooting their own stings. Falsehood is folly (says Homer) and liars and calumniators at last hurt none but themselves, even in this world. In the next, 'tis charity to say, God have mercy on them! They were the devil's vicegerents upon earth, who is the father of lies, and I fear has a right to dispose of his children.

I've had an occasion to make these Reflections of late, much juster[2] than from any thing that concerns my writings; for it is one that concerns my morals, and (which I ought to be as tender of as my own) the good character of another very innocent person,[3] who I'm sure shares your friendship no less than I do. ⌐You too are brought into the story so falsely, that I think it but just to appeal against the injustice to yourself singly, as a full and worthy judge and evidence too! A very confident asseveration has been made, which has spread over the town, that your god-daughter Miss Patty and I lived 2 or 3 years since in a manner that was reported to you as giving scandal to many: that upon your writing to me upon it I consulted with her, and sent you an excusive alleviating answer; but did after that, privately and of myself write to you a full confession; how much I myself disapproved the way of life, and owning the prejudice done her, charging it on herself, and declaring that I wished to break off what I acted against my conscience, &c.; and that she, being at the same time spoken to by a lady of your acquaintance,[4] at your instigation, did absolutely deny to alter any part of her conduct, were it ever so disreputable or exceptionable. Upon this villanous lying tale, it is farther added by the same hand, that I brought her acquainted with a noble lord, and into an intimacy with some others, merely to get quit of her myself, being moved in consciousness by what you and I had conferred together, and playing this base part to get off.

⌐You will bless yourself at so vile a wickedness, who very well (I dare say) remember the truth of what then past, and the satisfaction you expressed I gave you (and Mrs Caryll also expressed the same thing

---

[1] part-liv'd] short-liv'd *1735-42.* (An obvious miswriting by the scribe.)

[2] much juster] must juster *MS.* (an obvious error of the scribe): much more justly *1735-42.*

[3] In a scandal-loving age it was inevitable that the relations of Pope and Martha Blount should be subjects of comment. Obviously Pope had to omit this matter when publishing the letter: the surprising thing is that he should print even the first sentence of the paragraph. To see how he bridged the gap of omitted paragraphs see Pope to Dr. Arbuthnot, 10 Sept. 1725 (the fabricated text).

[4] Mrs. Caryll. At Mapledurham is preserved a letter from Mrs. Caryll to Martha (dated 15 Mar. [1723?]) which bears out completely what Pope says as to the satisfactory explanations that had then been made to the Carylls. See Sherburn, *Early Career,* p. 294.

to her kinswoman) upon that head. God knows upon what motives
any one should malign a sincere and virtuous friendship! I wish those
very people had never led her into any thing more liable to objection,
or more dangerous to a good mind, than I hope my conversation or
kindness are. She has in reality had less of it these two years past than
ever since I knew her; and truly when she has it, 'tis almost wholly
a preachment, which I think necessary, against the ill consequences
of another sort of company, which they by their good will would
always keep; and she, in compliance and for quiet sake keeps more
than you or I could wish.

⌐To deal with you like a friend, openly:¬ you know 'tis the ⌐whole¬
misfortune of that family to be governed like a ship—that is,¹ the head
guided by the tail, and that by every wind that blows in it.²

⌐God is my witness I am as much a friend to her soul as to her
person: the good qualities of the former made me her friend.¬ No
creature has better natural dispositions, or would act more rightly or
reasonably in every duty, did she act by herself, or from herself.

⌐I thank you for that hint about my satirical unguarded Stroke on
the French.³ I own it an unguarded one, and meant but as a jest. I
wish for many hours of talk with you on that and many other Subjects.
I had read *Mariamne*⁴ before our friend sent it, having formerly had
some correspondence (about the poem on the League) with its author.
I agree entirely with you on that subject—I know nothing of the
writer on the paintings, &c., of Rome, whom you enquire of. I thank
God, that Mr Congreve⁵ who is dead is not my friend of that name—
I am glad of what you say, of your Cosen Cope, tho' I've heard
nothing from her very lately.

⌐Dear Sir, adieu; my best wishes ever attend you, and more than
[can] be crowded into this paper. | Yours Affectionately | A: P.¬

POPE *to* THE EARL OF OXFORD   27 *December* 1725

Longleat Portland Papers, xii

My Lord,—I recoverd Dean Swifts Letter but yesterday, which I
inclose. I cannot enough acknowledge your Lordships goodness in
many instances, particularly this you mention of thinking to invite me
to Downhall: But that you shoud so much as doubt my real desires
of following you to Any place (were it to the Tower itself) I take as a

---

¹ that is] I mean *1735–42*.   ² The fabricated letter ends with this phrase.
³ Concerning the boy-king. See to Caryll, 23 Nov. [1725].
⁴ Not Fenton's play (acted in 1723) but Voltaire's of the same title, which Bolingbroke
had sent to Pope. See Bolingbroke to Pope, 18 Feb. 1724/5. Pope's statement about a
correspondence before 1725 is surprising. *La Ligue* (1723) was brought out in England as
La Henriade in 1728, when Voltaire was in England.
⁵ Col. Congreve, who died 18 Nov. 1725.—Elwin.

little allay, to that pleasure your Memory of me gives me. Then, my Lord, to cut short all speeches the best way, by Actions, I beg you to send your horses & a chariot to Hodson on Saturday next. Mr Bridgman & I will be there (God willing) by eleven a clock, & proceed directly to You. I have learn'd from Mr Priors Ballad,[1] that we ought to Inn at the black bull in that town, but what I am to say to the Land-lady, or Ostler, or Chambermaid, I will inform myself from Mr Morley. I intreat my Mother's & my humblest Services may be acceptable to my Lady Oxford, & to your Lordship. I am sincerely & with the greatest Satisfaction in the prospect of waiting on you both,

My Lord, | Your most obliged & ever | obedient faithful Servant | A. Pope.

Decr. 27th 1725.

Address: To the Right Honourable | the Earl of Oxford, at | Down-Hall: | Essex.

[*In another hand*:] By Harlow | Bagg

Postmark: /DE [The day is illegible.]

POPE *to* BROOME   30 *December* 1725

Elwin–Courthope, viii. 109

Dec. 30, 1725.

Dear Broome,—Though a thousand businesses which I am inevitably engaged in, of very different natures, may hinder very often my telling how constantly you are in my memory, yet I assure you your share in it is greater than seems compatible with such a number of avocations. Fenton took pity of me and promised to write for me, which I think a prodigious instance of his friendship, but indeed he had the gout, and was sedate enough to have sat and corresponded with all mankind, like the picture you see before the Turkish Spy. I received to-day the notes on lib. 18 and 23, and the sooner we have the small remainder—what a happy word is that—the better. I am obliged to pass part of the Christmas with my Lord Oxford at poor Prior's house at Down Hall;[2] but I will return, God willing, in a week. My mother, as you will conclude from this, is much recovered, and fit again to see and wel-come you. I have put your verses to me into a Miscellany,[3] which will come out in two or three months; and, since you did not think fit to alter one or two extravagant things in my praise, I have done it myself,[4]

---

[1] Prior's *Down Hall*; *A Ballad* (1723) 'sings' the exploits of Prior and Morley journeying from London to Down Hall. In line 58 they arrive 'At a Town they call *Hodsdon*, the Sign of the *Bull*', but as to the colour of the bull Prior is silent. 'Hodson' is surely Hoddesdon.
[2] After Prior's death the house reverted to Lord Oxford, who had helped the poet buy it.
[3] The fifth edition of his own and Lintot's *Miscellany Poems* (1726).
[4] See Pope to Broome, 22 Nov. [1725].

and given you a little modesty, as well as shown you I have some myself. The twenty-third book is in the press, and you must not take it ill if I use it freely. Indeed, as I think we ought to mend the farther we go, and especially to support our author towards the end of the journey, I have much altered, and, I hope, not a little amended it. I have been ill, but believe the spring's advance will set me up again. Nothing, I promise you, will so well please me in its return, as that I hope it will bring you to my shades and solitudes, which, though within ten miles of London, and flanked by two courts on each side,[1] shall be a solitude for us. The longer I live, the more I find I must drive from me the idle, the gaudy, and the busy part of the world, to leave what remains of my life free to the good, and the serious, and the learned part, in which, my nature directed, and my experience taught me, my pleasure is to consist. I cannot say this, without showing at the same time how much I am, or would be, dear Broome, your faithful affectionate servant.

[1] Richmond and Hampton Court; or Richmond and Kew on the one hand and Hampton Court and Windsor on the other.

This year is remarkable for the completed publication of the *Odyssey*, which involved the difficult and discreditable misrepresentation of the amount of aid Pope had received. Fenton was annoyed that his name was mentioned at all in the final note, and Broome was hurt that his part in the task was minimized. Hence a definite worsening of the friendly relations of the collaborators. Joseph Spence's *Essay on Pope's Odyssey* seemed a delightful voice in a chorus which in general devalued the *Odyssey*. Unpleasant also was Curll's publication in *Miscellanea*, vol. i (July 1726), of Pope's early letters to Henry Cromwell; but that publication probably led Pope later to consider publishing other letters. In September he suffered a badly cut hand and was nearly drowned when he was overturned in a coach in the Crane near Whitton.

The most agreeable event of the year was the visit of Jonathan Swift, who arrived in London about the middle of March and left on 15 August. Pope's villa was the scene of much summer hospitality, and the friends rambled to other houses often. *Gulliver's Travels* was published on 28 October 1726, about two months after Swift had returned to Dublin. Many letters report its immediate popularity.

BROOME *to* POPE   2 *January* 1725/6

Elwin–Courthope, viii. 110

Sturston, Jan. 2, 1725[–26].

Dear Mr. Pope,—*Jamque opus exegi.*[1] Huzza! I have finished the notes on the Odyssey. *Non ego sanius bacchabor Edonis!*[2] What a pile of useless commentators stand before me. Begone to the pastry-cook's or jakes! What a brave fellow am I, author of four-and-twenty books of notes. Hercules is nobody; he cleansed but one, I four-and-twenty Augæan stables. Methinks I am like Hannibal at the top of all the Alps, at the head of legions of critics, and look back with pleasure upon the dirty and difficult ways I have passed, and now come pouring down with my volumes upon poor England! But alas! there is an index still behind. I an Hannibal! I an Hercules! I am rather Jack the Giant-killer, who, when he had eat the whole body of the ox, the tail hung out of his mouth. Well! *dabit deus his quoque finem.*[3] By this time I suppose you think me distracted, and expect to hear soon that I am admitted among the exalted genii of Bedlam.

The lazy Mr. Fenton has obeyed your commands, and wrote for the notes in a huge long letter, of at least three lines. I am now in

[1] Ovid, *Metamorphoses*, xv. 871.   [2] Horace, *Carmina*, II. vii. 26–27.
[3] *Aeneid*, i. 199.

hopes he will not lose the use of writing and speaking. I will tell you a true story: when he was with me at Sturston he often fished; this gave him an opportunity of sitting still and being silent; but he left it off because the fish bit. He could not bear the fatigue of pulling up the rod and baiting the hook.

Mr. Southerne wants an epilogue, and will oblige me to write it. I am sorry he brings his play on the stage. His bays are withered with extreme age.[1] From what I heard of it with you at Sir Clement Cottrell's, it cannot bear water, and the lead of my epilogue fastened to the end of it will add to its alacrity in sinking. Mr. Southerne's fire is abated, and no wonder, when philosophers tell us that the warmth and glory of the sun abates by age. It requires some skill to know when to leave off writing.

N.B. Let Mr. Fenton and you take notice that I write this epilogue upon this express condition, that it shall not be spoken, if Mr. Southerne can procure one by another hand; if not, I will do myself the honour to attend the old bard, and hold up the train of his comedy in Drury.

Dear sir, I sincerely assure you that the chief satisfaction I have in the conclusion of the Odyssey arises from the certainty that my name will be read with yours by posterity. This will be a lamp that will cast a glory over my ***[2] and adorn it when I am no longer [living].

POPE *to* FORTESCUE   5 *January* [1725/6]

1797 (Polwhele, i. 324)

Down-Hall, in Essex, Jan. 5th

I had writ the post after my receipt of yours, but it followed me thirty miles beyond London, where I have spent part of the Christmas. I yet hope this will find you; and yet I wish the very next day you may begin your journey, because, sincerely, I cannot see you too soon. I am rejoiced that your gout left you the day after I did: may it never return! tho' it bring many compliments along with it. For let my friends wish me as long a life as they please, I should not wish it to myself with the allay of great or much pain. My old lord Dorset said very well in that case, the tenure is not worth the fine.—I hope the joys of a marriage, both to those who possess, and to you who procure (modestly speaking) will obliterate all those melancholy thoughts. I wish the new couple all felicity.[3] And pray make haste to town with the remainder of your family, and put them into the like happy condition with all speed. I had lately an opportunity of telling my Lord

---

[1] For Southerne's *Money the Mistress* (acted late in February) an epilogue by George Jeffreys was preferred to Broome's. Southerne, now 65, lived to the age of 85.
[2] A word or two is here worn away.—Elwin.   [3] The marriage is unidentified.

Harcourt what we had missed of, when at Sir W's. and of making him the complement of his cyder merchants. His reply was, that he desired to treat with you further, both in that capacity and in your other of a lawyer. To which purpose I have promised to bring you to dine with him as soon as you return to town, which I earnestly expect, and doubt not you will improve the acquaintance with each other. After thanking you for your kind letter, and returning you my mother's services, (who is pretty well,) I have only to add, that I will not fail upon my return to town to make all your compliments to Mrs. Howard, and to assure you, I am, with truth, dear sir, your ever affectionate friend and servant, | A. Pope.

Address: To Wm. Fortescue, esq. at Fallapit, near Totnes, Devon.
Frank: Oxford.

POPE *to* THE EARL OF OXFORD   7 *January* 1725/6

Longleat Portland Papers xii

My Lord,—I write this from Your own house, and at the Bed-side of Mr Morley, whom first yours & my Lady Oxfords letters, & next my Informing him how much you were concernd for him, has half recover'd. Your Letters lye on his bed, which he reads for his morning & evening prayer. This frosty weather keeps his leg in pain, when it is drest especially, but as to his spirits, they are to be Envy'd. He tells me he sees no company, and therfore I believe he talks or sings to himself, he is so much alive.

You may think I deserve less the character of a grateful man than I do, from any expression I can use of the Real Satisfaction I receivd at Downhall. I am sincerely the better pleasd that the Weather hinderd me from seeing any thing but what I came to see, yourself, & my Lady. I must be allowd to say I know Some Beauties preferable far to those of Nature itself; I mean those which a Good man gives to his own Mind, and are much greater Improvements upon Nature than the best you can make at Downhall.

I have the satisfaction to hear at my arrival in town that my Mother is pretty well. That all Health & happiness may be continued and increasd to your Lordship & your whole family, is, & always will be the hearty wish of | My Lord | Your most faithfull | obligd humble Servant | A. Pope.

Dover street. | Jan. 7th | 1725/6

Endorsement (in Lord Oxford's hand): R at Down Hall | Janu. 9. 1725/6

FENTON *to* BROOME   13 *January* [1725/6]

Elwin–Courthope, viii. 112

Jan. 13, [1726].

Before I was favoured with your last, which brought with it an epilogue for Mr. Southerne's play, he had got one from Mr. Jeffreys,[1]
so that I will observe the direction you gave about suppressing yours,
which is a very arch one.[2] I wish, *entre nous*, that there may be occasion for any at all, for I perceive he meets with some difficulties at
Lincoln's Inn House. I have not seen above two scenes of his comedy,
in which I find the old man was too visible; and, because I could not
counterfeit a transport, he has looked a little cold upon me ever since.
So dangerous a thing it is, without one had Gyges' ring, to look upon
the productions of most poets.

Mr. Pope is just gone from me. He desired me to send you his
service, and begs the remainder of the notes by the first opportunity.
He proposes to have the work published before spring;[3] and the
season is so severe that I cannot in reason expect you here much sooner;
but I hope you will not fail of coming before the work is out, that we
may agree about the manner of being mentioned as assistants.

In your next, pray send me word what edition of Milton your old
one is, and in what year it was printed. I am now revising his Life,
which is prefixed to the last edition, which I wrote in a hurry the last
summer,[4] and there is now another beautiful impression coming out
in octavo, for which I am preparing it a little more correct. I am still
confined by the gout, but, I thank God, without much pain, and the
weather is so bad that I am less sensible of the want of my shoes. I am
ever, dear Broome, your affectionate humble servant.

Do you intend to translate that passage of the death of Talus from
Apollonius?[5]

POPE *to* CARYLL   19 *January* 1725/6

Add. 28618

Twittenham Jan. 19. 1725–6.

I had much sooner acknowledged a Letter so worthy of you as your
last, in which you show so just and honorable a regard to truth
(which ought to be above all friends, if the old saying be good, *amicus*

---

[1] George Jeffreys (1678–1755), author and man about town, cousin of the 1st Duke of
Chandos, in Feb. 1724 had produced a tragedy *Edwin* that ran four nights.

[2] The conclusion of Broome's epilogue is printed (p. 164) in his *Poems* in 1739, but not in
1727.

[3] Volumes iv and v were advertised ('This Week will be publish'd') in the *Evening Post*,
11–14 June 1726.

[4] Fenton's Life of Milton was included in editions of the poet in 1725 and 1727, and
frequently thereafter.   [5] See Fenton to Broome, 20 Nov. [1725].

Plato sed magis amica veritas) and at the same time to your friends also. I never doubted the entire falsity of what was said relating to you any more than of what related to myself; I am as confident of your honor as of my own. Let lies perish and be confounded, and the authors of 'em, if not forgiven, be despised. So we men say, but I'm afraid women cannot: and your injured kinswoman is made too uneasy by these sinister practices, which especially from one's own family are terrible. *M[is]eremini mei saltem vos, amici mei! propinqui mei adversum me steterunt*[1] are terms she may too justly complain in, tho she keeps all in silence and suffers, not opening her lips.

Talking of one sufferer puts me in mind of another, whom I remember you told me you were willing to assist, whenever she was settled abroad. I had three days since a long letter from poor Mrs Cope[2] from Bar-sur-Aube en Champagne, where she tells me she has stayed several months in hopes of her brother's coming there (as he gave her assurance) to live together, but she knows no more of him yet than the first day she arrived, nor hears when, or how, he can assist her, insomuch that the little money I sent her half a year since, was actually all gone then and she really wanted bread when I remitted her a little more this Christmasse. I wish I could serve her farther, but really cannot wholly supply her being out of pocket of every farthing I sent her this last twelvemonth. I wish you could remit her something for I believe she never needed it more than at this juncture.

I have been very ill ever since my journey into Essex[3] last Christmasse but hope now by the help of a little physic for a few days more to recover, and live your affectionate servant some years more. I received the ten pounds on your note. I hope 'twill not be long before you pass some time as usual in this part of the world, and I hope still more that some of that time may be passed at this place which is as much improved since you saw it, as its owner is worse and more decayed. We may then talk at large over many things, and particularly I wish to hear what charge that can be, which, you say, has been proposed against you in any spiritual or celestial, or terrestrial court; for indeed I, who have known you so long, can have no notion of any such. If I live, or if my mother lives in health, or if it pleases God to remove her, I shall once more see Ladyholt. Pray make my compliments to the lady who wrote the last part of your kind letter, and to all your family. Many good New Years to you all. | Your ever affect. servant. | A. P.

The two friends you enquire after, who are my assistants, are Mr Fenton and Mr Broome.[4]

---

[1] A typical combination by Pope of two texts: Job xix. 21 and possibly Psalm xxxvii (or xxxviii), 11.   [2] On Mrs. Cope see *The Athenaeum*, 22 July 1854.

[3] His visit to Lord Oxford at Down Hall.

[4] Pope in his letter of 23 Nov. [1725] had mentioned the help of 'my two friends' without naming them.

POPE *to* JOHN MORLEY[1]   19 *January* 1725/6

Longleat Portland Papers xii (Harleian transcript)

It was a great pleasure to me to leave you so well recover'd and (as I may say) upon your Legs again. A Man that is so apt to run about to serve his friends ought never, sure, to be laid up as you have been. It must however have taught you to be more cautious for the future how you Venture at a Great Stake, and to walk warily with many other Moral and political lessons, when You that know Ground better than any Man in England have been thus mis-staken. If my Lord and Lady Oxford's Letters, which you us'd as daily plaisters to your wound, had not heal'd it up already; I might hope this which I send, would have some effect: Theirs I apprehend gave you vanity, and therefore increased your Proud flesh; mine may humble you, and take it down—I am eating the oysters you sent (pickled). St Peter never tasted so good, tho' he was a fisherman all his life. I would not advise you to use such diet, nor yet to eat Eringo roots (their near Neighbours, at Colchester): These things would put your body into some disorder at this time, when you lye so much on your back. Besides Dr Cottesworth says, your flesh is young, like a fellows of five and twenty.— Pray write something to satisfy Posterity (in the account of your Life) that Down-Hall was the ancient name of the place, and that it did not receive that appellation from throwing You Down, in which case it may come hereafter to be call'd Down-Morley. After all, I fancy you lay in so long, only to receive Visits, and Letters, and Homages, and Messages, in the greater State: to hear the Condolements of Countesses and Dutchesses; and to see the Diamonds of Beauties Sparkle at your Bedside. You are so little accustomed to take your rest, or to be still, that now you come to find the Sweets of it. I wish you don't do like the Indian King, who when first he got into a soft Bed, resolved he would never get up agen. If so, we will all come to your Couchee, and the Wits of the Time shall be set at work to make your Epitaph, without one word of a Resurrection. But if your natural and usual Impatience to serve others, and that Impetuosity so peculiar to your Self, prevail over your present habit of Repose; the next journey you take to buy Land for a Poet, I promise to accompany you, be as active as you will: And upon all other journies and projects whatsoever of yours, I will at least accompany you with my best wishes for your Success.

I am Dear Sir | Your very affectionate | and hearty humble Servant | A. Pope.

Jan: 19th 1725/6

Endorsement: by Mr Pope. [In Oxford's hand.]

[1] A second transcript of this letter is found in Portland Papers xvii, f. 132. The variants between the two are negligible.

POPE *to* BROOME   20 *January* [1725/6]

Elwin–Courthope, viii. 113

Jan. 20,[1] [1726].

Your last, very last, packet happily arrived two days ago. I wish you joy, and myself; we have been married now these three years, and dragged on our common load with daily and mutual labour and constancy, lightening each other's toil, and friends to the last. We want only now a glorious epiphonema, and crown to our work. Why should we not go together in triumph, and demand the bacon flitch at Dunmow,[2] or some such signal reward? Or shall I, like a good husband, write your epitaph, and celebrate your great obedience, compliance, and wife-like virtues; while you, in your turn, make a kind will at the conclusion of your career, and express all the kindness you can to your beloved yoke-fellow? Something must be done at the close of this work by us both, as a monument equally of friendship and of justice to each other. In the meantime, send me what you call a sort of discourse or criticism,[3] that I may judge if it may have place here, or something else in the room of it. I have considered the thing thoroughly, and when we meet, you shall know my thoughts at large. I must only at present warn you of one point, which it is necessary you should take some care of. I find upon comparing your notes with Dacier's, many of them much more directly, indeed, entirely copied from her—besides what she takes from Eustathius—than I expected, or than is consistent with the plan I laid down, and the declaration I made in the introduction to the notes on the Iliad, which you also declare, in yours to these on the Odyssey, to make your model. This must, in fairness, be acknowledged before you conclude,[4] in a period to this effect,—that you have sometimes made as free use of Madame Dacier, as she did of Eustathius, which you never could design should be concealed, her work being in everybody's hands, whereas that of Eustathius lay wrapped in his original from all but a few learned. It is the best excuse I can think of, for the fact is so, which till very lately I never imagined, and was indeed surprised at.

As soon as the greater part, or as an entire volume of the work is printed, I will send you the sheets, and desire you to continue the

---

[1] The date is from the postmark.—Elwin.

[2] At Dunmow a flitch of bacon might be awarded to any married couple who had not for a year and a day quarrelled.

[3] Broome's discourse was not used in the *Odyssey*, and he printed it as a discourse prefatory to his *Poems* (1727).

[4] Neither Pope nor Broome had been scrupulous in acknowledgements of this sort, but at the end of the *Odyssey*, vol. v (1726), p. 285, Broome remarks: 'I have sometimes used Madam *Dacier* as she has done others, in transcribing some of her Remarks without particularizing them; but indeed it was through inadvertence only that her name is sometimes omitted at the bottom of the note.'

errata. As far as you went before, I have kept by me. Dear sir, I wish
you unnumbered happy new years and every one happier than the last.
My mother and I are sincerely yours. Fenton I see often, and hope
ere long we shall all joyfully meet, &c. *Haec olim meminisse juvabit.*[1]

POPE *to* THE EARL OF OXFORD   22 *January* 1725/6

Longleat Portland Papers xii

Jan. 22d 1725.

My Lord,—Your Letter gave me a real pleasure in the news of the
good health of all at Downhall, a place that I shall always wish all
blessings to, & particularly that of a warm Sun and fair weather to
gild its Groves, & give Verdure to its walks: which I will, if it please
God, your Lordship, & my Lady, (this Speech methinks is in the
manner of Mr Wanley)[2] Revisit, another season. For my own part I
declare, I likd my Lodging so well (both the Apartment above, & the
closet below) that I am utterly against Gibbs,[3] & all his Adherents for
Demolition. The rooms when I look up to the Cieling, appear very
lofty; & surely they are large enough, when both Lady Margaret has
room to run about all the morning, in her chamber, & Mr Thomas[4]
to sport with Bridgman, in his. I fear he will grow fat, now, for want
of Exercise, unless he betakes himself to hard study and painful preaching; the latter whereof at least I advise him against, as to no purpose;
and the former he stands in no need of. But, whether he studies or
plays, I am much his Servant. I wish I were at breakfast with you
now, over a Tea table that is void of Scandal: We have none such
here in town, & The only Speech I have heard without any, is the
King's.[5] I hope your Lordship will have some curiosity to hear, tho'
not that, at least the Comments upon it, & be speedily at London. For
I fear if you stay a little longer, the weather will so mend, & Downhall
so Improve, that we shall not see you at all. I hope Lady Oxford has
health enough to come to Town, or according to the modern Constitution of Ladies, she must be very ill indeed: but she is of so particular
a make, & so errant a Wife, & so meer a Good Woman, that little is
to be hopd of her as a fine Lady. You are e'en a couple so fit for one
another, that the world is not fit for you: I'm half afraid you'll just
pass thro this, with a contempt of all you see in it, & get into a better.

The favor, my Lord, of your letters is what I deserve, only by one
title, that I have a just value for them: Till you move this way, I beg

---

[1] *Aeneid,* i. 203.   [2] Humphrey Wanley, Oxford's librarian.
[3] James Gibbs (1682–1754), the famous architect of St. Martin's-in-the-Fields and of the
Radcliffe Camera, was employed by Oxford at Wimpole and Down Hall.
[4] Oxford's chaplain, Timothy Thomas.
[5] On 20 Jan. 1725/6 the King 'made a most gracious Speech to both Houses'. See *Hist.
Reg.* xi. 43–44.

the continuance of 'em and of your belief that I am sincerely & with the truest Esteem & honour, | My Lord | Your most Obligd & | most obedient Servant | A. Pope.

My Mother is highly sensible of the favor both of your Lordship's and Lady Oxfords Memory, and with respect, your Servant.

Address: To | The Right Honble the Earl of | Oxford, at Downhall, in | Essex.
Postmark: 22/IA.

FENTON *to* BROOME   29 *January* [1725/6]
Elwin–Courthope, viii. 115
                                                      Jan. 29, [1726].

Dear Mr. Broome,—I thank you heartily for favouring me with your two last letters,[1] and have now time only to inform you that the morning after I received your last, I called on Mr. Pope, but found company with him, so I could not enter into the affair so fully as I intended.[2] However, I informed him that you intended to be soon in town on account of your brother's marriage. His answer was that he wanted to see you, and the sooner the better, in which I entirely concur, and wish you a good journey. As to the epilogue, if I mention anything of it to Mr. Southerne, he may desire to have it to print with his play—so I leave the matter to yourself. My humble service to Mrs. Broome and all friends concludes in haste from yours faithfully.

Is not your edition of Milton the second?

POPE *to* BROOME[3]   [1725/6]
Elwin–Courthope, viii. 115
                                                Sunday Evening.

I beg both yours and Mr. Fenton's company to Twitnam, on Tuesday morning, or at least yours, if he will not. But I hope he is of a better mind. You will find me at Dr. Arbuthnot's at eleven o'clock. I am ever truly his and, dear sir, your faithful servant.

I am very ill again to-night.

POPE *to* BROOME   [1726]
Elwin–Courthope, viii. 116
                                                     [1726]

I hoped to have been able to see you after you had dined at Lord Cornwallis's, but I am forced to attend upon a sick friend out of town,

---

[1] Not preserved.
[2] i.e. the arranging a meeting of the collaborators to settle accounts.
[3] Given this chronological position 'at a venture' by Elwin, this letter seems to fall at a time in the spring when Broome came to town for his brother's wedding.

from whence I very much fear I cannot return to-night so as to find you before it be very late; and if you hold your design of travelling to-morrow, that will be inconvenient to you. If by any accident you stay longer, pray acquaint me, or be so kind as to drink chocolate here, the earlier the better, to-morrow, before I go home; or go home with me, or tell me and I will rise early and come to you in Fleet Street by eight o'clock. Though it be what I am hardly ever able to do, I will do it. I would fain contrive any way to have more of you. If we miss to meet, God bless you, and write to me speedily. All that concerns you, concerns me, who am truly and sincerely, dear sir, yours.

Apollonius is sent with this letter to my Lord Cornwallis's.

POPE *to* CARYLL   [*February* 1725/6]

Add. 28618

I had much sooner answered a letter of the nature of your last, which is not on the one hand more a proof of your Christianity than on the other of your friendship (since written at so melancholy a juncture)[1] but that my own illness, which had been dangerous a little before, was thought more so upon a relapse, out of which, however, it has pleased God to recover me. I am not so fit for him, as I hope and confide those are, whom he sooner takes to himself, especially when he takes 'em from parents such as you, to whom the blessings promised to such as serve him would surely never be denied to continue, did not his wisdom know it was best other ways. Your own citation from Job says all that can be said on these subjects, *Deus dedit, Deus abstulit.* To which let me add a very comfortable passage in the Book of Wisdom of Solomon on occasion of what we call untimely and early death. It is in the 4th Chapter of that noble book from verse 7 to 17.

Another reason (to say true) that made me defer my letter to you was that, at that season, I knew no words could have any effect on a mind like yours. No thoughts could be added to your own, that could be of a reasonable resigning kind: and to have said nothing, or little, had been (seemingly at least) but an unfriendly return to the notice you had given me of your grief. But I hope that ere now, the best physician (next to that immortal one I have been speaking of) I mean time, has laid his hands and spread some lenitives upon your wound; the only relief which humane nature is susceptible of in such deep ones, being first a sort of stupefaction, and after a kind of composure, proceeding from the excess of the pain its self. Upon the most violent strokes one rather faints than groans; Heaven in this is merciful, even in the frame of our constitution; but then how infinitely more in the

---

[1] Mr. Caryll's son Henry died on the 30th of January 1726.—Elwin.

comforts it opens to us from the views of another, happier life, both
to our friends and to ourselves, in which alone is to be found lasting
rest, real comfort, and solid enjoyment of any Good.

I wish I could ever (as I will endeavour from this time to do) find
any person of merit enough to be linked to a family I so much esteem;
what I fear may render my wish ineffectual is my very small acquaintance with those of the religion which I believe you would think
essential to such an alliance.[1] I am sure no creature more sincerely
desires to be serviceable to you, in that or any particular which regards
your happiness or contentment.

I rejoice that your charity has been beforehand with my request in
relation to Mrs Cope. Indeed 'tis a good act, and such as doubtless
attract to us the benedictions of him, who will ask us no question sooner
at the great day (not even if we believed in him?) than, if we cloathed
the naked, gave drink to the thirsty, &c.—which he has directly told
us will be taken as done to himself.

Be assured my earnest prayers attend you, and your family; for I
am truly, as always | dear sir | your affect: faithfull friend | and ser-
vant | A: P:

†POPE *to* MRS. ——[2]

1735

It is with infinite satisfaction I am made acquainted that your brother
will at last prove your relation, and has entertain'd such sentiments as
become him in your concern. I have been prepar'd for this by degrees,
having several times receiv'd from Mrs. ——[3] that which is one of the
greatest pleasures, the knowledge that others enter'd into my own
sentiments concerning you. I ever was of opinion that you wanted
no more to be vindicated than to be known⌐: and like Truth, cou'd
appear no where but you must conquer⌐. As I have often condol'd
with you in your adversities, so I have a right which but few can
pretend to, of congratulating on the prospect of your better fortunes;
and I hope for the future to have the concern I have felt for you over-
paid in your felicities. Tho' you modestly say the world has left you,
yet I verily believe it is coming to you again as fast as it can: For to
give the world its due, it is always very fond of Merit when 'tis past

---

[1] Whether or not Pope aided the arrangement, Edward Caryll did marry, early in 1730,
one of Pope's 'very small acquaintance' of the religion, the daughter of his neighbour, Nathaniel
Pigott, barrister-at-law.—Elwin.

[2] This letter to Mrs. Weston, Mrs. Cope, or some other worthy but hitherto unappre-
ciated lady appears in all Pope's editions. In texts of 1737–42 two omissions (here in half-
brackets) represent the major textual changes. The letter is undatable, but Mrs. Cope's
brother was slowly showing his sister some humanity early in 1726, and so the letter is
placed there.　　　　　　　　　　　　　　　　　　　[3] Probably Mrs. Caryll.

its power to oppose it. Therefore if you should take[1] it into favour again upon its repentance, and continue in it, ⌜you would be so far from leading what is commonly call'd an unsettled life, (and what you with too much unjust severity call a Vagabond Life,) that the wise cou'd only look upon you as a Prince in a progress, who travels to gain the affections he has not, or to fix those he already has; which he effectually does wherever he shews himself.⌝ But if you are re-solv'd in revenge to rob the world of so much example as you may afford it, I believe your design will be vain; for even in a Monastery your devotions cannot carry you so far toward the next world as to make This lose the sight of you, but you'll be like a Star, that while it is fix'd to Heaven shines over all the Earth.

Wheresoever Providence shall dispose of the most valuable thing I know, I shall ever follow you with my sincerest wishes, and my best thoughts will be perpetually waiting upon you, when you never hear of me or them. Your own guardian Angels cannot be more con-stant, nor more silent. I beg you will never cease to think me your friend, that you may not be guilty of that which you never yet knew to commit, an Injustice. As I have hitherto been so in spite of the world, so hereafter, if it be possible you shou'd ever be more opposed, and more deserted, I should only be so much the more | Your faithful, &c.

POPE *to* FORTESCUE   17 *February* 1725/6

1817 (Warner)

Twitenham, Feb. 17, 1726.

I was sorry I missed of you the other day when you called; I was gone to Mrs. Howard's, as I told you. I send you part of what wholly belongs to you, and, as the world's justice goes, that is a fair composi-tion; I mean some of the Devonshire pease. If the ring be done, pray give it the bearer. I intend to wear it for life, as a melancholy memo-randum of a most honest, worthy man. I told you I dined t'other day at Sir Robert Walpole's. A thing has happened since which gives me uneasiness, from the indiscretion of one who dined there at the same time; one of the most innocent words that ever I dropped in my life, has been reported out of that conversation, which might reasonably *seem* odd, if ever it comes to Sir R.'s ears. I will tell it you the next time we meet; as I would him, if I had seen him since; and t'was not (otherwise) of weight enough to trouble him about. We live in un-lucky times, when half one's friends are enemies to the other, and

---

[1] From 1737 to 1742 this sentence read, 'Therefore if you can, take it into favour again upon its repentance, and continue in it.' The rest of the sentence of 1735 was omitted thereafter.

consequently care not that any equal moderate man should have more friends than they themselves have. Believe me, dear Sir, | Most affectionately your's, | A. Pope.

Address: To William Fortescue, Esq.

POPE *to* THE EARL OF OXFORD   3 *March* 1725/6

Longleat Portland Papers xii

Twitenham: | March 3d 1725/6

My Lord,—The Satisfaction I take in writing to you, ever since you allowd me the honour of it, would prompt me to employ your time more frequently this way, did I not know how very well you spend every moment, & (by an Experience I shall always agreeably remember) how happy to live in your own family; So happily, that tis a kind of Injury to take your very Thought away from it, in sending you any news, or troubling you with any notices that are foreign to it. I did however write you a very long letter, almost 3 weeks ago, which (by the last your Lordship favord me with) I believe the Floods carried away, which I'm told stopt the Post in many Countries. Now the face of the Earth is seen again, & now the Snows are gone away, and every Green thing appears above the waters, I'm pleasd to think your Bowling-green is one of the first of those green things I envy you the pleasure of creating, when one month's time will give you all your Idæas in lively colours, responsive to your expectation. It is now a season of the Year, when to plant, is in a manner but to say, Let it be! and it is done. I am therfore afraid, you will really stay in the Country these 2 months, & if so, I must desire to have a lodging either in my Garret at Downhall, or in some hollow Tree in the Wood. For my part, I am much less pleasingly imployd, being to write a Preface,[1] the thing that of all writings I hate; as indeed most folks do to be brought to an Account of themselves & their evil doings; That I fear may be my case; but if it were not, it is not much less irksome to a good and honest man, to be put upon declarations of what he has done well or honorably: For when a man has written well, he shoud no more prate about it, than when he has acted well. My present business is something like that of the Tatler's formerly, who found it needful to advertise the publick that if his writings appeard *Dull*, it was so *By Design*. For I am going to tell the world, that if they don't keep quite awake over part of my Homer, it is because I

---

[1] He means, rather, the Postscript that he appended at the end of the *Odyssey*, v (1726), 289–317, which is one of Pope's most interesting discussions of problems of poetic style. Much of the letter echoes the thought of the Postscript, and since some phrases are taken verbatim from it, one assumes this moment as the time of its composition.

thought it my duty to observe a certain mediocrity of Style, agreeable to Conversation and Dialogue, which is calld the Narrative, and ought to be low, being put into the mouths of persons not of the highest condition, or of a person acting in the disguise of a poor Wanderer, & speaking in that character of consequence; as Ulysses must in reason be supposed to do, or Ulysses was not the Wise man we are to take him for. Nothing is so ridiculous as the lofty or poetical Style in such parts, which yet many Poets (& no very mean ones) are often guilty of, especially in our modern Tragedy, where one continued Sameness of Diction runs thro' all their characters; and our best Actors from hence have got the custom, of speaking constantly the most indifferent things in a pompous elevated voice; 'tis not so properly Speaking as Vociferating. This goes even to their pronouncing of *Proper Names* those of the Greeks & Romans they sound as if there were some great Energy and mightiness of meaning in the very syllables of Fabius, Antony & Metellus, &c. In like manner our modern Poets preserve a painful Equality of Fustian, throughout their whole Epic or Tragic works, like travelling all along on the Ridge of a Hill; which is not half so pleasant as sometimes rising, & sometimes descending gently into the Vale, as the Way leads, and as the End of the journey directs. To write thus upon low subjects is really the true Sublime of Ridicule, tis the Sublime of Don Quixote; but tis strange men should not see, it is by no means so of the humbler and narrative parts of Poetry: It leaves no distinction between the Language of the Gods, which is when the Muse or the Gods speak, and that of men, in the Conversation & Dialogues. Even in set Harangues or Orations, this painted, florid Style would be ridiculous: Tully & Demosthenes spoke often figuratively, but not poetically, and the very figures of Oratory are vastly different from those of Poetry: Still it is (even in them) much below that Language of the Gods which I was speaking of.

But I have forgot myself, & run you half into my Preface without intending it. I beg your Lordships pardon, and only wish, in return, you would tell me as much of any thing that runs in your mind so as this does in mine: I'm sure it will be better worth reading. I am ashamd to add more than my sincerest respects to Lady Oxford, and to beg the continuance of your favours upon the best title I can pretend to, that of my being with the most esteem | My Lord, | Your most obligd & most | obedient Servant | A. Pope.

Endorsement (in Oxford's hand): Mr. Pope. march 3. 1725/6. R. | march 6. at Down Hall.

THE EARL OF OXFORD *to* POPE   10 *March* 1725/6

Longleat Portland Papers xii

Down Hall. March. 10. 1725/6

Sir,—I was extreamly glad to see your hand writing upon the outside of a letter but when I opened it I had double pleasure in having a letter from you of some length being in great hopes you are better in your Health by that circumstance for though I had rather converse with you then any man living yet I would not purchas it at so dear a rate as that it should put you to any pain. I congratulate you that you are come so near an end of your great work as to be upon the preface I belive you will have more quiet and ease now that Load is off your shoulders, I do not know anybody that is so able in all respects to give an account of themselves as you are all that I suspect is that as other writers say too much for & of themselves you will go to the other extream and say too little you cannot say too much. the letter you mention to have wrote to me about three Weeks ago I never received, I regret the loss of it very much as I do anything that comes from you;

My Bowling green is near finisht, I have planted trees round my spring, I have fallen my wood that is the underwood which does not look so ill as I suspected and was affraid it would, it will be the finer for it in a little while.

Since I saw you I found among some papers I was sorting which were my Fathers[1] your Translation of one of Dr Donnes Satyrs I think I did mention to you that I had formerly seen it & you expressed a desire to see it again, I will send it to you when & where you please, I do not care to trust it by the post because he lost your letter to me. I live in hopes we shall this year have a Summer and one great motive for my wishing one is that I may enjoy your company both at Wimpole and this place, I hope mrs Pope is well please to be so kind as to make my compliments to her. My Wife is your humble Servant and mrs Popes I am with most sincere esteem | Sir | Your most affectionate | humble Servant | Oxford.

I hope I shall hear from you soon.—

POPE *to* THE EARL OF OXFORD   22 *March* 1725/6

Longleat Portland Papers xii

London: March 22 | 1725/6

My Lord,—I designed to acknowledge in a fuller manner the honour of yours of the tenth, but just as I was sitting down to write, I had

[1] Lord Oxford's discovery of the 'translation' of one of Donne's satires (the second?) among his father's papers bears out Pope's statement—doubted by Elwin (*Works of Pope*, iii. 424)—that the version was made at an early date. The matter is set right in Professor Butt's comment, Twickenham ed., iv, pp. xli-xliii.

notice that a person was come to London who demanded my immediate Repair thither,[1] and to acquaint your Lordship with some thing relating to him made me defer my letter. He is in perfect health & spirits, the joy of all here who know him, as he was eleven years ago, & I never receivd a more sensible satisfaction than in having been now 2 days with him. It was agreed that I should only notify his arrival to you, & if there be any hopes of you here, we hope your Lordship will soon let us know when we may be so happy as to see the day of your return? I apprehend it is not so near as he thinks, from your never mentioning it in your last. I wish I could promise to myself and to the Dean of St Patrick's, to accompany him to Downhall in case your Lordship cannot leave that place which I fear is too beautiful already to admit you to quit it for us; Ill fortune will have it, that this very fortnight my Book[2] must be finished at the press: And the Dean I believe, (if I can judge his temper by his respect to you) will hardly (in that case) stay for me. I wish your Lordship would fancy there is some good or other to be done here, in publick, or in private; & then I'm confident you would come up with all speed.

I will not take the Manuscript of Donne's Satyr but from your own hands, somewhere: I rejoice first & principally in your own & Lady Oxfords health, secondly in the finishing of your works in the wood & Bowling green. I have just turfed a little Bridgmannick Theatre myself. It was done by a detachment of His workmen from the Prince's,[3] all at a stroke, & it is yet unpayd for, but that's nothing with a Poetical Genius—I must conclude by saying, I am well, tho not perfectly so well as before my illness: I am always equally, with sincere respect | Your Lordships faithful Servant | A. Pope.

We shall all be undone in the Stocks. I should not have minded it if I had dyed; but as I am like to live, I want somebody to give me an Estate in Land. Pray ask Morley.

Address: To the Right Honorable the | Earl of Oxford
Endorsement: March. 22. 1725/6. | Mr Pope

POPE *to* THE EARL OF OXFORD[4]   *26 March 1726*
Longleat Portland Papers xii
                                    March 26. | Saturday | 1726.

The Dean of St Patricks went this Saturday to my Lord Bolingbrokes at Dawley near Uxbridge, to stay some days Probably his return

---

1 Dean Swift had reached London about the middle of March, and lodged in Bury Street, 'next door to the Royal Chair', close to the lodgings of his friend Charles Ford.
2 The *Odyssey*.
3 Bridgeman probably had men working for the Prince of Wales at Richmond.
4 Though unsigned the letter is in Pope's hand.

to London may be in a week, He lodges in Berry street next door to
the Royal chair.

Address: To be left at my Lord Oxford's in | Doverstreet.
     (*In another hand*:) For youer | Lordship | Speed
Endorsement: Mr Pope | March 26. 1726

POPE *to* FORTESCUE   2 *April* [1726]

1797 (Polwhele, i. 322)

                                                       Twitnam, April 2d

I began a letter to you about a fortnight past, which Gay was to finish,
and accordingly put it in his pocket, I believe, for I never since could
find it here. If you received it, it would look odly enough, for intending to fill a page, I had left a large blank, and probably he sent it you
just as it was. I have ever since been engaged in country houses and
gardens, with one friend or other, and know nothing of the town, but
that Bowry gave my mother sometimes an account of the state of the
family, and of their drink. Dr. Swift is come into England, who is
now with me, and with whom I am to ramble again to lord Oxford's
and lord Bathurst's, and other places. Dr. Arbuthnot has led him a
course thro' the town, with lord Chesterfield, Mr. Pulteney, &c. Lord
Peterborow and Lord Harcourt propose to carry him to Sir R. Walpole,
and I to Mrs. Howard, &c. I wish you were here to know him. I have
just now a very ill-timed misfortune, a lame thigh, which keeps me
from these parties; but I hope, since so many of my friends' prayers
are on this occasion joined to my own, that I may be blest with a
speedy recovery, and make one amongst them. Many good wishes of
mine attend you! May no similar accident, such as a fall from your
horse by day, or a sprain in your back by night, retard your return to
us! Pray acquaint me, more largely than you did in your last concise
letter, and in a style more suitable to the length and duration of a
pleader and writer in law, of all your fortunes since we parted. In each
and all of which be assured, no man takes a truer part, and more wishes
your welfare and prosperity, than, dear Sir, your faithful, ever affec-
tionate servant, | A. Pope.

Address: To Wm. Fortescue, esq.

POPE *to* THE EARL OF OXFORD   3 *April* [1726]

Longleat Portland Papers xii

                                                       London Apr. 3d

My Lord,—I acquainted your Lordship in a very great hurry by 2
or 3 lines of all that I then knew of the Dean's motions, which paper

I left at Doverstreet. He has since been at Twitenham, in expectation of hearing further of your Lordships movements, & we were not without hopes you might call att Doverstreet, before your further Summer journies to Wimpole &c. I find the Dean had nothing in his view, in coming to England for a few months, but the seeing his friends, & principally to wait on you in relation to Lord Oxfords papers.[1] When ever you write, he will be heard of either at Twitenham, or at his lodgings in Berrystreet next door to the Royal Chair; or at Dr. Arbuthnot's. We hope my Lady Oxford & Lady Margaret continue in perfect health. I have something to trouble you with in regard to Lady Margaret; which is to ask your leave in the name of a Friend of mine, to prefix a few Verses to her before a new Edition of Waller, which is a very correct & beautiful one in Quarto, publishd by him. A Request of this nature relating to a Dedication, is what I never made in my life but once before; to your Lordships Father; & what I shall never make again; but I believe This will be no disgrace to the Family, as Verses go; And the person who is ambitious of doing it, wants to testify his Gratitude to you for a favor he already owes you, (though a Stranger to your Lordship.) Yet upon the whole, I would not mention this at all, if Mr Fenton were not as Good a Man, as he is a Poet: And if your Lordship any way, or my Lady, disapprove of it, you may look upon it as a thing not mentiond at all, & there will be an end of it. The Gentleman really means no more than that he truly honours you, & thinks himself (as I said before) obligd to you.

I cannot get Homer printed till the end of this month, which vexes me. I long to see your Lordship. I wish you all sort of happiness, & the accomplishment of every wish you can form. My Mother is my Lady's & your most faithful Servant. B[e] (I beg you) the same of me, as long as I am | A. Pope.

Address: To the Right Honorable, the | Earl of Oxford.

Endorsement: Mr Pope | Apl 3. 1726

POPE *to* BROOME   16 *April* 1726

Elwin–Courthope, viii. 116

                                        Twitnam, April 16, 1726.

I have received from you but one letter, which consisted but of three or four words. I am truly sorry for your illness. As to my own health,

---

[1] In July 1724 (Ball, iii. 196–7) Swift had suggested writing the life of Robert, Earl of Oxford, if the son found personal papers that would serve for materials. The second Earl replied (Ball, iii. 221–2) that there was a great mass of relevant papers, '. . . but give me leave to say that if you do not come into England nothing can be done'. Now Swift has come, and, perhaps disappointed that Lord Oxford has not rushed to town to greet him, has gone to Dawley to visit his other idol, Bolingbroke.

it is not yet confirmed, nor am I quite down, but more fatigued with less business than I used to be with greater, when I had strength. It is not to be imagined with what sickly reluctance I have at last finished my postscript to Homer. I would not mortify you with the trouble of an index, feeling so much what a toil it is to write against one's will. But an exact errata is of absolute necessity; in order whereto, I have bid Lintot send you as many sheets as are dry from the press. I believe you will have all but the very last. Pray send the errata with all speed.

I am heartily glad of your boy,[1] and of all that pleases you. Our services attend Mrs. Broome. My mother is ill of a rheumatism. I had writ to you sooner, but that I had expected to hear from you, and something, I thought, was to be allowed to the time of your christening, entertaining, gossiping, visiting your neighbors, &c. I fear you go too thin clad these northeasterly days, and that may endanger agues. I wish your lot were in a fairer ground nearer the warmth of London and its fires. This I wish for more reasons than one, being sincerely, dear sir, your ever affectionate friend and servant.

Fenton is going to Cambridge.

†POPE *to* EDWARD DIGBY[2] 21 *April* 1726

1737

April 21, 1726.

I have a great inclination to write to you, tho' I cannot by writing, any more than I could by words, express what part I bear in your sufferings. Nature and Esteem in you are join'd to aggravate your affliction:[3] the latter I have in a degree equal even to yours, and a tye of friendship approaches near to the tenderness of nature: yet God knows, no man living is less fit to comfort you, as no man is more deeply sensible than my self of the greatness of the loss. That very virtue, which secures his present state from all the sorrows incident to ours, does but aggrandise our sensation of its being remov'd from our sight, from our affection, and from our imitation; for the friendship and society of good men does not only make us happier, but it makes us better. Their death does but complete their felicity before our own, who probably are not yet arriv'd to that degree of perfec-

---

[1] On 15 March 1726 a son, Charles John, was born to the Broomes.—Elwin.

[2] The text of the Roberts octavo (1737 a) is here given. Other octavos follow it faithfully, and the variants in the quarto and folio of 1737 are negligible, except for a possible misprint in the date, which in those editions becomes 29 Apr. For a possible omission from the original letter see below.

[3] Pope's friend the Hon. Robert Digby had died on 19 Apr. 1726. If he died in London, the date of Pope's letter may well be the 21st. If he died in the country, the 29th might be more plausible.

tion which merits an immediate reward. That your dear brother and my dear friend was so, I take his very removal to be a proof; Providence would certainly lend virtuous men to a world that so much wants them, as long as in its justice to them it could spare them to us. May my soul be with those who have meant well and have acted well to that meaning! and I doubt not, if this prayer be granted, I shall be with him. Let us preserve his memory in the way he would best like, by recollecting what his behaviour would have been, in every incident of our lives to come, and doing in each just as we think he would have done: so we shall have him always before our eyes, and in our minds, and (what is more) in our lives and manners. I hope when we shall meet him next we shall be more of a piece with him, and consequently not to be ever more separated from him.[1] I will add but one word that relates to what remains of your self and me, since so valued a part of us is gone: it is to beg you to accept as yours by inheritance, of the vacancy he has left in a heart, which (while he could fill it with such hopes, wishes and affections for him as suited a mortal creature) was truly and warmly his; and shall (I assure you in the sincerity of sorrow for my own loss) be faithfully at your service while I continue to love his memory, that is, while I continue to be my self.

THE EARL OF OXFORD *to* POPE   22 *April* 1726

Longleat Portland Papers, xii

Wimpole. April. 22. 1726

Sir,—I am very much concerned I have not returned you my acknowledgements for your last kind and obliging letter   as to what you mention, in relation to peggy I leave it to you to do as you think proper for I know you can do nothing improperly,   I have a very good opinion of mr Fenton and have a regard for him, I shall be well satisfied with what ever you do in this affair & I leave [it] to you and I belive my Wife will be of my mind.

I am extreamly busie at this place but I will not tell you what I am doing nor of my designs till you come to the place and see it with

---

[1] The Harvard College Library has in its Gay Collection two volumes of Pope's *Works in Prose* (1737, 1741) in large paper folio, which in 1741 the poet gave to a friend who on the title-page of the 1741 volume inscribed: 'Ex Dono Authoris Alexr Pope. 1741.' Both volumes contain the dated (1755) bookplate of a family resident at Coleshill and allied to the Digbys.

At this point in the text is entered (p. 184) in a contemporary hand the following marginal addition to the text: 'I doubt not (as far as human reason can pretend to certainty) that we shal see, & know each other hereafter, to the greater Comfort of ourselves, & greater Glory of our Maker.—in the Orig: M.S.' It is arguable whether (assuming the sentence to be genuine) Pope omitted it as superfluous in view of the preceding sentence or as doctrinally indiscreet. In either case it is an interesting omission. Its discovery is due to Professor V. A. Dearing.

your own eyes and you shall have power to alter and I am sure that will be amending, anything I shall think of.

The very sudden death of old mr Bridgeman[1] has obliged me to stay longer than I thought to do which has prevented me the great pleasure of waiting upon the Dean which I much long to do I beg you will make my compliments to him   I hope to do it Soon, for my regard to him is very great. my humble Service to mrs pope

you should have had this some time since but I hope you will excuse this omission as well as many more which I fear I am guilty of, but I assure you I am with true respect | Your most obedient & | affectionate humble servant | Oxford.

FENTON *to* BROOME   20 *May* 1726

Elwin–Courthope, viii. 117

Trinity Hall, May 20, 1726.

Dear Mr. Broome,—I think I told you when I saw you in London of Mr. Trumbull's intended journey to Cambridge.[2] We came hither a few days since, and Sir Clement Cottrell was so good as to favour us with his company. He is returned to Twickenham; and, after about two months' stay here, we shall be setting out for Windsor Forest, so that the shortness of the time, and my horse not being yet out of Staffordshire, will I fear prevent my seeing Sturston this summer, but I flatter myself with seeing you here for two or three days before we leave the university.

The week before I came away from London Sir Clement and I visited Mr. Pope, who gave me an account of the postscript,[3] but took no notice of what you hinted to me. It unfortunately happened that he had company when we came, so that all our conversation ran on indifferent subjects. I find the clamour here is as great both against him and the work as it was last winter in London.[4] I shall see Dr. Newcome

[1] Very possibly the father of Pope's friend, Charles, who was at times employed by Lord Oxford.

[2] Young Trumbull was entering the University as a student, and Fenton evidently stayed in Cambridge with him.

[3] To the *Odyssey*. If one is to take literally Pope's remarks upon the Postscript in his letter to Broome, 4 June, the Postscript was just being written now. In a letter to Lord Oxford of 3 Mar. 1725/6 Pope speaks of writing a 'Preface', when he was very likely beginning work on this Postscript.

[4] As Elwin indicates, there was complaint about the quality of the paper and typography. Such complaints seem somewhat disingenuous, though Lintot may have palmed off slightly inferior paper along with that carefully stipulated by Pope in the indenture. Dr. Newcome had complained in a letter to Broome quoted by Elwin that 'Mr. Pope gives us but indifferent paper and margin and is too much bent on the profitable'. Dr. Newcome was not a subscriber, and consequently may have got bad paper from Lintot for which Pope was not responsible. The attack in *The London Journal*, 17 July 1725, has already (ii. 339) been mentioned. Such attacks were motivated in part by mere prejudice against Pope.

the beginning of next week, when I will not fail of drinking your health, though you owe me a letter. My humble service to Mrs. Broome, Mr. Burlington, and all our friends concludes in most affectionately.

Mr. Trumbull presents his service.

POPE *to* BROOME   4 *June* [1726]

Elwin–Courthope, viii. 118

                    [1]June 4, [1726].

I was in so great a hurry when I received yours, that I only bid Lintot to acquaint you of our receipt of the errata, &c. I have had a long and troublesome disorder upon me of the piles, which has put me more out of humour than out of health. And, as if it were fatal to me to be sedentary to no purpose, I had a hundred impertinent people continually coming to me, that were as troublesome as gnats in this season, and brought about me by the same cause, fine weather. I will one time or other of my life run away from my own home, and try if there be no such thing as living to one's self even in Suffolk. I fancy there too one should be encompassed about with clergymen of your acquaintance, and invitations and compotations,[2] the common effects of good-nature in a country-seat. Moreover, you will be getting more children, and I might fall just upon a christening time.

A long postscript relating to critical affairs, which I have taken it into my head to write since we met last, has retarded till now the publication of Homer. I will take care to send your number of books as before, the moment it is ready for delivery. But order this as you will by a line to me.

Your Miscellany[3] must be carefully and correctly done, and above all have no idle or too common thoughts or subjects, since the best versification in the world, and the most poetical dress whatever, will avail little without a sober fund of sense and good thought. I will be very sincere with you in that and all other things you shall confide to my trust. I have no intention at present of employing myself in anything that can interfere in the least with my overlooking yours.

Mr. Fenton promised to write to me as soon as he was settled at

---

 [1] Elwin inferred this date from the postmark.

 [2] In a letter to Lord Cornwallis, quoted by Elwin (viii. 118), Broome remarks, 'We in the country are a kind of thirsty plants that require much moisture to keep us alive.'

 [3] In 1727 Lintot published Broome's *Poems on Several Occasions*. Pope's fifth edition of *Miscellaneous Poems and Translations* (1726, 1727), so he assures Broome, need not interfere with the additional publication by Broome. Elwin says that Lintot gave Broome £35 for the volume (though Elwin gives a wrong title to the book). Later, when in 1735 (Broome to Pope, 1 Dec. 1735) Broome wished to reprint, Lintot insisted that it be at Broome's cost. There was a reprint in 1739.

Cambridge. I have not yet heard from him. If I go to Wimpole this summer, as I believe I shall, with my Lord Oxford, we may meet there

I wish your little son the continuance of life and health. I wish you all joys and felicities of life, and am yours very affectionately.

There is a book lately published at Oxford, called an Essay on Pope's Odyssey,[1] which you will have reason to be pleased with. Lintot, I hope, has sent it you.

FENTON *to* BROOME   10 *June* 1726

Elwin–Courthope, viii. 120

June 10, 1726.

I hope my good friend Mr. Broome will never so much as in thought accuse me of being a lazy correspondent, when I am so expeditious in my answer, notwithstanding you are a letter in arrear, unless you plead acquittance by the merit of one being brought by honest Mr. Needham, whose company I heartily wished to have enjoyed longer. As for my seeing Sturston this summer, my dear friend, you must not expect it, for the reasons which I gave you in my last; and, therefore, do you resolve on seeing Cambridge as soon, and contrive to stay as long, as possibly you can. I wish matters might be ordered so that Mr. Pope could give you the meeting, but his journey to Wimpole is so very uncertain that it would be in vain to endeavour to make an appointment.

I have sent the Essay[2] you wrote for, but have not read it over; but, upon a transient view, it appears to be writ with so much candour that I fancy the world will say that we have employed a friend to fight booty against us, or perhaps that it is one of our own productions. If, after so strict and deliberate an examination of the work, they can find no more nor greater faults than they have yet discovered, they will criticise me into a much better opinion of the translation than I should otherwise have entertained.

You mistake my intentions very much when you think I design to settle in a college.[3] If I spend the next summer in this way of life, it

---

[1] With his *Essay on Pope's Odyssey* Joseph Spence (1699–1768), one of Pope's most dis-interested and devoted friends, enters the poet's life. The *Essay* consists of five 'evenings' or dialogues, one for each of the volumes of the *Odyssey*. When Pope wrote this letter the first three dialogues had appeared; the last two were advertised in Aug. 1727. Before publica-tion of these last Pope made the acquaintance of the young Fellow of New College and even revised the MS. of the last two dialogues, but without excessive pruning of adverse comment. See *Notes & Queries*, 1 S. i (1850), 396. The original MS. is now in the possession of Mr. James M. Osborn of Yale University. Dr. Johnson's comment on this *Essay* in his Life of Pope is deservedly well known.   [2] Spence's *Essay on Pope's Odyssey*.

[3] As a non-juror Fenton would be ineligible for any university appointment; but apparently he might live in college as governor of young Trumbull.

will be the utmost that I propose. Heat of party and little intrigues cannot be agreeable, even to a disinterested bystander. I have seen your old friend Dr. Tudway but once. He is grown forty years older than he was when you were here; but, old as he is, I am so much awed with his superior genius that I have not attempted to make a pun[1] since I have been in Cambridge. Adieu, and believe me to be, with the greatest sincerity, your affectionate humble servant.

POPE *to* CARYLL[2]   [1726]

Add. 28618

I thought it a very long time I did not hear from you, and was going to write again just when I received yours. I shall be much pleased to see you here *en famille*, but pray tell me the time (if you can) it being else a great uncertainty whether I may not be abroad, or have strangers with me; for indeed my house is too like the house of a patriarch in the Old Testament, receiving all comers: whereas I can easily at a little warning contrive it so that nobody shall molest the enjoyment I propose of your company, and heartily desire. I thank you for your offer of venison and shall be glad of some. Why not send it so as it may make part of your entertainment here when you come?

I send inclosed [a] receipt, upon sending which to Mr Jervais's the Painter's you will have the books delivered to the bearer. I thank you for the congratulation upon the conclusion of that laborious book, which (first and last) has cost me as much pains as the *Iliad*.

What you tell me of Mrs Cope being at last met by her brother is a thing I am rejoiced at; even tho' his affairs may not be as I wish, yet it will doubtless be some addition of comfort to her besides his company. I wish that too common verse may not be applicable to them:

> Solamen miseris socios habuisse doloris.

The last time I heard from her she was extremely dejected, which is about 6 weeks past. I beg you sometimes to commend me and my service to Lady Mary Caryll. My best wishes attend her and her charge; your family has had a long and lasting right to mine. Believe me, dear sir | Your ever affectionat | Friend and servant | A: P:

---

1 Thomas Tudway, Professor of Music at Cambridge, was famous for his puns, one of which in 1706, made at the expense of Queen Anne, caused him to be temporarily deprived of all his college posts and from 'all degrees taken and to be taken'. He was more permanently distinguished for his great collection of early Anglican music, made for the Harleian Library. He died in Nov. 1726.

2 Pope's house was much frequented in 1726 when Swift was an attraction to visitors. Since the *Odyssey*, vols. iv and v were being distributed after 10 June 1726, that fact also places the letter chronologically. Elwin wrongly dated it in 1725.

SWIFT *and* POPE *to* THE EARL OF OXFORD 3 *July* 1726

Portland MSS. Harley Letters

My Lord,—Mr Pope by writing first hath limited me to what space you see. He prescribes all our Visits without our knoledge, and Mr Gay and I find our selves often engaged for three or four days to come, and we neither of us dare dispute his Pleasure; Accordingly this morning we go to Lord Bathurst, on Tuesday Company is to dine here, however I will certainly attend Your Lordship towards the End of the Week. It is too true to my sorrow, that I have not many Weeks to stay in England, and besides I have some Business that will keep me severall Days in my Journey. I confess I squandered away these four months, as People do their Lives, in neglecting their chief Business, which in me was to see and discourse with Your Lordship as often as I could, wherein however I am not so faulty as unfortunate, by Your Long Absence. I am with the greatest Respect | My Lord, Your Lordships most | obedient humble Servant | Jonath. Swift

Twitenham. Jul. 3d | 1726.

[Swift writes at the top of the leaf: Pope's note follows below:]

My Lord,—Indeed you are very unreasonable. I never knew you so before. You say you will quarrel with me if I keep the Dean here, & let nobody see him. Pray what hinders you? *Here we are to be seen*, is the Motto over my house, but it is so written that none but such as are worthy & Enlightend can understand it. Pray show that you do any day after Thursday.

Address [in Pope's hand]: To the Right Honorable | the Earl of Oxford, in | Dover-street.

THE EARL OF OXFORD *to* POPE 17 *July* 1726

Longleat Portland Papers, xii

July. 17. 1726. | Dover Street.

Sir,—according to my promise I write to you to let you know you will not have a troublesome guest this Week pray tell mr Dean he has not kept his word with me, I would not miss a line of his writing nor willingly a moment of his conversation that he could allow me.

now you three are Togather[1] I often think of the lines wrote in old times which begin

Pope Parnel and Gay the Doctor & Dean[2]

---

[1] Pope, Gay, and Swift were at Pope's villa in Twickenham—which Lord Oxford here speaks of as Swift's 'country house'.

[2] The line is the first of the rhymed letter sent by the Scriblerians to Robert, Earl of Oxford, on 20 Mar. 1713/14. See i. 216.

Only poor parnel is gone and I regret him the less because by being the editor of his poems you had an opportunity of making the finest copy of Verses and the greatest compliment that ever was paid by a poet to any man.—

I shall go out of town the end of the Week for two days. | my humble Service to the Dean

I do not wonder that he likes his country house   I doubt he will not come to town, I wish he would take such a strong fancy for the place as to bring him soon back from Ireland or rather to keep him from going there again.

I am | your most | affectionate | humble Servant | Oxford

my Service to mr Gay

CHRISTOPHER PITT *to* SPENCE   18 *July* 1726

1776 (*Additions*)

July 18, Blandford, 1726.

Dear Jo,—I am entering into proposals with a bookseller for printing a little miscellany of my own performances, consisting of some originals and select Translations.[1] I beg you to be altogether silent in the matter. Mr. Pope has used so little of the 23d Odyssey that I gave Dr. Younge, that if I put it in among the rest I shall hardly incur any danger of the penalty concerning the patent. However, I will not presume to publish a single line of it after Mr. Pope's Translation, if you advise me (as I desire you to do sincerely) to the contrary. I shall send you a small specimen of my Translation, which if you approve of, I can assure you the remainder of the book is not inferior to it.[2]

This is enough in conscience for this time; besides I am desired by Mr. Pope or Mr. Lintot, I don't know which, to write to Mr. Pope on a certain affair.[3]

POPE *to* CHRISTOPHER PITT[4]   23 *July* 1726

1797 (Warton)

Twitenham, near Hampton-Court, July 23, 1726.

Sir,—I received a letter from you with satisfaction, having long been

---

[1] In 1727 Lintot published *Poems and Translations*, By Christopher Pitt, M.A., Late Fellow of New College in Oxford. The volume did not contain any translation from Homer. It is supposed that Pitt had through Dr. Young sent to Pope a translation of *Odyssey* xxiii, of which Pope made some use in revising the work of Broome. In the letter to Spence, Pitt enclosed the first fifty lines of his translation (here omitted). They show no close relation to any phrase in the Pope–Broome version.

[2] At this point in the letter were inscribed the fifty lines of Pitt's translation mentioned in note 1. They are printed in the *Additions to the Works of Pope*, i (1776), 192–5, and by Elwin, x. 127–8.   [3] See Pope to Pitt, 23 July 1726.

[4] In printing this letter Warton gives no clue as to its source. The original has not been traced.

desirous of any occasion of testifying my regard for you, and particularly of acknowledging the pleasure your Version of Vida's Poetick[1] had afforded me. I had it not indeed from your bookseller, but read it with eagerness, and think it both a correct and spirited translation. I am pleased to have been (as you tell me) the occasion of your undertaking that work: that is some sort of merit; and, if I have any in me, it really consists in an earnest desire to promote and produce, as far as I can, that of others. But as to my being the publisher, or any way concerned in reviewing or recommending of Lintot's Miscellany, it is what I never did in my life, though he (like the rest of his tribe) makes a very free use of my name. He has often reprinted my things, and so scurvily, that, finding he was doing so again, I corrected the sheets as far as they went, of my own only. And, being told by him that he had two or three copies of yours, (which you also had formerly sent me (as he said) through his hands), I obliged him to write for your consent, before he made use of them. This was all: your second book[2] he has just now delivered to me, the inscription of which to myself I will take care he shall leave out; and either return the rest of your verses to him, or not, as you shall like best.

I am obliged to you, Sir, for expressing a much higher opinion of me than I know I deserve: the freedom with which you write is yet what obliges and pleases me more; and it is with sincerity that I say, I would rather be thought by every ingenious man in the world, his servant, than his rival. | I am, etc.

*BOLINGBROKE to THE THREE YAHOOS OF TWICKENHAM[3]　　　23 *July* 1726

Add. 4805

Jonathan, Alexander, John, most excellent Triumvirs of Parnassus, tho' you are probably very indifferent where I am, or what I am doing, yet I resolve to beleive the contrary. I perswade myself that you have sent att least fifteen times within this fortnight at Dawley farm, and that you are extreamly mortify'd att my long Silence. to relieve you therefore from this great anxiety of mind, I can do no less than write a few lines to you, and I please myself beforehand with the vast pleasure which this Epistle must needs give you. that I may add to this pleasure, & give you further proofs of my beneficent temper, I will likewise

---

[1] Published in 1725.

[2] Presumably the *Poems and Translations*, published in Feb. 1727, and now sent (?) to Pope in sheets. Possibly the verses 'To Mr. Pope on his Translation of Homer's Iliad' (which mention also the work on the *Odyssey*), printed on pp. 172–6, were intended as an 'inscription' to Pope. They remind one of Dr. Johnson's advice to Mrs. Hannah More on economy in flattery.

[3] Printed hitherto only in editions of Swift's correspondence.

inform you that I shall be in your neighbourhood again by the end of next week, by which time I hope that Jonathan's imagination of business will be succeeded by some imagination more becoming a Professour of that divine Science, La Bagatelle. Adieu Jonathan, Alexander, John. mirth be with you. From the Banks of the Severne July the 23d 1726.

Address: To the three Yahoos of | Twittenham

Endorsement [Swift's hand]: Ld Bolingbroke | 1726 July 23 [and again] Ld Bolingb.

†SWIFT *to* POPE[1]   4 [August] 1726
1740

London, May 4, 1726.

I had rather live in forty Islands than under the frequent disquiets of hearing you are out of order. I always apprehend it most after a great dinner; for the least Transgression of yours, if it be only two bits and one sup more than your stint, is a great debauch; for which you certainly pay more than those sots who are carry'd dead drunk to bed. My Lord Peterborow spoiled every body's dinner, but especially mine, with telling us that you were detained by sickness. Pray let me have three lines under any hand or pothook that will give me a better account of your health; which concerns me more than others, because I love and esteem you for reasons that most others have little to do with, and would be the same although you had never touched a pen, further than with writing to me.

I am gathering up my luggage, and preparing for my journey: I will endeavour to think of you as little as I can, and when I write to you, I will strive not to think of you; this I intend in return to your kindness; and further, I know no body has dealt with me so cruelly as you, the consequences of which usage I fear will last as long as my life, for so long shall I be (in spite of my heart) entirely Yours.

FENTON *to* BROOME   7 *August* 1726

Elwin–Courthope, viii. 121

Easthampstead Park, Aug. 7, 1726.

Dear Mr. Broome,—Two or three days since, and not sooner, I was favoured with yours of the 25th of July, which had been kept at Mr. Tonson's till he had an opportunity of sending it by a packet. For the future pray direct for me at this place, near Ockingham in Berkshire, by Ockingham bag.

---

[1] This letter was printed by Pope, 1740–2, always under the date of 4 May; but since Swift is preparing for his departure from England, the date must be an error. Probably in transcribing Swift's writing of *Aug.* the three letters became *May*.

I had always so ill an opinion of your post-scribing to the Odyssey that I was not surprised with anything in it but the mention of my own name, which heartily vexes me, and is, I think, a license that deserves a worse epithet than I have it in my nature to give it.[1] I was in a pretty confusion at Cambridge when Dr. Newcome told me of it after I had retired to the extremest brink of veracity to decline the suspicion of being concerned in the undertaking. But let it go.

I find you are come to a resolution about printing your Miscellany, and though the present age does not seem to have a keen appetite for poetry, I question not but they will be kindly received, and much better by posterity. But what magic does that scoundrel Lintot carry about him to engage you to be his chap?—a wretch that uses everybody's character with contempt, and not above six weeks since in conversation with ***.[2] An excellent blade to converse with when it is really a misfortune to be known to Curll or him barely by sight. I heartily wish you do not find cause to repent it in vain; for St. Chrysostom says— oh, that Bernard should ever bring St. Chrysostom into one's head— repentance avails us for nothing else but sin. I bear no malice to the fellow, and had not mentioned him on this occasion but to convince you that for your own sake it will not be at all proper for me to revise your poems for such a ———,[3] to put what construction he pleases upon it. *And have you not too much reason to be sensible that a reviser may purloin more merit from an author than he should honestly claim?*[4] As to the verses which you intend to inscribe to me, all the opinion I can form about them is that you are not content to be reckoned a top-writer in this age, but are resolved to rival the greatest wit in the last, by showing that you can write as well as he upon Nothing.[5] As you intend them for a monument, pray let them be an image of our friendship—plain and unaffected,—and do not mistake me for a man that either deserves or desires the name of a poet, but who is with true esteem and sincerity your faithfully affectionate humble servant.

[1] Strictly speaking Broome did not 'post-scribe': the Postscript is by Pope; but at the end of the last note to the *Odyssey* Broome did assume responsibility for the misstatements concerning the collaboration. Fenton clearly blames Pope rather than Broome for the mention of his name. Elwin (viii. 92 n.) quotes from a copy of the Proposals, preserved perhaps among the Broome papers that he used, a passage concerning the collaborators, in which Pope says, 'One of them enjoins me to conceal his name; the other is the Rev. Mr. Broome...' Not until the publication in June 1726 of the last volumes did Fenton's connexion become known—to his evident embarrassment.

[2] A line at the bottom of the sheet is here torn away.—Elwin.

[3] The dash is in the original.—Elwin. (Evidently words failed Fenton.)

[4] Pope is intended: he was the reviser of Broome's translation, and claimed (as his own) more books of the *Odyssey* than he had translated.

[5] Broome's *Poems* (1727 and thereafter) contained 'An Epistle to my Friend Mr. Elijah Fenton, 1726'. Fenton jokes about the lines 'Upon Nothing' by 'the greatest wit of the last' age, the Earl of Rochester.

†POPE *to* HUGH BETHEL   9 *August* 1726
1737
                                                     Aug. 9. 1726.

I never am unmindful of those I think so well of as your self; their
number is not so great as to confound one's memory. Nor ought you
to decline writing to me, upon an imagination that I am much employ'd by other people. For tho' my house is like the house of a
Patriarch of old, standing by the highway side and receiving all
travellers,¹ nevertheless I seldom go to bed without the reflection, that
one's chief business is to be really at home: and I agree with you in
your opinion of company, amusements, and all the silly things which
mankind wou'd fain make pleasures of, when in truth they are labour
and sorrow.

I condole with you on the death of your Relation, the E. of C.² as
on the fate of a mortal man: Esteem I never had for him, but concern
and humanity I had: the latter was due to the infirmity of his last
period, tho' the former was not due to the triumphant and vain part
of his course. He certainly knew himself best at last, and knew best
the little value of others, whose neglect of him whom they so grossly
follow'd and flatter'd in the former scene of his life, shew'd them as
worthless as they cou'd imagine him to be, were he all that his worst
enemies believ'd of him. For my own part, I am sorry for his death,
and wish he had lived long enough to see so much of the faithlessness
of the world, as to have been above the mad ambition of governing
such wretches as he must have found it to be compos'd of.

Tho' you cou'd have no great value for this Great Man, yet
acquaintance itself, the custom of seeing the face, or entring under the
roof, of one that walks along with us in the common way of the world,
is enough to create a wish at least for his being above ground, and a
degree of uneasiness at his removal. 'Tis the loss of an object familiar
to us: I should hardly care to have an old post pull'd up, that I remember'd ever since I was a child. And add to this the reflection (in
the case of such as were not the best of their Species) what their condition in another life may be, it is yet a more important motive for our
concern and compassion. To say the truth, either in the case of death
or life, almost every body and every thing is a cause or object for
humanity, even prosperity itself, and health itself, so many weak pitiful
incidentals attend on them.

I am sorry any relation of yours is ill, whoever it be, for you don't

---

¹ During this summer Pope kept open house for Swift's friends. See Pope to Caryll
[June–July 1726] for similar phrasing.
² The first Earl of Cadogan died 17 July 1726. He was a cousin of Bethel's mother.
Pope's account of him here is, naturally, more kindly than the line (89) in his Epistle to
Lord Bathurst. Cadogan's attitude towards Atterbury probably prejudiced Pope.

name the person. But I conclude it is one of those to whose houses you tell me you are going, for I know no invitation with you is so strong as when any one is in distress, or in want of your assistance: The strongest proof in the world of this, was your attendance on the late Earl.

I have been very melancholy for the loss of Mr. Blount.[1] Whoever has any portion of good nature will suffer on these occasions, but a good mind rewards its own sufferings. I hope to trouble you as little as possible, if it be my fate to go before you. I am of old Ennius his mind, *Nemo me decoret lachrymis*[2]—I am but a *Lodger* here: this is not an abiding City. I am only to stay out my lease, for what has Perpetuity and mortal man to do with each other? But I could be glad you would take up with an Inn at Twitenham, as long as I am Host of it: if not, I would take up freely with any Inn of yours.—Adieu, dear Sir: Let us while away this life; and (if we can) meet in another.

POPE *to* THE EARL OF OXFORD   [15 *August* 1726]

Longleat Portland Papers, xii

[Aug: 15. 1726][3]

My Lord,—I send the History[4] by the Servant, in which I am sure you will take no small delight. I beg your Lordship not to return it till I come for it myself, tho I'm impatient to read it again. Unless you will be so good one day this fine season to bring it.

Believe me My Lord, with | the truest Esteem & regard | Your Lordships most | faithfull humble | Servant | A. Pope

Address: To the Rt. Hon. the | Earl of Oxford

†POPE *to* SWIFT   22 *August* 1726

1740

Aug. 22. 1726.

Many a short sigh you cost me the day I left you, and many more you will cost me, till the day you return. I really walk'd about like a man banish'd, and when I came home, found it no home. 'Tis a sensation like that of a limb lopp'd off, one is trying every minute unawares to use it, and finds it is not. I may say you have used me more cruelly than you have done any other man; you have made it more impossible for me to live at ease without you: Habitude itself would

---

[1] Edward Blount of Blagden died 17 July 1726.
[2] In Cicero, *Tusculan Disputations*, I. xv. 34 (a favourite tag.).
[3] The date is written in by Lord Oxford.
[4] Swift's *History of the Four Last Years of the Queen*, which was passed about in MS. during this summer and later. It was first printed in 1758.

have done that, if I had less friendship in my nature than I have. Besides my natural memory of you, you have made a local one, which presents you to me in every place I frequent: I shall never more think of Lord Cobham's, the woods of Ciceter, or the pleasing prospect of Byberry,[1] but your Idea must be join'd with 'em; nor see one seat in my own garden, or one room in my own house, without a Phantome of you, sitting or walking before me. I travell'd with you to Chester, I felt the extream heat of the weather, the inns, the roads, the confinement and closeness of the uneasy coach, and wish'd a hundred times I had either a Deanery or a horse in my gift. In real truth, I have felt my soul peevish ever since with all about me, from a warm uneasy desire after you. I am gone out of myself to no purpose, and cannot catch you. *Inhiat in pedes*[2] was not more properly apply'd to a poor dog after a hare, than to me with regard to your departure. I wish I could think no more of it, but lye down and sleep till we meet again, and let that day (how far soever off it be) be the morrow. Since I cannot, may it be my amends that every thing you wish may attend you where you are, and that you may find every friend you have there in the state you wish him or her; so that your visit to us may have no other effect, than the progress of a rich man to a remote estate, which he finds greater than he expected; which knowledge only serves to make him live happier where he is, with no disagreeable prospect if ever he should chuse to remove. May this be your state till it become what I wish. But indeed I cannot express the warmth, with which I wish you all things, and myself you. Indeed you are engraved elsewhere than on the Cups you sent me, (with so kind an inscription) and I might throw them into the Thames without injury to the giver. I am not pleas'd with them, but take them very kindly too: And had I suspected any such usage from you, I should have enjoyed your company less than I really did, for at this rate I may say

Nec tecum possum vivere, nec sine te.

I will bring you over just such another present, when I go to the Deanery of St. Patrick's; which I promise you to do, if ever I am enabled to return your kindness. *Donarem Pateras,*[3] &c. Till then I'll drink (or Gay shall drink) daily healths to you, and I'll add to your inscription the old Roman Vow for years to come, VOTIS X.

---

[1] Apparently a visit to this Cotswold village was very memorable to Pope. While Pope was in September unable to use his hand in writing, he and his friends devised a 'Cheddar' letter to Swift, which included prose, verse, sketches, and maps. Swift speaks of the map of Bibury sent when he replied to the Cheddar letter on 15 Oct. 1726.

[2] Translated as 'Devours the scent' in 1741 Dab; as 'Gaping after his Game' in 1741 Lc (Curll).

[3] Horace, *Carmina*, IV. 8. 1. Translated in 1741 Dab as 'I would make you a present of Dishes.' Curll does not translate here.

VOTIS XX. My Mother's age gives me authority to hope it for yours.

[1]All those of your friends whom I have seen are constant in their remembrance and good wishes to you. Only the Doctor I have never been able to see since. Poor Congreve is desperately ill of the gout. Lord Bolingbroke bids me again tell you, he will take as a letter to himself, and reply to, every one that you shall write to Gay or me; so that we hope you will not be deterr'd from writing to some of us, by an imagination that all will expect it. | Yours, &c.

POPE *to* BROOME   23 *August* 1726

Elwin–Courthope, viii. 124

Aug. 23, 1726.

To begin with business,—the note of 100*l*. I wish you had rather acquainted me you wanted it, than put it into another person's hands.[2] I received yours but this day, having been three days from home, as I often am, you know, so that on so short a warning it might naturally enough have been difficult to assign a prompt payment on sight. As to sending Mr. Jervas for it, I should have been very sorry, because we have no accounts together, and I no right to charge or trouble him with my proper debts. But you may recollect the only reason of my giving you my note, instead of money, at all, was that a great part of my subscriptions would not immediately be paid in, as in fact some hundred pounds are yet unpaid; and as soon as I received more, I should have evened with you, without a demand. However, I have credit with Mr. Mead, the goldsmith, in Fleet Street, upon whom I will draw the hundred pounds whenever your agent brings my own note hither to Twitnam, or leaves it with Mr. Mead for that end,— and so all accounts between us will be at an end as soon as you please.

For your Miscellany, I am ready to look over it when you send it, and shall deal with you sincerely. I am glad you have commemorated Mr. Fenton.[3] No man living better deserves the character of an honest and ingenious man; no one I would sooner depend upon for all the parts of a good writer and good friend—free from the vanities and weaknesses of both; whose honour and trust, I dare say, are as sacred as his writings are blameless in morality, and whose life and conduct are as correct as they. I would have you methinks correct the proofs of

---

[1] This last paragraph, found in the clandestine volume and in Faulkner's octavo of 1741, was omitted by Pope from the folios and quartos of that year and from his later editions.

[2] In *The Dunciad* (1729), iii. 328 n., Pope announced that he had 'gratified' Broome with 'a present of all those books for which his own interest could procure him Subscribers, to the value of *One hundred*' pounds in addition to the £500 paid for translating. Here Broome is collecting £100.

[3] By addressing an Epistle to him—to be printed in Broome's *Poems*.

your poems yourself, nothing being easier than to have them by post: not but that either Fenton or I will do it, if you like it so better.

If you will send any correspondent you have for the two books of Homer, they shall be left directed for you at Mr. Jervas's. I did not send them before, knowing you corresponded with Lintot, who could at any time, on your order, have sent them, as he delivers many. I wish yourself and boy all health, and all your wishes. I have no more room. Yours.

BROOME *to* FENTON   26 *August* 1726

Elwin–Courthope, viii. 125

Aug. 26, 1726.

Dear Fenton,—I do not at all blame your refusal to revise my poems. I have taken so much care of them that if they be dull they will be correctly dull. I well know if they be saved from condemnation it must be by their own merit. As a protestant poet I expect no salvation from your extraordinary works of supererogation, and as you hint I can fully affirm that Pope has revised away some reputation due to me and you in regard to Homer. Pray in the name of goodness what does he mean in the postscript to the Odyssey by affirming some parts of the tenth and fifteenth books are not by his hand?[1] I declare I saw them daily as he translated daily when I was at Twickenham. The secret is, some parts of those books are a little heavy, and he is resolved as he robbed us of seven of our books to do us a greater injury by repaying us in base coin. His dulness is bright enough to be our glory. He is king of Parnassus, and claims what is good in our translation by pre-rogative royal. The mines of gold and silver belong to the monarch, as privileges of his supremacy, but coarser metals are left for the use of the owner of the soil. But in the meantime where is his veracity? One time or other the truth shall be publicly known. Till then I give him leave to shine like a candle in the dark, which is lighted up to its own diminution, and shines only to go out in a stink.

In a short time I will send you the verses I promised to inscribe to your name.[2] I intend them as a memorial of the friendship I bear you, and the uninterrupted amity that has subsisted so many years. May this copy at least live to posterity.

[1] Broome was mistaken here. Pope is making a quiet bow to an unannounced helper, Henry Layng, a young graduate of Oxford and protégé of Lord Bathurst. Elwin states (viii. 125) that the first 156 lines of Book X and the first 320 of Book XV are lacking in the Homer MSS. now in the British Museum, and supposedly these are the parts Layng translated. See the note on this matter by Professor A. Warren, *RES*, viii (1932), 77–82. Broome visited Twickenham in the spring of 1724, but hardly stayed long enough to justify his account of seeing much daily translation.

[2] The Epistle to Fenton, printed in Broome's *Poems* (1727).

My Miscellany advances apace. When I cast my eye over these dear offsprings of my brains I look upon the book as a kind of parish register, in which both those who live and those who die are entered promiscuously. If the critics rail at them I am resolved not to believe one word they say. Nature has furnished us poetasters with a secret mental glass that beautifies every line. I have one ready against the publication. You tell me you doubt not but my poetry will be well received by posterity. What! does a dead muse, like a dead saint, work more miracles in the grave than when living? Besides, is it not a mighty comfort to hope for a reversion of fame when I am insensible of it? It is just such a comfort as to expect a sprig of rosemary will be thrown into my coffin when I cannot enjoy its sweetness. But to be serious, I will take care that nothing obscene or ill-natured escape me. The wittiest poetry in the world loses all value if it raises an unchaste thought in a virtuous heart, or a pain in a deserving one. Let all such poetry be banished the British as well as the Platonic commonwealth. Poetry is but ingenious trifling; let us not make it criminal and scandalous. Dear Fenton, yours eternally.

POPE to MRS. CÆSAR[1]   28 *August* [1726?]
Rousham

Twitnam Augst 28th

Madam,—Besides the pleasure of telling you & Mr Cæsar how truly I am your Servant, I have an occasion to trouble you with an affair of which you know more than myself, as I believe. I received the inclosed from a Lady whom I suppose to be of your acquaintance. I beg you to inform her (since I see by the date, she lives at Hertford) that I have sent the 3 books as she requird, to Wyat the Book seller's, and I have added the 2 last also, which I desire her acceptance of. I am entirely a Stranger to the circumstances she mentions, but sincerely concern'd for the misfortune of such a change to any person; If it be, as she says, that to make the second payment were an Imprudence *in her condition*, I fear the having made the first may *now* be so too; and You will oblige me if you can find any Decent way of returning those three guineas, which I will righteously repay you.[2] I am troubled at such an instance of Want as this seems to be, in one who has (probably) the honour to be known to You, & consequently must be a Concern to you also. Believe me, Madam, with the sincerest regard & best wishes

[1] A contemporary transcript of this letter exists among the MSS. in Trinity College, Dublin.

[2] The episode here presented should be weighed when critics are inclined to accuse Pope of being parsimonious about the *Odyssey*.

to you all (not forgetting Mrs Madan) | Your faithful obliged Servant A. Pope.

Address: To [1]*Mrs Cæsar, at Bening-|ton near | Hertford
Frank: Oxford
Postmark: AV/28

POPE *to* CARYLL   30 *August* [1726]

Add. 28618

I did not intend to have challenged your kind offer of venison till you were the bearer of it yourself in your way to Essex; but I have hoped for you in vain this month; and yesterday meeting Dr Cockbourne, he told me you should not be this way till towards Michaelmas. I will therefore be so free as to desire (if it suit with your conveniency, and if this arrive at you time enough) to send me some directed to Mr Gay's lodgings in Whitehall, over the Gate, by Friday night; for I am to have some very particular company on Saturday, to whom I would always help to make myself welcome. But I apprehend the warning I give is too sudden and short. If so, there is no help for it, and the next convenient day will serve directed to Mr Jervas's in Cleveland Court.

I congratulate you on what is done in relation to Lord Seafort,[2] as I have a true concern for any related to your family. Sir Harry Bedingfield is but just gone to France and his lady is in town, so that if you would make a stronger compliment to her,[3] you may now do it here. I must insist upon your making as long a stay as you possibly can with me, whenever you come. A few hours will not serve, much less a few hours in the hurry of a traveller, to recollect half of the very heads we have to talk upon. I am truly sorry for our valuable friend Mr Blount,[4] of whose many virtues we had an experience of so many years. As for Mr Pulteney,[5] he is recovered and now in my neighbourhood. I will make him know the concern you expressed for him this very day; for I have not yet congratulated him.

I am greatly beholden to you for your good wishes (as to a patriarch) but yet more for your good opinion of my having any such title to 'em.

---

[1] The asterisk here is a sly repetition of the compliment paid when the lady's name was starred among the subscribers to the *Odyssey*.

[2] William, 5th Earl of Seaforth, brother of Lady Mary Caryll, had supported the Pretender in 1715, and had been attainted thereafter. Dissatisfied with his treatment by the Pretender in France (where Seaforth lived), he had recently (June 1726) secured a partial pardon.

[3] Lady Bedingfield was the sister of Pope's friend the Earl of Burlington.

[4] Edward Blount died in July of this year.

[5] Lady Hervey (*Suffolk Correspondence*, i. 205) was happy over the recovery 'of our common friend dear Mr. Pulteney' as early as 10 Aug. Pulteney became less dear to the Herveys presently! He lived at times in Sussex, and even leased Ladyholt. Ashley-on-Thames was another place of residence.

I really long to see a true patriarch, *the lappet of whose shoe I am not worthy to loose,* and to observe once before I die, the increase of all your herds, flocks, and plantations, &c., at Lady holt. Believe me with all respect | Dear sir | yours, and all yours. | A: P:

Augst 30th | Tuesday.

†SWIFT *to* POPE   [*August* 1726]
1740

¹Oct. 30, 1727

The first letter I writ after my landing was to Mr. Gay, but it would have been wiser to direct it to Tonson or Lintot, to whom I believe his lodgings are better known than to the runners of the Post office. In that Letter you will find what a quick change I made in seven days from London to the Deanery, thro' many nations and languages unknown to the civilized world. And I have often reflected in how few hours, with a swift horse or a strong gale, a man may come among a people as unknown to him as the Antipodes. If I did not know you more by your conversation and kindness than by your letter, I might be base enough to suspect, that in point of friendship you acted like some Philosopher who writ much better upon Virtue than they practiced it. In answer, I can only swear that you have taught me to dream, which I had not done in twelve years further than by inexpressible nonsense; but now I can every night distinctly see Twitenham, and the Grotto, and Dawley, and Mrs. B.² and many other et cetera's, and it is but three nights since I beat Mrs. Pope. I must needs confess, that the pleasure I take in thinking on you is very much lessened by the pain I am in about your health: You pay dearly for the great talents God hath given you; and for the consequences of them in the esteem and distinction you receive from mankind, unless you can provide a tolerable stock of health; in which pursuit I cannot much commend your conduct, but rather entreat you would mend it by following the advice of my Lord Bolingbroke and your other Physicians. When you talk'd of Cups and Impressions, it came into my head to imitate you in quoting scripture, not to your advantage; I mean what was said to David by one of his brothers: "I knew thy pride and the naughtiness³ of thy heart;" so I remember it grieved your soul to see me pay a penny more than my club at an inn, when you had maintained me three months at bed and board; for which if I had dealt with you in

---

¹ The Dublin editions (1741 Dab) have the superscription, 'Dublin, Oct. 30, 1727,' which Pope had assigned the letter in the 1740 printing. That date is obviously impossible. Swift's return in 1727 was slow, not quick; and his gift of cups dates in 1726. Mist's *Weekly Journal*, 3 Sept. 1726, gives an account of his welcome to Dublin under date of 25 Aug. 1726.

² Dawley, and Mrs. B. and] Dawley, and many *1741 Labc*; *1742 Lbc, Da.* Mrs. B[lount], that is, is not mentioned in any London texts of this letter.

³ 1 Sam. xvii. 28. The Dublin editions of 1741 print *haughtiness* for *naughtiness*.

the Smithfield way it would have cost me a hundred pounds, for I live worse here upon more. Did you ever consider that I am for life almost twice as rich as you, and pay no rent, and drink French wine twice as cheap as you do Port, and have neither coach, chair, nor mother? As to the world, I think you ought to say to it with St. Paul, *if we have sown unto you spiritual things, is it a great thing if we shall reap your carnal things?*[1] this is more proper still if you consider the French word *spiritual*, in which sense the world ought to pay you better than they do. If you made me a present of a thousand pound, I would not allow my self to be in your debt; and if I made you a present of two, I would not allow my self to be out of it. But I have not half your pride: witness what Mr. Gay says in his letter, that I was censured for begging Presents, tho' I limited them to ten shillings⌐, and tho' I forgave Sir R— W— a thousand pound, *multa gemens*⌐.[2] I see no reason, (at least my friendship and vanity see none) why you should not give me a visit, when you shall happen to be disengaged: I will send a person to Chester to take care of you, and you shall be used by the best folks we have here, as well as civility and good nature can contrive; I believe local motion will be no ill physick, and I will have your coming inscribed on my Tomb, and recorded in never-dying verse.

I thank Mrs. Pope for her prayers, but I know the mystery. A person of my acquaintance who used to correspond with the last great Duke of Tuscany,[3] shewing one of the Duke's letters to a friend, and professing great sense of his Highnesses friendship, read this passage out of the letters, *I would give one of my fingers to procure your real good.* The person to whom this was read, and who knew the Duke well, said, the meaning of *real good* was only that the other might turn a good Catholick: pray ask Mrs. Pope whether this story is applicable to her and me? I pray God bless her, for I am sure she is a good christian, and (which is almost as rare) a good Woman. | Adieu.

---

†POPE *to* SWIFT   3 *September* 1726

1740

                                         Sept. 3, 1726.

Yours to Mr. Gay gave me greater satisfaction than that to me (tho' that gave me a great deal) for to hear you were safe at your journey's

---

[1] 1 Cor. ix. 11. *Spirituel* of course means witty.

[2] Omitted in the London editions except the reissue of 1740 (i.e. 1742 La). On 8 July 1726 Swift had written Sheridan, 'I never asked for my thousand pounds . . . though I mentioned it to the Princess the last time I saw her; but I bid her tell Walpole, I scorned to ask him for it.' Bolingbroke in his brief moment of power before the death of Queen Anne had ordered payment to Swift of £1,000 to cover the expenses of settling into his deanery. Upon the death of the Queen the new government refused to honour the order.

[3] This may have been Sir Andrew Fountaine, who was intimate with the Grand Duke of Tuscany, and was formerly among the familiar companions of Swift.—Elwin.

end, exceeds the account of your fatigues while in the way to it: otherwise believe me, every tittle of each is important to me, which sets any one thing before my eyes that happens to you. I writ you a long letter, which I guess reach'd you the day after your arrival; since then I had a conference with Sir ———[1] who exprest his desire of having seen you again before you left us: He said he observed a willingness in you to live among us; which I did not deny; but at the same time told him, you had no such design in your coming this time, which was meerly to see a few of those you loved: but that indeed all those wished it, and particularly Lord Peterborow and myself, who wish'd you lov'd Ireland less, had you any reason to love England more. I said nothing but what I think wou'd induce any man to be as fond of you as I, plain Truth, (did they know either it, or you.) I can't help thinking, (when I consider the whole, short List of our friends) that none of 'em except you and I are qualify'd for the Mountains of Wales. The Dr. goes to Cards, Gay to Court; one loses money, one loses his time. Another of our friends labours to be unambitious, but he labours in an unwilling soil. One Lady you like has too much of France to be fit for Wales: Another is too much a subject to Princes and Potentates, to relish that wild Taste of liberty and poverty. Mr. Congreve is too sick to bear a thin air; and she[2] that leads him too rich to enjoy any thing. Lord Peterborow can go to any climate, but never stay in any. Lord Bathurst is too great an husbandman to like barren hills, except they are his own to improve. Mr. Bethel indeed is too good and too honest to live in the world, but yet 'tis fit, for its example, he should. We are left to ourselves in my opinion, and may live where we please, in Wales, Dublin, or Bermudas: And for me, I assure you I love the world so well, and it loves me so well, that I care not in what part of it I pass the rest of my days. I see no sunshine but in the face of a friend.

I had a glympse of a letter of yours lately, by which I find you are (like the vulgar) apter to think well of people out of power, than of people in power; perhaps 'tis a mistake, but however there's something in it generous. Mr. **[3] takes it extreme kindly, I can perceive, and he has a great mind to thank you for that good opinion, for which I believe he is only to thank his ill fortune: for if I am not in an error, he would rather be in power, than out.

To shew you how fit I am to live in the mountains, I will with great truth apply to myself an old sentence. "Those that are in, may abide in; and those that are out, may abide out: yet to me, those that

---

[1] Curll (1741 Lc) fills this blank with the name of Sir W. Wyndham, but obviously Walpole is intended.
[2] Henrietta, Dutchess of Marlborough jun.—Curll (1741 Lc).   [3] Wm. Pulteney.

are in shall be as those that are out, and those that are out shall be as those that are in."[1]

I am indifferent as to all those matters, but I miss you as much as I did the first day, when (with a short sigh) I parted. Wherever you are, (or on the mountains of Wales, or on the coast of Dublin,

> ——Tu mihi, magni superas dum saxa Timavi,
> Sive oram Illyrici legis æquoris——)[2]

I am, and ever shall be Yours, &c.[3]

POPE *to* BROOME   5 *September* 1726

Elwin–Courthope, viii. 128

Sept. 5, 1726.

I had some reason to be displeased at your publishing my note to you, as I may call it, in so many hands, and having actually first given it to a lord[4] I am a stranger to, and he to another, an agent—whether belonging to him or not I know not—before you so much as acquainted me with your design to demand the immediate payment. The person, whoever he was, was in so much haste that he went to Mr. Mead's a day before I could write him any order to pay it, he happening to be one day out of town, after which he came to my house, without any warning—which a post letter might have given me—to confine myself at home to wait on him. My mother told him I should return at night, but he has neither called here since, nor at Mr. Mead's, nor writ, nor left any direction at either place where he may be sent to. I conclude from hence, you have not been paid the money by Lord Cornwallis beforehand, or by this agent, so that it is you that trust them, not they you, which unless you know your man very well, might be not quite so safe, as if you had still trusted me who gave it. Be it as it will, that is not my business. I am discharged equally to whomsoever it is paid by your order, but I own I am vexed at its being managed by you in so precipitate a manner that I may seem deficient to two persons at least,

---

[1] Curll adds a note to this:

> 'Tis all one to *me*; or to *me* 'tis all one,
> Who is *in*, or who's *out*, or whoe'er is *undone*.

[2] Virgil, *Eclogues*, viii. 6–7. Translated in the Dublin editions but not in Curll's:

> Whether *Timavus* or the *Illyrian* Coast,
> Whatever Land or Sea thy Presence boast.—Dryden.

[3] Curll in a footnote adds a rhymed subscription (his own?):

> Believe me, *Swift*, with *Wish* most fervent,
> To be your most obedient *Servant*. (1741 Lc)

[4] Probably Lord Cornwallis. Pope seems justifiably irritated at Broome's lack of warning that he was drawing upon Pope for £100. Broome, on the other hand, evidently was right in thinking it time he was paid for his heavy work on the *Odyssey*.

if not to ten, supposing the man into whose hands you have committed my note make it a complaint to others that he has been twice to receive it to no purpose. If he be yet in town, you ought to acquaint him, in my justification, how this came about, and to tell him that if he will give himself the trouble to call once more at Mr. Mead's, or to leave word there where he may be found, the money shall be paid on delivery of my note, with his receipt of so much for your use. If he be gone out of town, as I have already taken in the money at some loss to accommodate you so instantly, and it lies ready, I think I cannot do better with part of it than pay what I yet owe to Mr. Fenton, whose occasions I fear may be as pressing, though he has never named it to me, nor possibly ever would till I sent it him, which without instigation I should soon have done to both of you. Your speedy orders in this are necessary, that I may do the one or the other. In your case it will be sufficient for you to write to the agent only, that you and I may have no more of this between us, who, in my opinion, ought to correspond rather on more polite subjects. *Let not such things,* as the apostle saith, *be so much as named amongst ye.*[1]

In earnest, dear Broome, you were a little inconsiderate, but be assured I shall not quarrel with you for anything you cannot help. Something is due from each of us to the other as friends,—I hope a great deal,—for on my side I have done my best to prove myself so, and I assure you I am above imagining the contrary of you. Suspicion is not of my nature, wherever a *trust* of any kind is *deserved* as well as *bestowed.* So you may depend upon me as, very sincerely ever, your affectionate faithful friend and servant.

FENTON *to* BROOME   7 *September* 1726

Elwin–Courthope, viii. 130

Sept. 7, 1726.

Dear Mr. Broome,—Since I was favoured with your last I have had a gentle return of the gout, at which time I am very little disposed to correspond with my best friends, and its visiting me so early makes me apprehensive that I shall have its company the greatest part of the next winter. I cannot believe that verse had ever the power to charm away diseases. If it ever had I might have expected a cure from the epistle you have addressed to me, for which I return you thanks, and am only sorry that it is too much above the subject, but it being *non tam de me quam supra me scripta,* I have the greater liberty to criticise it. It is indeed a very fine one, but I think in some places you may touch it over to advantage. Whilst I am writing this I have company with me,

---

[1] The apostle (Ephes. v. 3), as Elwin remarked appropriately, said this of other matters than debts due to a creditor.

and cannot be so particular as I would be. At present I remember that in reading it I did not like Homeric; it has a burlesque sound. "Hyde and Plato *lay*,"—should it not be in the present tense? I should like the simile of Ulysses' winds better if you had not had one out of the same poem not long before.[1] The wags may say that you do it to advertise the work which you had a share in. Perhaps there is too much delicacy in this objection, but it prevailed with me to strike out of my dedication to Waller[2] an allusion that would have been very *à-propos*. I want much to see you in town that we may read over the epistle and my dedication together. I hope you intend to fill up the vacancy where a character of eloquence is intended with Sir T. Hanmer's name.[3] Whatever name is intended I can never consent to have it begin with a W.[4] I beg that in this particular you will not fail to oblige me.

I have read the collection of letters you mentioned,[5] and was delighted with nothing more than that air of sincerity, those professions of esteem and respect, and that deference paid to his friend's judgment in poetry which I have sometimes seen expressed to others, and I doubt not with the same cordial affection. If they are read in that light they will be very entertaining and useful in the present age, but, in the next, Cicero, Pliny, and Voiture may regain their reputation.

On the change of weather Lady Judith begins to talk of London, but I believe it will be the middle of October before we go. I shall be pretty much taken up then with scribbling some notes for Waller. However I will spare time if possibly I can to revise your imitations of Milton. What I have seen of yours in the Miscellany need no correction. Too much handling of verses is apt to wear off the natural gloss, as I could give many instances in Garth and Prior. In your next inform me when you shall be in town, and when you design to put your poems to the press. My humble services as usual conclude in haste with sincere sincerity, from your affectionate humble servant.

Mr. Trumbull presents his service to you.

[1] In revising his Epistle to Fenton in the light of these strictures Broome kept *Homeric* (a new word in his day), which obviously advertised their connexion with the *Odyssey*—which Fenton had no desire to display.

[2] The Dedication to his Waller (1729) was to Lady Margaret Harley. See Pope to Lord Oxford, 3 Apr. 1726.

[3] Broome preferred Compton, then Speaker of the House of Commons, since Hanmer had apparently been critical of Broome (see Pope to Broome, 28 Dec. 1723) and was not at all a close friend.

[4] Broome did not mention Walpole in the questioned passage, but elsewhere in the Epistle gave him praise that may not have pleased Fenton.

[5] Curll's *Miscellanea*, vol. i, had appeared late in July 1726, though dated on the title-page 1727. It contained Pope's letters to Cromwell, upon which Fenton is here pleased to be ironical.

VOLTAIRE *to* POPE[1]   [*September* 1726]

1769 (Ruffhead, pp. 212–13)

Sir,—I hear this moment of your sad adventure. That water you fell
in, was not Hippocrene's water, otherwise it would have respected
you. Indeed I am concerned beyond expression for the danger you have
been in, and more for your wounds. Is it possible that those fingers
which have written the Rape of the Lock, and the Criticism, which
have dressed Homer so becomingly in an English coat, should have
been so barbarously treated. Let the hand of Dennis, or of your poetasters be cut off. Yours is sacred. I hope, Sir, you are now perfectly
recovered, really your accident concerns me as much as all the disasters
of a master ought to affect his scholar, I am sincerely, Sir, with the
admiration which you deserve, | Your most humble servant, | Voltaire.

In my Lord Bolingbroke's house, | Friday at noon.

GAY *to* SWIFT   16 *September* 1726

Add. 4805

Since I wrote last I have been always upon the ramble; I have been
in Oxfordshire with the Duke & Dutchess of Queensberry and at
Petersam & wheresoever they would carry me; but as they will go to
Wiltshire without me on Tuesday next for two or three months, I
believe I shall then have finish'd my travells for this Year, & shall not
go farther from London than now and then to Twickenham. I saw
Mr Pope on Sunday, who hath lately escap'd a very great danger, but
is very much wounded across his right hand; Coming home in the
dark about a week ago alone in my Lord Bolingbroke's coach from
Dawley, he was overturn'd where a bridge had been broken down near
Whitton about a mile from his own house, he was thrown into the
river with the glasses of the coach up, & was up to the knots of his
perriwig in water; The footman broke the glass to draw him out, by
which he thinks he receiv'd the cut across his hand. He was afraid he
should have lost the use of his little finger & the next to it; but the
surgeon whom he sent for last Sunday from London to examine it,

---

[1] When printed by Ruffhead—the first publication known—this letter had no date
beyond that given ('Friday') in the subscription. But in Ruffhead's context the letter is
quoted after a mention of the letter from Pope to Swift, 16 Nov. 1726; and in reprinting,
Warton (Pope's *Works*, i [1797], p. xxxvii) gave the letter that date. Unfortunately in
neither Old Style nor New was the 16th Friday, and it seems improbable from the tone of the
letter that Voltaire was writing two months after the accident.

Voltaire may be writing from Dawley or from Bolingbroke's house in Pall Mall. Friday,
9 Sept., seems a plausible date. The letter was printed, in a text verbally identical with that
of Ruffhead, in *The Athenaeum*, 4 Aug. 1860, there transcribed 'from the original in the
hands of Dr. Macro, of Norton, near Bury, in Suffolk'.

told him, that his fingers were safe, that there were two nerves cut, but no tendon. He was in very good health, & very good spirits, and the wound in a fair way of being soon heal'd. The instructions you sent me to communicate to the Doctor about the Singer, I transcrib'd from your own Letter and sent to him, for at that time he was going every other day to Windsor park[1] to visit Mr Congreve who hath been extreamly ill, but is now recovered, so that I was prevented from seeing of him by going out of town myself. I din'd & sup'd on Monday last with Lord & Lady Bolingbroke at Lord Berkeley's at Cranford & return'd to London with the Duke & Dutchess of Queensberry on Tuesday by two a Clock in the morning, you are remember'd always with great respect by all your acquaintance, and every one of them wishes for your return. The Lottery begins to be drawn on Monday next, but my week of attendance will be the first in October. I am oblig'd to follow the Gravers to make them dispatch my plates for the Fables, for without it I find they proceed but very slowly. I take your advice in this, as I wish to do in all things, and frequently revise my work in order to finish it as well as I can. Mr Pulteney takes the Letter you sent him in the kindest manner, and I believe he is, except a few excursions, fixt in town for the winter. As for the particular affair that you want to be inform'd in,[2] we are as yet wholy in the dark, but Mr Pope will follow your instructions. Mr Lancelot sent for the Spectacles you left behind you, which were deliver'd to him. Mr Jervas's sheets are sent home to him mended, finely wash'd, & neatly folded up.[3] I intend to see Mr Pope to morrow[4] or on Sunday. I have not seen Mrs Howard a great while, which you know must be a great mortification & self-denial, but in my case 'tis particularly unhappy that a man cannot contrive to be in two places at the same time; If I could, while you are there, one of them should be always Dublin, but after all, tis a Silly thing to be with a friend by halves, so that I will give up all thoughts of bringing this project to perfection, if you will contrive that we shall meet again soon. I am | Dear Sir | Your most oblig'd & affectionate | friend & Servant | J G.

London Sept. 16. 1726.

Address: To | the Revd Dr Swift Dean of | St Patricks in | Dublin. | Ireland
Postmark: 17/SE

Endorsements (2 in Swift's hand): Mr Gay. Sept 16th 1726

1 The residence of Henrietta, Duchess of Marlborough.
2 Presumably the affair of *Gulliver's Travels*, published a month later.
3 Gay had borrowed linen of Jervas while Swift lodged with him in the summer.
4 Gay is writing on a Friday. Pope's accident must have happened between Monday the 5th and Sunday the 11th. On the 5th he wrote to Broome (and could write); on the 11th Gay saw him in his damaged condition.

ARBUTHNOT *to* SWIFT   [*c. 20 September* 1726]

Add. 4805

I have been ballancing Dear sir these three days whether I should
write to you first? Laying aside the superiority of your dignity, I
thought a notification was due to me as well as to two others of my
friends. then I considered that this was done in the publick newes with
all the formalitys of Reception of a Lord Lieutenant. I reflected on
the dependancy of Ireland, but said I what if my friend should dispute
this? then I considered that Letters were allwayes introduced at first
from the civiliz'd to the Barbarous Kingdom . . . in short my affection,
& the pleasure of corresponding with my dear friend prevail'd, & since
you most disdainfully & Barbarously confined me to two lines a month,
I was resolv'd to plague you with twenty times that Number. Tho I
think it was a sort of a Compliment to be suppos'd capable of saying any
thing in two lines. The Gascoygne asked only to speak one word to
the ffrench King which the King confining him to, he Brought a
paper & said *signez* & not a word more. Your negotiation with the
singing man is in the hands of my daughter Nancy who I can assure
you, will neglect nothing that concerns you. She has wrote about it.
I beleive you did not gett receipts for your subscribers,[1] which they
ought to have had, however I shall Lodge the names with Mr Tonson
that they may call for the books. Mr Pope has been in hazard of his
life by drowning, coming Late two weeks ago from Lord Bolingbroke's in his Coach & Six a Bridge on a little River[2] being broke
down they were obligd to go through the water which was not too
high but the Coach was overturnd in it & the Glass being up, which
he could not break nor get down, he was very near drowned; for the
footman was stuck in the mud, & could hardly come in time to help
him he had that common with Horace, that it was occasioned by
the trunk of a tree but it was trunco Rhaeda illapsa neq₃ faunus
fatum dextra levabat for he was wounded in the left hand,[3] but thank
god without any danger but by the cutting of a Large vessel lost a
great dale of blood. I have been with Mrs Howard who has had a
most intolerable pain in one side of her head. I had a great dale of discourse with your freind her Royal Highness. She insisted upon your
witt & good Conversation. I told her R. Highness that was not what I
valu'd you for, but for being a sincere honest man & speaking truth

[1] Subscribers probably to Arbuthnot's *Tables of Ancient Coins*, &c., published by Tonson
in 1727. No list of subscribers is given in copies seen.
[2] The Crane, near Whitton. After the accident Pope was taken to the house of his legal
friend Nathaniel Pigott, who lived near by. For an account of the rescue see *The Harvard
Library Bulletin*, ii (1948), 121–3.
[3] We have the word of Pope, Gay, and Bolingbroke, and the evidence of Pope's use of
amanuenses to prove that it was the poet's right hand that was injured. Arbuthnot bases his
witticism on Horace's *Carmina*, II. xvii. 27–29, and makes it more apt perhaps by saying *left*.

when others were afraid to speak it. I have been for near three weeks together every day at the Duchess of Marlborough's with Mr Congreve who has been like to dye with a fever, & the gout in his stomach, but he is better, & like to do well. My Brother was like to be cast away, going to France   there was a ship lost just by him. I write this in a dull Humor, but with most sincere affection to an ungratefull man as you are that minds every body more than me [   ] My dear freind [   ]¹

Endorsements (2 by Swift): Dr Arbuthnot | 1726

POPE *to* THE EARL OF OXFORD²   21 *September* 1726

Longleat Portland Papers, xii

My Lord,—I was verry near my hopes of being able to see your Lp., when an unexpected cold intirely disabled me, threw me into perfect torment by settling in the same arm, and yet deprives me of any use of my hand: I cannot however but find this way of expressing my vexation at the disappointment, and as it is too true of writers that however disabled they will still be writing on, I feel a particular strong inclination at this verry time to sign my self in this wretched manner, but with great Sincerity | My Lord | Your most faith|full Servant | A. Pope.

Septbr 21. 1726

I beg you to send me by the bearer (who is a safe hand) the manuscript History, which my confinement will make me read with great attention and pleasure, you shall have it again whenever you will come and fetch it.

Address: To the Right Honble the Earl | of Oxford
Endorsement: Mr Pope not his own | Hand | Sept 21. 1726

BOLINGBROKE *to* SWIFT   22 *September* 1726

Add. 4805

London Sep. the 22d 1726

A Bookseller, who says he is going in a few days to Dublin, calls here, & offers to carry a letter to you. I cannot resist the temptation of writing to you, tho' I have nothing to say more by this conveyance than I should have by that of the post, tho' I have lately clubb'd with Pope to make up a most elegant Epistle to you in prose & verse, &

---

¹ The end of the letter is torn away. On the blank side Swift has entered the incomes of the various episcopal sees.
² The letter is in the hand of an amanuensis, probably Gay. Part of the subscription ('Your most faithfull Servant') and the signature are by Pope himself.

tho' I writ the other day the first paragraph of that Cheddar letter which is preparing for you.[1] the only excuse then which I can plead for writing now is that the letter will cost you nothing. have you heard of the accident which befel poor Pope in going lately from me? A Bridg was down, the coach forc'd to go thro' the water, the Bank Steep, an hole on one side, a block of timber on the other, the night as dark as pitch, in short he overturned, the fall was broke by the water, but the glasses were up, & he might have been drownd if one of my men[2] had not broke a glass & pull'd him out thro the window. his right hand was Severely cut; but the surgeon thinks him in no danger of losing the use of his fingers. however he had lately had very great pains in that arm from the shoulder downwards, which might create a Suspicion that some of the glass remain'd still in the flesh. StAndré says there is none.[3] if so, these pains are owing to a cold he took in a fit of gallantry which carry'd him across the water to see Mrs Howard, who has been extremely ill, but is much better. just as I am writing I hear that Dr Arbuthnot says that Popes pains are Rheumatick, & have no relation to his wound. he suffers very much I will endeavour to see him tomorrow. let us hear from you as often as you can afford to write. I would say something to you of myself, if I had any good thing to say, but I am much in the same way in which you left me, eternally busy about trifles, disagreeable in themselves, but render'd supportable by their end, which is to enable me to bury my Self from the world, who cannot be more tir'd of me than I am of it, in an agreeable Sepulchre. I hope to bring this about by next Spring, & shall be glad to see you att my funeral. Adieu.

Endorsement (by Swift): Ld Bolinge | Sept 22d 1726

GAY *to* SWIFT[4]   [*September* 1726]

Add. 4805

As We cannot enjoy any good thing without your partaking of it, Accept of the following receipt for Stewing Veal

Take a knuckle of Veal,
You may buy it, or steal,

---

[1] i.e. a letter of composite origin. See Gay to Swift, 22 Oct. 1726 (here ii. 409). The authors were Pope, Gay, Bolingbroke, Mrs. Howard, Pulteney, and possibly Arbuthnot. The earlier 'elegant epistle' written with Pope seems to have disappeared.

[2] Phil Hanaus. See Pope to J. Brinsden, Nov. [1740].

[3] Nathaniel St. André, a Swiss anatomist patronized by the Court. Presently he lost his reputation when in November of this year he investigated and supported the claims of Mary Tofts of Godalming, who pretended to give birth to rabbits.

[4] Gay's letter to Swift, 22 Oct. 1726, proves that these verses were a part of the 'Cheddar letter'—the only part, apparently, to be preserved. Ault has argued with plausibility (*New Light*, pp. 225–30) that the lines actually by Pope are in Gay's hand only because of the disability resulting from Pope's accident.

In a few peices cut it,
In a Stewing pan put it,
Salt, pepper and mace
Must season this knuckle,
Then what's join'd to a place,[1]   [1] Vulg. Salary.
With other Herbs muckle;
That which killed King Will,[2]   [2] Suppos'd sorrell
And what never stands still,[3]   [3] This is byDr | Bentley
Some sprigs of that bed[4]   thought to be | Time,
Where Children are bred,   or Thyme.
Which much you will mend, if   [4] Parsley. Vide Cham-
Both Spinnage and Endive,   berlain.
And Lettuce and Beet,
With Marygold meet;
Put no water at all,
For it maketh things small:
Which, lest it should happen,
A close cover clap on;
Put this pot of [5]Wood's mettle   [5] Of this composition
In a hot boiling kettle,   see the Works of the
And there let it be,   Copper farthing Dean.
(Mark the doctrine I teach)
About—let me see—
Thrice as long as you [6]preach   [6] Which we suppose to
So skimming the fat off,   be near four hours.
Say Grace with your hat off,
O then, with what rapture
Will it fill Dean & Chapter!

POPE *to* HILL[1]   [*September* 1726?]

1751 (Hill)

The little Thing which you take so kindly, is but a very small Part of
what I owe you; and whatever my Studies, or (to use a properer Word)
Idleness, are capable of producing, ought to be returned you in mere
Gratitude for the Pleasure I have received from your own Writings:
In which give me Leave to say, your good Will to me in particular,
is as distinguishable, as the Obligation you lay on the Publick in general.
I am very happy in the Envy and silly Attacks of such People, as have
awakened the Generosity of so powerful a Defender. Nor am I
ashamed of those Weaknesses of mine, which they have exposed in

---

[1] First printed in *A Collection of Letters never before Printed: written ... to the late Aaron Hill*, 1751, pp. 1–3. It is dated through the reference in the last paragraph to Pope's cut hand, received in the accident of this month.

Print[1] (the greatest of which was my thinking too candidly of them, to whom I wrote my Letters with so much unguarded Friendliness, and Freedom), since you have found a Way to turn those Weaknesses into Virtue, by your partial Regard of them. The Eye of Candour, like the Sun, makes all the Beauties which it sees; it gives Colour and Brightness to the meanest Objects purely by looking on them. I agree with you, that there is a Pleasure in seeing the Nature and Temper of Men in the plainest Undress; but few Men are of Consequence enough to deserve, or reward, that Curiosity. I shall indeed (and so will all Mankind) be highly pleased to see the Great Czar of *Muscovy* in this Light, drawn by himself, like an antient Master, in rough Strokes, without heightening, or shadowing: What a Satisfaction to behold that perfect Likeness, without Art, Affectation, or even the Gloss of Colouring, with a noble Neglect of all that Finishing and Smoothing, which any other Hand would have been obliged to bestow on so principal a Figure? I write this to a Man whose Judgment I am certain of, and therefore am as certain you will give the World this great Depositum, just as you have received it: There will be no Danger of your dressing this *Mars* too finely, whose Armour is not Gold, but Adamant, and whose Stile in all Probability is much more strong, than it is polish'd. I congratulate you, that this great Treasure is fallen into your Hands;[2] and I congratulate all *Europe*, that it is to be delivered to them through the Hands of one, who will think it Sacrilege to touch upon, much less to alter, any great Lines of such an Original.

I can make you no better Return for your great Compliment upon me (which it would be Arrogance in me to shew to any other, and dangerous even to remember myself) but by telling you, that it is Honour enough to reward all my Studies, to find my Character and Reputation is Part of the Care of that Person, to whom the Fame and Glory of *Peter Alexiowitz* was committed.

Sir,—I am forced to make use of another Hand than my own in this Letter, having received a Wound cross all the Veins of my right Hand, by which the Tendons of two Fingers are separated; however, it was a Fine paid for my Life, which has been very narrowly saved, and which may now continue me some Years longer, | Dear Sir, | Your most faithful, affectionate, | and obliged Servant, | A. Pope.

[1] His letters to Henry Cromwell, 'exposed' in Curll's *Miscellanea*.
[2] Peter the Great had died in 1725, and because of Hill's earlier tribute to him in *The Northern Star* (1720), the Empress had sent to Hill some papers to be used in a life.

406   *Pope to the Earl of Oxford, 27 September 1726*

POPE *to* THE EARL OF OXFORD[1]   [27 *September* 1726]

Longleat Portland Papers, xii

My Lord,—I should be very glad, if it agree with Your Conveniency,
to see your Lordship on thursday because it is a day sooner than friday.
If Lady Oxford does not find this season agreeable enough to go by
water, (which I much apprehend) & hath nothing better to do by
land, My Mother & I should be equally oblig'd to her.

I am | My Lord | Your most obliged Humble | servant   A. Pope.

Tuesday morning. | Sepr 27. 1726.

Address: To | The Right Honble | The Earl of Oxford & Mortimer | In
Dover Street.
Endorsement: From Mr Pope but not | his own Hand | Sept 27. 1726

SWIFT *to* POPE AND GAY   15 *October* 1726

Longleat Portland Papers, xiii

I received your Map and Pictures, by the latter I could not find out
the Originals, and your map is as much Caricatura of Biberry, as the
others must be of I don't know who.

As for your tripartite Letter, which begins with his Lordship[2] I
think (Gentry) it should be Settled what foot we are upon, and how
you intend we are to live together in Absence, His Lordship takes the
Office of a Critick, and is in a dozen Lines acting a Critick telling me
of a very indifferent Letter. Is it imagined that I must be always lean-
ing upon one Hand while I am writing with the other, Always upon
the *qui vive* and the *Slip Slop* instead of an honest plain Letter which
onely Should contain in more words Si vales bene est and me ama ut &c
I have Since writ him a much longer and a more indifferent Letter
which will cost him two dosen lines at least to find fault with, and will
be so much Matter for an Answer, aliquisq malo fuit usus &c However as to the writing Part, you Shall no more complain for I can
mend my Hand better than my Head. But may I never think again if I
think three Seconds whenever I write to the best or the worst of you.
Let Builders and Ministers think till they have not a Peny left in their
Pockets, or a Friend in the World. Besides I am so busy with railing
at those odious Beasts you send us for all Employments, that I can
think of nothing else. Breed a man a dosen year in a Coal pit, he Shall
pass his time well enough among his Fellows, but Send him to Light

---

[1] The whole letter is written by an amanuensis, apparently John Gay. The date at the
end of the letter is entered by Lord Oxford. The 27th was Tuesday.
[2] Bolingbroke.

for a few Months then down with him again; and try what a Correspondent he will be—I take you in order, the next is my Landlord
at Whitehall,[1] who treats me with [such] kindness and Domesticity,
that he is laying in a Double Stock of Wine. He is to return my Lord
Chesterfield thanks for the Honor I receive in his remembring me.
He is to make Mr Stopford be received by all who deserve it in the
best manner possible and to thank Mr Rawlinson &c but as for Tom
the water fool[2] I think he treats me with little Respect, therefor upon
Mature thoughts, I conclude it below me to return his Complement
and he must polish his manners before I will do him a good Office to
Mr Popes Maid.

To Speak in the Second Person, I would advise you to inquire dili-
gently whether the Mice who eat up your Buttons were whigs or
Toryes,[3] or whether of the Court or Country Party. Plutarch tells us
that Diogenes was Encouraged to Continue in the Study of Philosophy
by a Mouse if this be true by parallell reasoning, you Should have
enemyes at Court, and probably Mrs Howard sent those Mice to eat
your Buttons, as the readyist Instruments to make you a heathen
Philosopher; But if mice be like Rats who haunt onely Ships that are
not in danger of Sinking, then you are Safe enough, and they may
perhaps be Some of Knight Roberts Mice[4] to pay you a Visit I would
be Glad to know whether your Buttons were green; if So then they
must have been pontic mice, which as Olavs Magnus[5] assures us
always devours whatever is green and it never flourishes again, Upon
the whole, Pliny allows them to have been always an ill omen;[6] and
therefore you should be advised to prepare against it either by Averrun-
cation or Traps, for the latter you may consult Avicen.[7]—The last
Part of your Part relates to my Twitenham Host therefore I shall
answer it to him you ought to give me Joy that I was not present to be
overturned with you, in answer let me say, that I am ready to Stand
or fall with you as long as I live, however I believe my Weight would
have Saved us all if it had been rightly applyed; I am so far of your
Opinion that life is good for nothing otherwise than for the Love we
have to our Friends, that I think the easiest way of dying is so to
Contrive Matters as not to have one Friend left in the World; and
perhaps it would be no ill Amendment to add, nor an Enemy neither.
I hope you jest when you Say you have lost two Fingers, and it is so
bad and provoking a Jest, that if I did not love you I should wish it

[1] Gay entertained Swift in his Whitehall lodgings.
[2] Possibly, as Ball thought, Pope's waterman, Bowry.
[3] In *Gulliver*, ii, ch. iii, the Brobdingnagian king, says Gulliver, 'stroking me gently
asked me whether I were a Whig or a Tory'.
[4] Sir Robert Walpole's mice.
[5] *Gentium Septentrionalium Historiae Breviarium* (1652), lib. xviii, c. xvi.
[6] *Hist. Nat.* viii. 82.
[7] The *De Animalibus* of Avicen yields little about traps. Is Swift joking?

were true. Neither are your Hopes worth a Rush a Lawyer, a
Usurer, a Physicion, a Minister a Senator, a Judge must open their
Hand before they Shut it else they will go off empty handed. But other
Letters tell me you have onely lost Some Blood which you can ill
Spare, for you had nothing to Venture except Blood and Bones. I am
mustring as I told you all the little things in verse that I think may be
Safely printed, but I give you despotick Power to tear as many as you
please. I now turn to Mr Gay. I desire you will let me know where I
am to direct to Lord B;[1] when I am disposed towards him; I desire
he may onely See the most indifferent Part of this Letter, and lastly
to make my Acknoledgment to Mr Poltiney[2] for his Letter, and that
nothing hinders me from writing again, but the Fear that his Civilityes
would engage him in a very Useless Correspondence; or if you think
he did expect a Second Letter, I would readily do it, although I am
ever at a loss in dealing with Persons too civil, for I have a Cloud of
Witnesses with My Lord Bolingbroke at their Head to prove I never
practiced or possessed Such a Talent as Civility, which Sir Wm
Windham knew well enough when he refused to make any Returns
to what I writ to him before I left you wherein he knew me better
than Mr Polteney does although what I did was a pure Effect of
Friend Ship, Brotherly Love, Esteem and Concern. I have received
a Box with the Spectacles but by whose Care they were conveyed I
know not I onely desire that My Lord Bolingbroke may be assured
the Spectacles were for two old Cozens and not for me. Mr Ford is
just landed after a Months raking by the Way with Some of his Tory
Lords, for want of whom he must here Sink into Spleen as he uses to do.
I am going to try your Receit of the Knuckle of Veal, and I wish the
measure of Ingredients may prove better than of the Verses, but I
want the other of a Chicken in a wooden Boul from Mrs Howard,
upon which you may likewise exercise your Poetry, for the Ladys here
object against both, but they Swear that a Sauce Pan cannot get into
a Kettle, and therefore they resolve to change it into a deep Earthen
Pot. This day I was forced to dine upon Eggs alone, that I might have
time to write my Letter, This is all I have leisure to Say at present

Upon four dismal stories in the Doctor's Letter,
relating to four of my Friends

Here four of you got mischances to plague you
Friend Congreve a Feaver, Friend Howard an Ague
Friend Pope overturnd by driving too fast away
And Robin at Sea had like to be cast away

---

[1] Gay in his answer to this letter (22 Oct.) pretends doubt as to whether Swift refers to
Burlington or Bathurst—but gives him in a casual postscript Bolingbroke's Pall Mall address.
[2] William Pulteney.

But, alas, the pour Dean neither Shudders nor burns
No Sea overwhelms him, no Coach overturns
Though his Claret is bad, and he foots it on Stones
Yet he gets home at night with Health and whole Bones.

Octbr 15th 1726

GAY *to* SWIFT   22 *October* 1726

Add. 4805

Before I say one word to you, give me leave to say something of the
other Gentleman's Affair. The Letter was sent, and the answer was,
that every thing was finish'd, & concluded according to orders; and
that it would be publickly known to be so in a very few days, so that
I think there can be no occasion for his writing any more about this
Affair.[1]

The Letter you wrote to Mr Pope was not receiv'd 'till eleven or
twelve days after date, and the Post Office we suppose have very
vigilant Officers, for they had taken care to make him pay for a double
Letter. I wish I could tell you that the cutting of the tendons of two
of his fingers was a joke, but it is really so. The wound is quite heal'd;
his hand is still weak, and the two fingers drop downwards as I told
you before, but I hope it will be very little troublesome or detrimental
to him.

In Answer to our Letter of Maps, Pictures & receipts, you call it a
tripartite Letter; If you will examine it once again, you will find
some Lines of Mrs Howard, & some of Mr Pulteney which you have
not taken the least notice of. The receipt of the Veal [is] of Monsieur
Davoux Mr Pulteney's Cook,[2] and it hath been approv'd of at one of
our Twickenham entertainments. The difficulty of the Saucepan, I
believe you will find is owing to a negligence in perusing the manuscript, for if I remember right it is there call'd a Stew-pan. Your
Earthen Vessel provided it is close stopt, I allow to be a good suc-
cedaneum. As to the boiling Chickens in a Wooden Bowle, I shall
be quite asham'd to consult Mrs Howard upon your account; who
thinks herself entirely neglected by you in your not writing to her, as
you promis'd; However Let her take it as she will, to serve a friend I
will venture to ask it of her; The Prince and his family come[3] to settle
in town to morrow. That Mr Pulteney expected an answer to his
Letter & would be extreamly pleas'd to hear from you is very certain,
for I have heard him talk of it with expectation for above a fortnight.
I have of late been very much out of order with a slight feaver, which

---

[1] The affair of *Gulliver's Travels*?
[2] Ault (*New Light*, p. 230) gives the prose recipe.
[3] From Richmond, where they had spent the summer.

I am not yet quite free from; it was occasion'd by a cold, which my Attendance at the Guildhall improv'd.[1] I have not a friend who hath got any thing under my Administration but the Dutchess of Queensberry who hath had a benefit of a thousand pounds. Your mentioning Mr Rollison so kindly will, I know, give him much pleasure, for he always talks of you with great regard and the strongest terms of friendship; He hath of late been ill of a feaver, but is recover'd so as to go abroad to take the Air.

If the Gravers keep their word with me, I shall be able to publish my Fables soon after Christmas. The Doctor's book is entirely printed off,[2] & will be very soon publish'd. I believe you will expect that I should give you some account how I have spent my time since you left me. I have attended my distrest friend at Twickenham, & been his Emanuensis, which you know is no idle Charge, & I have read about half Virgil, & half Spenser's Fairy Queen. I still despise Court Preferments so that I lose no time upon attendance on great men, and still can find amusement enough without Quadrille, which here is the Universal Employment of Life. I thought you would be glad to hear from me, so that I determin'd not to stir out of my lodgings till I had answer'd your Letter, and I think I shall very probably hear more of the matter which I mention in the first paragraph of this Letter as soon as I go abroad, for I expect it every day. We have no news as yet of Mr Stopfort, Mr Rollinson told me he shall know of his arrival, & will send me word. Lord Bolingbroke hath been to make a visit to Sir William Wyndham; I hear he is return'd, but I have not seen him. If I had been in a better State of health, & Mrs Howard were not to come to town to morrow, I would have gone to Mr Pope's to day to have din'd with him there on Monday. You ask me how to address to Lord B when you are dispos'd to write to him. If you mean Lord Burlington, he is not yet return'd from France, but is expected every day. If you mean Lord Bathurst he is in Glocestershire & makes but a very short stay; so that if you direct to one of them in St James's Square, or to the other at Burlington house in Piccadilly your Letter will find them. I will make your Compliments to Lord Chesterfield & Mr Pulteney, and I beg you in return to make mine to Mr Ford. Next Week I shall have a new coat & new Buttons for the Birth-day, though I dont know but a turn-coat might have been more for my advantage. | Yours most sincerely & affectionately.

Whitehall. Octr 22. 1726.

I hear that Lord Bolingbroke will be in town at his house in Pell-mell next week.

---

[1] As commissioner of the lottery.
[2] *Tables of Ancient Coins, Weights, and Measures,* 1727.

DR. ARBUTHNOT *to* THE EARL OF OXFORD[1]

Longleat Portland Papers, xiii   16 *November* 1726

My Noble Lord,—I am sorry the bad weather allows your lordship
so much time for study in the Country. Tho I reckon that ev'n in the
most serene day, one can hardly leave Guliver. There has been a vast
dem[and] for Guliver the first impression was sold off in a moment
every body has been mightily delighted with him, I had the honor to
wait on her R. Highness when she had just come to that passage of
the Hobling prince, which her Highness Laugh'd at. Minesterial folks
say the book is a pleasant humorous book & it was pity he descended
so low, as some Little satyr, that is too particular some Folks that I
know went immediately to their Maps to look for Lillypott, &
reckond it a fault in their Maps not to have sett down. Lord Scar-
borrow Mett with a Sea Captain that Knew Guliver but he said the
bookseller was mistaken in placing his habitation at Rothereth for he
was sure he livd at Wapping. in short the Book has made very good
diversion to all the town It was not possible for me at this Time to
send the Ballad but your lordship shall have it ther are a hundred incor-
rect Copys of it about town. I have just now transcribed the substance
of the paper of Quadrille.[2] I fancy there will be some comical papers
about Guliver. I have seen a pretty good Epistle from Guliver's wife
to him in the Stile of ovid. I happen to be so unlucky as to have twenty
things to do this moment else your lordship should have had the
Ballad & for the same reason I hope you will be so good as to forgive
this hasty & hardly legible scrawl being with the utmost respect | My
Lord | Your lordships most faithfull | Sincere | servant | Jo: Arbuthnott

London: Novr 16 1726

Endorsement: Dr Arbuthnott | London Nov. 16 1726

---

†POPE *to* SWIFT[3]   16 *November* 1726

1740
                                                           Nov. 16, 1726.

I have resolved to take time; and in spite of all misfortunes and demurs,

---

1 The amusing comment on the reception of *Gulliver* throws some light on the verses
appended to the second edition of that work. See Ault, *New Light*, pp. 231–42. Ault
thought the earliest extant allusion to the verses was found in Pope to Swift, 18 Feb. 1726/7;
but this letter together with that from Arbuthnot to Oxford, 23 Nov. 1726, implies a concern by Arbuthnot in these verses that undermines confidence in Mr. Ault's arguments that
the poems are by Pope. See Ball, iii. 356 for a similar letter, Arbuthnot to Swift.

2 The ballad might well be that about Nelly Bennet printed in the *Miscellanies* ('last
volume'), pp. 168–71. Arbuthnot's 'Ballad on Quadrille' also appeared in this 'last' volume
pp. 197–201.

3 In all editions of 1740–2 this letter is printed just after Gay's to Swift of 17 Nov. It
seems probable that the two letters were really one, and indeed the table of contents for the
quarto and folio of 1741 indicates as much.

which sickness, lameness, or disability of any kind can throw in my way, to write you (at intervals) a long letter. My two least fingers of one hand hang impediments to the others, like useless dependents, who only take up room, and never are active or assistant to our wants: I shall never be much the better for 'em—I congratulate you first upon what you call your Couzen's wonderful Book,[1] which is *publica trita manu*[2] at present, and I prophecy will be in future the admiration of all men. That countenance with which it is received by some statesmen, is delightful; I wish I could tell you how every single man looks upon it, to observe which has been my whole diversion this fortnight. I've never been a night in London since you left me, till now for this very end, and indeed it has fully answered my expectations.

I find no considerable man very angry at the book: some indeed think it rather too bold, and too general a Satire: but none that I hear of accuse it of particular reflections (I mean no persons of consequence, or good judgment; the mob of Critics, you know, always are desirous to apply Satire to those that they envy for being above them) so that you needed not to have been so secret upon this head. Motte[3] receiv'd the copy (he tells me) he knew not from whence, nor from whom, dropp'd at his house in the dark, from a Hackney-coach: by computing the time, I found it was after you left England,[4] so for my part, I suspend my judgment.

I'm pleas'd with the nature and quality of your Present to the Princess. The Irish stuff you sent to Mrs. H.[5] her R.H.[6] laid hold of, and has made up for her own use. Are you determin'd to be National in every thing, even in your civilities? you are the greatest Politician in Europe at this rate; but as you are a rational Politician, there's no great fear of you, you will never succeed.

Another thing in which you have pleased me, was what you say to Mr. P.[7] by which it seems to me that you value no man's civility above your own dignity, or your own reason. Surely, without flattery, you are now above all parties of men, and it is high time to be so, after twenty or thirty years observation of the great world.

Nullius addictus jurare in verba magistri.[8]

---

[1] Gulliver's cousin Richard Sympson was the supposed publisher of the *Travels*.

[2] Translated 'Worn or thumbed by the Hand of the Publick', in 1741 Dab. Curll (1741 Lc) renders it, 'Generally read'.   [3] Swift's (and Gulliver's) bookseller.

[4] It is perhaps possible from this letter that Pope himself dropped the MS. of *Gulliver* at Motte's door. Probably Charles Ford did it; he was in London for about a month after Swift left. See Swift to Pope and Gay, 15 Oct. 1726 (ii. 408).

[5] Footnoted 'Mrs. Howard, now Countess of Suffolk' in 1741 Dab.

[6] R.H.] Royal Highness *1741 Dab*. By this present Swift hoped to promote the Irish weaving industry.   [7] Mr. Pulteney.—Curll, 1741 Lc.

[8] Horace, *Epistles*, i. i. 14. Translated in a footnote: 'Sworn to no Party, to no Cause attacht.'—1741 Dab. Curll (1741 Lc) translates it, 'Not addicted to swear in the Words of another, how great soever the Personage'. The Royal Society, which took its motto from the verse, gave it still another turn of meaning.

I question not, many men would be of your intimacy, that you might be of their interest: But God forbid an honest or witty man should be of any, but that of his country. They have scoundrels enough to write for their passions and their designs; let us write for truth, for honour, and for posterity. If you must needs write about Politicks at all, (but perhaps 'tis full as wise to play the fool any other way) surely it ought to be so as to preserve the dignity and integrity of your character with those times to come, which will most impartially judge of them.

I wish you had writ to Lord Peterborow, no man is more affectionate toward you. Don't fancy none but Tories are your friends; for at that rate I must be, at most, but half your friend, and sincerely I am wholly so. Adieu, write often, and come soon, for many wish you well, and all would be glad of your company.

†GAY *to* SWIFT   17 *November* 1726

1740

Nov. 17. 1726.

About ten days ago a Book was publish'd here of the Travels of one Gulliver, which hath been the conversation of the whole town ever since: The whole impression sold in a week; and nothing is more diverting than to hear the different opinions people give of it, though all agree in liking it extreamly. 'Tis generally said that you are the Author, but I am told, the Bookseller declares he knows not from what hand it came. From the highest to the lowest it is universally read, from the Cabinet-council to the Nursery. The Politicians to a man agree, that it is free from particular reflections, but that the Satire on general societies of men is too severe. Not but we now and then meet with people of greater perspicuity, who are in search for particular applications in every leaf; and 'tis highly probable we shall have keys publish'd to give light into Gulliver's design. Your Lord ———[1] is the person who least approves it, blaming it as a design of evil consequence to depreciate human nature, at which it cannot be wondered that he takes most offence, being himself the most accomplish'd of his species, and so losing more than any other of that praise which is due both to the dignity and virtue of a man. Your friend, my Lord Harcourt, commends it very much, though he thinks in some places the matter too far carried. The Duchess Dowager of Marlborough is in raptures at it; she says she can dream of nothing else since she read it: she declares, that she hath now found out, that her whole life hath been lost in caressing the worst part of mankind, and treating the best as her foes; and that if she knew Gulliver, tho' he had been the worst enemy

[1] Bolingbroke.

she ever had, she would give up all her present acquaintance for his friendship. You may see by this, that you are not much injur'd by being suppos'd the Author of this piece. If you are, you have dis-oblig'd us, and two or three of your best friends, in not giving us the least hint of it while you were with us; and in particular Dr. Arbuth-not, who says it is ten thousand pitys he had not known it, he could have added such abundance of things upon every subject. Among Lady-critics, some have found out that Mr. Gulliver had a particular malice to maids of honour. Those of them who frequent the Church, say, his design is impious, and that it is an insult on Providence, by depreciating the works of the Creator. Notwithstanding I am told the Princess[1] hath read it with great pleasure. As to other Critics, they think the flying island is the least entertaining; and so great an opinion the town have of the impossibility of Gulliver's writing at all below himself, that 'tis agreed that part was not writ by the same hand, tho' this hath its defenders too. It hath pass'd Lords and Commons, *nemine contradicente*; and the whole town, men, women, and children are quite full of it.

Perhaps I may all this time be talking to you of a Book you have never seen, and which hath not yet reach'd Ireland; if it hath not, I believe what we have said will be sufficient to recommend it to your reading, and that you order me to send it to you.

But it will be much better to come over your self, and read it here, where you will have the pleasure of variety of commentators, to explain the difficult passages to you.

We all rejoyce that you have fixt the precise time of your coming to be *cum hirundine prima*; which we modern naturalists pronounce, ought to be reckon'd, contrary to Pliny in this northern latitude of fifty-two degrees, from the end of February, Styl Greg.[2] at farthest. But to us your friends, the coming of such a black swallow as you, will make a summer in the worst of seasons. We are no less glad at your mention of Twickenham and Dawley; and in town you know you have a lodging at Court.

The Princess is cloath'd in Irish silk; pray give our service to the Weavers. We are strangely surpriz'd to hear that the Bells in Ireland ring without your money;[3] I hope you do not write the thing that is not. We are afraid that B—[4] hath been guilty of that crime, that you (like a Houyhnhnm) have treated him as a Yahoo, and discarded him

---

[1] The late Queen Caroline.—1741 Dab.

[2] Or 'New Style' of the Gregorian Calendar, not adopted in England until 1752.

[3] Mist's *Weekly Journal*, 3 Sept. 1726, gives as Dublin news, under date of 25 Aug., an account of Swift's arrival: 'On this Occasion the Bells of St. Patrick's, and other Adjacent Churches, were rung, and large Bonfires made in the neighbouring Streets.'

[4] Curll (1741 Lc) thought this meant Bolingbroke; Elwin thinks it refers to a manservant discharged; Ball suggests that B is a misprint for P, and refers to Swift's agent, Proudfoot.

your service. I fear you do not understand these modish terms, which every creature now understands but your self.

You tell us your Wine is bad, and that the Clergy do not frequent your house, which we look upon to be tautology. The best advice we can give you is, to make them a present of your wine, and come away to better.

You fancy we envy you, but you are mistaken, we envy those you are with, for we cannot envy the man we love. Adieu.

FENTON *to* BROOME   22 *November* [1726]

Elwin–Courthope, viii. 132

Leicester Fields, Nov. 22, [1726].

For about six weeks before I left Windsor Forest I lived in daily expectation of a letter from Mr. Broome, and for this fortnight past which I have spent in town I have been still more impatient to hear from you. Here have I been tormented with St. Anthony's fire in my face and eyes, which will only just serve me to scrawl these two or three lines to inquire after you, which on second thoughts I had better not to have mentioned, since you may urge the trouble I shall have in reading for a reason why you will not write. Pope has called on me thrice, and thrice I saw him not, and I had a loving epistle from him in the country which still lies unanswered. Sir Clement is laid up by the surgeons, who have cut off from his back a large wen, which he used to complain of, but he is in a fair way to do well. Prithee let me hear soon from you, and for a peace-offering to atone for your former neglect, sacrifice a fat turkey to me to present to Lady Judith; and if Mr. Burlington could pick up a hare to bear it company I should be doubly obliged. My service to him, Mrs. Broome, and all friends as usual, must now conclude, for my eyes will hold out no longer. Yours ever.

Mr. Trumbull presents his service.

GAY *to* BRIGADIER JAMES DORMER   22 *November* 1726

Rousham

Though you have heard from me but once in form, it hath not been either for want of respect or friendship. I had the pleasure to hear of your health by the return of the fleet, and I really would have writ to you often, if I did not look upon myself as an unnecessary corre-spondence. I have as little prospect of being provided for as ever, so that I have not had the least good fortune to make me some amends for the loss of your company. I am about to publish a collection of

Fables entirely of my own invention to be dedicated to Prince William, they consist of fifty, and I am oblig'd to Mr Kent & Wootton for the Designs of the Plates. The Work is begun to be printed, and is delay'd only upon account of the Gravers, who are neither very good or expeditious. I believe you must have heard that Mr Pelham is married to Lady Katharine Manners. Tis said that Mr Arundell is married to Lady Fanny, but as he is in the country, I believe, 'tis only the conjecture of the town. We have a Book lately publish'd here which hath of late taken up the whole conversation of the town. Tis said to be writ by Swift. It is called, The travells of Lemuell Gulliver in two Volumes. It hath had a very great sale. People differ vastly in their Opinions of it, for some think it hath a great deal of wit, but others say it hath none at all. As it hath been publish'd about a month, I fancy you must have either heard of it, or seen it. We have a famous French Author in town, who upon a Quarrell with the Chevalier de Rohan is banish'd his Country. He hath been here about half a year, and begins to speak English very well. His name is Voltaire, the Author of Oedipe. He hath finish'd his Poem of the Ligue, which he intends to publish in England in Quarto with very fine copper plates which he hath got already grav'd by the best Gravers in Paris. I am told the Parliament will not sit till about the middle of January, so that the town is yet but thin. There is a set of Italian Comedians who act twice a week at the Opera house, but they are very little approv'd off, for the Harlequin is very indifferent, so that they find but small encouragement. I was at Rousham twice last summer in a visit which I find extreamly improv'd, and your Brother was with us once or twice at Middleton. Lord and Lady Burlington are return'd from Paris where they made a stay of about two months. Lord Chesterfield designs to take Lord Cadogan's house in case the Duke of Richmond does not go into it himself, in which as yet he is undetermin'd. All the Goods of my Lord Cadogan are to [be] dispos'd off by auction in the month of January next. You see, I send you the little trifling news of the town, I leave that of more consequence to others. I long for your company, but since I cannot have it, I wish I could be serviceable to you in any thing you will please to command me.

Dear Sir, | I am | Your most obedient and | most faithfull servant | J Gay.

Whitehall, near the Chappell.
Novemr 22, 1726.

Address: A Son Excellence | Mr Dormer Envoyé Extraordinaire | de sa Majesté Britannique | a Lisbonne | Portugal.
Endorsement: Mr Gay | Novr 22 OS. 1726

DR. ARBUTHNOT *to* THE EARL OF OXFORD[1]

23 November 1726

Longleat Portland Papers, xiii

My Noble Lord,—I am come home so late, that I have only time to thank your lordship for the Honor of your's & to keep my promise by enclosing the Ballad. the only copy that I have   I hope your lordship will see some copys of verses with the next Edition of Guliver. This with my wishes for your lordships health & prosperity & your speedy return to town is with the greatest respect From | My Lord | Your lordships Most faithfull | humble servant | Jo. Arbuthnott

London: Novr 23.

Endorsement: Dr Arbuthnot | Nov 23. 1726

†SWIFT *to* POPE[2]   [27] *November* 1726

1740

Dublin, Nov. 17, 1726

I am just come from answering a Letter of Mrs. Howard's[3] writ in such mystical terms, that I should never have found out the meaning, if a Book had not been sent me called *Gulliver's Travellers*,[4] of which you say so much in yours. I read the Book over, and in the second volume observe several passages which appear to be patch'd and altered, and the style of a different sort (unless I am much mistaken) Dr. Arbuthnot likes the Projectors least, others you tell me, the Flying island; some think it wrong to be so hard upon whole Bodies or Corporations, yet the general opinion is, that reflections on particular persons are most to be blam'd: so that in these cases, I think the best method is to let censure and opinion take their course. A Bishop here said, that book was full of improbable lies, and for his part, he hardly believed a word of it; and so much for Gulliver.

Going to England is a very good thing, if it were not attended with an ugly circumstance of returning to Ireland. It is a shame you do not persuade your ministers to keep me on that side, if it were but by a court expedient of keeping me in prison for a Plotter; but at the same time I must tell you, that such journeys very much shorten my life, for a month here is longer than six at Twickenham.

How comes friend Gay to be so tedious? another man can publish fifty-thousand Lies sooner than he can publish fifty Fables.

---

[1] See Arbuthnot to Lord Oxford, 16 Nov. 1726.
[2] Since Swift's answer to Mrs. Howard's 'Sieve Yahoo' letter is dated 27 Nov. (Ball, iii. 365), the first sentence of this letter indicates that the date printed in all early editions (17 Nov.) is wrong. Warton first saw the difficulty.
[3] Howard's] H—'s *1741 Lab*; *1742 Lbc*.   [4] Travellers] Travels *1741 Dab*.

I am just going to perform a very good office, it is to assist with the Arch-bishop,[1] in degrading a Parson who couples all our beggars, by which I shall make one happy man: and decide the great question of an indeleble character in favour of the principles in fashion; and this I hope you will represent to the Ministry in my favour, as a point of merit; so farewel till I return.

I am come back, and have deprived the parson, who by a law here is to be hanged the next couple he marries: he declared to us that he resolved to be hanged, only he desired that when he was to go to the gallows, the Arch-bishop would take off his Excommunication. Is not he a good Catholick? and yet he is but a Scotch-man. This is the only Irish event I ever troubled you with, and I think it deserves notice. Let me add, that if I were Gulliver's friend, I would desire all my acquaintance to give out that his copy[2] was basely mangled, and abused, and added to, and blotted out by the printer; for so to me it seems, in the second volume particularly. | Adieu.

POPE *to* CARYLL   5 *December* 1726
Add. 28618

5 Decr. 1726.

I send this after you, to show your good family that you were not dismissed from my house in the same manner as from other inns on the road; forgot as soon as you were bid Adieu and out of sight. I hope you found no difficulties or disasters in the way, and I'm sure you would find all satisfactions and comforts in each other at the end of the Journey. My mother's prayers attended you all, and those I hope might be of more efficacy than her sinful son's, tho' you had them too.

I now thank you under my hand for the kind token of ancient friendship, expressed in your verses on my late accident.

I want to know what faith you have in the miracle at Guildford;[3] not doubting but as you past thro' that town, you went as a philosopher to investigate, if not as a curious anatomist to inspect, that wonderful phenomenon. All London is now upon this occasion, as it generally is upon all others divided into factions about it.

Having had for some time past, and again of late, many instances and memorandums of my own mortality, as a man; and apprehending the same of my mortality as an author; I have seriously thought of consulting what is to come after me, in both regards: and to settle my

---

[1] Dr. William King,—1741 Dab.

[2] Vide Captain *Gulliver's* Letter to his Cousin *Sympson*, prefixed to *Gulliver's Travels*, printed by George Faulkner in Dublin.—1741 Dab.

[3] The miracle of the rabbit woman, Mary Tofts. Since Caryll lived not too far from the miracle town, Pope hoped for local opinion. Mrs. Tofts confessed her imposture on 7 Dec. Spence says Pope and Pulteney wrote a ballad on the subject, but the ballad seems unidentified. See Arbuthnot to Lord Oxford, 16 and 23 Nov. 1726, and Spence, p. 285.

whole accounts with posterity. In order to this I shall endeavour
forthwith to call in all such papers of mine as have been preserved too
partially by any of my friends, from my childhood to this present. And
as no one of that number, I'm sensible, has had more partiality to me
than yourself, or has had it longer, I will begin by entreating of you
to consult my fame, such as it is, and to help me to put out of Curl's
power any trifling remains of mine.[1] If therefore you have preserved
any verses or letters, I beg you to send them to me (as I will desire
every man to do whom I know to be my friend). I will review them,
and return whatever can do no hurt to either of us, or our memories,
or to any other particular man's character; but so much, as would
serve to bear testimony of my own love for good men, or theirs for
me, I would not but keep on all accounts, and shall think this very
article more to my reputation than all my works put together.

Dear sir, adieu: all felicity be yours, and be it extended to all you
love. My hand has done its best, and has forgot that it has ached this
quarter of an hour; for it has been near an hour's work to write this.
I am ever | dear sir | Your obliged affect. servant | A: P:

†SWIFT *to* POPE   5 *December* 1726

1740

December 5, 1726.

I believe the hurt in your hand affects me more than it does your self,
and with reason, because I may probably be a greater loser by it.
What have accidents to do with those who are neither jockeys, nor
fox-hunters, nor bullies, nor drunkards? And yet a rascally Groom
shall gallop a foundred horse ten miles upon a causeway, and get home
safe.

I am very much pleas'd that you approve what was sent, because I
remember to have heard a great man say, that nothing required more
judgment than making a present; which when it is done to those of
high rank, ought[2] to be of something that is not readily got for money.
You oblige me, and at the same time do me justice in what you observe
as to Mr. P.[3] Besides it is too late in life for me to act otherwise, and
therefore I follow a very easy road to virtue, and purchase it cheap.
If you will give me leave to join us, is not your life and mine a state
of power, and dependance a state of slavery? We care not three pence
whether a Prince or Minister will see us or no: We are not afraid of
having ill offices done us, nor are at the trouble of guarding our words
for fear of giving offence. I do agree that Riches are Liberty, but

---

[1] This request for the return of letters and verses is probably a considered reaction to
Curll's *Miscellanea* (2 v., July 1726 but dated on the title-page 1727), which had printed
Pope's letters to Cromwell.
[2] ought] out *1741* La (corrected in Lb).   [3] Mr. Pulteney.—Curll, *1741* Lc.

then we are put into the balance how long our apprenticeship is to last in acquiring them.

Since you have receiv'd the verses, I most earnestly intreat you to burn those which you do not approve, and in those few where you may not dislike some parts, blot out the rest, and sometimes (tho' it may be against the laziness of your nature) be so kind to make a few corrections, if the matter will bear them. I have some few of those things I call thoughts moral and diverting; if you please I will send the best I can pick from them, to add to the new volume.[1] I have reason to chuse the method you mention of mixing the several verses, and I hope thereby among the bad Critics to be entitled to more merit than is my due.

This moment I am so happy to have a letter from my Lord Peterborow, for which I entreat you will present him with my humble respects and thanks, tho' he all-to-be-Gullivers me by very strong insinuations. Tho' you despise Riddles, I am strongly tempted to send a parcel to be printed by themselves, and make a nine-penny jobb for the bookseller. There are some of my own, wherein I exceed mankind, *Mira Poemata!*[2] the most solemn that were ever seen; and some writ by others, admirable indeed, but far inferior to mine, but I will not praise my self. You approve that writer who laughs and makes others laugh; but why should I who hate the world, or you who do not love it, make it so happy? therefore I resolve from henceforth to handle only serious subjects, *nisi quid tu docte Trebati, Dissentis.*[3] | Yours, &c.

POPE *to* BROOME   5 *December* [1726]

Elwin–Courthope, viii. 133

Twitnam, Dec. 5, [1726].

It is a long time since I have been able to write, and my hand, as you now see, almost rivals your own for ill writing,—I say almost, for no man can pretend to equal you quite in this respect. I am obliged to you for a letter a month ago, and I would not employ another man's hand in hopes of doing this sooner, knowing well it would be a satisfaction to a friend like you to see by ocular demonstration how much I am recovered of that really disastrous accident. I hope you and yours are well. I shall always wish you so, both your offspring of the body and of the brain. I shall be glad to hear of your little one's health, in which I doubt not much of your spirit and health is concerned. Lintot tells me you have begun at the press, but showed me none of it. Mr. Fenton says you have not writ to him a long while. He has an inflammation in his face and eyes which, he says, hindered his being

---

[1] Of *Miscellanies*.   [2] Wonderful Poems.—1741 Dab.
[3] Horace, *Sermones*, ii. i. 78–79. Translated (1741 Dab): 'Unless you, and my learned Friend, differ in Opinion.'

able to overlook the press, as my lame hand did to correct it. But if in anything now I can serve or ease you, I am very ready, being faithfully—I hope I need no further proof to convince you—dear Broome, your affectionate friend and servant.

My mother is much yours.

POPE *to* THE EARL OF OXFORD   8 *December* 1726
Longleat Portland Papers, xii

My Lord,—I am not a little dissapointed at your long Absence. Yours was the first house I went to, at my first going to Town after my tedious confinement; Yours was the house I went to, at my second going; Equally in Vain. My Lady could not tell me when you would return; and therfore I must not pretend to complain that I knew not. Indeed my Lord I wish your return, & tho' I am glad to see you Imitate your great Father in every other thing, I am not quite pleased that you do so in living out of town all the winter, & in town all the Summer. I want you for many reasons; & among the rest, to hear what you say of a Book called Gullivers Travels; and to desire you to lend us, John Bull &c. for a good End, in order to put together this winter many scatterd pieces of the same kind, which are too good to be lost. I beg to have the pleasure of a line, that I may still think myself remember'd by you, and still have a pretence, & some sort of title, to assure you sometimes as I do now, that I am, with truth, respect, & affection, | My Lord | Your ever obligd | faithful humble Serv. | A. Pope.

Decr 8th 1726.

Address: To | The Right Honorable | the Earl of Oxford, to be | left in | Dover street | Piccadilly | London.
Endorsement: Mr Pope | Dec. 8. 1726
Postmark: 9/DE

*POPE *to* JAMES STOPFORD[1]   16 *December* [1726]
The Victoria and Albert Museum (transcript)

Twikenham, | Decr 16.

Sir,—The favour you seem'd to intend me of passing a day or two in my retirement (which at this time of year is truly one) gives me occasion to use you so confidently as to desire it, now, that the Weather

---

[1] The year is determined because Swift has urged Gay and Pope (15 Oct. 1726) to welcome Stopford on his return from the Continent, and because Stopford carries letters to Swift when he returns from England to Ireland in Feb. 1726/7. Stopford returned to London after the middle of October—at least Gay writes to Swift that there is as yet no news of him (22 Oct. 1726).

is in all the beauty of Winter. I look upon you as a long Acquaintance, thro' the merits of Dr Swift, which I beg you to impute to me. Perhaps you may move Dean Berkley or Mr Gay to attend you. I shall stay these 3 or 4 days, and wish you could also. I am with esteem & sincerity ever | yours | A. Pope.

Address: To the Revd Mr Stopford, | at the Prince's Sadler's, in | Pall mall. | London.

FENTON *to* BROOME   17 *December* 1726

Elwin–Courthope, viii. 134

Leicester Fields, Dec. 17, 1726.

Dear Mr. Broome,—I received your hare, and an excellent one it was, for which I return you thanks, and had sooner acknowledged the favour of your last letter, but delayed in expectation of some remarks on your verses,[1] which a friend of ours promised to make on condition that I would not mention his name. Most of them I think you will believe are just. He would have all that paragraph from "Envy, 'tis true," &c., to "From men to trees," quite struck out. For "*Me* humble joys," &c., he would have "*Thee.*" "Lesser than a saint," he thinks not proper English. What if you make it

> Superior to the monarch is the saint.

For

> While low the vale in useful beauty lies,
> They heaved their naked summits to the skies,

he alters,

> And while low vales in useful beauty lie,
> Heave their proud, naked summits to the sky.

He would leave out

> In honour as in place ye great transcend;
> An angel fall'n degenerates to a fiend.

He thinks, as I observed before, that Hyde and Plato *lay* is not English, —at least, to make it so you must put *mixed* for *mix* in the next verse. I refer all these observations to your own judgment, only, as to the first of them, I think the whole paragraph needs not be left out, but let it end with,

> And amidst monsters rises into day.

I am glad you give me hopes of seeing you so soon in town, by which time probably my health may allow me to spend some agreeable hours together. In the meantime, in answer to your query, whether or no

---

[1] When Broome's Epistle to Fenton was published (1727) in his *Poems*, only two of these suggestions were accepted. 'Lesser than a saint' and 'Hyde and Plato lay' were reformed.

we are at liberty to own the books of the Odyssey, &c., upon looking at what your name is set to at the end of the notes, and Mr. Pope's postscript, I think you have absolutely transferred your right at least, if not mine, which he by *punctually just* seems as positively to have accepted; so that, unless you resolve to break all measures with him, I think the best way for you is to let it rest as it does. And besides you have sung *Non nobis, Domine, non nobis,* so loudly, that I do not think my own worth owning, which, in truth, was one reason why I was so vexed to have my name mentioned. Adieu, dear Broome. Let me hear soon from you, which, with wishing you many Christmases, according to the old honest compliment, concludes in haste from yours ever.

POPE *to* CARYLL[1]   [1726–7]

Add. 28618

This cold weather has almost a second time disabled my hand; but I am under an obligation to write to you, not only because what you mention requires a speedy reply, but because I would not neglect while I have any, tho' ever so weak, ability. As to the former, dear sir, either keep or return the principal sum: I am perfectly satisfied with its being in your hands, just as I would, if I were so. But if it be more for your own conveniency to pay it, do. Let me but know soon, because if you do pay it, I can just at this juncture, employ it. If not, send me only a note for the interest: but the sooner I know your determination, the better, on the account just now mention'd, that I may order my little affairs accordingly.

For the letters, I am obliged to the care you have taken, in the endorsement and order you mention: however, I beg once more to see them. You cannot conceive the pain which Cromwell's partiality to those things (which only could occasion their coming into the public) has given me. I have desired the same thing of Mrs Blount,[2] with whose late worthy husband I entertained so long a correspondence, and of all others. Dear sir, I must give over; I cannot hold my Pen longer. You see my hand is strangely altered; but I do assure you my heart is not. With which I am, and ever shall be | your affect friend and | most obedient servant |

You suspect me unjustly as to Gulliver's book. Upon my word I never saw it, till printed.

Pray make Mrs Caryll, and the young Lady, remember me as I shall always do them.

---

[1] The letter is placed here since it is the answer of Pope to Caryll's reply to the letter of 5 Dec. Pope's hand is a second time disabled by the cold and rheumatism. The first time was the accident of September.   [2] The widow of Edward Blount, Esq.

The year 1727 is not one of great epistolary interest. Correspondences other than that with Lord Oxford are obviously very fragmentary. Except his lordship, no one received more than three letters from Pope that have since come to light. The literary work of the year was the publication of two volumes of prose miscellanies chiefly by Pope and Swift, and the preparation, involving difficulty, of a third (called 'the last') volume of miscellaneous verses, finally published in March 1728. Letters concerning non-literary matters show Pope, as usual, being helpful to several people—to the Governor of the Bermudas (Sir John Hope Bruce), to his old schoolmaster (Thomas Deane), to the relatives of his friend Craggs in their erection of a fitting monument in the Abbey, and to the new master of the mint (John Conduitt), who was publishing a posthumous work by Sir Isaac Newton. The most pleasurable event of the year was doubtless the visit of Dean Swift, which lasted from the end of April to the middle of September.

*POPE *to* DR. RICHARD TOWNE[1]   5 *January* [1726/7]
Arthur A. Houghton, Jr.

Twitenham, Jan. 5.

Sir,—I am obligd to you for the favor of yours, but concerned to find my Debt to you still unpaid, which either my Lord Peterborow, or Mrs Robinson, or both promisd me to discharge the first time they should see you: (I speak of three or four months agoe.) If you please to send your Servant to Mr Mead the Goldsmiths with the inclosed, it will be done.

My hand (as you may see by this Scrawling) is not quite recoverd: I am glad to have so much the use of it, as now to assure you I am, Sir | Your most obedient humble Servant, A. Pope.

Endorsement: Mr Pope | 1726(?)
And below in pencil: To Dr Towne

*POPE *to* JACOB TONSON, JR.   20 *January* 1726/7
Add. 28275

Jan. 20th | 1726/7

To Mr Tonson,—My Lord Oxford desires you to give the Bearer

[1] Dr. Towne, who had been in Barbados, came to London in 1726 to publish his *Treatise of the Diseases most Frequent in the West-Indies*. He apparently returned to Barbados late in 1728. See Voltaire's *Correspondence* (ed. L. Foulet, 1913), pp. 168 n. 2 and 113. Pope's connexion with the doctor is obscure. Towne may have attended Pope during the time when the poet's hand was injured. He was evidently a friend of Lord Peterborow, Mrs. Robinson, and Pope, as well as of Voltaire.

twelve of Dr Arbuthnots Books,[1] and pray send with them, one to
me. | Your humble Servant | A. Pope.

Endorsement (in Tonson's hand?): Dd Wm Williams—sent to my Lord
Oxford

*POPE *to* JAMES STOPFORD   *17 February* 1726/7

The Victoria and Albert Museum (Forster Collection transcript)

Tho I seemed under some doubt when I saw you, whether I could
comply with my own inclinations to meet you with Dr Arbuthnot to
morrow; I did really intend & hope to do it; but a violent cold pre-
vents me, tho' I had contrived to overcome my other difficulties. I
am truly sorry for it—I have little to say to you, but that I am almost
sorry I knew you at all since 'tis for so short a time; & I am glad to
have known you no longer if you must be no Older an Acquaintance.
But pray come again among us, happier than you went from us, I
mean richer, & more dignified, as well as Beneficed: I shall expect
the two good Deans, this time twelve month together. In the meantime enjoy Finglas, & make it a Bishoprick to yourself, in your contentment there.

I must desire your acceptance of the Odyssey: you seemed, I thought,
to like the Quarto; but if your Edition of the Iliad be the Best large
folio, I will get you the same of the Odyssey. Let Mr Gay know, &
we will find some way to send it.

Pray tell Dr Swift I forgot one question in my Letter to him,[2]
whether he likes the Cadenus & Vanessa be inserted in the new Collection,[3] or not? This pacquet for him contains some Seeds of Italian
Fennel & Brocoli;[4] a part of which I desire him to give you to propagate (according to the directions I have sent him herewith) in your
Garden.

---

[1] Doubtless Arbuthnot's *Tables of Ancient Coins*, &c., listed in Wilford's *Monthly Catalogue* (iii. 4) as published in this month.

[2] Stopford is about to start for Dublin and his parish of Finglas with letters for Swift
from Bolingbroke, Pope, and Gay. Pope published his own letter in 1741, obviously with a
wrong date. See the following letter.

[3] The projected new volume of *Miscellanies*.

[4] Among the Polwarth Papers in the Register House, Edinburgh, is a letter from Pope's
friend William Cleland to Lord Kimmergham, 1 Nov. 1728, which in part reads as follows:

> Sure you are Mistaken in saying Brocoli is a kind of asparagus or he is Mistaken in
> saying so. I have eat them I beleive oftner than he, and am more Mistaken then either of
> you if they are any thing but Italian sprouts or Coleworts if you please. I know they are
> the rarest thing of that kind to be had here for I remember Mr Pope was talking to a
> ffriend of his and Myne of a promise of some of that seed as the greatest ffavor My Lord
> Peterborough had done him. If I cannot gett some amongst my Italian ffriends (I went to
> one and Missing him at home this Morning ffound him at anothers but so deep in Musick
> I was not to be heard except I had sung my request to him) I hope Mr Pope will help me
> to some.

My Letter is also inclosed with it. Dear Sir adieu, & God bless you in all your Ways. | I am sincerely | Your most obli|ged & faithfull | affect. Servant, | A. Pope.

Feb. 17 | 1726.

Address: To the Revd Mr Stopford

†POPE *to* SWIFT¹   [*17 February* 1726/7]
1740
                                        March 8, 1726/7

Mr. Stopford will be the bearer of this letter, for whose acquaintance I am, among many other favours, obliged to you: and I think the acquaintance of so valuable, ingenious, and unaffected a man, to be none of the least obligations.

Our Miscellany is now quite printed. I am prodigiously pleas'd with this joint-volume, in which methinks we look like friends, side by side, serious and merry by turns, conversing interchangeably, and walking down hand in hand to posterity; not in the stiff forms of learned Authors, flattering each other, and setting the rest of mankind at nought: but in a free, un-important, natural, easy manner; diverting others just as we diverted ourselves. The third volume² consists of Verses, but I would chuse to print none but such as have some peculiarity, and may be distinguish'd for ours, from other writers. There's no end of making Books, Solomon said, and above all of making Miscellanies, which all men can make. For unless there be a character in every piece, like the mark of the Elect, I should not care to be one of the Twelve-thousand signed.

You receiv'd, I hope, some commendatory verses from a Horse and a Lilliputian, to Gulliver; and an heroic Epistle of Mrs. Gulliver.³ The Bookseller would fain have printed 'em before the second Edition of the Book, but I would not permit it without your approbation: nor do I much like them. You see how much like a Poet I write, and yet if you were with us, you'd be deep in Politicks. People are very

---

¹ Pope's editions (1740–42) printed this letter always under the impossible date of 8 Mar. 1726/7. What happened, almost certainly, is that Pope did not date his letter, but Swift did endorse the letter with the date received—which Pope eventually printed. Letters from Bolingbroke (17 Feb. 1726/7: Ball, iii. 379) and Gay (18 Feb. 1726/7: Ball, iii. 382) indicate the approximate date of Pope's writing. Ball was the first (iii. 380) to redate this letter, but since it was enclosed to Stopford on the 17th, it cannot be later than that day.
    The only textual variants occur in Curll's reprinting (1741 Lc), and they are negligible. A footnote in 1741 Da and Db identifies Stopford as 'Dr. James Stopford, Minister of Finglass'.
² Called upon publication over a year later (7 Mar. 1727/8) 'the Last Volume'. It will be much discussed by Swift and Pope during this year.
³ Presumably Pope was the author of some of these. Arbuthnot's letters to Lord Oxford in November of 1726 (here ii. 411, 417) indicate that he also was concerned in the series. See Ault, *New Light*, pp. 231–42.

warm, and very angry, very little to the purpose, but therefore the more warm and the more angry: *Non nostrum est, Tantas componere lites.*[1] I stay at Twitnam, without so much as reading news-papers, votes, or any other paltry pamphlets: Mr. Stopford will carry you a whole parcel of them, which are sent for your diversion, but not imitation. For my own part, methinks, I am at Glubdubdrib with none but Ancients and Spirits about me.

I am rather better than I use to be at this season, but my hand (tho' as you see, it has not lost its cunning) is frequently in very aukward sensations, rather than pain. But to convince you it is pretty well, it has done some mischief already, and just been strong enough to cut the other hand, while it was aiming to prune a fruit-tree.

Lady Bolingbroke has writ you a long, lively, letter, which will attend this; She had very bad health, he very good. Lord Peterborow has writ twice to you; we fancy some letters have been intercepted, or lost by accident. About ten thousand things I want to tell you: I wish you were as impatient to hear them, for if so, you would, you must come early this spring. Adieu. Let me have a line from you. I am vex'd at losing Mr. Stopford as soon as I knew him: but I thank God I have known him no longer. If every man one begins to value must settle in Ireland, pray make me know no more of 'em, and I forgive you this one.

*POPE to VISCOUNT HARCOURT   1 March 1726/7

Harcourt MSS.

Twitnam, March, 1st

My Lord,—I have a particular favour to beg of your Lordship, not only as it concerns a friend of mine who has been personally injured, but as it relates to what you ever have been more tender of, than any private concern, even of your friends; Publick Justice, & Equity. I earnestly desire your Lordship to be Present at an affair relating to a Complaint against the Governor of Bermudas,[2] of which they are to move for a Hearing, next Saturday, at the Privy Council. I have cause to believe it is such an affair, as will require the Notice of all honest men, and be no less agreeable to Your own Love of Justice, than to your particular favour so long shewn to all that is requested by | My Lord | Your most obligd, faithfull | Servant, | A. Pope.

Endorsement: Mr Pope | to | Lord Viscount Harcourt | 1 March 1726

[1] Translated in 1741 Dab as 'it is not mine such Factions to compose'. Cf. Virgil, *Eclogues*, iii. 108.

[2] Pope seems to be intervening in behalf of John Hope (afterwards Sir John Hope Bruce) who was presently replaced as governor by Captain Pitt. The replacement was announced in *The Historical Register* (xii [1727], Chronological Diary, 43) as of 2 Oct. 1727. Sir John or his sister Lady Wardlaw was the author of *Hardyknute*.

POPE *to* CARYLL   28 *March* [1727]
Add. 28618

March 28

Your letter makes me smile, by rallying me upon my silence in such a manner, and imputing it to the punctual payment of your debt. I delivered the bond, &c., in form to Mr Wright,[1] and writ you an epistle of a merry, not busy, kind, the week after. I find you never received it. I assure you, I never did, could, or can, or will quarrel with you. In particular I never took anything more kindly of you and your family than your last visit at Twittenham,[2] which methought was a renovation of the ancient acquaintance you and they have honoured me with. The subject of the letter which miscarried, was Mr Dean, my old master,[3] who had writ me one whereby I perceived his head happy in the highest self opinion, whatever became of his body. And hereupon writ you a dissertation proving it better for him to remain a prisoner than to have his liberty. I showed, that self-conceit is the same with respect to the philosopher, as a good conscience to a religious man, a perpetual feast, &c. But to be serious, I've told Mr Webb that I will contribute with Lord Dormer and you in what manner you shall agree to think most effectual for his relief.[4] My own judgment indeed is, that giving him a small yearly pension among us and others, even where he is, would keep him out of harms-way:

[1] Elwin tells us that Caryll repaid the £200 borrowed from Pope's father in 1710 on 5 Jan. 1727.

[2] On this visit see Pope to Caryll, 5 Dec. 1726.

[3] To Pope's character of his old master should be added the notices of his career which appeared at the time of his death in 1735. *The General Evening Post*, 15 Nov. 1735, gives the following:

> A few Days ago died, in the 108th Year of his Age, at Mrs. Wagstaff's in Suffolk Place, near St. George's Fields, Southwark, Mr. Thomas Dean, of Town Malden in Kent. He was twenty Years of Age when King Charles was beheaded; was formerly Fellow of University College in Oxford, and Professor of the Greek Tongue: He continued in the University till King James the Second's Reign, in which becoming a Roman Catholick, he was depriv'd at the Revolution, afterwards kept a Boarding School at St. Mary le Bon, Middlesex, and lately liv'd wholly upon charitable Contributions. He never made use of Spectacles, but could read the smallest Print within half a Year of his Death.

The Whitehall Evening Post, 18 Nov. 1735, corrected this account in some details:

> A few Days since died obscurely, Mr. Thomas Deane, formerly Fellow of University College in Oxford, where he was admitted at the Age of 15; in 1669, he proceeded in his Degrees in Arts, but was not Publick Professor in any Faculty or Language in that University: He was reconciled to the Church of Rome in 1685, being converted by Obadiah Walker, more than once in prison upon Account of his Religion, and the Notion of his being in Popish Orders: In 1691, Dec. 38 [*sic!*], he stood on the Pillory for concealing a Libel printed by one who lodg'd in the same House with him: During King James's Reign, he wrote some Pieces in Defence of the Roman Church, which were privately printed in the Lodgings of the Master of University College.

See also *Ath. Oxon.* (ed. Bliss), iv. 450.

[4] The fifth Baron Dormer had two sons who might have been Pope's schoolmates—as was Webb, who later married the widow of Henry Englefield.

which writing and publishing of books may bring him into. And that I find to be the project that bites him. He was all his life a dupe to some. project or other.

I heartily wish you all a very Holy Week, and a happy Easter.[1] Your god-daughter Patty does the same. I'm sincerely troubled at the frequent returns of your gout. I wish your health with all real heartiness: Is not that a better phrase than the modern compliment? I'm neither well, nor ill; that is, in truth, almost always my State, but always so employed and so dissipated by other people's affairs, as well as my own, that I live in a hurry of thought, and too often in a hurry of person. God send me better thoughts, and more sedate reflexions than this world generally allows me of late. I am charged too with the affairs of my relations, which among other vexations must excuse me to a reasonable friend, as I know (notwithstanding your raillery) you are, when I'm sometimes an ill correspondant. Adieu, and all good things attend you. | Dear sir | Your's faithfully | A: P:

When did you hear of Mrs Cope.

FENTON *to* BROOME   28 *March* 1727

Elwin–Courthope, viii. 135

March 28, 1727.

I have not my old excuse, dear Broome, of invincible laziness to plead for not answering your two letters sooner, but I have hurried up and down with university and country acquaintance ever since I saw you; but I hope I shall get out of this troublesome town in about a fortnight. In the meantime I divert myself with watching for your name in the newspapers,—not among the lean poetical advertisements, but in a more significant and substantial paragraph.[2] Prithee do not let your interest sleep. Every day furnishes fresh arguments why you should vigorously pursue your attack.

Mr. Tonson and I have talked over the affair of Virgil. He is not for having dissertations, as you and I intended, but would have the notes executed in the same method that you took in the Odyssey.[3]

Mr. Pope was with me this morning, and desired me to present his service to you. He told me that he hears little Harte the poet is dead in the country.[4] I spoke to Jacob to send you Dr. Arbuthnot's book

---

[1] Easter fell on 2 Apr. in 1727.

[2] Announcing the publication of Broome's *Poems on Several Occasions*, which were published in March.

[3] It argues that if Tonson employed Fenton on Shakespeare and Waller and considered at this time having Broome do Virgil for him, the collaboration on the *Odyssey* had hardly robbed them of fame.

[4] The Rev. Walter Harte (actually he died in 1774) was already a Pope protégé. In May of this year Lintot published for Harte his *Poems on Several Occasions*, which included

bound.[1] Why will you not cultivate a correspondence with him? It would be both useful and entertaining to you, and postage will cost nothing to either. Adieu. Give my service to your good spouse, and Mr. Burlington and everybody else whom you know I love or honour. Thine ever.

*POPE *to* VISCOUNT HARCOURT[2]   *April* 1727

Harcourt MSS.
                                                                    Wednesday.

My Lord,—I trouble your Lordship with the answer I had from the Attorney concerning the writings I sent for by your direction. What you judge proper to be done next by me in it, I beg your Lordship to inform me: If it require no greater haste I would gladly stay in the Country four or five days, but whenever you please to command me, I am nevertheless ready to go to town. If I had no other cause to wait on you, it is unfeignedly a sufficient one to me, to have the pleasure of assuring you My Lord with what truth & obligation I am | Your most faithfull & | obedient Servant | A. Pope

  My Mothers & my humblest Respects to Lady Harcourt.

Endorsement: Apr. 1727 | Mr Pope | To Lord Vicount | Harcourt

POPE *to* THE EARL OF OXFORD[3]   [22 *April* 1727]

Longleat Portland Papers, xii

My Lord,—I was under no small Vexation (as you might see, tho I think I bore it Heroically) the other day. I want to have some amends made *Me* for having used *You* so ill. Therfore on Monday I intend to dine with your Lordship, and (if I can) to bring the Dean with me, in full atonement. I am with faithful Esteem, with obligation,

---

complimentary verses to Pope. Item 128 of the Cunningham Sale (Sotheby's, 26 Feb. 1855) was an autograph letter dated 9 Feb. 1727 from Harte to an unidentified correspondent. In part it read: 'My miscellany is now entirely printed off, except two sheets of Divine Poems. I thought to have published much sooner, but as Mr. Pope was pleased to correct every page with his own hand, I could not hurry him.' Pope subscribed for four copies of the book.
  [1] Jacob Tonson had just published Arbuthnot's *Tables*.
  [2] Possibly this letter was written on Wednesday, 5 Apr.; for on 10 Apr. Pope signed certain papers relating to Motte's agreement to publish Miscellanies for Pope and Swift. It is also quite possible that the papers in question refer to the vexatious affairs of 'my relations', mentioned by Pope to Caryll (28 Mar. [1727]). The documents concerning the Miscellanies were printed in *The Gentleman's Magazine*, xliv (1855), 363. They are now preserved in the Pierpont Morgan Library of New York.
  [3] The date is subscribed in Oxford's hand. The 22nd was Saturday. Ball says that Swift, who had left Dublin on the 8th or 9th, reached Twickenham on the 22nd (Ball, iii. 386 n.). Possibly Pope is writing in anticipation of the Dean's arrival: hence the 'if I can'.

& Gratefulness, | My Lord | Your most obedient | humble Servant, | A. Pope.

Saturday | night. April. 22. 1727

POPE *to* THE EARL OF OXFORD[1]   [23 *April* 1727]

Longleat Portland Papers, xii

April. 23. 1727.

My Lord,—So good a figure as you say I made in distress, I assure you I like Prosperity much better, & such I should have accounted it to have had neither *Man* or *Woman* that day with us but your Self. We will put off our intended Joint Journey to London to morrow, & fix some other day (I believe it must be toward the End of the Week, or beginning of the next,) by what I perceive of the Idle Dean's great Businesses. I heartily am obligd to you My Lord, & beg my Lady Oxford will think me her most obedient Servant, as I hope with or without the Dean to tell you both very soon, rather than fail of which I will come with him a Second time. | Your Lordships Ever faithfully, | A. Pope.

They[2] are gone a fishing, or would send their Services.

POPE *to* BROOME   26 *April* 1727

Elwin–Courthope, viii. 136

April 26, 1727

I hoped you would have made good your promise to give me an account of your health after your return to Suffolk, which was but ill in town; but I have inquired of it several times from Mr. Fenton, who is now gone to Cambridge. I came again to London that week on purpose to see you; but you were set out the day before. I desired him to tell you this, and to assure you I was yours at all times. I should be glad to have a few lines from you when you are at leisure, to inform me of anything that pleases or concerns you, to whom I have a true affection, as well as a constant good wish for all you desire or pray for. I have not in form thanked you for your book,[3] but I was very much pleased with almost everything in it. One or two little things I thought too puerile, and remember were written when you were very young. If Lintot had shown them me, I would have advertised you of them; but they are but trifles. Now I mention Lintot, I do not know how he treats you, but he is the greatest scoundrel to me in the earth—I mean in foul language and noisy falsehoods of many sorts, the worst

---

[1] The date is in Lord Oxford's hand.   [2] Swift and Gay?
[3] Broome's *Poems* had been published late in March.

of which I reckon his endeavours to set people at variance by mere lies, as he has done to several of the subscribers to Homer, and I am convinced it was wholly from thence that those rumours so prejudicial both to you and me proceeded, which, had I not known your natural integrity and sincere good-nature, must have made me think of you in a manner very different from what I really do.[1] The fellow had the impudence the other day to affirm that I never told him you had any hand in the work till after his agreement was signed, than which you know nothing can be a more flagrant lie. I think you had a letter from him before expressly about your share in the work; I wish you had it by you; and I desire you to write me whatever you remember to the contrary of this falsehood, that it may help to undeceive anybody to whom he tells it. You are sensible this is a piece of downright justice to me as an honest man.[2]

I wish your health confirmed. Mine I fear never will be better; but if I cannot live long in myself, I would in my friends. I think Fenton more lively and more in vigour than I ever knew him. Sir Clement Cottrell is not so. He is expected here in a few days for the whole summer. As you have made one journey purely to the town without seeing this place, I expect you should make another to this place in particular, where you will find the worthy gentleman I mentioned, and one, who, I faithfully assure you, is in heart and with truth very affectionately yours.

My mother is your hearty servant.

FENTON *to* BROOME   3 *May 1727*

Elwin–Courthope, viii. 138

Trinity Hall, May 3, 1727.

Dear Mr. Broome,—I have been at Cambridge about a week or ten days. I found your old college in a terrible fracas on the death of good Dr. Jenkin. You have seen by the news how his preferments are disposed of.[3] I am afraid that our friend has raised abundance of enemies; but whether or no his conduct in the competition has given any just provocation, *nec scio, nec, si sciam, dicere vellem.*

---

[1] Pope is perhaps thinking of rumours rather than of printed attacks, though the newspapers did print a few attacks.

[2] With this remark as well as the preceding passage Pope is trying to get Broome to defend the collaboration publicly. Failure to do so may in part have led Pope to glance in the 'Bathos' at the 'one or two little things' that he thought puerile in Broome's *Poems*. See the 'Bathos' (published in the 'last' volume of the *Miscellanies* (7 Mar. 1727/8), esp. Ch. VII—and Broome's later comments in letters to Fenton.

[3] Dr. Robert Jenkin, Master of St. John's College, had died 7 Apr. 1727. 'Our friend' Dr. Newcome was a candidate to succeed Dr. Jenkin as master, but at this time failed of election. He became master in 1735.

Jacob Tonson told me he had heard from you before I left London, and I gave him a note of such books as occurred to my memory that might be serviceable to you in executing your design on Virgil. I like the additional verses you sent me.[1] What a pity it is that you printed that poem in your Miscellany! *Mutatis mutandis*, if it had been published on the siege of Gibraltar, it would have gained you a great deal of reputation.

I hope you will hold your resolution of seeing Cambridge this summer, though I will not desire that happiness before the commencement, for I am undertaking an expedition into Staffordshire about a fortnight hence, and propose to return to college in a month at furthest. Two hundred miles in a hot season! Think o' that, Mr. Broome, and never apply the epithet lazy more to a person of my activity. I hope, however, to have a line from you before I set out. I beg you to present my service as usual, and believe me to be ever most affectionately your faithful humble servant.

†CONGREVE *to* POPE[2]   6 *May* [1727]

1737

May 6.

I have the pleasure of your very kind letter, I have always been obliged to you for your friendship and concern for me, and am more affected with it, than I will take upon me to express in this letter. I do assure you there is no return wanting on my part, and am very sorry I had not the good luck to see the Dean before I left town: it is a great pleasure to me, and not a little vanity to think that he misses me. As to my health, which you are so kind to enquire after, it is not worse than in London: I am almost afraid yet to say that it is better, for I cannot reasonably expect much effect from these waters in so short a time: but in the main they seem to agree with me. Here is not one creature that I know, which next to the few I would chuse, contributes very much to my satisfaction. At the same time that I regret the want of your conversation, I please my self with thinking that you are where you first ought to be, and engaged where you cannot do too much. Pray give my humble service, and best wishes to your good mother. I am sorry you don't tell me how Mr. Gay does in his health; I should have been glad to have heard he was better. My young Amanuensis,

---

[1] The additional verses are not identified. The verses so unfortunately printed in Broome's *Poems* were possibly those on 'The Seat of the War in Flanders, chiefly with Relation to the Sieges'. This was 'written in 1710'; but *multis mutatis mutandis* it might have been applied to the siege of Gibraltar by the Spanish in 1727.

[2] The year must be either 1726 or 1727, and the latter seems far more probable. In 1726 Swift had arrived in London in March and thus Congreve might have seen him before leaving town. In 1727 Swift (going first to Twickenham) did not go to town until the end of April, when Congreve may already have gone to Bath. Gay's health was questionable early in 1727.

as you call him, I am afraid will prove but a wooden one: and you know *ex quovis ligno*,[1] &c. you will pardon Mrs. R—'s Pedantry, and believe me to be | Yours, &c.

P.S. By the inclosed you will see I am like to be impress'd, and enroll'd in the list of Mr. Curll's Authors;[2] but I thank God I shall have your company. I believe it is high time you should think of administring another *Emetick*.

POPE *to* CARYLL   10 *May* [1727]

Add. 28618

Twicknam May 10th

My mother's long indisposition has been the occasion that I writ to you no sooner, being unwilling to omit at the same time to give you an account of the statue you bid me enquire about. There is but one antique one of Diana, the rest are modern, and but ordinary. And indeed the ancient statue is not in a very gracefull posture.[3] You must have seen it, drawing an arrow out of a quiver over her shoulder, which renders the arm, in some views, so foreshortened as to appear a stump. It is also of a large size, perhaps too large for the area in which you design to place it. I ought to know exactly what the open space is, in which it must stand, for a proportion ought to be observed. Perhaps a Flora, or a Pan, or Fawn, might do, of which there are several sizes. The most common, of a midle size, will cost about ten pounds, in lead without the Pedestal and carriage.

I received last post a letter from Mrs Cope, by which I find her miseries are increased by a cancer in her breast, which makes it un-avoidable[4] for her to live far from Paris, for the necessary help of surgeons, and also casts her under greater wants to pay for it. Surely she is now, every day, a greater object of charity than other people. I must hope you will add something to her relief, since really that (which she tells me is almost all her subsistance), the little I yearly send her, cannot suffice, nor can I, in my own narrow fortune (you must needs be so sensible) increase it. Mr Robert Arbuthnot, out of friendship to me and his own natural generosity of mind, had been kinder to her than any body; nor is it in my power to make him any returns, which

---

[1] The full adage seems to be: *Ex quovis ligno Mercurius non fingitur*.

[2] What of Congreve's writing Curll now wished to print is uncertain. A second edition of *The Altar of Love* is listed by R. Straus (*The Unspeakable Curll*, p. 282) for 8 June. The first edition of this made-up volume had included at least three fugitive pieces by Pope. Possibly Congreve knew how to deter this publishing scavenger.

[3] The ancient Diana Pope has in mind is doubtless the Artemis long at Versailles and now in the Louvre. Professor Mason Hammond notes that some critics (Furtwängler and Urlichs, for example) have been more favourably impressed by the posture of the figure than was Pope.   [4] Pope evidently means *impossible*.

renders me uneasy. Letters to her must be directed to him. *Banquier a Paris*, is sufficient; and he'll faithfully convey to her any thing you think fit, in the best manner.

I hope you are long since perfectly recovered of the gout. I see and hear of nothing but sickness and death. God fit us for either. I am, dear sir, your family's, and your own faithful servant. | A: P:

POPE *to* FORTESCUE   16 *May* [1727]

Dr. Dallas Pratt

Twitnam May 16.

I should without compliment come to town any day you desired, on any account, as well as on so agreable an one as you propose; but (which I wonder my Communicative Waterman never told your people) my Mother has been & is Extremely ill, & dangerously so, of an Intermitting Fever, which requires my Constant attendance. Here is nobody with me but the *Dean of St Patricks*, who would hardly be here if he were not the Best-naturd & indulgent man I know; it is so melancholy a way of passing his time. I could be glad to see you, if you have a day of leisure, & indeed, there are few friends to whom I could make this request. I wish you & yours well & happy in every circumstance of life, & am | Truly dear Sir Yours. A. Pope.

†POPE *to* MRS. HOWARD[1]   20 *June* [1727]

1737

June 20.

We cannot omit taking this occasion to congratulate you upon the encrease of your family, for your Cow is this morning very happily deliver'd of the better sort, I mean a female calf; she is as like her mother as she can stare. All Knights Errants Palfreys were distinguish'd by lofty names: we see no reason why a Pastoral Lady's sheep and calves should want names of the softer sound; we have therefore given her the name of Caesar's wife, Calf-urnia; imagining, that as Romulus and Remus were suckled by a wolf, this Roman lady was

[1] The date offers problems. The year must be either 1726 or 1727, and the latter seems preferable. In 1726 the Prince and Princess (and hence Mrs. Howard) were already at Richmond for the summer; in 1727 they had been there, but had been compelled to return to town upon news of the death of George I, which came from the Continent on 14 June. In 1726 Swift was presumably at Twickenham, and would have been at Marble Hill on the birthday; in 1727 he was in London, but might be invited for Friday's feast. Even the day-date is wrong, for in 1726 the 20th was Monday, and in 1727, Tuesday. For the movements of the Prince and Princess see *Public State of Great Britain*, xxxi (1726), 643, and xxxiii (1727), 549.

In the *Suffolk Correspondence*, i. 233, is a letter of this same day from Martha Blount to Mrs Howard. It seems to indicate that Martha had been a neighbour—either at Ham or at Richmond—and now regrets the absence of Mrs. Howard.

suckled by a cow, from whence she took that name. In order to celebrate this birth-day, we had a cold dinner at Marble-hill, Mrs. Susan
offer'd us wine upon the occasion, and upon such an occasion we could
not refuse it. Our entertainment consisted of flesh and fish, and the
lettice of a greek Island, called Cos. We have some thoughts of dining
there to morrow, to celebrate the day after the birth-day, and on friday
to celebrate the day after that, where we intend to entertain Dean
Swift; because we think your hall the most delightful room in the
world except that where you are. If it was not for you, we would forswear all courts; and really it is the most mortifying thing in nature,
that we can neither get into the court to live with you, nor you get
into the country to live with us; so we will take up with what we can
get that belongs to you, and make ourselves as happy as we can, in
your house.

I hope we shall be brought into no worse company, when you come
to Richmond: for whatever, our friend Gay may wish as to getting
into Court, I disclaim it, and desire to see nothing of the court but
yourself, being wholly and solely | Yours, &c.

†POPE *to* HUGH BETHEL   24 *June* 1727
1737
                                                      June 24, 1727.

You are too humane and considerate, (things few people can be charged
with.) Do not say you will not expect letters from me; upon my word
I can no more forbear writing sometimes to you, than thinking often[1]
of you. I know the world too well, not to value you; who are an
example of acting, living and thinking, above it, and contrary to it.

I thank God for my Mother's unexpected recovery, tho' my hope
can rise no higher than from reprieve to reprieve, the small addition of
a few days to the many she has already seen. Yet so short and transitory
as this light is, it is all I have to warm or shine upon me; and when it
is out, there is nothing else that will live for me, or consume itself in
my service. But I wou'd have you think this is not the chief motive
of my concern about her: Gratitude is a cheap virtue, one may pay it
very punctually for it costs us nothing, but our memory of the good
done. And I owe her more good, than ever I can pay or she at this
age receive, if I could. I do not think the tranquillity of the mind ought
to be disturbed for many things in this world; but those offices that are
necessary duties either to our friends or our selves, will hardly prove
any breach of it; and as much as they take away from our indolence
and ease of body, will contribute to our peace and quiet of mind by
the content they give. They often afford the highest pleasure; and

---

[1] thinking often of you] thinking of you *1737e–1742*.

those who do not feel that, will hardly ever find another to match it, let them love themselves ever so dearly. At the same time it must be own'd, one meets with cruel disappointments in seeing so often the best endeavours ineffectual to make others happy, and very often (what is most cruel of all) thro' their own means. But still I affirm, those very disappointments of a virtuous man are greater pleasures, than the utmost gratifications and successes of a mere self-lover.

The great and sudden event[1] which has just now happened, puts the whole world (I mean this whole world) into a new state: The only use I have, shall, or wish to make of it, is to observe the Disparity of men from themselves in a weeks time: the desultory leaping and catching of new motions, new modes, new measures: and the strange spirit and life, with which men broken and disappointed resume their hopes, their sollicitations, their ambitions! It would be worth your while as a Philosopher, to be busy in these observations, and to come hither to see the fury and bustle of the Bees this hot season, without coming so near as to be stung by them. Yours, &c.

†MRS. E. THOMAS *to* CROMWELL[2]   27 *June* 1727

1735 (In Preface)

June 27, 1727.

After so long a silence, as the many and great oppressions I have sigh'd under has occasion'd, one is at a Loss how to begin a letter to so kind a friend as your self. But as it was always my resolution, if I must sink, to do it as decently [that is as silently] as I cou'd: so when I found my self plung'd into unforeseen, and unavoidable ruin, I retreated from the world, and in a manner buried my self in a dismal place, where I knew none, nor none knew me. In this dull unthinking way, I have protracted a lingring death, [for life it cannot be call'd] ever since you saw me, sequester'd from company, depriv'd of my books, and nothing left to converse with but the Letters of my dead, or absent friends, amongst which latter I always plac'd yours, and Mr. *Pope*'s in the first rank. I lent some of them indeed to an ingenious person, who was so delighted with the specimen, that he importuned me for a sight of the rest, which having obtained, he convey'd them to the Press, I must not say altogether with my consent, nor wholly without it. I thought them too good to be lost in oblivion, and had

---

[1] The death of King George I at Osnabrügge, 11 June 1727.

[2] Mrs. Thomas had sold the Pope–Cromwell letters to Curll, who in the summer of 1726 had published them in *Miscellanea* (postdated 1727). The lady now calls upon her former lover to witness that the letters were not, as Pope had charged, stolen, but had been given to her by Cromwell. See Cromwell to Pope, 6 July and 1 Aug. 1727. Both Mrs. Thomas and Cromwell were dead before 1735 when Pope printed these letters. The dates of these letters to and from Cromwell are perplexing: one would expect them all to date in July or August of 1726.

no cause to apprehend the disobliging of any. The publick, *viz.* all persons of taste and judgment, wou'd be pleas'd with so agreeable an amusement; Mr. *Cromwell* cou'd not be angry, since it was but justice to his merit, to publish the solemn, and private professions of Love, Gratitude, and Veneration, made him by so celebrated an Author; and surely Mr. *Pope* ought not to resent the publication, since the early pregnancy of his Genius was no dishonour to his character. And yet had either of you been ask'd, common modesty wou'd have oblig'd you to refuse, what you wou'd not be displeas'd with, if done without your knowledge: And besides to end all dispute, you had been pleas'd to make me a free gift of them, to do what I pleas'd with them: and every one knows that the person to whom a Letter is address'd, has the same right to dispose of it, as he has of goods purchas'd with his money. I doubt not but your generosity and honour will do me the right, of owning by a line, that I came honestly by them. I flatter my self, in a few months I shall again be visible to the world, and whenever thro' good providence that Turn shall happen, I shall joyfully acquaint you with it, there being none more truly your oblig'd Servant, than, Sir, | Your faithful, and | most humble Servant, | E. Thomas.

P.S. A Letter, Sir, directed to Mrs. *Thomas*, to be left at my house, will be safely transmitted to her, by | E. Curll.

POPE *to* BENJAMIN MOTTE   30 *June* [1727]

The Pierpont Morgan Library

Twitnam June 30.

Sir,—Send me next (after the sheet R. & this) the last sheet of Cadenus & Vanessa.[1] As to the first, & the Title to Vol. 4. &c. let that alone to the last, next winter: only let them print one halfsheet, for me, of the beginning of Cadenus. For we will let the Table alone, & leave room for some new additions to the verses. As to the Poem, which I will have to end the Volume, it will make 3 sheets at least; & will take Time till winter to finish it. It may then be published singly first, if proper, I'm sure it will be advantageous, so to do. ⌜but say not a word of it to any man⌝.[2]

The advertisement of Curl is a silly piece of Impertinence,[3] not worth notice, & it serves to tell every body what makes for my purpose & reputation, "That those Letters to Mr Cromwell were printed

---

[1] Pope and Swift are busy with the 'last' volume of their *Miscellanies* (the third in order of publication). The volume was not published until 8 Mar. 1728, but it was apparently well in hand except for 'The Progress of Dulness' (later rechristened *The Dunciad*), which was to end the volume. *Cadenus and Vanessa* was to be the first item in the volume. Volume iv was for various reasons postponed until 1732.

[2] This statement is added between the lines after the period.

[3] Curll's advertisement must have appeared in a newspaper not identified.

without My Consent or knowledge." The fact of *Cabinets being broke open & dead people's Closets ransackd . . is nevertheless true*, which this Scoundrel wishes to have applyd to *Cromwells Letters*, only to advance their Sale, tho' it was spoken of other Instances relating to the Dean's as well as mine.[1]

You shall begin printing the next Volume of Prose, when you will; the large new Treatise which I formerly told you of,[2] relating to Rhetoric & Poetry, being in great forwardness, & the rest ready.

I am very sincerely, (& so is the Dean) | Your affect. Servant | A. Pope.

I'm afraid you have not sent the Books[3] to Mr Congreve at Bath, for I recd a letter from him without mention of 'em. Pray enquire about it.

Pray send one Sett of the Miscellanies to Wm. Fortescue Esq. at his house in Bellyard, in my name.

Address: To Mr Motte.

---

†CROMWELL *to* POPE   6 *July* 1727

1735 (In Preface)

Epsom, July 6th, 1727.

When these Letters were first printed, I wond'red how *Curll* cou'd come by 'em, and cou'd not but laugh at the pompous title; since whatever you wrote to me was humour, and familiar Raillery. As soon as I came from *Epsom*, I heard you had been to see me, and I writ you a short letter from *Will*'s, that I long'd to see you. Mr. D—s, about that time, charg'd me, with giving 'em to a Mistress, which I positively denied; not in the least, at that time, thinking of it: but some time after, finding in the news-papers Letters from Lady *Packington*, Lady *Chudleigh*, and Mr. *Norris*,[4] to the same *Sapho* or *E. T.* I began to fear that I was guilty. I have never seen these Letters of *Curll*'s,

---

[1] The other instances may take Pope's memory (stimulated by Swift) back to Dec. 1717 when Curll had avowed the opening of the cabinets of the dead in advertising 'Letters, Poems, &c. Amorous, Satyrical and gallant. Which pass'd between Sir Andrew Fountain, Dr. Swift, that celebrated Toast Mrs. Anne Long . . . the Hon. the Lady Mary Chambers, and other persons of distinction. Now first publish'd from their respective originals, found in Mrs. Long's Cabinet since her Decease. Printed for E. Curll.' See *The Evening Post*, 3 Dec. 1717–7 Jan 1717/18. Also Teerinck, 610.

[2] The 'Bathos', which presently Pope used as prefatory to the poems included in the 'last' volume. The printing of 'the next volume' (1732) did not begin at this time.

[3] Presumably vols. i and ii of the *Miscellanies*, published within the month.

[4] On a fly-leaf of the Bodleian MSS. Rawlinson Letters 90 is written 'Original Letters under the Hands of Mr John Dryden, Charles Dryden, — Norris, — Pope, Lady Chudleigh, Mrs Thomas, Dr. Ed: Young.' Rawlinson was an antiquary who published through Curll, from whom he must have got these Cromwell letters, now in Bodley.

nor wou'd go to his shop about 'em; I have not seen this *Sapho*,[1] alias
E. T. these seven years;—her writing, *That I gave her 'em, to do what
she wou'd with 'em*, is straining the point too far: I thought not of it;
nor do I think she did then: But severe Necessity, which catches hold
of a Twig, has produc'd all this; which has lain hid, and forgot by me,
so many years. *Curll* sent me a Letter last week, desiring a positive
answer about this matter, but finding I wou'd give him none, he went
to *E. T.* and writ a Postscript, in her long romantick Letter, to direct
my Answer to his house, but they not expecting an Answer, sent a
young man to me, whose name, it seems, is *Pattisson*:[2] I told him, I
shou'd not write any thing, but I believ'd it might be so, as she writ
in her Letter. I am extremely concern'd, that my former Indiscretion
in putting 'em into the hands of this *Pretieuse*,[3] shou'd have given you
so much disturbance; for the last thing I shou'd do wou'd be to disoblige you; for whom I have ever preserv'd the greatest esteem, and
shall ever be, Sir, | Your faithful Friend and | most humble Servant, |
Henry Cromwell.

†CROMWELL *to* POPE   1 *August* 1727

1735 (In Preface)

August 1, 1727.

Tho' I writ my long Narrative from *Epsom* 'till I was tir'd, yet was I
not satisfied; lest any doubt shou'd rest upon your mind. I cou'd not
make protestations of my Innocence of a grievous crime; but I was
impatient 'till I came to Town, that I might send you those Letters,
as a clear evidence, that I was a perfect stranger to all their proceeding:
Shou'd I have protested against it, after the printing, it might have
been taken for an attempt to decry his purchase; and as the little
exception you have taken, has serv'd him to play his game upon us,
for these two years; a new incident from me might enable him to play
it on for two more:—The great value she expresses for all you write,
and her passion for having 'em, I believe, was what prevail'd upon
me to let her keep 'em. By the interval of twelve years at least, from
her possession, to the time of printing 'em, 'tis manifest, that I had not

---

[1] This passage makes it impossible to argue that Mrs. Thomas was not called Sappho
by Cromwell. She was perhaps more commonly called 'Corinna'.

[2] Since William Pattison died of smallpox in Curll's house on 11 July 1727, his visit to
Cromwell must have antedated 6 July by some days. Pattison's life, prefixed to his *Poetical
Works* (1728), is a vivid document in the methods of Grub-street existence. This posthumous volume, published by Curll, was dedicated to the Earl of Peterborow by 'Lucasia' [Lucy
Price?]. Pope subscribed, and one poem by Pattison is addressed to Pope. Lucasia speaks
of Walter Harte as Pattison's 'dear friend', a fact which may account for Pope's interest in
this predecessor of 'Adonais'.

[3] For *précieuse*.

the least ground to apprehend such a design: But as people in great straits, bring forth their hoards of old Gold, and most valued Jewels, so *Sapho* had recourse to her hid treasure of Letters, and play'd off, not only yours to me, but all those to herself (as the Lady's last-stake) into the Press.—As for me, I hope, when you shall cooly consider the many thousand instances of our being deluded by the Females, since that great Original of *Adam* by *Eve*, you will have a more favourable thought of the undesigning error of | Your faithful Friend, | and humble Servant, | Henry Cromwell.

---

*POPE *to* FORTESCUE[1]   5 *August* [1727]

Harvard University

Twitenham, Augst 5.

It's long that I designd to answer your very kind letter, but I have been upon a Ramble to Cambridge which with other *Diverticula*, took up 3 weeks. I returnd home but 2 days since, but in my Return waited on Sir R.W.[2] and told him, it was You that made me so troublesome at his Sunday-Tables, & disturbing to his Sabbath-days of Rest. I communicated to Mr Gulliver's Cousin, what had befallen to him at Salisbury Assizes; whereat, like a good Relation; he seemed much concerned; Especially at the wicked Lawyer's calling in question the Veracity of that worthy Captain. I wish you the Success, which I think you cannot fail of, in your Election, & all other Views, provided you keep yourself pure of hand, as a Lawyer ought, & innocent of Heart, as a true Devonian. The only Argument I have yet heard against your Integrity, is what John Gay told me, that you had suffered a certain Clerk to counterfeit your hand-writing, & insert into the Margins of our Miscellanies, certain vile & scandalous Remarks against some paragraphs in the Prophecy of the Mohocks,[3] which we do affirm to be added in the true Spirit of Prophecy, as having been fulfilled, before we did add the same.

In short, do not forget me, as I do not forget You: I mention you to Mrs Hd. &c. Do you keep my Memory fresh, (in the Pickle of good French wine) with Mr Edgcomb when you see him; or, in his absence with Parson Hunt & Bickford.[4] Adieu. Let us hear from you.

[1] The year seems sure, since the letter must postdate the publication of *Gulliver* and antedate Swift's comment on what happened at the assizes in his letter to Pope of 10 May 1728.

[2] Doubtless Sir Robert Walpole, to whom Fortescue was devoted, and with whom this letter serves to indicate Pope had at this time some intimacy.

[3] Motte had been told (30 June 1727) to send the two volumes of *Miscellanies* to Fortescue. The Prophecy in question appears in ii. 260–4.

[4] The three may perhaps be identified as Sir Richard Edgcumbe (later Baron Edgecumbe), one of Walpole's lieutenants; Jeremiah Hunt (1678–1744), who preached in Pinner's Hall; and Edmund Bickford, a legal friend of both Fortescue and Pope.

Be sober & vigilant. Take fees. Spend nothing of your own pocket.
Love me as I love you.

　　Thine in the Law, | A. P.
　　(not to say Gospel)

Address: To Wm Fortescue Esqr at | his house in Bell Yard, near | Lincolns-
Inne | London.

Postmark: 7/AV

SWIFT *to* THOMAS SHERIDAN   12 *August* 1727

Dodsley *Miscellanies*, x (1745), 112

　　　　　　　　　　　　　　　　　　Twickenham, Aug. 12, 1727

I am cleverly caught, if ever Gentleman was cleverly caught; for
three Days after I came to Town with Lord *Oxford* from *Cambridgeshire*,[1] which was ten Days ago, my old Deafness seized me, and hath
continued ever since with great Encrease; so that I am now Deafer
than ever you knew me, and yet a little less, I think, than I was Yesterday; but which is worse, about four[2] Days ago my Giddiness seized
me, and I was so very ill, that Yesterday I took a hearty Vomit, and
though I now totter, yet I think I am a Thought better; but what will
be the Event, I know not; one thing I know, that these deaf Fits use
to continue five or six Weeks, and I am resolved if it continues, or my
Giddiness, some Days longer, I will leave this Place, and remove to
Greenwich, or somewhere near *London*, and take my Cousin *Lancelot*
to be my Nurse. Our Friends know her; it is the same with *Pat Rolt*.
⌐If my Disorder should keep me longer than my Licence of Absence
lasts, I would have you get Mr. *Worral* to renew it; it will not expire
till the sixth or seventh of *October*, and I resolved to begin my Journey
Sept. 15th. Mr. *Worrall* will see by the Date of my Licence what
time the new one should commence; but he hath seven Weeks yet to
consider: I only speak in time⌐.[3] I am very uneasy here, because so
many of our Acquaintance come to see us, and I cannot be seen;
besides Mr. *Pope* is too sickly and complaisant; therefore I resolve to
go somewhere else. This is a little unlucky, my Head will not bear
writing long: I want to be at home, where I can turn you out, or let
you in, as I think best. The K— and Q— come in two Days to our
Neighbourhood; and there I shall be expected, and cannot go; which
however, is none of my Grievances, for I had rather be absent, and
have now too good an Excuse. I believe this Giddiness is the Disorder
that will at last get the better of me; but I had rather it should not be
now; and I hope and believe it will not, for I am now better than Yester-

---

[1] On this ramble to Cambridge see Pope to Fortescue, 5 Aug.
[2] Emended from *forty*, which Dodsley printed.
[3] These two sentences are omitted in Swift's *Works* (ed. Faulkner), viii (1746), 419.

day.———Since my Dinner my Giddiness is much better, and my Deafness a hair's breadth not so bad. 'Tis just as usual, worst in the Morning and at Evening. I will be very Temperate; and in the midst of Peaches, Figs, Nectarins, and Mulberries, I touch not a bit. I hope I shall however set out in the middle of *September*, as I design'd. ———This is a long Letter for an ill Head: So adieu. My Service to our two Friends and all others.

POPE *to* THE EARL OF OXFORD   [15 *August* 1727]

Longleat Portland Papers, xii

Tuesday morning. | [1]Aug. 15. 1727.

My Lord,—I am very much obliged for your kind writing to us. The Dean is so much out of order, & withall so deaf, that he has conversd with no body, & fled all Company. Dr Arbuthnot comes to him to day or to morrow; & I purpose to go with him to London, to wait on your Lordship within [the] time you mention. I had a favor to beg of my Lady Oxford, which this may be a proper time for. It was to bespeak my Lord Morpeth's Interest in getting my Agent, Clarke, imployd as an Auctioneer in the Sale of Lord Lechmere's Goods.[2] Which if she will please to recommend to Lady Morpeth I shall be glad for the Man is honest, & has turnd himself to this business—I long to see you, & will very speedily give myself that happiness.

My Lord | Your most faithful obligd | humble Servant | A. Pope.

Address: To the Rt. Honorable, the | Earl of Oxford, in | Dover street. | Piccadilly | London.

Endorsement: Mr. Pope | Augt 15. 1727

*WILLIAM PULTENEY *to* POPE[3]   [22 *August* 1727]

Add. 4805

I am obliged to you all for your compliments & when the Dean is well enough I hope to see you in Town. You will probably find me a much happyer man than when you saw me last, for I flatter my self that in an hour or two I shall be once more bless'd with a Son. Mrs

---

[1] The date 'Aug. 15. 1727' is in Oxford's hand. The 15th was Tuesday.

[2] Lord Lechmere had died suddenly 18 June 1727. His widow was Lord Morpeth's sister. Lady Morpeth was the only daughter of a niece of Lady Oxford's: since Lady Morpeth's mother had died while the daughter was still very young, it seems likely that Lady Oxford may have supervised the grand-niece's early life. The 'agent Clarke' may be mentioned in Aikman's letter to Pope [Apr. 1725]. He was possibly the bookseller whose name appears on some of Pope's title-pages later. Lord Lechmere doubtless left a library that might be sold.

[3] The date comes from the *Westminster Abbey Registers* (ed. J. L. Chester), p. 402 n., where we learn that Anna-Maria Pulteney was born on 22 Aug. 1727 (a Tuesday).

Pulteney is now in labour, if she does well, & brings me a Boy, I shall not care one sixpence how much longer Sir Robert governs England, or Horace governs France.

I am | Evers Yrs | W. P.

11 a clock | Tuesday Morn.

[1]*Endorsement*: Mr Pulteney to Mr Pope | 1727

POPE *to* THE EARL OF OXFORD   25 *August* 1727
Longleat Portland Papers, xii

Twickenham Aug. 25. 1727.

My Lord,—That I write so soon to your Lordship is not purely in complyance to your Command, to acquaint you with the Dean's State of health, (tho I am very sensible you have Friendlyness & Good nature enough, to render That a Matter of Concern to you) but equally from a just desire I shall always have, of assuring your Lordship, that You have Another man in the world no less, the less worthily your Servant; ~~That I write this so soon to you~~ I guess this will find you yet unsetled at Wimpole;[2] where I wish I were with you again. But indeed the person whose health you enquire after, is not at all on the mending hand. He was for two days only, better, & ever since very bad: and the attendance I owe him will keep me here till I see some alteration.

Many things have given me trouble, at a time when His ill health was enough to disquiet me. I have withdrawn my little stake from the Turmoil of the Stocks, & out of suspitions which gave me continued disquiet. But the same Inquietude pursues me upon a different account. What to do with it any other way? I am like a man that saves, & lays together, the Planks of a broken Ship, or a falling House; but knows not how to rebuild out of them, either one, or the other?

Our Miscellany of Poems will be published next October: Tis one of the Benefits this Nation will reap by the Coronation. The greatest I shall receive from it, will be the seeing Your Lordship again; Which in sincerity, I earnestly desire, & am, with Esteem & obligation, Your most obedient affectionate | & most humble Servant. A. Pope.

Address: To the Rt. Honble | the Earl of Oxford at | Welbeck | Nottinghamshire | By Mansfield | Bagg [Only through the word *at* is the address in Pope's hand.]

Endorsement: Mr Pope | Twickenham Augt 25 1727

Postmark: 26/AV

[1] The endorsement seems to be in Swift's hand.

[2] Evidently Pope (as usual?) sent this letter to Dover Street, to be forwarded to his lordship wherever he was. Pope thought him at Wimpole; the servant thought him at Welbeck; and actually he seems to have been at Down Hall. See *Hist. MSS. Comm. Portland Papers*, vi. 18.

POPE *to* THOMAS SHERIDAN　　*6 September* [1727]

Dodsley *Miscellaniees*, x (1745), 68–70

Sir,—I am both obliged and alarmed by your Letter. What you mention of a particular Friend of the Dean's being upon the brink of another World,[1] gives me great Pain; for it makes me, in Tenderness to him, wish him with you; and at the same time I fear he is not in a Condition to make the Journey: Tho' (to ease you as far as I can) his Physician and Friend, Dr. *Arbuthnot*, assures me he will soon be well. At present he is very Deaf, and more uneasy than I hop'd that Complaint alone wou'd have made him. I apprehend he has written to you in a melancholy Way, which has put you into a greater Fright, than (with God's Will) we may have any reason for. He talks of returning to *Ireland* in three Weeks, if he recovers sufficiently; if not, he will stay here this Winter. Upon Pretence of some very unavoidable Occasions, he went to *London* four Days since, where I see him as often as he will let me. I was extreamly concerned at his Opiniatrety in leaving me; but he shall not get rid of the Friend, tho' he may of his House. I have suggested to him the Remedy you mention: And I will not leave him a Day, till I see him better. I wish you could see us in *England* without manifest Inconvenience to yourself; tho' I heartily hope and believe, that our Friend will do well. I sincerely honour you for your Warmth of Affection where it is so justly merited; and am, both for his Sake and your own, with great Esteem, | Sir, | Your truly-affectionate | and obedient Servant, | A. Pope.

Twittenham, Sept. 6.

P.S. I have often desired the Dean to make known to you my Sense of the good Opinion you have exprest of me in your Letters. I am pleas'd to have an Opportunity of thanking you under my Hand, and I desire you to continue it to one who is no way ungrateful.

POPE *to* MRS. HOWARD　　[*October* 1727?]

Add. 22626

Friday.

Madam,—Your Letter unfeignedly gives me great disquiet. I do not Only *Say* that I have a True Concern for you: Indeed I feel it, many times, very many, when I say it not. I wish to God any method were

---

[1] Swift himself had recently received news of Stella's serious illness, and had left Twickenham 'where so much company came to us while I was so giddy and deaf'—as he wrote Sheridan on 2 Sept. On the last day of August Swift had gone to his cousin Lancelot's house to avoid company and perhaps recover from his giddiness. Before September was out, he was on his way to Dublin.

soon taken to put you out of this uneasy, tormenting, situation.¹ You, that I know feel even to Delicacy, upon several triffling occasions, must (I am sensible) do it to a deep degree, upon one so near & so tender to you. And yet, as to the Last thing that troubles you, (the odd usage of Mr H. to his Son) I would fain hope some Good may be derived from it. It may turn him to a Reflexion, that possibly his Mother may be yet worse used than himself; & make him think of some means to comfort himself in comforting her. If any Reasonable creature, (any creature more reasonable than his Horses, or his Hounds, or his Country Gentlemen) were but about him, sure some Good might arise from it?²

It is a trouble to me not to be able to see & talk to you while you stay at Kensington. I will not fail to wait on you at London the next week, And yet God knows, when I reflect how little use or Good I can be to you, but meerly in Wishes, it is a sort of Vexation to me to come near you.

As for Mrs Blount, I verily believe she thinks you would take little satisfaction, much less comfort, in seeing her; I am otherwise very confident she would have been with you. (tho I also remember she has talkd of getting to see you by any method she could modestly propose, for a week past) In earnest she is so much your sincere Servant to my certain knowledge, that she would Prefer it to all she can do here.

I should not have put any more troublesome things into your mind than you alredy have, & therfore wish I had not mention'd Mrs V.'s³ paper; which (after all) she has since sent to me: It amounts to about 23 pound more than I believe you have any cause to pay. This is the matter so Important. But sure tis a Family-fault; & the Widow, like a good woman is very sollicitous to perform the *Will of the Dead*, which was, to Impose upon you every way.

The Dean surely thinks me much more his Friend, than You are; since he has not told his melancholy to me, as he has to you;⁴ which (considering his longer knowledge of me) he might have judged would affect me with more uneasiness, & therfore suppress'd.

I am truly afflicted about him. I really feel for my friends. What

---

¹ The original letter has no date except *Friday* which is heavily written over another date. Croker vaguely says the troubles of Mrs. Howard were due to the 'violent and indelicate proceedings' of her husband. Quite possibly, at the time of the Coronation of George II Mr. Howard thought, all things considered, some honours or a place were his due. He apparently withdrew from Court at this time. Mr. Howard's brother, the 8th Earl, was desirous at this time of securing an Act to enable him to sell certain estates. The Act failed of passing in Parliament in early 1727, but received royal assent 28 May 1728.

² This stable-loving son, Henry (b. 1706; succeeded his father as 10th Earl of Suffolk in 1733) would indeed seem to be in need of 'reflexion'.

³ Thomas Vernon (d. 1726) had sold the land for Marble Hill. Mrs. V. is his widow.

⁴ See Swift to Mrs. Howard, Ball iii. 412, 413, 419.

does Gay do? or what will be done for him? I am very sincerely Your Wellwisher, & | Madam, your most obedient faithful | Servant A. Pope.

Pray let me have some Authority to tell your Maid at Marble hill, that you will continue her, because I promisd her to intercede with you. (as you remember by your own Order)

POPE *to* THE EARL OF OXFORD[1]　　[2 *October* 1727]

Longleat Portland Papers, xii

Octr 2: 1727 | Twickenham.

My Lord,—I had not the least Imagination of your Lordship or my Lady's being in town yet. I was 2 whole days sick there, but should nevertheless have waited on You or Her, sick, as usual. I am not certain yet of the Dean's health or arrival at Dublin, but believe the one, & hope the other. I will do myself the honour to wait on your Lordship before the Coronation. My Mother is your most obliged Servant. I am ever with all truth & respect | My Lord | Your most obedient faith|full servant | A. Pope.

I beg my Lady Oxfords acceptance of my most sincere Service.

Address: To | The Rt. Honble the Earl of | Oxford.

†POPE *to* SWIFT　　2 *October* 1727

1740

Oct. 2, 1727

It is a perfect trouble to me to write to you, and your kind letter left for me at Mr. Gay's affected me so much, that it made me like a girl. I can't tell what to say to you; I only feel that I wish you well in every circumstance of life: that 'tis almost as good to be hated, as to be loved, considering the pain it is to minds of any tender turn, to find themselves so utterly impotent to do any good, or give any ease to those who deserve most from us. I would very fain know, as soon as you recover your complaints, or any part of them. Would to God I could ease any of them, or had been able even to have alleviated any! I found I was not, and truly it grieved me. I was sorry to find you could think your self easier in any house than in mine, tho' at the same time I can allow for a tenderness in your way of thinking, even when it seem'd to want that tenderness. I can't explain my meaning, perhaps you know it: But the best way of convincing you of my indulgence, will be, if I live, to visit you in Ireland, and act there as much in my own way as you did

---

[1] In the superscription the date and place are written in by Lord Oxford.

here in yours. I will not leave your roof, if I am ill. To your bad health I fear there was added some disagreeable news from Ireland, which might occasion your so sudden departure:[1] For the last time I saw you at Hammersmith,[2] you assured me you would not leave us, unless your health grew better, this whole winter;[3] and I don't find it did so. I never comply'd so unwillingly in my life with any friend as with you, in staying so intirely from you: nor could I have had the constancy to do it, if you had not promised that before you went, we shou'd meet, and you would send to us all to come. I have given your remembrances to those you mention in yours: we are quite sorry for you, I mean for ourselves. I hope, as you do, that we shall meet in a more durable and more satisfactory state; but the less sure I am of that, the more I would indulge it in this. We are to believe, we shall have something better than even a friend, there, but certainly here we have nothing so good.

Adieu for this time; may you find every friend you go to as pleas'd and happy, as every friend you went from is sorry and troubled. | Yours, &c.

POPE *to* CARYLL   5 *October* 1727

Add. 28618

5 Octr. 1727.

You would have reason to accuse me of negligence in so long deferring to answer yours, if I had not been unwillingly guilty in the same way to all my friendly correspondents. Betwixt very ill health, and very much attention to some uneasy business and unforeseen accidents of life, both to my self and my nearest relations, I have been perfectly engaged, and in a manner soured to the world and all the engagements of mere amusement in it. I had indeed the company here constantly of Dr Swift, who made my retirement his own for near four months, and is but just gone for Ireland;[4] which necessarily prevented my going any journeys from home, further than for a day or so to London, and back again. You see the reason why it was not possible for me, with any preservation of the laws either of civility or hospitality, to see you at Ladyholt. I thank God my mother is tolerably well again; but I

---

[1] Swift's departure (on 18 Sept.) was apparently unannounced to his friends: in that sense it was sudden. But Pope wrote to Sheridan (6 Sept.) that Swift would start for Ireland in three weeks, if well enough—and that is about what he did, if we assume that the three weeks dated from the last day in August when he left Twickenham.

[2] at Hammersmith] *omitted in 1741 Labc; 1742 Lbc; Da.* Possibly Swift found that Mr. Lancelot's house in New Bond Street was too accessible to friends, and his appetite for complete withdrawal led him to adopt his original plan and remove to Hammersmith with Cousin Patty Rolt (Mrs. Lancelot) as nurse.

[3] The same editions that omitted 'at Hammersmith' placed the words 'this whole winter' after 'leave us'.

[4] Swift arrived about the middle of April, and he left London for Dublin about 18 Sept.

myself labor under a very ill state of health, which increases daily; my old complaints of the stomach are turned into an inveterate cholic, which seldom leaves me in any lively sensation of life for two days together. I had lately the honour of a letter from Lady Mary Caryll,[1] which I answered within this month. I hear poor Mrs Cope is in a dying condition. You give me no farther orders about the statue; I have since seen a Flora that I like well enough. If you acquaint me at what time, you shall be in town, I will go purposely thither to meet you. But if you could make this in your way, it would be doubly engaging.

You are too partial to me, in what you say occurred to you, upon a review of the letters I've troubled you with. This brings afresh into my mind a request I made you some months ago of seeing them once more;[2] for I have greatly before my eyes the fear of a rascally bookseller who has printed some, very unfit to see the light in many regards; and I would be glad at least to prevent the like usage for the future, both in respect to my friends and my self. I beg my truest services may attend your whole family. You see my handwriting is altered for the worse, since the accident I met with this time twelvemonth. Adieu. In the least bad weather it pains me. Believe me, dear sir | Your ever affect oblig'd friend | and servant　A: P:

POPE *to* BROOME　　　　　　　　[5 *October* 1727]

Elwin–Courthope, viii. 139

[3]Oct. 5, [1727]

It is true that it is a great while since I writ to you, and as true that I designed to have written long ago; but indeed, as I have often formerly told you, it is not in my power to promise any regular correspondence, from the multiplicity of avocations I daily labour under, as well as from that terrible one of almost every other day's sicknesses. I am truly concerned to hear you have had your share in the fever, so epidemical in most parts of England,—I say your share, because I know you feel for those under your care who have had it. I hope you in person will still escape it.

I thank you for informing me what share you have in those verses which pass under other names, it seems, among those of Cambridge—not only the whole poem of Waller, but those twelve stanzas of alcaics that end another.[4] I like these last particularly. I know nothing of

---

[1] From France presumably.

[2] Pope has not as yet got his letters back, nor does he yet know that Caryll is having transcripts made.　　[3] The date, Elwin says, is taken from the postmark.

[4] In *Gratulatio Academiæ Cantabrigiensis de Pace* (1713) Broome had contributed some hexameter verses that he signed, and apparently had written the sapphics signed by Edmund Waller, M.D. (a Fellow of St. John's), and had also done twelve alcaic stanzas for another contributor, possibly Dr. Christopher Anstey, Fellow of St. John's.

the king's going to Cambridge, nor have heard the least rumour to that effect. I wish you the honour you mention,[1] and any other honour that pleases you,—though I find you determine for that obscurity and retirement, which you have so long cultivated, whatever nominal honours you may be no enemy to.

I am very sorry I knew nothing of your being a day or two in town. If I had, you should not have inquired for me, but have seen me at whatever place you lodged,—if my health had permitted,— infallibly. I shall ever be glad to hear of your intentions towards literature, which, next to the solid happiness of health, I wish may be constant, for your satisfaction first, and next for that of others. I am always, dear sir, your affectionate friend and servant.

I never hear from Mr. Fenton. Is he as lazy towards you? I was one day at Cambridge,[2] and missed of him. My mother is yours faithfully.

MATHER BYLES to POPE[3]   7 *October* 1727

The New England Historical and Genealogical Society

New-England. Boston. | Oct. 7. 1727.

Sir,—You are doubtless wondring at the Novelty of an Epistle from the remote Shores where this dates its Origin; as well as from so obscure a Hand as that which subscribes it. But what Corner of the Earth so secret, as not to have heard the Fame of Mr POPE? Or who so retired as not to be acquainted with his admirable Compositions or so stupid as not to be ravished with them.

Fame after a Man is dead, has been by some ingenious Writers, compared to an Applause in some distant Region. If this be a just Similitude, you may take the pleasure of an admired Name in *America*, and of spreading a Transport over the Face of a New World: By which you may, in some measure, imagine the Renown in which your Name will flourish many Ages to come, and anticipate a Thousand Years of Futurity.

To let you see a little of the Reputation which you bear in these unknown Climates, and the Improvements we are making I transmit to you the inclosed[4] Poems: Assuring my self, tho' not of the Approba-

---

[1] The degree of LL.D. was to be conferred on Broome at the time of the King's visit in Apr. 1728.

[2] When on a ramble to Wimpole with Swift and Lord Oxford. See Pope to Fortescue, 5 Aug., and Swift to Sheridan, 12 Aug.

[3] Printed from Byles's own copy in his letterbook. It has been edited, with three additional letters from Byles to Pope, in *PMLA*, xlviii (1933), 68–69, by Professor Austin Warren. The letters indicate an appetite for lion-hunting and doubtless a genuine admiration. Pope answered this first letter, but no others apparently. He did send his works later to Mr. Byles.

[4] In the left margin Byles annotates the Poems as '*The* POEM *on* ETERNITY, *and the*

tion of your Judgement, yet of the Excess and Lenity of that Candour which is forever inseperable from a great Genius.

But not withstanding all these Representations of your Goodness, which my Imagination is able to form, I find it very difficult to suppress the Struggle of Passions which swells my Heart, while I am writing a Letter to so great a Man. I am at once urged by a generous Ambition to be known to you; and forbid by a trembling Consciousness of my own Unworthiness and Obscurity. Prompted by Desire; flush'd with Hope; or appal'd with Concern, I shall add to the Incorrectness which I would now most of all escape. In short, *Sir*, when I approach you, it is with a real Awe and Reverence like that which you have so humourously described in the *Guardian* upon Dedications.

How often have I been sooth'd and charmed with the ever-blooming Landscapes of your *Windsor-Forest*? And how does my very Soul melt away, at the soft Complaints of the languishing *Eloisa*? How frequently has the *Rape of the Lock* commanded the various passions of my Mind: Provoked Laughter; breathed a Tranquility; or inspired a Transport? And how have I been raised, and born away by the resistless Fire of the *Iliad*, as it gl[ow]s in your immortal Translation?

Permit me, *Sir*, to conclude my Lett[er] with asking the Favour of a few Lines from the Hand which has bless'd the World with s[uch] Divine Productions. If you thus honour [me], assure your self the Joys you will produce in me, will be inferior to none but the Poetick Raptures of your own Breast. Perhaps you will be disposed to smile, when I confess, that I have a more superstitious Ardor to see a Word written by your Pen, than ever *Tom Folio* in the Tatler, to see a Simile of *Virgil* with that Advantage. I am, | *Sir*, Your great Admirer, | and most obedient | Humble Servant.

Address: (given in the letter book before the letter) To Mr. ALEXANDER POPE. | To be left with Mr. *Bernard Lintot*, between | the Temple-Gates in Fleetstreet.

---

†SWIFT *to* POPE   12 *October* 1727

1740

Dublin, Oct. 12, 1727.

I have been long reasoning with my self upon the condition I am in, and in conclusion have thought it best to return to what fortune hath made my home; I have there[1] a large house, and servants and con-

ANSWER *to it*; *and also the Panegyrick on* MILTON: all printed in the Weekly JOURNAL.' The poems were printed in *The New England Weekly Journal*. The issue for 5 June 1727 has verses 'To my Friend: Occasioned by his Poem on Eternity' which contain something over forty lines in praise of Pope—about a third of the poem! This is the newspaper that Pope forwarded to Swift in his letter of 23 Mar. 1727/8, because of its mention of Capt. Jonath. Gulliver.   [1] there] here *1741 Dab.*

veniencies about me. I may be worse than I am, and I have no where to retire. I therefore thought it best to return to Ireland, rather than go to any distant place in England. Here is my maintainance, and here my convenience. If it pleases[1] God to restore me to my health, I shall readily make a third journey; if not, we must part as all human creatures have parted. You are the best and kindest friend in the world, and I know no body alive or dead to whom I am so much obliged; and if ever you made me angry, it was for your too much care about me. I have often wish'd that God almighty would be so easy to the weakness of mankind, as to let old friends be acquainted in another state; and if I were to write an Utopia for heaven, that would be one of my schemes. This wildness you must allow for, because I am giddy and deaf.

I find it more convenient to be sick here, without the vexation of making my friends uneasy; yet my giddiness alone would not have done, if that unsociable comfortless deafness had not quite tired me: And I believe I should have returned from the Inn,[2] if I had not feared it was only a short intermission, and the year was late, and my licence expiring. Surely besides all other faults, I should be a very ill judge, to doubt your friendship and kindness. But it hath pleased God that you are not in a state of health, to be mortified with the care and sickness of a friend: Two sick friends never did well together; such an office is fitter for servants and humble companions, to whom it is wholly indifferent whether we give them trouble or no. The case would be quite otherwise if you were with me; you could refuse to see any body; here is a large house where we need not hear each other if we were both sick. I have a race of orderly elderly people of both sexes at command, who are of no consequence, and have gifts proper for attending us; who can bawl when I am deaf, and tread softly when I am only giddy and would sleep.

I had another reason for my haste hither, which was changing my Agent, the old one having terribly involved my little affairs; to which however I am grown so indifferent, that I believe I shall lose two or three hundred pounds rather than plague my self with accompts: so that I am very well qualified to be a Lord, and put into Peter Walter's[3] hands.

Pray God continue and increase Mr. Congreve's amendment, though he does not deserve it like you, having been too lavish of that health which Nature gave him.

I hope my White-hall landlord[4] is nearer to a place than when I

---

[1] pleases] please *1741 Dab.*

[2] The Inn in Aldersgate Street, from which Swift took coach for Chester. See Gay and Pope to Swift, 22 Oct.

[3] A remarkable Westminster-Attorney.—Curll, 1741 Lc. His remarkable qualities are frequently displayed in the satires of Pope, Fielding, and others.

[4] Mr. Gay, with whom the Dean sometime lodged.—Swift, 1741 Dab.

left him; as the Preacher said, 'the day of judgment was nearer, than ever it had been before.'

Pray God send you health, *det Salutem, det opes, animam æquam ipse tibi parabis.*[1] You see Horace wished for money, as well as health; and I would hold a crown he kept a coach; and I shall never be a friend to the Court, till you do so too. | Yours, &c.

†POPE *to* GAY   16 *October* 1727

[1]735

²Twickenham, Oct. 16, 1727.

I have many years ago magnify'd in my own mind, and repeated to you, a ninth Beatitude, added to the eight in the Scripture; *Blessed is he who expects nothing, for he shall never be disappointed.*[3] I could find in my heart to congratulate you on this happy Dismission from all Court-Dependance; I dare say I shall find you the Better and the Honester Man for it, many years hence; very probably the health-fuller, and the chearfuller into the bargain. You are happily rid of many cursed ceremonies, as well as of many ill, and vicious habits, of which few or no men escape the Infection, who are hackney'd and tramelled in the ways of a Court. Princes indeed, and Peers (the Lackies of Princes) and Ladies (the Fools of Peers) will smile on you the less; but men of Worth, and real Friends, will look on you the better. There is a thing, the only thing which Kings and Queens cannot give you (for they have it not to give) *Liberty*, which is worth[4] all they have; and which, as yet, I hope[5] *Englishmen* need not ask from their hands. You will enjoy That, and your own Integrity, and the satisfactory Consciousness of having *not* merited such Graces from them, as they bestow only on the mean, servile, flattering, interested, and undeserving. The only steps to their favour are such complacencies, such compliances, such distant decorums, as delude them in their Vanities, or engage them in their Passions. He is their *Greatest* favourite, who

---

[1] Adapted from Horace, *Epistles*, i. xviii. 112; translated (in 1741 Dab) as 'Let *Jove* give Health, give Riches; you shall find | An inward Treasure in an equal Mind. | Duncan'. Curll (1741 Lc) makes another translation.

[2] In 1737e and thereafter the date is misprinted 'Oct. 6'.

[3] This letter is written in the first shock from the fact that Gay, whose friends as well as himself had expected a 'place' of dignity and substance for him when the new court was organized after the Coronation, had been offered the post of Gentleman Usher to the (two-year-old) Princess Louisa. They approved his prompt refusal of the post. Warton, Bowles, and others have thought this present letter extreme in tone; but Gay had been encouraged to expect much, and in a day when (presently) Cibber could be made Laureate, a high tone in commendation of Gay's action is understandable. The letter, printed three years after Gay's death, is one of Pope's strongest attacks on the corruption of patronage in his day.

[4] Liberty . . . worth] Liberty: But it is worth *1737 ba-bd.*

[5] I hope] I thank God *1737a–1742.*

Pope struggled with this sentence and its pronouns: not all his variant attempts need be given.

is their *Falsest*: and when a man, by such vile Gradations, arrives at the height of Grandeur and Power, he is then at best but in a circumstance to be *hated*, and in a condition to be *hanged*, for serving their Ends: So many a Minister has found it!

I believe you did not want Advice, in the letter you sent by my Lord *Grantham*.[1] I presume you writ it not, without: And you cou'd not have better, if I guess right at the person who agreed to your doing it, in respect to any *Decency* you ought to observe: for I take that person to be a perfect Judge of Decencies and Forms.[2] I am not without fears even on that person's account: I think it a bad Omen: but what have I to do with Court-Omens?—Dear *Gay*, adieu. I can only add a plain, uncourtly Speech: While you are no body's Servant, you may be any one's Friend; and as such I embrace you, in all conditions of life. While I have a shilling, you shall have six-pence, nay eight pence, if I can contrive to live upon a groat. I am faithfully | Your, &c.

†GAY *and* POPE *to* SWIFT[3]   22 *October* 1727

1740
                                                              Oct. 22, 1727

Though you went away from us so unexpectedly, and in so clandestine a manner; yet by several enquiries,[4] we have inform'd our selves of every thing that hath happen'd to you.

To our great joy you have told us your deafness left you at the Inn in Aldersgate-street:[5] No doubt your ears knew there was nothing worth hearing in England.

Our advices from Chester tell us, that you met Captain Lawson; the Captain was a man of veracity, and set sail at the time he told you; I really wish'd you had laid hold of that opportunity, for you had then been in Ireland the next day: Besides, as it is credibly reported, the Captain had a bottle or two of excellent claret in his Cabbin. You would not then have had the plague of that little smoaky room at Holy-head; but considering it was there you lost your giddiness, we have great reason to praise smoaky rooms for the future, and prescribe them in like cases to our friends. The maid of the house writes us word, that while you were there you were busy for ten days together writing

---

[1] Gay's letter declining the post offered would go to Henry, Earl of Grantham, Chamberlain to Queen Caroline.

[2] Would this person be Mrs. Howard?

[3] In his quarto and folio editions (1741 Lab) Pope omitted the first three paragraphs, and used the last two only, beginning with 'The Queen's family is at last settled'. The variants in texts are negligible, serving chiefly to adjust grammatical points.

[4] Evidently the news came by letter from Sheridan; but see Swift's 'Holyhead Journal', *Prose Works* (ed. Temple Scott), xi. 391–403, and *Poems* (ed. Sir H. Williams), ii. 418–23.

[5] See Swift's letter to Pope, 12 Oct. 1727 (here ii. 452).

continually—and that as Wat drew nearer and nearer to Ireland, he blunder'd more and more. By a scrap of paper left in this smoaky room, it seem'd as if the Book you was writing, was a most lamentable account of your travels; and really, had there been any wine in the house, the place would have not been so irksome. We were further told, that you set out, was driven back again by a storm, and lay in the ship all night. After the next setting sail, we were in great concern about you, because the weather grew very tempestuous. When to my great joy, and surprize, I receiv'd a letter from Carlingford in Ireland, which inform'd us that after many perils you were safely landed there. Had the oysters been good it would have been a comfortable refreshment after your fatigue. We compassionated you in your travels through that country of desolation and poverty in your way to Dublin, for it is a most dreadful circumstance to have lazy dull horses on a road where there is very bad or no Inns. When you carry a sample of English Apples next to Ireland, I beg you would either get them from Gutheridge[1] or Devonshire. Pray who was the Clergyman that met you at some distance from Dublin? because we could not learn his name. These are all the hints we could get of your long and dangerous journey, every step of which we shar'd your anxieties—and all that we have now left to comfort us, is to hear that you are in good health.

But why should we tell you what you know already? The Queen's family is at last settled, and in the list I was appointed Gentleman-usher to the Princess Louisa, the youngest Princess; which, upon account that I am so far advanc'd in life, I have declin'd accepting; and have endeavour'd, in the best manner I could, to make my excuses by a letter to her Majesty. So now all my expectations are vanish'd; and I have no prospect, but in depending wholly upon my self, and my own conduct. As I am us'd to disappointments I can bear them, but as I can have no more hopes, I can no more be disappointed, so that I am in a blessed condition.—You remember you were advising me to go into Newgate to finish my scenes[2] the more correctly—I now think I shall, for I have no attendance to hinder me; but my Opera is already finished. I leave the rest of this paper to Mr. Pope.

Gay is a free-man, and I writ him a long congratulatory letter upon it. Do you the same: It will mend him, and make him a better man than a Court could do. Horace might keep his coach in Augustus's time, if he pleas'd, but I won't in the time of our Augustus. My Poem[3] (which it grieves me that I dare not send you a copy of, for fear

---

[1] Goodrich (as the Dublin editions have it) and Devonshire might both produce excellent apples. Swift's ancestors lived in Goodrich and Gay's in Devonshire.

[2] i.e. in *The Beggar's Opera*.

[3] Curll (1741 Lc) avidly annotated the word as follows: 'The *Dunciad*. This Passage detects a most flagrant Falshood; for, in the *Notes*, it is positively asserted, that the *Dunciad* was *first* printed in *Ireland*; verifying a *good* old *English* Proverb, that,—*Liars ought to have*

of the Curl's and Dennis's of Ireland, and still more for fear of the worst of Traytors, our friends and Admirers) my Poem, I say, will shew you what a distinguishing age we lived in? Your name is in it, with some others under a mark of such ignominy as you will not much grieve to wear in that company. Adieu, and God bless you, and give you health and spirits.

> *Whether you chuse Cervantes' serious air,*
> *Or laugh and shake in Rablais' easy chair,*
> *Or in the graver Gown instruct mankind,*
> *Or silent, let thy morals tell thy mind.*

These two verses are over and above what I've said of you in the Poem. Adieu.

SWIFT *to* POPE   30 *October* 1727

See August 1726: ii. 393.

POPE *to* JOHN KNIGHT[1]   30 *October* 1727

Bowles (1806), x. 97–99.

I have this day received your second letter with the note of 55*l.* at Twitnam, and will next week go to town, where, as soon as the figure is set up, I will pay the statuary. Your excess of punctuality has cost you and me this alarm and trouble; for I might as well have done it myself, and stayed till you came to town for the money.

I must now express to you, with great truth, my concern for Mrs. Knight's danger;[2] which I first heard of the day after I had sent you my first letter. I hope in God her recovery is more and more confirmed: and I must tax you with a second piece of forgetfulness, in not saying

_____

good Memories.' One is surprised that Curll had no better evidence that *The Dunciad* was not first printed in Ireland. Pope could have replied that the MS. was sent over later to Dublin, but there was little object in replying.

1 The chronological relation of this letter to those to Mrs. Newsham of 9 July, 8 Aug., and 13 Oct., which Elwin placed also in 1727 is arguable. The three letters mentioned are in this present edition placed in 1724. Some of them might come even earlier perhaps. If all four of these letters are placed in 1727 (as Elwin arranged them), we must assume that as late as 8 Aug. 1727 the statuary was still at work on his clay model ('the model I begin to be satisfied with', Pope then writes) and that the marble statue was completed and boxed by 30 Oct. It is true that on 13 Oct. Pope wrote Mrs. Newsham, that 'Mr. Elliot . . . has bought . . . the marble for the statue, upon which the Italian is now at work.' If (as in this edition) the remark is dated 1724, the assumption is that *which* refers to *statue* (i.e., the model) and not to *marble*. If the letter is dated 1727, the time between the purchase of the stone and the completion of the work is too short. Apparently the health of Guelfi was not good—a fact that may account for the period of time (1724–7, or longer) taken on the whole monument.

2 The last paragraph of this letter indicates that the lady who is ill is the former Mrs. Newsham, now Mrs. Knight. She was a widow from 1724 to 1727 apparently.

one word of it when you writ last those three lines, with the note. Let me trouble you for one letter more, at your next leisure, about her. If I get more health than indeed I have yet, and if she recovers fast enough to bear one additional infirmity, that of a philosophical companion, half sour and half sick, I intend, in less than a fortnight, to make you and her a short visit. In which case I will first go to Lees (the Duchess of Buckingham's), and send you an information when I am there, that you either may take notice of, or not, as it shall be most convenient to you at that time.

I went to Burlington-house two days ago, where the statue is boxed up, ready for carriage, by Guelfi: he had sent me two letters in one day about Bird[1] again; that he would not make the box for it, etc. Whereupon I bid him, if Mr. B. did not come for it soon, to take the care upon himself of erecting it. But I since understand Guelfi is fallen sick: so Mr. Bird's care will be the more necessary. I wish to God it were once well set up: it will make the finest figure, I think, in the place; and it is the least part of honour due to the memory of a man who made the best in his station; and would, questionless, have made yet a better, had God allowed, what all mortals who rightly knew his virtues, earnestly, desired,—his longer stay among us.

I have nothing to add, but my sincerest wishes for the welfare of two of the nearest parts of him, his friend and his sister. I am truly, dear Sir, | Your affectionate, faithful servant.

Twitnam, Oct. 30, 1727.

My mother is Mrs. Knight's humble servant: so is Mrs. Patty Blount.

---

*JOHN CONDUITT *to* POPE[2]   8 *November* 1727

Yale University

Sr,—The kind promise you made me at Mrs Howard's encourages me to trouble you with the enclosed. You will easily conceive the pain I am in how to acquitt myself in dedicating to the Queen of a work of Sir Isaac Newton's which will carry the meanest performance that is joined to it into all parts of the learned world, & as the honour of the

---

[1] The sculptor Francis Bird would thus seem to have had a share in working on the monument.

[2] John Conduitt (1688–1737), who married Newton's niece, succeeded him as Master of the Mint, and became his literary executor, is here asking Pope's aid in drafting a dedication to the Queen of Newton's *Chronology of Ancient Kingdoms Amended*. Pope revised the dedication, and the work was published in 1728.

The letter is printed from Conduitt's rough draft, preserved with the MS. of the dedication. It is thought unnecessary to indicate all the phrasal revisions of the draft.

nation is in some measure concerned in every thing that relates to that
great man, I hope you will excuse my being so solicitous to have so
earnestly the opinion and assistance of one whose judgment & compositions deservedly hold the first place in it[1] Being doubtful my self
I have inserted the different turns I have given to some places trusting
to your goodness to determine which shall stand—If you will add to
diminish or alter any part of it with the same freedom with which I
have troubld you you will highly oblige, &c—

8 Novr 1727–

Address: To Alexdr Pope Esqr
Endorsement: Mr Conduit to A Pope

*POPE *to* JOHN CONDUITT[2]   10 *November* 1727

Yale University

Sir,—I make use of the liberty you gave me, of a free Criticisme, in
the Inclosed; without any formalityes, or asking an Excuse from you
in my Turn. I think nothing can be more proper than the first part of
your Dedication, which relates to the Author & the Work: Whatever
Thoughts flow from *that*, or take rise from *that*, render your Compliment to the Queen, (in my opinion) the more graceful as well as the
more just, (& proper for You, as a Relation, & intrusted with so
valuable a Depositum.) As to what depends not on *That*, I would only
wish, you avoided as much as possible, the Common Topicks of Dedications and Addresses: Your Real Subject, (I mean both Sir Isaac
Newton & her Majesty) will shine of themselves; and a Shortness, a
Dignity, and Plainness, will become them. For instance, I cannot but
think, that after you have said, that Sir *Isaac carryd Arts & Sciences
in a few years farther than all Others had in whole ages*; it flattens, if
not contradicts it, to add afterwards that *in the present Reign they may
be advanc'd to a much greater heigth*. I would omit that paragraph,
which I have markd between two Crosses X It takes very much from
the Praise of Sir I. N. and I fear unjustly, to imagine Any Prince's
Reign can *Make* Newtons, however it might *incourage*, or *admire* them.
    I mean in general only that I would shorten those parts which are
mere Panegyric, independent on the Occasion the Book & Author
give you; The Character of Sincerity which you so rightly touch upon

---

[1] The last part of this sentence (after 'great man') first read, 'you will not wonder that I
am exceedingly desirous to have the opinion of one whose judgment is acknowledged by all
to be the first genius in it for performance of this kind'. This is crossed through.
[2] This answers the letter from Conduitt immediately preceding. Pope obviously did not
work long on his suggested changes, and it may have irked him to phrase complements to
the King and Queen at a time when John Gay had not been provided for, and when Bolingbroke was disappointed that Walpole was being continued in power.

in the King, I would keep exactly as it is, and any thing in short, that is characteristical. I prefer, (since your commands are, that I should chuse what I like,) the Column on the right hand; Only in one place I think what you say of the Queens Encouragement of Arts is almost a repetition of the same thing elsewhere; I have markd it by inclosing that passage with a line & two Crosses X X The rest I believe may stand.

Upon the whole, I really approve it; and You ought to pardon my freedom, since you caused it. If I am ever so much in the wrong, it will be at least an instance of my good Intention. I am ashamed to be so particular in things of so little importance as my Objections, which are indeed very slight. But the apprehension that you might soon want the Papers, and the consciousness that I could not be serviceable enough to you to excuse a longer delay, made me write this, rather than wait for an opportunity of talking with you—Methinks you should end the Dedication with returning once more to Sir Isaac Newton. What little I've added, is only a Hint to that effect. I am sincerely of opinion that your Dedication is very just, and decent, and well-judg'd. I could wish it were Inlarged with some Memoirs & Character of him, as a private Man: I doubt not his Life & Manners would make as Great a Discovery of Virtue, & Goodness, & Rectitude of Heart, as his Works have done of Penetration and the utmost Stretch of human knowledge. I am | Sir | Your most obedient | humble Servant, | A. Pope.

Twickenham | Novr 10th. | 1727.

[1]Your Majesty does not think these Instructive and Entertaining Pursuits below your exalted Station; and are yourself a proof, that the abstruser Parts of them are not beyond the reach of your Sex. &c.

formed by such *Models*?

That *Liberty* & *Knowledge* (as this glorious prospect gives us reason to hope) may be equally and jointly prepetuated; and that the bright *Example* set in this Reign by the Royal Patrons of Both, may be transmitted with the Sceptre, to those of the same great Line: to the end that This Age may be as Illustrious, and this Nation as distinguishd, for every Other Felicity & Glory; as it is, and ever must be, for having been honourd with Such a Man as Sir Isaac Newton; is the most Sincere prayer of | Madam | May it please your Majesty | &c

Endorsement: Letter from Pope | to Conduit.

---

[1] Here after his signature Pope adds a page of suggestions not easily indicated in the MS. of the dedication. They modify passages on pp. xii–xiv of the dedication (quarto edition of 1728). The suggestions influenced Conduitt, who evidently agreed with Pope that the picture of 'Generations to come under a Royal Progeny, so descended, so educated, and formed by such *Patterns*' as the King and Queen was preferable to calling Hanoverian royalty 'Models'. Conduitt does not adopt all of Pope's retrenchments in flattery.

||SWIFT *to* GAY *and* POPE¹   23 *November* 1727

Longleat Portland Papers, xiii (Harleian transcript)

Dublin Novr 23d 1727.

⌐I had your double Letter² some time agoe, whereof the first and greatest part is of your ~~own~~ head, and contains a very exact account of my journey from London to this Place, wherever you got it, or whatever Familiar you dealt with. I did actually amuse my self with writing a Journal of my distresses and living at Holyhead at least when it grew dark, for then I never read. I did miss my passage from Chester, which would have saved much time weariness and money. I wanted wine for 4 days of the 8. I staid there. I did set out and was driven back, and all the other Circumstances—Carlingford, bad Horses, worse roads, and Welch apples are all true, and nothing but the Devil could have informed you, for I kept no Company but travelled alone. Or else it must be Poetical conjuring, as Homer recites the dreams of those who were killed in their Sleep. I heard nothing of the Q—'s family Settling, nor ever hear one Syllable of News any more than at Twitenham. Remember how I detested your three half penny worth of News at Whitehall, which made me think myself in a Coffee-House.⌐

I entirely approve your refusal of that Employment, and your writing to the Q— I am perfectly confident you have a firm Enemy in the Ministry. God forgive him, but not till he puts himself in a State to be forgiven. Upon reasoning with Myself, I should hope they are gone too far to discard you quite, and that they will give you something, which altho' much less than they ought will be as far as it is worth, better circumstantiated. And since you already just live, a middling help will make you just tolerable. Your lateness in Life (as you so soon call it) might be improper to begin the World with, but almost the oldest Men may hope to see Changes in a Court. A Minister is always Seventy, and you are thirty Years younger, and Cromwell himself did not begin to appear³ till he was older than you: ——I beg you will be thrifty and learn to value a shilling, which Dr Birch said was a serious thing. Get a stronger fence about your 1000ll, and throw the Inner fence into the Heap; and be advised by your Twitenham Landlord and me about an Annuity. You are [the] most refractory honest good natured Men I ever have known. I could argue out this Paper. I am very glad your Opera is finished; and hope your

---

¹ In the editions of 1740–2 Pope omitted the parts of this letter here placed in half-brackets. He added to the letter sections found in letters from Swift dated 26 Feb. 1727/8 and 28 Mar. 1728 (q.v.). Verbal changes in the parts of this letter—the second paragraph and part of the third—are negligible.
² The letter of Gay and Pope dated 22 Oct. 1727.
³ appear till] appear in the world until *1741 Dab.*

friends will join the readyer to make it succeed, because you are used by others so ill

┌Scene. Twitenham-house. Just after Dinner.┐

I have known Courts these 36 years, and know they differ, but in some things they are extreamly constant: First, in the trite old Maxim of a Minister never forgiving those he hath injured; secondly, in the insincerityes of those who would be thought the best Friends; thirdly, in the Love of fawning, cringing and Tale bearing. Fourthly in sacrificing those whom we realy wish well, to a point of Interest or Intrigue. Fifthly, in keeping every thing worth taking for those, who can do service or disservice.[1] ┌I could go on to four and twentythly. But with all the partiality of my Inclination, I cannot acquit this Characterized Person; it is against my original fundamental Maxims. I durst appeal to our friend at Dawly, tho' I know more than he, because I was a Subaltern, and have even deceived him to do more for some I did not over much value, then the other who pretends to have so strong a regard for our Friend. Neither will your mutato nomine &c satisfie me unless things are monstrously changed from what you taught me. For I was led to believe that the present unexpected scituation or Confirmation of things was brought about above 2 years ago by the intervention of that Person whose Character was drawn.[2] But if it be as you say, the fate of the Princess des Ursines ought to be rememberd[3]——As to Ireland, the Air of this House is good, and of the Kingdom very good, but the best fruits fall short a little. All things to Eat and drink except very few, better then in London, except you have 4000ll a year. The ridings and coachings a hundred times better in Winter. You may find about six rational, good, civil learned Easy Companions ~~among~~ of the Males; fewer of the females; but many civil, hospitable, and ready to admire and Adore. About a dozen tolerable he Companions, without impertinence. No Paulteneys[4] nor Dawleys nor Arbuthnots. A very good Apartment, good French Wine, and Port. and among the Extravagant, Hoch, Burgundy, Rackpunch &c but too dear for me. Onely I hope to have Cyder from Goodridge. If you like this Bill of Fare, and air, and Company; The

---

[1] The rest of this letter was omitted in the editions of 1740–2.

[2] Mrs. Howard's character had been drawn by Swift in the summer of 1727. It is dated 12 June in his *Prose Works* (ed. Temple Scott), xi. 147.

[3] This princess, situated in the court of Philip V of Spain somewhat as Mrs. Howard now was in the court of George II, was suddenly disgraced for reasons by no means clear, and expelled from Spain under melodramatic conditions in Dec. 1714. Swift exaggerated both the abilities and the influence of Mrs. Howard when he made this implied comparison. It may be suggested that if Pope (as Spence, p. 364, records) composed a character of Orsini, applicable to Sarah, Duchess of Marlborough, he presumably took the name from that of the powerful Princesse des Ursines, in Italian *Orsini*.

[4] For *Pulteney*, of course.

sea, the Towngates, and the Door of this House are open. You can have an Eighteen penny Chicken for 7 pence. I will send Dr Delany and Mr Stopfort as far as Chester to Conduct you and thus I have enterd your Chalenge. I repeated your Civilities to Dr Sheridan, who reced them as he ought, and resolves to get you all sorts of those foolish Wines your Caprices are so fond of; and has a garden 2 Miles off to amuse you with; but inconveniency is, it will have very good fruit in it. I desire you will present my most humble service to Sir Spencer Compton (or the Speaker[1] if he must be so) and desire he will perform his promise of giving me 3 or 4 Marseill's Figs, and some of his most early grapes, and do you get them put into boxes with Earth, and send them to Whitehall, and let them be kept cool and I will send for them .—My humble Service and kind remembrance to Mrs Pope, and to Patty Blount, and to Lord Bolingbroke, Lord Bathurst, Dr Arbuthnot and Family, Mr Lewis, and Mrs Howard, who must remember my Duty to the Queen, and to all others without naming, but you are to name them in a particular manner, especially to Mr Pulteney—Adieu, God bless you.[1]

POPE *to* JOHN KNIGHT[2]   24 *November* [1727]

Bowles (1806), x. 106–7

Twitnham, Nov. 24.

I had some view of seeing you in the country; but the weather proved so cold, that the Duchess of Bucks came back to town before I was ready to go to Lees. I am forced now to content myself with such informations of Mrs. Knight's state of health, as your people give me in Dover-street. If these be true, she is pretty well; and I hope the cheerfulness you two can give one another, will make all that bad seasons, ill air, and uncomfortable prospects can do, ineffectual to molest or cloud you. Here the most unhappy gay people are reduced to mere children's play, and childish sights, to divert them. They go every day to stare at a mock coronation on the stage, which is to be succeeded by a more ridiculous one of the Harlequins (almost as ridiculous a farce as the real state one of a coronation itself). After that, they hope for it again in a puppet-show, which is to recommend itself by another qualification, of having the exact portraits of the most con-

---

[1] In a moment of witty exasperation Swift had written to Mrs. Howard, 19 Aug. 1727: 'I make nothing of mistaking untoward for Howard; wellpull for Walpole; slily for Ilay . . . in writing Speaker, I put an *n* for a *p* . . .' Evidently Mrs. Howard or someone had reproached Swift in behalf of Compton (who was destined for higher things than the post of Speaker: within six weeks he was to be a lord, and within six months Earl of Wilmington). Swift was evidently friendly, and his abusive jokes are not to be taken too seriously.

[2] The talk of the 'mock coronation' (King George II was crowned in October of this year) and the finishing of the Craggs monument determine the year of this letter.

spicuous faces of our nobility in wax-work, so as to be known at sight, without Punch's help, or the master's pointing to each with his wand as they pass. So much for news! 'Tis what passes most material in this metropolis; till you, Sir, with your fellow-members, come to find us greater business after Christmas.

At last I have seen the statue up, and the statuary down at the same time. The poor man has not been out of bed since. I sent part of the money to him and offered him more, which he refused, till he has been at the Abbey, to do some little matter more to the hair (as I understand) and feet. The inscription on the urn is not done yet, though they (*promised*) it two months ago, and had the draught: but yesterday they sent to me again for it, which I can't conceive the meaning of, for I saw it scored on in the Abbey. I have sent it over again to Mr. Bird this day, however.

I shall think it a favour to hear of you both, when your leisure permits. Believe me a sincere well-wisher to you both, and (if you will allow me a higher title), dear Sir, | a faithful friend and affectionate servant.

My mother is well, and very much your's and Mrs. Knight's.

FENTON *to* BROOME   3 *December* [1727]
Elwin–Courthope, viii. 140

Easthampstead Park, Dec. 3, [1727].

Dear Mr. Broome,—Your letter rejoiced me much by letting me know that you are both in good health and good humour, the last of which I ingenuously confess not to deserve any share of for neglecting so long to answer your last. About a week after I received it we left Cambridge, and soon after my arrival here, where we shall continue about six weeks longer before we go to London, I was laid up by the gout, and the squire, who presents his service to you, was seized with the new fever.

As soon as I go to town I will not fail consulting with Sir Clement Cottrell about the affair you mentioned.[1] He is at present in an ill state of health, and his lady's mother lies dead in his house.[2] You know what kind of usage I long met with in my pursuits, which indeed were not so much suits for favour as for justice in desiring a bare equivalent for what I resigned. In the meantime I am glad to hear your spirits hold vigorous enough to call out your muse. What dost thou mean by talking of old age? Even I have lately writ a poem to a girl, which I have just sent to the press, with my name to it. It is the dedication of

---

[1] His preferment. Broome may have hoped to prevail on the friends of young Blount to exert their influence on his behalf.—Elwin.

[2] Sir Clement in 1716 had married Bridget Sherborn only daughter and heiress of Davenant and Mary Sherborn. The will of the mother-in-law was proved in 1727.

Waller to Lady Margaret Harley.¹ Nay, I have drawn the scenery for a tragedy, which I know not whether ever I shall finish, or let it see the light when it is finished; but I think it necessary for the health of the mind to void the little ebullitions of fancy. It is not writing that is ridiculous in a man of years, but the vanity of printing on all occasions. Blessed be the memory of the man, whoever he was, who said, *Quisquis erit vitae, scribam, color.²* Whenever I set up my chariot that sentence shall glitter on the panel. Ever yours.

POPE *to* THE EARL OF OXFORD   13 *December* 1727

Longleat Portland Papers, xii

Decr. 13. 1727.

My Lord,—The only day I had in Town (except another spent in sickness) since I had the pleasure to see you, I sent to your Lordships house, but you were pre-ingaged. The last Conversation I had with you, my Lord, was a very agreeable Proof to me, of your Interesting yourself in My Concerns & happiness, which I take to heart from you, as I ought. I very much wish to see you; and trouble you with this, only to desire to know, how long you shall continue in Town? that I may have the pleasure of coming once to wait on you & my Lady Oxford before you go any where: if my very bad Health will allow me. My mother still lives upon your Brawn, & is yours & my Ladys faithfull Servant, as I truly am, & ever will be.

My Lord, yours ever | A. Pope

Address: To the Right Honble the | Earl of Oxford & Mortimer, | in | Dover street | London.

Postmark: 14/DE

Endorsement: Mr Pope | Decr. 13. 1727

LORD BATHURST *to* POPE³   [1727]

Elwin–Courthope, viii. 331

Riskins, Friday Night

Whether this will find you at Twickenham or London is uncertain, but I have ordered my servant to try at both places. You gave me

---

¹ This appeared in Fenton's quarto edition of Waller, 1729. See above, ii. 374.

² Horace, *Sermones*, II. i. 60.

³ Elwin printed this letter as 'From the Oxford Papers'—presumably meaning from Longleat MSS. The present editor has not seen the letter. The date is relatively hypothetical. It should fall after the return of Lord Bolingbroke from exile and before Riskins was disposed of in 1735. The mention of 'these holidays', the sending of a coach (presumably warmer for a winter ride than Pope's small chariot), and the talk of Gay's preoccupation with his play—*The Beggar's Opera*—all seem to indicate the Christmas season of 1727/8 as a probable date. Doubtless Pope had many such invitations from Riskins. *The Beggar's Opera* (then in rehearsal?) was first performed 29 Jan. 1727/8. During the holiday season of 1727/8 Friday fell on 22 and 29 Dec. and 5 Jan.

hopes that you would come over to me these holidays, and since Lord
Bolingbroke has promised to come to me on Sunday next I hope it
will not be inconvenient to you to meet him that day. My servant
shall return to me to-morrow night, and if you will have my coach
sent to Twickenham it shall be with you early Sunday morning. If
you are in London, I will send it to attend you at Brentford at the
time and place you shall appoint. Thus with the punctuality of a true
prose man I endeavour to fix you; but there are some volatile spirits
that no art nor care can ever fix, and whilst I am writing this I despair
of its success. If John Gay is not very busy with his new play you may
possibly prevail upon him to come with you. I have never seen him since
he made a proselyte of Will Shippen.[1] Adieu. Come if you can and
be assured you can go nowhere else, and find a more sincere and
faithful servant.

POPE *to* THE EARL OF OXFORD   26 *December* 1727
Longleat Portland Papers, xii
                                        Twitenham, Decr. 26. 1727.

My Lord,—Since till this very Day it was never known, that Poets
receivd the same Prize as Horse Racers, or that Pegasus ever won the
Golden plate ev'n in ancient times in any of the Olympian Pythian
Isthmian or Nemean Games; I think It would be very natural &
poetical to acknowledge your Lordships fine Present by a Quotation
or Translation of the Beginning of Pindar; And to confess, that it is a
greater Prize than ever that Poet carryd off for his Verses. But I must
differ from his opinion, that *Gold is only the best thing next to Water.*
I would correct the passage thus, that Gold is the Best, & next Gold,
Wine, not water. Both which your Lordship has now given me the
First opportunity I ever had, to unite together.

I must have One Inscription upon it, which with me will outweigh
all Motto's whatever, That of your own Name, and which will do
me more Honour than Gold or pretious stones. Would you expect it
should be out of the Psalms?

Nomen tuum Dilectum super aurum & topazion.[2]

I am calld in so much haste to dinner, & I go to it with so much
appetite, to drink with my friends your Health in your own Bowl,
(*Pleno me proluam auro*)[3] That I can no more write, than I could tell
you if you were present (as I wish you were) how much & with what

---

[1] William Shippen, the Jacobite leader in Parliament, in 1727 had urged a notable reduc-
tion in the civil list. On such an issue Gay might, in his disappointment over getting no
good place, perfectly agree.

[2] Psalm cxviii. 127: 'Ideo dilexi mandata tua, super aurum & topazion'.

[3] Adapted from *Aeneid*, i. 739.

grateful sense of many favours superior to this I feel myself | My Lord |
Your Ever obliged faithfull | Servant | A. Pope.

If you have no Material objection to suffering that Epitaph on Jenny
of Mr Priors[1] to accompany some things of the same nature of the
Dean of St Patricks & mine, it is what would be very agreable to
him. He several times spoke of it to me to ask you. & I've just had a
letter from him about that Book.

Our most reall services to my Lady Oxford.

Address: To | the Right Honble the | Earl of Oxford.

Endorsement: Mr Pope | Twitenham Decr 26. 1727

POPE *to* THE EARL OF OXFORD[2]   28 *December* 1727

Longleat Portland Papers, xii

My Lord,—I am always, I may say every day, obliged to you: And to
hear of your Lordships & my Lady's health, ev'ry time you acquaint
me of it, is a fresh kindness, I wish it so sincerely.

I will write upon your Cup, *This is the Least thing Alex. Pope owed
to Edw. E. of Oxford*

If your objection to adding Jenny's Epit. to our Collection,[3] be
grounded on its being Own'd to be Mr Prior's, we need only set 2
initial Letters before it; But whatever you think right, I am sure I
shall do the same.

I drank yours Lady Oxfords & Lady Margaret's, long life & increase
of new & happy years, Sep'rately, & in divers liquors, whereof Mr
Gay may probably give your Lordship an account not greatly to my
advantage for it ended in Sal Volatile.

I am in a very indifferent state of health & afraid to go to Town as
yet; but before the end of the Christmass I shall think I've past a
very ill one, if I do not dine one day with you with the greatest Truth |
My Lord | Your most faithfull | obedient & affectionate | Servant. |
A. Pope.

Decr. 28. 1727

Address: To | The Rt. Hon. the Earl of | Oxford, & Mortimer.

Endorsement: Mr Pope | Decr 27. 1727

---

[1] Oxford evidently demurred, and 'Jinny the Just' had to wait almost two centuries for
publication.

[2] The subscribed date is in Pope's hand; the endorsement is that of a secretary: it is not
clear which is in error.

[3] Pope's eagerness to print 'Jinny the Just' was in part due to the merit of the poem and
in part due to the fact that he did not have enough appropriate verses to fill out a volume of
poetical *Miscellanies*, now that he had decided to print *The Dunciad* separately. He solved
the problem by including the *Bathos* as a prefatory prose introduction to the poems.

1728

The correspondence of this year is definitely more concerned with matters of publication than have been the letters of several years. The 'last' volume of the Swift–Pope *Miscellanies* appeared early in March, and *The Dunciad* followed late in May. Even before this form of *The Dunciad* appeared, the project of a burlesque critical edition of the poem was on foot, and much of the correspondence of the years concerns this project. Letters to or from Swift (or from Gay to Swift or Swift to Gay) are frequent. So also are letters from Fenton to Broome, Broome to Fenton, and from Pope to Broome. The mentions of Broome in the *Bathos* offended him deeply. Apart from these the leading correspondent is easily Lord Oxford, whose amanuenses are now busy in Pope's service on *The Dunciad Variorum*. In another year they will be at work on his letters. One may note that on 17 June of this year Pope wrote to Hugh Bethel asking Bethel to return all his letters.

The year was very bad for Pope's health, and by midsummer he had decided on a long stay at Bath. He set out in August, reached Bath about the 1st of September, and remained there for something like ten weeks. It was his first known visit to Bath since 1716, and his last during the lifetime of his mother. The waters did his health no good. At the end of the year Mrs. Pope seemed desperately ill.

POPE *to* THE EARL OF OXFORD[1] [1728–34]

Longleat Portland Papers, xii

My Lord,—I have only time to Embrace with joy the kind Proposal you are so obliging as to make, of dining here on Thursday. Be pleas'd to tell the Messenger Your Hour, & believe me Impatiently to expect it. I am, | My Lord, | Your most faithfull | & obedient Servant | A. Pope

My sincerest respects wait on my Lady Oxford, & Ldy Margaret.

Address: To the Rt Hon. the | Earl of Oxford.

POPE *to* SWIFT [? *January* 1727/8]

Longleat Portland Papers, xiii (Harleian transcript)

I have a mind to be in the Spleen and quarrel with half the accidents of my Life, they have so severally and successively hinder'd me from writing to you. First a Continuation of such very ill health that I

---

[1] Pope seems to begin sending 'service' to Lady Margaret in 1728 when she is thirteen years old. She married in 1734 and then became Duchess of Portland. This letter falls before that event, but is otherwise undatable.

cared not to give you such an Account as from your friendship, would
have been so uneasy to you, And which almost disabled me indeed
from giving it, by attacking me in that part which only qualifies one
to write. Then I was advised to a Journey, which gave me as Sore an
Ailment at the other end, and was no sooner crawld home, but I
found my Mother at the Gates of Death, we did not for two days
expect her life, and in that Day of trouble I really thought of flying
to You in my anguish, if it had pleased God to have taken her from
me. She is still very weak, but we think in a fair way (if there can be
such a thing at her Age) of Recovery. Pray do your utmost to preserve
the Friend that I shall have left, against that Loss arrives, which
cannot be far off. Dr Delany gave me a pleasure which I hope was not
ill grounded, in saying (since I heard from you) that your Deafness
was removed. The Season here is very sickly, and all honest men will
be dead, or in danger, by the meeting of your House. I have not seen
Lords B. B.[1] nor the Dr. nor Lewis, nor Gay, nor any body above
once since you writ last; Lord Bolingbroke not these 3 Months.
Naming Lewis, I should tell you that I've ten times spoken to Gay to
give him the Note to send to M.[2] and he was within this week so
careless as not to have done it. I will take it my self at my next going
to town, and see Mr L. write about it. The third Volume of the Miscellanies is coming out post now,[3] in which I have inserted the Treatise
περὶ βαθοῦς I have entirely Methodized and in a manner written, it
all, the Dr grew quite indolent in it, for something newer, I know not
what.[4] It will be a very Instructive piece. I want to see the Journal of
your Travels from Holyhead, which Mr Sheridan seems highly delighted with. And it grieves me to the Soul that I cannot send you my
Chef d'œuvre, the Poem of Dulness, which after I am dead and gone,
will be printed with a large Commentary, and letterd on the back,
Pope's Dulness. I send you however what most nearly relates to yourself,
the Inscription to it, which you must consider, re-consider, criticize,
hypercriticize, and consult about with Sheridan, Delany, and all the
Literati of (the Kingdom I mean) to render it less unworthy of you.

Incipit Propositio
Books and the Man I sing—&c.
Inscriptio

---

[1] Lords Bolingbroke, Bathurst, nor Dr. Arbuthnot.

[2] This is complicated: Gay was to give Lewis a note for M[otte?], and Pope will see Lewis
'write about it'. One suspects that Swift still is coy about admitting authorship of *Gulliver's
Travels*, and is making Lewis his agent.

[3] The third volume of the *Miscellanies* (called 'the last' on the title-page) appeared 7 Mar.
1727/8.

[4] The *Peri Bathous* had been in the making since the days (1713–14) of the Scriblerus
Club, if not earlier. In view of the hornets that it aroused Pope naturally at times denied
authorship of parts of it. See the edition of Edna L. Steeves (New York, 1952).

And Thou! whose Sence, whose Humour, and whose Rage
At once can teach, delight, and lash the Age!
Whether thou chuse Cervantes' serious Air,
Or laugh and shake in Rab'lais' easy chair,
Praise Courts and Monarchs, or extoll Mankind,
Or thy griev'd Country's copper Chains unbind:
Attend, whatever Title please thine ear,
Dean, Drapier, Bickerstaff, or Gulliver.
From thy Boeotia, lo! the Fog retires;
Yet grieve not thou at what our Isle acquires:
Here Dulness reigns with mighty wings outspread,
And brings the true Saturnian Age of Lead.   &c.

John Gay's Opera[1] is just on the point of Delivery. It may be call'd (considering its Subject) a Jayl-Delivery. Mr Congreve (with whom I have commemorated you) is anxious as to its Success, and so am I; whether it succeeds or not, it will make a great noise, but whether of Claps or Hisses I know not. At worst it is in its own nature a thing which he can *lose* no reputation by, as he lays none upon it.

Mrs Patty is very grateful for your Memory of her, but not a jot the wiser for another winter; It's hard Time should wrinkle faces, and not ripen heads. But she is a very honest Woman, and deserves to be whipt. To make her wise is more than you can do, but 'tis in your power by writing to her once in your life to make her proud, which is the best Suppliment for want of wisdom.

Courts I see not, Courtiers I know not, Kings I adore not, Queens I compliment not; so am never like to be in fashion, nor in dependance. I heartily join with you in pitying our poor Lady[2] for her unhappiness, and should only pity her more, if she had more of what we call Court happiness. I've seen her very seldome. I had lately many Compliments to you from Mr Morris, &c.[3] Pray make mine to all you think worth remembering, But I will not exclude Mrs Delany, Sheridan, & Stopfort, the latter of whom treats me the most kindly by never writing to me, which proves he thinks himself, as he is, secure of my remembrance. I wish I could make Dr[4] and Mr Sh. so uneasy by my not writing to 'em, as to bring them hither the sooner. As for yourself, you cannot be absent, go where you will. Do you but keep well and live, and if I keep well and live, we *must* meet. Adieu.

To mortify you, I acquaint you that I am a hundred pound a year richer,[5] than when you was here; And I owe it to no Great Man.

---

[1] *The Beggar's Opera*, first performed 29 Jan. 1727/8.
[2] Mrs. Howard.
[3] The '&c.' doubtless means Atterbury, whose son-in-law, Morice, had recently returned from France.   [4] Dr. Delany.
[5] The increase in Pope's income probably comes from investing a part of the money received from the *Odyssey*.

And I believe I am in as good health as you, and my Lord Oxford has given me a great Gold Cup and Salver, which quite eclypses your Silver ones.—

> micat inter omnes
> Harleium Sydus, quales inter ignes
> Luna minores[1]

(Send me an Inscription to grave at the bottome of it) I have also a fine Seal of Plato, with which I will not seal this Letter.

Endorsements (by the scribe): Verses
                (by Lord Oxford): Mr Pope to Dean Swift.

POPE *to* BROOME   9 *January* 1727/8

Elwin–Courthope, viii. 141

Jan. 9, 1728.

You please me not a little in seeming pleased with my letter, for I dare say you are what you seem. Nothing is more agreeable than the mutual reconnaissance of two well-meaning men, after they find that only ill-meaning men have endeavoured to set them at variance. I assure you, if you are as sincere as you express yourself, and as I believe, being so myself, you shall be convinced by every good office that shall be in my future power, that I am in earnest on my part by every testimony I can give you. But you should not have judged of me by the impertinence of other people, whose stories ought not to be weighed against my actions. Those were, or should have been, convincing. I meant you well in joining you with me in that task; I meant you well in securing to you a fair and candid opinion from the public, by not declaring at first what particular parts were yours, so lending the little credit I had to my friend; I meant you well in the share you received from me of your profits of a work which, without my personal interest, had been little worth your while; I meant you well in offering, if you remember, of my own free motive, to look over every piece you designed to publish in your Miscellany,—in giving, unasked, my advice as to your printing it, though afterwards the person into whose hands you fell,[2] by his blundering between us, created a misunderstanding. And I must say you should have taken facts as a proof of my friendliness, rather than words of any other whatever. Even a peevish saying or two

---

[1] Horace, *Carmina*, I. xii. 46–48. Line 47 is 'Iulium sidus velut inter ignes.'

[2] Lintot, here blamed unduly—though doubtless unfriendly to Pope hereafter—was obviously not the only cause of friction between Pope and Broome. In 1727 he had published for Walter Harte as well as for Broome, and had made no difficulties between Pope and Harte. One wonders a bit at Pope's tone in this letter in view of the inclusion of Broome in the *Peri Bathous*, which he must have forgotten (?).

of my own, when I was made to think myself injured by your imprudence,[1] for I never charged you with any wilful error, must not be considered as the truth of my heart. And God forgive the man who, merely to set two friends at distance, could steal a paper![2] You say he is one who does not love me. I dare say he either never knew me, or never can say he was hurt by me. I am glad such an one is not my friend. If he were, I should fear him worse than an enemy, who was capable of such an action.

As you would think it hard to have ascribed to yourself the idle or hotheaded things of some of your acquaintance, so be assured I should be sorry to have what Mr. J[ervas] may say imputed to me. I have formerly, and I will again desire his silence, but if I were able I would command it. Therefore be just to me, as I truly am to you. He never had countenance from me for so doing.

As to what L[intot] said, I lay as little stress upon it as you. It only gave me an opportunity, when you were silent, to assure you of my inclination for that friendship which I shall sincerely bear you, and doubt not of from you. I am, dear sir, your affectionate faithful friend.

POPE *to* BUCKLEY   26 *January* [1727/8]

Add. 33964

Sir,—I am very much obliged, and (which is, as the world goes, some thing extraordinary) very much pleased at the same time, by your Present: I have read your Account of your intended Edition of Thuanus with great Satisfaction.[3] It is some Comfort (I fancy) to great Genius's, & honest Transmitters of Facts to posterity, to see so much worthy Pains taken, to right them after their Deaths, & set their labours in the fullest and fairest light: And I believe, the Care of such an Editor as yourself, is All the Reward an honest & faithful Historian ever did, or could, hope to receive for his integrity: The *Iniquitas temporum* which you mention, will generally deprive him of all other.

These Men write for Posterity, and are of use to all Ages: But such Authors as He, whose poor present[4] you set too Great a value upon,

---

[1] His imprudence was his tendency to talk publicly of his work for Pope on the *Odyssey*.
[2] Lacking Broome's letter which told of this theft, we cannot even guess at the nature of the episode.
[3] The account was contained in a pamphlet by Buckley, *A Letter to Dr. Mead, concerning a new edition of Thuanus's History*, which had been circulated very early this year. It was the first of three such 'letters' to Dr. Mead. All three were translated into Latin and printed in the great edition of Thuanus which Buckley brought out in seven folio volumes in 1733, with a most distinguished list of subscribers. In this first *Letter to Dr. Mead* occurs a sentence (p. 24) alleging that *iniquitas temporum* kept Thou's friends from publishing a complete and authentic text in Paris.
[4] Pope's present of the *Odyssey* to Buckley.

write only for the present Ear, & are (as St. Paul expresses it) only as a Tinkling Cymbal.

I am, with thanks for your kind remembrance, | Sir | Your very humble | Servant, | A. Pope.

Twitnam, Jan. 26.

†BOLINGBROKE *and* POPE *to* SWIFT[1]   [*February* 1727/8]
1740

Pope charges himself with this letter; he has been here two days, he is now hurrying to London, he will hurry back to Twickenham in two days more, and before the end of the week he will be, for ought I know, at Dublin. In the mean time his *Dulness*[2] grows and flourishes as if he was there already. It will indeed be a noble work: the many will stare at it, the few will smile, and all his Patrons from Bickerstaff to Gulliver will rejoice, to see themselves adorn'd in that immortal piece.

I hear that you have had some return of your illness which carried you so suddenly from us (if indeed it was your own illness which made you in such haste to be at Dublin) Dear Swift take care of your health, I'll give you a receipt for it, *a la Montagne*, or which is better, *a la Bruyere. Nourisser bien votre corps; ne le fatiguer jamais: laisser rouiller l'esprit, meuble inutil, voire outil dangereux: Laisser sonner vos cloches le matin pour eveiller les chanoines, et pour faire dormir le Doyen d'un sommeil doux et profond, qui luy procure de beaux songes: Lever vous tard, et aller al' Eglise, pour vous faire payer d'avoir bien dormi et bien dejeuné.* As to myself (a person about whom I concern myself very little) I must say a word or two out of complaisance to you. I am in my farm, and here I shoot strong and tenacious roots: I have caught hold of the earth, (to use a Gardener's phrase) and neither my enemies nor my friends will find it an easy matter to transplant me again. Adieu, let me hear from you, at least of you: I love you for a thousand things, for none more than for the just esteem and love which you have for all the sons of Adam.

P. S.[3] According to Lord Bolingbroke's account I shall be at Dublin in three days. I cannot help adding a word, to desire you to expect my soul there with you by that time; but as for the jade of a body that is tack'd to it, I fear there will be no dragging it after. I assure you I have few friends here to detain me, and no powerful one at Court absolutely to forbid my journey.[4] I am told the Gynocracy are of

---

[1] There are no textual variants of importance.   [2] *The Dunciad* to be.
[3] By Pope.
[4] Queen Caroline was frequently called the real ruler of England by critics. Mrs. Howard in the summer of 1727 had in a sense 'forbid' Swift to go to France. See his letter to her, 21 Nov. 1730; Ball, iv. 182.

opinion, that they want no better writers than Cibber and the British Journalist;[1] so that we may live at quiet, and apply ourselves to our more abstruse studies. The only Courtiers I know, or have the honour to call my friends, are John Gay and Mr. Bowry;[2] the former is at present so employed in the elevated airs of his Opera, and the latter in the exaltation of his high dignity (that of her Majesty's Waterman) that I can scarce obtain a categorical answer from either to any thing I say to 'em. But the Opera succeeds extremely, to yours and my extreme satisfaction, of which he promises this post to give you a full account. I have been in a worse condition of health than ever, and think my immortality is very near out of my enjoyment: so it must be in you, and in posterity, to make me what amends you can for dying young. Adieu. While I am, I am yours. Pray love me, and take care of your self.

GAY *to* THE EARL OF OXFORD   12 *February* 1727/8

Longleat Portland Papers, xiii

My Lord,—I was last night to pay my duty to your Lordship, and to thank you for interesting yourself in so kind a manner in my behalf. I had heard before, that the King & Queen were to be present at Julius Cæsar on Friday, so that my intention was to acquaint your Lordship that I had fixt on thursday. As to the Boxes on that day, I fear by what I have heard about the town, they are taken up already, but if your Lordship would be so good as to send a servant to the Box-keeper, I hope I shall have the honour of Lady Oxford's presence in the very Box she chuses, for I know Mr Rich would upon all occasions be very glad to oblige your Lordship.

I am | My Lord | Your Lordship's | most obedient & | most oblig'd humble | Servant | J Gay

Whitehall | Monday morning.

Endorsement: Whitehall Feb: 12: 1727/8

GAY *to* SWIFT   15 *February* 1727/8

Add. 4805

I have deferr'd writing to you from time to time till I could give you an account of the Beggar's Opera. It is Acted at the Playhouse in Lincoln's Inn fields, with such success that the Playhouse hath been

---

[1] Pitt.—Curll (1741 Lc). *The British Journal* apparently had a new writer in 1728. Which of Pope's dunces he may have been is obscure. It is doubtful if William Arnall had yet taken over the journal. James Pitt is a possibility.

[2] Bowry had been Pope's waterman, and apparently still is.

crouded every night; to night is the fifteenth time of Acting, and 'tis thought it will run a fortnight longer. I have order'd Motte to send the Play to you the first opportunity. I made no interest either for approbation or money nor hath any body been prest to take tickets for my Benefit, notwithstanding which, I think I shall make an addition to my fortune of between six and seven hundred pounds. I know this account will give you pleasure, as I have push'd through this precarious Affair without servility or flattery. As to any favours from Great men I am in the same state you left me, but I am a great deal happier as I have no expectations. The Dutchess of Queensberry hath signaliz'd her friendship to me upon this occasion in such a conspicuous manner, that I hope (for her sake) you will take care to put your fork to all its proper uses, and suffer nobody for the f[uture] to put their knives in their mouths. Lord Cobham says that I should [have] printed it in Italian over against the English, that the Ladys might have understood what they read. The outlandish (as they now call it) Opera hath been so thin of late that some have call'd that the Beggars Opera, & if the run continues, I fear I shall have remonstrances drawn up against me by the Royal Academy of Musick.[1] As none of us have heard from you of late every one of us are in concern about your health. I beg we may hear from you soon. By my constant attendance on this affair I have almost worried myself into an ill state of health, but I intend in five or six days to go to our Country seat at Twickenham for a little air. Mr. Pope is very seldom in town. Mrs Howard frequently asks after you & desires her compliments to you; Mr George Arbuthnot, the Doctor's Brother, is married to Mrs Peggy Robinson.[2] I would write more, but as to night is for my Benefit, I am in a hurry to go out about business, | I am | Dear Sir | Your most affectionate | & obedient Servant, | J Gay.

Whitehall | Febr 15. 1727/8 | My Service to Dr. Delany

Address: To | The Reverend Dr Swift | Dean of St Patricks in | Dublin | Ireland

Postmark: 15/FE

Endorsements (in Swift's hand): Mr Gay | Feb. 15th 1727–8 | Mr Gay. | Feb. 22d; 1727–8 | Ansd May 11th 1728.

(in another hand): Leskibar blanc

---

[1] This organization sponsored and governed the Italian opera in the Haymarket.

[2] A sister of Anastasia; Anastasia is now privately married to the Earl of Peterborow.

SWIFT *to* GAY[1]   26 *February* 1727/8
Longleat Portland Papers, xiii (Harleian transcript)

Now.—Why does not Mr Pope publish his dullness, the rogues he mawles will dy of themselves in peace, and So will his friends, and So there will be neither punishment nor reward. Pray enquire how My Lord St John does   there is no mans health in Engld I am more concerned about then, his—I wonder whether you begin to tast the pleasure of independancy, or whether you do not Sometimes leer upon the Court oculo retorto; Will you now think of an annuity when you are two years older, and have doubled your purchase-money? Have you dedicated your opera and got the usuall dedication-fee, of 20 guinneas. How is the Doctor, does he not chide that you never called upon him for hints. Is My Lord Bol— at the moment I am writing, a planter, a Philosopher or a writer, Is Mr Pultaney in expectation of a Son, or My Lord Bathurst of an employment, or My Lord Oxford of a new old manuscript ⌐ask Mrs Howard whether She will take the remedy with which I twice perfectly cured my deafness, tho' I am again relapsed; and I will Send her the receit I Said Something of this to Mr Pope, Does W—[2] think you intended an affront to him in your opera. Pray God he may, for he has held the longest hand at hazard that ever fell to any Sharpers Share and keeps his run when the dice are changed: Present my most humble Service to the deliverer of this letter, for So he must be, and not Dr Delany; who Stole away without it; by an accedent—It is probable I have forgot Something of more moment than any thing here, My Service to Mr Pope & all friends.—adieu⌐— I bought your opera to day for 6 pence, a cursed print I find there is neither dedication nor preface, both which wants I approve it is in the grand goût.

SWIFT *to* MARTHA BLOUNT   29 *February* 1727/8
Stowe 755
                                    Dublin, Feb. 29th. 1727–8

Dear Patty,—I am told you have a mind to receive a Letter from me, which is a very undecent declaration in a young Lady, and almost a confession that you have a mind to write to me; for, as to the fancy of looking on me as a man sans consequence, it is what I will never understand. I am told likewise you grow every day younger and more

---

[1] Under date of 23 Nov. 1727 Pope printed in his editions of 1740–2 a composite letter, of which the third and fourth paragraphs came from this letter. Except for the long omission indicated here by half-brackets, this whole letter was used in the composite. See also 23 Nov. 1727 and (for the later paragraphs of the composite) 28 Mar. 1728.

[2] W— has been expanded in the Harleian transcript (by a later hand) to *Walpole*.

a fool, which is directly contrary to me, who grow wiser and older, and at this rate we shall never agree. I long to see you a London Lady where you are forcd to wear whole cloaths and visit in a chair, for which you must Starve next summer at Petersham with a mantow out at the sides; and spunge once a week at our house without ever inviting us in a whole Season to a cow-heel at home. I wish you would bring Mr Pope over with you when you come, but we will leave Mr Gay to his beggars and his operas till he is able to pay his club. How will you pass this Summer for want of a Squire to Ham-common and Walpole's lodge; for, as to Richmond lodge and Marble-hill they are abandond as much as Sir Spencer Compton.[1] And Mr Schutz's[2] coach that usd to give you so many a Set-down, is wheeled off to St James's. You must be forced to get a horse and gallop with Mrs Jansen and Miss Bedier.[3] Your greatest happiness is that you are out of the chiding of Mrs Howard and the Dean, but I suppose Mr Pope is so just as to pay our arears, and that you edify as much by him as by us, unless you are so happy that he now looks upon you as reprobate and a castaway, of which I think he hath given me some hints. However I would advise you to pass this Summer at Kensington where you will be near the Court, and out of his jurisdiction, where you will be teazed with no lectures of gravity and morality, and where you will have no other trouble than to get into the mercer's books, and take up a hundred pounds of your principal for quadrille. Monstrous indeed that a fine lady in the prime of life and gayety must take up with an antiquated Dean, an old Gentlewoman of fourscore,[4] and a sickly poet. I will stand by my dear Patty against the world; if Teresa beats you for your good, I will buy her a fine whip for the purpose. Tell me, have you been confined to your lodging this winter for want of chair-hire.—[Do you know that this unlucky Dr Delany came last night to the Deanery, and being denyed without my knowledge is gone to England this morning, and so I must send this by the Post. I bought your opera to day for 6 pence, so small printed that it will spoyl my eyes. I ordered you to send me your edition, but now you may keep it till you get an opportunity.] Patty: I will tell you a blunder. I am writing to Mr Gay,[5] and had almost finished the letter. But by a mistake I took up this instead of it and so the six lines in a hook are all to him, and therefore you must read them to him, for I will not be at the trouble to write them over again. My greatest concern in the matter is that I

---

[1] King George II had intended to make this favourite Walpole's successor, but Compton's lack of capability prevented his rise in 1727. He was presently to be created Earl of Wilmington.

[2] Augustus Schutz was a favourite courtier—and a friend of Patty Blount's.

[3] Probably a daughter of Sir Theodore Janssen, who had lost much of his large fortune in the South Sea scandal. *Miss* Bedier should, since called Miss, be either a child or a servant.

[4] Pope's mother.　　　　　　　　　　　　　　　　　　　　[5] The letter of 26 Feb.

am afraid I continue in love with you, which is hard after near six Months absence. I hope you have done with your rash and other little disorders, and that I shall see you a fine young healthy plump lady, and if Mr Pope chides you, threaten him that you will turn Heretick. Adieu dear Patty, and believe me to be one of your truest Friends and humblest Servants, and that since I can never live in England, my greatest happyness would be to have you and Mr Pope condemned during my life to live in Ireland, he at the Deanery, and you for reputation Sake just at next door, and I will give you eight dinners a week, and a whole half dozen of pint bottles of good french wine at your lodgings, a thing you could never expect to arrive at, and every year a suit of 14 penny stuff, that should not be worn out at the right side; and a chair costs but sixpence a jobb, and you shall have catholicity as much as you please, and the catholick Dean of St Patricks, as old again as I, to your Confessor. Adieu again dear Patty—

Address: To Patty Blount

MOTTE *to* REV. [R. ?] WOODFORD   12 March 1727/8

The Pierpont Morgan Library

Revd Sir,—The dispute with Mr Curll stands as follows:—For many years past he has made it his business to pick up straggling and imperfect Copies of Verses, which he has father'd upon Dr Swift or Mr Pope, or some other name of reputation. Some of these were really written by these Gentlemen, but publish'd by him without their knowledge and against their consent; and many Pieces were laid to their charge which they knew nothing of, and were so worthless that they had reason to be ashamed of them. To vindicate their Reputation they made a Collection of such things as were genuine, and have just now published them, having before for a valuable and substantial consideration made a formal Conveyance of the Copyright of them to me in May last.[1] On the Publication of them I receiv'd the following Letter from Curll:—

Mr. Motte,—I have carefully examin'd your new last volume of old Miscellanies; in the Art of Sinking, your Authors have printed the Project for advancing the Stage,[2] which is my copy; and most of the other pieces in the Volume have been by me published many Years ago. To-morrow night you'll find I have in some measure undeceiv'd the Town. And to do myself justice, will reprint what-

---

[1] The agreement was signed 29 March 1727. See *Gent. Mag.* xliv (1855), 363.
[2] As Chapter XVI of *The Art of Sinking in Poetry*.

ever is *New* in this last Volume as a just reprizal for what they have taken from me that is *Old*. | Yours, | E. Curll.

> However Swift and Pope agree,
> Nor they nor you shall bubble me.[1]

Q. Whether, in case he be in execution in the Court of King's Bench, that Court has not a power to curb him in such enormities?

I am, with grateful respect, | Your obliged humble servant, | B. Motte.

March 12, 1727–8.

GAY *to* SWIFT   20 *March* 1727/8

Add. 4805

I am extreamly sorry that your disorder is return'd, but as you have a medicine which hath twice remov'd [it] you I hope by this time, have again found the good effects of it. I have seen Dr Delany at my Lodgings, but as I have been for a few days with Mr Pulteney at Cashioberry I have not yet return'd his visit, I went with him to wait upon Lord Bathurst & Lord Bolingbroke both of whom desire me to make you their compliments. Lady Bolingbroke was very much out of order; and with my Lord is now at Doyley;[2] she expects a letter from you. Mrs Howard would gladly have the receipt you have found so much benefit by; she is happier than I have seen her ever since you left us, for she is free as to her conjugal affairs by articles of agreement. The Beggar's Opera hath now been acted thirty six times, and was as full the last night, as the first, and as yet there is not the least probability of a thin audience; though there is a discourse about the town that the Directors of the Royal Academy of Musick design to sollicite against it's being play'd on the *outlandish* Opera days, as it is now call'd. On the Benefit day of one of the Actresses last week one of the players falling sick they were oblig'd to give out another play or dismiss the Audience; A Play was given out, but the people call'd out for the Beggar's Opera, & they were forc'd to play it, or the Audience would not have stayed. I have got by all this success between seven & eight hundred pounds, and Rich[3] (deducting the whole charge of the House) hath clear'd already near four thousand pounds. In about a month I

---

[1] Curll loves to spice even his printed letters with these derisive couplets. They appear frequently in the introductory sections of his various volumes of *Mr. Pope's Literary Correspondence*. For example, in ii. 29 we have the triumphant lines:

> No longer now like Suppliants we come,
> E.C. makes War, and A.P. is the Drum.

[2] i.e. Dawley.

[3] John Rich (d. 1761) was the manager of the theatre in Lincoln's Inn Fields where *The Beggar's Opera* was being performed. According to the witticism of the day the success of the opera made 'Gay rich, and Rich gay'. Drury Lane had refused the play.

am going to the Bath with the Dutchess of Marlborough and Mr
Congreve; for I have no expectations of receiving any favours from
the Court. The Dutchess of Queensberry is in Wiltshire, where she
hath had the small pox in so favourable a way, that she had not above
seven or eight in her face; she is now perfectly recover'd. There is a
Mezzo-tinto Print publish'd to day of Polly,[1] the Heroine of the
Beggar's Opera, who was before unknown, & is now in so high vogue,
that I am in doubt, whether her fame does not surpass that of the
Opera itself. I would not have talk'd so much upon this subject, or
upon any thing that regards myself but to you; but as I know you
interest yourself so sincerely in every thing that concerns me, I believe
you would have blam'd me if I had said less. Your Singer[2] owes Dr
Arbuthnot some money, I have forgot the sum; I think it is two
Guineas; the Dr desir'd me to let you know it. I saw him last night
with Mr Lewis at Sr William Wyndham's, who if he had not the
Gout would have answer'd your Letter you sent him a year & a half
ago; he said this to me a week since; but he is now pretty well again,
& so may forget to write, for which reason, I ought to do him justice
and tell you that I think him a sincere well-wisher of yours. I have
not seen Mr Pope lately, but have heard that both he & Mrs Pope are
very well. I intend to see him at Twickenham on sunday next. I have
not drunk out the Gutheridge Cyder yet, but I have not so much as a
single pint of Port in my Cellar. I have bought two pair of Sheets
against your coming to town, so that we need not send any more to
Jervas upon that ac[count] I really miss you every day, and I would
be content th[at] yo[u shoul]d have one whole window to yourself, &
half [another] to have you again. | I am | Dear Sir | Yours most
affectionately.

You have a half years interest due at Lady-day, & now 'tis March
20th 1727/8

†POPE *to* SWIFT[3]   23 *March* 1727/8

1740

March 23, 1727-8.

I send you a very odd[4] thing, a paper printed in Boston in New

---

[1] Lavinia Fenton achieved fame as Polly. She speedily became the mistress of the 3rd
Duke of Bolton, who upon the death of his Duchess married (1751) 'Polly'. She was perhaps
the first actress to achieve such rank.

[2] As Swift's reply [28 Mar. 1728] explains, the reference is to William Fox, who was a
member of Swift's choir from 1727 until his death in 1734.—Ball. iv. 16 n.

[3] The Rev. Mather Byles had enclosed in a letter to Pope, 7 Oct. 1727, a copy of *The
New England Weekly Journal* for 5 June 1727. This issue of the Boston paper contained
verses by Byles complimenting Pope. It also contained a mention of 'Capt. Jonath. Gulliver,'
who was at this time member of the General Court ('Parliament') of the Province for the
town of Milton. It is an interesting coincidence that in the seventeenth century settlers in
the town of Milton included both Gullivers and Swifts.   [4] odd] old *1741 Dab.*

England, wherein you'll find a real person, a member of their Parliament, of the name of Jonathan Gulliver. If the fame of that Traveller has travel'd thither, it has travel'd very quick, to have folks christen'd already by the name of the supposed Author. But if you object, that no child so lately christen'd could be arrived at years of maturity to be elected into Parliament, I reply (to solve the Riddle) that the person is an *Anabaptist*, and not christen'd till full age, which sets all right. However it be, the accident is very singular, that these two names should be united.

Mr. Gay's Opera has acted near forty days running, and will certainly continue the whole season. So he has more than a fence about his thousand pounds: he'll soon be thinking of a fence about his two thousand. Shall no one of us live as we would wish each other to live? Shall he have no sure annuity,[1] you no settlement on this side, and I no prospect of getting to you on the other? This world is made for Cæsar —as Cato said,[2] for ambitious, false, or flattering people to domineer in: Nay they would not, by their good will, leave us our very books, thoughts, or words, in quiet. I despise the world yet, I assure you, more than either Gay or you, and the Court more than all the rest of the world. As for those Scriblers for whom you apprehend I would suppress my *Dulness*, (which by the way, for the future you are to call by a more pompous name, The *Dunceiad*) how much that nest of Hornets are my regard, will easily appear to you when you read the Treatise of the Bathos.

At all adventures, yours and my name shall stand linked as friends to posterity, both in verse and prose, and (as Tully calls it) in *consuetudine Studiorum*. Would to God our persons could but as well, and as surely, be inseparable! I find my other Tyes dropping from me; some worn off, some torn off, others relaxing daily: My greatest, both by duty, gratitude, and humanity, Time is shaking every moment, and it now hangs but by a thread! I am many years the older, for living so much with one so old; much the more helpless, for having been so long help'd and tended by her; much the more considerate and tender, for a daily commerce with one who requir'd me justly to be both to her; and consequently the more melancholy and thoughtful; and the less fit for others, who want only in a companion or a friend, to be amused or entertained. My constitution too has had its share of decay, as well as my spirits, and I am as much in the decline at forty as you at sixty. I believe we should be fit to live together, cou'd I get a little more health, which might make me not quite insupportable: Your Deafness wou'd agree with my Dulness; you wou'd not want me to speak when you could not hear. But God forbid you shou'd be as

---

[1] no sure annuity] no annuity *1741 Labc*; *1742 Lbc*.
[2] Addison's *Cato*, vi. 19.

destitute of the social comforts of life,[1] as I must when I lose my mother; or that ever you shou'd lose your more useful acquaintance so utterly, as to turn your thoughts to such a broken reed as I am, who could so ill supply your wants. I am extremely troubled at the returns of your deafness; you cannot be too particular in the accounts of your health to me; every thing you do or say in this kind obliges me, nay delights me, to see the justice you do me in thinking me concern'd in all your concerns; so that tho' the pleasantest thing you can tell me be that you are better or easier; next to that it pleases me that you make me the person you wou'd complain to.

As the obtaining the love of valuable men is the happiest end I know of this life, so the next felicity is to get rid of fools and scoundrels; which I can't but own to you was one part of my design in falling upon these Authors, whose incapacity is not greater than their insincerity, and of whom I have always found (if I may quote myself)

That each bad Author is as bad a Friend.

This Poem will rid me of those insects,

Cedite Romani Scriptores, cedite Graii,
Nescio quid *majus nascitur Iliade,*[2]

I mean than *my Iliad;* and I call it *Nescio quid,* which is a degree of modesty; but however if it silence these fellows, it must be something greater than any Iliad in Christendome. Adieu.

SWIFT *to* GAY[3]   28 *March* 1728

Longleat Portland Papers, xiii (Harleian transcript)

Dublin Mar 28th 1728

⌈I had yours of the 20th last night As to the remedy that twice cured my deafness, I would not take it the 3d time because it made me so tender that the least cold brought on my disorder again, which went of however without using it any more. This I say on Mrs Howards account, yet she shall have it if she pleases, I am now tolerable well but my fears of relapsing hang over me, and very much take down my mettle. I will write to my Lady Bolingbroke; but I would be glad

---

[1] This is Pope's first letter to Swift since the death of Stella (28 Jan. 1727/8), which he may here have in mind.

[2] Propertius, ii. 34, 65–66.

[3] The parts of this letter not placed in half-brackets were printed (1740–2) in the composite letter of 23 Nov. 1727 as paragraphs 5–10; i.e. as the last half of the letter. Paragraphs 1 and 2 had been taken from a letter actually of the date printed (q.v.), and 3 and 4 came from the letter of 26 Feb. 1727/8. Pope's carelessness in thus conflating three letters under the November date is seen in the fact that the composite deals with the success of Gay's opera, which any reader could know was not staged until two months later than the date of the composite.

first, that you would know from her whether she will have such Usquebagh as I can get, and how much, and whether the green or the yallow, (for there is no such thing as white) or will she leave all but the quantity to my discretion? We have your opera for 6d and⌐ we are as full of it pro modulo nostro as London can be continuall[1] acting, and house[2] Crammd, and the Lord Lieut[3] severall times there, laughing his heart out ⌐I wish you had sent me a Copy as I desired to oblige an honest Bookseller, it would have done Motte no hurt, for no English copy has been sold but the Dublin one has run prodigiously.⌐ I did not understand that the Scene of Locket and Peachum's quarrels was an imitation of one between Brutus and Cassius till I was told it; I wish Mackheath when he was going to be hang'd had imitated Alexdr the great when he was dying. I would have had his fellow rogues, desire his commands about a Successor, and he to answer, let it be the most worthy: &c, we hear a million of Storys about the opera, of the ancore[4] at the Song, *That was levelled at me*,[5] when 2 great Ministers were in a Box together, and all the world staring at them I am heartily glad your opera hath mended your purse though perhaps it may Spoyl your Court ⌐I think that rich rogue Rich Should in conscience make you a present of 2 or 3 hundred Guineas. I am impatient that Such a dog by Sitting Still Should get five times more than the Author. you told me a month ago of 700ll, and have you not quite made up the Eight yet, I know not your methods. how many third days are you allowd, and how much is each day worth, and what did you get for the Copy? Pray give one to Dr Delany for me,⌐ will you desire My Lord Bolingbrok Mr Pulteney and Mr Pope to command you to buy an annuity with two thousand pounds that you may laugh at Courts. and bid Ministers[6] kiss ⌐&c—and ten to one they will be ready to grease you when you are fat I hope your new Dutchess will treat you at the Bath, and that you will be too wise to lose your money at play:⌐ Ever preserve Some Spice of the Alderman[7] and prepare[8] against age and dulness and Sickness and coldness or death of friends. A whore has a ressource left that She can turn Bawd: but an old decayd Poet is a creature abandond and at mercy when he can find none. Get me likwise Polly's mezzo-tinto. Lord, how the School-boys at Westminster, and University Lads adore you at this juncture; have you made as many men laugh, as Ministers can make to weep? ⌐I am

---

[1] continuall] continually *all printed editions*.

[2] house] houses *all eds.*, 1740–2. Ball (iv. 20 n.) reprints from *Dublin Intelligence* of 23 Mar. 1727/8 an item indicating that boxes were sold out for '16 or 18 Nights to come'.

[3] Lord Carteret.—1741 Dab.   [4] ancore] applause *all editions*, 1740–2.

[5] See Air XXX (Act II) of *The Beggar's Opera*.

[6] Ministers kiss—] Ministers— *1741 Labc*; *1742 Lbc*.

[7] Curll (1741 Lc) adds a footnote *Barber*; but evidently Swift means 'some spice of the character of an alderman'—i.e. financial prudence.

[8] Oxford's scribe here wrote *proper*.

glad your Goddess-Dutchess[1] hath preserved a face which I never Saw Since it was on the shoulders of a girl. Doct Arburthnot[2] lent Fox the Singer whome he Sent me, 5 guinneas, and had his note, This note I took from the Doctr and payd him the 5 Guinneas honestly at his house in Cork Street over against my Lord Harvy's; If he lent the Fellow any other money without a note, I know nothing of it;⌐ I will excuse Sir Wm Windham[3] the trouble of a Letter. when Ambassadors came from Troy to condol with Tiberius upon the death of his Nephew, after two years. The Emperor answered that he likewise condoled with them for the untimely death of Hector.[4] I always loved and respected Sir Wm W.[5] very much, and do so Still as much as ever and it is a return Sufficient if he pleaseth to accept the offers of my most humble Service. ⌐I have 20 Dozen of Gudridge Syder as good as yours; which cost me 8 pounds, and if you will just cross the water heither from the Bath I will give you a Bottle of it every day. I had a Letter from Jo Taylor last Post, recommending one Waghern for my Quire.[6] He must be answered by your means, that I did admit him to a half place a year ago, or more, and have recommended him to the Dean of our other Cathedrall[7] to be taken in there But the man by his indiscretion is got So deep in debt, that I doubt he must run away back to England; as I Suppose he did from thence hither for the Same reason, This I would have Said to Mr Taynor without troubling him with a Letter; neither do I know his address unless it be to Bridewell My most humble Service to Mr Pulteney, and Mrs Howard, and Mr Pope, &c, and the Doctr. I hope Dr Delany hath Shown you the Tale writ by Mrs Barbar[8] a Citizen's wife here in praise of your Fables There is Something in it hard upon Mr Congreve, which I Sent to her (for I never Saw her) to change to Dryden, but She absolutely refused. I am now descended * * * * *⌐

⌐But I have not yet descended So low as a halfpenny, that indeed would be an indignity Tel D. Delany that our Town is full of Speculations about his Journey, and they have found outt three Ladyes for him One is Lady Rawden[9] of Irland another is a Daughter of Sir

---

[1] Queensberry, who had been reported as having smallpox.
[2] See Gay to Swift, 20 Mar. 1727/8.
[3] The clandestine volume (1740) printed 'Sir W— W—'. The Dublin editions (1741 Dab) printed 'Sr Wm Windham.' The London editions, except the reissue of 1740 (1742 La), printed 'Sir ——.'
[4] Suetonius, *Tiberius*, 52.
[5] Sir Wm W.] Sir William *1740, 1741 Dab.*   ] him *all London eds, 1741–2, except the reissue of 1740 (1742 La).*
[6] John Waghorne, appointed to Swift's choir in 1726, remained a member of it until his death in 1733.—Ball, iv. 22 n.   [7] Christ Church, Dublin.
[8] On Mrs. Mary Barber (1690?–1757) see *DNB*. The poem mentioned is called 'A True Tale', and before publication in 1735 in her *Poems on Several Occasions* the specific mention of Congreve disappeared.
[9] The widow of Sir John Rawdon of Moira, who speedily married another.—Ball.

Const Phipps,[1] and the third is a Lady who hath no name, but 600ll
a year estate. These conjectures entertained this Town, till your opera
drove them out So that I fear at present they are under little concern
whether he gets a wife or no—⌉ The Beggers Opera hath knockt
down Gulliver, I hope to see Popes Dullness knock down the Beggers
Opera, but not till it hath fully done its Jobbʳ, Say have not been told
how easy a thing it is to gett 800ll by two or three months writing An
Aldermans you could never failing of writing two or three Such trifles
every year˥[2] to expos vice and make people laugh with innocency does
more publick Service than all the Ministers of State from Adam to
Walpol, & So adieu

POPE *to* JOHN KNIGHT[3]   [1728]

Bowles (1806), x. 105

Sir,—I had very long ago found a day liable to no accident of prevent-
ing me from seeing yourself and Mrs. Knight; but for a very tedious
series of wretched ill health, that almost renders every day of my life
wearisome and vexatious. My mother too has relapsed twice or thrice;
and it is so melancholy to her to be quite alone, that I have in a manner
kept home entirely. Twice I endeavoured to find you, as I think, since
we last met. I wish it now; and, if I am not downright ill, will wait
on you both next week. Guelfi sent me a letter this post, to whom I
owed an arrear, thinking some things were wanting to be done, particularly to conceal better the joining of the urn. Pray send to him
about it, and tell him (it will save me writing, and my head aches
extremely), that, as soon as that is done, or if it be already done, I
will pay him.[4]

Be assured, dear Sir, of our hearty services to yourself and your
lady. | I am, etc.

I hope you have read the book of the Bathos, and the last volume
of our Miscellanies.

---

[1] To whom Delany had been chaplain.—Ball.

[2] The scribe made this passage hopelessly corrupt. Elwin amended it to read: 'They have
not been told how easy a thing it is to get 800*l.* by two or three months' writing. If you were
an alderman you could never fail of writing two or three such trifles every year.' There is no
conceivable antecedent for the initial *they*, and one doubts if Swift thought that being an
alderman aided literary facility! The passage was very likely confused in the original letter:
hence Pope omitted it.

[3] The postscript places the letter a moderate time after 7 Mar. 1727/8 when the 'last'
volume of the *Miscellanies* appeared.

[4] Craggs's monument had now been 'opened' to the public in the Abbey for some weeks.
This curious remark, together with earlier letters to Mrs. Newsham (now Mrs. Knight)
sounds as if a sum had been turned over to Pope who thereafter paid for the monument. See
Pope to J. Knight, 30 Oct. 1727.

POPE *to* MRS. KNIGHT[1]   [*Spring of* 1728]

Bowles (1806) x. 109–10

Madam,—I was unlucky not to be able to find you the only day I have
been in town: and the season now keeps me to the country, where all
the business I have in the world is to be. I was, if I could have seen
you, to have informed you of some curiosities (as I know you to like
things of that nature) in shells, corals, and mineral ores, and congela-
tions, which, I'm told, are very beautiful, and to be had at a very
reasonable rate. I heard of them by chance: they belong to one Mrs.
Dering, who brought them from the Indies, and lives at Mrs. Le
Grand's. If you care to see them, Mrs. Patty Blount will wait upon
you thither, and be glad of the opportunity of becoming better acquainted with you. I said something from you to her, which I have
forgot, and was to say something from her to you since, which I have
also forgot; but you may take my word it was very civil, very reasonable, and very well intended. I hope you will meet some way or other
upon better terms than silly civilities (as you desired, I know, to do):
if you don't meet at your own houses, let it be at mine. Pray acquaint
me how soon you can do me the favour you promised of a day! Assure
Mr. Knight of my hearty services, and believe me sincerely, Madam, |
Your, etc.

*POPE *to* MRS. KNIGHT   [1728?]

Mapledurham

Madam,—It happens, very much agst my hope & inclination, that I
must of necessity be out of town upon business all the next week: I
therfore beg you to defer the appointment with Mrs Blount till I see
you next. I am with real Truth, Esteem, & Obligation, Mr Knight's,
and | Madam | Yours. | A. Pope.

Friday|night.

Address: To | Mrs Knight. | Present

POPE *to* JOHN KNIGHT[2]   [1728?]

Bowles (1806), x. 108

Thursday, 7 in the Morning.

There has arisen such a tempest to-night, and in the morning is so

---

[1] A letter difficult if not impossible to date. Martha Blount has met Mrs. Knight, but is
not as yet 'well acquainted' with her. Yet in July of 1728 she visited the Knights at Gosfield,
and later letters indicate intimacy. To Mrs. Knight Pope would hardly say that all his business
(planting?) was in the country before the Craggs monument was finished in 1727?
[2] A letter that cannot be dated with certainty.

blustering, that I think it unreasonable to tax Mrs. Knight's good-nature at such a rate, as to expect her here to-day. If she were one of those fine ladies who *goes* no where but for her own sake, and for her own dear amusements, and visits those whom she would hang in her passion, or beggar in her play; why then I should not be sorry to see her soused and mortified one wet day in the country for it. But as she intends to please me, and as I gratefully wish her to be pleased, I will not expect her if the weather does not perfectly change, so as you may be here before one o'clock: and pray name any day whatever else (after to-morrow, on which I am indispensably engaged). Nevertheless, as for you, Sir, if you fear neither wind, nor thunder, nor storm, according to your wonted alacrity, come on horseback forthwith, and appoint your other day yourself in person. I am very truly Mrs. Knight's, and, dear Sir, | Your, etc.

FENTON *to* BROOME   3 *April* 1728
Elwin–Courthope, viii. 143
                                        Easthampstead Park, April 3, 1728.

Dear Mr. Broome,—In my next I suppose I must raise my style, and address to the reverend Dr. Broome, for I think it will be wrong in you to neglect this opportunity of taking your degree when the king visits Cambridge. I think however that you acted perfectly right in refusing the Devonshire preferment, and though great men are odd creatures, I cannot think that your refusal can bear an ill construction; in reason I am sure it ought not.

Do you ever correspond with our good friend Mr. Pope? I never hear of him but in the weekly chronicles. Mist had a very severe paper against him in the last journal, which seems to have been written by one who has studied and understands him.[1] In a little time I shall have frequent opportunities of seeing him; for after about a month's stay in London, whither we shall go the next week, Mr. Trumbull intends to spend two or three months at Twickenham. In the meantime continue to direct for me at Mr. Tonson's.

I am sorry to hear Mrs. Broome has had so severe a winter, which has been very sickly in these parts, though few have died. I have escaped with two or three pinches of the gout, which has served to keep me out of the dirt and wet a great part of the season. How go you

---

[1] In the spring of this year Mist's *Weekly Journal* contained several attacks on Pope, some of them by Theobald. Since the journal had a Tory, Jacobite bias, Pope in the first *Dunciad* retorted by saying that Theobald (a Whig) 'cackled to the Tories' in these attacks. The attack here mentioned appeared 30 Mar. 1728 with the title, 'An Essay on the Arts of a Poet's Sinking in Reputation'. It was presently reprinted in *A Compleat Collection of all the Verses, Essays, Letters and Advertisements, which have been occasioned by the Publication of three Volumes of Miscellanies, by Pope and Company* (15 June 1728).

on with your poem on Death?[1] You have heard of Johnny Gay's success with his mock opera, which has been both applauded and preached against. The town, I hear is divided about Miss Fenton, who acted his heroine.[2] Some take her to be my niece, others my ———, others think from a similitude in some features that she is my bastard.

> Qualibus in tenebris vitae, quantisque periclis
> Degitur hoc ævi, quodcunque est![3]

Dinner calls, adieu! Let me hear soon from you.

FENTON *to* BROOME   *7 April* [1728]

Elwin–Courthope, viii. 144

Easthampstead Park, April 7, [1728].

Dear Mr. Broome,— I have not yet seen any of these famous Miscellanies, and therefore was very much surprised to find by your last that you are traduced by a person from whom you could little expect, and have less deserved such ungenerous treatment. He has indeed discovered a keen appetite to quarrel with you, but I think *næ iste magno cum conatu magnas nugas dixerit.*[4] The *monstra natantia*, which you quote from Horace,[5] is translated by Mr. Dryden, "and monsters rolling in the deep." To which you may add that of Virgil, Æn. 6: *Et quæ marmoreo fert monstra sub æquore pontus,*[6] for all kinds of fish. Manilius is still fuller to your purpose. Lib. 4, v. 660.[7]

> Huic varias pestes diversaque monstra ferarum
> Concessit bellis *natura* infesta futuris
> Horrendos angues—
> Et vastos elephantas habet, sævosque leones, &c.

Cornelius Fronto, as I find him quoted by Vossius,[8] observes on the word monstrum, *consuetudo monstri nomen iis quasi proprium fecerit in quibus non servatur naturæ ordo*, which I think makes nothing against you when you are supported with so many incontestable authorities.

His other criticism appears to me just of a piece with this; but not

---

[1] In 1739 Broome included in his *Poems* 'A Poem on Death, To Thomas Marriot'.
[2] Miss Lavinia Fenton ('Polly'), afterwards Duchess of Bolton, was at this moment as notorious as she was charming.   [3] Lucretius, ii. 15–16.
[4] Terence, *Heauton*, IV. i. 8.   [5] Horace, *Carmina*, I. iii. 18.
[6] *Aeneid* vi. 729.
[7] *Astronomicon*, iv. 662–6 (Housman ed.).
[8] Vossius, *Etymologicon*, s.v. *monstrum*.
All this appeal to precedent in poetic diction is typical of the period. Pope obviously had quoted (*Bathos*, ch. vii) the couplet from Broome '(Thus Phoebus through the Zodiac takes his way, | And amidst monsters rises into day) partly in order to append *magnas nugas*;' i.e. the jocose observation that of the signs of the zodiac, 'There were only the centaur and the maid that could be esteemed out of nature.' What hurt, however, was the concluding quip about Broome's technique: 'What he found not monsters, he made so.'

having either your or his book by me, I cannot strictly examine it.[1] I cannot think it at all proper to send him the letter which you enclosed. He has challenged you to a public defence, and if you do not think it worth your while to take up the gauntlet, the sullen silence of Ajax will be the most manly revenge. Far be it from me to endeavour to spirit you up to the combat; but if it were my own case, I could not remain passive under such a provocation.

As to your query relating to myself after I quit Mr. Trumbull, with whom I shall continue till next winter at least, I intend to undertake another young gentleman if I meet with an agreeable offer; for I should disoblige my sister, who is my sheet anchor, if I lived out of business any where but with her. But before that time I hope I shall have an opportunity of chatting with you. I am ever, dear Broome, your faithful humble servant.

Let me hear soon from you whether we are to expect peace or war, and whether you would have your letter delivered. My service as usual. Direct to Mr. Tonson's.

P.S.—Mr. Waller, in the Battle of the Summer Islands, calls whales monsters in five or six places. Mr. Dryden, in his translation of the story of Meleager, calls the boar a monstrous foe. In the next line, "his tusk the monster grinds." It were endless to quote authors in your justification. What I quoted from Fronto respects the purity of prose, which has little relation to figurative poetical diction. Adieu.

BROOME *to* FENTON   3 *May* [1728]

Elwin–Courthope, viii. 146

May 3, [1728].

My Dear Friend Fenton,—You guess right. I am now dignified with the style of Doctor,[2] and as I do not find that it has made me one jot more wise or learned, I assure you it shall not make me one jot more proud. I affected not the title. As obscure as it is I was contented with my own name, having done nothing to disgrace it. But my friends told me they could ask with a better grace for a doctor, than a common clergyman, so I submitted, and the more willingly because it is no burthen to carry a feather. I really look upon the doctorate with a very indifferent eye, at best but as a bauble hung about me, to grace my second childhood of old age, as the like tinsel is made use of to please babies. If it really be of any service to me with regard to pre-

---

[1] This criticism concerns a passage from 'On the birthday of a Gentleman [Mr. Robert Trefusis] when three Years Old'. In 1727 Broome had added two couplets to the passage that further confounded the imagistic confusion that Pope had quoted from the text published in 1712 (by Pope as editor) in Lintot's Miscellany.

[2] In April, on the occasion of the king's visit to Cambridge, Broome had been made an LL.D.

ferment, you have as much reason to be glad of it as myself, and I bless God I am a doctor. It will then give me an opportunity of enjoying my friend Mr. Fenton as a sharer of it. I invite you to the participation of it, and the greatest pleasure I shall receive from it will be your dividing it with me. Our tempers suit very well, and it would be a sin for me to abound and you want.

> Utrumque nostrum, incredibili modo,
> Consentit astrum.[1]

We will then walk hand in hand down the declivity of life to the land where only I can forget you.

You ask me if I correspond with Mr. Pope. I do not. He has used me ill, he is ungrateful.[2] He has now raised a spirit against him which he will not easily conjure down. He now keeps his muse as wizards are said to keep tame devils, only to send them abroad to plague their neighbours. I often resemble him to an hedgehog; he wraps himself up in his down, lies snug and warm, and sets his bristles out against all mankind. Sure he is fond of being hated. I wonder he is not thrashed: but his littleness is his protection; no man shoots a wren. He should rather be whipped; and it was pleasant enough in Mr. Ambrose Philips to hang up a rod at Button's *in terrorem*, which scared away the little bard.[3]

I have seen Mr. Gay's mock opera. Johnny is a good-natured inoffensive man. I doubt not, therefore, but those lines against courts and ministers are drawn, at least aggravated, by Mr. Pope, who delights to paint every man in the worst colours. He wounds from behind Gay, and like Teucer in Homer, puts Gay in the front of the battle, and shoots his arrows lurking under the shield of Ajax.[4]

Pray write very soon, dear Fenton, to him who is yours inviolably

POPE *to* THE EARL OF OXFORD   6 *May* 1728

Longleat Portland Papers, xii

Twitenham. May 6. | 1728.

My Lord,—I had the honour of yours some time since, which the hope of finding you soon in Town prevented me from answering. I now am so immers'd in the Country & in Books, that unless your

---

[1] Horace, *Carmina*, II. xvii. 21–22.
[2] In chapter vii of his recently published *Bathos* Pope had included a couplet from Broome's Epistle to Fenton, and had passed (off-hand?) cruel jokes about it.
[3] Broome here anticipates the printed account of the episode given in *Pope Alexander's Supremacy* (published in May 1729). In writing to Lord Oxford (16 May 1729) Pope says of this attack, 'The book is writ by Burnet, and a person who has great obligations to me, and the cut is done by Ducket.'
[4] Here Broome echoes *A Complete Key to the Last New Farce The What D'ye Call It* (1715), which also concerned Ambrose Philips.

Lordship commands me to quit them for what Is really more valuable, (your conversation, in town or any place) I am like to stay some time here; at least longer than I would, or ought to delay acknowledging the very obliging care you are pleasd to show always for my health. I most gratefully wish your Lordship yours, & all sorts of felicity, being with great truth & Esteem | My Lord | Your most obligd, ever faithfull | Servant | A. Pope.

I desire to know how long you stay in town. My sincere respects to my Lady Oxford

Address: To the Rt. Honble the | Earl of Oxford, in | Dover street | Piccadilly | London.

Endorsement: Mr Pope | Twitenham May 6. 1728

Postmark: 8/MA

POPE to MRS. CÆSAR[1]   7 *May* [1728?]
Rousham

                                                   Twitenham, May 7.

Madam,—Your Goodness can never be enough admired; After my Omission this whole Winter to show you I was alive, how could you think it was possible I was to be seen in this World? Well, here I am, & here I shall rejoice to see you, with my Lord & Lady Oxford (if they are as Good as you)   I have indeed been very near seeing the other world, but the glympse I had of it was too short, to enable me positively to prefer it to This, especially while You continue to favour | Madam | Your very obliged & most | humble Servant | A. Pope.

I am much Mr Cæsar's | humble Servant.

Address: To Mrs Cæsar, in Poland | Street, near | Golden Square, | London.
[2]*Postmark*: ?/MA

MARTHA BLOUNT *to* SWIFT   7 *May* 1728
1768 (Deane Swift)

                                                        May 7, 1728.

Sir,—I am very much pleased with your letter, but I should have thought myself much more obliged, had you been less sincere, and not told me, I did not owe the favour entirely to your inclinations, but to an information that I had a mind to hear from you: and I mistrust

---

[1] The year is altogether hypothetical. Later letters this month show that 'the Caesarean majesty' and the Oxfords were trying to arrange a visit to Twickenham. Pope's health had been bad for several weeks.

[2] In the postmark the day is illegible.

you think even that as much as I deserve. If so, you really are not deserving of my repeated inquiries after you, and my constant good wishes and concern for your welfare; which merits some remembrance without the help of another. I can't say I have a great inclination to write to you, for I have no great vanity that way, at least not enough to support me above the fear of writing ill: but I would fain have you know how truly well I wish you.

I am sorry to hear no good account of your health: mine has been, since *Christmas* (at which time I had my fever and rash) neither well, nor ill enough to be taken notice of: but within these three weeks I have been sick in forms, and kept my bed for a week, and my chamber to this day.

This confinement, together with the mourning,[1] has enabled me to be very easy in my chair-hire: for a dyed black gown, and a scoured white one, have done my business very well; and they are now just fit for *Petersham*, where we talk of going in three weeks; and I am not without hopes I shall have the same squire[2] I had last year. I am very unwilling to change; and moreover I begin to fear I have no great prospect of getting any new danglers; and therefore, in order to make a tolerable figure, I shall endeavour to behave myself mighty well, that I may keep my old ones.

As a proof that I continue to be well received at *Court*, I will tell you where the royal family design to pass their *Summer*: two months at *Richmond-Lodge*, the same time at *Hampton Court*, and six weeks at *Windsor*. Mrs. *Howard* is well, and happier than ever you saw her; for her whole affair with her husband is ended to her satisfaction.

Dr. *Arbuthnot* I am very angry with: he neglects me for those he thinks finer ladies. Mr. *Gay*'s fame continues, but his riches are in a fair way of diminishing: he is gone to the *Bath*: I wish you were ordered there, for I believe that would carry Mr. *Pope*, who is always inclined to do more for his friends than himself. He is much out of order, and is told nothing is so likely to do him good.

My illness has prevented my writing to you sooner. If I was a favourite at *Court*, I would soon convince you that I am very sincerely your faithful friend and very humble servant, | M. B.

<hr/>

†SWIFT *to* POPE   10 *May* 1728

1740

Dublin, May 10, 1728.

I have with great pleasure shewn the New-England Newspaper with the two names Jonathan Gulliver, and I remember Mr. Fortescue

---

[1] For the death of King George I.   [2] Dr. Swift.—1768.

sent you an account from the assizes,[1] of one Lemuel Gulliver who had a Cause there,[2] and lost it on his ill reputation of being a liar; and these are not the only observations I have made upon odd strange accidents in trifles, which in things of great importance would have been matter for Historians. Mr. Gay's Opera hath been acted here twenty times, and my Lord Lieutenant[3] tells me it is very well perform'd; he hath seen it often, and approves it much.

You give a most melancholy account of your self, and which I do not approve. I reckon that a man subject like us to bodily infirmities, should only occasionally converse with great people, notwithstanding all their good qualities, easinesses, and kindnesses. There is another race which I prefer before them, as Beef and Mutton for constant dyet before Patridges: I mean a middle kind both for understanding and fortune, who are perfectly easy, never impertinent, complying in everything, ready to do a hundred little offices that you and I may often want, who dine and sit with me five times for once that I go to them, and whom I can tell without offence, that I am otherwise engaged at present. This you cannot expect from any of those that either you or I or both are acquainted with on your side; who are only fit for our healthy seasons, and have much business of their own. God forbid I should condemn you to Ireland (*Quanquam O!*)[4] and for England I despair; and indeed a change of affairs would come too late at my season of life, and might probably produce nothing on my behalf. You have kept Mrs. Pope longer, and have had her care beyond what from nature you could expect; not but her loss will be very sensible whenever it shall happen. I say one thing, that both summers and winters are milder here than with you; all things for life in general better for a middling fortune; you will have an absolute command of your company, with whatever obsequiousness or freedom you may expect or allow. I have an elderly housekeeper,[5] who hath been my *Walpole*[6] above thirty years, whenever I liv'd in this kingdom: I have the command of one or two villa's near this town: You have a warm apartment in this house, and two gardens for amusement. I have said enough, yet not half. Except absence from friends, I confess freely that I have no discontent at living here; besides what arises from a silly spirit of Liberty, which as it neither sowers my drink, nor hurts my meat, nor spoils my stomach farther than in imagination, so I resolve to throw it off.

You talk of this Dunciad, but I am impatient to have it *volare per*

---

[1] See Pope to Fortescue, 5 August [1727].

[2] 'There' refers to Salisbury assizes, not, as it seems, to New England.

[3] Lord Carteret,—1741 Dab.   [4] And yet I wish.—1741 Dab.

[5] Mrs. Brent.—1741 Dab.

[6] Prime Minister, or chief Manager.—1741 Dab. (The London editions omit the footnote, and print, except in 1740 and its reissue, *W–lp–le*.)

*ora*¹—there is now a vacancy for fame: the Beggars Opera hath done its task, *discedat uti conviva satur.*² | Adieu

POPE *to* THE EARL OF OXFORD³   [14 *May* 1728]
Longleat Portland Papers, xii

My Lord,—I beg you (without Ceremony or Apology) to make me Twelve Franks, for post Letters, in folio, any time this day. I will wait on your Lordship to morrow, and tell you my reason for this request. I am sick, but truly & for ever | Your Lordship's | Most faithful, | most obligd Servant | A. Pope.

Tuesday | morn: May: 14. 1728.

Address: To the Rt. Hon. | the | Earl | of Oxford [Address split because of trick folding of the paper.]
Endorsement: Mr Pope | Twickenham May 14. 1728

POPE *to* THE EARL OF OXFORD⁴   [17 *May* 1728]
Longleat Portland Papers, xii

My Lord,—I send you the Deans first book,⁵ & desire you to take a Copy of it, or keep the Original & give me one, (which you please.) I will desire the same, wherever you can procure (or I) the Other pamphlet in answer to the Memorial.

I hear nothing yet of her Caesarean Majesty. But I conclude I shall; & I hope it heartily, after the Bribe you have promised me of yours & my Lady's company.

I am with true Esteem, her Ladyships & My Lord | Your most faithfull | Servant | A. Pope

Friday. may 17. 1728.

Address: To the Rt. Hon. the Earl of | Oxford.
Endorsement: Mr Pope | May 17. 1728

¹ Published.—1741 Dab. *Georgics*, iii. 9.
² Let it depart, like a full-fed Guest.—1741 Dab. From Horace, *Sermones*, I. i. 119.
³ Pope gave only 'Tuesday morn' as date; the specific date is added in Lord Oxford's hand.
⁴ The entire date inserted at the end of the letter is in Lord Oxford's hand.
⁵ Presumably the first book of his *History of the Four Last Years of the Queen.* His 'Answer to the Memorial' was published in Dublin in March. *Mist's Weekly Journal*, 11 May 1728, reprinted an item, signed 'A.B.' and called 'A Memorial address'd to the Reverend Dean Swift'. A.B. writes from Dublin under date of 25 Mar. 1728.

*MATHER BYLES to POPE   18 *May* 1728

The New England Historical and Genealogical Society.

N. England. Boston may 18. 1728.

Sir,—Your generous Letter this Day opens to me, with a most agreeable surprize at the Condescension and Goodness expressed in it. It cannot but awaken every Sentiment of Joy and Gratitude in my Breast, that you seem not only willing to forgive my Impertinence, but even incour[a]ge my Desire of Addressing you with another Letter. A Gentleman who has done so much Honour to the Holy Writings,[1] will forgive me if I fall into a Thought upon this Occasion, very natural to my Function, and can think of no Simile applicable to my present Case more readily than that of *Solomon*. I hoped but a Pardon, and receive your Letter, your Compliments, and expect your Works for my Country: So he asked for Wisdom; but obtained with it, Length of Days, and Riches, and Honours.

We have in this Country several very fine Publick Libraries, to those who have not seen your vaster Collections; and among private ones, my own consists of several Thousands of the best ancient and Modern Writers: But, far from Flattery, I confess that no uninspired one ravishes me like Mr *Pope*. If you, *Sir*, feel a [more] Distinct Transport, in the Study of *Horace*, or *Virgil*, or o[u]r admired *Homer*, than I in your living pages, it is easy to determine, it proceeds from the Strength and Compass of your Soul, but by no means from the Superiority of your Author.

The Church to which I am related in this Town,[2] has a very noble Collection of Books belonging to it, for the Emolument of the Minister, the Scholars, and other Gentlemen of the Town; To which you will give me leave to add your most valuable present. If you direct it to me, you may depend upon my Fidelity to deliver it to the Publick Collection. Mr. *Lintot*, by your order, will be so good as to deliver it to Captain *Cary*, the Gentleman who brings you this Letter. Several of o[u]r principal Gentlemen both of Church and State here, I have informed of your generous offer, who crowded round your Epistle, with uncommon demonstrations of Curiosity & Delight.

I have already been charmed with most of your happy Compositions, but have not yet seen them all. Those I have seen are the following. In o[u]r Colledge Library, at *Cambridge*[3] (a Town about three miles from *Boston*) we have your Translation of the *Iliad* in 12mo and your Poems in a large Folio: In which is the only picture I have seen of you in a modern Dress,[4] tho your smaller pictures in a

[1] Alluding to *Messiah*.
[2] Byles was at this time a member of the Second (Old North) Congregation in Boston, Mass.
[3] Byles's son, Mather Jr., was librarian of Harvard College from 1755 to 1757.
[4] The engraved folding portrait in the *Poems* of 1717.

poetical one are frequent, and most of o[u]r Genteel Rooms are embellished with your large mezzotinto.[1] For my own Library, your *Iliad* glitters in a distinguished Box, and close by, your two Volumes of Miscellanies:[2] Besides what of your poetry is in the Sixth Volume of *Drydens* Miscellany; and of your prose in the *Tatler, Spectator,* and *Guardian,* which I would gladly know how, more infallibly, to distinguish. I have also borrowed and read the three first Volumes of your *Odyssey,* but could never learn that the Two last are yet in my Country. And tho' I have given orders to several of o[u]r Booksellers to send over for the whole lot compleat, they have not yet arrived.[3]

The polite and learned Part of my Country-men, agree with me, to look upon such exalted Genius's as Mr *Pope,* o' tother Side the inconceivable Breadth of Ocean, in the same Light, in which you behold the admired Classicks. We read you with Transport, and talk of you with Wonder. We look upon your Letter as you would upon the original parchment of *Homer.* We pay you a deference & veneration belonging to a Race of Superior Beings and you appear to our Imaginations, like so many Deities in Human Shape. But when we vote you all people of the Elyzium, we please our selves to fancy how much Mr *Pope* appears the Musæus of the shining Company

> Musæum ante omnes: medium nam plurima turba
> Hunc habet, atque humeris exstantem suscipit altis.[4]

Forgive me Impertinance if I beg leave to give you one Trouble more, and ask, who was the [Au]thor of the *Key* to the *Rape of the Lock?* and what was the true design of that satirical performance, The *Key?*

I can't forbear to express my Wishes, That we may both meet in that Future World, where the whole Conversation will be beautifull, rich, Sublime, like the Thoughts and the Language of your own immortal poetry.

I am, | *Sir,* | Your Admirer, | and most obliged, | humble Servant.

POPE *to* THE EARL OF OXFORD[5]   [20 *May* 1728]

Longleat Portland Papers, xii

My Lord,—Your most kind letter gave me abundant pleasure, & so indeed it ought, in recompence for my ill luck, of which it acquainted me, in missing the sight of you as you past by. I can't say how agreable You will make Wednesday; You will make Mrs Caesar spare me &

---

[1] Made in 1717 by I. Smith from a portrait by Kneller.
[2] (Lintot's) *Miscellaneous Poems,* 2 vols., 1712 or 1720.
[3] To this observation Pope responded with the gift of a set of the *Odyssey.*
[4] *Aeneid,* vi, 667–8.   [5] The date is added in Lord Oxford's hand.

my Poem,¹ & then you will work a miracle. I hope you have seen the Dunciad in print, which is more than I have done: you'l see I have spar'd Mattaire² at your request. I wish I could obey you in things of more *weight* than ever in Dulness, & dull Authors. I am with truth & lasting obligation | My Lord | Ever yours most | Faithfully | A. Pope.

May. 20: 1728.

Address: To the Rt. Hon. the | Earl of Oxford.

Endorsement: Mr Pope | May 20. 1728.

THE EARL OF OXFORD *to* POPE   27 *May* 1728

Longleat Portland Papers, xii
                                                    May: 27: 1728.

Sir,—By your favor I have this morning receved a packet from the Dean in which was some medals and a letter which I value more then a thousand medals. I shall write to him soon. many thanks for your kind entertainment, poor calphurnia³ got the gripes she stopt and we kept sweet and clean.—I have sent you the Transcript of the Deans book, I long for the other.—

I see curl has advertised a Key to the Dunciad,⁴ I have been asked for one by several   I wish the True one was come out. I go on Wenesday for Down Hall for a few days. I am with true respect & esteem sr | Your most affectionate | humble Servant | Oxford.

my humble Service to mrs Pope.

*POPE *to* LADY SARAH COWPER⁵   [30 *May* 1728]

Panshanger MSS.

The very particular Favour your Ladyship did me in calling at Twik'nam deserv'd an Acknowledgment which as soon as I came to

---

¹ *The Dunciad*. The poem was published 18 May 1728.

² Michael Maittaire (1668–1747) was a learned protégé of the Oxfords. Richardson's marginalia to Book III of *The Dunciad* indicate that after the passage about Wormius or H[earn] in the first edition of Book III it was designed to insert the lines:

> On yonder part what fogs of gathered air
> Involve the scene, there musefull sits Mattaire.

³ Apparently 'the Caesarean majesty' contrived without intention to make itself amusing in one way or another.

⁴ Curll followed the technique of Pope's *Dunciad*, published by 'A. Dodd', and late in May published his *Compleat Key to the Dunciad* with Mrs. Dodd's name on the title-page. The volume contains lists of books published by Curll.

⁵ The letter is found in vol. vi of Lady Sarah Cowper's Family Books, p. 299. It is printed from a transcript made by Sir Harold Williams, by kind permission of Lady Salmond. Lady Sarah Cowper was the daughter of Earl Cowper, the Lord Chancellor. The letter is dated by a marginal entry: 'May 30th Went with my Sister and Mrs. Lewis Mordaunt to Oxford.'

London I endeavour'd to pay you by waiting on you in Stretton Street: I was there last night ineffectually; and this day again, when I am told your L. is just gone for Oxford. Since you are there I hope to be forgiven if I presume so far upon your Good natural Memory of me (which I have so lately experienced by your obliging Enquiry after me) as to beg your Interest at that Place, for a Friend of mine and a very Ingenious Young Gentleman, as well as a Poetical one: Mr. Walter Harte of St. Mary Hall, who desires to be elected Fellow of Exeter Coll: I am inform'd if Mr. Atwell, my Lord your Brother's Tutor,[1] will use his power, it will be of vast Service to his Pretensions.[2]

Excuses or Apologies I will not make you. I believe no man of merit but will be proud to do any thing you ask.[3] I wish you could, that way, make any Trial whether I have any worth. I am very sure I am in the way to it, being sincerely your Ladyship's | respectful | and Humble Servant, | A. Pope.

Endorsement (at top): From Mr. Pope to me.

†SWIFT *to* POPE   1 *June* 1728
1740
                                                     June 1, 1728.

I look upon my Lord Bolingbroke and us two, as a peculiar Triumvirate, who have nothing to expect, or to fear; and so far fittest to converse with one another: Only he and I are a little subject to schemes, and often upon[4] very weak appearances, and this you have nothing to do with. I do profess without affectation, that your kind opinion of me as a Patriot (since you call it so) is what I do not deserve; because what I do is owing to perfect rage and resentment, and the mortifying sight of slavery, folly, and baseness about me, among which I am forc'd to live. And I will take my oath that you have more Virtue in an hour, than I in seven years; for you despise the follies, and hate the vices of mankind, without the least ill effect on your temper; and with regard to particular men, you are inclin'd always rather to think the better, whereas with me it is always directly contrary. I hope however, this is not in you from a superior principle of virtue, but from your situation, which hath made all parties and interests indifferent to you, who can be under no concern about high and low-church, Whig and Tory, or who is first Minister—Your long letter was the last I receiv'd 'till this by Dr. Delany,[5] although you mention another since. The

---

[1] Lord William Cowper was at this time an undergraduate of Exeter College.
[2] Apparently Harte did not secure this fellowship.
[3] These two sentences are badly separated in the letterbook, with no period after *you* and an illogical one after *merit*.
[4] and often upon] and one of us (I won't say which) upon *all London editions, 1741–2, except 1742* La.   [5] Unknown.

Dr. told me your secret about the Dunciad,[1] which does not please me, because it defers gratifying my vanity in the most tender point, and perhaps may wholly disappoint it. As to one of your enquiries, I am easy enough in great matters, but have a thousand paltry vexations in my little station, and the more contemptible, the more vexatious. There might be a Lutrin writ upon the tricks used by my Chapter to teize me. I do not converse with one creature of Station or Title, but I have a set of easy people whom I entertain when I have a mind; I have formerly describ'd them to you, but when you come you shall have the honours of the country as much as you please, and I shall on that account make a better figure, as long as I live. Pray God preserve Mrs. Pope for your sake and ease, I love and esteem her too much to wish it for her own: If I were five and twenty, I would wish to be of her age, to be as secure as she is of a better life. Mrs. P. B.[2] has writ[3] to me, and is one of the best Letter-writers I know; very good sense, civility and friendship, without any stiffness or constraint. The Dunciad has taken wind here, but if it had not, you are as much known here as in England, and the University lads will crowd to kiss the hem of your garment. I am griev'd to hear that my Lord Bolingbroke's ill health forc'd him to the Bath. Tell me, is not Temperance a necessary virtue for great men, since it is the parent of Ease and Liberty? so necessary for the use and improvement of the mind, and which philosophy allows to be the greatest felicities of life? I believe, had health been given so liberally to you, it would have been better husbanded, without shame to your parts.

POPE *to* THE EARL OF OXFORD[4]   [13 *June* 1728]
Longleat Portland Papers, xii

June. 13: 1728.

My Lord,—Your letter is very kind, and I will soon tell you so in person. My Mother is pretty well. I was at my heart with you at Down-hall, I fear that your Lordship has forgot the Extract out of Caxton's preface,[5] how he came by Virgil: I want it speedily, if you can conveniently get it. I have the punishment of the Dunciad & all my other sins, in my Head this day, the offending part suffers, but pray believe my Heart is free, & always | My Lord | Yours. | A. Pope.

My humble services to my Lady Oxford.

Address: To | the Rt. Honble the | Earl of Oxford.

Endorsement: Mr Pope | June 13. 1728

---

[1] The secret that a larger (*variorum*) edition was in preparation, and that the inscription of the poem to Swift was deferred to it.   [2] Mrs. Patty Blount *1741 Dab*.
[3] has writ] hath written *1741 Dab*.   [4] The date is entirely in Oxford's hand.
[5] Caxton's Preface was to serve as Appendix III in *The Dunciad* of 1729.

BROOME *to* FENTON   15 *June* [1728]

Elwin–Courthope, viii. 148

June 15, [1728].

Dear Fenton,—I am greatly obliged to you for your sensibility of the unjust usage I meet with from Mr. Pope. He abuses me unprovoked, but I have my revenge by knowing that it is an abuse. He may make me ridiculous, but at the same time he proves himself wicked and ungrateful. I grant he is much the better poet, but I am still his superior by being a better man. He has injured both you and me by lying in print, and attesting a falsehood with the solemnity of "to be punctually just." Is it to be punctually just to defraud you of two books of the Odyssey and me of five? I know his motive to this falsehood. He has taken a large subscription for the Odyssey, and paid us what he pleased, when at the same time he has a much less share in that work than myself, eight books of the verse and all the notes being mine. He, therefore, suppresses the truth, being ashamed to take so much money for other men's labours. You rightly observe in your last that he ought in prudence to have remembered the last paragraph in the Odyssey.[1] I add, he ought to remember it with fear, if he is afraid of being proved a dishonest man. In short, it is owing to my mercy that he is not scandalous. I have luckily preserved his letter of thanks to me upon the conclusion of my notes on the Iliad. It runs as follows: "I am seriously sensible of the kind expressions you use to me, and be assured I shall never forget the long and laborious things you undertook and discharged for my sake. It is really as reasonable that you should be congratulated on the finishing of my Homer as I myself. I have had the flowery walks of imagination to expatiate in. It is a spirited and lively task to be striving to raise one's self to the pitch of the most delightful of authors, while you have drudged in only removing the loads and clearing the rubbish heaped together by the negligence no less than by the industry of past pedants, whose very taste was generally so wrong that they toiled most on what was least worth; and to undo what they raised was the first thing to be done in order to do anything to the purpose. As you had no share in the pleasant, and so large an one in the disagreeable part of the work, I think this to be acknowledged in the strongest terms, as it highly exalts the merit of your friendship to me, that your task was a task of so much more pains than even credit. It was Hercules in the stable of Augeas, when the same Hercules was capable of so many better and more glorious labours. I can say nothing that equals my sense of it, in short, and therefore shall say very little, &c."

[1] Meaning, rather, the last 'observation' to Book XXIV, in which appeared, ostensibly above the signature of Broome himself, the misstatements as to the amount of help Pope had received from Fenton and Broome. Pope should remember—with fear of exposure.

Thus writes Mr. Pope, March 24, 1720, and I solemnly assure
you I never took one farthing for all that long and laborious task I
undertook and discharged for his sake, in my annotations upon his
Iliad. Now tell me, dear Fenton, considering all these circumstances,
am I unjust if I call him false and ungrateful? All the crime that I
have committed is saying he is no master of Greek; and I am so confident of this, that if he can translate ten lines of Eustathius I will own
myself unjust and unworthy.

I perceive by your letters that it is your opinion I should reply.
Cui bono? He will certainly make me riduculous, and what benefit will
arise to me to prove him ungrateful? No. I will dismiss him with the
sullen silence of Ajax, but will leave such memorials[1] behind me when
I die, that posterity shall be acquainted with his history. At present I
am not angry enough to be of that canine disposition to bite the stone
that strikes me. To speak ingenuously, I am not greatly moved at his
jokes, and he would be disappointed if he knew that he gives me no
more uneasiness. The other day I made a piece of a new Session of
Poets, by which you will see I can laugh at him

> Next in stepped a wight, a monkey of man,
> Through av'rice ill-clad, maliciously wan:
> With a book in his hand, to Apollo he bowed,
> And, raised on a tripod, thus sang out aloud.

Ody. 5.—A man, an outcast to the storm and wave,
>   It was my crime to pity and to save!
>   For this I mourn, till death, or dire disease,

II. 3.— Destroy those charms, whose crime it was to please.

> Apollo was pleased with the languishing strain,
> And cried, Who is this, what soft bard of the plain?
> How witty, how sweet! but why do I gaze so?
> 'Tis the ghost of Thersites repeating old Naso.
> The rhymer then cried, with astonishment moved,
> Who prates about Ovid? 'tis Homer improved.
> But why stand I here? Apollo is mad,
> I'll put him next week in my Dunciad, begad![2]

I have now, dear Fenton, opened my bosom to you with respect to
Mr. Pope; and I have found him what you always affirmed him to
be—a most insincere person; but I assure you that no one is more
sincere than myself, when I tell you that I am yours affectionately.

Pray my respects to Sir Clement Cottrell.

---

[1] In the absence of other evidence one must assume that Broome means that his letters
will tell the truth about the collaboration. Actually in his *Poems* of 1727 and 1739 he told
the truth in quiet footnotes.

[2] Broome was evidently in the mood for attack, but he seems neither to have completed
nor published this *Session*.

†POPE *to* HUGH BETHEL[1]   17 *June* 1728
1737

June 17, 1728.

After the publishing of my Boyish Letters to Mr. Cromwell, you will not wonder if I should forswear writing a letter again while I live; since I do not correspond with a friend upon the terms of any other free subject of this kingdom. But to you I can never be silent, or reserved; and I am sure my opinion of your heart is such, that I could open mine to you in no manner which I could fear the whole world should know. I could publish my own heart too, I will venture to say, for any mischief or malice there's in it; but a little too much folly or weakness might (I fear) appear, to make such a spectacle either instructive or agreeable to others.

I am reduced to beg of all my acquaintance to secure me from the like usage for the future, by returning me any letters of mine which they may have preserved; that I may not be hurt after my death by that which was the happiness of my life, their partiality and affection for me.

I have nothing of my self to tell you, only that I have had but indifferent health. I have not made a visit to London: Curiosity and the love of Dissipation dye apace in me. I am not glad nor sorry for it, but I am very sorry for those who have nothing else to live on.

I have read much, but writ no more. I have small hopes of doing good, no vanity in writing, and little ambition to please a world not very candid or deserving. If I can preserve the good opinion of a few friends, it is all I can expect, considering how little good I can do even to them to merit it. Few people have your candour, or are so willing to think well of another from whom they receive no benefit, and gratify no vanity. But of all the soft sensations, the greatest pleasure is to give and receive mutual Trust. It is by Belief and firm Hope, that men are made happy in this life, as well as in the other. My confidence in your good opinion, and dependance upon that of one or two more, is the chief cordial drop I taste, amidst the Insipid, the Disagreeable, the Cloying, or the Dead-sweet, which are the common draughts of life. Some pleasures are too pert, as well as others too flat, to be relish'd long: and vivacity in some cases is worse than dulness. Therefore indeed for many years I have not chosen my companions for any of the qualities in fashion, but almost intirely for that which is the most out-of-fashion, sincerity. Before I am aware of it, I am making your panegyrick, and perhaps my own too, for next to possessing the best of qualities is the esteeming and distinguishing those who possess it. I truly love and value you, and so I stop short.

---

[1] Found, without revision, in all of Pope's editions in or after 1737.

POPE *to* THE EARL OF OXFORD[1] 17 *June* [1728]

Longleat Portland Papers, xii

June the 17. | 1728.

My Lord,—I am so busy about a thing to gratify you with,[2] which I assure you is a more pleasing end than any other I propose (tho I have received a Command for the same thing from the Highest & most Powerful Person in this Kingdom)[3] that I can but just tell you I thank you for yours, & Dr Stratford[4] for his kind Concern about my person, which hath hitherto remaind as Unhurt (I thank God) as my Temper, by these Scoundrels. I shall see you in 2 days, and have a favor to beg of you in relation to writing. I am sincerely my Lady Oxfords, & | My Lord's | Ever obligd faithful | Servant | A. Pope.

Address: To the Rt. Hon. | Earl of Oxford.

Endorsement: Mr Pope / June 17. 1728

POPE *to* THE EARL OF OXFORD [25 *June* 1728]

Longleat Portland Papers, xii

Tuesday night.[5] | June : 25. 1728.

My Lord,—I have the satisfaction at length to procure you the Dean's second book:[6] I beg you as soon as you've taken a Copy, to send it (together with the other here inclosed) to Mr Daniel Pulteney at his house by St. James's: who is in haste for them in a day or two.

I was sorry not to be able once more to see you, while I was in town. I will endeavor it again in a few days. I am Ever with the most lasting obligation | Your Lordships most faithful | & most obedient Servant | A. Pope.

Endorsement: Mr Pope | June 25. 1728

---

1 The year is added to the date by Lord Oxford.

2 Oxford (27 May 1728) had wished for an authoritative *Key* to *The Dunciad*. Pope, rather, is working on an edition with footnotes that should explain—not all but some things.

3 The king himself was apparently much interested in *The Dunciad*, and when on 12 Mar. 1729 the variorum *Dunciad* was presented to the king by Sir Robert Walpole himself, His Majesty is said to have remarked that Pope was 'a very honest man'.

4 Dr. William Stratford of Christ Church, Oxford, was a close friend of Lord Oxford, and during the period following the publication of *The Dunciad* addressed letters concerning it to his lordship. These are printed by the Hist. MSS. Comm. among the *Portland Papers*, vii. 464–5. His concern about Pope's person was occasioned by a pamphlet published 2 June 1728 under the title, *A Pop upon Pope: Or, A true and faithful Account of a late horrid and barbarous Whipping committed on the Body of* Sauny Pope, *a Poet; as he was innocently walking in* Ham-Walks, *near the River of* Thames. . . . Pope at times blamed this attempt at revenge on Lady Mary Wortley Montagu.

5 Pope wrote simply 'Tuesday night'; the specific date is added in Oxford's hand.

6 On the Dean's book see Pope to Lord Oxford, 17 May 1728.

†POPE *to* SWIFT   28 *June* 1728
1740

Dawley, June 28, 1728.

I now hold the pen for my Lord Bolingbroke, who is reading your letter between two Haycocks, but his attention is sometimes[1] diverted by casting his eyes on the clouds, not in admiration of what you say, but for fear of a shower. He is pleas'd with your placing him in the Triumvirate between your self and me; tho' he says that he doubts he shall fare like Lepidus, while one of us runs away with all the power like Augustus, and another with all the pleasures like Anthony. It is upon a foresight of this, that he has fitted up his farm, and you will agree, that this scheme of retreat at least is not founded upon weak appearances. Upon his return from the Bath, all peccant humours, he finds, are purg'd out of him; and his great Temperance and Oeconomy are so signal, that the first is fit for my constitution, and the latter would enable you to lay up so much mony, as to buy a Bishoprick in England. As to the return of his health and vigour, were you here, you might enquire of his Hay-makers; but as to his temperance, I can answer that (for one whole day) we have had nothing for dinner but mutton-broth, beans and bacon, and a Barn-door fowl.

Now his Lordship is run after his Cart, I have a moment left to my self to tell you, that I overheard him yesterday agree with a Painter for 200 *l.* to paint his country-hall with Trophies of Rakes, spades, prongs, &c. and other ornaments merely to countenance his calling this place a Farm—now turn over a new leaf—

He bids me assure you he should be sorry not to have more schemes of kindness for his friends, than of ambition for himself: There, tho' his schemes may be weak, the motives at least are strong; and he says further, if you could bear as great a fall, and decrease of your revenues, as he knows by experience he can, you wou'd not live in Ireland an hour.

The Dunciad is going to be printed in all pomp, with the inscription, which makes me proudest. It will be attended with *Proeme, Prologomena, Testimonia Scriptorum, Index Authorum,* and Notes *Variorum.* As to the latter, I desire you to read over the Text, and make a few in any way you like best, whether dry raillery, upon the stile and way of commenting of trivial Critics; or humorous, upon the authors in the poem; or historical, of persons, places, times; or explanatory, or collecting the parallel passages of the Ancients. Adieu. I am pretty well, my Mother not ill, Dr. Arbuthnot vex'd with his fever by intervals; I am afraid he declines, and we shall lose a worthy man: I am troubled about him very much. | I am, &c.

[1] sometimes] somewhat *1742 Lbc.*

POPE *to* THE EARL OF OXFORD¹ [1 *July* 1728]

Longleat Portland Papers, xii

July: 1. 1728.

My Lord,—I now trouble you to get your Amanuensis to transcribe (in the paper I send & only in one column) this Preface written by a friend of mine.²

A very unforseen accident has obligd me to go a Journey for 9 or 10 days, so that I cannot wait on your Lordship in person till my Return, when I will come to thank you for this, & a hundred favors, done, & to be done, to | My Lord | Your most faithfull | humble Servant | A. Pope.

Endorsement: Mr Pope | July 1. 1728

†SWIFT *to* POPE 16 *July* 1728

1740

July 16, 1728.

I have often run over the *Dunciad* in an Irish edition (I suppose full of faults) which a gentleman sent me. The notes I could wish to be very large, in what relates to the persons concern'd; for I have long observ'd that twenty miles from London no body understands hints, initial letters, or town-facts and passages; and in a few years not even those who live in London. I would have the names of those scriblers printed indexically³ at the beginning or end of the Poem, with an account of their works, for the reader to refer to. I would have all the Parodies (as they are call'd) referred to the author⁴ they imitate— When I began this long paper, I thought I should have fill'd it with setting down the several passages I⁵ had mark'd in the edition I had, but I find it unnecessary, so many of them falling under the same rule. After twenty times reading the whole, I never in my opinion saw so much good satire, or more good sense, in so many lines. How it passes in Dublin I know not yet; but I am sure it will be a great disadvantage to the poem, that the persons and facts will not be understood, till an explanation comes out, and a very full one. I imagine it is not to be published till towards winter, when folks begin to gather in town.

---

¹ The date is in Lord Oxford's hand. The unforeseen accident and the journey are not known.

² The transcript was probably made from the 'Letter to the Publisher' eventually printed in *The Dunciad* of 1729 (pp. 5–15) as by William Cleland. The fact that the transcript was to leave one column vacant indicates that revision was contemplated.

³ This suggestion, like most others here made, was adopted by Pope. His notes were doubtless not explicit enough for Swift and many another reader.

⁴ author] authors *1741 Dab.*

⁵ passages I] passages which I *1741 Dab.* (The Dublin text was carefully revised.)

Again I insist, you must have your Asterisks fill'd up with some real names of real Dunces.

I am now reading your preceding letter, of June 28, and find that all I have advis'd above is mention'd there. I would be glad to know whether the quarto edition is to come out anonymously, as published by the Commentator, with all his pomp of prefaces, &c. and among complaints[1] of spurious editions?—I am thinking whether the Editor should not follow the old style of, This excellent author, &c. and refine in many places when you meant no refinement? and into the bargain take all the load of naming the dunces, their qualities, histories, and performances?[2]

As to your self, I doubt you want a spurrer-on to exercise and to amusements, but to talk of decay at your season of life is a jest. But you are not so regular as I. You are the most temperate man God-ward, and the most intemperate your self-ward, of most I have known. I suppose Mr. Gay will return from the Bath with twenty pounds more flesh, and two hundred less in money: Providence never design'd him to be above two and twenty, by his thoughtlessness and Cullibility. He hath as little foresight of age, sickness, poverty, or loss of admirers, as a girl of fifteen. By the way, I must observe, that my Lord Boling-broke (from the effects of his kindness to me) argues most sophistically: The fall from a million to an hundred-thousand pounds is not so great, as from eight hundred pounds a year to one: Besides, he is a controller of Fortune, and Poverty dares not look a great Minister in the face, under his lowest declension. I never knew him live so great and expensively as he hath done since his return from Exile; such mortals have resources that others are not able to comprehend. But God bless You, whose great genius has not so transported you as to leave you to the courtesy of mankind; for wealth is liberty, and liberty is a blessing fittest for a philosopher—and Gay is a slave just by two thousand pounds too little.—And Horace was of my mind,—and let my Lord contradict him if he dares.—

POPE *to* THE EARL OF OXFORD[3]   [17 *July* 1728]

Longleat Portland Papers, xii

My Lord,—I have reason to be ashamed of the trouble I have given

1 The clandestine text here printed *among* when probably *many* should have been printed. No later text at this point follows the text of 1740 (reissued as 1742 La). The Dublin texts read, most acceptably: 'with all the pomp of preface, &c. and many complaints....' The London texts preserve the faulty *among* but add *many*: 'with all the pomp of prefaces, &c. and among many complaints....'

2 Pope whole-heartedly adopted this pretence of commentators other than himself responsible for the notes. It led him to annotate recklessly so far as true facts were concerned.

3 Pope dated the letter 'Wednesday'. Lord Oxford in his endorsement identified the Wednesday as the 17th, and apparently added the 23rd as the day on which he either read or answered it.

you, & the Employment even of your Amanuensis, who has so many better things to do with your own papers. I will not send the next book¹ till next week, and hope about that time to have the pleasure of waiting on you myself, to thank your Lordship for the kind favour you did me here, & those you are continuing to do me, daily. I beg our humblest Services to my Lady Oxford, and am, with the sincerest Esteem, ever | Your Lordships most obligd | & most faithfull Servant | A. Pope.

Wednesday; July. 17. 1728.

July. 23 1728.

Address: To the Rt. Hon. the Earl of | Oxford.

Endorsement: Mr Pope | July 17. 1728

POPE *to* THE EARL OF OXFORD [25 *July* 1728]

Longleat Portland Papers, xii

Thursday. | July: 25: 1728.

My Lord,—Being to go from home this day, & your Lordship saying you would send me those papers, I write & leave this, to return you many thanks, and to convey to your hands the remainder of the Notes on the 2d. I can never enough express my Sense of such obligations as I have to you & which are of so pleasing a nature that they will make one of the greatest satisfactions of my life to come. God preserve your Lordship & all that is dear to you, Long. My sincere Services (with my Mothers) attend on yourself, my Lady, & Lady Margaret, I am, with the hope of sometimes hearing of your good health, ever My Lord | Your faithful & obedient Servant | A. Pope.

Address: To | The Rt. Hon. the Earl of | Oxford & Mortimer.

Endorsement: Mr Pope. | July 25. 1728

THE EARL OF OXFORD *to* SWIFT² 27 *July* 1728

Longleat Portland Papers, xiii (Harleian transcript)

July 27. 1728

Reverend Sir,—It is now compleat two Months since I receivd the favor of your letter and a very great one I esteem it, and also some Medals which were of use to me in my Collection   please to accept my thanks for them   Mr Clayton has been going this six weeks which was one reason of my not writing and I think I should not give you

---

¹ Pope is speaking of Book II of *The Dunciad*. See his next letter to Lord Oxford, 25 July.

² This copy of Oxford's letter was made on the blank verso of a cover addressed: 'To | The Right Honble the Earl of | Oxford at Down Hall Essex.'

the trouble of two letters upon the same Subject resolving to write by him when ever he went. I have heard some kind of Whisper as if the Dean of St Patricks would be in England this Winter   I wish he may but it is too good news to be true I fear. Mr Pope stands by himself Athanasius Contra Mundum; there is never a Newspaper comes out but he is favord with a letter; a poem and Epigram even to a Distich from the newmorous Herd of Dunces and Blockheads that are in and about London and the Suburbs there of. I saw him the other day   he is as to his health much of the Same as you left him   he has at last taken a resolution of going to the Bath this Season   I hope it will be of Service to him   my Wife and Peggy are much your humble Servants my Wife goes this next Season to the Bath   I hope it will do her good for the Badness of her Stomach   I hope this will find you very well where ever it be for I hear you often make excurtions into the Country   I shall be glad to hear that you are free from your Deafness you complaind of when you went out of England last.

I am Sir with true esteem | Your most Affectionate Humble | Servant | O

The medalion you mention is a | Curiosity but it is too high | prized for me

Endorsement: A Copy of a letter | to the Dean of St Patrick's | July 27. 1728

SPENCE *and* POPE *to* CHRISTOPHER PITT[1]

2 *August* 1728

1797 (Warton)

Twickenham, Aug. 2, 1728.

I am here, my dear Rector, in as delightly a situation for the world about me, and books, and conversation, as mortal man can wish to be. I can think of nothing at present that could add to it, except the hearing that you are very well, and entirely free from your old enemy the gout. I should not know how to leave this place, had not I the hopes of waiting upon you in a few weeks; but first I can assure you, I have a world of drudgery to go through. I had almost forgot one particular: when I was with our old friend, Mr. Pescod, the other day, he confirmed me in a thought I had, that the verses on an Old Beauty (she, you know, "who blooms in the winter of her days like Glastenbury Thorn") were written by you at New College. If they are yours, as I am very much persuaded they are, I beg you would be so good as to

---

[1] In printing this letter Warton adds the following: 'N.B. In a letter from Mr. Spence to Mr. Pitt, dated New College, November 12, 1728, are the following words, containing Mr. Pope's opinion of *Pitt's Virgil*. "Before this I gave you Mr. Pope's real sentiment on your first book; I dare say it was his real sentiment, because, as I told you, I took care to ask him the question before I had mentioned my being acquainted with you: and it was literally what I told you." '

send me a copy of them in your answer; which I beg may be as soon as possible, because, as you may easily imagine, I don't love to be many days without hearing from you. I desire this copy the rather, because I have been asked for it since I have been in town, and have none but a very incorrect copy at present. If you have any commands here, I beg you would favour me with them, as your most affectionate friend and servant, | Jo. Spence.

Sir,—I take this opportunity of assuring you, you have, at the place from whence this letter is dated, a friend and servant, | A. Pope.

†GAY *to* POPE   2 *August* 1728

1737

Aug. 2, 1728

'Twas two or three weeks ago that I writ you a letter: I might indeed have done it sooner; I thought of you every post-day upon that account, and every other day upon some account or other. I must beg you to give Mrs. B.[1] my sincere thanks for her kind way of thinking of me, which I have heard of more than once from our friend at court, who seem'd in the letter she writ to be in high health and spirits. Considering the multiplicity of the pleasures and delights that one is over-run with in those places, I wonder how any body hath health and spirits enough to support 'em: I am heartily glad she has, and whenever I hear so, I find it contributes to mine. You see I am not free from dependance, tho' I have less attendance than I had formerly; for a great deal of my own welfare still depends upon hers. Is the widow's house to be dispos'd of yet?[2] I have not given up my pretensions to the Dean; if it was to be parted with, I wish one of us had it: I hope you wish so too, and that Mrs. Blount and Mrs. Howard wish the same, and for the very same reason that I wish it. All I could hear of you of late hath been by advertisements in news-papers, by which one wou'd think the race of Curls was multiplied; and by the indignation such fellows show against you, that you have more merit than any body alive could have. Homer himself hath not been worse us'd by the French. I am to tell you that the Duchess[3] makes you her compliments, and is always inclin'd to like any thing you do; that Mr. Congreve admires, with me, your fortitude; and loves, not envys your performance, for we are not Dunces. Adieu.

---

[1] Mrs. B.] Mrs. Blount *1737b*.
[2] Some house by the Thames that Gay dreamed of buying so as to be near Pope and Mrs. Howard.
[3] Gay is at Bath with Congreve and Henrietta, Duchess of Marlborough.

THOMAS COOKE *to* POPE[1]   11 *August* 1728

Elwin–Courthope, x. 212

11 Aug., 1728

Sir,—Since I have been informed that you have expressed some resentment, on the supposition of my being the author of some scurrilous
Pieces, which have been lately printed in the Daily Papers, I think
it incumbent on me to make this declaration that I am not: neither am
I vain enough to think, if I had the inclination, that I have the power,
to invalidate a character so well established, and on so just a foundation,
as yours is. I hope you will hence conclude, that nothing but the high
opinion I entertain of you could have made me have given you and
myself this trouble; I call it a trouble to me, only because I am forced to
apologize for what I am not conscious of; and, at the same time, give
me leave to assure you there is none to whom I should be prouder to
write than to Mr. Pope, if I was satisfyed it would be received with
the same pleasure with which it would be sent. I must own I have
formerly wrote a poem of which I am now sincerely ashamed,[2] and
which, with some other trifling productions, I shall take an occasion
to disown, by declaring myself the author of nothing but what is contained in a collection of pieces, of verse and prose, now printing against
the winter. That I converse with many who have wrote against you
is true; for some of which I have a real respect, and for some as
sovereign a contempt as you can have. It is an unhappiness, I doubt
not, that yourself has been under to converse with those of whom you
have not entertained the most favourable thoughts; and, if I may
judge from the foolish freedoms which I know have been took with
your name of late, I believe you still lye under the same inconveniency;
but this is a subject improper to be any more than hinted in a letter.
I shall trouble you no farther, only to beg your acceptance of the mean
present[3] I have honoured myself to send you, and believe me studious
of approving myself, with an unfeigned regard, sir, your faithful
humble servt.

Westminster, Aug. 11, 1728.

[1] Printed by Elwin and Courthope from MSS. then in the possession of Mr. Murray,
publisher of the edition.

We lack Pope's replies to Cooke, but his attitude may be seen in his letters to or from Lord
Oxford, beginning in this month and running on to that of 20 Jan. 1728/9. Cooke was made
a Dunce in *The Dunciad* of 1729, and he almost appeared in the *Epistle to Dr. Arbuthnot*
(1735). See Pope's *Poems* (Twickenham ed.), iv. 99–100 and 353 for the comments of Professor Butt. In the MS. of the *Epistle* Cooke definitely appears. In his list of attacks appended
to *The Dunciad* of 1729 Pope ascribes to Cooke satirical reflections (Thersites) printed in
The Daily Journal of 23 Apr. 1728. See *The Dunciad* (ed. Sutherland), p. 209, n. 3.

[2] *The Battel of the Poets* (1725).

[3] Cooke's translation of Hesiod (2 v.) had appeared in February of this year.

POPE *to* THE EARL OF PETERBOROW   24 *August* 1728

See 24 August 1732.

POPE *to* THE EARL OF OXFORD[1]   [17 *August* 1728]

Longleat Portland Papers, xii

Saturday. | Aug: 1728.

My Lord,—I am just going my Journey, having hoped your return to town in vain, a few days since; while I might have had the happiness of just seeing you. I hope to find my Lady Oxford at Bath by the time I shall arrive there. I may wish at least to find your Lordship too.

I am now obligd to fly to your assistance in an affair that is troublesom to me, of a man I am utterly a stranger to, & of whose character I have heard very ill.[2] Yet the matter is this. He writes me the inclosed, which perhaps I should not quite slight, and yet I can hardly believe. You will judge, my Lord, of my Uneasiness which proceeds from a fear of doing the least wrong even to a man who by his own Confession has abused me unprovoked. I would not wrong him on the one hand, nor be Deceivd by him on the other, that is all.

I'm willing some person of probity should be witness to what I have writ to him, I know none such of his acquaintance, but Mr Westley, whom I desire your Lordship to procure to deliver it.[3] after you have read & approved it (not else:) and to give him also two books which he sent, but I must not receive. I am really ashamd to give your Lordship this trouble, but I can think of no other way, unless I make him no reply at all; which perhaps he would complain of as a Neglect of his repentance, or Implacability in me.

I've added a word or two to Mr. Westley as an excuse for not writing to the other in my own hand, which (to say truth) I don't care such sort of people should be acquainted with. But this you'l keep to yourself—

After again thanking you for the use of your amanuensis, I must acquaint your Lordship that I shall not need to give him any more trouble. I think I ought to tell you an extreme odd thing. that Some

[1] Pope simply dated 'Saturday'; but Lord Oxford added the month and year. The journey to Bath was evidently leisurely. Pope writes (4 Sept.) to Martha Blount, who is apparently staying with Mrs. Pope while Pope is away, that he visited Lord Cobham at Stowe (somewhat out of his way: hence he probably spent some days there), Col. Dormer at Rousham (one night), Mr. John Howe of Stowell the next night; and finally Sir William Codrington (and Bethel's sisters) at Dodington, where he spent more than one night. Hence he probably left home on the 18th; possibly on the 25th. One notes that Cooke (16 Sept.) says that Pope's letter to him was dated 17 Aug.

[2] Pope is forwarding Thomas Cooke's letter of the 11th to Lord Oxford.

[3] Samuel Wesley, older brother of the Methodists John and Charles, was usher at Westminster School.

of these Fellows have come to the knowledge, or have seen, some of those papers, which I can be very certain were never out of my hands, or shown to any but yourself: and there is a Paragraph printed in a late Daily-Journal, evidently quoted from those papers.[1] God knows how this could come about. But I thought it my duty to tell you the Fact, which I think could not possibly be meer chance, the Paragraph is so remarkable.

My Lord, I can use no expressions to show you, how sensible I am of all your kindnesses & distinctions, for which my life must continue a proof of my gratefulness. No *words* can excuse my freedom, but my *Heart* can; for I feel it daily wishing to be able to do you any service or Pleasure. Your most faithfully obligd Servant. | A. Pope.

I set out on Sunday.

Address: To | the Rt. Hon. the Earl of Oxford
Endorsement: Mr Pope | Saturday Augt 1728

‡POPE *to* [MARTHA BLOUNT?]²   [*September* 1728]

1737

.Cirencester.

It is a true saying that misfortunes alone prove one's friendships: they show us not only that of other people for us, but our own for them. We hardly know our selves any otherwise. I feel my being forc'd to this Bath-journey as a misfortune; and to follow my own welfare preferably to those I love, is indeed a new thing to me: my health has not usually got the better of my tendernesses and affections. I set out with a heavy heart, wishing I had done this thing the last season; for every day I defer it, the more I am in danger of that accident which I dread the most, my Mother's death (especially shou'd it happen while I am away.) And another Reflection pains me, that I have never

---

[1] See later Oxford letters of 10 and 14 Sept. Pope (14 Sept.) is fairly explicit as to his grounds for suspicion, but apparently all concerned were ultimately convinced that the parallels were coincidence.

[2] This is a most troublesome letter. In his editions of 1737–42 Pope printed it without date and without addressee. It is placed by him in a group of letters to or about John Gay; but since the letter following this in Pope's editions is about Gay's death and is presumably addressed to Miss Blount, this present letter may also be addressed to her. It seems to be a composite letter. The first paragraph fits into the journey to Bath in 1728; the rest of the letter contradicts the other letters of 1728 by representing Pope and Bathurst together at Cirencester. The latter parts of the letter may have been written later than the first paragraph, but the first paragraph fits into a series mentioned in the postscript to his letter to Miss Blount of 4 Sept. The first letter (written from Stowe) is lost; this is the second letter. The third (4 Sept.) gives an account of his resting-places in the journey of 1728, and does not mention Cirencester. The letter of 15 Sept. to Lord Bathurst indicates that Pope left Stowe on 2 Sept., and agrees with the letter of the 4th in mentioning the hospitality of Mr. Howe. The superscribed 'Cirencester' derives from the latter parts of the letter and does not fit 1728—or any year that might find Pope talking of his mother's health.

since I knew you been so long separated from you, as I now must be. Methinks we live to be more and more strangers, and every Year teaches you to live without me: This absence may, I fear, make my return less welcome and less wanted to you, than once it seem'd, even after but a fortnight. Time ought not in reason to diminish friendship, when it confirms the truth of it by experience.

The journey has a good deal disorder'd me, notwithstanding my resting place at Lord Bathurst's. My Lord is too much for me, he walks and is in spirits all day long: I rejoice to see him so. It is a right distinction, that I am happier in seeing my friends so many degrees above me, be it in fortune, health, or pleasures, than I can be in sharing either with them: for in these sort of enjoyments I cannot keep pace with 'em, any more than I can walk with a stronger man. I wonder to find I am a companion for none but old men, and forget that I am not a young fellow my self. The worst is, that reading and writing which I have still the greatest relish for, are growing painful to my eyes. But if I can preserve the good opinion of one or two friends, to such a degree, as to have their indulgence to my weaknesses, I will not complain of life: And if I could live to see you consult your ease and quiet by becoming independent on those who will never help you to either, I doubt not of finding the latter part of my life pleasanter than the former, or present. My uneasinesses of body I can bear; my chief uneasiness of mind is in your regard. You have a temper that wou'd make you *easy* and *beloved*, (which is all the happiness one needs to wish in this world) and content with moderate things. All your point is not to lose that Temper by sacrificing your self to others, out of a mistaken tenderness which hurts you, and profits not them. And this you must do soon, or it will be too late: Habit will make it as hard for you to live independent, as for L— to live out of a Court.

You must excuse me for observing what I think any defect in you: You grow too indolent, and give things up too easily: which would be otherwise, when you found and felt your self your own: Spirits wou'd come in, as ill-usage went out. While you live under a kind of perpetual dejection and oppression, nothing at all belongs to you, not your own *Humour*, nor your own *Sense*.

You can't conceive how much you would find resolution rise and chearfulness grow upon you, if you'd once try to live independent for two or three months. I never think tenderly of you but this comes across me, and therefore excuse my repeating it, for whenever I do not, I dissemble half that I think of you: Adieu, pray write, and be particular about your health.

POPE *to* MARTHA BLOUNT   4 *September* [1728]

Bowles (1806), x. 4–7

Bath, Sept. 4.

Dear Madam,—I thank you for many things, and particularly for your Letters. That which gave me an account of my mother's tolerable health, told me no more than three others told me; yet it satisfied me much more, as being from you. To think that a person whom we wish so much our friend as to take a concern in all that concerns us, should be cordially affected with things, is a greater and more tender pleasure than any of the same cares or testimonies from others. I left Lord Cobham's, as I told you,[1] not without a wish that yourself and Mrs. Howard had seen it with me. I passed by the door of my Lord Deloraine's, which is a neat stone-house, with a view of the Downs, but low situated. I can't help telling you one circumstance, that, as I travelled all alone, made me contemplative. I was drawn by a horse now employed by Lord C. in rolling the gardens, which was the same in former days on which the Earl of Derwentwater rid at Preston. It made me reflect, that man himself is as blind and unknowing of his fate, as the beast he bestrides: equally proud and prancing in his glory, and equally ignorant whither or to what he is running. I lay one night at Rousham,[2] which is the prettiest place for water-falls, jetts, ponds inclosed with beautiful scenes of green and hanging wood, that ever I saw. I lay next at Mr. Howe's, in Gloucestershire;[3] a fine thing of another kind, where Nature has done every thing, and luckily, for the master has ten children. But it might be made very grand, merely by taking away part of what is there already.

I called at Sir William Codrington's,[4] designing but for half a day, and it not being a mile out of the way; but found it impossible (without more violence than ought ever to be offered to good nature) to get from thence till just now. My reception there will furnish matter for a letter to Mr. Bethel. It was perfectly in his spirit: all his sisters, in the first place, insisted I should take physic, preparatory to the waters, and truly I made use of the time, place, and persons, to that end. My Lady Cox, the first night I lay there, mixed my electuary, Lady Codrington pounded sulphur, Mrs. Bridget Bethel ordered broth. Lady Cox marched first up-stairs with the physic in a gallipot; Lady Codrington

[1] In his first (unpreserved) letter to her; his second was from 'Cirencester;' this (as his postscript says) is his third.

[2] Rousham was the seat of Col. Dormer.

[3] Presumably John Grubham Howe of Stowell, younger brother of the 1st Viscount Howe. His niece Sophia Howe (d. 1726) had been maid of honour to Caroline Princess of Wales, and thus a friend of Pope's—as were all the maids of honour at that time.

[4] Pope's friendship with Sir William (of Durhams, near Bath) was doubtless due to Hugh Bethel. Lady Codrington (b. 1693), Lady Cox (b. 1691), and Bridget Bethel (b. 1692) were sisters of Hugh and Slingsby Bethel.

next, with the vial of oyle; Mrs. Bridget third, with pills; the fourth sister, with spoons and tea-cups. It would have rejoiced the ghost of Dr. Woodward[1] to have beheld this procession; and I should be inclined to think it might bring Mr. Bethel this way two hundred miles about, if I would promise but to do the same thing on my return home. By this means I have an opportunity of astonishing Dr. Arbuthnot, to see me begin the waters without any physic, and to set him and Mr. Gay in an uproar about me, and my wilfulness: I may even hope to be as famous as yourself. I was much pleased with what happened on Mr. B.'s sisters all taking physic some days together (which I was told there, and gives a perfect character of the great taste of the family to it). A country wench in the house thanked God heartily, that she was not born a gentlewoman, and declared she would not be one for the world. Their house is pretty enough, the situation romantic, covered with woody hills tumbling upon one another confusedly, and the garden makes a valley betwixt them, with some mounts and waterfalls.

I have experienced the fate of many promises, and many friends. Before I came hither, it was matter of contention who should carry me the journey! and at last, when it came to the point, I travelled every step of the way all alone. However, it was some comfort to me, that I really amused myself, and found not the length of the journey: it is a satisfaction to find that power in oneself, which one would not always owe to other helps and contingencies. I think I never passed a pleasanter, abating a few thoughts, with which I will not trouble you or any other friend; and which sit too near me to be totally banished by any company, amusement, or distance whatever.

When you say Mrs. Howard is well, I fear you don't (speak) of the pain in her face, but in general. I can't but think that Bath might give her blood a new turn, of which the Doctors here, I believe, will not despair. But I have yet seen none of them, nor any other creature. The first thing I have done is to sit down to write this. My next shall tell you who is here, etc. and what I find in the place. I am ever | Yours, etc.

Wednesday. Lord Peterborow is just arrived. I have writ you two letters before this.

THE EARL OF OXFORD *to* POPE[2]   10 *September* 1728

Longleat Portland Papers, xii

Dover Street. Sepr. 10: 1728.

Sir,—I received your letter with the parcel and letters, I sent to mr

---

[1] Dr. John Woodward (Dr. Fossile in *Three Hours after Marriage*) died 25 Apr. 1728.
[2] This is Lord Oxford's reply to Pope's letter of [17 Aug.].

Westleys House and he was gone into the country for the Holly-days, I have sent him the letters & parcel to be delivered up to him as soon as I came to Town which I belive has been done because he called upon me and I was not at home. This is the reason you had not an answer from me before this   you mention as if you had sent me mr Cooks letter to you but none came only your letter to mr Cook and to mr Westley

what you mention of a paragraph printed from those papers I had from you to have Transcribed I was much surprised at it and I did not see the paper nor what the paragraph is I cannot tell, I assure you I allways gave out only one sheet at a time and nobody else saw them the others were lockt up, and when wrote were examined by myself, I have examined my Servant and he declares no person what ever has seen the papers nor has he mentioned any thing of them or out of them to any person whatever, I shall desire that this affair should be cleared up, for it is of consequence to me.

I hope you are got safe to the Bath & that you will find great Benefit by it my Wife will soon be there.

I am with true respect sir | your most humble | Servant | Oxford.

my compliments to the Dr master Lewis & Gay if he be there.

I shall be glad to hear from you if you are so good   Direct to Dover street it will be sent where ever I am

Address: For | Alexander Pope Esqr | at | Bath
Frank: Oxford
Postmark: 10/SE

POPE *to* THE EARL OF OXFORD   14 *September* 1728

Longleat Portland Papers, xii

My Lord,—I little imagind when I sent that pacquet, that you were at Downhall, & that it was sent after you thither. I concluded you in London, and was grieving my self not to be able to pass one day with you before I set out for Bath. The hurry I was in (that being the Last day of my Stay) made me omit to inclose Cook's Letter, for your perusal: Twas a singular one enough. I also had not time to transcribe the paragraph I mentioned which was so like one in the Preface your Lordship was so good as to have writ out for me. It surprized both me & the author of that preface, when he saw it in a Daily Journal, which I have at home, but can't tell here where to procure, nor do I remember the Number. It was not however so literal, as to be more than a Con-jecture that they had seen ours; yet really if it happened by chance (as from what you say, I think it did) it was very odd. In the Preface is a passage[1] saying, "That the favor shown my writings by the Ladies, must vindicate 'em from the charge of Obscenity, the friendship shown the author by the *Clergy* from Prophaness, and a degree of Regard from the *Ministry*, from any inclination or suspicion of Treason." In the daily Journal it is said, that "This Author very little deserves what *he Boasts of*, the Countenance of the *Ladies*, the Friendship of the *Clergy*, and the Regard of the *Ministry*"—or words to that direct effect. which was a Boast never made by me or insinuated any where else but in That unprinted Preface. This was all, and I really fancy twas accidental, or possibly from something the gentleman who writ that preface[2] might chance to have said in company to my justification, & be again reported.

I did however think it my duty, to hint the bare suspition to you, that your Lordship might examine about it.

I heartily thank you, my Lord, for the kind concern you always take in my welfare. I can't say the Bath has yet operated much on my Complaint: I have drunk constantly & regularly, a fortnight. I also pump my lame hand, & it pains me pretty much. You may see it in the characters I write just now. I am forbid to use it much, or to hang down my head to write with the waters: They continue to make me giddy still. But nothing shall hinder me from sometimes testifying my obligations to your Lordship, both with Head & Hand, how much soever both may be out of order; as long as their Cunning[3] (as the Psalmists phrase is) remains; that is, as long as one can think, or the other can write.

I am truly glad to hear of my Lady Oxfords Coming, and will Hope, at least wish, your Lordship may not totally desert her while she stays here. I have made your Compliments to those you honour with your mention of 'em; and am (while I live) | My Lord | Your most faithfull, | and most gratefull, | humble Servant | A. Pope.

Bath, Sept. 14th 1728

Endorsement: Mr Pope | Bath Sept. 14. 1728

POPE *to* LORD BATHURST[4]   15 *September* [1728]
Cirencester

My Lord,—Plato saith, a Man in anger should not take the Lash (that

---

[1] This passage, possibly because of the episode here mentioned, was omitted before *The Dunciad* of 1729 was printed.

[2] One is led to guess that the Preface in question was 'A Letter to the Publisher', and that here Pope speaks of Cleland as 'the gentleman who writ that preface'. In the latter part of the 'Letter' remarks such as Pope here summarizes might have occurred.

[3] Pope recalls the King James version (cxxxvii. 5) rather than that of Douay.

[4] This letter contradicts the perplexing letter to Miss Blount which is here dated 4 Sept. 1728 (ii. 513) simply because its first paragraph fits no other possible place. In that letter

is the Pen) in his hand; and a certain Emperour (as I learn from Don Antonio de Guevara) used to count over the four & twenty Letters in such case before he spake. I have therfore thought it fit to count four & twenty days, before I would mention to your Lordship what has passd between us. I will keep my temper, & now only acquaint you, that I went according to your order (tho I receivd no further Invitation as you were pleasd to promise, by a Letter to Stow) to Cirencester in full & certain hopes of attending you to Bath. I stayd to the last day I could, namely the second of Sept.[1] I found you not, nor any Letter from you. so that had not Mr. Howe receivd me in my wandrings, I had been cast out in the Common, & reduced to feed like Nebuchadnezzar among the Beasts, and to travel on afterwards in the manner of Tom Coryate. However my Visit to your House was not wholly void of all Comfort to me: for I saw the Steeple of Ciceter stand on one side over it, and the great Vista in Oakley wood to the said Steeple by being widened beyond its former Hedges, borderd now only with some low thing which I took to be a Box-Edging on either side: Moreover I beheld with singular consolation the Back of the high Wood piercd thro, & every Tree that bore the least pretence to be Timber, totally cut down & done away. Wherby I see with delight not only the bare Prospect you have made, but also another, of the Necessity you are now reduced to, of raising some Building there: And I form to myself yet a third prospect, that you will so unwillingly & grudgingly undertake the said building, that it will be so small & inconsiderable as to oblige you to pull it down again another year, to erect a bigger & more adequate. Nevertheless my Lord (to prove I am not angry, but with a mixture of charity inclind to rectify, what I disapprove) I would not advise you to an obelisque which can bear no Diameter to fill so vast a Gap unless it literally touch'd the Skies; but rather to a solid Pyramid of 100 ft square, to the end there may be Something solid and Lasting of your works. As to the church Steeple, I am truly sorry for it, yet I would not however pull down the House. I would rather the Reformation began, as reformations always ought, at the church itself; not that I would wish the Body of it entirely taken away, but only the Steeple lower'd: This would bring matters to Some Uniformity, & the Dissenters & Quakers be greatly obliged, as

(here thought a composite) his stay at Cirencester was tiring; here he reproaches Bathurst for not being at home at all. The letter to Miss Blount of 4 Sept. narrates his progress to Bath, and does not mention any stay at Cirencester. In 1728 Mr. and Mrs. Erasmus Lewis were at Bath (as here mentioned). They were married in 1724, and she died after some years of invalidism in 1736. During these years Pope visited Bath only in 1728 and 1734. The year 1734 is impossible for the letter to Miss Blount of [3 Sept. 1728] because it mentions Mrs. Pope as still alive.

[1] This remark, dating Pope's departure from Stowe, without 'further invitation', is important in placing the letter in 1728. In other possible years Pope had left for Bath somewhat later in September.

it is the High-tower itself which above all they hold in abomination (wherby your Lordships Interest in the next Elections might vastly be strengthen'd) Certain it is, that Something extraordinary & *eclatant* must be done, if you would render yourself agreeable to the present Administration, which may be a convincing proof to all the world of the Conversion of one who has been so long, & so distinguished, a Patron of the Church of England. It would not be amiss, I further think, if your Lordship would also give some other evidence of your Capacity for a Statesman, and pretensions to make a greater Figure (in another House) than you yet have done; by breaking your Word with your Friends, &c. which, tho I never perceivd it but by one late Instance, I was exceedingly rejoyc'd to find was not entirely out of your power.

Mr Lewis is offended by your letters, for he is a Serious Man. But Mrs Lewis is the youngest & gayest Lady here: and would be an excellent Match for your Lordship, (as well as a noble Subject for You to prove that Vigor you have been so famous for) if my Lady cares to part with you. Pray tell my Lady, that either Mr Lewis or I have that Opinion of her Steddiness & Sobriety that we will take a Lodging for her here the moment She appoints, provided she pleases to write to us in her own hand, & witnessed to be her hand by the Young Ladies your Daughters, who are also sober persons: and provided it be not wrapt up, countersign'd or superscribed by your Lordship; in which case we shall suspect some fraud or insincere practises.

We shall both[1] leave this place for Cirencester on the last day of this month & be with you by dinner time on the first of October punctually. In the meantime believe me (my Lord) to forget all that is past, and to be with the very same Sincerity and Affection & Esteem which I have always felt in your regard, | My Lord | Your most faithfull | & most hearty | humble Servant, | A. Pope.

Bath Sept. 15th

FENTON *to* BROOME   15 *September* [1728]

Elwin–Courthope, viii. 152

Sept. 15, [1728].

Ζωὸν γόον "Εκτορα.—Hom.[2]

Quod optanti Divum promittere nemo
Auderet, volvenda dies en attulit ultro!—Virgil.[3]

Having thus cut a caper in Greek and Latin for joy to hear of thy

---

[1] 'Both' is a vague word, but it very likely means Pope and Gay. Since both men were in Bath until Pope left (about 12 Oct.), the journey to Cirencester was probably for a brief visit, perhaps for a day or so only. Possibly the journey never took place but was merely planned.

[2] *Iliad*, vi. 500.   [3] *Aeneid*, ix. 6–7.

life and health, let me change my style, and chide you for not employing some of your acquaintance in town to make the newswriters
contradict the report they spread of your death,[1] to recover your
friends from the pain they had given them. By the last post I had
a letter from our friend Mr. Blount,—whom my young Lady Cottrell
tells me is wonderfully improved with travelling,—who spoke of your
death with the tenderest concern imaginable. I believe before this
comes to your hands he will be married to one Mrs. Cornwallis,[2]
a young lady of a very good fortune and character; but though he used
to say whenever he married he would have a long-waisted wife to
lengthen the breed, this lady happens to be almost the head lower than
himself. I am sure you join with me in wishing him entirely happy.

Long live and flourish the Rector of Pulham.[3] Is not this upon
every account preferable to a long pilgrimage, or rather banishment
into Devonshire? I would not have thee to be either anxious in your
expectations, or troublesome to your patrons, without which I think
you may hold your eye fixed on Norwich whenever a prebend is vacant.
In the meantime, *tibi tuisque jucundus vive.* My humble service to
Widow Broome.[4] I am ever yours most affectionately.

Pope has been much colicked of late. He is now gone to the Bath.
Let me hear soon from you.

THOMAS COOKE *to* POPE   16 *September* 1728

Elwin–Courthope, x. 213

Sept. 16, 1728.

Sir,—I had by this day the favour of a letter from you, dated Augt 17,
by what accident it was kept so long from me I cannot judge.[5] If Mr.
Wesley had left it at my lodgings in Westminster I should not have
been two days without it. I am at present in the country, not far from
town, where a gentleman, who received the letter from Mr. Wesley,
was so kind to come purposely to give it me. You seem in your postscript to let your opinion of the sincerity of my professions depend on
the readyness of my answer. Assure yourself you should not have
wanted that testimony if I had had your letter sooner; nor shall I be

---

[1] *The Evening Post*, 29 Aug. 1728, had mistakenly reported that 'The Rev. William
Broome, who assisted Mr. Pope in his Notes on Homer, died last Week of a Fever at his
Living in Suffolk'.
[2] Henry Pope Blount and Mrs. Anne Cornwallis were married, according to *The Historica
Register*, on 19 Sept. 1728.
[3] Broome had secured by gift of the Crown the living of Pulham in Norfolk. It was reported (*Universal Spectator*, 23 Nov. 1728) to be worth 'about three hundred pounds *per
annum*'.
[4] 'Widow' is a joke, of course.
[5] The delay is amply explained in the letters of Pope and Lord Oxford, 10 and 14 Sept.
Lord Oxford's letter of 20 Jan. 1728/9 coupled with remarks Cooke here makes would seem
to indicate that Cooke was hiding from creditors at this time.

backward in discharging myself as I ought, in relation to your character, and at the same time preserve my honour in what I have professed in the hours of friendship, to other writers. I find you unluckily mistake the persons for whom I profess *a real friendship*; nor are they such as take those methods of writing slander in the dark. Your moral character I never heard attacked by any with whom I converse.[1] Mr. Moore who greatly shares my esteem, has often, since the Dunciad was published, spoke of you in terms which could come from none but a wellwisher and admirer. What Mr. Dennis has sayed passes as unregarded as the wind. I never reported that he should say he had a letter from you exhorting him to write against Cato, but that he should tell me Mr. Lintot had advised him to it from you. Give me leave here to express some resentment against the person whom I suspect must have told you that; and who at the same time was not sparing of many other calumnys against me; your prudence, I doubt not, will keep you from any want of a guardian in your conduct in your correspondence with any one; but I believe you will not think it amiss to be warned against the follys and insincerity of a person with whom you converse. I am credibly informed that a certain clergyman, this last summer, was very free with my character, and in a more extensive manner than was either gentlemanlike or pertinent. He went from London, after having received such benefits from me as he wanted, and was able to give, for the continuance of three or four months, with a resolution, I should think from what I heard, to return them with abuses. One great topic was what I had wrote five or six years ago; among the idleness and mistakes of which time were some few verses in commendation of him. Yet this person has since thought fit to print in his own name a translation of a small Greek poem, litterally my own, amidst a folio of his labours; which, without taking any notice of his, I shall print in the Collection of Poems which I mentioned in my last. You commend my design of leaving out that passage about you in the Battel of the Poets; I intend to omit the whole poem,[2] nor would I have it remembered that I was the author of it. Believe me, as I wrote this from my heart, so should I be sincerely proud of waiting on you where you shall appoint. I am, sir, your humble servant.

Direct to me at Mr. Hunter's, an undertaker in John Street, near Story's Passage, Numb. 1, Westminster.

---

[1] It must have been this remark that convicted Cooke of being a Dunce. In the 'Index of Things (including Authors)' found at the end of the quarto *Dunciad* of 1729 is the following entry: 'Cooke, (Tho.) abused Mr. *Pope*'s moral Character.' Cooke is mentioned in *Dunciad* (1729), ii. 130. See Pope's letter to Wesley, 6 Jan. 1728/9, here v. 6–7.

[2] Cooke changed his mind, evidently foreseeing his niche in *The Dunciad*. Within a month of the publication of *The Dunciad Variorum* (April 1729) Cooke published his volume of *Poems*, where was found an 'improved' form of the poem he had thought of omitting.

‡POPE *to* [FORTESCUE][1]   17 *September* [1728]
1737

Sep. 17

The gayety of your letter proves you are not so studious of Wealth as
many of your profession are, since you can derive matter of mirth from
want of business. You are none of those Lawyers who deserve the
motto of the devil, *Circuit quaerens quem devoret.*[2] But your *Circuit*
will at least procure you one of the greatest of temporal blessings,
Health. What an advantageous circumstance is it, for one that loves
rambling so well, to be a grave and reputable rambler? while (like your
fellower Circuiteer, the Sun) you travel the round of the earth and
behold all the iniquities under the heav'ns? You are much a superior
genius to me in rambling; you, like a Pigeon (to which I would sooner
compare a Lawyer than to a Hawk) can fly some hundred leagues at
a pitch; I, like a poor squirrel, am continually in motion indeed, but
it is about a cage of three foot: my little excursions are but like those
of a shopkeeper, who walks every day a mile or two before his own
door, but minds his business all the while. Your letter of the Cause
lately before you, I could not but communicate to some ladies of your
acquaintance. I am of opinion if you continued a correspondence of
the same sort during a whole Circuit, it could not fail to please the
sex, better than half the novels they read; there wou'd be in them what
they love above all things, a most happy union of Truth and Scandal.
I assure you the Bath affords nothing equal to it: It is on the contrary
full of grave and sad men, Mr. Baron S. Lord chief Justice A. Judge P.
and Counsellor B.[3] who has a large pimple on the tip of his nose, but
thinks it inconsistent with his gravity to wear a patch, notwithstanding
the precedent of an eminent Judge. I am, dear Sir, | Yours, &c.

†POPE *to* SWIFT[4]   12 [*October*] 1728
1740

Bath, Nov. 12, 1728.

I have past six weeks in quest of health, and found it not; but I found

---

[1] Pope is evidently writing from Bath, where he arrived on 4 Sept. 1728. In 1734, at
first sight the chief rival as year for this letter, he was probably setting out for Bath about the
17th. Fortescue is supposedly riding the circuit and not picking up much business. But since
September is late for assizes, one begins to suspect here a conflation of perhaps two letters—
a suspicion that is somewhat augmented by Pope's remarks (just after a ramble all the way
to Bath) comparing his little excursions to those of the shopkeeper. Perhaps 1715 is a possible
year for this letter.   [2] 1 Peter v. 8.
[3] The initials are difficult. No 'Chief Justice A' emerges at this general time. If 'Coun-
seller B' stands for Fortescue's and Pope's friend Bickford, one may note that he died in
June of 1732.
[4] The month printed as date in Pope's editions (1740–2) is clearly wrong; for he certainly
was back home before 12 Nov., and both this letter and that to Dr. Sheridan [12 Oct.] were
written at Bath, if we may accept the superscription.

the folly of sollicitude about it in a hundred instances; the contrariety of opinions and practices, the inability of physicians, the blind obedience of some patients, and as blind rebellion of others. I believe at a certain time of life, men are either fools or physicians, and[1] zealots or divines, for themselves.

It was much in my hopes that you intended us a winters visit, but last week I repented that wish, having been alarm'd with a report of your lying ill on the road from Ireland; from which I am just reliev'd by an assurance that you are still at Sir A——'s,[2] planting and building; two things that I envy you for, besides a third, which is the society of a valuable Lady: I conclude (tho' I know nothing of it) that you quarrel with her, and abuse her every day, if she is so. I wonder I hear of no Lampoons upon her, either made by yourself, or by others because you esteem her. I think it a vast pleasure that whenever two people of merit regard one another, so many scoundrels envy and are angry at them; 'tis bearing testimony to a merit they cannot reach; and if you knew the infinite content I have receiv'd of late, at the finding yours and my name constantly united in any silly scandal, I think you would go near to sing *Io Triumphe!*[3] and celebrate my happiness in verse; and I believe if you won't, I shall. The inscription to the Dunciad is now printed and inserted in the Poem. Do you care I shou'd say any thing farther how much that poem is yours? since certainly without you it had never been.[4] Would to God we were together for the rest of our lives! The whole weight of Scriblers would just serve to find us amusement, and not more. I hope you are too well employed to mind them: every stick you plant, and every stone you lay, is to some purpose; but the business of such lives as theirs is but to die daily, to labour, and raise nothing. I only wish we could comfort each other under our bodily infirmities, and let those who have so great a mind to have more Wit than we, win it and wear it. Give us but ease, health, peace, and fair weather![5] I think it is the best wish in the world, and you know whose it was. If I liv'd in Ireland, I fear the wet climate wou'd indanger more than my life, my humour, and health, I am so Atmospherical a creature—

---

[1] physicians, and] physicians for themselves, and *1741 Labc, 1742 Lcd.*

[2] Sir A——'s] Sir Arthur Acheson's *1741 Dab.* Sheridan had told Pope of the 'lampoons' actually written. The poems by Swift written at Market Hill (where he visited in 1728) are printed in the edition of Swift's *Poems* made by Sir H. Williams, pp. 845–908. 'My Lady's Lamentation and Complaint against the Dean, July 28, 1728' is among the most delightful, and is doubtless the 'lampoon' Sheridan had mentioned.

[3] An Expression of Congratulation among the Ancients after a Victory.—*1741 Dab.*

[4] Pope is somewhat too eager to involve Swift with himself as an ally against the Dunces. Swift had doubtless encouraged Pope in writing the poem during his visit of 1727; but to call Swift 'properly the Author of the Dunciad' (as he did in the following letter to Sheridan) was absurd.

[5] 'Health, peace, and fair weather' was the favourite wish of Swift's early patron Sir William Temple.

I must not omit acquainting you, that what you heard of the words spoken of you in the Drawing-room, was not true. The sayings of Princes are generally as ill related as the sayings of Wits. To such reports little of our regard shou'd be given, and less of our conduct influenc'd by them.

POPE *to* DR. SHERIDAN[1]   [12 *October* 1728]

1745 (Dodsley *Miscellanies*, x. 65)

Sir,—I thank you kindly for your News of the Dean of St. *Patricks*, for your *Persius*,[2] for every thing in your Letter. I will use my warmest Endeavours to serve Dr. *Whalley*.[3] Besides his own Merit, the Demerit of his Antagonist goes into the Scale, and the Dean tells me he is a Coadjutant of that Fool, *Smedley*. You *must have seen*, but you *cannot have read*, what he has lately publish'd against our Friend and Me.[4] The only Pleasure a bad Writer can give me, he has given, that of being abused with my Betters and my Friends. I am much pleas'd with most of the Intelligencers,[5] but I am a little piqued at the Author of 'em for not once doing me the Honour of a Mention upon so honourable an Occasion as being slandered by the Dunces, together with my Friend the Dean, who is properly the Author of the Dunciad: It had never been writ but at his Request, and for his Deafness: For had he been able to converse with me, do you think I had amus'd my Time so ill? I will not trouble you with Amendments to so imperfect an Edition as is now published; you'll soon see a better, with a full and true Commentary, setting all Mistakes right, and branding none but our own Cattle. Some very good Epigrams on the Gentlemen of the Dunciad have been sent me from *Oxford*, and others of the *London* Authors; if I had an Amanuensis (which is a thing neither I, nor my common Trifles are worth) you should have them with this. If your University or Town have produced any on this Subject, pray send 'em me, or keep them at least together, for another Day they may all meet.

I've writ to the Dean just now by Mr. *Elrington*,[6] who charges himself with this, and have inserted a Hint or two of his Libelling the

---

[1] The date is inferred from the corrected date of Pope's letter to Swift (which precedes this). The two were evidently written at approximately the same time.

[2] A literal translation in prose, published at Dublin, 1728.—Nichols–Elwin.

[3] Dr. Whaley, chaplain to Primate Lindsay, was now engaged in a suit for a valuable living. See Ball, iv, *passim*, and here especially, Swift to Pope, 6 Mar. 1728/9 and note.

[4] Dean Smedley was apparently responsible for the collection of pieces published about a week before Pope began his Bath journey under the title of *Gulliveriana*.

[5] *The Intelligencer* ran to 20 numbers in 1728–9, written chiefly by Swift and Sheridan. (Pope hopes for allies?)

[6] At the time of writing this letter the tragedian Thomas Elrington was appearing as a substitute for Booth at Drury Lane. Dr. William Van Lennep notes that the *Dublin Weekly Journal* tells us that Elrington returned to Dublin in May 1729. Hence he would seem not to be the Elrington here mentioned.

Lady of the Family; in as innocent a manner, as he does it, he will hardly suspect I had any Information of it.

Tho' I am a very ill Correspondent, I shall at all times be glad to have the Favour of a Line from you. My Eyesight is bad, my Head often in Pain, my Time strangely taken up. Were I my own Master (which I thank God I yet am, in all points but one, where Humanity only constrains me) I wou'd infallibly see *Ireland* before I die. But whether that, or many other of my little, tho' warm Designs will ever take Effect,

Caliginosa nocte premit Deus![1]

I am (wherever I am) the Dean's, and the Dean's Friends', and consequently faithfully, | Sir | Your affectionate Servant | A. Pope.

POPE *to* FORTESCUE[2]   [17 or 24 *October* 1728]

1880 (Lord Clermont)

Thursday

I am heartily glad to hear of your safe arrival in Town, and doubt not you will be pleasd that I am as safe at Twitnam. I came from the Bath 2 days since hither; & find my Mother tolerably well, as I hope you left all yours. I should be glad to see you in Town, but having been so long absent, have some necessary matters here for a few days which I would pursue, if you could find it suitable to your convenience to lye here on saturday & pass the Sunday together   Otherwise I will wait on you. In the meantime pray convey this Letter to Mrs[3] Howard, it is a Case that requires dispatch, as you will see, and I beg, if you can to favour it with any of the Board of Admiralty that you know: for I am convinced that he is ill used.[4] adieu dear Sir, till we meet. Pray give me a line by Bowrey. I have a thousand things to say to you.

Your Ever affectionate | Servant | A. Pope.

Address: To Wm Fortescue Esqr | Member of Parliament at his | house in Bell yard; | nr Lincolns inn fields | London

POPE *to* LORD BATHURST   7 *November* [1728]

Cirencester Park

My Lord,—I have long intended to write to you, to know from yourself what I now only hear by your Porter, that your Lordship and all yours

---

[1] Horace, *Carmina*, III. xxix. 30.
[2] The text comes from the *History of the Fortescue Family* (1880), i, opp. 156, where the author, Thomas Fortescue Clermont (Baron Clermont), prints a facsimile.

Fortescue (see address) was first elected to Parliament in 1727, but Pope did not go to Bath that year. In 1728 he returned about 12 Oct., so that the first Thursday after the return would be the 17th.   [3] Polwhele and Elwin wrongly print *Mr* for *Mrs*.
[4] The ill-used person is unidentified.

are in health. I am sure no man alive more sincerely wishes it; and really it ever has been a sort of Satisfaction to me, to know that those I love are Happier this way than myself. I do not think I ever shall enjoy any health four days together, for the remaining Sand I have to run. The Bath was tryed after all other remedies, as a last remedy, and that has proved totally ineffectuall. I never had more long or more violent Headakes, &c. than three fits since my return. I hope, my Lord, you find other fruits of the Bath and are now a Sound Man on the hills of Gloustershire: I could wish I were fit to be anywhere but in the chimney corner, and then I know what place and whose company I could most wish to be in at this time. Without flattery, I have so often found my self so perfectly easy, & my heart so much at rest, with You, that I could not take it into my head I could be troublesome to you even tho I've been often sick. I vow I have found myself happier in sickness with you, than in health with some who are not thought bad or disagreeable Company.

I have been but once at London since I saw you: where you was inquired after by all that I call my friends. The Duchess of Buckingham is at Leighs, wishing (she tells me) to execute your Lordships Schemes, but believing they must be left to the Duke's & your own Riper Judgment, seven years hence.[1] The writing to my Mother & me she has signed:[2] You will rejoice I know with me, that what You so warmly sollicited and contributed to, for my future Ease, is accomplished. If I live these hundred years, I shall never fancy, even in my jealous Old age, that I live too long upon You & Her. And if I live but one year, it would better please me to think an Obelisque might be added to your Garden, or a Pond to hers, with my money, than such a Hospital as Guy's[3] to the City, or such a Monument as Priors to Westminster.

Lord Bolingbroke & I commemorated you in our Cups one day at Dawley—(Farm I should say, & accordingly there are all the Insignia and Instruments of Husbandry painted now in the Hall,[4] that one could wish to see in the fields of the most industrious Farmer in Christendome.) He is gone with my Lady to London, who is rather better.

I have one pleasure left which I am now pursuing, & that is Planting, if making Sallad-beds can be so called. It passes away half my day; the rest I eat & sleep; for read I cannot, my eyes (since I was at Bath) being worse than ordinary. I want a book or two in your Lordships

---

[1] Young Duke Edmund (b. 1716) would be approaching his majority in seven years.

[2] The paper would probably concern the annuity purchased from the Duchess, payments on which caused some difficulties noted in later letters (e.g. Pope to Orrery, 23 July 1742).

[3] Pope evidently did not approve the architecture of the new hospital, which first received patients in 1725.

[4] On these 'murals' see Pope to Swift, 28 June 1728.

Library, but how to get at them I know not. I beg to hear at your leisure a word or two, and particularly if there be any probability of your making any Excursion this way, in which case I beg to meet you either at London or Riskings. My Mother joins in her most humble Services, with mine, to my Lady Bathurst & the young Ladies: And be pleas'd to believe me, with entire affection and true Esteem, always | My Lord | Yours faithfully, | A. Pope.

Twitenham | Novr. 7th

Address: To | The Right Honourable the Lord | Bathurst, in St. James' Square, | London.

POPE *to* BENJAMIN MOTTE[1]   *9 November* [1728]

The Pierpont Morgan Library

Novr the 9th

Mr Motte,—This is to acquaint you, in order that I may not be disappointed a Third time in the manner I last was, that at the time you desird, I will draw a bill of 25ll on you, namely the 16th of this instant, which I promisd the payment of, as of the remainder the beginning of next month. I found it very troublesom to borrow it the morning you left me; And I must acquaint you, that, trying to procure it of Dr Arbuthnot, he told me (what had I known before, I should have been more vex'd) that his family were made to wait for the payment of his 50ll six or seven times after he was at Bath—I am ashamed of it—

As I would do any thing in reason to make you easy, this was Ill done of you. The Dean does not come to England this Winter, as I was made to hope. As to what I promisd you of the Miscellanies, I will keep my word as you do with me, since it presuppos'd your observing the Conditions. It will be necessary to give Mr Gay a note for the remainder due, and what patience he pleases he may have, but since what I heard of Dr Arbuthnot, I will take it upon myself no further. I am | Your sincere Wellwisher | & Servant | A. Pope.

Address: To | Mr Motte, Bookseller, | at Temple Barr, | Fleetstreet. | London.

[1] This letter concerns Motte's failure to pay with any reasonable promptness what he owed the authors of the 'last' volume of the *Miscellanies*. For his agreement signed 29 Mar. 1727 see *The Gentleman's Magazine*, xliv (1855), 363. The matter was not completely regularized until 1729, and it explains Pope's lack of eagerness to let Motte publish the fourth volume of *Miscellanies* in 1732. Swift, in Dublin, was less aware of Motte's dilatory payments.

*POPE *to* JAMES STOPFORD   20 *November* 1728

The Victoria and Albert Museum (modern transcript)

Twiknham, Novr. 20th 1728.

The Testimony of your Remembrance & Friendship is highly grateful to me: the Share you must always bear in both of mine was but due to your merit; but let me add something that is my own, a great and unfeigned Affection & Inclination for you.

Your Present I thankfully accept. The Conjecture you make upon the Temple of Jupiter Olympius at Agrigentum, deserves the name of a Demonstration.[1] I am so pleased with it, that I design to draw with my own hand the Ichnography of it, pursuant to your Dissertation. You will look on it meerly as a proof how much I enter into your Opinion. I left it with Lord Bolingbroke to compare with Diodorus, who was not a little pleased with it. He assures you of his Esteem, & Desire to renew the pleasure he had in your Conversation, whenever our good fortune allows us to see you in this kingdom.

I will not fail to make the compliments as you desire in the meantime, pray believe me yours, & heartily wishing your welfare & felicity every way, My own health is bad, but my spirits make some amends for it: And, just as I find it in almost all other cases, so I am vastly more in Heart and Spirit, than in Powr or Act | Dear Sir, | Your really Obliged & | faithfull Servant | A Pope.

Address: To | The Reverend Mr Stopford, at | Col. Butler's in Dawson street | Dublin

*MATHER BYLES *to* POPE   25 *November* 1728

The New England Historical and Genealogical Society

Boston. N.E. Nov. 25. 1728.

Sir,—It is now near six Months since I did my self the Honour of addressing you with a second Letter:[2] But whither ever it came to your Hands, I have not as yet had the Happiness to learn. In the Letter with which you so soothed and gratified my Ambition, you were pleased to make a generous offer of your Works to our Publick Library, if I could contrive for their safe Conveyance. This I endeavoured by expressing my Desires in an Answer, that you would leave them at Mr. *Lintot*'s Shop, where I would direct one Capt *Cary* to call for them. By a Mistake he has Disappointed me; for which Reason I have directed another Person, [Mr. Samuel Sewal, a Merchant of *New*

---

[1] The 'conjecture' was doubtless of the informal sort that Pope himself loved. Stopford is not known to have published any observations on the temple.

[2] One letter was all Pope wrote to Mr. Byles, but the Boston parson hoped for more still.

England]¹ to call at the same place, if you think it convenient to leave them there for him to receive. I hope the Gentleman will wait on you himself as I have appointed him, in Order to receive your Commands, and present you my most humble Service.

Since I last wrote you, I have with the greatest Satisfaction perused several of your Pieces, which I had not before mett with. The Countrey has just received three Volumes of Miscellanies to which are affixed your Name, and Dr. *Swift*'s. His Excellency our Governour *Burnet* has also obliged me with the *Dunciad*,² and a Key to it: But whither the Key be written by a Friend or an Enemy I found something difficult to determine. In *Lintots* Miscellanies I find a set of inimitable *Verses to the Memory of an unfortunate Young Lady*: What would I not give to know who she was, and the remarkable circumstances of her History. But I presume too far, and must ask Your Pardon for my Impertinance.

By the Verses which accompany this Letter you will see how Little we may pretend to the Inspiration of the Muses, in these unharmonious climates.³ However, suffer me in Justice to my Native Countrey, to assert our *Taste* for the polite Studies, at the same Time that I am obliged to acknowledge our *Unskilfullness* in them. There can need no proof of this, when I have said how we are charmed with the admired productions of your immortal pen. It is the best complement I can pay the learned Part of my Countreymen, to declare in what a raised Strain they speak of the unrivalled Sallies of your sublime Genius. In Short, *Sir*, we can *relish*, what we are unable to *produce*, and *admire* where we can by no means *imitate*

But I would by no means be tedious, nor trespass upon that Time which is designed the Glory of the present Age, and the Transport and Wonder of all Posterity. Permit me so far to applaud my own Judgement, as to Subscribe my self | Sir, | Your perpetual Reader | And Admirer.

POPE *to* THE EARL OF OXFORD⁴   [*27 November* 1728]

Longleat Portland Papers, xii

Wednesday: | ten a clock
Nov: 27: 1728.

My Lord,—I am just got hither, and very desirous (as I am always) of waiting on You. Some physick I've taken hinders me this morning,

---

¹ The brackets are Byles's own.

² Governor Burnet was William, son of the Bishop, and brother of Pope's enemy Thomas, who was identifiable in *The Dunciad* (1728), iii. 135–42.

³ At this point a marginal note identifies the verses as 'The Poems on the Death of K. George I. and on the Arrival of Governour Burnet'.

⁴ The date ('Nov: 27: 1728') is written in by Lord Oxford. The endorsed date is in his clerk's hand.

but if at dinner your Lordship happens to be totally un-ingagd, I beg leave to attend you. Will you allow me, My Lord, to desire, if it be no way inconvenient, that Mr Westley may be there whose acquaintance I am willing to improve.[1] If any other time will be less troublesome to you, your Lordship has but to command me, who am with the truest respect & obligation, Ever | My Lord | Your most faithfull | & obedient Servant | A. Pope.

Address: To the Rt. Honble the Earl | of Oxford.
Endorsement: Mr Pope | Novr 27. 1728

*POPE to BUCKLEY[2]   [1728–9?]

1885 (Hist. MSS. Comm.)

                         Thursday evening. Twitnam

I have not been long returned from my rambles; the only day I was in town I dined with Dr. Mead and enquiring after you found you had scarce seen him since we met there last. I hope your health is as good as I wish it. I send the books you favoured me with and will shew you the effect of them in the paper I have drawn up whenever you have leisure. I suppose you keep the same days in town, or shall you reside there constantly? pray acquaint,

    Dear Sir your very sincere and affectionate servant, | A Pope.

POPE to FORTESCUE[3]   [*November–December* 1728]

The Historical Society of Pennsylvania

I am so ill to day with the Headake & Wind, that I am utterly incapable of Company or supping, or even conversing with any Comfort. I must lye in an arm chair till Bed time & the Motion of a Chair makes me quite sick. I'm sorry to be now twice disapointed of you. I'll come to morrow after noon or night & take my Chance. I am Ever Truly Yours | A. Pope.

Address: To | Mr Fortescue in | Bell Yard

[1] One suspects that Pope wished to talk over with Wesley and Lord Oxford the problem of Thomas Cooke's worthiness for a place in *The Dunciad*.

[2] The text was printed by the Hist. MSS. Comm. from the MSS. of Capt. Stewart of Alltrodyn in their *Tenth Report*, Appendix IV, p. 142.

Not surely datable, the letter seems to concern a conference about some paper Pope has been drawing up to help Buckley on his edition of Thuanus. Pope had returned from his Bath expedition in Oct. 1728. The year 1715, suggested in the Report of the Hist. MSS. Comm., is impossible, since Pope did not live at Twickenham then.

[3] Unfortunately this letter might have been written at almost any time in Pope's career; but since its contents agree with the letter immediately following it is placed here.

POPE *to* FORTESCUE¹   [*Late* 1728]

Harvard University

Twickenham, | Friday.

I am in the condition of an old fellow of Threescore, with a Complica-
tion of Diseases upon me; A constant Headake; ruind Tone of the
Stomach; the Piles; a Vomiting & Looseness; & an Excess of Wind.
Some of these succeed, the moment I get quit of the others: & upon
the whole, indeed I am in a very uncomfortable way. I could have
wishd to see you, but cannot. I wish you all health whereever you go.
Pray, if you can, do not forget to try to procure the annuity for life for
1000ll which I recommended to you in behalf of a Lady of our acquaintance. Make my services to all yours, as acceptable, as they are
sincere. I am ever | Dear Sir yours affectionately | A. Pope.

If you have an opportunity, pray give my Services to Sir R. W.² whom
I will wait upon the first Sunday I am able.

Address: To | Mr Fortescue.

*POPE *to* FORTESCUE³   [?*December* 1728]

Harvard University

I can't but write these two words to thank you for all favors, & to wish
you a good journey, if you must go so soon as the End of the week: if
not, I shall see you again with pleasure. You'l be kind, in writing me
a word what you can do in my poor Sisters affairs, who is much
affected by them. I send you (the Least of my debts) half a Guinea by
the bearer. Adieu dear Sir. I have a very bad Headake. | Ever yours, |
A. Pope.

Address: To Wm. Fortescue Esqr.

*POPE *to* LORD BATHURST   [*December* 1728]

The Huntington Library

My dear Lord,—I have never felt more melancholy than since I last
wrote to you. But in the midst of it, tis a contentment to me to find

¹ The date of the letter is uncertain, but since the annuity for Mrs. Blount was purchased
before the middle of May, this placing seems probable. See Pope to Fortescue [15 May 1729].
The letter antedates at least some of the troubles of Mrs. Rackett, and the journey to Devonshire mentioned also in the following letter to Fortescue.

² Sir Robert Walpole.

³ The affairs of Pope's 'poor sister' Mrs. Rackett became confused when she began administration of the estate of her late husband, Charles. Letters of administration were granted
7 Nov. 1728. See *The Athenaeum*, 30 May 1857 (p. 694). The letter could have been written
any time thereafter for several years.

You so easy, so happy! Quisque est Faber suae fortunae[1] is, in part, true; but not where Affections & Passions predominate. Philosophy flourishes only in a free state of mind: It serves us to bully with in Health: Those who have their hearts touchd will find their Heads but weak. I have been on the brink of losing such a Friend as Nature only can make; a Mother (I fear I shall lose her yet) and such another as Custom & Habit, the second nature, have render'd as necessary to me as a Limb. If poor Gay were gone, I should feel as if I wanted an Arm:[2] Tis not that one every day wants to use one's Left, but one nevertheless shou'd be missing it when one did not use it. But we all hope that Gay is in a fair way of recovery, tho he has been just in the jaws of Death; but (that I may say something in your stile) he was grown so lean that Death thought him not worth swallowing. In earnest, he is in danger of a Consumption, & no poor creature had ever a narrower escape.

I believe your Lordship will think I have really been troubled, and sufferd a Dejection which I think no other Loss, or its prospect, can so justly cause; Almost all others are retrievable in a degree, but that of Friends is not.

It pleases me that you fancy you writ to me before. May Friendship claim the powers of Piety, and be said to be exerted always, even without the Act? & so my Lord, you write always, as St. Paul says one may Pray always?

As much as you give into Philosophy, I incline to the side of Religion: It was ever so, your Lordship well remembers. Yet I am glad to find among the topicks of your Lordships own Panegyrick, One, that I can refer rather to the latter than the former; I mean Charity to the Poor, which the Philosophers ascribe to a meaner principle namely our compliance [with] Human weakness & Compassion on seeing the miseries of another, (and which the Stoicks held rather a Frailty than a Virtue) whereas Riders Almanack and other Christian authors call it a Christmas virtue, and give you some hopes at this time of the year to get Heaven by it.—As the whole passage contains some other useful, seasonable, nay (which comes nearer to your Lordships bosome) rural, domestic, and physical observations, I shall transcribe it from the book which is just brought me, verbatim, with applications to yourself in particular.

"This is the best time to fell Timber" (if you have any in Oaklywood) "Let Fowlers mind their game" (be sure you pot some woodcocks and bring up to town) "Let a warm fire and a Cup of Nectar [Styre Cyder] be thy Bath" (that is, go not to the Bath at this Season,

---

[1] Adapted from Sallust, *Ad Caesarem Senem De Re Publica Oratio,* i. 2.

[2] In Nov. 1728 both Mrs. Pope and Gay had been seriously ill. Gay's illness serves to date the letter approximately.

tho no body else does) "Let thy Kitchen be thy apothecarys shop, hot meats and broth thy Physic; and a wellspread Table the proof of thy charity to thy poor neighbors," (especially the Vicar.)

Rider's Alm. obs. on Decr.

I do not perceive this excellent author, or any other sound Philosopher, mentions mony as an Ingredient to well-living; or else I would accept your Bill. But I would much rather see you than that; and if this wish will bring you a day the sooner, let the other alone till you come. Adieu, my Lord, I wish I had you at Riskins: So do many more here—Lord Bolingbroke admires your wisdom—Sequitur, non passibus æquis:[1] whereas others can do no more than behold it, and cry out—Vestigia semper adora!

I beg the Ladies acceptance of my faithfull Wishes for them of many happy new years, and am with great truth & affection ever

My Lord | Your most obedient Servant | A Pope

I beg you will put Mr Howe[2] in mind that I am his servant.
Prince Frederic wonders he has not seen you.[3]

Address: To the Right Honorable | the Lord Bathurst, at | Cirencester: | Glocestershire.
Endorsement [in a small, old hand]: Mr. Pope | no date

*POPE to THE EARL OF BURLINGTON[4]

Chatsworth

[23 *December* 1728]

Twitnam. Decr. 23.

My Lord,—I had sooner troubled you with the papers you so kindly offerd to show Mr. Fazakerly, and with them taken the opportunity to give both your Lordship and my Lady my thanks for a Humanity, which (I have long known of you, and now find of Her) neither of you are too great to exercise to the Sick: I may now add to that word, the Unfortunate; for ever since, my poor Mother seems to have been dying; tho' not quite yet at the point of expiring, but hourly expected. I shall, indeed my Lord, at all times be sensible of your favour, tho accidents may prevent my repeating so often as I would, the assurances

---

[1] *Aeneid*, ii. 724.

[2] Mr. Howe of Stowell had given Pope shelter early in September, when Bathurst was unexpectedly from home. See To Bathurst, 15 Sept. 1728.

[3] Frederick, Prince of Wales, first came to England in Dec. 1728, and doubtless was wondering about other matters than Lord Bathurst. Pope coyly is saying that Bathurst's loyal duty is to come to Town to pay his respects to the newly arrived Prince—and thus gratify Pope's desire of seeing his lordship.

[4] The illness of Pope's mother and the submission of papers (the text and apparatus of *The Dunciad Variorum*) to the skilful legal eye of Nicholas Fazakerley, who could warn Pope of dangers of libel, date this letter so far as the year is concerned.

of it; And, with great truth & respect, ever be | My Lord | Your most obligd & most | obedient Servant, | A. Pope.

I am really in so much trouble I hardly know what I say, these are what Mr Kent sent me some days since; The book I can't attend, & have beggd a Friend to correct ye press for me, who has made some mistakes.[1]

Address: To the Right Honorable, the Earl of Burlington

POPE *to* THE EARL OF OXFORD[2]   [28 *December* 1728]

Longleat Portland Papers, xii

Saturday. | Dec: 28. 1728.

My Lord,—It was with regret I let your Servant go without a line, in thanks for your always-obliging, always-kind, regard to my Mother. I have myself been ill 3 days; As for her, she is still in danger, yet I hope not without possibility of recovery: Recovery indeed is too bold a word for Her Age, but of Lingering on some little time, or rather Dying Longer.

My faithful Services to my Lady Oxford & Lady Margaret: whose health I hope is confirmd to your wishes. I shall ever be with the sincerest respect & obligation | My Lord | Your faithfull & | most humble Servant, | A. Pope

Address: To the Rt. Hon. the Earl | of Oxford.

Endorsement: Mr Pope | Decr. 28. 1728

---

[1] If this book is not still *The Dunciad Variorum*, it is difficult to identify. William Kent had no clear connexion with *The Dunciad*, but the first page of the volume has a head-piece that looks much like his work, and he may have submitted other designs to Pope.

[2] The specific date is Lord Oxford's addition to Pope's 'Saturday'.

PRINTED IN
GREAT BRITAIN
AT THE
UNIVERSITY PRESS
OXFORD
BY
CHARLES BATEY
PRINTER
TO THE
UNIVERSITY